MEDIEVAL ENGLAND: TOWNS, COMMERCE AND CRAFTS 1086–1348

Social and Economic History of England

Edited by Asa Briggs

Anglo-Saxon England and the Norman Conquest (2nd Edition)
  H. R. Loyn

Medieval England: Rural Society and Economic Change 1086–1348
  E. Miller and J. Hatcher

Medieval England: Towns, Commerce and Crafts, 1086–1348
  E. Miller and J. Hatcher

The Late Medieval Economy

The Age of Plunder 1500–1547   *W. G. Hoskins*

The Age of Elizabeth 1547–1603 (2nd Edition)   *D. M. Palliser*

The Vital Century: England's Economy 1714–1815
  John Rule

Albion's People: English Society, 1714–1815   *John Rule*

MEDIEVAL ENGLAND:
Towns, Commerce and Crafts
1086–1348

Edward Miller

Sometime Master of Fitzwilliam College, Cambridge

and

John Hatcher

Reader in Economic and Social History,
University of Cambridge and Fellow of Corpus Christi College,
Cambridge

Longman
London and New York

Longman Group Limited,
Longman House, Burnt Mill, Harlow,
Essex CM20 2JE, England
and Associated Companies throughout the world.

*Published in the United States of America
by Longman Publishing, New York*

© Longman Group Limited 1995

First published 1995

ISBN 0 582 485487 CSD
ISBN 0 582 485495 PPR

British Library Cataloguing-in-Publication Data
A catalogue record for this book is available from the British Library

Library of Congress Cataloging-in-Publication Data
Miller, Edward, 1915–
    Medieval England. Towns, commerce, and crafts, 1086–1348 / Edward
Miller and John Hatcher.
        p.   cm. – (Social and economic history of England)
    "Intended as a complement to Medieval England. Rural society and
economic change, 1086–1348" – Pref.
    Includes bibliographical references and index.
    ISBN 0–582–48548–7 (CSD). –ISBN 0–582–48549–5 (PPR)
    1. England— Social conditions –1066-1485.   2. England – Economic
conditions – 1066-1485.   I. Hatcher, John.   II. Miller, Edward,
1915–   Medieval England.   III. Title.   IV. Title: Medieval England.
V Series.
HN385.M487   1995
306'.0942'0902 – dc20   94–31297
                                                                    CIP

Set by 8 in 10/12pt New Baskerville
Produced by Longman Singapore Publishers (Pte) Ltd.
Printed in Singapore

Contents

List of maps	vii
List of abbreviations	viii
A note on medieval English measures and money	xi
Preface and acknowledgements	xiii
Map of medieval England	xvi
1. Domesday Book and beyond	1
Crafts and craftsmen	2
Trade and traders	10
Urban beginnings	18
Conquest and consequences	38
The king's rights and the Domesday economy	44
The Anglo-Saxon legacy	49
2. Medieval industries	51
Some characteristics of medieval industries	52
Some industrial raw materials: wood, leather and clay	56
Mining and smelting	58
The consumer goods industries	74
Special cases: i. the building trades	85
Special cases: ii. the textile industry	93
Industrial specialization and its limits	128
3. The inland trade	135
The background of commerce	137
Communications	144
Transport costs	149
Markets and marketing	155

Fairs 166
Markets, fairs and urban development 176

4. Overseas trade 181

The thirteenth century and before 182
Changes in England's commerce, *c.* 1303–1348 210
The rise of an English merchant class 225

5. Medieval English towns 255

Some features of medieval English towns 257
A period of urban growth, 1086–1348 263
Boroughs and towns 279
Municipal development 290
Town governments 308
English towns in the early fourteenth century 320

6. Medieval townsfolk 323

Towns and their inhabitants 324
The limits of urban solidarity 356
The quality of urban life 389

7. England under the three Edwards, 1272–1348 393

The economic and social background, 1086–1300 393
England before the Black Death: forces of change,
  c. 1300–48 409
England before the Black Death: economic
  problems, *c.* 1300–1348 418
Crisis or equilibrium? 426

Select Bibliography 430
Index 457

List of maps

1. The leading towns of medieval England (including
    some lesser places discussed in the text)   xvi
2. Early development of the borough of Cambridge   24
3. Clothing towns paying fines for the exemption from
    the assize of cloth, 1202   101
4. Principal points of commercial contact between
    England and Western Europe, *c.* 1300
    (a) The North Sea trade   199
    (b) The northern and southern trades   205
5. The expansion of Bristol, *c.* 1066–1250   266
6. Progress of urbanization: Oxfordshire and
    Gloucestershire, 1086–1348   276

List of abbreviations

The following are the principal abbreviations used in the notes and bibliography.

AA	*Archaeologia Aeliana.*
AHEW	Finberg, H.P.R. and Thirsk, J., general eds, *Agrarian History of England and Wales.*
AHR	*Agricultural History Review.*
Arch. Soc.	Archaeological Society.
Arch. and NH Soc.	Archaeological and Natural History Society.
BARSEH	British Academy Records of Social and Economic History.
BBC 1042–1216	Ballard, A., ed., *British Borough Charters, 1042–1216.*
BBC 1216–1307	Ballard, A. and Tait, J., eds, *British Borough Charters, 1216–1307.*
Beresford, *New Towns*	Beresford, M.W., *New Towns of the Middle Ages: Town Plantation in England, Wales and Gascony.*
Cal. Docs. Scot.	Bain, J., ed., *Calendar of Documents relating to Scotland.*
Cal. Inq. Misc.	*Calendar of Inquisitions, Miscellaneous.*
Carus-Wilson, *MMV*	Carus-Wilson, E.M., *Medieval Merchant Venturers.*
CBA	Council for British Archaeology.
CCR	*Calendar of Close Rolls.*
CEcH	Postan, M.M. *et al.*, eds, *Cambridge Economic History of Europe.*

CLB	Sharpe, R.R., ed., *Calendar of Letter Books of the City of London.*
Close R.	*Close Rolls.*
CLR	*Calendar of Liberate Rolls.*
CPR	*Calendar of Patent Rolls.*
CRR	*Curia Regis Rolls preserved in the PRO.*
CUL	Cambridge University Library.
Dd.	Farley, A., ed., *Domesday Book seu Liber Censualis.*
EcHR	*Economic History Review.*
EHD	Douglas, D.C., general ed., *English Historical Documents.*
EHR	*English Historical Review.*
EYC	Farrer, W. and Clay, C.T., eds, *Early Yorkshire Charters.*
Fryde, *Studies*	Fryde, E.B., *Studies in Medieval Trade and Finance.*
HMC	Royal Commission on Historical Manuscripts.
Keene, *Survey*	Keene, D., *A Survey of Medieval Winchester.*
Med. Arch.	*Medieval Archaeology.*
Mon. Angl.	Dugdale, W., *Monasticon Anglicanum.*
NCH	Bateson, E. *et al.*, *A History of Northumberland.*
n.d.	no date
North. Hist.	*Northern History.*
NS	New Series.
Pat. R.	*Patent Rolls.*
PCAS	*Proceedings of the Cambridge Antiquarian Society.*
PP	*Past and Present.*
PQW	Illingworth, W. and Caley, J., eds, *Placita de Quo Warranto.*
PRO	Public Record Office.
RCHM (England)	Royal Commission on Historical Monuments, England.
Rec. Comm.	Record Commission.
Reg. Antiquissimum	Foster, C.W. and Major, K., eds, *Registrum Antiquissimum of the Cathedral Church of Lincoln.*
Regesta	Davis, H.W.C. *et al.*, eds, *Regesta Regum Anglo-Normannorum.*

Reynolds, *Introduction*	Reynolds, S., *An Introduction to the History of English Medieval Towns.*
RLC	Hardy, T.D., ed., *Rotuli Litterarum Clausarum in Turri Londinensi Asservati.*
RLP	Hardy, T.D., ed., *Rotuli Litterarum Patentium in Turri Londinensi Asservati, 1201–1216.*
Rot. Hundr.	Illingworth, W. and Caley, J., eds, *Rotuli Hundredorum.*
Rot. Parl.	*Rotuli Parliamentorum*, 6 vols. 1783.
Stubbs, *Select Charters*	Stubbs, W., ed., *Select Charters and other Illustrations of English Constitutional History from the Earliest Times to the Reign of Edward I.*
TRHS	*Transactions of the Royal Historical Society.*
VCH	*Victoria History of the Counties of England.*
VSWG	*Vierteljahrschrift für Sozial- und Wirtschaftsgeschichte.*
YAJ	*Yorkshire Archaeological Journal*
YAS	Yorkshire Archaeological Society.
YB	*Year Book.*

Throughout this book place of publication is London unless it is stated to be elsewhere.

A note on medieval English measures and money

While the money circulating in England was strictly controlled by the crown throughout our period, the measures in common use were subject to much local diversity despite government endeavours to promote uniformity. In what follows we have used contemporary statements of measure even though we cannot always be sure that they conformed to the official standard. Indeed, the dimensions of those measures which did conform to official standards sometimes changed over time and deviated significantly from their modern equivalents. To add to the complexity, the dimensions of measures which bore the same name could vary from commodity to commodity; thus a gallon of wine was likely to have been smaller than a gallon of ale, and a quarter of coal larger than a quarter of wheat. At the same time, because even the names of these measures may now sometimes be unfamiliar to readers, we have listed the most important of them below, together with their approximate modern metric equivalents. A selection of 'Tracts and Table Books relating to English Weights and Measures' was published by H. Hall and F.J. Nicholas in *Camden Miscellany*, XV, Camden Society, 3rd ser. XLI (1929). Those readers wishing to investigate further the history of metrology are invited to begin with R.D. Connor, *The Weights and Measures of England* (HMSO, 1987).

1.   Measures (general)

Weight

1 pound			(lb. – 0.45 kg)
14 lb	=	1 stone	(st – 6.35 kg)
8 st	=	1 hundredweight	(cwt – 50.8 kg)
20 cwt	=	1 ton	(1.02 metric tonnes)

Volume

1 gallon			(4.55 litres)
8 gallons	=	1 bushel	(36.37 litres)
8 bushels	=	1 quarter	(*c.* 291 litres)

Length

1 inch			(2.54 cm)
12 inches	=	1 foot	(ft = 0.305 m)
3 ft	=	1 yard	(yd = 0.9144 m)
1,760 yards	=	1 mile	(*c.* 1.61 km)

Area

1 square yard			(0.84 sq m)
4,840 sq yd	=	1 acre	(0.40 hectares)

2. **Measures (some particular commodities)**

Wool	1 sack	=	364 lb	=	*c.* 260 fleeces
Hides	1 last	=	20 dickers; 1 dicker	=	10 skins
Wine	1 tun	=	252 gallons		

Cloth The standard broadcloth was 24 yd long × 1½ –2 yd wide, though in practice there was much diversity, as was the case with other varieties of cloth. The dimensions of worsteds were even more varied, but the single worsted was valued for customs purposes at about one fourteenth of a broadcloth.

3. **Value**

12 pence (d.)	=	1 shilling (s.)	=	5 new pence (p.)
13s. 4d.	=	1 mark	=	66.7 p.
20s.	=	1 pound (£)	=	100 p.

The value of money in the middle ages is not easily expressed in present-day terms, since the prices of commodities have changed at widely different rates over the intervening centuries. In the 1290s a pound would have purchased somewhere between half and two-thirds of a ton of wheat, and more than 150 days' work from an agricultural labourer. By 1991 the price of wheat had risen between seventy- and ninety-fold, but the hourly remuneration of an agricultural labourer had risen more than six thousand-fold.

Preface and acknowledgements

This book is intended as a complement to *Medieval England: Rural Society and Economic Change, 1086–1348*, even though other inescapable commitments have meant that it appears more tardily than we had hoped. Since each volume is designed to be read independently there are some overlaps between the two volumes and, in particular, the final chapter of the present volume seeks to present some general conclusions about the character and achievements of the medieval English economy. As in the earlier volume we have located places in the historic counties or other English districts; and we have used the medieval monetary system and medieval measures, although we have thought it wise to include brief notes on both. In the preparation of this volume we have accumulated many obligations. We are indebted to Catherine E. Byfield for turning our drafts into acceptable copy, and to the help given to us by the staff of Longman Higher Education. As in the first volume the notes and bibliography, as well as indicating to the reader a sample of the relevant source material which is available, point (although less than completely) to the debts we have incurred to very many scholars who have laboured in this field. In a few cases our debt is particularly extensive. One of us, over a period of many years, has enjoyed intermittent opportunities of discussing some of the matters treated here with three friends – Rodney Hilton, Edmund Fryde and the late David Farmer; and the other has benefited from the ability to share ideas with Mark Bailey. We have long realised that our enquiries in many respects were taking a parallel course to those engaging Richard Britnell. It was some relief to find, when his *Commercialisation of English Society* was published, that his findings did not seriously diverge from our own and that its publication came in time for us to take some account of them. In a more general sense, too, our long-term indebtedness to the work of M.M. Postan and E.M. Carus-Wilson has not diminished with the passage of time, although responsibility for our conclusions, of course, is solely our own.

April 1994   E.M.
                                                                        J.H.

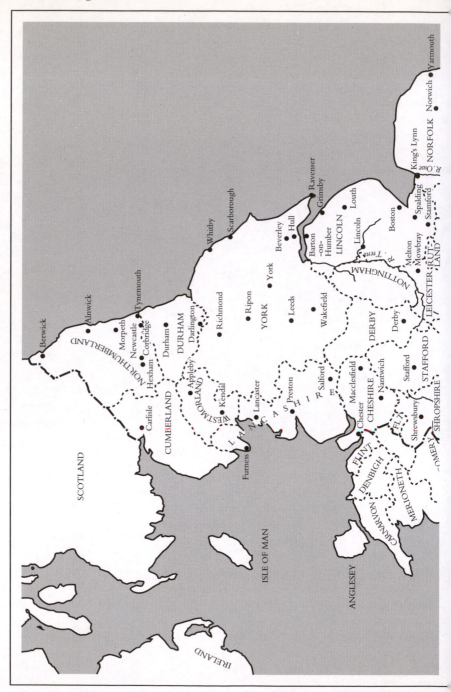

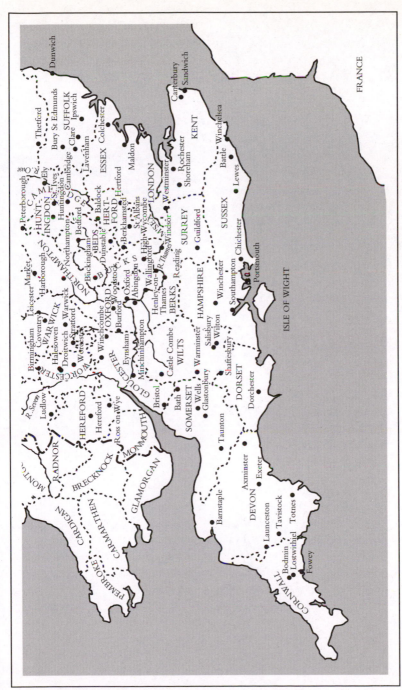

Map 1 The leading towns of medieval England (including some lesser places discussed in the text)

CHAPTER ONE
Domesday Book and Beyond

The Anglo-Saxon chronicler's account of the proceedings of the Domesday commissioners in 1086 makes clear the bias of their investigations. They were sent 'all over England into every shire . . . to ascertain . . . how much land and livestock the king himself owned in the country', and 'how much each man who was a land-holder here in England had in land and livestock', so that the shameful fact was that not an ox or a cow or a pig escaped notice in their record.[1] Their prime concern, in other words, was with a pro-foundly rural world, a bias which reflected the realities of eleventh-century England. This was not, however, the whole truth about England at that time, and indeed Domesday Book tells us something about communities which had urban features and, occa-sionally, about men engaged in other than agricultural occupations. These notices, unfortunately, are fleeting, inconsistent and often enigmatic; and the record of urban groups is seriously incomplete, if only because the towns may not have been part of the original scope of the enquiry. In consequence, the Domesday entries for towns represent a 'haphazard and incomplete' transfer of old mate-rials relating to the dues which boroughs owed to the king or sheriff. A further result is that the Domesday information about towns principally relates to things as they had been in or before 1066 and provides nothing like the systematic description of urban communities which the commissioners assembled for rural manors in 1086. For some places, moreover, including London, Winchester

---

[1] G.N. Garmonsway, trans., *The Anglo-Saxon Chronicle*, p. 216.

and probably Coventry, there are no entries at all; and the information given about others, including Bristol, is of the slightest.[2]

Domesday, all the same, offers a point of departure, although it needs to be supplemented wherever possible with evidence from the sparse written records of late Anglo-Saxon England, from coins which have survived in some quantity, and perhaps most of all from the findings of archaeologists which are the most likely source of genuinely new information. The historian's need to cast his net widely is all the greater because the many signs of economic and social development in the pre-Conquest generations have become increasingly clear to us. A recent suggestion that these generations experienced a 'first English industrial revolution'[3] is almost certainly an exaggeration; but the period from the ninth century onwards witnessed urban and industrial expansion, together with an intensification of agricultural production, which together enabled the England the Normans conquered to support a substantially larger population than it had in King Alfred's day. These developments of the late Saxon centuries were a prelude to many of the features revealed, however imperfectly, by Domesday Book, and they enable us to fill, although necessarily tentatively, some of the many gaps in that record.[4]

1. CRAFTS AND CRAFTSMEN

Domesday at once makes abundantly clear that much of what might be described as industry had nothing to do with towns. Right through the Anglo-Saxon centuries, indeed, a high proportion of craftsmen had been villagers. Smiths, for example, were indispensable for making and maintaining many of the tools and implements required by farmers, and by 1066 a smith was the one 'rural specialist' to be found in most villages.[5] Not every smith, of course, was a village blacksmith of this sort. There were slave smiths, at least

---

[2] S.P.J. Harvey, 'Recent Domesday studies', *EHR*, xcv (1980), pp. 127–8; *idem*, 'Domesday Book and Anglo-Norman governance', *TRHS*, 5th ser. xxv (1975), p. 178; for Coventry, R.H.C. Davis, *The Early History of Coventry*, pp. 16–18.
[3] R. Hodges, *The Anglo-Saxon Achievement*, pp. 150, 177.
[4] The Domesday evidence relating to towns and non-agricultural occupations has been systematically digested by H.C. Darby and his colleagues in the Domesday geographies listed in the bibliography. What follows, where no other reference is given, depends principally on these volumes.
[5] H.R. Loyn, *Anglo-Saxon England and the Norman Conquest*, pp. 107–9.

in the north, who were probably tied to the service of a particular lord or lady; there were a few urban specialists like Spileman the sword-maker who occupied a tenement in Winchester; and in a few places there were little concentrations of smiths – eight at Glastonbury and a sufficient number to pay substantial rents at Green's Norton and Towcester (Northants.) – possibly to provide central services for a wealthy landlord or staffing for an incipient iron manufacturing centre. Smiths, in turn, imply the existence of iron miners and smelters of whom archaeologists have uncovered traces in at least 29 of the 41 English counties, although Domesday tells us little of them. There are stray references to smelting in Hampshire, Sussex and Wiltshire; there were iron mines around Rhuddlan over the Welsh border with Cheshire; rents of iron were paid in Dorset, Somerset and Gloucestershire; there were iron workers at Moulton (Devon) and Hessle (Yorks.); and there were ironworks at Corby and elsewhere in Northamptonshire as well as at Castle Bytham (Lincs.).[6] Other branches of mining are still more rarely mentioned. Domesday records lead miners and rents of lead in Derbyshire, but not elsewhere; and tin leaves scarcely a trace in any early record.[7]

Many of these country smiths, miners and metal workers, like their successors later in the middle ages, are likely to have been part-time specialists, combining their craft with small-scale farming. Their individual and aggregate production, too, was doubtless meagre. There were, of course, other rural craftsmen in the Domesday countryside, although their traces are even fainter. Quarries, for instance, were noted at Taynton (Oxon.) and at four places in Sussex, that at Bignor supplying millstones; and potters were recorded at Westbury (Wilts.), Haresfield (Glos.) and Bladon (Oxon.), representing a good deal less than a full directory of eleventh-century rural pottery-making. Archaeologists have found potters' kilns in at least five Norfolk villages and at Michelmersh (Hants.); Domesday place names indicate the presence of potters at Potterton (Yorks.) and Potterne (Wilts.); and it has been suggested that much of the Saxo-Norman St Neots ware was made locally in villages over a wide area of eastern England, and that the expansion of

---

[6] H.H.E. Craster, 'Some Anglo-Saxon records of the see of Durham', *AA*, 4th ser. I (1925), p. 189 (a slave smith); for specialists, M. Biddle, ed., *Winchester in the Early Middle Ages*, p. 68, and D.M. Wilson, ed., *The Archaeology of Anglo-Saxon England*, pp. 263–4.
[7] J. Hatcher, *English Tin Production and Trade before 1550*, pp. 17–18; H.C. Darby, *Domesday England*, pp. 266. 268.

the industry in East Anglia and the Midlands in the eleventh century may have taken place largely in villages rather than, as earlier, in towns. There are also signs of a similar development in the same period in the south-west Midlands and parts of Wessex, for demand there was increasingly met by producers serving only a restricted area with hand-formed articles, by contrast with the wheel-thrown pots widely distributed from fewer manufacturing centres in the tenth century. Industrial expansion, in other words, often took place in a rural context.[8]

Domesday Book is even less informative about the countrymen and countrywomen who spun the yarn and wove the cloth needed both by ordinary folk and their betters. Many of these rural textile workers were doubtless, like many rural smiths and miners, farmer-craftsmen rather than craftsmen pure and simple, and as such they are not distinguished in the ranks of eleventh-century villagers. On the other hand, we do have certain knowledge of one west country estate in the eleventh century which possessed the equipment needed for cloth making, and it is likely that it would have been available in most manorial centres and many other households besides. Those who used the manorial equipment may sometimes have been slaves, for the property bequeathed by a tenth-century Dorset lady included a slave weaver and a slave seamstress (both women), and Eadred the weaver and his family were freed from slavery at Durham in the eleventh century. We are again reminded that a good deal of 'industrial' production, apart from being imperfectly distinguished from agriculture, was to some degree a matter of household self-supply. Just as, in the making of pottery, 'simple household production' gave place only slowly to production by specialist craftsmen, so much cloth was made for domestic use by slaves or servants in the headquarters of large estates; and in lesser households 'homespuns were produced in the home by and for the family'.[9] At the very least, it can be said that textile skills were indigenous in the Anglo-Saxon countryside.

---

[8] J.G. Hurst, 'Saxo-Norman pottery in East Anglia', *PCAS*, LI (1958), pp. 39, 60-1; P.V. Addyman, 'Late Saxon settlements in the St Neots area', *PCAS*, LXIV (1973), p. 82; M.R. McCarthy and C.M. Brooks, *Medieval Pottery in Britain, AD 900–1600*, pp. 88, 139–205.

[9] *Ibid.*, pp. 60–3; Wilson, ed., *The Archaeology of Anglo-Saxon England*, pp. 271–3; Loyn, *Anglo-Saxon England and the Norman Conquest*, pp. 117–18; D. Whitelock, ed., *Anglo-Saxon Wills*, p. 10; Craster, 'Some Anglo-Saxon records of the see of Durham', p. 190; P. Walton, 'Textiles, cordage and raw fibre from 16–22 Coppergate', in P.V. Addyman, ed., *Archaeology of York*, XVII(5), pp. 412–13.

Non-agricultural occupations were only of major importance in relatively few country places, but exceptional in this respect were the locations where salt was made by evaporation from sea water or from brine from inland springs. Salt was an indispensable commodity. As the salter in Ælfric's *Colloquy* pointed out, without him cellars and storehouses would be empty, for salt was needed to preserve meat and butter and cheese, as well as to season vegetables. It also generated revenue for kings and landlords, a fact which won its production attention in Domesday Book, which records salterns scattered along the coasts from Lincolnshire to the Bude estuary in North Cornwall. In some places they were so numerous they must have needed considerable bodies of workers.[10] There were 180 salterns, for instance, in the Marshland of north-west Norfolk, where the settlement which would become the town of King's Lynn may already have been forming on the spoil heaps deposited by the salters, whose activities in this way literally raised land from the sea. Many of these salterns were appendages of agricultural estates, like that which was entered under the manor of Nether Wallop in the interior of Hampshire, although doubtless the saltern itself lay near the coast. Presumably it was designed to meet the desmene requirements of that manor; and the Count of Mortain and his household may have consumed at least part of the salt produced in his manor of Studland (Dorset), with its 32 attached salterns. Salters, too, probably often worked only part-time at this trade, for salt boiling was mainly a summer activity; and in north Norfolk some salters may have brought sheep with them to graze on the salt marshes during the production season. This coastal industry remained close to the farming world.[11]

The same is true to some extent of the inland salt industry, although that centred on the Droitwich (Worcs.) brine springs does have a somewhat more specialized appearance. The Droitwich industry was well known to William of Malmesbury and Domesday has much to say about it, and by that time it was already old. In the ninth century Droitwich was known as Saltwic and there were royal taxes on the distribution of its product; and as early as the eighth

---

[10] P.H. Sawyer and I.N. Wood, eds, *Early Medieval Kingship*, Leeds, 1977, p. 147. The eastern and south-eastern salterns are mapped in H.C. Darby, ed., *A New Historical Geography of England*, p. 64.
[11] D.M. Owen, ed., *The Making of King's Lynn*, pp. 5-8; *idem*, 'Bishop's Lynn: the first century of a new town', *Proc. of the Battle Conference on Anglo-Norman Studies*, II (1980), pp. 141–53; *Dd*, I, ff. 38d, 79d–80.

century there had been salt 'furnaces' there.[12] In 1086, however, there were villeins as well as burgesses at Droitwich; some burgesses owed mowing services; and many of the Droitwich *salinae* were appurtenances of rural manors lying both in the neighbourhood and widely scattered over the West Midlands. Again the ties between industrial activity and agricultural society were very close. The same seems to be true of the salt industry of Nantwich, Middlewich and Northwich in Cheshire. These 'wiches' may have been 'little manufacturing enclaves in the midst of an agricultural district'; but we cannot be sure that the salters were full-time specialists and the salt-houses were certainly manorial appendages. At Nantwich, for example, the earl of Chester had his own salt-house attached to his manor of Acton, and many men of the *patria*, the surrounding countryside, also had salt-houses there, just as thegns did at Northwich. The earl's Nantwich salt-house, moreover, supplied his household throughout the year, although some salt might be left over for sale. Rural lordship, in other words, provided a framework for the industry; and it was geared to domestic self-supply as well as the market.[13]

The salt industry once again illustrates Domesday's patchy enumeration of rural craftsmen. Because many salters were part-time farmers they are noticed as craftsmen only if, in that capacity, they made a direct contribution to royal or seignorial revenues. They are, for example, rarely mentioned in connection with coastal salterns except occasionally in Devon and Cornwall. Notices of some other rural craftsmen are equally sporadic or even non-existent. We hear nothing of village tanners, tailors or shoemakers, who occur regularly in manorial records a few generations later; and the single carpenter recorded (in Herefordshire) was surely not unique at a time when wood was the principal material for most building and for agricultural tools and implements.[14] As we have seen, too, the Domesday record of rural potters is clearly incomplete, and that for millers is even more inadequate. The single miller entered for Cheshire, Herefordshire, Sussex and Shropshire respectively, together with three in Worcestershire and a 'keeper' of a mill in

---

[12] R.R. Darlington, ed., *The Vita Wulfstani of William of Malmesbury*, Camden 3rd ser. XL (1928), pp. 35–6; F.E. Harmer, ed., *Select English Historical Documents of the Ninth and Tenth Centuries*, pp. 22–3; H.P.R. Finberg, *The Early Charters of the West Midlands*, nos 237, 265, 268.

[13] J. Tait, ed., *The Domesday Survey of Cheshire*, Chetham Soc., NS LXXV (1916), p. 40; *Dd*, I, f. 268.

[14] Wilson, ed., *Archaeology of Anglo-Saxon England*, pp. 253–4.

Derbyshire, hardly represents an exhaustive enumeration given that there were some 5,624 mills in 3,463 of the 9,250 Domesday manors.[15] No doubt, as archaeological finds make clear, in many places grain continued to be ground by hand in querns; but to a significant extent mills, mostly driven by water power, had superseded hand grinding by 1086. The resources and authority of manorial lords were probably all but indispensable for the construction and maintenance of water mills and their associated mill races. Some mills may have been designed primarily to satisfy the domestic needs of seignorial households, like that at Catsfield (Sussex) which was for 'serving the hall', the manor house; but the revenues which lords got from some mills in 1086 suggest that many of them were already seignorial monopolies which tenants might be required to use and pay for doing so. The spread of corn mills in the late Anglo-Saxon centuries, therefore, is from one point of view an aspect of the consolidation of landlordship; but its scale also makes it, from the economic point of view, 'one of the greatest achievements' of those centuries.[16]

If the supersession of the hand-quern by the water mill (and sometimes by the horse mill) was one technical advance inherited by Norman England, there were others in pottery-making. As a consequence of the Anglo-Saxon invasions some parts of the country for the time being ceased to use pottery and even where production continued, up-draught kilns and the potter's wheel disappeared. They did not re-appear in East Anglia until the seventh century, spreading to other parts of eastern England by the ninth century and to much of the rest of the country by the tenth century, although without totally replacing hand-formed and clamp-fired products. By the tenth century, however, the industry had grown to an extent which must imply a greatly increased aggregate output, so that pottery was in everyday use at every level of society, and at least in many locations workshop production had taken the place of the simple household production of the early Saxon period.[17]

---

[15] *Ibid.*, pp. 275–6. These figures represent orders of magnitude only. Darby has demonstrated the difficulty involved in counting mills, like anything else, in Domesday Book, and concludes that the total of mills in 1086 (including urban installations) was '6,000 or rather more': *Domesday England*, pp. 272–3, 361, and cf. R.A. Holt, *The Mills of Medieval England*, pp. 3–5.

[16] *Dd*, I, f. 18; Darby, *Domesday England*, p. 270 citing J.H. Clapham's judgement; H.P.R. Finberg, ed., *AHEW*, I (ii), pp. 498–9.

[17] H.E.J. Le Patourel, 'Pottery as evidence for social and economic change', in P.H. Sawyer, ed., *Medieval Settlement*, p. 173; J.G. Hurst, 'The pottery', in Wilson, ed., *Archaeology of Anglo-Saxon England*, pp. 283–4, 314; McCarthy and Brooks, *Medieval Pottery in Britain*, pp. 60–7.

Other evidence of technological advance is far from plentiful. Industrial development in Anglo-Saxon England seems, on the whole, to have been quantitative rather than qualitative, a good deal of it a by-product of agricultural expansion and the consolidation of lordship, with more advanced methods of production only partially supplanting methods that were older and less advanced. On the other hand, communities were developing which housed concentrations of industrial producers which were both larger and more diverse than those to be found in country places. Of these we catch occasional glimpses in Domesday Book and its satellites. There were enough bakers and brewers at Canterbury, Stamford, Hereford and Chester for these crafts to be subject to regulations (those at Canterbury having been ordained of ancient time); and at Canterbury there were also enough drapers and shoemakers for them to owe an annual payment of 30s. Gloucester and Hereford may have been exceptionally active centres of iron-working, and Thetford, Derby and perhaps Arundel of corn milling; but the only description of urban diversity in Domesday is the account of the new town which developed between 1066 and 1086 on former ploughland on the western edge of Bury St Edmunds (Suffolk). At the latter date it was peopled by 75 bakers, brewers, tailors, washerwomen, shoemakers, robe-makers, cooks, porters and despencers 'who daily wait upon the saint and the abbot and the bretheren'. This list may be something less than a full enumeration of the crafts of Norman Bury St Edmunds, but the diversity of its occupations is clear.[18]

Documentary evidence to supplement Domesday's is also sparse. A Winchester survey records a few of the pre-Conquest holders of property there: they included a number of moneyers (one a goldsmith), two herring-mongers, a shoemaker, a glover, a soap-maker, a hosier, a blacksmith, a hay-merchant and a ladder-maker, as well as Spileman the sword-maker; and street names suggest that there were concentrations of tanners and shield-makers in Winchester by the late tenth century. The archaeological record also attests the presence of tanners, as well as of smiths capable of producing high-quality metal work and of potters, some of whose output may have been good enough to meet the demands of the king's

---

[18] A. Ballard, ed., *An Eleventh-Century Inquisition of St Augustine's, Canterbury*, pp. 8–9; R.R. Darlington, ed., *Cartulary of Darley Abbey*, Derbyshire Arch. and NH Soc., 2 vols, 1945, I, p. xlvi; *Dd*, II, f. 372; M.W. Beresford and J.K.S. St Joseph, *Medieval England: an Aerial Survey*, pp. 215–17.

court.[19] Archaeology, indeed, provides evidence that a concentration of crafts was already a feature of the urbanizing process in the middle Saxon period. Eighth-century *Hamwih*, just to the north of medieval Southampton, was the home of craftsmen working in wood and bone and metals, and also probably of weavers (a fragment of whose work has survived) and potters producing the local ware which is much in evidence. Middle Saxon Ipswich leaves a similar impression: of a 'cottage industry' of spinners, weavers, leather workers, metal workers and workers in bone and antler, all overshadowed by the potteries of the Carr Street area already working on something like a mass-production scale.[20] Rather later, Anglo-Scandinavian York affords evidence of leather-working (including a tannery measuring 90ft by 17ft); the working of jet, amber, iron, lead, copper alloy, gold and silver; glass-working and the turning of wooden bowls and cups; the working of bone and antler, and cloth-making and dyeing. By late Anglo-Saxon times the output of the Lincoln potteries consisted of wares that were 'mass produced to a considerable degree of uniformity and standardization'; Thetford (Norfolk) had a veritable 'artisans' quarter' on the south side of the Little Ouse; and there was the familiar concentration of crafts at Gloucester – shoemakers, cobblers, silversmiths, glass-workers, weavers, blacksmiths, and potters whose products were marketed not only locally but also in Worcester and Hereford.[21]

The material remains, of course, do not permit us to count craftsmen or measure their output; but they do provide backing for the impression conveyed by such written sources as we have of a growth and diversification of industrial production, especially from the ninth century onwards, at a time when agricultural expansion was enlarging the resources of customers for its products. We no longer need, therefore, automatically think of imports when we read of exotic bequests in Anglo-Saxon wills: swords, armlets, necklaces, silver cups, gold headbands, tapestries. After all, St Cuthbert's stole

---

[19] Biddle, ed., *Winchester in the Early Middle Ages*, pp. 34–6, 39–40, 43, 49–50, 56–7, 60, 67–8, 427–8, 433–4; McCarthy and Brooks, *Medieval Pottery in Britain*, p. 62.

[20] P.H. Holdsworth, 'Saxon Southampton: a new review', *Med. Arch*, XX (1976), pp. 41–51; M. Brisbane, 'Hamwic (Saxon Southampton)', in R. Hodges and B. Hobley, eds, *The Rebirth of Towns in the West, AD 700–1050*, p. 104; K. Wade, 'Ipswich', in *ibid.*, pp. 95–6.

[21] R.A. Hall, 'York 700–1050', in *ibid.*, p. 130; J. Radley, 'Economic aspects of Anglo-Danish York', *Med. Arch.* XV (1971), pp. 43–52; McCarthy and Brooks, *Medieval Pottery in Britain*, p. 147;' B.K. Davidson, 'The late Saxon town of Thetford', *Med. Arch.* XI (1967), pp. 189–94; C. Heighway, 'Saxon Gloucester', in J. Haslam, ed., *Anglo-Saxon Towns in Southern England*, p. 377.

and maniple and the Bayeux tapestry still testify to the skills of English embroideresses; and the plunder King William despatched to all the lands which furnished troops for his invading army is evidence that he found rich accoutrements in many of the houses and churches of the land he conquered.[22] Many craft products of the mid-eleventh century, of course, may have been produced in manorial or monastic households, and others by farmer-craftsmen. The growing number of full-time and independent industrial workers, therefore, is an inadequate indicator of the scale of economic development in Anglo-Saxon England. On the other hand, the fact that there were more communities comprising men and women more or less exclusively dependent upon craft industries for their livelihood was a no less significant aspect of that development.

2. TRADE AND TRADERS

Craftsmen both in town and country, of course, were also likely to be traders, selling their products to the members of their own community or to the inhabitants of their own neighbourhood. The economy of eleventh-century England was in no way an 'economy without markets': Domesday, indeed, lists a good number of markets, although as unsystematically as it lists many other things. Some were in places with few pretensions to any urban character: at Bampton (Oxon.), Titchfield (Hants.), Otterton (Devon), and Melton Mowbray (Leics.); but others were in settlements which may be classed as boroughs. The market at Ilchester (Somerset) was worth the not inconsiderable sum of £11 a year to the king; at Tewkesbury (Glos.) a new burgess colony appears to be associated with the market; the 42 inhabitants of the new borough developing at the gate of Tutbury castle (Staffs.) were said to live *de mercato suo tantum*; and in Suffolk burgesses at Beccles are mentioned in the context of the market and at Eye dwelt in the market.[23] Tenth-century Anglo-Saxon kings even tried to confine trade to boroughs: the attempt was less than successful, but it reveals an assumption that the developing urban centres should be trading communities.

[22] Whitelock, ed., *Anglo-Saxon Wills*, pp. 14, 26–8, 63–5; D. Talbot Rice, *English Art, 871–1100*, Oxford, 1952, pp. 2–3, 245–7; E.A. Freeman, *History of the Norman Conquest*, 2nd edn, IV, Oxford, 1876, p. 62.
[23] *Dd*, I, ff. 86d, 163–3d, 284d; II, ff. 319d, 369d-70.

One reason was that, because they were relatively populous compared to most villages, they needed little colonies of tradesmen to process and retail much of the food they consumed and to provide other necessities like clothing, footwear, tools, domestic utensils and the like. Townsfolk, in other words, were often mutual suppliers of each other's needs. This was especially true of provision traders, like the Canterbury bakers and brewers or the butchers whose stalls in the York Shambles get a passing mention in Domesday; but archaeological finds make it clear that the same was true of other craftsmen, including weavers, jewellers, and workers in metal and leather and wood at York. Towns, in important respects, were self-supplying communities; but, at the same time and to varying degrees, they depended upon a network of exchanges with their hinterlands both for customers and for food supplies their own fields could not provide and materials for their crafts. A statement of dues received by the archbishop of York in c. 1080 suggests much coming and going between the city and its hinterland: fish coming in by the River Foss, horses and carts loaded with merchandise (no doubt including grain or other foodstuffs) entering from every quarter, and merchants making purchases in the city.[24] Once again archaeology supports the written record. Bone, antlers and especially metals are often likely to have been materials imported into the city; and from an early date town-made pottery was found in country places. Ipswich ware, for example, has turned up in virtually every Middle Saxon site in East Anglia; and later, urban development at Thetford and Norwich was probably stimulated by the market which town craftsmen found for consumer goods, like pottery, among the peasantry of their surrounding countryside.[25]

Some of these exchanges clearly imply the existence of a communications network which could be used for bulk consignments and for goods which a person or a packhorse could carry. Some of this traffic, of course, went by water: York got fish supplies by the River Foss; Abingdon abbey's navigation rights on the Thames, enabling it to get a store of herrings among other things, went back to pre-Conquest times; and finds along the Lincolnshire coast and the rivers draining into the Wash may imply that water transport was one of the ways in which Stamford-ware pottery was distributed. Domesday itself affords evidence of the comings and goings of

[24] *VCH City of York*, p. 20.
[25] Wade, 'Ipswich', p. 96; J. Campbell, 'Norwich', in M.D. Lobel, ed., *Atlas of Historic Towns*, II, pp. 5–6.

coastal vessels (including 24 from Hastings) in the creeks and havens of Lincolnshire.[26] Much trading, however, must have relied upon roads and trackways overland. Some were totally unimproved and had to keep to the higher ground to avoid terrain liable to waterlogging; but in addition there were *stræts*, often inherited from the Roman network and therefore paved. Their military origin and continued utility in war is indicated by the fact that even in the twelfth century the Anglo-Saxon name for a main road meant literally 'army street';[27] but new needs made additions to the inherited pattern of communications necessary. The development of salt production at Droitwich, for instance, called for 'salt roads' along which salt was distributed over much of Midland England; and the growth of Chester may well have owed something to the fact that it was a focus of the salt ways leading west from the Cheshire wiches.[28] The 'salt roads' and other new lines of communication may not have been of high quality, but it is interesting to note that the twelfth-century *Leges Edwardi Confessoris* drew a distinction between these 'ways' (*viae*) and the 'great roads', the arterial links like Ermine and Watling Streets and the Fosse and Icknield Ways. It was the *viae* which led from borough to borough and along them 'men go to market and about their other affairs'.[29]

The communications network, however rudimentary it was, served the needs of the basic exchanges between towns and their hinterlands, but also of an inter-regional trade of which we catch occasional glimpses. Pottery, because it leaves sherds for archaeologists to exhume, provides some of them. Even in the late eighth century Ipswich ware reached London and Canterbury as well as East Anglia; St Neots, Stamford, Thetford and Torksey wares have been found in Anglo-Danish York; Stamford ware has also been identified at Beverley, Lincoln, Thetford, Cambridge, Oxford, Norwich, Warwick, Worcester and Gloucester among other places; and even Winchester pottery, though it was less widely distributed, seems to have reached Gloucester and possibly Hereford. At Worcester, it is true, Stamford and other wares obtained from a

[26] J. Stevenson, ed., *Chron. Monasterii de Abingdon*, II, p. 95; *Regesta*, II, no. 937; McCarthy and Brooks, *Medieval Pottery in Britain*, p. 86; *Dd*, I, f. 375d.
[27] M.O.H. Carver, ed., 'Medieval Worcester: an archaeological framework', *Trans. Worcs. Arch. Soc.*, 3rd ser. VII (1980), p. 45.
[28] H.C. Darby and I.B. Terrett, *Domesday Geography of Midland England*, pp. 255–6, for the midland 'salt roads'; A.T. Thacker, 'Early medieval Chester', in Hodges and Hobley, eds, *Rebirth of Towns in the West*, pp. 122–3.
[29] D.M. Stenton, 'Communications', in A. Lane Poole, ed., *Medieval England*, I, pp. 197–8.

distance became of less importance from the mid-eleventh century onwards, the greater prominence of pottery from the city's locality reflecting the more general spread of industrial activity throughout the country by the time of the Norman Conquest.[30] Commodities other than salt and pottery also entered into inter-regional trading. Herrings, for example, can be smoked or salted as well as eaten fresh, and it seems likely that the harvest of the North Sea herring fisheries was widely distributed. As we have seen herrings reached inland markets by the way of the Thames, and there are a number of indications that they represented big business for some towns of eastern England. An eleventh-century document from Christ Church, Canterbury, makes clear Sandwich's dependence upon the herring season, and the port in 1086 owed a rent of 40,000 herrings a year to the monks' kitchen. The rent is hardly likely to have been the sum total of the catches by the men of Sandwich, for there must have been some to be traded for their own livelihood; and we must suspect similar contributions to the fish trade are implied by the fact that in 1086 Beccles owed a rent of 60,000 herrings, and Dunwich one of 68,000 herrings each year.[31]

International trade also had a long history by King William's time. There were cross-Channel links between Quentovic and south-east England even in the seventh century; and in the eighth and ninth centuries the ports of eastern and south-eastern England were part of a Frisian trading region centred on Dorestad from which Frisian merchants went to York and London in the eighth century, and doubtless also to other English *wics* (trading towns) like Ipswich, Fordwich and *Hamwih*. Nor was the traffic only one-way. Charlemagne in 796 offered protection to English traders in the Frankish kingdom and it is likely that there were Englishmen among those who, 'seeking gain, not serving religion', mingled with pilgrims to avoid paying tolls on their merchandise. The fact that Offa of Mercia, when he reformed the English currency, took

---

[30] Hodges, *The Anglo-Saxon Achievement*, pp. 134–5; Radley, 'Economic aspects of Anglo-Danish York', pp. 51–2; J.G. Hurst, 'Saxo-Norman pottery in East Anglia', *PCAS*, XLIX (1956), pp. 47–8; Carver, ed., 'Medieval Worcester', pp. 223–5; P. Rahtz, 'The archaeology of the West Mercian towns', in A. Dornier, ed., *Mercian Studies*, pp. 122, 127; and see the select gazetteer in McCarthy and Brooks, *Medieval Pottery in Britain*, pp. 137–205, for the period from the tenth to the twelfth centuries.

[31] A.J. Robertson, ed., *Anglo-Saxon Charters*, no. 91; *Dd*, I, f. 3; II, ff. 311d-12, 370.

Carolingian money as his model, indicates the closeness of the economic ties between England and Carolingian Europe.[32]

The succeeding Viking age imposed severe strains upon those links, but despite some recent arguments it is hard to believe that England's external trade diminished in late Saxon times or that a revival of commercial ties with the German and French kingdoms had to wait until 1025 or later.[33] Ipswich and Southampton may have been shadows of their former selves, but York and Norwich grew; and if it is true that imported pottery lost ground to locally produced wares, that may simply reflect a spread of relatively more developed industrial production in England which was in no way incompatible with a continuing diversification of England's commercial connections. In particular, the traditional links with Carolingian Europe were complemented by closer ties with Scandinavia, reaching fullest development in the years of Cnut's northern empire (1016–35). York's principal commercial ties, for instance, were with Scandinavia and the Scandinavian colonies in Scotland and Ireland, but they extended via the Baltic and the Russian routes to Byzantium and even Samarkand, suggesting places of origin for some of the fragments of silk found in the Coppergate excavations.[34] Similar indications of commercial diversification, however, are also evident elsewhere. Pottery finds at Exeter suggest that urban growth there was associated with a developing trade with western France; from the tenth century onwards Chester developed as a port for the Anglo-Irish trade; and before that century was over English merchants were to be found at the fairs of Pavia.[35] Most of the evidence suggests, nonetheless, that in the late Anglo-Saxon period as earlier England's main commercial ties were with north-western France, the Low Countries and the Rhineland, the lands with which England also had close political, religious and cultural contacts during the tenth century. Anglo-Baltic trade was probably at its peak during the half century or so before the Norman Conquest, which helps to explain why the English currency provided a model for the coinages of the Scandinavian kingdoms; but

[32] Sawyer and Wood, eds, *Early Medieval Kingship*, pp. 150–2; P.H. Sawyer, *Kings and Vikings*, 1982, p. 70; R. Latouche, *Les origines de l'économie occidentale*, pp. 197–8; A. Lewis, *The Northern Seas*, pp. 203–4; *EHD*, I, pp. 781–2.

[33] As Hodges appears to suggest: *The Anglo-Saxon Achievement*, pp. 164–5.

[34] Hall, 'York 700–1050', p. 130; Walton, 'Textiles, cordage and raw fibre from 16–22 Coppergate', pp. 419–20.

[35] J. Allen *et al.*, 'Saxon Exeter', in Haslam, ed., *Anglo-Saxon Towns in Southern England*, pp. 404–5; Thacker, 'Early medieval Chester', pp. 122–3; R.S. Lopez, 'An aristocracy of money in the early middle ages', *Speculum*, XXVIII (1953), pp. 21–2.

14

by the 1020s weight standards in Flanders were moving in conformity to those with England, another reflection of close commercial relationships.[36]

So far as the character of England's trade was concerned, Ælfric, abbot of Eynsham, in c. 1000, catalogued some of the goods which merchants brought into the country: fine fabrics and garments, gold and jewels, dyestuffs, wine, oil. Many imports, clearly, were designed for the rich man's market. A list of tolls levied at London's Billingsgate wharf about the same time, however, mentions imports of wood and fish as well as of cloth, wine and pepper, affording rather less than proof that much of London's cross-Channel trade was in 'bulk goods of an ordinary, not luxury kind'; but obviously it did not consist of luxuries alone.[37] Archaeologists have also demonstrated that there were some imports of pottery; it is likely that the men of Rouen were already bringing in 'wine and fat fish' as they did later; some wine was being bought at the Paris fairs even in the tenth century; and Domesday attests an import of marten skins from Ireland. In 1066 England's import trade, although our knowledge of it is far from complete, was clearly diversified.[38]

The evidence for exports is equally fragmentary; but Bristol sent slaves to Ireland, wheat and cloth were apparently shipped to Scandinavia, there seems to have been some demand for English cheese in France and Flanders, and English merchants took woollen and linen cloth, canvas, swords, tin and horses to Pavia.[39] England's exports to Flanders and the Rhineland seem also to have been diverse. English tin may have been reaching Cologne, Liège, Huy and Dinant before 1066, and it was possibly through an English friend that a southern German abbot got a stock of lead at the end of the tenth century.[40] It is doubtful, on the other hand, whether

[36] F.M. Stenton, *Anglo-Saxon England*, pp. 533–5; P. Nightingale, 'The evolution of weight standards and the creation of new monetary and commercial links in northern Europe from the tenth century to the twelfth century', *EcHR*, 2nd ser. xxxviii (1985), pp. 199–200.
[37] Loyn, *Anglo-Saxon England and the Norman Conquest*, pp. 96–100; P.H. Sawyer, *From Roman Britain to Norman England*, p. 232. For the Billingsgate toll-list, A.J. Robertson, ed., *Laws of the Kings of England from Edmund to Henry I*, pp. 70–3.
[38] F.E. Harmer, ed., *Anglo-Saxon Writs*, p. 467; *Regesta*, iii, no. 729; R. Doehaerd, 'Ce qu'on vendait et comment on le vendait dans le Bassin Parisien', *Annales ESC*, ii (1947), pp. 274–9; *Dd*, i, f. 262d.
[39] Darlington, ed., *The Vita Wulfstani*, pp. 42–4, 90–1; Lewis, *The Northern Seas*, p. 428; Loyn, *Anglo-Saxon England and the Norman Conquest*, p. 100; R. Doehaerd, *Le haut moyen âge occidental: économies et sociétés*, p. 280.
[40] A. Joris, *La ville de Huy au moyen âge*, Paris, 1959, pp. 235, 243; M. Lombard, *Espaces et reseaux du haut moyen âge*, Paris, 1972, pp. 78–9; H. van Werveke, *Miscellanea Medievalia*, pp. 42–3.

any or all these exports would have sufficed to pay for expensive imports and, at the same time, generate an inflow of enough silver to support England's large and stable currency. To meet these requirements England's most likely compensatory export may have been wool.[41] The close monetary links between England and Flanders perhaps suggest a reciprocal commercial relationship going back at least to the early eleventh century and the pre-eminence of Flanders in cloth-making, recognized in the third quarter of the century, may already have depended in some degree on the use of English wool. If so, it is not surprising that the sea-faring merchants of Flanders, according to an account of one of St Bavo's miracles recorded before 1010, dealt especially with England.[42]

This account underlines the fact that overseas merchants were responsible for much of England's overseas trade. The Billingsgate toll-list also reveals merchants from Flanders in the port of London, together with others from the Rhineland and north-west France; the men of Rouen had their own wharf in London before 1066; a life of St Oswald speaks of Danes coming to York from every quarter; and the privileges Danes and Norwegians enjoyed in London in the twelfth century are likely to have been established in Cnut's and the Confessor's times.[43] Yet Englishmen, too, traded overseas. King Alfred's preface to the translation of Orosius suggests that even in the ninth century Englishmen as well as Vikings voyaged from England to the Baltic; in the late tenth and early eleventh centuries English merchants were found in the Paris region, at Pavia and even in Rome; and Abbot Ælfric's merchant was a man who went in his ship and brought back precious things. Overseas trading, indeed, could be an avenue to social promotion, for 'if a trader prospered, that he crossed thrice the open sea at his own expense, he was afterwards entitled to the right of a thegn'.[44]

Overseas trade and traders, of course, were concentrated mainly in the ports, but from ports travelling merchants delivered imported goods to inland markets, other secondary currents of trade were involved in collecting goods for export, and the widespread distribution of some industrial products (like Stamford pottery) must have

---

[41] As Sawyer suggests, *From Roman Britain to Norman England*, p. 233 and cf. Nightingale, 'The evolution of weight standards', p. 199; but for a contrary view, T.H. Lloyd, *The English Wool Trade in the Middle Ages*, pp. 1–2.
[42] Van Werveke, *Miscellanea Medievalia*, p. 5.
[43] Harmer, ed., *Anglo-Saxon Writs*, p. 467; Stenton, *Anglo-Saxon England*, pp. 533–4.
[44] Lewis, *The Northern Seas*, pp. 301–2; W. Cunningham, *Growth of English Industry and Commerce*, I, p. 132; *EHD*, I, p. 432.

owed something to the activities of middlemen. By the tenth and eleventh centuries, therefore, England had developed a 'hierarchy of markets',[45] many of them in the growing urban communities which were commercial centres for their surrounding countryside. This role explains why legislation of the second quarter of the tenth century confined minting to towns. In the late Saxon period there were moneyers in some 60–70 centres, although naturally they were more numerous and active in large towns than in small. This decentralization of minting enabled monetary relations to penetrate rural society as well as the world of commerce even though, in the countryside, both great men and small were to a large extent self-suppliers, paid many of their dues in kind or by service, and often secured what they wanted by barter. Nonetheless, by the time the Normans came, a monetary economy had attained some maturity in England, making that country a focus of economic expansion in the north European area to which merchants were giving a measure of unity.[46]

Another feature of this monetary economy was that, while minting was decentralized, the currency itself was under strict royal control from the tenth century onwards. 'One coinage is to be current throughout all the king's dominion', Edgar decreed in c. 959–63; the bullion content of the silver pennies which constituted the circulating medium, and the time-table of periodic recoinages, were centrally determined; and by 1066 the dies by which the coins were struck were produced solely in London.[47] Other royal powers, as well as this control over money, also might have economic implications. They included rights to control trade and to draw profit from this control in the form of tolls and other dues. Because trade generated revenue, moreover, kings sought to confine as much of it as possible to boroughs which, as royal military and administrative centres, provided facilities for revenue collection. Since many of these boroughs were towns, or grew into towns, royal lordship constituted a large part of the framework of early urban development in England.

---

[45] Hodges, *The Anglo-Saxon Achievement*, pp. 156–7.

[46] *EHD*, I, p. 384; Loyn, *Anglo-Saxon England and the Norman Conquest*, pp. 127–9; Nightingale, 'The evolution of weight standards', pp. 200–1, 208–9; R.H. Britnell, *The Commercialisation of English Society, 1000–1500*, pp. 29–31, 35.

[47] *EHD*, I, p. 397; M.H. Dolley, 'The coins', in Wilson, ed., *Archaeology of Anglo-Saxon England*, pp. 358, 362–3.

3. URBAN BEGINNINGS

(a) Boroughs and towns

Domesday Book describes about a hundred places as boroughs (or in a few cases as cities) or as having at least some inhabitants who were burgesses.[48] They varied so greatly in character that it is hard to believe that the words borough and burgess were used with much technical rigour. Many boroughs were evidently very small (although some of the entries, especially in the highly abbreviated first volume of Domesday, may be seriously incomplete);[49] and particularly in the small towns of southern England, like Bedwyn (Wilts.), it is difficult to disentangle the burghal element from the agrarian complex in which it was embedded. As we have already seen, moreover, for a number of important centres Domesday either provides no information at all or entries which preclude even a guess at their populations.[50] On the other hand, in 1086, despite much urban depopulation during the preceding twenty years, about 19 places (including Cambridge) may have had *c.* 1,000–2,500 inhabitants; another nine (Oxford, Wallingford, Canterbury, Gloucester, Stamford, Grantham, Thetford, Dunwich and Bury St Edmunds) *c.* 2,500–5,000; and York, Lincoln, Norwich and probably Winchester over 5,000.[51] These figures may not fully support the view that England in 1066 had been 'one of the most highly urbanized parts of Europe', but clearly a hierarchy of urban communities, recognizably different 'from the ordinary run of agricultural villages and hamlets', was an integral part of the social fabric.[52]

The urban developments revealed by Domesday, of course, already had a long history. England, like many other western lands,

---

[48] The figure is that given by S. Reynolds, *Introduction to the History of Medieval English Towns*, p. 36.
[49] S.P.J. Harvey, 'Evidence for settlement study: Domesday Book', in Sawyer, ed., *Medieval Settlement*, pp. 196–7; *idem*, 'Recent Domesday studies', p. 128. Consequently, estimates of town populations derived from Domesday must be regarded as minima: Darby, *Domesday England*, pp. 291–5.
[50] *Dd*, I, ff. 64d, 183.
[51] For Winchester, which is omitted from Domesday Book, see Biddle, ed., *Winchester in the Early Middle Ages*, pp. 467–9 and for Gloucester, for which no Domesday figure is calculable, H. Ellis, *General Introduction to Domesday Book*, II, p. 446 for a total of 518 burgesses in *c.* 1100. Other figures are drawn from H.C. Darby's Domesday geographies and are given with all the cautionary reservations he would have recommended.
[52] Sawyer, *From Roman Britain to Norman England*, pp. 204, 219; S. Reynolds, 'Towns in Domesday Book', in J.C. Holt, *Domesday Studies*, p. 300.

experienced a 'ruralization of the ancient city' when the Roman dominion collapsed, so that there were open spaces under cultivation within the walls of sixth-century London, probable breaks in the occupation of Worcester and Canterbury, and the transformation of ninth-century Roman Gloucester into an agricultural estate or estates. Whatever occupation there was of Chester, too, even as late as the tenth century, was 'the occupation of a Roman ruin'.[53] Symptoms of urban revival, however, became evident from the seventh century onwards at places where lines of communication intersected or where people congregated: adjoining the sites of royal residences like Tamworth, or of royal manors where hundred courts were held, or where minsters and monasteries like Amesbury, Malmesbury and Wilton were established, or where a bishop had his seat. Winchester was 'a royal and ecclesiastical community' from an early date, although it was hardly a town in any proper sense before the late ninth century; but the walled area of Canterbury was reoccupied after St Augustine established his church there, and the church seems to have preserved the Roman fortress area at York from 627 onwards. The precinct of St Paul's, and later a Mercian royal palace at Cripplegate, kept what had been Roman London alive at a time when urban London, what Bede called 'an emporium of many people coming by land and sea', lay outside the city along the axis of the Strand.[54]

What was happening in, or rather outside, Roman London had parallels in the growth of coastal wics on both sides of the North Sea, which in England included places with a long-term economic importance like York (*Eoforwic*), Ipswich, Sandwich, and Southampton (*Hamwih*). Southampton by the eighth century was an international *mercimonia*, an international trade centre as well as the home of various manufacturing crafts; its economic importance is indicated by the fact that it was *Hamwih*, not Winchester, which gave Hampshire its name.[55] York, too, by that time was exhibiting a

---

[53] Doehaerd, *Le haut moyen âge occidental*, p. 124; Hodges and Hobley, eds, *Rebirth of Towns in the West*, pp. 69, 117, 126; Carver, ed., 'Medieval Worcester', pp. 1–3; Haslam, ed., *Anglo-Saxon Towns in Southern England*, pp. 5, 364–5; C. Heighway, *Anglo-Saxon Gloucestershire*, Gloucester, 1987, pp. 146, 154.

[54] Britnell, *Commercialisation of English Society*, pp. 20–2; P. Rahtz, 'Archaeology of the West Mercian towns', pp. 111–14; Haslam, ed., *Anglo-Saxon Towns in Southern England*, pp. 5, 89, 136–9; Biddle, ed., *Winchester in the Early Middle Ages*, p. 450; R. Hall, 'The making of Domesday York', in D. Hooke, ed., *Anglo-Saxon Settlements*, pp. 237–8; Hodges and Hobley, eds, *Rebirth of Towns in the West*, pp. 69–73.

[55] Haslam, ed., *Anglo-Saxon Towns in Southern England*, pp. 159–60, 335; Hodges, *The Anglo-Saxon Achievement*, pp. 80–7; L. Keen, '*Illa mercimonia que dicitur Hamwih*', *Archaeologia Atlantica*, I (1975), pp. 168–70, 178–82.

similar potential for economic and urban development; but, in most of England, the decisive phase in early urban history only came in the time of the Vikings and the West Saxon reconquest of England. The Danish conquests in eastern England were organized around 'boroughs', most of them the county towns of the future (Lincoln, Nottingham, Derby, Leicester, Northampton, Huntingdon, Cambridge and Bedford) and already displaying some urban characteristics. At Cambridge, however, the Danes seem to have established their own *burh*: an area defended by ditches to the south of the Roman fort and straddling the river, suggesting that it was regarded as a centre for trade by land and water as well as a fortress; and at Northampton a 'dramatic intensification' of urban activities may have begun at this time.[56]

King Alfred, his successors and his daughter (the 'lady of the Mercians') contributed to the urbanizing process by the measures they took to defend their territories and the lands they regained from the Vikings. They established a defensive network of fortified *burhs* in Wessex and Mercia: some in Roman or even Iron Age forts, some in existing towns and some on new sites. The *burh* at Winchester was established within the old Roman walls, Worcester's fortifications were built by order of the lady of the Mercians although they enclosed a community which already had a market and streets, while Cricklade and Oxford may have been new settlements on land carved from royal estates.[57] Even London was uprooted from the Strand and re-established, probably by Alfred, within the defences of the old Roman city. The regime of fortified boroughs was extended as the West Saxon dominion expanded, some being planted cheek by jowl with Danish boroughs in order to control them. This seems to have been the case at Stamford, and probably at Bedford and Cambridge, giving this last town a triple origin: a resettled Roman fortress on Castle Hill, a Danish borough focused on the bridge, and a West Saxon tenth-century *burh* around the market place.[58]

To establish a place as a *burh*, of course, did not automatically

[56] J. Haslam, 'The development and topography of Saxon Cambridge', *PCAS*, LXXII (1984), pp. 17–20; Dornier, ed., *Mercian Studies*, p. 148.

[57] *EHD*, I, p. 498; Haslam, ed., *Anglo-Saxon Towns in Southern England*, pp. 106–10; *VCH Oxon.*, IV, pp. 5–7.

[58] A. Vince, 'The economic basis of Anglo-Saxon London', in Hodges and Hobley, eds, *Rebirth of Towns in the West*, p. 92; A.G. Rosser, *Medieval Westminster, 1200–1540*, p. 12; *EHD*, I, p. 198; J. Hassall and D. Baker, 'Bedford: aspects of town origin and development', *Beds. Arch. Jnl.*, IX (1974), p. 78; Haslam, 'The development and topography of Saxon Cambridge', p. 20.

create a town. Some boroughs had urban features from the start, but some never acquired them and others, after promising beginnings, relapsed into being mere villages. Some *burhs*, therefore, cannot be identified with certainty; the *burh* at Pilton (Devon) was replaced by Barnstaple in the tenth century; and Frome and Milverton (Somerset) had ceased effectively to be *burhs* by 1086.[59] The age of *burh*-founding was nevertheless decisive in the history of many medieval English towns. The central planning involved in their establishment often left its mark, as at Winchester and Wallingford, in their planned lay-out, and in the city of London the earliest street grid in the Cheapside area seems to have been laid out after the focus of settlement moved back within the Roman defences from the Strand.[60] Because *burhs* were royal foundations, moreover, English kings had what was, for the time, a unique authority in the development of urban life, which they used to expand the functions of *burhs* well beyond their original strategic and military role. Many of them became the administrative centres of their surrounding territories, and their economic development was deliberately promoted, the better to support their roles as fortresses and centres of administration. King Athelstan (924–39) not only required *burh* fortifications to be made good, but also ordered that trade and minting should be confined to those *burhs* which were *ports*, towns in the strict sense. It was evidently the royal intention to make *burhs* into commercial centres supplied with the currency that would make trade possible.[61]

The fruits of this policy were soon manifested. At Cambridge, the new southern *burh* centred on the market place had a mint by Edgar's reign and, with its long stretch of river frontage, was clearly regarded as an inland port; Winchester's principal street by the early tenth century was called *ceap strǣt* (Market Street); and London's Cheapside apparently originated as a collection of food markets.[62] Of course other things than royal artifice contributed to the development of properly urban communities. Churches played

---

[59] W.G. Hoskins, *Devon*, p. 327; J. Tait, *The Medieval English Borough*, p. 55.

[60] M. Biddle and D. Hill, 'Late Saxon planned towns', *Antiquaries Jnl.*, LI (1971), pp. 70–85; K. Rodwell, ed., *Historic Towns in Oxfordshire*, pp. 15–17, 133, 155; B. Hobley, 'Lundenwic and Lundenburh', in Hodges and Hobley, eds, *Rebirth of Towns in the West*, pp. 73–7.

[61] *EHD*, I, p. 354; D. Hill, 'Towns as structures and functioning communities', in D. Hooke, ed., *Anglo-Saxon Settlements*, pp. 202–7.

[62] Haslam, 'Development and topography of Saxon Cambridge', pp. 20–3; D. Hinton, *Alfred's Kingdom*, 1977, p. 60; C.N.L. Brooke and G. Keir, *London 800–1216*, pp. 172–7.

their part: the settlement established early in the eleventh century on the rocky peninsula at Durham as a resting place for St Cuthbert's body was soon capable of repulsing Scottish invaders; St Albans was perhaps a deliberate plantation by the abbey in the tenth century which drew settlement away from Roman Verulamium across the river; and Bishop Æthelwold's foundation at Abingdon led to a diversion of the Thames for the convenience of traders and the laying out of a market place at the abbey gate, where ten merchants dwelt in 1086.[63] At the same time urban development from the ninth century onwards was also conditioned by what was happening in the countryside: a growing population and expanding settlement, enlarging food production and providing some recruits for the ranks of townsfolk, and the consolidation of a class of landlords capable of organizing production on a sufficient scale to furnish significant marketable surpluses. A more numerous peasantry and landlords with more resources, in turn, made greater demands upon urban goods and services. The trade that mattered most in 1066 was not that to distant places or in exotic goods upon which Abbot Ælfric dwelt; rather it was a bread and butter trade, involving an exchange of the produce of agriculture and stock-farming for the products of simple craft industries. It was not solely conducted in towns. The rate of economic expansion was sufficient to generate some development of minor markets and doubtless there were many informal exchanges within and between villages; but also there was enough trade to turn some *burhs* into towns properly so-called and to give birth to some towns which had never been *burhs*.

Urban communities grew, therefore, during the generations before the Norman Conquest, and did so despite fires (inevitably destructive when most buildings were made of wood) or armies like the Danish force which sacked Norwich in 1004. Yet Norwich grew, nonetheless, as a number of smaller settlements were fused together. In *c.* 900 the settled area had covered about 50 acres; but this doubled by *c.* 1000 and doubled again by 1066 to accommodate a population of at least 5,000 and possibly nearer 10,000. At Winchester, too, where there may have been three or four distinct settlements within the walls in the ninth century and large open

---

[63] M.W. Beresford, *New Towns of the Middle Ages*, pp. 326–7; W.E. Kapelle, *The Norman Conquest of the North*, 1979, pp. 25–38; Haslam, ed., *Anglo-Saxon Towns in Southern England*, pp. 63, 73; *Dd*, I, f. 58d.

spaces, some of them cultivated, similar tendencies were soon evident. Large tenements were subdivided and open spaces were occupied, first along the High Street (the market area) and the streets leading to the gates, and later along the streets radiating from these axes. There was even some suburban development, perhaps from as early as the first half of the tenth century, and the western suburb was intensively occupied by 1066.[64] There are many similar signs of growth and consolidation elsewhere. By 1066 the various components that went into the making of the borough of Cambridge had been fused together (although there was still an undeveloped 'green belt' between the West Saxon *burh* round the market and the older constituents of the town); but it was this newest part of the town which accommodated perhaps 70 per cent of Cambridge's 400 or so houses.[65] Oxford had grown even more rapidly, for it perhaps had a thousand houses and eleven churches; and there had been suburban development in other places than Winchester: at Hereford, Chester and Stafford, at Lincoln across the river to the south and on the hillsides to east and west, and at York over the Foss along Walmgate.[66] Churches had also multiplied in many towns. There were at least five Saxon churches in addition to the cathedral at Worcester, there were ten churches in the royal parts of Gloucester by c. 1100, most of Exeter's medieval churches existed by that time, and at least half of Canterbury's twelfth-century churches were of pre-Conquest origin. There were four or five churches even at Shrewsbury although the Domesday borough there was 'a group of interconnected villages and townships' rather than a town proper.[67]

The influence of general economic expansion upon urban growth is particularly clear at Thetford. First heard of when a Danish army wintered there in 869, Thetford was a *burh* by 952; but the site of the Anglo-Saxon town on the Suffolk bank of the Little Ouse shows little of the planned character of many early boroughs. It had grown, nevertheless, until it stretched along the river bank for

[64] J. Campbell, 'Norwich', in Lobel, ed., *Atlas of Historic Towns*, II, pp. 5–6; A. Carter, 'The Anglo-Saxon origins of Norwich', *Anglo-Saxon England*, VII (1978), pp. 199–202; Biddle, ed., *Winchester in the Early Middle Ages*, pp. 265–6, 450–6.

[65] Haslam, 'The development and topography of Saxon Cambridge', pp. 20–3; *VCH Cambs.*, III, pp. 4, 111–13.

[66] *VCH Oxon.*, IV, p. 10; Dornier, ed., *Mercian Studies*, p. 126; J.W.F. Hill, *Medieval Lincoln*, p. 35; Hall, 'York 700–1050', p. 130.

[67] Carver, ed., 'Medieval Worcester', pp. 7, 116–19; Haslam, ed., *Anglo-Saxon Towns in Southern England*, pp. 375, 398; M.O.H. Carver, 'Early Shrewsbury: an archaeological definition', *Trans. Shropshire Arch. Soc.*, LIX (1969–74), pp. 249, 253.

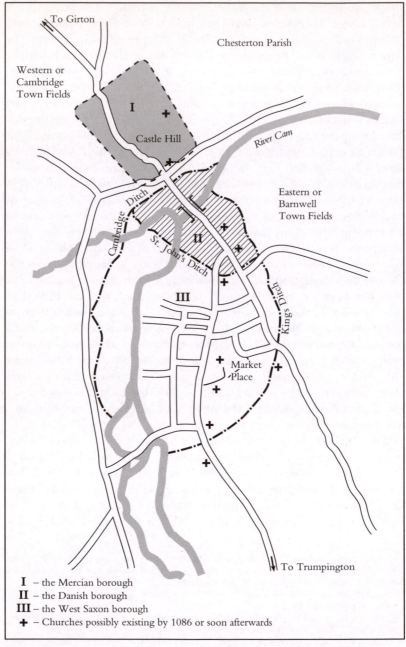

To Girton

Chesterton Parish

Western or
Cambridge
Town Fields

I

Castle Hill

River Cam

Cambridge Ditch

St. John's Ditch

Eastern or
Barnwell
Town Fields

II

III

King's Ditch

Market
Place

To Trumpington

I – the Mercian borough
II – the Danish borough
III – the West Saxon borough
+ – Churches possibly existing by 1086 or soon afterwards

Map 2 Early development of the borough of Cambridge (based on Haslam, 'The development and topography of Saxon Cambridge')

a mile or so; it had a mint by King Edgar's time; and its population included textile and metal workers as well as numerous potters. Possibly it may have been an administrative centre even before the East Anglian bishops were established there in the period 1072–*c*. 1095, for Thetford was said to share with Cambridge, Norwich and Ipswich an importance for the registration of property transfers; but its markets and its manufactures are as likely as its administrative role to have persuaded Ely, Bury St Edmunds, Ramsey and Thorney abbeys to acquire property there in the tenth and eleventh centuries. Thetford suffered severely at the hands of Danish armies in 1004 and 1009, and may have been smaller in 1066 than it had been earlier, but even so it accommodated 943 burgesses and a dozen churches. Although there was agricultural land within its bounds, Thetford was basically an urban community.[68]

(b) Domesday boroughs

The cities and boroughs which the Norman invaders took over in 1066 in many cases already had a long history and they had grown up in an essentially agrarian world. It is reasonable to suppose that, in the tenth and eleventh centuries as in later times, their growing populations were largely recruited from the rural areas surrounding them; and indeed the personal names of many pre-Conquest property holders in Winchester suggest that they were recent immigrants from Hampshire and other Wessex villages.[69] Nor were burgesses of necessity totally divorced from agricultural concerns. As Maitland pointed out long ago, 'Cambridge had fields . . . as the neighbouring villages had fields' – in fact two sets of fields which had probably been carved out of the territory of a large royal estate centred on the village of Chesterton to support respectively the eighth-century Mercian *burh* on Castle Hill and the southern *burh* set up after the West Saxon conquest of Cambridge in 917.[70] Particularly in early

---

[68] Garmonsway, trans., *The Anglo-Saxon Chronicle*, pp. 70–1, 112; E.O. Blake, ed., *Liber Eliensis*, pp. 92–3, 100; *Dd*, II, ff. 118d-19; Harmer, ed., *Anglo-Saxon Writs*, no. 56; Robertson, ed., *Anglo-Saxon Charters*, p. 252. On Thetford generally, see Reynolds, *Introduction to the History of English Medieval Towns*, p. 38 and Wilson, ed., *Archaeology of Anglo-Saxon England*, pp. 138–9, 314–20.

[69] Biddle, ed., *Winchester in the Early Middle Ages*, p. 463.

[70] F.W. Maitland, *Township and Borough*, pp. 4–5; *Dd*, I, f. 189. We have followed here Haslam's persuasive hypothesis: 'The development and topography of Saxon Cambridge', esp. pp. 23–6.

days, after all, fields might be as essential as fortifications if *burhs* were to fulfil their role as fortresses: the possession of fields might be some guarantee that those who manned the fortifications would be fed. There were, admittedly, towns without fields. Oxford had no arable, though it did have extramural pastures; sometimes, perhaps, magnates appropriated town lands (perhaps this was the origin of the bishop's manor 'around the gate' at Hereford or of the bishop of Lincoln's and Countess Judith's suburban manors at Leicester); in other cases, like that of Dorchester, the borough may have been so imperfectly differentiated from the rural community in which it had developed that no specific borough fields were ever designated for it.[71] As the lord of a borough, too, the king might give away town fields or portions of them; perhaps that was what Edgar was doing in 968 when he granted three hides near Wilton, formerly belonging to a merchant, to the nunnery there.[72]

There were still plenty of town fields, however, in 1086. The citizens of York cultivated six ploughlands, though they belonged to the archbishop; Lincoln had fields outside the city, Stamford some 1,000 acres of arable, and Derby's burgesses twelve ploughlands; there were burgess landholders at Norwich, Thetford and Ipswich (although with 40 acres only in this last place); and Colchester had some 1,300 acres of farmland, although doubtless much of it lay in the town's banlieu which later was distinguished from the borough.[73] It was also another feature of these Colchester fields that they were very unequally distributed among the 276 burgesses there. A small elite of some eight per cent of them each had twenty acres of land or more; only a third of them had five acres or above, and 45 per cent of them held houses but no land. Clearly a substantial part of Colchester's population got its living, wholly or in part, by other means than agriculture.[74] There were also parallels elsewhere to the situation in Colchester. Only fourteen out of Derby's 243 Domesday burgesses were said to be landholders, and only 21 of the king's 720 burgesses at Thetford. At Maldon (Essex), too, only fifteen of the holders of 180 inhabited messuages possessed land, the rest having 'no more than their houses in the borough', although in some cases

---

[71] *Dd*, I, ff. 154, 182d, 230–30d; Haslam, ed., *Anglo-Saxon Towns in Southern England*, pp. 236–7.
[72] *Ibid.*, pp. 127–8; Finberg, *Early Charters of Wessex*, no. 305.
[73] *Dd*, I, ff. 100, 280, 298, 336–6d; II, ff. 104–6, 116–16d, 119, 290; R.H. Britnell, *Growth and Decline in Colchester*, pp. 16–17.
[74] Tait, *Medieval English Borough*, pp. 73–4.

they may have been among the owners of the considerable amount
of livestock in the townsfolk's possession. Perhaps the Domesday
entries for two smaller places, Berkhamsted and St Albans (Herts.),
have a similar significance. They had 52 and 46 burgesses respectively, but in each case only a notional 60 acres of land, yet
Berkhamsted rendered £4 for toll and St Albans £11 4s. for tolls and
other payments. It looks as though trading bulked larger than farming in their economic life.[75] At Ipswich, too, where there was only 40
acres of land for 538 burgesses, surely 'nothing but an abundance of
urban employment can explain these figures'.[76] Many Domesday
boroughs, in brief, and still more Domesday burgesses no longer
relied upon the town fields for their daily bread. They relied instead
upon the surrounding countryside to provide for many of their
needs as well as markets for their manufactures and their commerce. This interdependence had become a general feature of
much of England's economy in the period of expansion during the
post-Alfredian age.

The ties between town and country, however, were not only commercial. While the king was the predominant lord of most
Domesday boroughs, his lordship was not exclusive. A few towns
were already virtually private boroughs, like those developing at the
gates of abbeys like St Albans, Abingdon or Bury St Edmunds; but
more commonly, and especially in the older and larger boroughs,
what Maitland called 'tenurial heterogeneity' was the rule. Lordship
over burgesses and borough tenements, in other words, was shared
between the king and various bishops, abbots, earls and other landowners. At Norwich, for instance, while most burgesses were directly
subject to the king, in 1066 Archbishop Stigand had possessed jurisdictional and seignorial authority over 50 burgesses and Earl Harold
over 32 more.[77] In some places these private lords of burgesses and
burghal property were important and numerous. At Leicester in
1086 Hugh de Grandmesnil, the greatest of the Leicestershire barons, had many more houses than the king, and others with property
there included the archbishop of York, two abbots, Earl Hugh of
Chester and the Countess Judith. Some of these private lords also
had judicial powers over enclaves within towns; and the fact that

[75] *Dd*, i, ff. 135d, 136d; ii, ff. 5d-6.
[76] Tait, *Medieval English Borough*, p. 71.
[77] *Dd*, ii, f. 116.

they were the lords of burgesses created many links between towns and country places. At Leicester 97 of the houses and 37 of the burgesses were said to 'pertain' to some 25 rural manors. What that entailed is illustrated by entries for Calne (Wilts.). There were 45 burgesses on the king's land there, but in addition 25 burgesses owed 25s. a year to the manor of Calne church, held by one Nigel, three others made annual payments to the manors of Ernulf de Hesding and Richard de Poynant in Calstone Wellington, and a house in the town made a similar payment to the bishop of Salisbury's manor in Bishops Cannings. Townsmen and town houses, in other words, provided revenue for country landlords.[78]

Many links of this sort between town and country reflect the stages through which the Domesday boroughs evolved. Ecclesiastical lordship over townsfolk was sometimes rooted in the church's role, at York and Canterbury for instance, in preserving some degree of proto-urban life in old Roman centres, although by 1086 it more frequently attested the way in which minsters and monasteries had attracted traders and craftsmen to their gates. The dominant position of the king in so many towns, on the other hand, is accounted for in part by the fact that very often they grew up within or near the centres of royal estates, but also by royal policies from King Alfred's time onwards to establish *burhs* as the military, administrative and ultimately the economic centres of districts. These policies, however, also had the effect of dissipating superiority over townsfolk and town property. By giving *burhs* a military role, for instance, kings gave country landowners a role in urban life. They were required, at least temporarily, to reside in *burhs* in order to defend them, as King Alfred's thegns were summoned to man the south-western *burhs* when a Danish army struck westward to the Severn; at Oxford, there are indications that the walled area was initially partitioned among the thegns of the surrounding countryside, who would have needed town houses in order to fulfil their garrison duties or in which to station retainers to do so in their stead; and even in 1086 various landowners held 'mural mansions' in Oxford, so-called because, 'if the need arises and the king commands, they repair the wall'. A

---

[78] *Dd*, I, ff. 64d, 66, 70, 73, 230.

'garrison theory', as part explanation of how the Domesday boroughs had evolved, still has a measure of validity.[79]

As time passed, however, landlords acquired town houses for other reasons than military duty. One was the developing role of boroughs as district administrative centres. Ely abbey may have been encouraged to acquire a 'well built dwelling' in Cambridge, together with land in the town fields, because of the frequency with which it used tribunals meeting in the town in order to validate its titles to Cambridgeshire land. The king also needed officials to supervise these administrative proceedings, some of whom were clearly men of substance like Æthelwine, reeve of Winchester before 1012, who held a spacious tenement near the city market with room enough for his own church as well as his dwelling; or like the thegn Ælfgar, who was a reeve of Æthelred II's, to whom the king granted an urban property in Cricklade which he apparently annexed to a country estate at Moredon in Rodbourne Cheney (Wilts.).[80] At the same time, the economic development of towns in the tenth and eleventh centuries increased the demand for town property, encouraging landlords from the country to acquire it as lodgings for their visits to town, or as bases for the sale of manorial produce and making purchases in town markets. It might also be a straightforward investment, as Domesday suggests in its record of the payments made by town tenements annexed to rural manors.[81] Because they were sources of income urban as well as rural holdings were granted by kings to monasteries in need of funds, as Edgar gave tenements in Winchester to Abingdon, or to thegns as rewards for service, as Æthelred II gave his thegn, Æthelweard, nine messuages in that same city. There was also a growing market in town as well as country property. Edgar granted land in Herefordshire and a house in Hereford to a thegn 'for his acceptable money'; Bishop Theodred of London (942–51) purchased a house in Ipswich and Archbishop Ælfric of Canterbury (995–1005) a house in Canterbury; and most of Ely's acquisitions in Cambridge were bought.[82] Important

---

[79] S. Keynes and M. Lapidge, trans., *Alfred the Great: Asser's Life of King Alfred and other Contemporary Sources*, Harmondsworth, 1983, pp. 115–16; *Dd*, I, f. 154; *VCH Oxon*, IV, pp. 8–9.

[80] Blake, ed., *Liber Eliensis*, pp. 83, 88, 95–6, 97; Finberg, *Early Charters of Wessex*, no. 150; Biddle, ed., *Winchester in the Early Middle Ages*, pp. 37–8, 340–2, 424; Stevenson, ed., *Chron. Monasterii de Abingdon*, I, pp. 377–82.

[81] As Sawyer points out: *From Roman Britain to Norman England*, p. 210.

[82] *EHD*, I, pp. 514–16, 537; Finberg, *Early Charters of Wessex*, no. 138; Whitelock, ed., *Anglo-Saxon Wills*, pp. 4–5, 52; Blake, ed., *Liber Eliensis*, pp. 95–6.

landowners with substantial urban estates, like Tochi son of Auti who had a hall, 30 messuages and $2^{1}/_{2}$ churches in Lincoln in 1066, may well have accumulated them over time; but clearly they yielded revenue. From his 30 messuages Tochi not only got the nominal rent (*landgable*) due to the king, but also *locationem*, the right to let them and receive the commercial rent which letting produced.[83]

This was a right which became more profitable as town populations grew. Initially, as we have seen, there was much empty space within towns. At Winchester, for instance, there were vacant areas in Tanner Street well into the tenth century, although by the mid-eleventh century it was fully built up; and in many towns, at least initially, urban haws, messuages or tenements were generously large. One given to a reeve of Winchester, later called Godbegot and provided with its own private church, seems to have extended over half an acre, and similarly spacious tenements seem to have been not uncommon in the city.[84] Winchester was by no means unusual in this respect. In London the soke of Aldermanbury, a name meaning the 'fortified manor of the alderman', may have been a survival of a similar urban holding; it has been suggested that the early Gloucester haws were several acres in extent; and one haw within the walls of Worcester in 904 apparently occupied a three-acre site. There was room within tenements like these for private chapels as well as gardens; and the fact that so many town churches were originally proprietary establishments possibly carries with it the implication that their first establishment had been within large urban messuages of this sort.[85]

(c) Borough social structures

Domesday is sometimes quite explicit about the way in which towns were filling up. At Nottingham eleven houses had been built on three messuages, at Guildford 175 tenants occupied 75 haws, in the abbey's portion of Shaftesbury 151 burgesses seem to be living in 111 house-sites.[86] The crowding of people into a small space, so

[83] C.W. Foster and T. Longley, eds, *The Lincolnshire Domesday and the Lindsey Survey*, p. 2 (also p. xxx for a different interpretation of this entry by F.M. Stenton).

[84] Haslam, ed., *Anglo-Saxon Towns in Southern England*, pp. 158–9; Biddle, ed., *Winchester in the Early Middle Ages*, pp. 340–2.

[85] Haslam, ed., *Anglo-Saxon Towns in Southern England*, pp. 307, 364; Carver, ed., 'Medieval Worcester', pp. 40, 49; Finberg, *Early Charters of the West Midlands*, no. 272; Wilson, ed., *Archaeology of Anglo-Saxon England*, p. 133.

[86] *Dd*, I, ff. 30, 75, 280.

characteristic of medieval towns, was already becoming evident by 1066. It is much harder, however, to define with any accuracy the social characteristics of their inhabitants. They were, as we have seen, in no way sharply differentiated from the rural world of their day. There were town fields in many places; there were burgesses ploughing the land (*terram laborantes*) at Totnes and Shrewsbury, although they may have lived outside these towns; and country land-owners not only had town property but sometimes helped to manage a town's affairs, as Æthelwine did whose bequest to Abingdon abbey shows he had an estate at Lyford (Berks.), but also a haw in Oxford (which included St Martin's Church) 'in which he himself dwelt'. At Cambridge there was even a group of resident thegns who established a gild in the city for their mutual aid and support, although they were 'clearly men of substance likely to hold estates in various parts of the country'.[87] For such men, as for men of similar standing in Roman Britain, urban living is likely to have been a 'seasonal activity' governed by calls for garrison duty, suit of court and so forth. Some of their subordinates, often called *cnihts*, were perhaps more continuously resident and may have played a part in the life of some English towns similar to that played by the *ministeriales* in many continental cities.[88] We hear of *cnihts* in various places, including Exeter and Cambridge (where the thegns were evi-dently concerned about keeping their *cnihts* in order); and sometimes the *cnihts* had their own gild. The London *cnihtengild* sur-vived into the twelfth century; there was another at Canterbury by the mid-ninth century; and at Winchester the *cnihts* had one or even two halls 'where they used to drink their gild'. We know little enough about these bodies, and they lived long enough to suffer many changes; but what little we know is perhaps enough to suggest that the subordinates of landlords, as well as landlords, had their parts to play in the early development of English towns.[89]

An even greater part was played by men who were first and fore-most the agents of the king, who needed resident reeves in towns to collect royal revenues and to safeguard royal interests. In Domesday Hereford, for example, the king's reeve had in 1066 collected the

---

[87] *Dd*, I, ff. 108d, 253; R. Welldon Finn, *Introduction to Domesday Book*, 1963, p. 161; Stevenson, ed., *Chron. Monasterii de Abingdon*, I, pp. 439–41; *VCH Oxon.*, IV, p. 384; *EHD*, I, pp. 557–8.

[88] S. Frere, *Britannia*, 1974, p. 276; Haslam, *Anglo-Saxon Towns in Southern England*, p. 62.

[89] *EHD*, I, pp. 558–9; Harmer, ed., *Anglo-Saxon Writs*, pp. 532–5; F.M. Stenton, *The First Century of English Feudalism*, 2nd edn, Oxford, 1961, p. 135; *idem*, *Anglo-Saxon England*, pp. 519–20; Biddle, ed., *Winchester in the Early Middle Ages*, pp. 34, 39, 335.

various 'customs' due from the city, and paid over £12 to the king and £6 to the local earl (who here, as in many other places, was entitled to one-third of the revenue towns produced). At Hereford, obviously, the reeve 'farmed' the borough revenues: that is paid over a fixed round sum rather than accounting in detail for many miscellaneous receipts. The reeve of Hereford also had to sell the house of any burgess who wished to leave the city and to take over the house of a burgess too poor to meet his obligations, making sure that it did not stand empty so that the king lacked the service due from it. No doubt this is a less than exhaustive list of the reeve's duties. At Chester, for example, he had a role in keeping the peace, bought marten skins on the king's behalf, enforced rules against false measures and the brewing of bad ale, and made arrangements for the repair of the town walls and bridge. Domesday all too rarely gives details of this sort, but clearly borough reeves, like the sheriff in the county, were very much the king's maids-of-all-work in their towns.[90]

About who these reeves were there is even less information. Some may have been burgesses; but the portreeve of Canterbury at the opening of the twelfth century was William Cauvel, a Norman whom Archbishop Anselm addressed as his friend, who married a knight's daughter and with her got land outside Canterbury to be held by knight service, and who acquired further property in or near the city by grant of the archbishop and the cathedral priory.[91] There is nothing very bourgeois about William Cauvel, although he may have been a special case: a Norman entrusted with the task of consolidating the invaders' hold upon a key city. On the other hand, he is not an entirely dissimilar sort of man to some of the Anglo-Saxon thegns who played ministerial roles in late Anglo-Saxon boroughs.

Men of a similar type appear sometimes to have occupied two other town offices: those of 'lawman' and moneyer. Lawmen are found only in some towns situated in those parts of the country which had been subjected to Viking rule, including Lincoln, Stamford, Cambridge, York and possibly Chester. By 1086 they had perhaps lost much of an earlier collective role, but they were representative of a traditional Scandinavian institution: the presence in popular courts of panels of men capable of laying down what the law was and applying it to particular cases.[92] At Stamford and

[90] *Dd*, I, ff. 179, 262d; Tait, *Medieval English Borough*, pp. 143–4.

[91] W.J. Urry, *Canterbury under the Angevin Kings*, pp. 62–4, 83, 385–7; F.R.H. Du Boulay, *The Lordship of Canterbury*, p. 74.

[92] P. Foote and D.M. Wilson, *The Viking Achievement: the Society and Culture of Early Medieval Scandinavia*, 1970, pp. 90–2; Stenton, *Anglo-Saxon England*, p. 525; Tait, *Medieval English Borough*, p. 43.

Lincoln, however, the Domesday lawmen appear clearly to be privileged groups, with jurisdictional powers over their property and dependants; and equally clearly they were men of property. At Stamford all but one of the lawmen held more than a single dwelling in the town, and one had seventeen messuages and a half share of a mill. At Lincoln, where the lawman's office seems clearly to be hereditary, no details are given of the lawmen's city property, but some of them certainly had interests outside the walls. Sortebrand in 1086 had inherited a hide of land in the city's fields and had himself made acquisitions in Burton-by-Lincoln, South Carlton and Metheringham; Godric son of Eddeva in 1066 had also held in Burton-by-Lincoln; and Walraven the lawman may have been the man of that name with sokeland and a small manor in Canwick. It may also be significant that in 1086 Sortebrand's lands were entered in Domesday under the rubric 'the lands of Sortebrand and other thegns'.[93] Some York lawmen seem also to have been men of a like sort. Ulviet son of Forne was a hereditary lawman of the city in 1106, and Ralph and Thomas, who were apparently Ulviet's sons, were clearly men of property. Ralph held land and houses in York, as Thomas did; but the latter also acquired land held by military service from Amfrid de Chancy and paid Henry I a hunting horse in 1130 to be confirmed as alderman of the York gild merchant. This need carry no implication that either Thomas or his progenitors were merchants: rather, like William Cauvel of Canterbury and Sortebrand of Lincoln, he seems to belong to a property-owning ministerial class which, even when possessed of country estates, played leading parts in the running of towns.[94]

Some of the moneyers to be found in the Domesday boroughs appear to have been men of a similar type. Minting was not organized everywhere in the same way. In some cases the burgesses took responsibility for the operations of the mint in their town for a fixed annual payment to the king, while in others the moneyers themselves 'farmed' the mint in a similar manner and in others again the moneyers simply owed a payment to the king on the occasion of the regular recoinages. At the same time, the Anglo-Saxon word *mynetere* appears to have been used for two distinct types of person. It designated either a craftsman who actually struck the coins or a man, probably of higher standing, who organized and supervised

---

[93] *Dd*, I, ff. 336–6d, 368d, 370d, 376–6d; Foster and Longley, eds, *The Lincolnshire Domesday*, p. xxix; Hill, *Medieval Lincoln*, pp. 31, 40.
[94] *VCH City of York*, pp. 21, 32.

the process of minting.[95] One royal moneyer of this latter type about whom something is known was Deorman, a member of a family of moneyers active in London from Æthelred's reign (979–1013) to the twelfth century. It is perhaps an indication of his ministerial position that he appears in the Hertfordshire Domesday among the king's thegns and that the Conqueror referred to him as his 'man'. Royal appreciation of his services, as well perhaps as shrewd investment, may account for the fact that Deorman figures in Domesday as a holder of property: possibly at Colchester, and certainly at Islington (Middlesex) and at Watton and Walkern (Herts.). Appreciation of him, however, was not restricted to the king, for he was a tenant of the archbishop of Canterbury at Keston (Kent) and was probably the *Dirman* entered in a list of the archbishop's knights at the end of the eleventh century. His grandson eventually married a kinswoman of the first earl of Pembroke, but Deorman's own utility to Archbishop Lanfranc is likely to have been as a man of business rather than a soldier.[96]

Other members of this ministerial class make fleeting appearances in the records. Algar, who had held Islington before Deorman, had been 'King Edward's man' and a London moneyer; the Confessor's goldsmith, Theodoric, was listed in 1086 among the king's thegns or 'ministers' with estates in Surrey, Berkshire and Oxfordshire;[97] and Odo of Winchester, who may have been a moneyer and, from his name, have occupied a ministerial position in that city, had by 1086 acquired a solid territorial base. As a king's thegn he held some eight estates in Hampshire, Berkshire and Wiltshire, as well as borough property in Southampton, Cricklade and Winchester itself.[98] Men like these clearly played an important part in the life of towns, even though its details are difficult to discern. Their weight in town affairs, however, was occasionally recognized. Thomas son of Ulviet and William Cauvel seem to have headed the gilds merchant at York and Canterbury; and one of Deorman's sons, another moneyer called Ordgar, in 1125 was a

---

[95] Loyn, *Anglo-Saxon England and the Norman Conquest*, pp. 129–30; for this and what follows, P. Nightingale, 'Some London moneyers and references to the organization of English mints in the eleventh century', *Numismatic Chron.*, CXLII (1982), pp. 38–50.
[96] *Dd*, I, f. 142; *Regesta*, I, no. 84; D.C. Douglas, ed., *The Domesday Monachorum of Christ Church, Canterbury*, pp. 62–3, 105.
[97] *Dd*, I, ff. 36d, 63, 160d.
[98] Biddle, ed., *Winchester in the Early Middle Ages*, p. 421; *Dd*, I, ff. 44d, 49d, 52, 63d, 73d.

member of the London *cnihtengild*, 'burgesses of London from that old descent of noble English knights'.[99]

This ministerial class, of course, was a small minority only in the ranks of burgesses; and most burgesses were increasingly clearly differentiated from villagers despite the fact that many towns had fields and many townsfolk had close ties with country places. This differentiation was a matter not only of the occupations which predominantly engaged townsmen and villagers, but also of their status and obligations. Burgesses, unlike many villagers, seem to have been regarded as freeholders, even though at Tamworth some burgesses owed labour services at Drayton Bassett (Staffs.) like the villeins of that manor. It was perhaps more compatible with freedom that some Oxford burgesses owed military service, and perhaps even that some Shrewsbury men acted as guards for the king when he visited that town or assisted him when he went hunting.[100] Burgesses also, of course, paid general taxes like virtually everyone else; but their principal obligations were the payment of money rents for their burgages to the king, a private lord or both, judicial penalties, and tolls on trading or the transit of merchandise. It is in this respect that they are representative of that cash economy which was focused particularly upon boroughs and their markets.

Domesday Book offers no very coherent picture about the customary rules governing borough communities, but the conclusion has been drawn that 'all the essential features which distinguished the burgess tenure of the middle ages had been developed in the Old English borough'.[101] Burgages seem usually to have been heritable, and indeed one of the promises the Conqueror made to the Londoners was that 'every child shall be his father's heir after his father's day'. It also appears that such tenements were alienable, even if (as at Hereford) sales had to be effected through the king's reeve. Both heritability and alienability, and an indication of the scale of the property market, are implied by the Gloucester survey of c. 1100, showing that 97 of the king's burgesses were living in inherited houses and a similar number in houses which they had bought. Even at that date we must not underrate the scale of the market for town properties.[102]

[99] *EHD*, II, pp. 950–1.
[100] *Dd*, I, ff. 154, 246d, 252.
[101] Stenton, *Anglo-Saxon England*, pp. 522–3.
[102] *EHD*, II, p. 945; *Dd*, I, f. 179; Ellis, *General Introduction to Domesday Book*, II, p. 446.

(d) Borough administration

A precise picture of how towns were managed is no more easily
obtainable from Domesday and other contemporary sources than
any clear impression of borough society. Some of them, as we have
seen, were still federations of settlements rather than coherent communities; and even where that was not so it was common for the
king to share administrative powers, and the profits from them, with
other lords. At Canterbury, for example, the king's jurisdiction did
not extend to the property of the cathedral or St Augustine's abbey;
and at York the archbishop had 'full custom' and 'as much as the
king has in his own shires' from one of the seven shires into which
the city was divided. At Lincoln and Stamford, moreover, the lawmen had similar immunities in respect of their own houses and
tenants; and at Oxford in 1086 Robert d'Oilly's 42 inhabited houses
seem to have been held as one manor together with the church of St
Peter-in-the-East. Privileged urban estates like this are most evident
in London. Some landowners like Chertsey abbey enjoyed jurisdiction over their city property by pre-Conquest royal concessions; and
we may suspect that the Ealdred who gave his name to Aldersgate
and the Billing who gave his name to Billingsgate had enjoyed similar liberties. These franchises represented 'a most formidable
obstacle to any ubiquitous city jurisdiction'.[103]

In most boroughs, however, the principal authority by 1066, and
therefore the main share of the profit that flowed from it, belonged
to the king. The earls of the districts in which boroughs were situated in many cases continued to receive a share of the revenue from
boroughs, but any authority they had possessed in them had long
been weakening; while that of the sheriffs, increasingly the king's
most important administrative representatives in the localities, had
probably grown. Within boroughs, however, the most continuously
present representative of royal authority is likely to have been the
portreeve. Much of his authority was financial. Generally what a borough owed to the king had been formalized as a fixed round sum
per year, a 'farm': to secure the resources to pay it the portreeve collected the various charges due from the town and townsfolk, and
sometimes paid the earl his share of the town revenues before paying the king's portion to the sheriff or even directly to the king

---

[103] *Dd*, I, ff. 2, 158, 298; Harmer, ed., *Anglo-Saxon Writs*, no. 43; D.M. Stenton, ed.,
Preparatory to Anglo-Saxon England, pp. 33–4.

himself.[104] Because he was a finance officer the portreeve figures in the records from time to time for his extortions. At Canterbury, if the Norman portreeve was castigated by Archbishop Anselm for having moved the market, his English predecessor was remembered for having levied 'custom' from exempt church property; and at Gloucester in c. 1100 both sheriff and portreeve were said to have taken illegal exactions for their own profit over and above those lawfully owed to the king.[105]

An important source of the revenues which kings derived from boroughs was the penalties and forfeitures imposed by courts; and, as the officer responsible for their collection, the portreeve was a natural officer for whatever courts were held in boroughs. The nature of these courts is often far from clear. At Cambridge, in the late tenth century, those present included not only the lawmen and the citizens, but *hundredani* (perhaps countrymen from the surrounding hundreds); and the court's business extended to dealing with titles to land outside the city and even in the Isle of Ely.[106] By 1066, on the other hand, many boroughs had courts which may properly be described as borough courts, mostly 'hundredal courts adapted to the needs of burgesses' and thus fitting the growing urban communities into a local government pattern to which the West Saxon monarchy gave a measure of national uniformity.[107] Burghal developments from King Alfred's time onwards helped to elevate the status of portreeves as the king's ministers within boroughs. When *burhs* were links in a defensive network, it is not surprising to find a thegn acting as the reeve of Winchester; and it is hardly less surprising that a Norman knight was the reeve of Canterbury when the Normans were still consolidating their hold on England. Our few scraps of information about the early reeves of London perhaps have similar implications. One of them in c. 1054 witnessed a charter in the company of the bishop and many thegns from within and without the city; the portreeve of London may also have been sheriff of Middlesex even in Edward the Confessor's first years; and after the Conquest a Norman baron as notable as Geoffrey de Mandeville seems to have been both portreeve of London and sheriff of Middlesex.[108]

---

[104] Tait, *Medieval English Borough*, pp. 143–8.
[105] Urry, *Canterbury under the Angevin Kings*, p. 83; Ballard, ed., *An Eleventh-Century Inquisition*, pp. 7–8; Ellis, *General Introduction to Domesday Book*, II, p. 446.
[106] Blake, ed., *Liber Eliensis*, pp. 83, 88, 97; Tait, *Medieval English Borough*, pp. 41–3.
[107] *Ibid.*, pp. 46–62.
[108] Robertson, ed., *Anglo-Saxon Charters*, no. 116; Harmer, ed., *Anglo-Saxon Writs*, p. 50; Brooke and Keir, *London 800–1216*, pp. 193–4.

Portreeves, therefore, were often neither bourgeois nor representative of the burgesses: in principle they were officers of the king. This did not mean that burgesses lacked a capacity for self-expression. Domesday tells us that the burgesses of Sandwich and Wallingford 'testified' on certain matters, and that the burgesses of York and all the burgesses of Lincoln 'said' certain things. They also complained loudly and clearly: the burgesses of Nottingham that they were no longer allowed to fish in the Trent, and the English burgesses of Shrewsbury because it was 'very hard on them' that they had to pay as much tax as formerly despite the destruction of many houses and the exemptions accorded to French settlers in the town and to the burgesses the earl had given to his newly founded abbey. Before 1066, too, the burgesses of Lincoln collectively witnessed Earl Leofric's endowment of the minster at Stow St Mary's, and in 1086 the burgesses of Oxford held their pasture outside the walls *communiter*.[109] Towns evidently had a degree of corporate potentiality: there was a 'gildhall of the burgesses' at Dover and perhaps some sort of embryonic borough treasury there to account for the profits of justice in the town which the king had granted to the burgesses in return for an undertaking to do naval service; Northampton, too, perhaps had some sort of financial organization, for the burgesses there seem to have been responsible for paying over to the county sheriff the borough's 'farm'; and in a number of places lawmen or *judices* or *seniores*, empowered to declare what the law was on particular issues, did much to shape the custom of their boroughs.[110] All this does not take us far along the road to the corporate borough, but even in this world in which lordship dominated a few hesitant steps had already been taken.

4. CONQUEST AND CONSEQUENCES

The economic effects of the Norman Conquest in those areas with which this volume is concerned were frequently contradictory. Some, immediately at least, were adverse. Conquest, almost inevitably, entailed some dislocation of economic life at home, relations

---

[109] Welldon Finn, *Introduction to Domesday Book*, p. 67; *Dd*, i, ff. 3, 56, 154, 252, 280, 298, 336; Robertson, ed., *Anglo-Saxon Charters*, no. 115.
[110] S. Reynolds, 'Towns in Domesday Book', in Holt, ed., *Domesday Studies*, pp. 306–7; *Dd*, i, ff. 1, 219; Tait, *Medieval English Borough*, pp. 119–20, 123–9.

with the Baltic lands were initially hostile, and those with Flanders were scarcely better. Some branches of commerce suffered, therefore, and so did production as a consequence of rebellions and military campaigns. The salt output of the Cheshire wiches in 1086 was worth less than a third of its value in 1066.[111] Nor were the new masters of the English towns necessarily enlightened urban landlords. Their limited aristocratic notion of what a town was – a fortress and little more – is illustrated by the depiction of places like Rennes in the Bayeux tapestry as settlements reduced to a tower or castle set on the summit of a motte. Apart from that, the king and magnates were as avaricious in their dealings with townsfolk as with their rural tenants. Time and time again what towns paid was increased even when they had suffered much damage since the Confessor's time. Between 1066 and 1086 what Totnes paid was increased from £3 to £8 and what Hertford paid from £7 10s. to £20; Oxford in 1066 owed £20 and six sesters of honey together with a further £10 for Earl Ælfgar's mill, but by 1086 it was paying £60 yearly; and the value of Buckingham had gone up from £10 to £16 even though Buckingham was 'as primitive as any county borough could be'. The Normans tightened the screw on their urban properties just as they did on many of their rural manors, and both got hard terms from King William and his followers.[112]

Town property, moreover, was as liable as country property to damage and forcible expropriation at the hands of the conquerors, especially in the course of the many troubles marking the early Norman years. Picot, the sheriff of Cambridgeshire, was not only a notable plunderer of Ely abbey: he seized some of the common pasture of the burgesses of Cambridge and then abstracted more in order to build three mills. At Norwich, too, the oppressions of the sheriff, Waleran, were perhaps one of the reasons for some burgesses fleeing the city for Beccles and other places, although Earl Ralph's forfeiture, fires and the king's taxes were contributory causes of their departure and the 'wasting' of their houses. A still commoner cause of 'waste' houses was their demolition to clear sites for castles, those fortresses within burghal fortresses needed to overawe a conquered land. At York one of the city's seven 'shires' was totally 'wasted' to accommodate two Norman castles, and apparently

[111] Lewis, *The Northern Seas*, pp. 470–3; Darby, *Domesday England*, p. 261.
[112] J. Le Goff, ed., *La France urbaine*, II, p. 44; *Dd*, I, ff. 108d, 132, 143, 154; H.C. Darby and E.M.G. Campbell, *Domesday Geography of South-East England*, pp. 178–9; Garmonsway, trans., *The Anglo-Saxon Chronicle*, p. 218.

1,029 out of 1,607 messuages were wholly or partially 'waste' in 1086. York's involvement in northern rebellions and Scandinavian invasions, of course, made it especially unfortunate; but many other places had fewer occupied houses in 1086 than in 1066. At Exeter 48 houses had been destroyed since the king's coming to England; at Oxford 478 houses were 'so wasted and destroyed that they cannot pay geld'; at Shrewsbury 51 messuages had been taken over for the earl's castle and another 50 were 'waste'. Ipswich is unlikely to have been the only town where some burgesses had been turned into 'poor burgesses' who 'can only pay towards the king's geld one penny per head'.[113]

Urban contraction, however, was neither universal nor necessarily of long duration. In the south-east, perhaps as a result of closer commercial links with France, numbers of houses and burgesses seemingly increased between 1066 and 1086 at Pevensey, Sandwich and Chichester; the value of tolls at Dover grew almost threefold; a new borough was established at Rye; and 65 Frenchmen and 31 Englishmen were newly settled at Southampton. Town growth, too, was soon resumed at Winchester, fostered by heavy investment in building and by royal expenditure in a place where King William regularly 'wore his royal crown . . . as often as he was in England'.[114] There were similar signs of urban progress in other parts of the country. The Domesday burgesses at Tewkesbury look like newcomers and by 1086 castle boroughs were developing at Clifford and Wigmore; French burgesses had reinforced the remaining Englishmen at Gloucester, Shrewsbury and Norwich; if there were 'waste' messuages at Nottingham and Northampton, 'new boroughs' had been added to the existing settlements there; at Bury St Edmunds agricultural land had been diverted to urban use, and at Lincoln Colsuain had built two churches and 36 houses on 'waste land which the king gave him'. Long-term urban growth seems to have been resumed by 1086 in many, and perhaps in most, parts of the country.[115]

---

[113] *Dd*, I, ff. 100, 154, 189, 252, 298; II, ff. 117d, 290; *VCH City of York*, p. 22. Counting urban dwellings in Domesday is, of course, a hazardous exercise, but an impression of the short-term effects of the Conquest on towns can be got from C. Stephenson's list of urban *mansiones* in 1066 and 1086: *Borough and Town*, p. 221.

[114] *Dd*, I, ff. 2, 17, 17d, 23, 52; Darby, *Domesday England*, pp. 299–300; Garmonsway, trans., *The Anglo-Saxon Chronicle*, p. 219; M. Biddle, 'Early Norman Winchester', in Holt, ed., *Domesday Studies*, pp. 328–9.

[115] *Dd*, I, ff. 163d, 183–3d, 219, 252, 280, 336d; II, f. 118; Ellis, *General Introduction to Domesday Book*, II, p. 446; Hill, *Medieval Lincoln*, pp. 48, 133–4.

That this should be so is in no way inexplicable. Domesday manorial values in 1086 were often higher than they had been in the
early days of Norman rule or even in the Confessor's day, reflecting
not only the Norman avarice of which the Anglo-Saxon chronicler
complained but also their capacity, as conquerors, to revise relationships in rural society to their own advantage. Since landowners were
the principal spending classes, the increased revenues they could
wring from their estates were likely to result in an increased aggregate demand for the commodities which craftsmen and merchants
could provide. Not surprisingly, therefore, there were soon signs of
boroughs growing up at castle gates and, in existing boroughs, of
compensatory development to make good some of the housing lost
to make room for castles or for other reasons. At Nottingham, for
example, the sheriff 'established 13 houses on the earl's land, which
were not there before, in the new borough', and apparently located
in the space between the old borough and the castle; and it seems
likely that the 48 merchants' houses, together with dwellings for
knights and bordars, belonging to William Peverel were in the same
area, for William was constable of the castle.[116] The church also contributed to a rising demand for urban goods and services. Many old
monastic communities grew, in some cases quite dramatically, in the
years which followed the Conquest, and among new foundations
were those at Selby, Shrewsbury, Chester, Spalding, Colchester and,
of course, Battle. Monasteries, like rich men's households and feudal garrisons, made demands upon the sorts of provision that towns
could supply. The new urban development at Bury St Edmunds
accommodated a group 'waiting on St Edmund, the abbot and the
brothers', and by *c.* 1114 a very similar group of burgesses was established at Battle abbey's gate.[117]

The development of England's overseas commerce had also been
resumed without too much delay after the Conquest. The resumption of urban growth in the south-east and the establishment of
French burgesses in a number of English boroughs point in all
probability to strengthened commercial ties within the cross-
Channel Norman 'empire' which the Conquest had created. The

[116] *Dd*, I, f. 280; Stephenson, *Borough and Town*, pp. 196–7; Beresford and St Joseph, *Medieval England: an Aerial Survey*, pp. 176–8; W. Barley and I.F. Straw, 'Nottingham', in Lobel, ed., *Atlas of Historic Towns*, I, pp. 2–3.
[117] D. Knowles, *The Monastic Order in England: a History of its Development from the Times of St Dunstan to the Fourth Lateran Council, 943–1216*, pp. 126–9; Beresford and St Joseph, *Medieval England: an Aerial Survey*, pp. 215–17; E. Searle, *Lordship and Community*, pp. 69–76.

importance of these ties, indeed, may initially have been enhanced by comparison with those with Flanders, the Rhineland and Scandinavia. None of these connections, however, was ever totally severed; and that with Flanders and the Rhineland was old and well-established, it had been reinforced in 1044 when St Peter's abbey in Ghent acquired Warmsacre on the London waterfront, and it drew strength from the fact that the post-1066 ruling class included significant elements from Flanders and Lorraine. By Rufus's reign relations with Flanders were again close, at the opening of the twelfth century Flemish merchants were making regular voyages to England to buy wool, and in 1127 communications with Flanders were good enough for news of the murder of Count Charles the Good to have shocked Londoners only two days after it happened.[118]

Ultimately, therefore, the Norman Conquest served to strengthen the economic tendencies which had been at work in England since the late ninth century: urban growth, increased specialization in trade and manufacture, more production (including more agricultural production) directed towards markets. To measure how far these tendencies had gone by 1086 is another matter. It has been suggested that the volume of currency in circulation at different points in time might provide an index of their progress, but attempts to establish what the money supply was have not achieved total agreement and, in any case, the implications of these estimates are themselves debatable.[119] At first sight the proportion of the Domesday population living in towns might appear to be a more hopeful indicator, and one 'liberal' estimate puts this at around one Englishman in ten.[120] Even if that figure could be accepted with confidence, however, it would probably be wrong to regard it as a measure of that part of the population engaged in the commercial, industrial and service occupations which would ultimately be regarded as characteristically urban. The borough entries in Domesday are haphazard and incomplete; a proportion of borough

---

[118] P. Grierson, 'England and Flanders before the Norman Conquest', *TRHS*, 4th ser. XXIII (1941), pp. 104–5; 'Miracula S. Mariae Laudunensis', in J.P. Migne, ed., *Patrologia Latina*, 217 vols, Paris, 1844–55, CLV, cols 975–7; Galbert of Bruges, *The Murder of Charles the Good, Count of Flanders*, trans. J.B. Ross, New York, 1967, p. 113.

[119] P.H. Sawyer, 'The wealth of England in the eleventh century', *TRHS*, 5th ser. XV (1965), pp. 153–9; but see P. Grierson's cautionary remarks, 'The volume of Anglo-Saxon coinage', *EcHR*, 2nd ser. XX (1967), pp. 157–60.

[120] Sawyer, 'The wealth of England', pp. 163–4; Loyn, *Anglo-Saxon England and the Norman Conquest*, p. 398.

inhabitants had interests that at least in part were agricultural; and an unknowable number of countrymen depended to some degree upon trade and industry for their livelihoods. What can be said is, that if one-tenth of the Domesday population were townsmen, while this is low compared with modern industrial societies, it is relatively high for the agrarian societies of the middle ages. The implication seems to be that the development of town life and of an exchange economy, as it is summed up in Domesday, had been substantial.

At the same time, one result of the Norman Conquest was some strengthening of the influence of the dominant landowning class in towns. Their urban property rights were often extended in the aftermath of conquest. Even before 1066, too, a few towns had effectively been private boroughs subject to ecclesiastical lordship: Bury St Edmunds, Durham, St Albans, Fordwich given to St Augustine's abbey, Canterbury, and Sandwich controlled by Canterbury cathedral priory. Private lordship over boroughs, including some former royal boroughs, was extended under the new Norman rulers. The Conqueror relinquished Totnes to Judhael, and Rufus granted away Bath, Warwick and Northampton.[121] Still commoner were private borough foundation, especially as we have seen in connection with new Norman castles and new monastic foundations. The capacity of Norman magnates to harness for their own advantage the forces making for urban growth was also illustrated at Launceston in Cornwall. The Domesday settlement of that name, which had possessed a market and at least at times a mint, belonged to the canons of St Stephen's, but before 1086 the count of Mortain moved the market to his castle at *Dunhevet* more than half a mile away. In the mid-twelfth century the older settlement was still claimed by the canons to be a 'free borough'; but in fact it was around the count's castle and market that the medieval town of Launceston grew up.[122] The Norman kings preserved much of the lordship their Old English predecessors had possessed in the older English boroughs; but especially in new towns private urban lordship had made undoubted progress by the end of the eleventh century.

---

[121] *Ibid.*, pp. 390–1; Robertson, ed., *Anglo-Saxon Charters*, no. 91; *Dd*, I, f. 108d; Tait, *Medieval English Borough*, pp. 140–1, 154–5.
[122] R.C. van Caenegem, ed., *English Lawsuits from William I to Richard I*, I, no. 332; *Dd*, I, ff. 120d, 121d; Beresford and St Joseph, *Medieval England: an Aerial Survey*, pp. 220–2; M.W. Beresford, *New Towns of the Middle Ages*, pp. 180, 216.

5. THE KING'S RIGHTS AND THE DOMESDAY ECONOMY

The authority which the Norman kings inherited in the boroughs endowed them with some powers of economic intervention in the commercial and industrial life of the country, although their scope to do so was narrow because their stake in the boroughs consisted very largely of proprietary rights in the exercise of which fiscal considerations were apt to predominate. At the same time, two other royal rights had more general economic implications. The first was royal control of the 'managed currency' of late Anglo-Saxon England. In the exercise of that control fiscal considerations might be brought to bear, for in the frequent recoinages before 1066 more coins were often struck from a given weight of silver, yielding a profit to the king's treasury. At the same time these recoinages made possible an adjustment of the currency to the changing values of bullion and seem to have displayed a measure of sensitivity to international parities in north-western Europe. In these respects royal monetary policies served England's international economic needs while, at the same time, providing the country with a very substantial money supply for that day. One estimate puts it at a circulating medium worth £60,000–£80,000 early in the eleventh century, although at that time it may have been inflated by the need to provide enough coin for the payment of very heavy taxes. In the Conqueror's time the value of the coin in circulation may have been less, and was perhaps worth £25,000–£37,500. Even so, a large part of the population paid taxes to William I, although perhaps at a somewhat lower rate than under Æthelred II and Cnut, and after taxes were paid there was a currency balance available for the market needs of the domestic exchange economy.[123] At the same time, in one respect the Conqueror made a change in the Confessor's policies. He continued to order recoinages at frequent intervals, but he abandoned alterations in the silver content of the coins his mints issued. Because those alterations had yielded a profit he did not, of course, abandon them gratuitously. In return for his refraining to

---

[123] Stenton, ed., *Preparatory to Anglo-Saxon England*, p. 374; Grierson, 'The volume of Anglo-Saxon coinage', pp. 159–60; Sawyer, 'The wealth of England', p. 153; J. Campbell, 'Observations on English government from the tenth to the twelfth centuries', *TRHS*, 5th ser. xxv (1975), pp. 39–41; Nightingale, 'The evolution of weight standards', pp. 194–201; D.M. Metcalf, 'Continuity and change in English monetary history, *c.* 973–1086', *British Numismatic Jnl.*, L (1980), pp. 20–49; LI (1981), pp. 52–90. On these matters we are much indebted to N.K. Mayhew's counsel.

exercise an established royal right he levied a new tax, the common *monetagium*, in boroughs and counties alike. It is not a tax about which we know much, for Henry I abolished it in 1100 as part of the package of concessions which secured him the throne. The Conqueror, however, honoured his promise that the standard of the currency would be preserved, as did his successors. England in consequence, very unusually in the Europe of those days, enjoyed a period of currency stability lasting until 1279.[124]

The king's control over money in one sense was a fiscal authority, one of his sources of revenue, although other sources were much more important. Probably most important for William I, as for other members of the Norman ruling class, were agricultural estates. In 1086 there was *terra regis* in every county the Domesday commissioners surveyed except Cheshire and Shropshire. These estates furnished the king with revenue in cash or kind, or as at Houghton Regis (Beds.) in both: for Houghton owed the king, in addition to some 'small customs', a sum of £30 each year, and provisions, in the form of wheat, honey and other things, sufficient to supply the court for half a day.[125] This royal land fund in the long run was something of a wasting asset, for royal lands were granted away to subjects to buy service or political support and to churches to secure the salvation of royal souls. In the Conqueror's time, however, this may not have seemed a pressing concern: the king's demesnes were swollen by confiscated estates, so that he had much more land than the Confessor had possessed. In addition King William, as a conqueror, was less likely than his predecessor to feel restraints of custom upon the way he managed the lands he kept: indeed, like other Norman lords, he was said to have 'farmed his land as dearly as he might'. Royal grants of land, therefore, did much to shape the structure of landowning society in Norman England, while the king's own demands as a landlord influenced the prosperity of numerous peasant villagers. His lordship, moreover, extended over most of the developing towns, so that his fiscal exactions also influenced the fortunes of townsfolk; and the fact that this lordship was so firmly based and in large measure preserved by the Conqueror, at least in the more important towns, gave the monarchy an exceptional influence over town development in medieval England compared to other western lands.

---

[124] D.J.A. Matthew, *The Norman Conquest*, 1966, pp. 250–2; P. Grierson, 'Sterling', in R.H.M. Dolley, ed., *Anglo-Saxon Coins*, pp. 274–5; *EHD*, II, p. 401.
[125] *Dd*, I, f. 209d.

A second unique royal right, in addition to control over money, inherited and preserved by the Conqueror was one exceptional in the contemporary west, a right to levy what Domesday called 'the common geld . . . from which no man escapes' – a general direct tax on the community at large.[126] The geld, as it appears in Domesday Book, was a property tax for which both towns and rural areas were rated at so many taxable units (hides, carucates, sulungs), the unit depending on the part of the country in which a place lay. Individual landholders and property owners contributed towards the total sum demanded of their town or village according to their share of the community's assets. The development of this system to the point at which the Normans took it over is imperfectly documented and therefore imperfectly known; but, while it absorbed a number of earlier elements, it seems to have been a response to Scandinavian attacks on England in the late tenth and early eleventh centuries, and particularly the need to raise large sums to buy off the invaders. If the Anglo-Saxon Chronicle is to be believed, some of these figures were very large indeed – imposts that were so heavy that they were 'fully capable of transmuting a whole nation'. Not surprisingly they have generated much discussion, the details of which have no place here.[127] In any case, before the Norman Conquest the system was subject to a variety of modifications. Under Cnut geld was levied regularly, or at least frequently, to finance the consolidation of the Anglo-Danish state and, in particular, its military and naval forces. It became in fact an army tax (heregeld) rather than danegeld, a tax to buy off invaders. It continued to be a tax which 'oppressed all the English people' until in 1051 Edward the Confessor is said to have abolished it; but whether its suspension was of long duration is a matter of some doubt. It was recalled in 1086 how payment was made when 'the geld was given in King Edward's time commonly throughout Berkshire'; and certainly the Conqueror collected it, periodically and perhaps even annually.[128]

---

[126] *Ibid.*, f. 30.

[127] For recent contributions to the long-running debate about the plausibility of these figures, see M.K. Lawson, 'Levels of taxation in the reigns of Æthelred II and Cnut', *EHR*, CIV (1989), pp. 385–406; *idem*, 'Danegeld and heregeld once more', *EHR*, CV (1990), pp. 951–61; J. Gillingham, 'Levels of danegeld and heregeld in the early eleventh century', *EHR*, CIV (1989), pp. 373–84; and *idem*, 'Chronicles and coins as evidence for levels of tribute and taxation in late tenth- and early eleventh-century England', *EHR*, CV (1990), pp. 939–50.

[128] P. Vinogradoff, *English Society in the Eleventh Century*, p. 141; *EHD*, II, p. 120; F. Barlow, *Edward the Confessor*, pp. 106, 155; *Dd*, I, f. 56d; J.A. Green, 'The last century of danegeld', *EHR*, XCVI (1981), pp. 241–2.

The geld, therefore, continued to oppress all the English people, especially when, as in 1083–4, it was a 'great and heavy tax' taken at the rate of 6s. on the hide. The Conqueror, in consequence, faced demands from powerful men and from devastated districts for its reduction or even abolition, and in fact by 1086 'sweeping reductions' of liability had often been achieved. Some tenants-in-chief, in particular, seem to have secured exemption both for their manorial demesnes and for all who lived on their demesne manors.[129] Concessions of this sort, moreover, were not new in 1083–4. A Northamptonshire geld account, probably dating from the 1070s, shows that the county's assessment had already been cut from its early eleventh-century level by some 18 per cent before 1066; and after the Conquest about one-third of this reduced liability was remitted because 'inland' (seignorial demesnes) was exempted from tax. Similarly, in the south-western counties in 1085–6 exemptions reduced the total by 31 per cent from what it would have been in earlier days, and less than two-thirds of that total was actually collected. Not surprisingly the processes of collecting this particular levy had to be supplemented by a special 'geld inquest' conducted by the Domesday commissioners, or that Bishop Robert of Hereford lamented that 'the whole land was vexed by calamities coming from the collection of the king's money'.[130]

The conclusion to be drawn therefore, is that the efficiency of the fiscal system which the Normans inherited should not be exaggerated, even though it may have had 'no parallel in the Dark Ages'.[131] The capacity of the landowning classes to secure their own advantage limited its effectiveness, their ability to do so strengthened by the fact that the monarchy depended upon their political and military support, and by the absence of any sense that paying taxes was any part of the service they owed the king. In the Conqueror's time there were some 'superficial attempts at revision' of assessments, but nonetheless the potential yield of the geld continued to fall. This, at least in part, was the background of a remarkable enterprise for its time, the Domesday survey. It established and put on record for most of England the ownership and value of agricultural estates,

---

[129] *EHD*, II, p. 160; S. Painter, *Studies in the History of the English Feudal Barony*, pp. 74–5; S.P.J. Harvey, 'Taxation and the economy', in Holt, ed., *Domesday Studies*, pp. 257–60.

[130] J.H. Round, *Feudal England*, pp. 231–7; Welldon Finn, *Domesday Studies: the Liber Exoniensis*, pp. 105–10; V.H. Galbraith, *The Making of Domesday Book*, 1961, pp. 43, 88, 91–6.

[131] Stenton, *Anglo-Saxon England*, p. 640.

and a more disjointed evaluation of the king's stake in urban communities; and it may have been intended to provide the information necessary for 'a new fiscal rating system to raise taxation in a more effective manner'.[132] It is probably anachronistic to suggest, on the basis of much sophisticated statistical analysis, that in Domesday Anglo-Norman government displayed a capacity to 'assess and record the taxable capacity of English manors accurately';[133] but hard-headed English jurors were perhaps capable of making a reasonable estimate of the value and potentialities of their own neighbourhoods, even if they were inclined conveniently to conclude that a hide of land was worth £1. In the event, however, the Domesday inquest failed to change the basis of geld assessments, which continued to be founded on manorial assessments which Domesday put on record and which go back, with some modifications, to the late Anglo-Saxon rating system. It may, on the other hand, have checked the headlong pace of exemptions in the early Norman years and set limits to the erosion of taxable values revealed by the geld accounts of that time.[134]

The Norman kings, therefore, retained the power to tax won by the Old English rulers. Henry I used that power regularly, and in 1129–30 the geld raised some £2,400, about 10 per cent of the receipts of his exchequer that year. This was a modest sum compared with monstrous tributes collected in the early eleventh century, but it was still not a contribution to the king's financial needs to be despised.[135] The way the Norman kings exercised this power, however, had social and economic results which were undesigned and unforeseen. The exemptions secured by landlords transferred an increasing share of the tax burden especially to the peasantry; and in combination with 'avaricious' demands for higher rents and heavier services this depressed their fortunes to an extent which may still be remembered in the popular seventeenth-century notion that conquerors imposed a 'Norman yoke' upon the country. Even Domesday Book at times suggests that manors and manorial tenants were excessively exploited. It was something which might

---

[132] Harvey, 'Domesday Book and Anglo-Norman governance', pp. 181–3.
[133] J. McDonald and G.D. Snooks, 'Were the tax assessments of Domesday artificial? The case of Essex', *EcHR*, 2nd ser. xxxviii (1985), pp. 352–72
[134] Harvey, 'Taxation and the economy', pp. 251–2; Green, 'The last century of danegeld', pp. 243–52.
[135] *Ibid.*, pp. 252–4.

concern the king since it could affect their capacity to contribute to his taxes.[136]

6. THE ANGLO-SAXON LEGACY

The features of the Domesday economy which have been the principal concerns of this chapter, of course, in no way call in question the fact that Norman England rested upon overwhelmingly rural foundations. As many as nine out of ten persons may have been country folk whose labours were devoted primarily to satisfying their own subsistence needs from the land they cultivated; many of the greatest men of the kingdom depended directly upon the produce of their estates for many of their consumption requirements; the bishops and monastic communities serving the great churches were no less rooted in the soil and local churches were sustained, at least in part, by tithes of agricultural produce; and many of the services needed by government and subjects alike were purchased not with money but by concessions of land. Yet eleventh-century England, as we have seen, was a wealthy country by the standards of the time; its inhabitants were involved in trade both locally and internationally, and in manufacturing aimed at both local and wider markets; and towns and boroughs had developed, at least in part, as centres of non-agricultural economic life. These sectors of the economy, moreover, had been expanding, along with the country's agricultural base and the number of its people, since King Alfred's day. By the tenth century, too, there was a national currency, the provision of which had become an accepted royal function; and by the end of that century a national system of taxation, capable of producing large sums for the crown, was in place. Both illustrate the fact that, in the England the Normans conquered, elements of a money economy had penetrated deep into society, even though many goods were still got by barter and, for many things and not least for land, men paid by service rather than in cash.

These last features of the Domesday economy are indications of the fact that the commercialization of English society had progressed only so far, with much still to be achieved in the proliferation and expansion of markets and towns, in the scale and

---

[136] Harvey, 'Taxation and the economy', pp. 256, 262–3.

regularity of trading contacts, and in the quantity and diversity of the commodities that were produced, bought and sold. In the course of the two and a half centuries after the Domesday inquest the population of England grew approximately threefold to a level which may not have been surpassed until the eighteenth century. In order to support so many people, an achievement remarkable in itself, economic advances which were qualitative as well as quantitative were requisite. The expansion of the agricultural economy, an essential element in these advances, was surveyed in the first volume of this work; but the provision of new marketing facilities and incentives to increase production which went beyond the satisfaction of the consumption needs of those who worked on the land were no less vital. The development of primary and secondary industries, therefore, the spread of urbanization, improvements in transport, and a growing availability of financial and administrative services were also central features of this period of medieval economic expansion. These non-agrarian elements in England's economy and society between the Conquest and the Black Death constitute the subject matter of the chapters which follow.

CHAPTER TWO
Medieval Industries

The economic environment of the twelfth and thirteenth centuries was in many ways unfavourable to industrial development. Most families depended principally upon agriculture for their living and enjoyed incomes which were commonly low, and which fluctuated with the yield of crops, the fertility of livestock and the visitations of animal diseases. The peasant majority, therefore, disposed of scant surplus resources above what was needed for its subsistence; and rural families, to a much greater extent than in more recent times, were self-suppliers of goods other than foodstuffs. On the other hand, of course, some manufactured or fashioned goods were essential even to the poorest peasant farm or household; and the limited purchasing power of the many was to some extent complemented by the wealth of the few – churches, landowners and in due course rich merchants, who were customers for grand buildings, fine clothing, furred garments, plate and jewellery, arms and armour, even splendid accoutrements for their horses, to say nothing of wines and spices, heavy expenditure upon which was a mark of the truly wealthy.[1] The demands of the rich sucked in manufactured imports (quality textiles, metal goods, pottery, for example); but they also called for English craftsmen of exceptional skills, as well as for men of lesser talents to serve their more basic needs and those of their households.

It is also relevant in this connection that, while before the fourteenth century England sent relatively small quantities of manufactured goods overseas, most of the needs of most English

---

[1] C. Dyer, *Standards of Living in the Later Middle Ages*, pp. 62–3.

folk were satisfied by native products. The long-term growth of the country's total population, therefore, called for an increase of its industrial as well as of its agricultural output. Despite the relative poverty of many villagers and townsfolk, in consequence, everything suggests that the volume of industrial goods being produced in early fourteenth-century England was significantly greater than it had been in early Norman times. Furthermore, because technological advances in industry had been relatively restricted, the handicraft character of most industrial activity remained the rule and increased industrial output called for something like a parallel increase in the number of those employed, full-time or part-time, to achieve it.

It is an altogether different matter, however, to attribute any sort of dimensions to this expansion. The problem is one of evidence. The great record-keeping institutions of the middle ages were the large agricultural estates of the churches and the lay nobility. By contrast, even in the fourteenth century, records kept by merchants, like William de la Pole's wool accounts or Gilbert Maghfeld's ledger, are wholly exceptional survivals. So far as records that have come down to us are concerned, industrial producers, and the merchants who organized some branches of industrial production, are as silent as the medieval peasant. The reasons are straightforward enough: industrial units were normally small, they called for little in the way of managerial staff accounting for their responsibilities, and therefore little record-keeping was entailed. Where records were kept they have seldom survived. Before looking at the indications of development in the various branches of medieval industry, therefore, it may be best to review certain basic characteristics of the medieval industrial scene.

1. SOME CHARACTERISTICS OF MEDIEVAL INDUSTRIES

Some of those characteristics survived only slightly modified in the better documented early modern centuries. Much of Tudor and Stuart industrial production, for instance, continued to be conducted in small-scale units, often literally domestic in character and possessing little in the way of fixed capital. Differentiation between industry and agriculture was also incomplete, for small farmers were sometimes part-time craftsmen and town craftsmen sometimes had agricultural interests. Many industrial producers, too, were also traders, especially for the purpose of marketing their own products.[2] These features of the early modern economy derive from the fact that the markets served by many craftsmen were local and restricted. Whenever markets expanded, calling for an expansion of production, the ways in which production was organized might also need modification.

In the middle ages some insights into the organization of industrial production can be got from the few surviving detailed urban tax assessments, which provide inventories and valuations of goods in the possession of individuals. Of course some goods were doubtless successfully concealed from the taxors and others were officially exempt from taxation, but returns for taxes assessed in 1296 and 1301 at Colchester illustrate the information that can be derived from these records.[3] They suggest, first, that Colchester traders and craftsmen were usually men and women of very modest means. Of those who can be recognized as belonging to these categories in 1301, none had goods worth more than £10, only seven had goods worth more than £5, and about two-thirds had goods worth £1 or less. Secondly, industrial equipment and materials normally made only a small contribution to these valuations. Gilbert Agote, for instance, apparently had some involvement in cloth-making, but his wool stock, fulling shears and wool cards were worth only 10s. out of the total value of £8 13s. 8d. placed on his goods. His household possessions, the grain in his granary, and particularly his horse, pig, two cows, four bullocks and 60 sheep were much more valuable. Obviously Gilbert was more a farmer than a textile worker. Thirdly, capital goods made relatively small contributions to these valuations. A baker's troughs and utensils were worth only 1s. 10d. out of a total assessment of £2 4s. 8d. and a barber's bowls only 3s. 6d. out of a total of £3 4s. 4d. Knives and choppers belonging to one butcher were valued at 6d. and to another at 9d., although those belonging to William Proveale were put at 1s. 4d. and he also had salting tubs worth 1s. 3d. A carpenter's axes, adzes, square and plane were valued at only 1s.; and dyers' vats were worth as much as 2s. 6d. and as little as 9d. While the tools and the stock of iron belonging to

[2] L.A. Clarkson, *The Pre-Industrial Economy of England*,1971, pp. 97–105; G. Unwin, *Industrial Organization in the XVI*[th] *and XVII*[th] *Centuries*, Oxford, 1904, pp. 9–14.
[3] On these records, see J.F. Willard, *Parliamentary Taxes on Personal Property, 1290–1334*, pp. 75–7; and J.F. Hadwin, 'The medieval lay subsidies and economic history', *EcHR*, 2nd ser. XXXVI (1983), pp. 202–3; the Colchester returns are in *Rot. Parl.*, I, pp. 228–36, 243–65.

one smith were valued at £1, the comparable figure for another was only 2s. 6d. Few craftsmen had tools or equipment of any great worth.

Two further impressions are conveyed by the Colchester assessments. One is that a craftsman's place of business was often closely associated with his dwelling. We hear of goods located in a man's house, his chamber and his kitchen, as well as in his tan-yard, brew-house, dye-yard or bakery; but even when separate working premises are noticed they look like an extension of domestic living space. Secondly, it was common for more capital to be tied up in raw materials, or in goods in the process of manufacture or awaiting sale, than in tools and equipment. This was especially true of tanning, inevitably a lengthy process.[4] Hides and bark in one tanner's tan-yard were valued at £1 13s. 4d., in another's at £1 3s. and in those of others at 16s. and £1 10s.; in Henry Pakeman's yard the figure was as high as £4 6s. 8d. By contrast Henry's vats and troughs were valued at only 10s. and those of the other tanners at between 3s. and 6s. 8d. Similar disparities were evident in other crafts. A baker's stock of wheat was worth much more than his 'utensils'; a dyer, with a dye-vat worth 1s. 5d., possessed cloth and wood-ash worth 16s. 8d.; and William Proveale the butcher, whose knives, chopper and salting tubs were worth less than 3s., had meat, tallow, lard and oil in his shop valued at £3 10s. As for a man who made wool combs for textile workers, no value at all was set on his tools, but his stock of wood, iron and finished combs was worth 15s. 8d.

The imprecision of occupational demarcations is equally evident at Colchester. Gilbert Agote seems to have been a small farmer who dabbled in cloth-making, but other taxpayers, who were first and foremost craftsmen, also had some agricultural interests. A baker had a pig and a barber a horse as well, a dyer had a couple of cows, and a smith a heifer, eight sheep, four lambs and two pigs. Nor was the line between crafts and agriculture the only one which was blurred. Ranulf Steleger was principally a butcher, but he also had a stock of wool (with which, perhaps, he set the women of his household to spinning), and barrels and vats for brewing. Spinning and brewing, indeed, were common secondary occupations. Among those with stocks of wool, in addition to weavers and fullers and Margery le Chaloner, were butchers, a glazier and a small-time merchant; and part-time brewers included a baker, a barber, a dyer, a

---

[4] L.A. Clarkson, 'The organization of the English leather industry in the late sixteenth and seventeenth centuries', *EcHR*, 2nd ser. XIII (1960), pp. 246–7.

couple of mercers, a couple of tanners, and the versatile Margery le Chaloner. William Pentecost is also of interest in this connection. His craft is not stated, but his goods included a little wool, a piece of russet cloth, a pair of fuller's shears and a wool card. He may have been a fuller, in which case he undertook other finishing processes, including carding to raise the nap and shearing. He may also have had a loom, for this was one of the items exempted from assessment,[5] in which case his household, like West Riding households in the sixteenth century, may have undertaken all stages of cloth-making from spinning the wool into yarn to finishing the woven cloth.

Colchester, of course, was a relatively small town with a restricted market, conditions which limited the division of labour and the demarcation between industrial processes. These were much more marked in larger towns by the fourteenth century, and most marked of all in London, by far the largest English urban community. There the various stages in producing a given commodity were more likely each to be the province of a distinct craft, so that, in cloth-making for instance, weavers, fullers, shearmen and dyers each had their own role and craft organization. This progress of the division of labour, at the same time, made a co-ordinating role essential. In the London textile industry this was provided in part by the dyers, but more particularly by the burellers. The latter, originally makers of the coarse cloth called burels, were already described in 1225 as 'men of London who *cause burels to be made*', turning the London weavers into their 'piece-work employees'. In a very similar manner the skinners came to employ the tawyers, and the cutlers the sheathers and bladesmiths.[6] This developing hierarchy of crafts, however, did little to alter the essential features of medieval industry: the smallness of most of its individual units, the low levels of fixed capital, its labour intensiveness, its mainly domestic context. There were inevitably differences between the branches of industry, but in the middle ages as in early modern times there was also a good deal of uniformity.[7]

[5] Cf. the peasant's plough: Willard, *Parliamentary Taxes on Personal Property*, p. 80.
[6] Carus-Wilson, *MMV*, pp. 234–5; G. Williams, *Medieval London: from Commune to Capital*, pp. 175–6; G. Unwin, *Gilds and Companies of London*, p. 73.
[7] Clarkson, *The Pre-Industrial Economy of England*, p. 97.

2. SOME INDUSTRIAL RAW MATERIALS: WOOD, LEATHER AND CLAY

Many of the materials craftsmen used were nature's or the farmer's bounty: the grain that was baked into bread or brewed into ale, the wool that was woven into cloth or blankets, the skins that were turned into furs or leather goods, and the produce of England's extensive woodlands. Wood had a great diversity of uses. It was the most important building material; it went into the making of an almost infinite variety of tools, agricultural and other implements, pieces of furniture, dishes and table ware, and of course carts and boats and ships; it was the major fuel, whether burned directly or as charcoal; and turned into potash it was indispensable to dyers. Felling and sawing timber were probably seldom specialist activities, but something to which virtually all countryfolk could turn their hands; and charcoal-burning, too, was often a subsidiary occupation of small-holding farmers. The men who bought licences for this purpose in Inglewood Forest (Cumberland), for instance, usually did so for only part of the year, and they were often owners of pigs or other livestock. In the West Riding, on the other hand, some charcoal-burners may have been itinerant specialists, moving with their families from site to site where they could find wood to burn. These are areas of medieval life upon which light is only beginning to be thrown.[8]

Animal skins, too, provided raw materials for a wide range of uses, but only after being submitted to preparatory treatments which transformed raw hides into leather or furs or even parchment. Tanners, skinners and leatherdressers were widely dispersed crafts. They are found in country places near the flocks and herds on which they relied, like a couple of tanners, each with his little store of tanned hides, living in a hamlet of Eaton Socon (Beds.) in 1297. They are also found on the staff of some Cistercian monastic establishments: indeed, Fountains abbey (Yorks.) still had its tannery at the end of the middle ages and, in the thirteenth century, Beaulieu abbey (Hants.) had departments making parchment from calf and sheep skins, tanning hides of every sort to make leather, and treating lamb skins to be turned into furred hoods and coverlets. There were also numerous leather workers in towns: at least thirteen

---

[8] J. Birrell, 'Peasant craftsmen in the medieval forest', *AHR*, XVII (1969). esp. pp. 96–7; M.L. Faull and S.A. Moorhouse, eds, *West Yorkshire: an Archaeological Survey*, III, pp. 783–5.

tanners paid tax in Colchester in 1301 and there were 30 tanners or more at Beverley in 1366. The trade in livestock which supplied towns with meat also ensured a regular supply of hides.[9] As the Beaulieu accounts show, skins could be prepared in a variety of ways. They might be tanned, i.e. soaked in an infusion of oak bark after preliminary treatment to remove the hair. This soaking was often for a prolonged period and afterwards the tanned hides might need oiling and shaving before they were ready for use, tasks sometimes carried out by the separate craft of curriers. Other hides were tawed rather than tanned, i.e. they were treated with oil or alum to produce a lighter leather; and others that were to be turned into furs had to be pared to remove the flesh, oiled, stretched, suppled and in some cases sheared to give a dense and even fur. These preparatory stages of dealing with animal skins called for a variety of skills, but generally only for modest investment. The units of production were normally essentially domestic; the Eaton Socon tanners in 1297 may also have engaged in small-scale farming; and the fact that hides were tawed at Beaulieu's St Leonard's grange as well as in its central workshop may imply that leatherdressing was not exclusively a specialist craft.

The work-force of the leather crafts in towns, by contrast, was composed mainly of specialists, and was notorious for polluting water supplies and for the stench which arose from its operations. It was the latter which, at Winchester, led to the banishment of tanners to places which were down-wind of the town centre.[10] Pottery-making, on the other hand, and also the making of tiles and bricks which was assuming a growing importance by the fourteenth century, were often tied to country locations in order to secure supplies of suitable clay, although Beverley had a flourishing brickmaking industry by the fourteenth century and Hull's brickyard goes back at least to 1303 and had become a municipal enterprise by 1321.[11] There is little evidence about the supplies of clay for these brickyards, but it seems clear that country potters and tilers commonly provided their own. Admittedly a Lincolnshire woman, in 1364, leased two crofts so that she could dig and sell clay;

[9] D.J.H. Michelmore, ed., *The Fountains Abbey Lease Book*, YAS Rec. Ser., CXL (1981), p. 243; A.T. Gayton, ed., *The Taxation of 1297*, p. 24; S.F. Hockey, ed., *The Account Book of Beaulieu Abbey*, pp. 195–8, 211–13, 226–8; *VCH East Riding*, VI, p. 41.
[10] L.F. Salzman, *English Industries of the Middle Ages*, pp. 247–9; E.M. Veale, *The English Fur Trade in the Later Middle Ages*, pp. 25–7; Keene, *Survey*, I, p. 287.
[11] *VCH East Riding*, I, p. 56; R. Horrox, ed., *Select Rentals and Accounts of Medieval Hull*, pp. 56, 59.

but potters at Longbridge Deverill (Wilts.) paid rent for clay dug from their holdings, as did a Broomley (Northumberland) potter for 'clay from the land to make jars' and three others at Broomhaugh in the same country for clay and fuel from Styford woods.[12]

3. MINING AND SMELTING

The industries providing essential metals and fossil fuels have attracted rather more attention than the other primary industries, perhaps as much as anything because of the part they were to play in Britain's industrial future. They were essentially rural industries, for their locations depended upon the availability of deposits and, in the case of smelting, of timber to provide fuel – a good reason for Henry III's order in 1229 that forges should 'itinerate' through Chippenham Forest (Wilts.) to make iron from any iron ore which might be found there.[13] Mining and smelting, therefore, generated employment in many poor and thinly settled regions. Furthermore, because kings and other lords found that, in order to attract labour and increase their own profit by expanding output, it was wise to be moderate in the demands they made on those engaged in these industries, they were also apt to give rise to highly independent communities. By the fourteenth century the mining areas broadly coincided with those of later times. The extraction of silver and copper were of limited importance, but tin mining had long been established in Devon and Cornwall, and lead was mined in Derbyshire, in the Pennine dales of Yorkshire, Durham and Northumberland, in the Mendips and in Shropshire. Iron was worked wherever deposits existed and often for mainly local markets (a mine at Rookhope (Durham) provided St Giles's Hospital with iron to make ploughs and other things needed for its estate there);[14] but there was also iron-working on a much larger scale in the Forest of Dean and, by the fourteenth century in the Sussex and Kentish Weald. Mineral coal, finally, seldom mentioned before the thirteenth century, was being extracted from relatively superficial

---

[12] *NCH*, VI, pp. 145, 262; M.R. McCarthy and C.M. Brooks, *Medieval Pottery in Britain*, pp. 14–15.
[13] *Close R.*, 1227–31, p. 268.
[14] W. Greenwell, ed., *Boldon Book*, Appx. p. xlvi.

deposits in many parts of the country, but primacy already clearly belonged to Northumberland and Durham.

(a) Output

The evidence for the development of these basic industries is unsatisfactory and incomplete, but in the case of tin mining in Devon and Cornwall royal taxes levied on output suggest an increase from 50–65 tons annually in the 1150s to 300–350 tons in the 1190s. Heavier taxes imposed in 1198–99 temporarily reversed this rising trend, but it was soon resumed. By 1214 output was above 600 tons and the crown revenue from it reached £800.[15] There are also indications that the output of lead was growing in this same period. That of the Derbyshire mines appears to have reached something like a high point late in the twelfth century, when revenue from the Peak Forest mines was ten times what it had been in 1170; and indications of the exploitation of lead deposits elsewhere multiply. The 'Carlisle' (Alston Moor) mines were let for around £100 a year as early as the mid-twelfth century (although this figure may have been inflated by the fact that there were some silver as well as lead deposits in the region). Shropshire lead mines, too, were operating by the 1180s; in 1189 the bishop of Bath and Wells was licensed to mine lead in his Somerset lands (the first specific mention of the Mendip mines); and in 1214 the bishop of Durham drew £500 from mining in his lands, doubtless for lead and iron and a little coal as well as silver. In Yorkshire, Fountains and Byland abbeys were also getting lead from the Forest of Nidderdale, and a 'free mining' district was developing in Swaledale which provided some lead for building work at the great abbey of Clairvaux in Burgundy.[16]

Explanations of this late twelfth-century expansion of mining are less easy to achieve with any certainty; but lead was mainly used for roofing, pipes, gutters and so forth, so that demand for it at home and abroad was intensified by the spread of large stone buildings financed by the rising incomes of landlords – that 'white mantle' of new cathedrals, abbeys, churches, castles, palaces and manor houses clothing England and other western lands. This building boom may

[15] J. Hatcher, *English Tin Production and Trade before 1550*, pp. 18–21, 152–5.
[16] Salzman, *English Industries of the Middle Ages*, p. 39; J.W. Gough, *The Mines of Mendip*, p. 49; S. Painter, *Studies in the History of the English Feudal Barony*, p. 165; I.S.W. Blanchard, 'Derbyshire lead production, 1195–1505', *Derbys. Arch. Jnl.*, XCI (1971), pp. 122–5; D.E. Greenway, ed., *Charters of the Honour of Mowbray, 1107–1191*, nos. 48, 102–3; R. Fieldhouse and B. Jennings, *A History of Richmond and Swaledale*, p. 62.

also have quickened the demand for tin as an ingredient of common alloys like bronze, bell-metal and pewter. It is all the more surprising that thirteenth-century evidence, such as it is, suggests that twelfth-century expansion did not continue and may even have been reversed. Records of tin output are lacking for most of the century, but when they reappear in 1301 the combined production of Devon and Cornwall was little more than half what it had been in 1214. The evidence for lead output is even less satisfactory, for it was mined in so many places that faltering production at one centre might be more than balanced by rising production elsewhere. Derbyshire output at the Peak Forest mines, however, does appear to have contracted in the first half of the century, and in the county as a whole the general trend between the late twelfth and the late thirteenth centuries appears to have been downwards. If these impressions are correct, the output of Derbyshire lead and of south-western tin may have followed very similar courses.[17]

Part of the explanation of thirteenth-century trends in tin and lead production may lie in the opening up of competitive mines in central Europe; but whatever the explanation signs of recovery were clear from the opening of the fourteenth century. By the 1330s Cornish tin production reached a new peak and lead output in parts of the Derbyshire field may have doubled between 1300 and 1340. This increased activity probably reflected growing demand from various quarters. English builders continued to be customers for lead (Dunstanburgh castle got 360 stones of lead from Newcastle in 1348–51 and the canons of Exeter cathedral sent as far as to Boston fair for lead for the cathedral roof); but alien merchants were also in the market for this metal. It accounted for about 30 per cent by value of their shipments from Hull in 1304–9, and lead was also being shipped overseas from Boston and King's Lynn at this time. There had also long been a strong overseas demand for tin. Bayonne merchants accepted it in satisfaction of Edward I's debts to them in 1298 and in the 1330s Florentine merchants exported substantial quantities of it. There was also an active home market for tin. Supplies of it were available in King's Lynn in 1345–46 for casting the new bells for Ely cathedral; and there was an increasing call for both lead and tin from the pewter industry, which was beginning to serve a general household market. Specialist pewterers had

---

[17] Hatcher, *English Tin Production and Trade*, p. 156; Blanchard, 'Derbyshire lead production', pp. 124–5.

established themselves in London by 1311 and in York by the mid-century.[18]

At the same time, the basic and most indispensable metal was iron. It was essential for agricultural and industrial tools and implements, for horse shoes and wheel tyres, for kitchen hearths and utensils, for an infinity of building uses, and of course for the accoutrements of war. These were good reasons for iron being worked and traded even in the darkest days of the so-called Dark Ages, but only in the mid-twelfth century do crown purchases begin to provide some sort of picture of the industry. They included axes, spades, nails and arrow-heads as well as iron for smiths to fashion, and in 1194 50,000 horse shoes. Most of these supplies came from the Forest of Dean, which has been described as the Birmingham of the late twelfth century; and the connection between war and the development of the iron industry is evident enough. At the same time more peaceful demands encouraged a more dispersed development of the industry designed mainly to meet local needs.[19] In Yorkshire monasteries of the new orders were among the pioneers. Rievaulx had an iron mine and forges near Barnsley by c. 1150 and, later in the century, mines near Wakefield together with forges and workshops to smelt the ore and make utensils and other things necessary for the abbey. Fountains and Byland, too, mined iron as well as lead in Niddersdale; and early in the thirteenth century the canons of Guisborough had an iron mine and forges at Glaisdale in the North Yorkshire moors.[20]

By the end of the thirteenth century this diversified industry was established in every part of the country where ore could be dug and fuel was available to smelt it, including even the relatively undeveloped parts of northern England. Even a random selection of sources reveals that the honour of Richmond had a mine in Wensleydale, Peter de Brus seven forges at Danby in Cleveland, the earl of Cornwall at least four forges in Knaresborough Forest which brought in £35 17s. in 1296–97. Further north, in Northumberland,

---

[18] A.M. Erskine, ed., *Accounts of the Fabric of Exeter Cathedral, 1279–1353*, I, pp. 19, 50, 61; *NCH*, II, p. 28; T.H. Lloyd, *Alien Merchants in England in the High Middle Ages*, pp. 45, 48; N.S.B. Gras, *The Early English Customs System*, pp. 278–9, 281–2; *CPR, 1292–1301*, p. 326; Hatcher, *English Tin Production and Trade*, p. 93; F.R. Chapman, ed., *Sacrist Rolls of Ely (1291–1360)*, II, pp. 138–9; J. Hatcher and T.C. Barker, *A History of British Pewter*, pp. 37–41, 79–80.

[19] *VCH Glos.*, II, pp. 215–19; Salzman, *English Industries of the Middle Ages*, pp. 21–40.

[20] *EYC*, III, no. 53; J.C. Atkinson, ed., *Cartularium Abbathiae de Rievalle*, nos. 100–1; Greenway, ed., *Charters of the Honour of Mowbray*, nos. 48, 102–3; W. Brown, ed., *Cartularium Prioratus de Gyseburne*, I, pp. 105, 111–12.

Gilbert de Umfraville had forges at Elsdon in 1245; in Lancashire a Rossendale forge was leased for £3 in 1295 and ore-smithies at Colne for £8 16s. 8d. in 1323. By that time, too, the forges in Rothwell park, near Leeds, had frightened away the herons and the sparrow hawks and even the bees, so that there was little honey or wax to be got.[21] Such places, of course, cannot be compared as centres of production with the Forest of Dean, where the 60 or so forges operating in 1282 may have been responsible for a fifth or a sixth of the country's total iron output.[22] In the meantime, however, the demands of London and the crown were fostering large-scale development in the Weald. Sussex was providing the king with horse shoes and nails in 1254, by 1266 the town of Lewes levied a toll on iron coming in from the Weald, the king's smith bought Wealden iron in 1276, and Wealden smiths supplied London ironmongers with cart tyres in 1300 and the army for a campaign in Scotland with horse shoes in 1327. About that time, too, Elizabeth de Burgh's officials were organizing iron works at Tudeley, near Tonbridge (Kent), where production averaged 200 blooms a year in 1330–34 and reached 600 blooms in 1335. The expansion of the Wealden industry was well under way, although the technological advances of the fifteenth and sixteenth centuries were needed for its full development.[23]

It is impossible to establish the total output of so diverse an industry, although one estimate has put the increase in the number of bloomeries between 1086 and 1300 at five-fold and their output in 1300 at c. 1,000 tons.[24] What at least is clear, however, is that the domestic production of iron fell some way short of satisfying demand, leaving a gap to be filled by imports from Normandy, Biscay, Spain and the Baltic, again possibly totalling some 1,000 tons a year in the early fourteenth century.[25] Such relatively high import

[21] W. Brown, ed., *Yorkshire Inquisitions*, I, YAS Rec. Ser., XII (1892), nos. 82, 130; L.M. Midgley, ed., *Minsters' Accounts of the Earldom of Cornwall, 1296–1297*, II, pp. 187–8; J. Hodgson, *History of Northumberland*, II(1), p. 85n; W. Farrer, ed., *Court Rolls of the Honour of Clitheroe*, 3 vols, Manchester, 1897–1913, I, p. 483; PRO DL 29/1/1; Faull and Moorhouse, eds, *West Yorkshire: an Archaeological Survey*, III, p. 780.
[22] R.H. Hilton, *A Medieval Society: the West Midlands at the end of the Thirteenth Century*, pp. 215–16.
[23] E. Straker, *Wealden Iron*, pp. 33–4; H.C. Darby, ed., *A New Historical Geography of England*, p. 228.
[24] S. Pollard and A.E. Crossley, *The Wealth of England, 1085–1966*, p. 44.
[25] W.R. Childs, 'England's iron trade in the fifteenth century', *EcHR*, 2nd ser. XXXIV (1981), pp. 39–41; and for Hanseatic and Biscayan iron, P. Dollinger, *La Hanse (XIIᵉ–XVIIᵉ siècles)*, pp. 276, 282, 294–5, 304; and R.H. Bautier, *Economic Development of Medieval Europe*, 1971, p. 128.

figures may have more than one explanation. Some imported iron, perhaps especially that from Spain, may have been better suited than the domestic product for purposes like the making of arms, armour and steel, while other imports may have enjoyed the advantage of relative cheapness. By 1300, in fact, competition from imports may have been exercising a depressing influence on home production in some places where, in the first half of the fourteenth century, the industry was contracting or at least ceasing to expand. Production seems to have ceased around Skipton in Yorkshire and to have been much reduced in Knaresborough Forest and Duffield Frith (Derbys.); and iron production even in the Forest of Dean was declining before the Black Death. A contributory influence in some places may have been shortage of fuel, as woodlands were depleted, pushing up domestic production costs. The story was perhaps different in the Weald; but in general, for whatever reasons, the trends of iron output seem to have varied somewhat from those of tin and lead production.[26]

Coal production, too, had its distinctive chronology. It was a late developing industry, for the prime fuels were (and continued to be) wood, peat and, especially for industrial purposes, charcoal. It had nevertheless been appreciated at least since Roman times that 'sea-coal' (the term used to distinguish mineral coal from charcoal) was a fuel well suited to the smith and especially for lime-burning. The long-term advance of land in agricultural use also adversely affected supplies of wood fuel eventually in many parts of England, encouraging the greater use of coal where it was available locally;[27] and a growing insufficiency of traditional fuels became increasingly noticeable in towns lacking an abundance of woodland in their hinterlands. London, in particular, began to experience scarcity in the later thirteenth century, so that the capital was precocious in its use of coal. Supplies came directly and relatively cheaply by sea from Tyneside, and probably long antedated the first mention of 'Sea-coals Lane' in 1228. Under the stimulus of this London market commercial exploitation of outcrops on the north side of the Tyne valley made considerable progress during the second half of the thirteenth century, and by the mid-fourteenth century collieries had

[26] H.R. Schubert, *History of the British Iron and Steel Industry*, pp. 111–15; J.E. Thorold Rogers, *A History of Agriculture and Prices in England*, I, pp. 424, 454; Hilton, *A Medieval Society*, p. 216.
[27] J. Birrell, 'Common rights in the medieval forest', *Past and Present*, no. 117 (1987); K.P. Whitney, 'The woodland economy of Kent', *AHR*, xxxviii (1990).

multiplied on both sides of the river. As a consequence, in 1281, Newcastle as the main port of outlet for this coalfield was said to be worth double the £100 a year for which King John had granted the town to its burgesses; and the roads leading westward from Newcastle had been rendered unsafe in many places by the numerous coal workings along their courses.[28]

A similar expansion of coal-mining, although on a smaller scale, took place in other districts where deposits outcropped close to the surface, and exploitation gathered pace in the early fourteenth century as demand for fuel increased and the uses to which coal could be put multiplied. Even though coal was normally expensive away from the coalfields, it was used more and more widely in building processes for the burning of lime and plaster, as was the case in thirteenth-century London. It was also one of the fuels used in casting bronze and bell-metal, for sea-coal as well as charcoal fired the hearths for heating the metal from which the bells of Ely cathedral were cast; it was employed in salt boiling, as at Cowpen (Northumberland) where a colliery was worked in association with saltpans; and it was used by smiths whenever the quality of the finished ironwork was deemed more important than cheapness of fabrication.[29] Where wood fuel was especially scarce, as in London, brewers and dyers, too, turned to coal. Because it did not burn well in the wide fireplaces designed for wood, however, coal made relatively little headway as a domestic fuel, although the monks of Durham installed iron chimneys to enable it to be burned in their hall and it provided heating for many of the domestic rooms of Lindisfarne priory (Northumberland). By the fourteenth century there was also a small export trade in coal, for members of one of Newcastle's bourgeois dynasties, the Scotts, shipped coal to Flanders before 1350 as well as exploiting mines at Benwell (Northumberland). Small quantities of coal, too, were shipped into and out of the ports of southern and western England in the early fourteenth century, probably to meet the demands of discerning smiths.[30]

[28] *NCH*, XIII, pp. 25–8; R.L. Galloway, *Annals of Mining and the Coal Trade*, I, pp. 21, 29–30; W. Page, ed., *Three Early Assize Rolls for the County of Northumberland*, p. 103. Newcastle received a levy of 1d. on every 4 qrs. of sea-coal bought in or shipped from the town: A.J. Lilburn, 'The pipe rolls of Edward I', *AA*, 4th ser. XXXVI (1958), p. 286.
[29] J.B. Blake, 'The medieval coal trade of north-east England', *North. Hist.*, II (1967), pp. 2–8, 13–16; Chapman, ed., *Sacrist Rolls of Ely*, II, pp. 122, 138–9; *NCH*, IX, pp. 223–4.
[30] *VCH Durham*, II, p. 322; E. Miller, 'Rulers of thirteenth-century towns: the cases of York and Newcastle upon Tyne', *Thirteenth-Century England*, I (1986), p. 139; C. Platt, *Medieval Southampton*, p. 83; N.D. Harding, ed., *Bristol Charters, 1155–1373*, p. 113

Not every influence, however, favoured expansion, and the growth of the industry during our period must not be overstated. In towns coal could be unpopular as a pollutant. Henry III's queen in 1257 found coal smoke hanging so heavily in the air around Nottingham castle that she cut short her visit and withdrew to the more salubrious environment of Tutbury. From the 1280s, too, a series of attempts were made to compel London lime-burners, brewers and dyers, who had lately changed over from wood to coal, to revert to their former fuel because of the danger to health from the intolerable smell and infection of the air arising from their coal-fired kilns and vats. A widespread adoption of coal as a domestic fuel, therefore, had to await late Tudor times, when firewood had become even scarcer and more expensive, and when the 'multitude of chimneys lately erected' came to characterise English skylines.[31]

There seems no doubt, however, that an overall expansion of mining output in all its branches was achieved between 1100 and 1350, even though it was not necessarily continuous or dramatic by the standards of later times. Some mining, like manorial agriculture, was intended for the self-supply of landlords on whose lands it was conducted: this was, as we have seen, the acknowledged purpose of some early monastic iron mines in Yorkshire; in 1268–69 iron from mines at Bolton went to Cockermouth castle (Cumberland) to make nails, plough parts and tyres for cartwheels; and as late as 1384 the keeper of Bamburgh castle (Northumberland) was instructed to mine enough coal for those dwelling in the castle, although any surplus was to be sold.[32] Although more and more mining was aimed at the market, this self-supplying motive continued to limit the ambitions of some mine-owners. Nor was mining necessarily a fully specialist occupation. Most of the men who dug ironstone and 'sea-coal' in the bondlands of the manor of Wakefield were probably also agricultural tenants; certainly Adam Isbell, who sank coal-pits in the high road at Stanley, apparently raised pigs on some scale. The lead miners of south-west Northumberland, too, look like migratory part-timers. The archbishop of York in 1320 assumed that they would work the Allendale mines only in summer, and the Alston miners were regarded as incomers who, while at work, would find accommodation in 'lodges' or shielings, just like the summer

---

[31] H.R. Luard, ed., *Annales Monastici*, III, p. 105; *CPR*, 1281–92, pp. 29, 296; *CCR*, 1302–7, pp. 537, 549; L. Withington, ed., *Elizabethan England: from a Description of England by William Harrison*, Scott Library, London, n.d., p. 119

[32] PRO SC 6/824/7; *NCH*, I, p. 152 and note.

herdsmen who came up to the high moorland pastures for the grazing season. Even in the tin mines of Devon and Cornwall, which in good times might employ 6,000–8,000 tinners, many were migratory workers who spent part of the year in farming or other occupations; and even full-time tinners might carry on a little farming on the side.[33]

(b)   Technology

If mining, in these various ways, continued to be embedded in agricultural England, technological considerations might also limit the scale of enterprises. How modest these were in coal mining is suggested by the rents paid for mines, even in the north-east. The £333 6s. 8d. paid to the bishop of Durham in 1356 for five mines at Whickham and Gateshead (Durham) was altogether exceptional. Tynemouth priory's income from its mines in Northumberland in 1291 was just over £3; its Hartley mines in the late thirteenth century brought in only 13s. 4d. annually and its Cowpen mine £1 13s. 4d. in 1315. Some mines were worth even less: 10s. for a mine at Trawden (Lancs.) in 1296 or 5s. for a Staffordshire mine in 1291 and a South Yorkshire mine in 1321.[34] The range of returns might reflect different forms of operation. The simplest way of mining coal was to gather that which was washed up on the seashore, something Newminster was empowered to do on the Blyth estuary in Northumberland in 1236. Open-cast mining, like that practised in the Forest of Dean and the Wakefield area in the thirteenth century, was probably only a little more advanced and demanded only modest investment. Where surface deposits were not available, however, it might be necessary to exploit underground seams, often accomplished by means of 'bee-hive' or 'bell' pits: i.e. by sinking a shaft into the seam and widening it out at the bottom until as much coal had been extracted as was possible without causing the shaft to collapse (although the many mining casualties indicate that this was not always avoided). Deeper and more elaborate workings, on the

---

[33] S.S. Walker, ed., *Court Rolls of the Manor of Wakefield, 1331–3*, pp. 40, 45, 108, 110, 114, 183, 206; J. Raine, ed., *The Register or Rolls of Walter Gray, Archbishop of York*, Surtees Soc., LVI (1872), pp. 236–7; Hodgson, *History of Northumberland*, II(3), pp. 47, 49–51; Hatcher, *English Tin Production and Trade*, p. 47; *idem, Rural Economy and Society in the Duchy of Cornwall, 1300–1500*, pp. 30–6, 92–3.
[34] *VCH Durham*, II, p. 322; J. Brand, *History and Antiquities of Newcastle upon Tyne*, II, p. 591; *NCH.*, IX, pp. 101, 104, 223; *VCH Staffs.*, II, p. 449; *VCH Yorks.*, II, p. 339; PRO DL 29/1/1.

other hand, are in evidence in some places. The increasingly frequent reference in Durham to water-gates, the local name for underground drainage channels, suggest deep mining of which there are many other indications; an entry on a Wakefield court roll in 1311 suggests that coal was being mined in galleries radiating from a central shaft; and at Cossall (Notts.) in 1316 a lease of a mine specified that the drainage gutter (*le sowe*) should be kept in good repair, and allowed for the possibility that mining might be interrupted by the presence of *le dampe*, a combination of carbon dioxide and nitrogen. Most coal mining continued to be a small-scale and primitive, as well as a dangerous, industry throughout this period, but there are signs that its expansion was accompanied by an increase in the size of some mines and a few modest technological advances.[35]

Other branches of mining displayed similar features. Some tin, for example, was certainly being mined by the mid-fourteenth century, although the commonest method of extracting tin was by 'streaming', i.e. by using water to sift the ore from the debris in which it was embedded. For deposits close to the surface this method could be cheaper than mining proper and produced better tin, but drainage trenches to carry water and waste from the workings had to be dug and, since an adequate water supply was essential, this might have to be brought by conduit over a considerable distance or even entail the diversion of a river. How extensive some of these works were is indicated by complaints about the damage done to farmland and, in 1356, to Lostwithiel harbour (Cornwall) by debris discharged from stream-works.[36]

Because of the nature of the deposits lead had usually to be mined, generally by sinking a shaft into the seam which could then be widened out into a trench. The essential requirements then were for hoists or windlasses to raise the ore and waste to the surface, and to keep the workings free from water.[37] Again, small-scale units of production were the rule except where, as in the royal mines in Devon, the deposits contained silver as well as lead. Their disposition made deep mining essential, and government hunger for bullion around 1300 seemed to make heavy investment justifiable.

[35] J.T. Fowler, ed., *Chartularium Abbathiae de Novo Monasterio*, p. 55; *NCH*, XIII, p. 25; *VCH Durham*, II, p. 322; Faull and Moorhouse, eds, *West Yorkshire; an Archaeological Survey*, I, p. 43; III, p. 778; HMC, *Report on the Manuscripts of Lord Middleton*, p. 88.
[36] Hatcher, *English Tin Production and Trade*, pp. 44–6; G.R. Lewis, *The Stannaries: A Study of the English Tin Mines*, pp. 1–7.
[37] I.S.W. Blanchard, 'Stannator Fabulosus', *AHR*, XXII (1974).

The most productive mines were at Bere Alston which, at the peak of their activity, employed over 700 miners, pumpmen, carpenters, smiths, chandlers, sawyers, ore-washers, ore-roasters, refiners, charcoal-burners and carters. They produced, in addition to some lead, silver worth about £800 annually in 1292–97 and rising to £1,773 in 1305, but thereafter output declined rapidly to only £70's worth of silver in 1347. Their early productivity was made possible by advanced drainage techniques to supplement the traditional gangs of water-drawers bailing out the mines with leather buckets. Much of the drainage was now done through adits: gutters cut from the lowest points of a mine to a still lower outlet on the surface of a hill-side, often at very considerable expense. In 1297 a hundred tinners were ordered to be recruited to construct adits for the king's Devon mines; and in 1327 the cost of improvement at the Birland mine in that county, including a new drain from the mine to the sea, was estimated to be £1,000. In fact the Birland adit may never have been constructed, but it is testimony to a scale of royal mining which, like royal building, was much larger than any known private enterprise. Even so, most royal investment went into hiring labour rather than the purchase of capital equipment. The latter – timber props, ropes, baskets, buckets, shovels, wedges, barrows, carts, winches, candles and so forth – were mainly low-cost items; the heavy expenditure was on the wages of workers.[38]

Smelting equipment was hardly more elaborate or costly. The itinerant forges for smelting iron, for instance, seem to have been ordinary blacksmith's forges with cup-shaped crucibles in which the molten iron was accumulated, and the hearths were sited in exposed spots where the prevailing winds would provide a draught for the fire. Lead and tin were also smelted in rudimentary structures, which inevitably were not particularly efficient, so that ore required more than one smelting before it was acceptably pure. This was formally recognized in the tin stannaries in the late twelfth century. A first smelting, using a peat fire close to the mine, produced rough clumps of impure metal and slag; it was the second smelting which produced the refined metal called white tin.[39] Before the mid-fourteenth century, however, there were some signs of technical advance. Bellows operated by hand or foot (or by waterwheels at the

---

[38] Lewis, *The Stannaries*, pp. 192–4; Salzman, *English Industries of the Middle Ages*, pp. 63–4; *idem*, 'Mines and stannaries', in J.F. Willard, W.A. Morris and W.H. Dunham, eds, *The English Government at Work, 1327–1336*, III, pp. 88–104.
[39] Lewis, *The Stannaries*, pp. 16–17; the late twelfth-century royal tax was assessed on the product of the first smelting: Hatcher, *English Tin Production and Trade*, pp. 18–19.

Devon silver mines) produced artificial blast in place of reliance on the wind, and some furnaces could be rotated to take advantage of changing winds. Tin-smelting was increasingly concentrated in 'blowing houses' of granite and thatch with water-driven bellows; and water power was probably also sometimes used to crush ore. Such improvements increased the output of furnaces and the amount of metal yielded by a given quantity of ore. This may be reflected in the rents some Yorkshire forges commanded. Even in the thirteenth century an iron forge at Blubberhouses was leased for £25 a year and others at Henkstank, working for only part of the year, for £10 and £17 18s. Early in the following century in the Wakefield area, where bellows were certainly in use to provide blast, forges were let at 14s. and 15s. a week, and one in Sowerby Forest brought in £9 12s. a year. Although they probably covered free access to woodlands for fuel, these were substantial amounts when compared with the modest rents paid for many coal mines.[40]

(c)   Mining communities

Other than technological influences, of course, also shaped the organization of mining and smelting. First, the privileges secured by many mining groups combined with extensive rural under-employment to assure these industries of a steady stream of both independent workers and hired labourers. Secondly, however, the speculative character of many enterprises and the fact that most miners lacked capital resources made their independence precarious. The result was that much of the profit arising from their labour found its way into the hands of others, and by no means least the landlords (including the crown) of the land on which they worked. Silver mines apart, landlords by 1300 seldom exploited mines directly; they took their profit from the industry in various other ways. Coal and iron mines, and the forges associated with the latter were commonly leased, but tin and lead mining were subject to levies on output. In the stannaries coinage duty was assessed on the amount of tin produced, while lead miners owed their lords a share of their output called 'lot' (a thirteenth in the High Peak and a ninth at Alston). Sometimes, too, lords had a right to pre-empt the produce

---

[40] Salzman, *English Industries of the Middle Ages*, p. 59; C. Gill, ed., *Dartmoor: a New Study*, Newton Abbot, 1970, p. 104; J.L. Bolton, *The Medieval English Economy, 1050–1500*, p. 168; Faull and Moorhouse, eds, *West Yorkshire: an Archaeological Survey*, III, pp. 780–2.

of mines at an agreed price, a right exercised intermittently in the stannaries, but commuted in Derbyshire before the end of the thirteenth century in return for an additional tax on lead output called 'cope'.[41]

Because many of the profits which landlords drew from mining depended upon output, they encouraged increased production by granting privileges to miners. The revenue the crown drew from the stannaries, for example, which rose to almost £3,000 a year in the 1330s, then and earlier won for tinners a series of charters which established them as an independent community free of most seigno-rial and many royal impositions. Their earliest known charter, in 1201, confirmed to them sweeping rights to dig tin and turves in any man's land and to divert streams for their works, and also exempted them from being claimed as villeins. They were to be subject only to the jurisdiction of a Warden of the Stannaries, a jurisdiction which came to be exercised by an independent stannary court. In 1305, too, the tinners were exempted from most taxes, as well as from tolls and market dues throughout the south-west. These privileges must have offered encouragement even to the poorest villein seeking to become his own master or, at least, a free-lance labourer.[42]

Other mining communities were less privileged, but 'free miners' in Derbyshire, in Mendip and on Alston Moor had some analogous liberties, originally by custom but, by the thirteenth century, usually buttressed by royal confirmation. They were free to prospect where they would except in churchyards, in gardens or on high roads, although in Mendip they needed the permission of the lord of the soil, but that could not be unreasonably withheld. They could also cut the timber they needed whoever the owner was; they had a right of access from their mines to the nearest high road; and they were subject to the jurisdiction of their own courts the officers of which, at least at Alston, were chosen from their own ranks.[43] Much mining, of course, went on outside this framework of privilege, including most coal and iron mining; and it is anyhow, given the sheer diversity of mining communities, difficult to determine how much privileges contributed to the expansion of the industry. The

[41] Midgley, ed., *Ministers' Accounts of the Earldom of Cornwall*, II, pp. 187–8; Blanchard, 'Derbyshire lead production', p. 120; Gough, *The Mines of Mendip*, pp. 51–2; Salzman, *English Industries of the Middle Ages*, p. 50; Hatcher, *English Tin Production and Trade*, p. 6.
[42] *Ibid.*, pp. 48–9.
[43] Salzman, *English Industries of the Middle Ages*, pp. 37–8, 43–9; Hodgson, *History of Northumberland* III(2), pp. 47–51; *VCH Derbys.*, II, pp. 326–8; *VCH Somerset*, II, pp. 367–9.

labour force of mines included full-time and part-time, permanent and casual, self-employed and hired workers. Independent miners worked their claims individually, or in association with partners, or they employed labourers who might be paid a fixed wage, or a share of the product, or a combination of the two. If some mine labourers were attracted by the opportunities the industry offered, moreover, others were conscripts. To expand silver mining in Devon, Edward I in 1295 sent commissioners to recruit miners in Cheshire, Derbyshire, Shropshire, Gloucestershire and Somerset; and a few years later 384 miners were secured for the Devon mines in the Peak District and 35 from Wales. Even chronic rural under-employment was insufficient, without a measure of compulsion, to make a sudden expansion of mining possible.[44]

The 'free miner's' position also made him vulnerable. The search for and extraction of ore were speculative enterprises which, even if successful, called for much expenditure of labour and money before yielding a return. Most miners, too, lacked capital resources and commercial expertise, and most units of production were small, all of which made for the subordination of free miners as well as labourers to dealers and entrepreneurs with access to capital and to markets beyond the reach of working miners. The lessees of the Whickham mines from the bishop of Durham in 1356 were a knight and the rector of the parish church, and their lease suggests that the mines would be staffed by hired labourers and that the coal produced would find its way to ships on the Tyne. Entrepreneurs were also to be found in the West Riding iron industry: men like John and Thomas Culpon of Sowerby who had mines and forges in a number of different townships employing servants as miners, charcoal-burners and smiths, whose fines they paid when they cut firewood without licence.[45] Merchants from Derby, too, a town which was the main market for Derbyshire iron, controlled various branches of the industry, making knives on a 'putting out' basis within the town and some of them owning country forges. Derby and Chesterfield were also markets for Derbyshire lead, some of which was exported through Boston and the Humber ports as early as the twelfth century, but for which London had become a principal

[44] Salzman, *English Industries of the Middle Ages*, p. 64; in 1296 miners were to be impressed for the Devon mines in Cheshire, Denbighshire, Derbyshire, Gloucestershire and Dorset: *CCR*, 1288–96, p. 504.
[45] Faull and Moorhouse, eds, *West Yorkshire: an Archaeological Survey*, III, pp. 781–3; Walker, ed., *Court Rolls of the Manor of Wakefield, 1331–3*, p. 48.

destination by the fourteenth century. The range over which Derbyshire lead was distributed presupposes the existence of well-organized mercantile services.[46]

In like manner the first extant stannary document, in 1198, clearly distinguishes among stannary men between miners, ore-dealers, tin-dealers and smelters; and an early fourteenth-century petition asserts that merchants were accustomed to advance money to the tinners on the security of future deliveries of tin, an assertion abundantly supported by debt cases in the stannary court rolls.[47] The contemporary coinage rolls, which record the amounts of tin presented for tax, also make clear that the tin trade was dominated by merchants and that few working tinners retained possession of their tin long enough to pay taxes on it. In 1300–1 a dozen merchants handled over 60 per cent of Cornish tin and five merchants 40 per cent of it, while in 1301–2 five merchants handled over 50 per cent of it. A single merchant, Gerard de Villiers, paid £358 duty on some 80 tons of tin which, after duty was paid, was worth around £1,000. Little is known of de Villiers except that he was a Lostwithiel merchant and shipowner who engaged in overseas trade: possibly his stake in tinning was not very great. Roger Blake and his son John are another matter. Their advances to tinners (and perhaps their loans to the Black Prince) may have brought them much profit, for when John Blake committed suicide soon after inheriting his father's estate he had fourteen burgages in Bodmin and Lostwithiel as well as much rural property. Michael Trenewith, about the same time, as well as being a notable entrepreneur, was perhaps representative of a semi-criminal element in the stannaries. He owned tin-works, dealt in tin and loaned money to tinners; but he was also involved in smuggling, wrecking, fraud and coercion. In 1342 he, his son and a group of tin merchants were accused of seizing a number of tin-workings and 'compelling tinners to work for them for little more than a penny every other day', despite the fact that 'the tin won by a man daily is worth 20d.'. The analogy with what happened in 'frontier' mining areas elsewhere in the world in later times is irresistible.

The independent miner's freedom, therefore, was a fragile thing and, because labour was plentiful, his rewards were small. The available evidence suggests that around 1300 the annual output per working tinner in Devon amounted to 145–237 lb and in Cornwall (where total production was higher and the work-force rather more

---

[46] *VCH Derbys.*, II, pp. 323–4, 346, 356–8; *PQW*, p. 138.
[47] For this and what follows: Hatcher, *English Tin Production and Trade*, pp. 43–88.

specialized) to 400–450 lb, worth respectively at the retail prices then current 12s.–27s. and 33s.–37s. From these returns, however, there has to be deducted coinage duty (2s.–5s. in Devon and 13s.–15s. in Cornwall), the costs of capital equipment, smelting and transport, and the profits of dealers and merchants. What was left for the working miners, even allowing for the fact that many of them were part-timers, was pitifully little. Judging from the royal silver mines labourers fared no better. They were paid no more than agricultural or building labourers (i.e. 1d. or $1^1/_2$d. a day); there is no sign that they were supplied with food; and the payment of wages was often long in arrears. On at least one occasion, too, the silver miners were forced to strike in the face of attempts to reduce their wages.[48]

The characteristic medieval mining or smelting unit, then, was small, with limited capital equipment, and capable of being exploited by working miners or smelters either as individuals or in family and small partnership groups. This was a pattern of production compatible with a limited degree of specialization, for many miners and smelters also engaged in other economic activities (and especially in small-scale agriculture). While there were mines owned by entrepreneurs and worked by labourers, few such operations had numerous work-forces, and those which did, like the king's silver mines, were totally exceptional. There are indications, nevertheless, that the output of metals increased over time, even if not necessarily continuously, to meet the demands of a growing population and of landowners as builders for the metals needed for building. At the same time, while the outlets for metals and coal were often very local, there was also some expansion of markets. This had been true of lead and tin from an early date, but Tyneside coal was fouling the air of London before 1300 and is found in southern ports soon afterwards and bound for the Continent across the North Sea. Even the iron for making the horse shoes which Exeter cathedral regularly bought in the early fourteenth century at Lopen fair in Somerset did not necessarily come from local mines. Coal and iron miners, like tinners and lead miners, might need the services of merchants to reach their customers.[49]

[48] For wage rates, see Salzman, *English Industries of the Middle Ages*, p. 49 and Hatcher, *Rural Economy and Society in the Duchy of Cornwall*, p. 291. Salzman concludes 'even allowing for the possible cheapness of living in the west country, it is difficult to see how the miners lived': 'Mines and stannaries', pp. 72–3.

[49] C.M. Fraser, 'The life and death of John Denton', *AA*, 4th ser. XXXVII (1959), p. 319; *idem*, 'The pattern of trade in the north-east of England, 1265–1350', *North. Hist.*, IV (1969), pp. 64–5; Erskine, ed., *Accounts of the Fabric of Exeter Cathedral*, I, pp. 14, 33, 103–4.

Merchants sometimes intervened in production as well as distribution. Advances from merchants might bridge the gap between prospecting for ore and the sale of the refined metal, turning the miner into the merchant's debtor. A need for advances was particularly acute for tinners because, to prevent them evading the payment of duty, they were only allowed to sell tin at Midsummer and Michaelmas; and wherever miners depended heavily on advances they became captives of the traders who controlled their access to markets. Direct investment by merchants in production was probably less common; but some dealers in iron in Derby organized the production of iron consumer goods and some dealers in tin seem to have had a hand in the organization of tin mining and smelting. Commercial control over the extractive industries and the working up of their products was growing by the mid-fourteenth century. This explains why the Blakes and Michael Trenewith were conspicuously wealthy Cornishmen and why, by that time on Tyneside, a few precursors of the later Hostmen can already be identified.

4. THE CONSUMER GOODS INDUSTRIES

It would, however, be anachronistic to make too much of the medieval extractive industries, however important they were in some localities. If we return to the early fourteenth-century Colchester taxpayers, where we can be reasonably certain of their occupations about a quarter were small traders mostly in the ordinary run of consumption goods (food, fish, mercery, wine), which they doubtless sold mainly to their fellow townsfolk. About a hundred or so taxpayers made as well as sold goods, probably mainly to local customers, although some leather and textile workers, the two most numerous groups, may have served more distant markets. Even among leather workers, on the other hand, there were more cobblers and shoemakers than other crafts and a quarter of the textile workers were tailors, crafts with strictly limited horizons. After leather and textile workers, furthermore, the most numerous group of Colchester's 'manufacturing craftsmen' belonged to the provision trades: they were bakers and butchers, cooks and alewives, millers and mustardmakers.

The prominence of provision traders at Colchester is in no way unusual. Where their occupations are known about a quarter of

York citizens in 1307–49 followed these trades, with bakers, butchers, cooks and fishmongers well to the fore. There is also much in the records to give backing to Andrew Borde's dictum that 'ale for an Englishman is a natural drink'. Brewing was commonly a bye-occupation, in which women were unusually prominent, but the number of people engaged in it was very high. In medieval Norwich fines for breaches of the rules governing the trade were a major source of municipal revenue; at Faversham in 1327 there were 84 ale-wives among the 252 tallage payers; and few if any villages lacked at least a few brewers. Some villages, too, also had specialist butchers who, on the Ramsey abbey estate, paid a few pence or capons for licence to pursue that calling.[50] Even in towns, however, most provision traders were in a small way of business. At Colchester over half of them had goods valued at under £1 and only two had goods worth £5 or more – both butchers who were also farmers. There were, of course, wholesale provision traders in the larger towns and in London particularly, some of them wealthy men clearly different in kind from the general body of shopkeeping craftsmen and retailers.[51] They belong to the world of merchants and their wealth has to be measured against the wealth of merchants. The leading London vintners and grocers and fishmongers clearly disposed of resources of a different order to those of even the most prosperous Colchester butcher or, for that matter, of the great majority of shopkeepers in the capital itself.

Among provision trades those of salters and millers have a special character. Salt continued to be produced from sea-water at coastal salterns stretching from Ross, Warkworth and Cowpen in the far north-east to the furthest south-west,[52] and from brine pits at the inland wiches of Cheshire and Worcestershire. The parts of Lincolnshire and of the Norfolk marshland bordering the Wash were particularly active centres of the coastal industry. The salterns lay close to the sea and needed to be large enough to provide storage space for the salt produced and for the saturated sand from which the salters made a salt solution which was boiled down in large lead pans, using peat dug from fen turbaries as fuel. The

---

[50] *VCH City of York*, pp. 114–16; Salzman, *English Industries of the Middle Ages*, pp. 285, 287, 290; Keene, *Survey*, I, pp. 265–7; W. Hudson and J.C. Tingey, eds, *Records of the City of Norwich*, I, p. cxxxviii; W.O. Ault, ed., *Court Rolls of the Abbey of Ramsey and the Honour of Clare*, pp. 184, 187, 190 etc.

[51] Unwin, *Gilds and Companies of London*, pp. 74–5.

[52] *NCH*, I, p. 405; V, pp. 139–42; VII, pp. 426–3; IX, pp. 224, 314; J.H. Bettey, *Wessex from A.D. 1000*, Regional History of England, 1986, pp. 326–7.

salters usually rented their salterns, and sometimes also the relatively costly boiling pans. Some of them, too, leased agricultural land and, still more frequently, common rights for their oxen, essential for carting salt and sand; at Wrangle (Lincs.) in *c.* 1200 each saltern was assumed to need six oxen for its operation. The salters' rents were often paid in salt, the bishop of Ely getting about 920 bushels of salt in 1251 from this source at his manor of Terrington (Norfolk) and Thomas of Multon some 660 bushels in 1315 from his lands at Fleet (Lincs.).[53] Some salterns might employ labourers who in Lincolnshire were said to have been paid 15d. per week before 1349, less than the rate laid down for building craftsmen in 1351 but better than that for their mates.[54] In general, the salters are perhaps to be compared with many miners in that their work was seasonal and some of them were also small farmers.

The inland wiches displayed more diversity and a rather more elaborate organization, although the 'machinery of the industry' (lead boiling pans and salt-houses in which to accommodate them) was much the same as on the coasts. At Droitwich from 1215 the burgesses of the town themselves controlled the industry in return for an annual payment to the crown as high as the borough farm of Newcastle upon Tyne, and which they raised by taxing the salters. In Cheshire, by contrast, various taxes were levied on output and were paid to whoever was the lord of the wich.[55] At Droitwich the salters apparently owned their salt-houses, but in Cheshire some were owner-occupiers and others lessees. These centres of saltmaking became almost purely industrial towns, their main business creating a good deal of ancillary employment for carpenters, leadsmiths and the like.[56] Inland and coastal salt production also brought into existence a class of middlemen salt traders. Much of the salt produced on the east coast was used to preserve the herring harvest of the

---

[53] F.M. Stenton, ed., *Documents Illustrative of the Social and Economic History of the Danelaw*, no. 526; R. Ransford, ed., *Early Charters of Waltham Abbey*, no. 443; Caius College Ms. 485/489, ff. 198–200; H.E. Hallam, *Settlement and Society: a Study of the Early Agrarian History of South Lincolnshire*, Cambridge, 1965, pp. 77–8; *idem*, 'Salt-making in the Lincolnshire Fenland in the middle ages', *Reports and Papers of the Lincs. Archit. and Arch. Soc.*, NS VIII (1959–60), pp. 95, 111.

[54] E.H. Rudkin and D.M. Owen, 'The medieval salt industry in the Lindsey marshland', *ibid.*, p. 81; A.R. Bridbury, *England and the Salt Trade*, p. 37; L.F. Salzman, *Building in England down to 1540*, p. 72.

[55] J. Varley, ed., *A Middlewich Chartulary*, I, pp. 37–8; E.K. Berry, 'Droitwich and its salt industry, 1215–1700', *Univ. of Birmingham Hist. Jnl.*, VI (1957–8), pp. 40, 51; H.J. Hewitt, *Cheshire under the Three Edwards*, pp. 66–9.

[56] Berry, 'Droitwich and its salt industry', pp. 48–9; Varley, ed., *A Middlewich Chartulary*, pp. 38–4, 42, 80; Hilton, *A Medieval Society*, p. 175.

North Sea and needed to be transferred to the ports where catches were landed; while to serve domestic consumers innumerable 'salt ways' stretched out from Cheshire into Yorkshire, Lancashire and Derbyshire, and from Droitwich westward beyond the River Teme, east beyond Chipping Norton, and south to Lechlade and Old Sodbury.[57] It is much more difficult to establish trends in output. Foreign merchants exported some salt from east-coast ports, but in amounts which appear to be declining in the first half of the four-teenth century, although this may merely reflect the falling share of England's trade shipped by aliens. There does appear to have been a contemporary increase of salt imports, particularly into Scarborough, Hull and King's Lynn and mainly from western France, possibly indicating reduced production on the east coast; but there is no sign that there was any long-term check to rising production at Droitwich, and all the Cheshire wiches continued to be very active. Despite the rise in England's population since 1086, most of England's salt in 1349 was still home-made.[58]

Milling takes us into a very different world. Here the principal concern must be corn milling, although in 1278–79 Adam of Stratton built a new apple mill at Sevenhampton (Wilts.), one of many places where cider was made. Most villages and all towns, how-ever, needed facilities to grind flour, meal and malt. These were not always mechanized. As late as 1332 the St Albans abbey tenants at Codicote (Herts.) bought a licence to use hand mills and, about the same time, a Wakefield man had 'mills in his house constantly grinding malt';[59] but by then most milling had been mechanized. Much of the provision for this purpose was made by manorial lords or by municipal authorities for the good reason that they alone were likely to possess the resources needed to construct and maintain mills. To move one Hampshire mill in 1210–11, it is true, cost only 50s., and much later a wattle and daub mill was built at Cuxham (Oxon.) for £2; but even new windmills, which were cheaper to con-struct than water mills, usually cost £10–£20 (£12 in the case of Adam of Stratton's windmill at Sevenhampton in 1285–86).

---

[57] Bridbury, *England and the Salt Trade*, p. 23; Hallam, *Settlement and Society*, p. 200; Rudkin and Owen, 'The medieval salt industry in the Lindsey marshland', pp. 83–4; Hewitt, *Cheshire under the Three Edwards*, pp. 66–9; Hilton, *A Medieval Society*, p. 12.
[58] Bridbury, *England and the Salt Trade*, p. 30; Darby, ed., *A New Historical Geography of England*, p. 173; Berry, 'Droitwich and its salt industry', p. 51.
[59] A.E. Levett, *Studies in Manorial History*, Oxford, 1938, pp. 352, 359; Walker, ed., *Court Rolls of the Manor of Wakefield, 1331–3*, pp. 6, 184.

Expenditure on milling capacity was often very considerable. The bishop of Winchester spent nearly £114 on new mills at Southwark in 1210–11 and timber worth £61 was supplied from Sherwood Forest for the water mill with which Edward I equipped the town of Hull. While manorial tenants might be required to provide much of the labour for the maintenance of mills, especially in northern England, lords often contributed substantially to the costs which maintenance entailed, and particularly to those for the replacement of expensive items of mill equipment like millstones, the price of which doubled between the early thirteenth century and the Black Death. These costs absorbed some 24 per cent of the income which the bishop of Winchester got from the mill at Bitterne (Hants.) in the decade beginning in 1283, and 14 per cent of that from the mill at Downton (Wilts.).[60]

The management of mills usually involved one or other of two arrangements, both of which were represented in the manor of Wakefield in 1348. In three of the townships of the manor the mills were demised to Thomas Culpon for a fixed payment of £5 for the year; but the Cartworth and Holmfirth mills, because they could not be let for as much as in previous years, were in the hands of two men who were presumably paid employees who would account for the proceeds of their custody.[61] Farming out mills to lessees was probably the most common practice: it was adopted by Adam of Stratton at Sevenhampton, by Merton College at Cuxham, and by the bishop of Ely in most of his manors in 1251; and the castle mills at Oxford, ownership of which was shared between the city and the crown, were also usually leased. On the other hand, at Taunton in 1251–52 the bishop kept ten of the twelve mills in hand, and payments in kind for grinding grain at them furnished him with some 559 qr. of wheat, rye, meal and malt. The millers in charge of the largest of these mills may well have been full-time employees; but many manorial millers combined that office with tenure of an agricultural holding. One man, who had half the mill at Little Abington (Cambs.) early in the thirteenth century, also had a half virgate and

[60] P.D.A. Harvey, *A Medieval Oxfordshire Village*, pp. 140–1; N.R. Holt, ed., *Pipe Rolls of the Bishopric of Winchester, 1210–11*, pp. 131, 157–8; M.W. Farr, ed., *Accounts and Surveys of the Wiltshire Lands of Adam de Stratton*, p. 163; *VCH East Riding*, I, pp. 18–19; *CCR*, 1302–7, p. 64; D. Austin, ed., *Boldon Book*, p. 36 for the duty of tenants to provide labour on the mills of Aucklandshire; R.A. Holt, *The Mills of Medieval England*, p. 177; J. Langdon, 'Water-mills and windmills in the West Midlands', *EcHR*, 2nd ser. XLIV (1991), pp. 436–7; D.L. Farmer, 'Millstones for medieval manors', *AHR*, XL (1992), pp. 104–9.
[61] H.M. Jewell, ed., *Court Rolls of the Manor of Wakefield, 1348–50*, p. 11.

presumably was a villein, for he could be sold with all his progeny if the lord alienated the mill.[62]

Milling grain saw the most widespread application of power to industrial production during the middle ages. The power involved might literally be horse-power. On the Ely manors at Fen Ditton and Wisbech in 1251 customary tenants were obliged to grind their corn at the bishop's horse-mills even though there were windmills in both places and a water mill, too, at Fen Ditton. Horse-mills were still operating in these places, and at Ely, in 1299; but even in 1251 the 'town mill' at Bridgham (Norfolk) and the mills in many other places were water mills.[63] From the late twelfth century onwards notices of windmills also multiply, Herbert the dean even setting one up in the banlieu of Bury St Edmunds, much to the fury of Abbot Samson. They seem to have spread particularly rapidly in the late thirteenth century, and by the early fourteenth century they may have accounted for 12 per cent of all mills in the West Midlands. They were, however, supplements rather than alternatives to water mills, since the latter, although they called for heavier capital investment, were likely to generate a significantly larger income for their owners.[64]

A long-term increase in milling capacity, therefore, seems clear, for not only were there more mills by the early fourteenth century, but the spread of windmills made it possible to establish them in places ill-provided with water-power. Investment for this purpose seems to have been particularly heavy in many areas in the middle years of the thirteenth century, but perhaps came somewhat later in some colonizing regions like the Cambridgeshire and Norfolk marshlands. In England as a whole the number of mills at work perhaps doubled between 1086 and the early fourteenth century to 12,000, or it may even have attained 15,000 if full account is taken of greatly expanded provision required in the exceptionally active colonizing areas like the north and the south-west.[65] Not only were

[62] *VCH Oxon.*, IV, pp. 328–9; T.J. Hunt, ed., *Medieval Customs of the Manors of Taunton and Bradford on Tone*, Somerset Rec. Soc., LXVI (1962), pp. xlvii–viii; Ransford, ed., *Early Charters of Waltham Abbey*, nos. 167, 171–2.
[63] Caius College Ms. 485/489, ff. 120d, 268; BL Cott. Claudius C XI, f. 73; PRO SC 6/1132/10.
[64] H.E. Butler, ed., *Chronicle of Jocelin of Brakelond*, pp. 59–60; Holt, *Mills of Medieval England*, pp. 34–5; Langdon, 'Water-mills and windmills in the West Midlands', pp. 432–4.
[65] Caius College Ms. 485/489, *passim* (1251); PRO SC 6/1132/10 (1298–9); Holt, *Mills of Medieval England*, pp. 3–5, 115; Langdon, 'Water-mills and windmills of the West Midlands', pp. 424, 440–1.

mills more numerous, moreover, but many of them produced increasing revenues suggesting more intensive use. This was not universally so: on the Ely estates receipts from the Little Downham and Little Gransden mills fell or remained stationary between 1251 and 1299; but those from Haddenham and Ely mills doubled or more than doubled, and receipts at Fen Ditton (perhaps reflecting the manor's role as a collecting centre for grain from much of the bishop's Cambridgeshire estate) rose from just over £4 to £26. Nor did an increase in mill revenues necessarily cease after 1299. The water mill the bishop of Ely acquired at Great Shelford shortly before 1251 was let in 1299 for £5 a year, a figure which had risen to £10 by 1322–26 although it then came tumbling down to £6 13s. 4d. in 1327. Even so, this was a better return than in 1299, and it was three times the combined values of the Great and Little Shelford mills in 1086.[66]

More numerous and busier mills not only augmented the incomes of landlords: they also offered expanding opportunities to small-scale entrepreneurs. Where lords kept mills in hand the millers employed to operate them, who were often paid largely in kind from the toll-corn levied from those whose corn was ground there, probably fared no better or worse than other manorial *famuli*. The miller who 'farmed' a mill, on the other hand, might find his returns increasing as output increased, although the rapid adjustments of the rent paid by the Great Shelford miller in the 1320s suggest that payments responded quite quickly to changing circumstances. The farmers of manorial mills, moreover, enjoyed positions which had some advantages. Most manorial tenants were compelled to grind their corn at them and to pay a proportion of the corn they brought in (which might be as low as a twenty-fourth or as high as a thirteenth) for the miller's services; and what the miller got, as Chaucer well knew, could be surreptitiously augmented:

> Wel coude he stelen corn, and tollen thryes.

Even more than bakers, butchers and brewers, upon whom civic and manorial authorities kept a wary eye, millers were viewed with eternal suspicion. The point is neatly made in two drawings preserved in an early fourteenth-century manuscript. One shows a woman bringing in her corn to be ground; but on the next page, no doubt after

---

[66] For Great Shelford, *Dd*, I, f. 191 and PRO SC 6/1132/14–15, 1133/1.

experience of the miller's exactions, she is seen setting fire to the mill.[67]

The consumer goods industries, of course, were not limited to the provision trades, as the occupations, where these are known or can be presumed, of York freemen between 1307 and 1349 or of Colchester taxpayers in 1301 make clear. In each place about a third of those listed look like manufacturing craftsmen making up goods for direct sale to customers. At York the largest groups were leather and metal workers. There were more cobblers and shoemakers than representatives of any other craft, but also numerous glovers, saddlers, armourers, cutlers, girdlers, goldsmiths, smiths and lorimers. Second in numbers to the cobblers, however, were the tailors, and the clothing trades were also represented by hosiers. Finally, citizens also engaged in a number of miscellaneous crafts, of which bowyers, coopers and potters were the most important, but others were cartwrights, shipwrights, chandlers, ropers, hatters, horners and arrowsmiths. The Colchester taxpayers in 1301 were inevitably less diverse, for Colchester was a much smaller place; but again the largest group consisted of cobblers and shoemakers, followed by smiths and then by tailors. There were also a few glovers, some coopers, some lorimers and other metal workers, half a dozen bowyers and at least one potter. It is also noticeable that nearly 80 per cent of these craftsmen were assessed on goods worth less than £1, and none of them had goods worth over £5. Evidently most of them had no great wealth.

The modest standing of most craftsmen reflects their circumstances. The great majority of them, who in town or village made up consumer goods from cloth or leather or metal or wood or horn, relied principally upon local supplies of raw materials; and they found their customers in their own community or in its near neighbourhood. Usually they bought their materials directly, themselves fashioned them into goods for retail sale, and then sold them directly once more to customers. The work of fashioning them required only a few simple tools. A Colchester smith in 1301 had in his smithy hammers, an anvil and other tools valued, together with his little stock of iron, at only £1; and a wheelwright's two axes and two planes were only reckoned to be worth 1s. 6d. Even a specialist, like the Beaulieu abbey parchment-maker (who also did a little book-

[67] H.S. Bennett, *Life on the England Manor: a Study of Peasant Conditions, 1150–1400*, Cambridge, 1937, p. 133; P. Basing, *Trades and Crafts in Medieval Manuscripts*, p. 42.

81

binding), was apparently capable of working as a solitary individual; and goldsmiths, some of them aristocrats among craftsmen, seem hardly better equipped than ordinary smiths. A fourteenth-century painting of St Dunstan working as a goldsmith gives him as his sole equipment, apart from a stool on which to sit, an anvil and a double-headed hammer. The workshops of this sort of craftsmen could be accommodated in their houses, even though in London these were commonly cramped and built 'on narrow frontages in small, narrow streets'. Where shops as well as workshops were necessary, they were often 'no more than stalls projecting from the house-front'; the ground-floor front of a dwelling house sometimes served both as shop and workshop, or goods might be sold from a front shutter folded down in business hours to project into the street. The medieval craftsman generally, in fact, 'carried his skill in his hands', and not in expensive premises or equipment. The skinner who made up sometimes costly furs, for instance, needed only chests for storage, a trestle table, a stool, a pair of scissors, a knife, and needle and thread.[68]

The mention of goldsmiths and skinners, however, is a reminder that there were some craftsmen whose market was not that for everyday consumables, but one for individually styled products which would attract kings and prelates and noblemen and rich merchants. Most towns of any size had a few craftsmen capable of meeting the needs of the rich, but inevitably they were most numerous in London which, by the fourteenth century, was the principal seat of government and a magnet periodically for most of the great men of England. It is significant that in 1319 the London goldsmiths, in terms of taxable wealth, were the only manufacturing craft with 'a standing comparable to that of merchants', although they were hardly the only craftsmen serving a rich man's market. Some tailors probably made a better class of garment, some vestment-makers and embroiderers probably catered for discriminating customers, and some saddlers, armourers, fan-makers, jewellers and makers of mazer bowls probably turned out products of exceptional quality. Even so, the equipment they needed was little, if at all, more elaborate than that used by craftsmen serving the mass market. In either

---

[68] *Rot. Parl.*, I, p. 254; Hockey, ed., *Account Book of Beaulieu Abbey*, pp. 37–8, 195–8; T.F. Reddaway and L.E.M. Walker, *The Early History of the Goldsmiths' Company, 1327–1509*, plate 2 and pp. 14–16; Basing, *Trades and Crafts in Medieval Manuscripts*, pp. 46–7; Veale, *The English Fur Trade in the Later Middle Ages*, p. 33.

case, therefore, the unit of production was small and essentially domestic.[69]

The earliest ordinances of the York girdlers, drawn up in 1307, clearly reflect some of the characteristics of craft production. Girdlers were to 'work in no place but in their houses and . . . to work of their own goods'. They were allowed to put out work to bucklemakers, who were treated as 'common servants' of the girdlers' craft, but the master girdler himself had few helpers. He was allowed only a single apprentice who should 'abide with his master for four years at the least', and he was forbidden to take any 'stranger' into his service who had not served an apprenticeship in girdlercraft elsewhere.[70] A master and his family, with a single apprentice and at most a journeyman or two, with a little outside help from the bucklemakers, is the industrial unit envisaged here, although in London some were rather larger. The rules of the cordwainers in 1271 limited the number of 'servants' a master might employ to eight, and in 1309–12 many craftsmen of no great substance had two or more apprentices. Even so, production under the eye of the master in his own house remained the norm, and the cordwainers' rules forbade masters to give out work to servants to do in their own homes. Putting work out, none the less, was relatively common in London, especially when production involved a series of craft operations. Harness-making, for instance, was a matter not only for saddlers, but for lorimers who worked bits and bridles, joiners who made saddle-bows, and painters who decorated them. The outcome was a hierarchy of crafts, with saddlers providing many of the materials for the others and disposing of the finished product: they were 'the men of capital operating at the point of sale' and standing to the other crafts as quasi-employers. This was a pattern of organization which was reproduced elsewhere, for we also find ironmongers putting out work to nailers and smiths, and cutlers standing as employers to bladesmiths and sheathers.[71]

London, of course, was exceptional in the extent of the division of labour there, the diversity of its organized crafts, and the need of its craftsmen for commercial services in the distribution of their industrial products. Comparable services, however, were also needed elsewhere. The 79 cutlers taxed at Thaxted (Essex) in 1381, for

---

[69] E. Ekwall, ed., *Two Early London Subsidy Rolls*, pp. 100, 205–350.
[70] M. Sellars, ed., *York Memorandum Book*, I, pp. 180–1.
[71] Unwin, *Gilds and Companies of London*, pp. 83–7; Ekwall, ed., *Two Early London Subsidy Rolls*, pp. 75–7; *CLB, D*, pp. 96–179; Williams, *Medieval London*, pp. 177, 188.

example, must have needed some supplies of iron, and some customers for the knives they made, from outside their own locality.[72] Industrial expansion, in fact, had various levels. Much of it was purely quantitative: more people needed more manufactured commodities just as they needed more foodstuffs, a need satisfied by more craftsmen, many of them based in villages and serving markets which were literally parochial. Much of the expansion of pottery manufacture, made necessary by the fact that its products were in normal use by all classes in every part of the country, took place in the countryside, and most rural potteries had a restricted range of distribution (archaeologists have suggested a radius of 20–25 miles, a day's carting).[73] Villagers, therefore, as the inhabitants of the remote Northumbrian township of West Whelpington did, relied on pottery supplies from no great distance; but some potteries served much wider markets and must have relied upon distributive services to do so. Scarborough wares, for instance, were sold widely in northern England, as well as in Scotland, the northern isles and even in Flanders; the numerous medieval potteries at Chilvers Coton (Staffs.) must have served customers beyond those in neighbouring Nuneaton; and the potteries at Kingston on Thames came to be one of London's sources of supply.[74]

It is an advantage that pottery, even when it survives only as sherds, can often be traced back to its source and, within limits, dated. Markets for other consumer goods are less easily established, but here again some were not of necessity merely local. Special circumstances might contribute to that end; the fact that York was so often the king's forward base during the Scottish wars enlarged the circle of customers for the tailors, saddlers, bowyers and the smiths who made swords and arrow-heads of York itself and other Yorkshire towns. Specialist centres of production were developing. Northampton in 1266 was already a home of the boot and shoe industry, for Henry III ordered 150 pairs of shoes there to be given as alms; and by the fourteenth century rope-making, especially for naval stores, was the staple industry of Bridport, drawing supplies of

---

[72] K.C. Newton, *Thaxted in the Fourteenth Century*, pp. 20–1.

[73] McCarthy and Brooks, *Medieval Pottery in Britain*, pp. 69–74, 76–7; H.E.J. Le Patourel, 'Pottery as evidence for social and economic change', in P.H. Sawyer, ed., *Medieval Settlement*, p. 174; J.G. Hurst, 'White Castle and the dating of medieval pottery', *Med. Arch.*, VI–VII (1962–3), p. 147.

[74] D.H. Evans and M.G. Jarrett, 'The deserted village of West Whelpington, Northumberland', *AA*, 5th ser. xv (1987), p. 269; McCarthy and Brooks, *Medieval Pottery in Britain*, pp. 73–4, 94, 228–9, 309–11, 368.

flax and hemp from places widely scattered over Dorset.[75] Wider markets and increased output might demand more capital investment, especially in the provision of raw materials and the distribution of manufactured goods; but in many respects pottery manufacture was not untypical of the consumer goods industries of the central middle ages. There were few significant technological advances (although there was perhaps some shift from wood to coal as fuel, and wheel-throwing and better controlled firing became almost universal). A great deal of pottery was made, however, for a very restricted market, the basic production unit was the nuclear family with perhaps a servant or two, and judging by the fact that potters figure only rarely in the lay subsidy returns their craft was not beyond the reach even of the poorer among the villagers.[76] Even town manufacturing craftsmen, whatever their craft, with sufficient resources to be assessed for taxation were unlikely to rank among the richer townsfolk. Characteristically they were handicraftsmen, engaged in small-scale production within a domestic framework.

5.   SPECIAL CASES: I. THE BUILDING TRADES

The building trades fit these general characteristics of medieval industry less than perfectly. Representatives of these trades are found everywhere: most towns supported settled groups of building workers; Beaulieu abbey had a full-time master carpenter and master plumber; and a country manor like Cuxham could count on finding local workers to build and roof a hall, to cut wooden shingles, and to thatch the oat grange and other buildings.[77] Builders, too, disposed of few mechanical aids, although slings and hoists might be used to lift heavy weights and the erection of a crane was a necessary preliminary to starting the 'new work' at Ely cathedral in 1322–23.[78] For the most part, however, building was a matter for hand-tools

---

[75] H. Swanson, *Medieval Artisans*, pp. 48, 69–71, 101–2, 104; Salzman, *English Industries of the Middle Ages*, p. 257; J. Pahl, 'The rope and net industry of Bridport', *Proc. Dorset NH and Arch. Soc.*, LXXXII (1960), pp. 143–5.

[76] McCarthy and Brooks, *Medieval Pottery in Britain*, pp. 76–80.

[77] H. Swanson, *Building Craftsmen in Late Medieval York*, pp. 9–14; Hockey, ed., *Account Book of Beaulieu Abbey*, pp. 204–5; P.D.A. Harvey, ed., *Manorial Records of Cuxham, Oxfordshire, c. 1200–1359*, pp. 234, 269, 376.

[78] Salzman, *Building in England*, pp. 322–4; Chapman, ed., *Sacrist Rolls of Ely*, II, p. 33.

and depended upon the craftsman's skilled hand, supported by the toil of 'mates', of youngsters learning the trade and of a good deal of less skilled labour. In such respects building differed little from other industries. Many building workers, on the other hand, were more mobile than most craftsmen; most of the capital costs of building were borne by the customer; and even master craftsmen commonly worked for wages, which might include rations and accommodations, but the principal (and often the only) element was a money payment.[79]

Building work covered a range of activities from minor repairs to the erection of castles and churches, some of which have survived as memorials of the medieval builder's art. Repairs and minor modifications were the most continuous building activity. On most manors there were charges to be entered virtually every year under the rubric *custus domorum*, if only the wages of a carpenter or thatcher for a few days and the cost of timber or nails or other materials. Periodically, however, lords built a new barn or byre or house; and in towns agreements were sometimes drawn up to develop whole sites. In 1310 a London carpenter undertook to build three shops with two storeys above them in St Michael's parish in Cornmarket, a job he estimated would take four months; and in 1335 the parishioners of St Martin's in Coney Street, York, contracted with another carpenter to build, in a little over three months, a row of six or seven houses under one roof in St Martin's Lane.[80] Such commissions called for the employment of more labour over a longer period than repairing jobs, which in major establishments like abbeys and castles would probably be carried out by a small full-time staff. The building of castles and the great churches was another matter, for there work might continue for many years and demand the services of large bodies of workers. They were not the typical building enterprises of the middle ages, but most is known about them because they were undertaken for men and institutions which kept records.

Even lesser building operations, however, required a diversity of skills. The manorial buildings at Cuxham, for instance, regularly needed the employment, usually only for a few days at a time, of men who, without being specialists, could saw timber, make mortar, or thatch and tile a roof. These were perhaps the sort of modest accomplishments that peasant villagers acquired by experience, but

[79] Swanson, *Medieval Artisans*, p. 85.
[80] Salzman, *Building in England*, pp. 418–19, 430–2.

86

for some tasks specialists had to be engaged. They included skilled thatchers and tilers, occasionally smiths and plumbers, and more rarely a mason to repair a sewer, a garden wall or a dovecote. The building specialist most regularly hired, on the other hand, both in town and country, was a carpenter. Carpenters at Cuxham, as well as repairing buildings and sawing timber, put up granaries, cartsheds, piggeries and henhouses, and rebuilt the hall and solar of the manor house. Larger building enterprises, of course, called for the co-operation of a range of crafts, but what distinguished them most of all were the sheer number of workers involved. The work force at Caernarvon castle in the summer of 1295 rose to 528 in one week, and that of Windsor in the spring of 1344 to 710.[81]

These grand buildings were of stone, and here the mason comes into his own. Among masons it became increasingly common to distinguish between those who set the stones, the 'free masons' who cut and dressed the stones and were 'the superior branch of the craft', and a specialized craft of monumental masons who may already have contributed to St Hugh's buildings at Lincoln cathedral at the end of the twelfth century and a veritable dynasty of whom, the Canons of Corfe, left their mark in Purbeck marble in monuments ranging from the Eleanor crosses of the 1290s to the images provided for Westminster Hall in 1385. All the same, the place of the mason in the history of medieval building should not be exaggerated. Stone houses were sufficiently exceptional among domestic buildings to be mentioned as such in thirteenth-century charters.[82] Most buildings were of wood, or were wooden-framed infilled with daub, and even on the 'new work' at Ely (the octagon, the adjoining parts of the choir and the Lady Chapel), while masons were the largest group of workmen in 1322–26, they were outnumbered by carpenters ten years later. On major enterprises especially, moreover, both masons and carpenters had to be reinforced by representatives of other crafts: tilers, slaters and thatchers for roofing, or plumbers if the roof was to be of lead and to provide guttering and water pipes, glaziers and painters, plasterers and daubers, carvers and turners, and of course smiths who, as the Exeter cathedral building accounts demonstrate, were wonderfully versatile. There they made iron-work for windows, hinges for a

---

[81] *Ibid.*, pp. 35–6; Harvey, ed., *Manorial Records of Cuxham*, pp. 234, 252, 285, 319, 338, 356, 376, 416.

[82] E.g. 'the Jews' house' in Lincoln and Hugh fitzLefwin's house on the corner of Coney Street and Stonegate in York: J.W.F. Hill, *Medieval Lincoln*, pp. 234–7; *EYC*, I, nos. 242, 246–7.

clock, a little clapper for a bell called Peter, the surrounds of the
eagle on the pulpit, and the binding for a coffer in the exchequer,
and besides they kept the tools of the other workers in repair. In the
background were quarrymen, sawyers preparing timber, and carters
and boatmen providing transport. At Ely, too, a tile-works was set up
to make bricks, and bells were founded by a bell-founder from
Gloucester.[83]

Even towns were often unable to supply all the skilled labour
needed for major enterprises. How labour was recruited for them is
seldom clear, except when kings used prerogative powers to impress
building workers in much the same way as they sometimes
impressed miners. Many building workers, in consequence, and
stone-masons especially, were apt to be peripatetic and to need
accommodation once they had been assembled. This explains why
masons tended to be organized, not in the craft gilds which developed among settled workers, but in temporary 'lodges', i.e. in more
or less involuntary associations brought together for a particular job.
The 'lodge' was primarily a workshop for dressing stone, but it also
served as a dining room, a place for taking the midday nap allowed
in summer, and often as a dormitory – all uses encouraging association among its users. Some castles and cathedrals had more or less
permanent 'lodges', but elsewhere it was common for temporary
accommodation to be improvised as the need arose.[84] Incomers
other than masons might be brought in for major projects. For the
'new work' at Ely, as we have seen, a bell-founder was recruited from
Gloucester; Master Thomas the carpenter, much used in the king's
service, came over from Newport (Essex) to advise; William de
Hurle, another carpenter used by the king, probably came up from
London; and the services of Walter the painter were shared by Ely
and the lady of Clare. These, of course, were men of exceptional
skills, but the fact that a building labour-force was often an improvised one perhaps helps to explain some of the criticisms directed at
the workers employed at York minster in 1345: their pilfering of
materials, their mutual quarrels, the failure of some masons to obey

[83] D.L. Douie and H. Farmer, eds, *Magna Vita Sancti Hugonis*, Medieval Texts, 2 vols,
1961–2, pp. xxxvii–viii; Salzman, *Building in England*, pp. 30–3, 91–5, 130, 134, 147,
165; idem, *English Industries of the Middle Ages*, p. 120; Erskine, ed., *Accounts of the Fabric
of Exeter Cathedral*, II, pp. xvii–xxiv; Chapman, ed., *Sacrist Rolls of Ely*, II, pp. 67, 122,
136–9.
[84] G.P. Jones, in *CEcH*, II, pp. 785–6; Salzman, *Building in England*, pp. 33–40, 45.

the master mason's orders, and the latter's inability either to restrain them or to discipline them properly.[85]

The organization of building projects obviously depended on their scale. Modest enterprises called for little organization, although contracts like those for London shops or the houses in St Martin's Lane, York, specified in some detail what their owners wanted. It is also possible that reaction against some past romantic assumptions about the role of non-professionals in the design of cathedrals and monastic churches has gone too far. There is a case to be made, for example, for accepting the contemporary attribution to Alan of Walsingham, sacrist of Ely, of the conception of the octagon, the chief glory of the 'new work'.[86] On the other hand, the mark of the professional is no less evident. An early fourteenth-century drawing, for instance, depicts King Offa of Mercia, as builder of St Albans, consulting a master mason whose enormous pair of compasses indicate his ability to draw up plans and mark out foundations on the ground. For large projects, in other words, men who are not inappropriately described as architects were needed to contribute to building design, to provide plans for others to work from, and to superintend their execution. Financial management was usually in other hands (those of the sacrist at Ely or of the keeper of the works at Exeter); but at Exeter cathedral the master mason planned and directed building work, allocated tasks to the labour-force, was chiefly responsible for selecting and assembling materials, and probably recruited labour. Most 'architects' were either master masons or master carpenters, and like their successors in later times they often had a number of irons in the fire simultaneously. When Richard de Farlegh was put in charge of the fabric at Salisbury cathedral in 1334 it was recognized that he had other commitments at Bath and Reading; and Master Thomas of Whitney, master mason at Exeter cathedral 1316–42, was also engaged at one time and another at Wells, Winchester, Malmesbury, Exeter castle and Merton College, Oxford. Men like this were well rewarded: Exeter cathedral paid Master Thomas a fee of £6 or £6 13s. 4d. a year, and when William de Hoton succeeded his father in a similar position at

[85] *Ibid.*, pp. 54–5; Chapman, ed., *Sacrist Rolls of Ely*, I, pp. 21–2, 45–7; II, p. 99.
[86] N. Pevsner makes a persuasive case: *The Buildings of England, Cambridgeshire*, Harmondsworth, 1954, pp. 281–2.

York minster in 1351 he got £10 a year and a promise of the rever-
sion of the house which had been provided for his father.[87]

The rewards of rank-and-file building workers, of course, were
much smaller. Average daily wages during the century before the
Black Death have been calculated to be 3d.–4d. for a craftsman and
$1^1/_2$d.–2d. for a labourer – i.e. assuming full employment 1s.
6d.–2s. and 9d.–1s. respectively for a six-day week.[88] Realities, however, were somewhat more complicated. Some workers, at Ely for
example, got part of their reward in the form of food 'at the lord's
table'; wages were lower in winter when hours of work were necessarily shorter (in 1299 1s. $10^1/_2$d. a week for the best paid Exeter
mason compared with 2s. 3d. in summer); and feast days when no
work was done meant no pay. Employment was also highly precarious. In November 1252 a blunt warning went out at Windsor castle:
'because there are many more workmen . . . than is necessary, from
whose work by reason of the shortness of the days . . . the king
derives little profit, the king wills that the greater part of them be
discharged, together with the painters . . . since they cannot work
properly by reason of the dampness of winter time'. The number of
employees on major building projects, therefore, fluctuated wildly:
there were, for example, between 15 and 210 masons at work on
Windsor castle in the spring of 1344, and between 17 and 401
labourers. Daily and even weekly wage rates, in consequence, are an
imperfect guide to the annual earnings of building workers. Of the
masons working on Exeter cathedral in 1299–1300, one was
employed for 46 weeks for £5 7s. $2^1/_2$d., another for 31 weeks for
£2 13s. $2^1/_2$d., and yet another for a mere nine weeks for 15s. 4d.
The difference is that between relative affluence and evident
penury unless alternative employment was available. These were
the realities of life for men who, according to York regulations in
1352, 'ought to begin work on all working days in summer . . . at
sunrise', and whose day thereafter was prescribed in detail until (as

[87] Basing, *Trades and Crafts in Medieval Manuscripts*, pp. 67–8; Salzman, *Building in
England*, pp. 24–5, 45; Erskine, ed., *Accounts of the Fabric of Exeter Cathedral*, II, pp.
xix–xxi. Elias of Dereham was perhaps an 'architect' who was neither mason nor carpenter, but rather a clerk and 'administrator familiar with building processes'; he may
have advised on the design for Salisbury cathedral and was entrusted with the construction of the king's hall at Winchester by Henry III: Salzman, *Building in England*,
pp. 9–10; P.H. Brieger, *English Art, 1216–1307*, Oxford, 1956, pp. 18–19.
[88] E.H. Phelps Brown and S.V. Hopkins, 'Seven centuries of building wages', in E.M.
Carus-Wilson, ed., *Essays in Economic History*, II, pp. 168–78.

the monks of Beaulieu put it) it ended only with the setting of the sun.[89]

The relatively low rewards of building workers, combined with the intermittent nature of their employment, perhaps explains why so many of them seem to have been poor even by comparison with other artisans.[90] Their low rewards also served to keep down building costs, since labour accounted for a high proportion of them. In 1338 a timber-framed house in Cambridge, apparently erected on existing stone foundations, cost £23 to build, a total of which wages of carpenters, sawyers and plasterers accounted for 40 per cent. The proportion might even be higher in more elaborate buildings: 60 per cent, for instance, of the expenditure on the 'new work' at Ely in those years for which accounts survive. Building, like other medieval industries, was clearly labour intensive; but it also demanded what was, for the time, high levels of capital expenditure. For men of modest means £23 spent on a timber-framed house in Cambridge, or £22 on building three London shops, or the £40 spent by parishioners on building a little row of houses in York, or the £50 needed to replace five shops with a capacious London tavern, even the £9 5s. 4d. expended by a London skinner on a new house and outbuildings in 1308, were not inconsiderable sums. And, of course, there were building enterprises of an altogether different order. In 1313–14 Thomas of Lancaster spent some £1,900 on his castles (£1,343 on his Derbyshire castle at Melbourne alone); the 'new work' at Ely was said to have cost £2,400 by 1342; and work on Exeter cathedral may have cost in the order of £6,000 in the period 1299–1326. The king's works were more expensive still: the cost of castles in Wales alone for Edward I has been estimated to be around £80,000 over a period of twenty-five years.[91]

Building was a continuous activity, but there were periods of special intensity. In the generation or two after 1066 most of the Saxon cathedrals and abbey churches were reconstructed and buildings

[89] Chapman, ed., *Sacrist Rolls of Ely*, II, p. 47; Erskine, ed., *Accounts of the Fabric of Exeter Cathedral*, I, pp. 175–7; Salzman, *Building in England*, pp. 35–6, 56–7, 59; Hockey, ed., *Acount Book of Beaulieu Abbey*, pp. 202–3. Work continued until dusk only in winter; in summer it normally ceased at 7 p.m., implying a 10½ hour day when allowance is made for meal-breaks: H.M. Colvin, ed., *Building Accounts of Henry III*, pp. 9–10.
[90] Swanson, *Medieval Artisans*, p. 84.
[91] Salzman, *Building in England*, pp. 206–7, 417–19, 430–4; J.R. Maddicott, *Thomas of Lancaster, 1307–1322: a Study in the Reign of Edward II*, Oxford, 1970, pp. 25–6; *VCH Cambs.*, IV, p. 64; Erskine, ed., *Accounts of the Fabric of Exeter Cathedral*, I, *passim*; Brieger, *English Art, 1216–1307*, p. 264.

were provided for many new monastic foundations. In the twelfth century stone castles multiplied and new monastic orders needed churches and accommodation; in some places the 'great rebuilding' of parish churches began in the late twelfth century and continued until the Black Death; and Edward I built new towns at Hull and Winchelsea as well as castles in Wales.[92] These spurts of activity were linked by more consistent demands for the services of builders as population increased and new towns were established; new building fashions gave rise to calls for new churches; and new wealth generated by high farming led to demands for grander and more comfortable dwelling places. Not all of this building, of course, was necessarily either sound or durable; even major buildings collapsed as the central tower at Ely did one night in 1322. When so many buildings, too, were timber structures fire was an ever present hazard; and much of the provision for ordinary folk took the form of 'flimsy, do-it-yourself structures'. The building stock, therefore, had continuously to be renewed, and even in villages archaeologists are revealing 'a complex of superimposed buildings' suggesting that they were replaced 'about every generation'. At this humble level skilled craftsmen may have made some contribution to the building effort, but it also offered opportunities for ordinary villagers to develop some elementary building skills.[93]

The history of the building trades between 1086 and 1349, then, like that of many other trades, is one of expansion and development. In the first place, the pool of trained craftsmen was enlarged. Some of the crude mason's work of the early Norman age perhaps points at that time to a shortage of trained workers in stone. As time passed, however, that shortage seems to have been made good and the skills of other building crafts were refined. Basic techniques probably changed relatively little, but the necessary skills became more widely diffused. Secondly, because building was a labour-intensive industry demanding the services of numerous labourers as well as of skilled craftsmen, it provided itself some of the opportunities for the diffusion of

---

[92] D. Talbot Rice, *English Art, 871–1100*, Oxford, 1952, p. 72; T.S.R. Boase, *English Art, 1100–1215*, Oxford, 1953, p. 198; W.G. Hoskins, *Midland England: a Survey of the Country between the Chilterns and the Trent*, 1949, pp. 24–9; M.W. Beresford and J.K.S. St Joseph, *Medieval England: An Aerial Survey*, pp. 231–2, 238–41.

[93] *VCH Cambs.*, IV, p. 62; M.W. Beresford and J.G. Hurst, 'Wharram Percy: a case study in microtopography', in Sawyer, ed., *Medieval Settlement*, pp. 122–3.

skills. At a bread and butter level, too, chances to earn wages in the less skilled branches of the industry, however poor the wage and however brief the engagement, were not to be despised at a time when, in town and country alike, under-employment was chronic and many families existed very near to the margins of subsistence.

6. SPECIAL CASES: II. THE TEXTILE INDUSTRY

The textile industry was again a special case, because the manufacture of the materials from which clothing, bed-clothing and wall-hangings were made served basic and universal consumer needs, so that it necessarily had to cater for a mass market. Textile workers, therefore, were found virtually everywhere – in town and in country and in all parts of the land. Most of them, like other craftsmen, served mainly local markets, but influences were at work to expand the horizons of some of them. In addition to the common man's market for homespun there was a much smaller, but better documented, 'fashion' market for fabrics superior in quality or more arresting in colour. This market was often much less local in character and in serving it some centres of production gained a competitive advantage because they were better organized, displayed higher levels of skill, or had access to especially good raw materials. The craftsmen working for this market often needed commercial services to link them with distant customers and access to capital resources to bridge the more extended interval between production and sale. Cloth-making, furthermore, involved a chain of processes in order to turn raw wool into the finished fabric. A single individual, with the help of his family, might be capable of carrying out all of them; but almost inevitably each process tended to become the province of a specific craft, especially when markets expanded and more efficient production was needed to capture them. In such circumstances entrepreneurs to organize and co-ordinate the successive stages of production became necessary, a role often assumed by the merchants who linked the industry to its markets.

(a) Cloth-making and its costs

It is necessary, therefore, to say a little more about the processes of cloth-making.[94] The industry had several branches. Linen cloth was made from vegetable fibres (especially flax) in locations as far apart as Norfolk and Herefordshire. The king's wardrobe was able to buy nearly a thousand yards of English linen in 1336; there were probably linen weavers in York throughout the middle ages; but Wilton, where Henry III bought linen for napkins and tablecloths, and perhaps Aylsham (Norfolk), were among the few specialist linen towns.[95] For king and subjects alike, however, the cloth that mattered most was woollen cloth.

Its making was a lengthy affair. First the wool had to be sorted, beaten and washed to remove impurities, then carded or combed according to its staple, and spun into yarn. All of these were commonly women's work and hand operations, for even spinners still often used the age-old distaff and spindle: the spinning wheel was well enough known to be illustrated in a fourteenth-century English manuscript, but it was in nothing like general use before Tudor times.[96] The yarn then passed to the weavers, many of whom initially probably used the traditional warp-weighted upright looms, although there is no sign of them in medieval Winchester by contrast with the villages around the city. By the thirteenth century, however, these looms were being superseded by horizontal looms fitted with a shedding mechanism operated by pedals. The horizontal loom was more expensive and required more space; but it gave greater scope for varying the tightness and fineness of the weave, and it substantially increased the weaver's productivity. It replaced the older types of loom only slowly and incompletely, and the variety of thirteenth-century fabrics probably owed a great deal to the variety of the looms on which they were woven; but the fact that more and more of the looms in use were more expensive, took up more

---

[94] Succinctly described by E.M. Carus-Wilson, 'The Woollen Industry before 1550', in *CEcH*, II, pp. 636–9. What follows relies heavily upon this and other writings of Carus-Wilson's, the most significant contributions to the early history of the textile industry by any English scholar. On manufacturing processes, see also Bolton, *The Medieval English Economy*, pp. 153–5 and P.J. Bowden, *The Wool Trade in Tudor and Stuart England*, 1962, pp. 41–3.

[95] Salzman, *English Industries of the Middle Ages*, pp. 328–40; *CLR*, 1226–40, pp. 34, 116, 192; P. Walton, 'Textiles, cordage and raw fibre from 16–22 Coppergate', in P.V. Addyman, ed., *Archaeology of York*, XVII(5), pp. 422–3.

[96] C. Singer, E.J. Holmyard and A.R. Hall, eds, *History of Technology*, II, 1955, p. 202; Swanson, *Medieval Artisans*, pp. 30–2; Basing, *Trades and Crafts in Medieval Manuscripts*, p. 80.

room, and were more productive speeded up the long-term process of removing textile production from the housewife's domestic domain into the workshops of professional weavers, even though some horizontal looms clearly operated in contexts which were essentially domestic.[97]

Weaving was not the end of the production process, especially for the broadcloths which became England's staple. Most cloth (apart from light fabrics like worsteds) was fulled: i.e. felted by soaking it in an alkaline detergent in which it was trampled by human feet, or beaten with sticks, or from the late twelfth century onwards pounded by wooden hammers driven by water power (the fulling mill of which more will need to be said). Each cloth was then dried and stretched to the appropriate dimensions on a tenter, the nap was raised with teasels, and the surface was trimmed with a large pair of shears. Finally, at some stage unless the cloth was to be sold or worn 'white', either the raw wool or the yarn or the woven and fulled cloth was dyed. Here the art lay in the choice of dye-stuffs, their mixture where appropriate, and the treatment of the fabric for the optimum time. At the same time, because dyeing was often the last of the finishing processes, it might fall to the dyer to market the finished product.

Information about the costs of cloth-making is a good deal less than satisfactory. Some details relating to the making of winter 'white' (i.e. undyed) cloth at Beaulieu abbey in an average year in *c.* 1270, and of dyed cloth at the Westminster manor of Laleham (Middlesex) in the 1290s, have survived and seem to offer some chance of comparing production costs. Too much weight, however, cannot be given to this information for a variety of reasons, although for lack of better an analysis of the costs of producing undyed cloth in the two places is set out in Table 2.1. The figures certainly need to be treated with many reservations. Some errors may have crept into the Beaulieu record, so that certain amendments need to be tentatively suggested; and actual production costs there in 1269–70, although again the record of them may be imperfect, were about 15 per cent higher than in the 'average' year. The Laleham material, too, consists of rough notes which are almost certainly incomplete, we do not know whether Laleham cloths were

---

[97] A. Woodger, 'The eclipse of the burel weaver: some technological developments of the thirteenth century', *Textile History*, XII (1981), pp. 59–76; Keene, *Survey*, I, p. 298; Swanson, *Medieval Artisans*, pp. 32–3; Walton, 'Textiles, cordage and raw fibre from 16–22 Coppergate', pp. 386–8; Basing, *Trades and Crafts in Medieval Manuscripts*, p. 81.

of the same size as those made at Beaulieu, it may be incorrect to set the whole of the weaver's remuneration against the cost of the six cloths he produced for the abbey since he seems to have been hired out to others when there was no work for him on the manor, and the cost of the wool he used (even when adjusted to take account of that taken from the manor store) seems low when compared with this element in costs at Beaulieu or in fifteenth-century Flanders.[98] The figures also exclude the substantial cost of dyeing Laleham cloth, which amounted to 21 per cent of total production costs and 30 per cent of manufacturing costs.

When all these reservations have been made, however, and in default of more satisfactory evidence, the figures are perhaps suggestive in certain respects. It looks as though both at Beaulieu and Laleham the costs of preparing and spinning the wool were relatively high. It also seems that weaving was a less expensive operation, indeed especially so at Beaulieu; that fulling and related finishing processes were not conspicuously expensive; but that at Laleham dyeing added not inconsiderably to the cost of the finished product. The distribution of costs would also suggest that the provision of woollen yarn for the weaver must have made the heaviest demands for labour, since this work was done by low-paid workers.

Table 2.1. Percentage distribution of the costs of producing 'white' cloth at Beaulieu abbey in *c.* 1270 and at Laleham in c. 1294–5[99]

| | Total production costs | | Manufacturing costs | |
	Beaulieu	Laleham	Beaulieu	Laleham
Wool	57	35	–	–
Preparation & spinning	32	29	75	45
Weaving	4	23	9	35
Fulling and finishing	7	13	16	20
Cost per cloth	£1 9s. 7^{1}/4d.	£1 10s. 9^{1}/2d.	12s. 7^{3}/4d.	19s. 7d.

[98] Hockey, ed., *Account Book of Beaulieu Abbey*, pp. 214–15, 219–21; T.H. Lloyd, 'Some costs of cloth manufacture in thirteenth-century England', *Textile History*, I (1968–70), pp. 233–6. In the Beaulieu account the details do not add up to the total given, and it has been assumed that a cost of 2s. 3^{1}/2d. for combing the wool used for the weft may have been omitted; and in the Laleham accounts some of the wool used to make 6 cloths seems to have been taken from stock, the value of which has been assumed to be the same as that of additional wool which was bought.

[99] J. Munro, 'Industrial protectionism in medieval Flanders', in H.A. Miskmin, D. Herlihy and A.D. Udovich, eds, *The Medieval City*, 1977, Table 13.2, suggests that in Flanders in the late middle ages wool accounted for about two-thirds of the costs of cloth-making.

Beaulieu and Laleham fabrics, of course, cannot be taken as representative of thirteenth-century English textiles. The former in particular looks like a relatively cheap cloth, and certainly it did not receive expensive finishing.[100] One of the most difficult problems in the history of cloth-making, in fact, is the sheer variety of the industry's products, a variety illustrated by purchases for the king's wardrobe in 1264–65. They included cheap London burels, possibly looser and irregular weaves made on the traditional vertical looms. Other purchases were very variously priced. These differences might sometimes reflect variations in the length and width of cloth in the bolts in which it was sold in the wholesale market in which the king dealt. In 1264–65 London burels were 40 yards long, but Lincoln greens were only 39 yards and Beverley cloths varied between 34 and 41 yards. Two generations later there were 'short' scarlets 23 yards long (although these came from Bruges) and 'long' scarlets 28 yards in length. Not surprisingly, therefore, the king in 1264–65 bought by the yard rather than by the cloth. Cloths also differed in finish, quality and colour, matters about which the records tell us little except to the extent that they are reflected in variations of price. These variations were quite considerable. In 1264–65 Lincoln green cost 3s.–3s. 2d. a yard, but Beverley green could be got for only 1s. 10d.; and a whole bolt of Lincoln green cost £6 3s. 6d. compared with £3 11s. 6d. for Beverley green.[101]

The variety of textile products and their prices means we can never be absolutely sure that we are comparing like with like. It also makes difficult any attempt to establish the trend of textile prices over time, a basically important matter for the standards of living of those who bought the industry's products, the rewards of those who engaged in it, and for its competitive position. There may have been a rise in the price of the cheapest cloth, for burel for the king's alms cost $6\frac{1}{2}$d. a yard at Winchester in 1173, while grey cloth bought there for the same purpose in 1244 cost 7d.–8d. a yard; on the other hand, the

---

[100] The account book sets the cost of winter cloth at 1s. $2\frac{1}{4}$d. and gray cloth at 1s. $3\frac{1}{4}$d. a yard. Presumably, if it had been marketed, it would have sold for rather more than that, but in any case it was a dearer fabric than Oxford russets and London burels which could be got for 8d.–11d. a yard (e.g. *CLR*, 1226–40, pp. 159, 215, 319), although these may have been narrower than the Beaulieu cloths, which were the standard 2 yards wide. In any event the latter were relatively inexpensive compared to Lincoln scarlets, which sold at up to 6s. 8d. a yard or Lincoln greens at 3s. or more a yard: PRO E 101/350/4. So much for A.R. Bridbury's gratuitous assumption about Beaulieu's 'presumably exacting standards': *Medieval English Clothmaking*, p. 2.

[101] PRO E 101/340/4, 383/2. At Beaulieu, too, winter cloths were 25 yards long, but summer cloths were 30 yards: *Account Book of Beaulieu Abbey*, pp. 214–15.

price of London burels seems to have altered little during Henry III's reign, perhaps suggesting that, if prices had risen, the main impact had come by the early thirteenth century.[102] At the other end of the quality scale, by contrast, Lincoln scarlet seems to have been obtainable for about 6s. 8d. a yard alike in 1182 and in *c.* 1300.[103] These indicators are too few for very confident conclusions, but there seems no strong evidence for any marked increase of textile prices in the thirteenth century, despite the rising cost of wool. Technological advances like the spread of horizontal looms and of fulling mills may have combined with a wider diffusion of the industry itself to intensify competition, and to make the course of cloth prices rather different from that for land and for basic foodstuffs.

(b)   The twelfth-century industry

The importance of the medieval textile industry makes necessary some attempt to chart its history.[104] Cloth-making, as we have seen, was an ancient occupation in villages and manorial centres, as well as in developing towns, long before 1066; and the fuller evidence available by c. 1200 is sufficient to show that, as elsewhere in the medieval west, cloth-making skills were traditional in the English countryside.[105] A random sample of manorial and official documents from around 1200 reveals men called 'the weaver' or 'the fuller' in almost every English county; and it is particularly interesting to find them attested at Lavenham in Suffolk and at Avening and Minchinhampton in Gloucester, which were to become notable cloth-making centres in due course.[106] What the evidence suggests, in fact, is that at that time, over much of the English countryside, relatively isolated weavers and fullers are to be found working

---

[102] *Pipe Roll*, 18 Henry II, p. 8; *CLR*, 1240–5, p. 263. London burels were bought at 8d. a yard in 1239 and the 1260s: *CLR*, 1226–40, p. 407; 1260–67, p. 224; PRO E 101/350/4.

[103] *Pipe Roll*, 28 Henry II, p. 50; PRO E 101/354/23. Lincoln green was also bought for 3s. a yard in both 1182 and 1264–65: PRO E 101/350/4.

[104] See in general E. Miller, 'The fortunes of the English textile industry in the thirteenth century', *EcHR*, 2nd ser. XVIII (1965), pp. 64–82 and A.R. Bridbury, *Medieval English Clothmaking*, pp. 1–46.

[105] A point rightly stressed by Bridbury, *Medieval English Clothmaking*, pp. 22–3 and cf. Miller, 'Fortunes of the English textile industry', p. 67.

[106] To the sources listed *ibid.*, p. 67n. may be added H. Hall, ed., *Pipe Roll of the Bishopric of Winchester, 1208–9*; N.R. Holt, ed., *Pipe Roll of the Bishopric of Winchester 1210–11*; M. Chibnall, ed., *Charters and Custumals of the Abbey of Holy Trinity, Caen; Reg. Antiquissimum*, IV, no. 1156 and V, no. 1464; R.H.C. Davis, ed., *Kalendar of Abbot Samson of Bury St Edmunds and related Documents*, pp. 21, 38, 51, 59, 101.

mainly to supply the needs of their neighbours.[107] These rural specialists leave traces in the records from Henry I's time, for we hear of a fuller and possibly a weaver at Thornton Parva (Suffolk) in *c.* 1130, of a fuller at *Withmere* near Stafford in *c.* 1118, and of a fuller at Barton-on-Humber in *c.* 1140.[108] Similar specialists were necessary, although possibly in greater numbers, to supply the needs of developing towns. At the start of the twelfth century there was a weaver at Battle (Sussex); there was another in 1185 in the Templars' new town at Baldock (Herts.); weavers, fullers and dyers were mentioned in the foundation charter of Egremont (Cumberland) in c. 1202; and of the 78 inhabitants of Newark (Notts.) with occupational surnames in c. 1175 ten were weavers and two were fullers.[109]

Newark by 1175, in fact, may have attained a more advanced degree of specialization, enabling its cloth workers to supply markets more extensive than their own neighbourhood. Towns which succeeded in doing so might produce high-quality fabrics aimed at national or even international markets; or they might concentrate on the production of relatively cheap and ordinary fabrics, or on marketing rural textiles of a similar quality, in quantities large enough to supply markets beyond their own localities. These cheaper lines, including burels and russets, were sometimes traded in considerable quantities. In 1218 Marlborough and Bedwyn (Wilts.), as well as London, were recognized centres of burel production; in 1172 Henry II bought 2,000 yards of burel for his army in Ireland as well as cloth for like purposes in Oxford; bulk purchases of burels were also made in Kent and at Gloucester; and of cheap cloth for the king's almsgiving in Yorkshire. The expansion of markets for ordinary fabrics, although we catch only occasional glimpses of it, was probably as significant as the growth of markets for better quality products.[110]

---

[107] E.M. Carus-Wilson, 'The woollen industry before 1550', in *VCH Wilts.*, IV, pp. 115–47.
[108] D.C. Douglas, ed., *Feudal Documents from the Abbey of Bury St Edmunds*, p. 115; C.G.O. Bridgeman, ed., 'Burton abbey twelfth-century surveys', *William Salt Arch. Soc. Collections* (1916), p. 221; Stenton, ed., *Documents Illustrative of the Social and Economic History of the Danelaw*, no. 473.
[109] E. Searle, ed., *Chronicle of Battle Abbey*, p. 52; B.A. Lees, ed., *Records of the Templars in England in the Twelfth Century*, p. 69; *BBC, 1042–1216*, p. 160; M.W. Barley, ed., *Documents relating to the Manor and Soke of Newark on Trent*, Thoroton Soc. Rec. Ser., XVI (1956).
[110] Carus-Wilson, *MMV*, p. 215; *Pipe Roll*, 18 Henry II, pp. 18, 84 and 9 John, p. 31; T. D. Hardy, ed., *Rotuli de Liberate, Misis et Praestitis*, p. 121.

A pointer to some of the principal centres of cloth-making by the end of the century is provided by a list of fines paid by 28 towns in 1202 to be exempted from rules enacted in 1196 prescribing standard dimensions for cloth offered for sale.[111] The fines varied in amount, variations which perhaps bore some relationship to a town's importance as a manufacturing centre, although no doubt a very rough and ready one. The list, too, is less than a complete directory of clothing towns; it does not, for example, include either Marlborough or Oxford. If the information contained in it is mapped, however, a few general conclusions are suggested. First, the clothing towns *par excellence* seem to have been Lincoln and York, with Newcastle upon Tyne, Beverley, Leicester, Northampton and Winchester also ranking as important centres. Secondly, there was a concentration of cloth-making in the eastern plain of England and, to a somewhat lesser extent, in the West Midlands, between Gloucester and Coventry. Thirdly, the fines paid by many of the towns probably reflected their roles as distributors of cloth manufactured in neighbouring villages as well as within their walls.

The evidence afforded by the fines of 1202 can be amplified and supplemented by many of scraps of twelfth-century evidence. In the north-east, for instance, the burgesses of Newcastle were already claiming the sole right to make, dye and retail cloth there as early as Henry I's reign, and the York weavers secured a charter from Henry II in 1163. In Yorkshire, at least, there is also evidence of cloth workers in a number of smaller centres including Malton, Thirsk, Scarborough, Ripon and Knaresborough, as well as Beverley.[112] Further south, in Lincolnshire, the industry was solidly established in Stamford and Lincoln. The latter town, indeed, already had a gild of weavers in 1130 and was clearly a centre of quality production. Henry II bought scarlets and greens there, and King John accepted similar cloths as part of a fine the city made to recover its forfeited liberties.[113] It is no less clear that the industry was well established in the East Midlands. Nottingham and Huntingdon had gilds of weavers by Henry II's reign; Leicester dyers were prominent members of the town's gild merchant towards the end of the twelfth

---

[111] *Pipe Roll*, 4 John, p. xx, corrected in certain particulars from details in the text of the roll. Bridbury's doubt about the assumption that originally the assize applied only to English cloth seems fully justified: *Medieval English Clothmaking*, p. 106.

[112] *EYC*, I, no. 349; A.F. Leach, ed., *Beverley Town Documents*, p. 135; *Pipe Roll*, 32 Henry II, p. 70; 13 John, p. 89; *BBC, 1042–1216*, p. 211.

[113] *VCH Lincs.*, II, p. 305; *Pipe Roll*, 31 Henry I, pp. 109, 114; 26 Henry II, p. 48; 28 Henry II, p. 560; 31 Henry II, pp. 80–1; 13 John, p. 61.

Map 3 Clothing towns paying fines for exemption from the assize of cloth, 1202 (based on information in Pipe Roll, 4 John)

century and Leicester merchants imported woad for the dyers to use; Derby weavers early in the thirteenth century got monopoly rights of manufacture in their town and its hinterland like those acquired in 1157 by the weavers of Nottingham; and Northampton produced cloth good enough for the king to buy it.[114] The stage of the industry's development in East Anglia is less clear. One chronicler thought that the citizens of twelfth-century Norwich were 'for the most part weavers', but their craft probably took second place to the leather trades; if woad came in through Ipswich it does not seem to have supplied a large-scale industry; and Bury St Edmunds, with its fair, may have been more important as a distributive than as a manufacturing centre even though there were old women there who 'came out with distaffs . . . abusing the cellarer' and fullers who sold cloth to the abbey.[115]

The development of the industry in the Thames Valley area likewise does not seem to have gone very far, even though Newbury had a fulling mill in 1205;[116] but Kent was perhaps another matter. Canterbury claimed monopolistic rights of cloth manufacture in 1237 which may have been of long standing; at least fourteen cloth workers are named in the city's rentals and charters between 1153 and 1206; and the city may have been the source of the burels bought for the queen in Kent in 1207.[117] There is also no doubt about the antiquity of the London industry, for there was a weavers' gild there in Henry I's reign and London was the most consistent source of supply for the king's household (although some of what it supplied may have been imported or made elsewhere in England) in the reign of Henry II.[118] The extent of the industry in the West Midlands, on the other hand, may have been underrated. That it was established in Gloucester and Worcester is clear, but some towns which did not pay fines in 1202 certainly had cloth workers. Bristol

[114] *Pipe Roll*, 16 Henry II, p. 23; 25 Henry II, p. 61; 3 John, p. 259; 4 John, p. 40; 6 John, p. 186; 7 John, p. 74; 11 John, p. 182; W.J. Ashley, *Introduction to English Economic History and Theory*, i(1), pp. 81–2; *VCH Derbys.*, ii, p. 163; C.J. Billson, *Medieval Leicester*, pp. 127–8; *BBC, 1042–1216*, p. 169. Royal agents attending Northampton fair early in the thirteenth century may also have bought there cloth from overseas or elsewhere in England: C.A. Markham and J.C. Cox, eds, *Records of the Borough of Northampton*, i, p. 34.
[115] Hudson and Tingey, eds, *Records of the City of Norwich*, ii, p. xii; Butler, ed., *Chronicle of Jocelin of Brakelond*, pp. 99, 103; G. Unwin, *Studies in Economic History*, ed. R.H. Tawney, 1927, p. 262.
[116] *Pipe Roll*, 9 Richard I, p. 240; *VCH Berks.*, i, p. 388.
[117] W.J. Urry, *Canterbury under the Angevin Kings*, pp. 121, 131, 221–382; *Pipe Roll*, 9 John, p. 31.
[118] Unwin, *Gilds and Companies of London*, pp. 42–5; *Pipe Roll*, 10 Henry II, p. 20; 12 Henry II, p. 130; 13 Henry II, pp. 1–3; 16 Henry II, p. 15; 17 Henry II, p. 147 etc.

supplied the king with cloth of a reasonable quality; Oxford was a source of relatively cheap fabrics, but its weavers' gild went back to the reign of Henry I; and Bruges merchants claimed they had bought cloth at Shrewsbury from King John's time and, in the years 1209–20, drapers and dyers were members of Shrewsbury's gild merchant. The absence of weavers from its membership may merely imply that, there as elsewhere, they were not eligible.[119]

The evidence, finally, for the southern counties is less than satisfactory. Only Winchester and Exeter fined in 1202, and Exeter in 1215–16 supplied the bishop of Winchester with green and blue cloth of reasonable quality. These were not, however, the only clothing towns of the region. Taunton also supplied the bishop of Winchester with cloth, although it was cheaper than that which he got at Exeter; Marlborough and Bedwyn burels had a more than local reputation by 1218; and regulations governing the Marlborough weavers a decade or so earlier have been preserved.[120] Only the Winchester industry, however, has left more than occasional information. The city had gilds of fullers and weavers by the reign of Henry I; under Henry II the Winchester weavers paid as much to the crown for their gild as the London weavers did; and cloth workers (including dyers) were not infrequently mentioned in the late twelfth-century records of the city. Possibly the Winchester industry produced cloth of a range of qualities, for while Henry II bought bulk consignments of cheap burels there both he and John also purchased fabrics suitable as gifts for the king of France's daughter or for the countess of Gloucester. These costlier textiles, however, may have both been brought from elsewhere in England, or even from overseas, for sale at Winchester fair which, judging by the income the bishop got from it, reached a high point of activity in the reign of Richard I.[121]

It seems clear, therefore, that some parts of the twelfth-century English textile industry had outgrown a local framework. Some large purchasers, like the king and the bishop of Winchester, dealt directly with suppliers in distant towns; and Winchester fair was not the only one serving something like a national market, for cloth was also on

---

[119] *Pipe Roll*, 18 Henry II, p. 18; 19 Henry II, p. 165; 21 Henry II, p. 11; T.D. Hardy, ed., *Rotuli de Liberate, Misis et Praestitis*, pp. 94, 119, 121, 141; *CRR*, XI, pl. 1266; W. Cunningham, 'The gild merchant of Shrewsbury', *TRHS*, NS IX (1895), pp. 99–117.

[120] T.J. Hunt, 'Some notes on the cloth trade in Taunton in the thirteenth century', *Proc. Somerset Arch. and NH Soc.*, CI–II (1956–7), pp. 89ff.; Holt, ed., *Pipe Roll of the Bishopric of Winchester, 1210–11*, p. 173; Leach, ed., *Beverley Town Documents*, p. 134.

[121] Biddle, ed., *Winchester in the Early Middle Ages*, pp. 286, 427, 435, 438; *Pipe Roll*, 17 Henry II, p. 34; 18 Henry II, p. 84; 8 John, p. 149; *RLC*, I, pp. 145, 620.

sale at St Ives fair (Hunts.) in 1198 and King John made substantial cloth purchases there in 1212.[122] The cloth that was traded to these wider markets included cheaper lines like the russets and burels supplied by Oxford, London and Winchester, and also fabrics of much better quality like those produced by Lincoln and other towns. Nor were markets only those at home. By 1200 English cloth appeared regularly in Genoa and from Genoa it was re-exported to Sicily, the prices it commanded suggesting that much of it was high quality. The fact that it was reaching the Mediterranean makes it likely that it also found its way to markets elsewhere in western Europe. The quantities exported were probably not very large, but by 1200 some export opportunities supplemented the home demand which was satisfied for the most part by the cloth workers of English towns and villages.[123]

The expansion of the market for textiles also left its mark upon the organization of the English urban industry. Certain 'laws of the weavers and fullers' have survived from the years around 1200 which make clear how economically dependent these manufacturing craftsmen were at Oxford, Beverley, Marlborough, Winchester and Lincoln. They were forbidden to undertake the finishing stages of cloth production, to sell cloth either wholesale or retail, and at Oxford even to weave or full cloth without the consent of the *prudhommes*, the leading citizens. Economic dependence was reinforced by rules making them second-class members of their town communities. They could not bear witness against free citizens, they were themselves ineligible for the freedom of their town, and, as a Lincoln judgement put it, they 'had no law or community with free citizens'. To become a freeman of Winchester and Marlborough, in fact, a fuller or weaver had to abandon his craft, a rule the citizens of Winchester said they got from London. In *c.* 1190, too, Northampton weavers (in company with children's nurses) were precluded from breaking their contracts or departing in anger and ill-will, and the fifteenth-century Northampton weavers' ordinances may echo an ancient injunction when they are told to have their

[122] *Pipe Roll*, 10 Richard I, p. 161; 14 John, pp. 43–4.

[123] R. Doehaerd, *Relations commerciales entre Gênes, la Belgique et l'Outremont*, I, pp. 176–7; II, nos. 51–2, 68, 75, 77–8, 88, 90, 202, 216, 241, 286; also R. Reynolds, 'The market for northern textiles in Genoa', *Revue Belge*, VIII (1935), pp. 840–1. There were, of course, also some cloth exports into England: below, pp. 193–4.

'customable drinking . . . without any confederacies making'.[124] The fact that there were virtually no weavers or fullers among the early members of the gilds merchant at Shrewsbury and Leicester may suggest that there, too, they were denied 'law or community with free citizens'; and the royal licences obtained for their gilds by the weavers of York, Huntingdon and Nottingham may have been designed at least in part to compensate for their lack of rights in their own communities.

The economic implications of the rules governing the textile crafts emerge clearly at Marlborough. They were only to weave or work for the *prudhommes* of the town, they were not to go outside the town to trade, and they could sell what they made only to merchants of the town.[125] Cloth production and access to the markets for it, in other words, were controlled by a commercial group to whom the manufacturing crafts were subordinate. This controlling group may have included some dyers, for their responsibility for what was often a final production process put them in a favourable position to market the finished product. Perhaps Henry Costein of Leicester was a case in point, for he imported woad, was a leading member of the gild merchant, and witnessed charters of the earl and countess.[126] Dyers, on the other hand, are unlikely to have been the only members of the developing entrepreneurial class. The Winchester and Marlborough customs envisage weavers and fullers thriving to such an extent that they could abandon their craft and take to the cloth trade; and the tantalizing glimpses we get of other dealers in cloth perhaps suggest that often they were simply men willing to do business wherever there was money to be made. Robert Cause and Ralph of Colchester from Lincoln may have been among their number. Ralph was bailiff of the city in the 1170s; both were pledges for men who owed money to Aaron, a famous and wealthy Lincoln Jew; and both were capable of fulfilling large orders for cloth from the king in the 1180s. It is not unreasonable to suppose that, in order to meet

---

[124] Carus-Wilson's treatment of this question is definitive: *CEcH*, II, pp. 640–2 and *MMV*, pp. 233–8. See also Leach, ed., *Beverley Town Documents*, pp. 134–5; Hill, *Medieval Lincoln*, pp. 188–9; *CRR*, I, pp. 259–60; G. Rose and W. Illingworth, eds, *Abbreviatio Placitorum, Richard I – Edward II*, Rec. Comm., 1811, p. 65; M. Bateson, ed., *Borough Customs*, I, pp. 215–16; Markham and Cox, eds, *Records of Northampton*, I, p. 269.
[125] Leach, ed., *Beverley Town Documents*, I, p. 134.
[126] *Pipe Roll*, 7 John, p. 34; M. Bateson, ed., *Records of the Borough of Leicester*, I, pp. 6, 11, 34–5, 39.

such demands, they needed to put out work to weavers and fullers and to buy up cloth produced by independent artisans.[127]

This context is also significant for an understanding of the character of the twelfth-century textile gilds, which was different in important respects from that of the craft gilds of later times. They owed their existence and rights not to the municipal authorities but to the king, and in recognition of that fact they owed an annual payment at the exchequer. They were not, in other words, like the later crafts, instruments of municipal government, one good reason why towns treated them with a suspicion enhanced by the likelihood that merchants, to whom the manufacturing craftsmen were subordinated, would occupy positions of power in towns. It is not surprising, therefore, that in 1202 the mayor and citizens of London persuaded King John to suppress the weavers' gild there by promising a higher annual payment to the exchequer than the weavers had made. The London weavers secured a restoration of their gild within a few years, but what the episode makes clear is that what was at issue was not only the weavers' right to form themselves into an organized body to regulate their craft, but also for its members to enjoy a monopoly of the craft. At Oxford that monopoly extended not only to the town but also to the countryside for five miles around it; and the York gild, together with 'others of the same craft' in various other Yorkshire boroughs, were accorded sole rights of manufacture throughout the county.[128] By John's reign gilds of textile workers of this sort were also beginning to appear in private as well as royal boroughs, for the earl of Leicester had accorded analogous privileges to the Leicester fullers.[129]

The right of manufacturing craftsmen, in brief, with royal backing to establish their own organization, the members of which had exclusive right to produce cloth in a town and sometimes in a rather larger area, was their response to the economic dependence and the legal inferiority which the developing entrepreneurial class and municipal governments sought to impose on them. The monopolistic rights claimed by gildsmen were designed to prevent entrepreneurs turning to alternative sources of labour within towns,

---

[127] Carus-Wilson, *MMV*, p. 234; *Pipe Roll*, 30 Henry II, p. 14; 31 Henry II, pp. 80–1; 32 Henry II, p. 70; Hill, *Medieval Lincoln*, pp. 219, 379. Ralph of Colchester's wife had property of her own and was referred to as 'the lady Maud of Colchester' in *c*. 1195. Their son Adam was also to be bailiff of Lincoln early in the thirteenth century: *Reg. Antiquissimum*, VIII, nos. 2316, 2336 and p. 199.

[128] *CLB, C*, p. 55; *CLB, D*, pp. 221–2; Unwin, *Gilds and Companies of London*, pp. 45–6; *EYC*, I, no. 349; *VCH Oxon.*, IV, p. 316.

[129] *Pipe Roll*, 11 John, pp. 24–5.

and where these extended into the surrounding countryside to pre-clude town merchants from finding in the traditional rural industry an alternative source of supply, especially of cheaper fabrics. At the same time, the 'laws of the weavers and fullers' backed by a few other pieces of supporting evidence also suggest that by c. 1200 commercial entrepreneurs were firmly in control of a good deal of cloth production and probably of still more cloth marketing.

(c)   The thirteenth-century industry

It is reasonable to regard the twelfth-century development of the cloth industry as responses to growing demand from a growing population, the increased incomes received by many landlords (especially late in the century), and an expansion of western commerce offering new export opportunities. The respective impact of these various influences cannot be measured, but it seems likely that the industry's growth was governed principally by increased demand at home. It is significant in this respect that, in 1086, the south and east of England had been more heavily populated than the north and the west; and that, despite the recolonization of Yorkshire, the balance of wealth was still heavily tipped towards the south and east in 1334.[130] The evidence for a growth of textile output was also most marked in these same parts of the country. Even so, continuous growth was not assured everywhere, for by the opening of the thirteenth century disquieting symptoms were evident in some urban centres particularly. The Winchester weavers failed to make the payment they owed at the exchequer in 1198, and by 1202 both they and the fullers were in arrears 'on account of poverty', while by 1214 the York weavers had failed to make their payment to the crown for six of the preceding years. The reasons for these difficulties were not necessarily identical; for Henry II had raised the sum he demanded from the Winchester weavers, prompting a flight of the industry into the countryside or to the bishop's suburb, while the problem at York may have been competition from country industry. Whatever the explanation, the poverty of weavers in these towns in King John's reign presaged more general difficulties to come.[131]

Those difficulties arose despite the fact that during the thirteenth century continued growth of population and of the incomes of

[130] Darby, *Domesday England*, pp. 92–4; *idem*, ed., *A New Historical Geography of England*, pp. 137–43.
[131] Miller, 'Fortunes of the English textile industry', pp. 69–70.

landlords must have meant that domestic market for cloth continued to grow. A significant share of that market, however, was supplied by Flemings and Brabançons, who doubtless supplied to their English customers (as they did to customers in the Mediterranean lands) both the cheaper varieties of cloth that would be bought by ordinary folk and by lords and ladies buying to provide liveries for their servants, and higher quality fabrics. Because a good deal of the English urban industry had been geared to the supply of this quality market, it was especially affected by quality imports. The volume of imports must not be exaggerated. They have been estimated to have supplied one cloth for every 600 inhabitants of England in the decade before the outbreak of the Hundred Years' War.[132] The alien share of the English market, however, may have been rather larger a generation or two earlier, their bias towards the quality end of the market affected town industries particularly, and the increasing domination of Flemish products in western Europe also reduced the capacity of English urban cloth workers to develop, or even to retain, export markets they had seemed to be winning when the thirteenth century opened.

Exports of English cloth, of course, did not cease completely. In the mid-thirteenth century English 'stamfords' and York cloth were sold in Genoa, Venice and Montpellier; Northampton cloth was still subject to duties in Genoa in 1308; cloth from York, Stamford and Beverley was shipped to Spain in 1272; and English cloth was reaching Pisa in 1305. Only after 1303, however, do the customs accounts enable us to make any sort of estimate of the volume of these exports, and even then only of those that were shipped by alien merchants. The summary accounts suggest that, in the years 1303–9, they were exporting on average just under 400 broadcloths per year, mainly from Hull, Boston and London. On the other hand, a detailed account of the customs collected at Boston during eight months in 1303 shows that the summary accounts seriously understate the real volume of exports. The latter accounts record only the duty paid on broadcloths, which during those months were worth £1,150; but in addition 'straits', worsteds and other fabrics were exported, which paid duty as general merchandise and which brought the total value of textiles exported (according to the official

---

[132] P. Chorley, 'The cloth exports of Flanders and northern France during the thirteenth century', *EcHR*, 2nd ser. XL (1987), pp. 350, 359, 370–1; R.H. Britnell, 'England and Northern Italy in the early fourteenth century', *TRHS*, 5th ser. XXXIX (1989), pp. 177–8.

valuations) in this period nearer to £3,000.[133] Since this takes no account of cloth exported by denizen merchants there is some likelihood that English textile exports at this time have been unduly minimized. That is not to say, however, that they matched the volume of cloth imports into England during much of the thirteenth century. The cloth going overseas from Boston, Southampton and Bristol at the opening of the fourteenth century, moreover, consisted mainly of ordinary broadcloths (to say nothing of 'straits' and worsteds) by contrast with the fine scarlets which centres like Lincoln had earlier sent overseas. A good deal of the trade represented by the exports recorded in the early fourteenth-century customs accounts, in fact, may be a new trade in rather cheaper fabrics rather than a survival of that older commerce which had taken English cloth to Genoa a century earlier.[134]

Given this background it is perhaps not surprising that, in many towns, the textile workers were in difficulties during the thirteenth century. Between 1202 and 1309 the accumulated arrears of the annual payment of £10 which the York weavers owed at the exchequer climbed to £790; by 1285 weavers had largely deserted Winchester for the bishop's suburban liberty; the number of weavers in Oxford, said once to have been 60, was alleged to have fallen to fifteen by 1275 and to seven by 1290; and in 1251 the Huntingdon weavers were unable to pay the king the sum they owed him to have their gild.[135] In this last case the failure of the weavers to meet their obligations was in part at least due to the fact that they had not received their customary contribution from the weavers of St Neots, but more general influences were also at work. First, since textile gilds were concerned to protect the rewards of their members and to buttress them with monopoly, town cloth making tended to be a high-cost industry to the detriment of its competitive position. Secondly, as municipalities achieved a large measure of independence, they were apt to treat the industry as a source of municipal income. At Winchester the charges levied on looms by the city were said to be one of the reasons for weavers moving out to the bishop's

[133] P. Chorley, 'English cloth exports during the thirteenth and early fourteenth centuries: the continental evidence', *Historical Research*, LXI (1988), pp. 2–5; Miller, 'Fortunes of the English textile industry', pp. 70–1; T.H. Lloyd, *Alien Merchants in England*, Appx. I; Gras, *Early English Customs System*, pp. 273–88. Only round figures can be got from the Boston account in 1303 since, in many entries, cloth is bracketed with other commodities for the purpose of valuation.

[134] *Ibid.*, pp. 346–73.

[135] Miller, 'Fortunes of the English textile industry', p. 70; and for Huntingdon, PRO E 368/25, m. 14.

liberty, and the fullers there paid more to the city in the thirteenth century than they had owed to the king in the twelfth. At Northampton, too, one reason alleged for cloth workers deserting the town was that they bore an undue share of common charges.[136] Finally, in many cases, the town industry faced rural competition. In 1227 the York weavers attributed their inability to pay their dues to the king to the fact that 'divers men in divers places in that county, elsewhere than in the city, . . . make dyed and rayed cloths', a complaint which became a recurrent theme on their part; and ten years later it was held that the making and dyeing of cloth at Littlebourne and Sturry (Kent) were prejudicial to the cloth workers of Canterbury.[137]

Rural competition has been attributed, at least in part, to a technological innovation: the mechanization of the fulling process, giving a cost advantage to country places with swift flowing streams which could be harnessed to drive fulling mills.[138] There are difficulties in accepting that this was a principal cause of major changes in the location of the industry. That many fulling mills were built from the late twelfth century onwards is not, of course, in question, or that many of them were in country districts, like the Lake District or Cornwall, where cloth-making was not of major importance (although some were also constructed on the verges of towns like those at Winchester built perhaps by private individuals or possibly by the city's fullers or by the civic authorities). The rural mills often look like attempts by landlords to extract some profit from traditional country cloth-making, and neither their number nor their profitability should be exaggerated. In the West Midlands, in the generation before the Black Death, they accounted for only one mill in twelve; and in Lancashire in 1311 a Burnley fulling mill was worth 5s. (a twentieth of what the corn mill brought in) and one at Colne 6s. 8d., one at Manchester yielded 13s. 4d. in 1322, and the fulling mill at Hornby in the Lune valley was valued at 20s. 6d. in 1286, 6s. 8d. in 1319 and 13s. 4d. in 1335.[139] Undoubtedly, by somewhat reducing production costs, fulling mills could have given some

---

[136] Biddle, ed., *Winchester in the Early Middle Ages*, pp. 512, 516; Keene, *Survey*, I, pp. 296–7; *Rot. Hundr.*, II, pp. 2–3.

[137] *RLC*, II, p. 176; *Close R.*, 1234–37, p. 422; *CCR*, 1302–7, p. 134.

[138] Carus-Wilson, *MMV*, pp. 183–209; but for contrary views, Miller, 'Fortunes of the English textile industry', pp. 70–7; Holt, *Mills of Medieval England*, pp. 155–8; and Langdon, 'Water-mills and windmills in the West Midlands', pp. 434–5.

[139] Keene, *Survey*, I, pp. 306–7; II, p. 1083; W. Farrer, ed., *Lancashire Inquests*, I, p. 245; II, pp. 6–7, 36–8, 60, 187; III, pp. 39–41, 57–8; PRO DL 29/1/2, C 133/42/5.

economic advantage to country cloth workers; but the superior skills of some urban craftsmen may have told on the other side. Where water supplies were limited the fact that returns from corn mills were higher in most cases than from fulling mills might well determine the investment decisions of landlords, and the impact of mechanization was limited by the fact that fulling does not appear to have been one of the more costly production processes. For these reasons the mechanization of fulling is likely to have confirmed, rather than initiated major changes in, the locations of the industry in rural England.

It is true, on the other hand, that on occasion townsmen themselves may have stimulated the development of rural competition. The charges and disabilities which municipal authorities placed upon cloth workers might persuade the latter to desert their town for the countryside; certainly that was what the few remaining Oxford weavers were threatening to do in 1290. Probably more important, however, was a deliberate encouragement of rural manufacture. That encouragement may sometimes have come from lords. In 1228 the abbey was said to have set up looms for weavers in Peterborough to the detriment of the industry of neighbouring Stamford, and in 1230 the abbot of Westminster had weavers at Islip contrary to the monopolistic privileges of the Oxford gild.[140] Patronage of rural cloth making, however, also came from town merchants. In 1275 weavers at Islip, and also at Beckley and Cowley, were working looms provided for them by a group of Oxford notables;[141] and there were also Leicester merchants with fulling mills outside the town and Lincoln merchants who were buying up country cloth for dyeing. If the industrial balance between town and country was changing, that change was contrived at least in part by urban capital.[142]

The control of the industry by merchants within towns, of course, was still more comprehensive and has been graphically described using the exceptional range of surviving sources from Leicester.[143] Cloth-making there in the mid-thirteenth century was directed by

---

[140] *Rot. Parl.*, I, p. 50; *CRR*, XIII, pl. 406; C. Robinson, ed., *Memoranda Roll of the King's Remembrancer, 1230–31*, Pipe Roll Soc., NS XI (1933), p. 89.
[141] H. Jenkinson and B. Fermoy, eds, *Select Cases in the Exchequer of Pleas*, Selden Soc., XLVIII (1932), pl. 134; and for some details about this group, E. Miller, 'English town patricians, c. 1200–1350', in A. Guarducci, ed., *Gerarchie Economiche e Gerarchie Sociali, secolo XII–XVIII*, p. 224.
[142] Bateson, ed., *Records of the Borough of Leicester*, I, p. 91; Hill, *Medieval Lincoln*, pp. 403–4.
[143] By Carus-Wilson, *MMV*, pp. 228–34.

entrepreneurs like Henry Houghil and Richard Shilton. They bought wool and had it washed and dyed; they gave it out to carders and spinners; they employed 'weavers and fullers throughout the town, under stringent supervision, at piece-rates fixed by them-selves'; and they sold the finished cloth at the great fairs of eastern England. The economic power of these men of capital, with the gild merchant which they dominated as their instrument, was reinforced by the disabilities of the craftsmen. Weavers could not weave for strangers without the permission of the gild merchant, and that could only be given if no Leicester man would offer them work; when the weavers made certain rules about weaving they were annulled as contrary to the common interests of the gild merchant; and when the fullers held a 'morning-speech' (meeting) without members of the gild merchant being present they were held to have transgressed. Manufacturing craftsmen also continued to be excluded from the gild merchant. In 1264 Nicholas Chaluner was fined for failing to put away weaving when he became a member of that body, a penalty which moved him to abuse the mayor and the 'community of the gild' for which he was threatened with 'excom-munication' (i.e. exclusion from the gild's community). As late as 1276 he still kept weaver's work in his house, and it was ordered that he should lose his gild membership for ever. In fact he was able to buy it back in 1280, although his plea that he had lost it through ignorance was more than a little disingenuous.[144]

The control exercised by commercial interests over cloth-making at Leicester was all the more effective because the manufacturing craftsmen had very limited powers of self-regulation. In London, on the other hand, the weavers had a well-established gild organization buttressed by a royal charter; but there, too, an entrepreneurial group emerged, especially in the persons of the burellers who could be described, in 1225, as the 'men of London *who cause* burels to be made'. It was not easy for manufacturing craftsmen, in the face of these quasi-employers and of the city government concerned to assert its authority, to preserve their powers of self-regulation. Rules promulgated for fulling in 1298 distinguished between the owners of cloth and the weavers, fullers and dyers who sent them to be fulled, suggesting that these latter craftsmen were mainly employed on a putting-out basis; and it is significant that the largest group among those who authorized the rules were burellers.[145] A period of more

[144] Bateson, ed., *Records of the Borough of Leicester*, I, pp. 104–6, 168–9.
[145] Carus-Wilson, *MMV*, p. 234; H.T. Riley, ed., *Munimenta Gildhallae Londoniensis: Liber Custumarum*, pp. 128–9; *CLB, C*, pp. 51–2.

open confrontation began in 1300, with the burellers playing for the support of the city authorities by alleging that the weavers' gild had usurped powers belonging to the mayor. Their interests as employers, however, were no less clear: they accused the weavers of having ordained a compulsory holiday from Christmas to 2 February, of reducing the number of looms in the city, and of raising charges for weaving two-fold or more. The city government obligingly held these actions to be prejudicial to the community of London and the mistery of burellers, and set up a nicely unbalanced committee to draw up new ordinances for the weavers. These forbade a weaver to stop work when he quarrelled with a bureller, set aside a rule that at least four days of work was needed to weave a 40-yard length of cloth, made 6 January the end of the Christmas holiday, and abolished all fixed charges for weaving, ordering that these should be whatever could be agreed between individual weavers and whoever engaged them. Only the gildsmen's monopoly of weaving was preserved for the time being, for that was guaranteed by the king's charter; but the economic dependence of the weavers upon men who 'caused burels to be made' was significantly reinforced.[146]

A similar dependence of manufacturing craftsmen is found in other clothing towns and was often backed by municipal governments. At Oxford, in the mid-century, the city laid down rules governing cloth making by the 'lesser commune'; at Winchester in *c.* 1275, where fullers and weavers were assumed to be excluded from the city's franchise, what a weaver could charge for his work was prescribed by the city; and in the small towns of Yorkshire in the 1270s, although there were fullers and weavers selling cloth direct at Pontefract, Yarm and Leeds, dyers (from whose ranks the controlling entrepreneurial class was often recruited) were particularly prominent among those who sold cloth at Pickering, Skipton and Pontefract.[147] At Newcastle upon Tyne at the opening of the fourteenth century, too, the 'rich burgesses ... by sinister collusion among themselves' refused to let the 'poor burgesses' sell retail the cloth they had made, although there judgement was given for the latter on the grounds that the town charters gave equal trading rights to all burgesses.[148] At Lincoln a weavers' gild validated by royal

[146] A.H. Thomas, ed., *Cal. of Early Mayor's Court Rolls*, pp. 53–5; Riley, ed., *Liber Custumarum*, I, pp. 121–6; Unwin, *Industrial Organization in the XVIth and XVIIth Centuries*, pp. 29–30.
[147] *Cal. Inq. Misc.*, I, no. 238; J.S. Furley, ed., *Ancient Usages of the City of Winchester*, pp. 29–30; *Rot. Hundr.*, I, pp. 106, 108, 112, 119, 127, 133.
[148] C.M. Fraser, 'Medieval trading restrictions in the North-East', *AA*, 4th ser. XXXIX (1961), pp. 138–9, 147–50; Miller, 'Rulers of thirteenth-century towns', pp. 133–4.

charters may for a time have given them some protection, but as in London their defences were crumbling by the middle of the fourteenth century. The city's entrepreneurs went behind the backs of the gildsmen; for, while free weavers all but disappeared, 'many citizens kept hired weavers working cloths for sale'. The economic dependence of these hired weavers was likely to be complete.[149]

In the English countryside at the end of the thirteenth century there were still 'simple folk making cloth for themselves with their own wool';[150] and a high proportion of rural clothworkers probably dealt with customers direct in restricted and localized markets. The domestic mass market, in fact, was one which to a very large extent the traditional cloth industry of the English countryside and small towns was capable of satisfying; and the demand for its products grew as England's population grew. Circumstances during the thirteenth century, therefore, favoured the expansion of the rural industry, especially because its costs were lower in many cases than those of the urban industry. The fortunes of the rural industry inevitably varied from place to place; but places which had inhabitants with appropriate skills, access to raw materials of adequate quality, a sufficient degree of under-employment to provide hands especially for the highly labour-intensive preliminary manufacturing processes, and perhaps available water-power to drive fulling mills, might be well placed to expand production and even to serve markets beyond their own locality. Where that happened there was a tendency for clothworkers to become dependent upon entrepreneurs, who provided capital and commercial services which facilitated the processes of production and distribution. These entrepreneurs were likely to be town merchants, and in this manner townsmen probably contributed significantly to industrial expansion in some parts of the thirteenth-century countryside.

(d)   The cloth industry in c. 1300

The available evidence about the locations where cloth was made in *c.* 1300 is infinitely more plentiful than in earlier times, and it shows how widespread cloth making was. Northumberland cuts no great figure, although clearly cloth was made in Newcastle, Hexham and Alnwick and there were occasional rural fulling mills like that on the

---

[149] Hill, *Medieval Lincoln*, pp. 326–7; *CPR*, 1348–50, pp. 120–1.
[150] H.R. Luard, ed., *Annales Monastici*, IV, p. 531 (referring to Worcestershire).

Newminster estate at Sturton grange.[151] The north-western counties, by contrast, were replete with fulling mills, although most were of small value and presumably served merely local needs.[152] Exceptions were the mills at Cockermouth, leased for £12 6s. 8d. in 1268, and Kendal, said to be worth £5 6s. 8d. in 1275. Kendal also had a dye house, and the industry there possibly served a market wider than the town's immediate neighbourhood.[153] In Lancashire, too, there were a number of dye-houses and fulling mills, although that at Ellel, near Lancaster, was for the cloth which the canons of Cockermouth had made for their own use.[154] Yorkshire, however, continued to be the main clothmaking county in the north. The York and Beverley weavers, despite their evident difficulties, continued to make cloth which was sold in the great fairs throughout England and supplied Henry III's court;[155] there were cloth workers in many smaller towns like Northallerton, Pickering, Pontefract and Leeds; and before 1300 there was an embryo cloth market at Wakefield, a weaver at Batley in 1248, and in the second half of the century cloth workers along the Calder valley as far west as Halifax and Sowerby. There were even two weavers in a village as remote as Bentham in the Wenning valley. Some of the foundations of the West Riding industry of the future were being laid.[156]

In the eastern counties, judging by the distribution of craft surnames in 1279, there was also a scatter of rural cloth workers in Cambridgeshire, Huntingdonshire and north Buckinghamshire; there were drapers selling cloth in Cambridge in 1260; and Bedford had men with textile craft names in 1297. There do not appear, however, to have been any major centres of cloth production in these counties, and the same seems to be true of Derbyshire, although an Ashbourne fuller left his memorial in the records when he built a

---

[151] *NCH*, III, p. 31; V, pp. 252, 350, 456.

[152] The list in Carus-Wilson, *MMV*, p. 195 can easily be extended; e.g. the pre-1307 mills at Bolton near Cockermouth, on Derwentfells above Derwentwater, at Kirkoswald and in Liddell Forest: PRO SC 6/824/7; C 133/15/2 and 31/3; *Cal. Docs. Scot.*, I, no. 2665.

[153] PRO SC 6/824/7, C 133/5/10.

[154] *VCH Lancs.*, II, p. 376; Farrer, ed., *Lancashire. Inquests*, I, p. 219; PRO C 133/42/5; W. Farrer, ed., *Chartulary of Cockersand Abbey*, III(1), Chetham Soc., NS LVI (1905), p. 779.

[155] Here and elsewhere, where no reference is given, evidence is drawn from the printed close, patent and liberate rolls.

[156] *Rot. Hundr.*, I, pp. 106–33; *VCH Yorks.*, II, pp. 407–8; H. Heaton, *The Yorkshire Woollen and Worsted Industries*, p. 6; M.W. Beresford and G.R.J. Jones, *Leeds and its Region*, p. 134; Faull and Moorhouse, *West Yorkshire: an Archaeological Survey*, II, p. 502; BL Cott. Vesp. E. XIX, f. 42; Farrer, ed., *Cockersand Chartulary*, III(2), pp. 952–3.

privy on the public highroad.[157] Leicester, Nottingham and Northampton, by contrast, supplied cloth to the king and sent their merchants to the great fairs: indeed, so many merchants in Leicester's case that no pleas were entertained in the town courts during the season in which the fairs were held. Northampton, as well as producing cloth, also enjoyed a reputation for its dyers, both London and Nottingham apparently sending cloth there to be dyed. By 1279, however, urban cloth making at Northampton may have been contracting, although a spread of rural fulling mills perhaps suggests that the industry was expanding in the surrounding countryside. Finally, across the Warwickshire border, many Coventry men in the twelfth and thirteenth centuries had surnames suggesting employment in the textile crafts; the industry there probably made a slow start, but it seems to have expanded more or less steadily until it attained its fourteenth-century peaks.[158]

The cloth workers with the highest reputation in the thirteenth century, on the other hand, were those of the Lincolnshire towns, and of Lincoln and Stamford particularly. Even at the end of the century Edward I still bought Lincoln scarlet and cloth from Stamford, and probably some of the scarlets exported from Boston in 1303 were made in these towns. Lincoln merchants, too, were found at all the great fairs selling greens, murrey and russets as well as scarlets; and one Stamford notable in the 1270s, Ralph de Stoke, was certainly organizing cloth making there on a putting-out basis. Stamford seems also to have manufactured some worsted fabrics by the early fourteenth century, perhaps in an attempt to meet demand from the new markets being opened up by Hanseatic shipping.[159]

In parts of East Anglia, too, the type of cloth produced was changing and a rural industry geared to the supply of distant markets was developing. Norwich continued to be a clothing town throughout the thirteenth century, its fullers even establishing a clandestine gild in 1293; but it produced broadcloths of the traditional sort and, in the period 1285–1311 cloth-making seems still to have been less important than the leather trades. Norwich, in other words, looks as though it was a more important centre for the cloth trade and for

---

[157] W.M. Palmer, ed., *The Assizes at Cambridge, AD 1260*, Linton, 1930, pp. 5, 42; Gaydon, ed., *The Taxation of 1297*, pp. 96–101; *Rot. Hundr.*, II, p. 295.

[158] Bateson, ed., *Records of the Borough of Leicester*, I, pp. 74, 77–80, 84–5, 95, 126–7, 162–3; *VCH Northants*, III, p. 26; *Rot. Hundr.*, II, pp. 2–3 (*molendina solaria* should presumably be *molendina folaria*); *VCH Warks.*, VIII, p. 153.

[159] PRO E 101/352/23, 360/22, 362/31; *Rot. Hundr.*, I, pp. 352–3, 396; A. Rogers, ed., *The Making of Stamford*, p. 46.

cloth finishing than for the primary manufacturing processes.[160] There are clear signs, however, of an expanding rural cloth industry about this time, with places like North Walsham, Scottow, Tunstead, Worstead and Aylsham launched on a course of development which made them conspicuously wealthier than neighbouring places in 1334.[161] They produced mainly the lighter and cheaper fabrics which took their name from Worstead, and which were already included in cloth shipments from Great Yarmouth and perhaps from King's Lynn in the early fourteenth century. Possibly, too, the Norfolk industry was already sending worsteds for sale at Northampton and supplying the London market, for the flow of Norfolk immigrants into London, which ultimately makes a study of the London mercers 'like thumbing a Norfolk directory', was in full flood. Many of them, too, came from significant places: in the period 1292–1308 they included William from Scottow, Robert from Worstead, and John Rak from Aylsham to be apprenticed to another man of Norfolk extraction, John from Foulsham.[162]

Further south cloth was made in all the larger boroughs of Suffolk and Essex without any of them being a major manufacturing centre. Bury St Edmunds, although its fair attracted cloth merchants from as far away as Beverley, was perhaps an unfavourable environment for industrial development given the abbey's power over the town; the tax returns of 1296 and 1301 do not suggest that Colchester was primarily a clothing town, even though Henry III bought russet cloth there for his valets; and in 1282 cloth workers were not especially numerous at Ipswich, some men with stocks of cloth being probably dealers rather than makers. Among these Hugh Golding was pre-eminent. His goods included cloth worth £76; but clearly he was a man of diverse interests, for he also had malt worth £40 and wood worth £10.[163] At the same time, cloth was not only made in the

---

[160] *Rot. Hundr.*, I, p. 531; Hudson and Tingey, eds, *Records of Norwich*, II, pp. xxii–iii, 209ff.; W. Hudson, ed., *Leet Jurisdiction in Norwich*, p. 30; E. Lipson, *History of the Woollen and Worsted Industries*, p. 222; U. Priestley, ed., *Men of Property: an Analysis of the Norwich Enrolled Deeds, 1285–1311*, Norwich, 1983, pp. 24–5.

[161] For the worsted villages in 1329, *CPR*, 1327–30, p. 424; and for their assessments, R.E. Glasscock, ed., *The Lay Subsidy of 1334*, pp. 192–208.

[162] Lloyd, *Alien Merchants in England*, pp. 49–51; Markham and Cox, eds, *Records of Northampton*, I, pp. 58–9; Williams, *Medieval London*, p. 138; E. Ekwall, *Studies on the Population of Medieval London*, pp. 36, 55–6, 82, 89.

[163] R.S. Gottfried, *Bury St Edmunds and the Urban Crisis, 1290–1539*, pp. 105–7; *Close R.*, 1247–51, pp. 198–9; R.H. Britnell, *Growth and Decline in Colchester, 1300–1525*, pp. 13–14; E. Powell, 'The taxation of Ipswich for the Welsh War of 1282', *Proc. Suffolk Institute of Archaeology*, XII (1906), pp. 137–57; Unwin, *Studies in Economic History*, p. 263.

larger towns: the goods shipped from Ipswich in *c.* 1300 included cloths of Coggeshall, Maldon and Sudbury, and there is evidence for a development of cloth-making at Halstead and along the Stour valley from Haverhill to Clare. In the second quarter of the thirteenth century there was 'a virtual flood of textile tradesmen into the record' in Essex, often in villages developing into small towns, although they might depend upon Colchester and Sudbury for outlets for their production. Growth may have been rather slower after that, but the industry was firmly grounded in this region. Unlike Norfolk, it produced traditional woollens, mostly of modest quality like the Colchester russets which could be bought for $10\frac{1}{2}$d. a yard or the burels which were Hugh Golding's main stock-in-trade in Ipswich in 1282.[164]

The south-eastern and home counties on the whole saw only a limited growth of cloth-making. London continued to produce some cloth, mostly at the lower end of the quality range; while in Kent some cloth was made in 1227 at Dartford and other small towns as well as Canterbury, and there were fulling mills around Cranbrook. In Berkshire cloth workers were fairly numerous in Reading and Wallingford, Wallingford and Abingdon merchants sold cloth in the great eastern fairs, and Henry III bought a little cheap cloth at Abingdon. Merchants from High Wycombe (Bucks.), Berkhamsted (Herts.) and Cricklade (North Wilts.) also sold cloth to the court, as did St Albans merchants at St Ives, Bury St Edmunds and Winchester fairs; and St Albans abbey spent heavily on its fulling mill during the thirteenth century. Attempts to compel the citizens to use it (and of course to pay for doing so), however, gave rise to intermittent guerilla warfare which probably did little to encourage industrial development.[165]

Further west, Winchester continued to be a major cloth market throughout the thirteenth century, although cloth-making in the city probably declined as the industry moved out into the suburbs and the countryside. There is also mention of cloth merchants at Andover (Hants.), Salisbury, Wilton, Marlborough and Devizes (Wilts.). Salisbury in 1297 provided Edward I with blues and russets to make saddle cloths; and there were small groups of cloth workers

---

[164] T. Twiss, ed., *The Black Book of the Admiralty*, II, p. 187; M. Gervers, 'The textile industry in Essex in the late twelfth and thirteenth centuries', *Essex Archaeology and History*, XX (1989), esp. pp. 38–9, 41–5; *CLR*, 1251–60, p. 280; Powell, 'The taxation of Ipswich', p. 142.
[165] *VCH Kent*, III, pp. 403–4; M. Clanchy, ed., *The Roll and Writ File of the Berkshire Eyre of 1248*, nos. 1041, 1050; *Close R.*, 1247–51, pp. 198–9; Carus-Wilson, *MMV*, pp. 201–3.

in towns like Malmesbury and Colerne. The spread of fulling mills in rural Hampshire, in the Vale of Kennet, and along the Bradford Avon and Salisbury Avon likewise indicates a developing country industry, which like the towns mostly produced cheap fabrics principally for local markets.[166] Further west still the bishop of Winchester built a fulling mill at Taunton in 1218–19, although his return from it was much reduced by 1272 as other mills were set up in the surrounding countryside. Taunton merchants, however, probably controlled much of the cloth trade in the area; while in Devon, at the beginning of the century, Exeter had supplied good quality cloth for the bishop of Winchester's knights and, somewhat later, Totnes furnished 'gross russet' for the king's bed and sent its merchants to the Winchester fair. There were also fulling mills at Honiton, Tiverton, Barnstaple and Crediton; and the annals of crime or disaster, like the presentments of two lady weavers from Buckland (one for murder and the other for a theft of shoes), afford glimpses of a small-scale and mainly rural industry. Some of the growth points of the future Devon industry, however, were already in existence.[167]

In the West Midlands Oxford appears initially to have been the main centre of cloth production. It was capable of meeting substantial orders from the court for cheap russets and its merchants did business at St Ives, Northampton, Stamford and Winchester fairs.[168] If the Oxford industry contracted in the course of the thirteenth century, a village industry was developing in the surrounding countryside, sometimes with active encouragement from Oxford merchants. From the 1279 Hundred Rolls we get the impression of little groups of textile workers around Thame, around Chipping Norton and most notably around Witney. Further afield, the distribution of fulling mills by the early fourteenth century suggests the existence of a country industry capable of meeting more than local demands in the southern Cotswolds around Cirencester, in the northern Cotswolds around Winchcombe and Northleach, and in northern Worcestershire around Kidderminster.[169] At Worcester, Shrewsbury, Stratford-upon-Avon, and even Gloucester, and in the

---

[166] C.A.F. Meekings, ed., *Crown Pleas of the Wiltshire Eyre, 1249*, p. 41; BL Add. Ms. 7965, f. 16d; Carus-Wilson, in *VCH Wilts.*, IV, pp. 115–47. The location of fulling mills is indicated by the map in Darby, ed., *A New Historical Geography of England*, p. 113.

[167] Hunt, 'Some notes on the cloth trade in Taunton', pp. 89–107; *Close R.*, 1253–54, p. 176; W.G. Hoskins, *Devon*, pp. 124–5; H. Summerson, ed., *Crown Pleas of the Devon Eyre of 1238*, pll. 51, 328, 531, 555, 579.

[168] E.g., *CLR*, 1226–40, pp. 215, 319; 1251–60, p. 461; 1260–67, p. 126.

[169] *Rot. Hundr.*, II, pp. 689, 698, 701–2; Hilton, *A Medieval Society*, pp. 209–12.

Stroud Valley where so much cloth was to be made later, the industry still mainly served local markets; but some concentration of the finishing trades in the towns is suggested by the prominence of dyers in Gloucester deeds in the period 1180–1320 and of dyers and shearmen among members of the Shrewsbury gild merchant. Bristol, however, may have been exceptional among western towns. Men with surnames derived from the textile crafts were the largest group among Bristol tallage payers in 1312–13, and the cloth exported from Bristol in the first decade of the fourteenth century may have been in part of its own manufacture as well as from its hinterland.[170]

The thirteenth-century cloth industry, then, failed to realize some of its twelfth-century promise, losing some ground both in home and overseas markets, especially for better quality products and in the face of Flemish competition. Those who suffered most as a consequence were the town cloth workers, and particularly those towns in the east of the country, in which so much of English quality production had been concentrated. At the same time places like Oxford and Winchester, which produced lower quality fabrics, also experienced hard times. There the reason may have been that the traditional industry of the countryside, especially when it was organized and financed by urban commercial capital, was increasingly capable of competing with town crafts, the costs of which were kept up by the defensive efforts of the textile gilds and by the charges which municipal authorities placed on manufacturing craftsmen. The tribulations of the town cloth workers, however, were not the only feature of the time. First, it seems clear that the rural textile industry was expanding. Much of it did not cater for markets very far from home, but it is probable that some cloth woven in villages was included in the consignments which town merchants carried for sale to the fairs. Secondly, the merchants and cloth workers serving more local markets had to cater for an increased demand as population grew, even though the competition from imports meant that this increase was more marked for fabrics at the cheaper end of the market. Finally, in a few places – East Anglia and the Cotswolds, for example – a mainly country industry displayed a capacity to open up new and extended markets. To achieve this the cloth workers needed the commercial services provided by town merchants such as

---

[170] *Ibid.*, pp. 194–8; E.M. Carus-Wilson, 'The first half century of the borough of Stratford-upon-Avon', *EcHR*, 2nd ser. XVIII (1965), pp. 55–6; *idem*, 'Evidences of industrial growth on some fifteenth-century manors', *EcHR*, 2nd ser. XII (1959), p. 193; C.H. Drinkwater, 'The merchants' gild of Shrewsbury', *Trans. Shropshire Arch. and NH Soc.*, 2nd ser. VIII (1896) and XII (1900).

those which were available in Yarmouth, Ipswich and Bristol. By 1300 these developments were pointing the way to still more significant economic changes in the fourteenth century.

(e)   Cloth-making in c. 1300–1348

The signs of change did not appear with any rapidity. In the early years of the new century much is still heard about the difficulties of cloth workers; at Oxford and Leicester mention of cloth-making largely fades from the record; and in London dyers sent cloth out of the city for fulling. In London, too, battles continued between their employers and the weavers, whose restrictive practices were said in 1321 to have resulted in a steep fall in the number of working looms and a rise in the cost of weaving 'for their own profit and to the common detriment of the people'. In 1335 the gildsmen's monopoly of weaving was finally ended, any freeman being allowed to set up looms in his house. Something of the same sort probably happened at Lincoln where, by 1348, there were few independent weavers, but many citizens maintained hired weavers working cloth for sale. At Northampton, by contrast, weavers were said in 1334 to have disappeared completely.[171]

Tales of the disasters which had befallen vested interests like gildsmen, of course, need to be taken with a grain of salt, and in fact town industries seldom totally collapsed. Despite the troubles in London Edward II's agents were able to buy 'cloths of Candlewick Street' there down to the end of the reign; in 1319 Beverley could supply high quality *perse* worth as much as 6s. a yard; and even Cambridge had half a dozen riotous shearmen in the 1320s.[172] The fortunes of the industry in the villages and smaller towns are harder to determine. Rural England, in the aftermath of the agrarian crises of 1315–22, was not perhaps a very favourable environment for industrial development. The very few instances of cloth sales recorded in debt litigation entered on the Wakefield court rolls in the 1330s, and the fact that the wool sales mentioned were in little more than penny packets, possibly indicate a period of arrested development in the West Riding; and when the payments made by High Wycombe weavers for their looms were fixed in 1316 the object may have been to give them support in hard times. On the other hand,

[171] Bateson, ed., *Records of the Borough of Leicester*, I, p. 347; *CLB, D*, pp. 239–40; Riley, ed., *Liber Custumarum*, I, pp. 416–24; *CPR*, 1348–50, p. 120; *Rot. Parl.*, II, pp. 85–6.
[172] PRO E 101/380/14, 381/9, 382/2; Heaton, *Yorkshire Woollen and Worsted Industries*, p. 4; *CPR*, 1321–24, pp. 151–3.

Merton College built a fulling mill at its south Oxfordshire manor at Cuxham in 1312 which, save for a few years in the late 1320s when it fell into disrepair, was regularly let for 13s. 4d. a year down to 1349.[173] The occupational surnames of Suffolk taxpayers in 1327, too, suggest the presence of fullers in many villages and small towns in that county and relatively numerous weavers in Sudbury, Lavenham and Hadleigh; and if in the 1320s alien exports of English cloth from the east coast ports were decreasing, shipments from Bristol by foreigners were larger than they had been at the beginning of the century, Dartmouth and the neighbouring ports exported not inconsiderable quantities of inexpensive textiles, and an Exeter merchant setting out for Bordeaux in 1328 loaded his ship with cloth as well as with money and other goods. The industry may have continued to grow in the south-west, and even the fall in alien exports from eastern England may in part reflect the fact that denizen merchants were capturing a growing share of this branch, like other branches, of England's trade. Since denizens paid no customs on these exports, however, that is not something which can be measured.[174]

Signs of a continuing growth of cloth manufacture are clearest in Norfolk. Both alien and denizen merchants complained in 1314 that they were often deceived about the dimensions of aylshams and worsteds sold in Norwich, and in the following year one of the king's yeomen was appointed to enforce regulations concerning the standard length and width of cloths in respect of worsteds as well as other fabrics. The appointment opened a period of conflict between Norfolk clothmakers and government agents, the details of which make clear that the cloth mainly at issue, worsted, was made, not in Norwich, but in small towns and villages to the north. Norwich certainly made cloth, and indeed it seems to have been in the first half of the fourteenth century that clothmaking replaced the leather trades as the city's principal industry. Much of its output, however, consisted of traditional broadcloths, and its main role in the developing worsted industry was as a centre of distribution. The varied types of cloth which the Norfolk industry was capable of supplying is

---

[173] Walker, ed., *Court Rolls of the Manor of Wakefield, 1331–3*, pp. 164, 217; C. Gross, *The Gild Merchant*, II, p. 277; L.J. Ashford, *History of High Wycombe*, p. 41; Harvey, *A Medieval Oxfordshire Village*, pp. 37, 142; *idem*, ed., *Manorial Records of Cuxham*, pp. 352, 356, 372, 376.
[174] S.H.A. Hervey, ed., *Suffolk in 1327*, *passim*; E.M. Carus-Wilson, ed., *Overseas Trade of Bristol in the Later Middle Ages*, pp. 167–77; Gras, *Early English Customs System*, pp. 394–8; *CCR*, 1327–30, p. 243.

reflected in the cargo shipped out of Yarmouth by Norwich and Yarmouth merchants in 1333: it consisted of five scarlets, 41 other cloths, over 200 worsted cloths and fourteen coverlets.[175]

By the 1330s, however, the expansion of English output was becoming general rather than local. Home demand for basic textiles may well have increased as the mass of the population benefited from sharply falling food prices at this time; and the problems faced by overseas cloth workers also enabled English makers of better quality cloth to capture a greater share in the home market and to develop a stake in the export trade, sending overseas in 1347–48 more than 4,400 broadcloths as well as large shipments of worsteds.[176] The most consistently effective influence which favoured English producers was government exploitation of English wool exports for fiscal purposes, made all the more effective in this respect because much of the best cloth produced in the Low Countries, which had dominated European markets, was made from English wool, and by the fact that the cost of wool was the single largest item in cloth-making costs. High export duties on English wool, therefore, inflated the costs of overseas producers, while English cloth workers were able to buy wool without this surcharge and English merchants paid no duty on cloth exported until 1347. Wool export duties, of course, were not new in the 1330s; but manufacturers in the Low Countries had perhaps been able to absorb the relatively moderate wool custom imposed in 1275, and the impact of the increased duty on alien exports imposed in 1303 was perhaps partly offset by the increased share of wool exports handled by denizens. The massive and long-term increases in duties from 1336 to finance Edward III's war with France, which raised the cost of exported wool by as much as 45 per cent, were another matter altogether. Fiscal influences were abetted by interruption of trade as a result of embargoes and naval operations, by policies designed to encourage English folk to wear English cloth, and even by attempts to persuade skilled foreign cloth workers to settle in England; while the defensive and protectionist measures adopted by Flemish crafts perhaps enhanced the competitive advantage of the relatively low-cost English industry.[177]

[175] *Rot. Parl.*, I, p. 292; Williams, *Medieval London*, pp. 136–40; *CPR*, 1313–17, p. 344; 1327–30, pp. 297, 424; *CCR*, 1333–37, p. 125; M.W. Atkin and H. Sutermeister, 'Excavations in Norwich, 1977–8', *Norfolk Archaeology*, XXXVII (1978), pp. 39–40.
[176] Gras, *Early English Customs System*, pp. 414–34.
[177] Munro, 'Industrial protectionism in medieval Flanders', p. 231; *idem*, 'Industrial transformations in the north-west European textile trades', in B.M.S. Campbell, ed., *Before the Black Death*, pp. 134–8; *CPR*, 1324–27, p. 268; 1327–30, pp. 98–9.

The signs of an expansion of the industry, therefore, multiply in the second quarter of the fourteenth century. In west Yorkshire, for instance, the Wakefield debt litigation differed markedly in 1348–50 from that a couple of decades earlier. Debts for small quantities of wool and cloth were of much more frequent occurrence: the impression is that a small-scale industry was mushrooming.[178] The growing number of textile craftsmen admitted to the freedom of the city also suggests a revival of urban industry in York. Between 1272 and 1326, although admittedly the freemen's register is less than complete, on average one such craftsman was admitted every other year, no weaver appeared among the freemen until 1318, and then no other until 1324. By contrast, in 1327–50, seven textile craftsmen on average were admitted every two years and more than a third of them were weavers. In the 1340s two weavers were being admitted every year, including a couple of Brabanters and a Fleming as well as men with northern roots in Beverley, Fangfoss, Hartlepool, Pocklington and Thirsk.[179]

There are similar indications of expansion elsewhere. Lincoln continued to be a clothing town, perhaps because new entrepreneurs were breaking down restrictions imposed by the city's ancient weavers' gild; the industry of Norwich and its neighbourhood went on growing; and Canterbury re-emerged as a cloth-making centre, perhaps providing some of the textiles shipped from Sandwich, probably to Gascony, in 1348–49.[180] Industrial expansion appears, if anything, to have been even more marked further west. Much cloth was marketed in Gloucester in the 1350s; a weaver and a chaloner became freemen of Exeter in the 1340s, perhaps indicating that the manufacturing side of the industry there was growing in prestige; and, if only on a modest scale, there was a revival of cloth-making at Winchester in the 1330s and 1340s. It would soon again be a centre of the industry, but as a producer of broadcloths rather than the cheap burels which were its earlier staple.[181] Bristol, too, made as well as traded cloth. In 1346 the city enacted much legislation relating to its weavers and fullers, the weavers' regulations apparently reiterating or amending ancient usages, but the fullers' rules were

---

[178] Jewell, ed., *Court Rolls of the Manor of Wakefield, 1348–50, passim.*
[179] F. Collins, ed., *Register of the Freemen of the City of York*, I, pp. 1–44.
[180] Gras, *Early English Customs System*, p. 418.
[181] H.L. Gray, 'The production and export of English woollens in the fourteenth century', *EHR*, XXXIX (1924), pp. 21–2; M.M. Rowe and A.M. Jackson, eds, *Exeter Freemen, 1266–1967*, pp. 9–30; Keene, *Survey*, I, pp. 296–8, 315; K.H. Rogers, 'Salisbury', in Lobel, *Atlas of Historic Towns*, I, p. 6.

'newly made', perhaps indicating formal recognition of their gild for the first time.[182] This legislation probably marked an attempt to impose order on a situation created by a period of very rapid development of textile manufacture in Bristol, stimulated by export merchants like Thomas Blanket, who caused weaving instruments, weavers and other workmen to be brought into his house, where he set them to work.[183]

As in East Anglia and Yorkshire, however, industrial development in the west of England was to be found in villages as well as towns. By 1340, for example, Castle Combe on the Wiltshire–Gloucestershire border, which was to become one of the classical industrial villages, already had a fulling mill; and in 1332 over fifty Wiltshire taxpayers had surnames taken from the textile crafts. It may also be significant that most of those called weaver or fuller were villagers, but that half those called dyer and the solitary shearman were in towns, large or small (Salisbury, Wilton, Calne, Cricklade and Marlborough). Perhaps a measure of collaboration had been established, with villagers carrying out many of the primary stages of cloth production, but relying on urban centres to finish their products and provide market outlets.[184]

In the 1350s some of the accounts have survived that were kept by officials called aulnagers, appointed to exercise quality control of (and levy a tax on) cloths offered for sale.[185] They afford an overview of the industry in the mid-century even though too much cannot be expected of them. Evasion was no doubt widespread in the case of an industry largely scattered over the countryside; but, more important, the completeness of the aulnagers' accounts was seriously affected by major exemptions from the scope of their scrutiny. These included worsteds and probably other cheap and non-standard fabrics, cloths less than 13–14 yards long (i.e. half the prescribed standard length), and cloths made for the producer's own use or for that of his household. The aulnagers, in brief, must have had no concern with much of the cloth produced for the home market, and

---

[182] Gray, 'The production and export of English woollens', p. 34; Gras, *Early English Customs System*, pp. 414–34; F.B. Bickley, ed., *Little Red Book of Bristol*, II, pp. 1–6, 10–14.
[183] *CCR*, 1339–41, p. 311. For Thomas Blanket and his family, Bickley, ed., *Little Red Book of Bristol*, I, pp. 20–1, 26, 221–6 and Gras, *Early English Customs System*, p. 420.
[184] Carus-Wilson, 'Evidences of industrial growth on some fifteenth-century manors', p. 198; D.A. Crowley, ed., *The Wiltshire Tax List of 1332, passim.*
[185] Their content was summarized long ago by Gray, 'The production and export of English woollens', pp. 21–2 and there is a useful digest in Bridbury, *Medieval English Clothmaking*, p. 114.

the 15,000–16,000 cloths a year recorded on their accounts in the 1350s were a part only of a very much larger output of textiles. The information the accounts give, too, is fullest for regions producing for export or for relatively extensive markets at home.[186] They suggest that the principal region manufacturing broadcloth stretched from Southampton and Winchester, via Salisbury and the southern Cotswolds, to Bristol and Gloucester, followed by the area centred on London (the south-eastern counties, Essex, Suffolk and Norfolk); but Lincoln and Lincolnshire were still large producers, with York and Yorkshire some way behind. From the accounts and other sources it is clear that in the mid-fourteenth century, however, Lincoln and York, like Salisbury, Bristol, London, Winchester, Canterbury, Bath and Gloucester, were centres for cloth-marketing and cloth manufacture of some importance. By contrast, Oxford, Northampton, Nottingham, Leicester and Stamford seem to have lost much of their earlier prominence.

The available evidence, in its nature, tells us very little about the mass market for textiles and how it was served. Yet a population which rose to perhaps six millions or more, despite much general poverty, must have generated a very large demand for the industry's products. Clothing and bed-coverings for ordinary folk no doubt had to last for many a year, and most were undoubtedly of poor quality and rudimentary colour, ranging down in price to a mere 6d. a yard; but it is not impossible to conceive of a home demand equivalent to 150,000–200,000 standard cloths measuring 24 yards in length and 2 yards in width. Such a figure puts into perspective England's participation in international trading in textiles. Exports of broadcloths in 1347–48 totalled only about 4,400, supplemented by worsted equivalent to about 500 more;[187] and early in the century, before native products had ousted them from some parts of the home market, imports had probably amounted only to 15,000–16,000 cloths a year or a little more. It seems likely, therefore, that much of the increase in cloth production in the 1330s and 1340s was directed towards satisfying demand at home, not only to replace imports but at a time when falling food prices increased

---

[186] *Ibid.*, pp. 52–6.
[187] Figures based on Gras, *Early English Customs System*, p. 415; E.M. Carus-Wilson and O. Coleman, *England's Export Trade, 1275–1547*, pp. 75, 200; Bridbury, *Medieval English Clothmaking*, p. 118.

disposable incomes and when the French and Scottish wars generated demands for army clothing.[188] A growing commercialization of the rural cloth industry also becomes increasingly evident. The proliferation of weekly markets throughout the country enabled yarn and cloth surplus to local needs to be sold, and gave even remote country craftsmen greater access to raw materials, especially dyestuffs, from distant places. In consequence, the quality of some cloth produced in the countryside may have risen, and the mechanism was in place which made possible its passage into the hands of merchants for sale in urban markets or even with a view to export.

The progress made by England's cloth industry by 1349, on the other hand, must not be exaggerated. It has rightly been stressed that, even in the mid-1350s, 'English clothmaking, although successfully launched into exporting, was still struggling . . . to win its home markets from foreign competition', and only with difficulty did cloth exports exceed 10,000 cloths a year. The reviving export trade evident by the 1340s, moreover, was mostly very different from that in the high-quality fabrics which had gone to Italy and Iberia early in the thirteenth century or in the English scarlets which had been held in such high repute in Germany. On the contrary, fourteenth-century exports 'competed for cheapness at the lower end of the international market'.[189] Nor should the retreat of the woollen industries in the Low Countries be antedated. Their pre-eminence in many international markets continued well into the late fourteenth century and beyond. English producers using the best English wools may have enjoyed a cost advantage of 25–35 per cent over their rivals on the other side of the North Sea, but the latter strove mightily to preserve the predominance they had enjoyed for so long in international markets. Even in England the standard of excellence was that set in Flanders, for the mark of Chaucer's wife of Bath's skill in cloth-making was that she surpassed those engaged in these trades in Ypres and Ghent. Even so, by the mid-century foundations had been laid for a continued expansion of English cloth production and for the surges of English cloth exports which would take them above 40,000 cloths a year by the 1390s.

---

[188] The estimate of total imports is Bridbury's: *ibid.*, p. 38; for army demand, cf. Carus-Wilson, *MMV*, pp. 242–3.
[189] Bridbury, *Medieval English Clothmaking*, p. 48; Chorley, 'English cloth exports during the thirteenth and early fourteenth centuries', pp. 9–10.

7. INDUSTRIAL SPECIALIZATION AND ITS LIMITS

In conclusion it is appropriate to return to certain matters raised at the beginning of this chapter. The industrial developments in England between the Norman Conquest and the Black Death can be looked upon as part of a process of economic specialization, marked by the growth in the number and size of communities depending upon activities other than agriculture for their livelihood. Such communities, of course, had been developing long before 1066, but in the ensuing generations most of them became larger and new towns were added to their numbers. Towns will concern us in due course, but in the countryside both before and after 1066 agriculture and handicrafts were complementary rather than competing ways of making a living. Some villagers sought seasonal employment away from home as fishermen or miners or salt-boilers; and more still derived at least part of their income from a craft, even to the extent of taking their name from it while also undertaking a little farming. Gilbert 'the shoemaker' of Ashfield Magna (Suffolk) in 1283 was a case in point. There is no doubt that Gilbert made shoes, for his store of them accounted for a third of the value of his taxable goods; but he also had four ewes and a little stock of grain from an arable holding.[190] Village craftsmen, in fact, helped to make villages self-supplying communities in things other than basic foodstuffs. Ale-wives and bakers, often in considerable numbers, are found in most places;[191] but many villages also housed suppliers of leather goods, of clay pots and platters, of wooden furniture and table ware, of farm tools and implements, of metal articles made in the smithy, and of woollen cloth and blankets. Villages, as well as being communities of farmers, also held reserves of men and women with industrial skills.

The distribution of villagers with craft surnames is an illustration of these facts. Some of these names, of course, became hereditary, so that not every man called 'the baker' baked or 'the miller' milled, but even so an ancestor must have followed the trade from which his descendant took his name. Craft surnames, therefore, present a guide to the diversity of rural crafts even if they do not permit us to count craftsmen at any particular point in time. The court rolls of Halesowen illustrate what this information can tell us for the years

---

[190] Powell, ed., *A Suffolk Hundred in 1283*, Table I.
[191] 18 ale-wives and 14 bakers were presented at Littleport (Cambs.) in 1321: F.W. Maitland and W.P. Baildon, eds, *The Court Baron*, p. 111.

1270–1307.[192] Although there was a little monastic borough at Halesowen, most of the parish consisted of scattered rural settlements. In them are found the usual ale-wives, bakers and millers, but also Agnes Gachard weaving linen cloth, sawyers and carpenters and charcoal burners in the woodlands, even miners digging for 'seacoal'. The abbot of Hales, indeed, leased one mine for £4 a year, a good deal more than many Tyneside mines brought in, and a son promised to provide his widowed mother with five cart-loads of 'seacoal' each year. In these instances our evidence is specific, but the craft surnames recorded on the rolls provide a more complete picture of the diversity of industrial activity in the parish. It is summarised in Table 2.2.[193] Even though not everyone with these names was engaged in the appropriate occupation, some certainly were. Philip Simond 'called the smith' rented a plot of land on which to build a smithy and paid part of his rent in horseshoes; Richard the mason failed to finish building the lord's hall on time; and a tree was delivered to Henry the turner from which he was to make cups.

This material makes certain things clear. Even when millers and brewers are left out of the account, to say nothing of mercers,

Table 2.2 Craft surnames occurring in the Halesowen court rolls, 1270–1307

Craft group	Individual craftsmen	Minimum number of persons	Percentage of total craftsmen
Provision trades	Baker (8), cook (7), salter (1)	16	19
Woodworking	Carpenter (5), cartwright (1), charcoal-burner (1), cooper (2), turner (3), fletcher (1), wheelwright (2)	15	18
Building	Mason (3), slater (2)	5	6
Cloth-making	Chaloner (1), flaxbeater (1), spinner (1), dyer (6), weaver (5)	14	16
Clothing trades	Tailor (1)	1	1
Metal working	Smith (22), goldsmith (1), ironmonger (1), tinker (1)	25	29
Leather working	Skinner (2), shoemaker (6), tanner (1)	9	11

[192] J. Amphlett and S.G. Hamilton, eds, *Court Rolls of the Manor of Hales*; for the borough of Halesowen, Z. Razi, *Life, Marriage and Death in a Medieval Parish*, pp. 5–6 and R.H. Hilton, *Class Conflict and the Crisis of Feudalism*, pp. 199–202.
[193] Men and women called the brewer and the miller are omitted from Tables 2.2–2.3.

merchants and 'leeches', the diversity of non-agricultural employ-ments in Halesowen was considerable. Not all the craftsmen listed here, of course, were totally divorced from farming: Richard the cooper, for example, may have made barrels, but he certainly brewed ale, had a horse which strayed, and rescued his wandering cattle by force when they were impounded. It is curious, indeed, with so much straying stock, that leatherworkers appear to have been rel-atively few; but as might be expected in a well wooded area woodworkers appear frequently and, of all Halesowen men with craft surnames, those called 'the smith' were the most numerous. Many of them were no doubt blacksmiths of the classic sort who provided indispensable services for their agricultural neighbours. Two of them, on the other hand, were called Balismith implying, it has been suggested, that 'they took their hearths about with them instead of working at a fixed one at home'. Perhaps they were itinerant metal workers, like the sole tinker mentioned in the rolls, doing repairs and making goods for sale. There are also indications either that the abbot of Hales was anxious to attract smiths to his manor or that smiths from elsewhere desired to settle there. In 1305 a smith from Edgbaston was granted a building plot at Ridgacre, and in the fol-lowing year a smith from Shenstone near Kidderminster was granted a similar concession in the parish. There are perhaps glimpses here of an early stage in the development of the West Midlands' metallur-gical industries.[194]

A comparable diversity of industrial employment is evident else-where in the medieval English countryside. Suffolk tax returns in 1327 list numerous rural taxpayers who took their names from a wide range of crafts, including those of ploughwright, ropemaker, ewermaker and potter, although most prominent were those who took their name from cloth-making (weaver, fuller, chaloner, shear-man, dyer) or cloth dealing (draper). This last feature of the returns is hardly surprising when, half a century earlier, there were taxpayers called fuller or weaver in a group of villages to the north of Bury St Edmunds in which cloth-making never became a major source of employment. The details of their assessment, at the same time, sug-gest that they were not necessarily full-time specialists. Adam 'the fuller' at Stanton, for instance, rented two acres of land as a

---

[194] Amphlett and Hamilton, eds, *Court Rolls of the Manor of Hales*, pp. xcv, 120n., 516, 531.

subtenant, and in 1283 he had a small store of grain, one beast and a solitary ewe.[195]

Parallels may be found in other parts of the country. In Wiltshire in 1332, even when taxpayers whose names suggest that they may have been millers, smiths and cloth workers are ignored, some 250 others had surnames suggesting employment in about 40 other craft occupations; and in Bedfordshire in 1297 taxpayers with craft sur-names occur reasonably frequently. In some instances, too, it is clear that they practised the craft from which they took their names: a car-penter's goods, for example, included a stock of timber, a roper's a supply of hemp, and a smith's iron, steel and charcoal. The evidence of surnames also suggests that diversity of occupations in the Northumbrian countryside in 1296 was as great as that to be found a generation later in Suffolk. Smiths were the most numerous country craftsmen, with carpenters and brewers not far behind. There were also other workers in metals, leather and building workers, and of course provision traders and the usual sprinkle of cloth workers (although many fewer than in Suffolk). Three taxpayers were also called collier, two of them at Cambois. Northumberland lay on the frontiers of the expanding medieval economy, but in these respects its villages showed many similarities to villages further south.[196]

In this connection the information provided by the 1297 Hundred Rolls is of special interest because of its comprehensive-ness. What this source tells us about villagers stated to be craftsmen or who had craft surnames in Cambridgeshire, numbering in all nearly 450, is summarized in Table 2.3 (once again omitting brewers and millers). The spread of craftsmen and the relative importance of the main trades is not basically dissimilar to that revealed by the Halesowen court rolls. In both areas carpenters were the most numerous woodworkers (and might often have more accurately been assigned to the building trades); village blacksmiths were the overwhelming majority of metal workers; and shoemakers were the predominant representatives of the leather crafts. In Cambridgeshire, however, by contrast with Halesowen, tailors greatly outnumbered members of the cloth-making crafts; but then, as

---

[195] Hervey, ed., *Suffolk in 1327*; Powell, ed., *A Suffolk Hundred in 1283*.
[196] Crowley, ed., *The Wiltshire Tax List of 1332*; Gaydon, ed., *The Taxation of 1297*; C.M. Fraser, ed., *The Northumberland Lay Subsidy Roll of 1296*.

Table 2.3 Village craftsmen and villagers with craft surnames in
Cambridgeshire, 1279

Craft group	Individual craftsmen	Total	Percentage of total
Provision trades	Cook (35), poulterer (4), fisherman (23), baker (21), saucer (3), spicer (2), butcher (1)	89	20
Woodworking	Carpenter (45), shipwright (3), cooper (13), turner (3), wright (5)	69	16
Building	Mason (10)	10	2
Clothworking	Fuller (12), weaver (22), chaloner (2)	36	8
Clothing trades	Tailor (49)	49	11
Metalworking	Smith (143), ironmonger (2), cutler (1), lorimer (1), goldsmith (2)	149	33
Leather trades	Shoemaker (20), tanner (8), skinner (4), glover (2)	34	8
Miscellaneous	Roper (2), soaper (2), potter (4), barber (2)	10	2

Daniel Defoe was to observe later, Cambridgeshire was not much
taken up in manufacturing or famed for industry.[197]

These instances of country craftsmen have mainly been drawn
from the years around 1300 because evidence of them has become
reasonably plentiful by that time; but this does not imply that they
were a novelty, even though with the growth of population the number of artisans which rural communities could support would be
likely to increase. If we go back to 1256, however, the rolls of the
king's justices in Shropshire reveal once more numerous village
smiths and millers, the usual range of provision traders, carpenters
and turners and a charcoal-burner in the wooded areas, masons and
a tiler and a quarryman, tailors (but no cloth workers), goldsmiths
and skinners and shoemakers and potters.[198] Even earlier still more
random samples have a familiar appearance. The manor of the nuns
of Holy Trinity, Caen, at Felstead (Essex) early in the thirteenth century accommodated a cook, two turners, a cooper, a fuller, a weaver,
three smiths, a skinner, a harness-maker and two shoemakers; and

[197] *Rot. Hundr.*, II, pp. 393–589. About 7 per cent of Cambridgeshire villagers with
craft surnames were women. Taken at their face value these would suggest that
women engaged in a diversity of crafts, including those of smith and miller. Women
appear to have been especially prominent, however, in only two occupations: a third
of the villagers called brewer were women and nearly half of those called weavers.
There was no-one, on the other hand, called spinster despite the fact that spinning
was largely women's work.
[198] A. Harding, ed., *Roll of the Shropshire Eyre of 1256.*

there was a similar range of occupations there and in the abbey's other manors at Horstead (Norfolk), Avening and Minchinhampton (Glos.) in *c.* 1170. Doubtless these craftsmen worked for a local clientele, but the fact that at Felstead some of them had houses 'in the market place before the abbess's door' perhaps suggests that they also supplied the nuns. The evidence of the Holy Trinity surveys is also compatible with that of the charters of Lincoln cathedral in the twelfth and early thirteenth centuries which preserve a record of some 70 men with craft surnames in about 40 villages. The most numerous were carpenters (one splendidly Latinized as *lignifaber*, woodsmith), followed closely by smiths; but there were also bakers, cooks, a butcher, a number of tailors, occasional ironmongers, a glazier, a tanner, a wheelwright, a potter, a turner, and at least two weavers. Some of them, too, like the tenants of Holy Trinity, had some agricultural interests as well as industrial skills.[199]

The country craftsmen of the late twelfth and thirteenth centuries, of course, were following traditions manifest long before 1066 for some individuals, or even groups of individuals, to specialize, at least partially, in manufacture and trading rather than in the production of basic foodstuffs. Their willingness to do so created the urban communities of the middle ages, but it also continued to be evident in the countryside. Some industrial occupations of necessity were almost totally rural. Miners, for instance, had to go where the deposits were, and charcoal-burners had to seek out woodland; but almost every village had at least a few people who spent at least part of their time serving the needs of their agricultural neighbours for iron tools and parts for implements, for shoes and garments, for ale and daily bread, and for a score of other things. Many village craftsmen were not total specialists any more than every townsman was totally divorced from a concern with agriculture; but the industrial expansion of the twelfth and thirteenth centuries, which was essential to meet the demands of a growing population, took place in the country as well as in the towns. Many villagers, therefore, possessed industrial skills which might, as in towns, be acquired through apprenticeship. One fatherless young man at Stamfordham (Northumberland) himself saw to it that he was so equipped. In 1307 he granted a messuage and four acres of land to a mason of that village on condition that the latter would maintain him for a term of nine years and instruct him in the mason's mistery *more*

[199] Chibnall, *Charters and Custumals of the Abbey of Holy Trinity, Caen*; *Registrum Antiquissimum*, IV–VII.

apprenticii. It was for this reason that villages could provide towns with some recruits possessed of technical skills, as well as with some industrial products which enabled urban entrepreneurs to cut their costs and expand their businesses.[200]

Sometimes, of course, increased rural industrial activity transformed the character of a village. In 1327 cloth workers were thicker on the ground in Lavenham and Long Melford than in the ordinary run of Suffolk villages; in the fourteenth century there was an extraordinary concentration of cutlers at Thaxted; in 1334 Norfolk clothing villages like Worstead paid much more in taxes than neighbouring places. In 1297, too, taxpayers with craft surnames or who were assessed on merchandise were numerous enough at Luton and Leighton Buzzard to distinguish these places from the majority of Bedfordshire villages; and the fact that a quarter of Wakefield taxpayers were assessed on tannery goods makes it unlikely that tanning there catered merely for a narrowly local market.[201] The outcome was not, in every case, the creation of new towns or of communities which thereafter remained urban: Worstead, for example, today is classed as a parish and village. It also seems to be probable that the increase of taxable values in England between 1086 and 1334 reflected in the main an expansion of agricultural exploitation and colonization of what in 1086 had been under-developed parts of the English countryside. There was still little sign in 1334 that industrial development had augmented the wealth of whole regions in the way that, in the later middle ages, the fortunes of the South-West, the Cotswolds, East Anglia and the West Riding were so strikingly advanced.[202] Even before 1349, however, manufacture had become a major ingredient of the economy in some country districts like the worsted villages of Norfolk, and some manors like Luton or Wakefield or even Lavenham were growing into towns in the proper sense of that word. This rural dimension is an essential part of England's industrial history in the medieval centuries.

[200] *NCH*, XII, p. 311.
[201] Gaydon, ed., *The Taxation of 1297*, pp. 74–90; W. Brown, ed., *Yorkshire Lay Subsidy, being a Ninth collected in 25 Edward I, 1297.*
[202] H.C. Darby *et al.*, 'The changing geographical distribution of wealth in England, 1086–1334–1525', *Jnl. of Historical Geography*, V (1979), pp. 249–61; *AHEW*, III, pp. 27–9, 52, 149–51.

CHAPTER THREE
The Inland Trade

In English villages during the twelfth and thirteenth centuries, as in peasant societies at all times and in all places, 'the first concern of the productive units [was] to grow food crops to feed themselves'.[1] Self-supply, moreover, was not a preoccupation solely of the peasantry. The earliest surviving accounts for the bishop of Winchester's estate, in 1208–9, show oats being dispatched, doubtless for the bishop's horses, from Burghclere and High Clere (Hants.) to Marlborough and to his palace at Wolvesey, timber from Fareham (Hants.) to his residence at Marwell, and pigs in large numbers from Wargrave (Berks.) to his larders at Wolvesey and in London. Later in the century, in 1278–9, livestock was sent from the Earl Marshal's manor of Kennet (Cambs.) for the earl's household in London, in 1280 four cows and a consignment of rabbits to the earl's residence at Hanworth (Norfolk) against Christmas, in 1289–90 geese, capons, and hens to his castle at Framlingham (Suffolk), and in 1297–98 a boar, ten wethers and ten ewes to provide victuals for the earl while attending parliament. In 1299–1300, on the other hand the earl and countess visited the manor and ate up some of the wheat crop, 34 wethers and four ewes. Later still, in the early decades of the fourteenth century, many pigs were driven from Great Shelford to the bishop of Ely's larder at Ely, and wheat and malt were taken to Balsham and Willingham for his use; and the Harston manor of a much smaller landowner, the judge Robert of Madingley, supplied his household at Chesterton, on the other side of Cambridge, with

---

[1] D. Thorner, 'Peasant economy as a category in economic history', *Deuxième Conférence internationale d'histoire économique: Aix-en-Provence (1962)*, II, p. 291.

wheat, mixed corn, geese, capons and other poultry, and large numbers of eggs.[2] The extent to which landowners and landowning
corporations could draw upon the resources of their estates to satisfy
many of their basic needs explains why, at Winchester, the religious
establishments of the city (by contrast with the king's household during its periodic but irregular visits) made limited demands upon the
city's markets, and therefore contributed only to a limited extent to
the city's economic development.[3]

Self-supply, too, was not merely a matter of agricultural produce.
Estate workshops and craftsmen often supplied a variety of articles
which otherwise would have had to be purchased. At Beaulieu and
Fountains, as we have seen, cloth and leather and other necessities
were produced by domestic artisans, although admittedly Cistercian
houses were apt to take self-sufficiency further than other monastic
establishments; but in most villages manorial blacksmiths fashioned
many of the tools and implements needed for demesne agriculture,
and ordinary villagers tackled many of the tasks required to keep
manorial buildings and equipment in working order. Even in Tudor
times, moreover, Fitzherbert and Tusser assumed that the good hus-
bandman would do much more than care for his livestock and
cultivate his land: he might do his own butchering, in 'dirty
December' he would get 'grindstone and whetstone to tool that is
dull', and when he 'sitteth by the fire and hath nothing to do, then
may he make [forks and rakes] ready, and tooth the rake with dry
withy wood'.[4]

On the other hand, the prevalence of self-supply even in respect
of foodstuffs needs to be kept in proportion. Most demesnes were
cultivated with the market in mind; the poorest peasants and labourers needed to buy in the market in order to procure subsistence; a
small minority of peasant households blessed with substantial land-
holdings willingly sold their agricultural surpluses; and for the
majority, with less ample resources, the sale of produce even at the
expense of subsistence was often a necessity imposed upon them by
requirements to pay rent and other charges to their lords. Many circumstances, in fact, generated exchanges at all social levels and, at
the same time, brought into existence institutions and facilities
through which those exchanges could be conducted. Between the
Norman Conquest and the Black Death, and to a degree becoming

[2] H. Hall, ed., *The Pipe Roll of the Bishopric of Winchester, 1208–9*, pp. 7, 26, 30; PRO SC
6/768/8, 11, 14, 19, 20; 1132/14, 15; BL Add. Roll, 18522.

[3] Keene, *Survey*, I, pp. 103–4.

4 D. Hartley, ed., *Thomas Tusser: his Good Points of Husbandry*, 1931, pp. 106–7, 117–19.

more marked over time, exchange relationships linked England to other lands, towns to other towns and to the countryside around them, and villages to each other and to town markets and even to other countries. The influence of trade was felt throughout English society, so that the circumstances which generated exchanges are of prime importance for an understanding of the dynamics of the medieval economy.

1. THE BACKGROUND OF COMMERCE

In certain respects trade was a response to the fact that resources and productive capacity differed from one part of the country to another. Climate, topography and soil types all varied widely, and consequently the suitability of different regions for raising animals or crops. Some lowland regions, for example, might have cereals to spare, and in some upland districts there might be animals or animal products surplus to the needs of their inhabitants. Some inter-regional points of contact, indeed, are recognizable: Bolton fair, for instance, the principal outlet for the earl of Lincoln's Lancashire cattle farms, or Corbridge fair in Northumberland, where there was an established cattle market by 1278 when the bursar of Durham priory bought 50 young beasts there.[5] To the extent that farmers on the thin but well-watered upland soils of the north and west were able to specialize in pastoral farming and buy in the grain they needed, their land was being put to its most productive use. There were also other significant disparities of natural resources. Iron and mineral coal deposits were fairly widely distributed, but many parts of the country lacked them; timber may have been becoming scarce in some areas even in 1086;[6] and lead and tin were to be found only in a few localities. Some requirements, therefore, could only be met through trade, as an extreme case illustrates. When lead was needed for work on Exeter cathedral in 1301–2 it was bought at Boston fair in Lincolnshire, doubtless having reached Boston from the Peak

---

[5] PRO DL 29/1/2; *NCH*, x, pp. 35, 102–3, 146–7; J.T. Fowler, ed., *Account Rolls of the Abbey of Durham*, II, p. 488.
[6] The map showing the distribution of woodland in H.C. Darby, *Domesday England*, p. 193 suggests relative scarcity in much of East Anglia and Lincolnshire as well as in some parts of southern England.

District of Derbyshire. From Boston it was shipped around the coast to Devon.[7]

Trade was also generated by other influences, including a distribution of wealth which enabled the few to indulge in conspicuous consumption. The households of the rich, with their numerous servants and bands of retainers, made heavy demands not only on their manors and estate workshops but on suppliers both in England and overseas. Robert Grosseteste in advising the countess of Lincoln about the management of her affairs, reminded her that, after full advantage had been taken of the produce of her manors, there were still 'wine and wax and wardrobe' to be bought at various fairs.[8] The great household depended upon both commerce and self-supply, sometimes making arrangements which combined both. Beaulieu abbey sent its own ship to Gascony for wine, but at least on occasion it loaded it with grain for sale in order to offset the cost of the return cargo; and it also had an establishment at Great Yarmouth in Norfolk at which herrings were bought for curing before being sent on to the abbey kitchen.[9]

The dependence of great households upon the market, however, is not in doubt, nor is the very wide range of their requirements which was met in this way. In the mid-thirteenth century, the household of Simon de Montfort's wife bought grain from local dealers, especially in the pre-harvest period when manorial stocks were depleted; and also beef, mutton, pork, venison, large amounts of poultry, and fish in even larger quantities – including salt herrings (consumed at the rate of 400–1,000 a day in Lent), whale, sturgeon, pike as a special treat, oysters, lampreys and, when in the vicinity of Dover, mackerel, mullet, salmon, plaice, crayfish and crabs. The spice account, too, attests purchases of ginger, cinnamon, cloves, galingale, saffron, cumin, sugar at 1s.–2s. a pound, Spanish rice and almonds, dates, raisins and figs. Then there were purchases of eggs and dairy produce, onions and garlic, apples and pears, wax, wine in substantial quantities, ale when domestic supplies ran out in the summer, and of course clothing and jewellery. The servants of the Countess Eleanor paid many visits to the market place.[10]

[7] A.M. Erskine, ed., *Accounts of the Fabric of Exeter Cathedral, 1279-1353*, I, p. 19.

[8] D. Oschinsky, ed., *Walter of Henley and other Treatises on Estate Management and Accounting*, pp. 399, 411.

[9] S.F. Hockey, ed., *Account Book of Beaulieu Abbey*, pp. 170–1, 190; *CPR*, 1272–81, p. 457.

[10] M. Wade Labarge, *A Baronial Household in the Thirteenth Century*,1967, pp. 70–115, 129–49.

Of medieval rich men the king was the biggest buyer of all. In the year 1301–2 Edward I's great wardrobe spent nearly £800 on cloth alone; in 1315 Edward II ran up a bill of almost £600 with a single London skinner; and his queen had 150 gallons of ale bought for her household in a single day in 1312, purchased 1,800 oysters for herself and her damsels in the latter months of 1311, and acquired horses in the course of that year at a cost of some £37. Over and above she had four silver basins made for her by a London gold-smith (using mainly worn-out plate for materials) and got gifts from her husband which included jewels worth £40 and six cloths of gold. Noblemen and members of the religious elite were also lavish spend-ers. When the earl of Lancaster visited Leicester in *c.* 1270 wax, spices, meat, oats, bread, pasties, ale, herrings and other fish, coal and cloth were bought for him at a cost of over £223, and purchases for the earl of Lincoln's household in the year 1304–5 involved an expenditure of ten times that sum. In addition to basic foodstuffs they included spices, figs, raisins, wine, harness, a silver gilt serpent, chaplets of pearls, cloths of gold, silks for the earl's summer livery, cloth for his servants' liveries, a green tent for his hunting, and red and green saddle cloths embroidered with his arms. Patterns of expenditure by ecclesiastical dignitaries were not dissimilar. The household steward of the abbot of Westminster in 1289–90 bought a good deal of plate, spices and rare fruits, white wine for the abbot and red for his *familia*, cloth for winter and summer liveries at a cost of some £65, oxen and pigs to supplement supplies from the abbey's manors, a great deal of fish, and also candles, parchment, horse-shoes, harness, and pigments to decorate the chamber of the abbot's mother. A few years earlier the cellarer of Battle abbey expended over £183 in a year on food and drink, with fish as his principal pur-chase, but he also bought almonds and raisins, figs and garlic, pepper and saffron, cumin and rice. The particulars of household expenditure endorse the conclusion that the largest items were for food and drink, with an emphasis on meat and fish as especially characteristic of an aristocratic diet. A taste for wine and spices, how-ever, was hardly less evident, or for that matter a liking for luxury clothing or articles of adornment.[11]

---

[11] PRO E 101/18/379; E.M. Veale, *The English Fur Trade in the Later Middle Ages*, pp. 53–4; F.D. Blackley and G. Hermansen, eds, *The Household Book of Queen Isabella of England*, pp. 25, 31, 119, 223, 227, 233; M. Bateson, ed., *Records of the Borough of Leicester*, I, pp. 126–7; PRO DL 29/1/2; B.F. Harvey, ed., *Documents Illustrating the Rule of Walter of Wenlok, Abbot of Westminster*, pp. 159–92; E. Searle and B. Ross, eds, *Cellarer's Rolls of Battle Abbey, 1275–1513*, pp. 43–6; C.C. Dyer, *Standards of Living in the Later Middle Ages*, pp. 55–8, 72–9.

Manorial lords had other necessary expenses. The reeve of Beaulieu abbey's manor at Inglesham (Wilts.) in 1269–70, for example, bought various iron parts for ploughs and carts, harness for draught animals, cartwheels and axles and grease to lubricate them, and forks and other tools required for work in the fields. Jars, dishes, plates and pitchers were also purchased for the *curia* together with replacement livestock, a change of seed-corn, and cheese to go with bread baked in the manor as food for boonworkers in harvest time. Similar expenditures were incurred at the abbey's grange at Coxwell (Berks.) and, in addition, ale, fish and other foodstuffs were bought for monks and lay brothers staying there. As early as 1208–9 agents of the bishop of Winchester travelled far in order to meet the needs of his manors: to Wales (as well as to Devizes) to buy horses for his estates in Wiltshire and Oxfordshire as well as for his Hampshire stud-farm, and to Lincolnshire to purchase rams and other sheep for his flocks in Wiltshire and Surrey. Manorial agriculture, especially for landlords with wide-ranging interests, involved much buying, as well as selling, in many market places.[12]

Sales, on the other hand, far outweighed purchases, particularly from the opening of the thirteenth century onwards as manorial lords geared their enterprises to the production of marketable surpluses. In the case of the Winchester manors these were substantial even at an early date: over 4,000 qr. of grain in 1208–9 and 6,900 qr. in 1210–11 (admittedly an amount swollen by stocks left over from previous years).[13] Nor was the bishop of Winchester exceptional save in the magnitude of his sales. The demesne of the bishop of Ely's manor at Great Shelford was not particularly large, but in 1322–23 nearly 200 qr. of grain and malt were sold from the 250 acres under crops, and 140–150 qr. annually on average in the 1320s. Marketing the grain crop, in fact, was a major preoccupation of estate officials, which explains why the reeve of Combe (Hants.) went to Andover and Newbury markets on 17 occasions in 1306–7 and the reeve of Cuxham travelled to Henley market 17 times in 1290–91, 20 times in 1291–92 and 21 times in 1293–94.[14] Much less is known about the

---

[12] Hockey, ed., *Account Book of Beaulieu Abbey*, pp. 69–70, 90–1; Hall, ed., *Pipe Roll of the Bishopric of Winchester, 1208–9*, pp. 7–8, 17, 22, 36, 38, 54.

[13] *Ibid.*, pp. xliv–xlv: income from sales was nearly £438 (here and elsewhere we have accepted Hubert Hall's computations from the 1208–9 pipe roll); N.R. Holt, ed., *Pipe Roll of the Bishopric of Winchester, 1210–11*, especially pp. 69, 83, 127–8, 165–6, 173–5.

[14] PRO SC 6/1132/14, 15; M. Chibnall, ed., *Select Documents of the English Lands of the Abbey of Bec*, p. 149; P.D.A. Harvey, ed., *Manorial Records of Cuxham, Oxfordshire, c. 1200–1359*, pp. 216, 237.

commercial activities of smaller landlords, but there is no reason to suppose that they were either more or less market-orientated than their betters. Lionel de Bradenham's serjeant at Langenhoe (Essex), for instance, appeared regularly in Colchester market, Lionel himself on occasion made contracts with grain buyers, and on average 30 per cent of the wheat grown at Langenhoe was sold each year.[15]

Nor should attention only be concentrated upon grain. In 1208–9 the bishop of Winchester sold 26 horses, 146 oxen and other cattle, 1,277 sheep and lambs, 20 goats and 118 hens; and there were also substantial sales of animal products, including 4,135 cheeses, 2,800 eggs, 320 hides, 4,567 sheep and goat skins, and the fleeces of 13,496 sheep and 3,523 lambs. Receipts from sales of livestock, hides, skins, wool and cheese were about £290, a figure that is about two-thirds of the income coming from the sale of grain that year. Other major landlords drew income from similar sources. In 1263–64 80 wethers, 297 ewes, 35 lambs, 49 stones of cheese and 37 sacks of wool were sold from the Holderness estate of Isabella de Forz; and in the following year wool sales went up to 42 sacks, producing £212 13s. 4d. A generation later, in 1304–5, the earl of Lincoln's agents in the Honour of Pontefract sold 14$^{1}/_{2}$ sacks of wool for £116, horses worth £20, and 583 sheep; his stockman in Blackburnshire sold 213 oxen, 168 cows and five bulls; and in addition revenue was also received from sales of timber at Cridling and Altofts, of sea-coal at Scales, and of 1$^{3}/_{4}$ million peat turves at Whitgift. At about the same time, in the south of England at Sevenhampton, Isabella de Forz and later Adam of Stratton derived modest profits from the sale of apples and of the cider pressed from them.[16]

Men bought and sold for many reasons other than straightforward business or consumption. Even the rich at times might face an urgent need to raise money. The politically prominent were likely periodically to incur heavy fines for pardon or privilege, and an incoming bishop might have to restock a large estate after a vacancy during which it had been subjected to royal spoliation. Smaller landlords were under no less frequent pressure to raise the wind – to pay taxes, to meet wages, or just to support a degree of extravagance.[17]

---

[15] R.H. Britnell, 'Production for the market on a small fourteenth-century estate', *EcHR*, 2nd ser. XIX (1966), pp. 380–7; *idem*, 'Minor landlords in England and medieval agrarian capitalism', *Past and Present*, no. 89 (1980), pp. 3–22.
[16] Hall, ed., *Pipe Roll of the Bishopric of Winchester, 1208–9*, pp. xlii–xlviii; M.W. Farr, ed., *Accounts and Surveys of the Wiltshire Lands of Adam of Stratton*, pp. 31, 92; PRO SC 6/1078/8 and DL 29/1/2.
[17] For small landlords cf. Britnell, 'Minor landlords in England', p. 19.

The spread of marketing, however, was also a response to the needs and enterprise of families still lower in the social scale. While some peasant farmers had surpluses to sell, other villagers produced insufficient for the needs of their families: the latter may have provided some of the customers for the grain which the reeve of Cuxham sold *in curia* rather than taking it to Henley market, or for that sold from Lionel de Bradenham's barns at Langenhoe.[18] Villagers, too, had to raise money to meet needs which their lands could not directly supply – for clothing, salt, pots and pans, iron for tools and implements, not all of which could necessarily be obtained by barter. Most manorial tenants, furthermore, even those landless or nearly landless, had to find cash for rents, entry fines, court amercements, payments in lieu of labour services, and seignorial and royal taxes. Some of the cash required might come from wages or the profits of a rural craft, but a large part must have come from receipts from sales of produce, sales that were not only enforced but which might be at the expense of consumption. The peasantry's financial burdens, as well as their spirit of enterprise, forced them to be (like their betters) farmers for the market.

The burgeoning network of exchanges was nourished by many additional streams which swelled those springing directly from villages and seignorial estates. The small, but already well-established urban sector in 1066 grew substantially at least down to the early fourteenth century. Towns and villages acquiring urban characteristics relied, no doubt to varying degrees, upon their rural hinterlands for food and raw materials, offering in return to their country neighbours the commercial, industrial and other services which principally engaged townsfolk. The very existence of towns, however, depended upon exchanges, and all of them in their diverse ways were trading towns. Their increasing populations, moreover, both enhanced the potential rewards of agricultural producers and encouraged farmers to adopt more entrepreneurial attitudes towards the management of their land; and in turn a more positively commercial exploitation of farmland, especially by those with large surpluses to sell, augmented incomes from land and the capacity of those who received them to consume non-agricultural products. In the last resort, moreover, since a large part of the cash incomes of landlords was derived ultimately from the petty commercial

[18] Harvey, ed., *Manorial Records of Cuxham*, pp. 267–8; Britnell, 'Production for the market', p. 382.

transactions of peasants, even the meanest tenant had to generate cash in order to meet his lord's demands.

The expanding network of exchanges was not limited to those within the country. The tastes of the wealthier and more sophisticated English consumers increasingly extended to goods which were neither home-grown nor homespun, and markets for some English products (wool, tin and lead, for example) became increasingly international. These domestic developments, and their parallels in other countries, provided the stimulus for an international commercial expansion which bestowed upon western Europe a certain economic unity. When merchants from Spain, Toulouse, Normandy, Flanders and the German Empire attended Winchester fair in 1224, England had already been absorbed into that international economy; in 1300, when it took as much as a quarter of Gascon wine exports, and when it was the view of the common folk of Flanders that 'without the coming of the English into Flanders and the passing of the Flemish into England, we cannot profitably trade', it was an indispensable part of it.[19]

This overseas trade inevitably has attracted much attention because it is intrinsically important, but also because it attracted regulation and because it could be taxed. By the mid-fourteenth century, indeed, taxes on overseas trade were a major source of revenue for the English crown. That trade, therefore, has left a rich deposit of records including some which, from the late thirteenth century, can provide quantitative information about the goods entering or leaving England's ports. Overseas trade we must look at in due time, but the inland trade has a logical priority. In the first place, the overwhelming majority of commercial transactions involved neither imports nor exports: most of them were relatively short-range dealings in English products by small men engaged in commerce only in a small way. Unfortunately, however, this is the sort of trade which leaves little in the way of records. Secondly, even overseas trade depended upon a network of transactions within the country. Exotic goods from distant lands needed a pre-existing distributive apparatus in order to find their way to English customers; and goods destined for export, especially those that were small men's produce, had to be collected and bulked before they were put to sea. The inland trade, in brief, provided the broad base for the commercial economy of the central middle ages.

[19] *RLC*, I, p. 620; M.K. James, *Studies in the Medieval Wine Trade*, pp. 9–10; H.R. Luard, ed., *Flores Historiarum*, III, p. 290.

2. COMMUNICATIONS

The development of the inland trade was dependent upon the avail-ability, the cost and the security of communications, as well as upon general economic and social circumstances. Among the means of communication the medieval road system has not enjoyed a high reputation. The lack of general arrangements for making and main-taining roads has been stressed, so that 'the king's highway made and maintained itself'; and certainly many people treated roads in ways which showed little concern for their proper purpose. A mill was built out over the road at Stanwell (Middlesex), wells were dug in the road from Egham to Staines, trenches were dug across the Fosse Way in Leicestershire, and the abbot of St Mary's dug up the road from York to neighbouring Huntingdon. Royal commissioners, on the other hand, tried to check such anti-social behaviour, and so did manorial courts. At Walsoken (Norfolk) one Joseph was arraigned for a trench in the highroad 'to the damage of passers by and the hurt of his neighbours', and at Stanley (Yorks.) Adam Isbell was presented for sinking coal pits in the road. There were also occa-sional road-making schemes, like the building of Egham causeway (Surrey) in Henry III's reign and the making of three great roads to Hull in the early fourteenth century.[20] In fact, goods moved by road over both long and short distances, so that by the fourteenth cen-tury, in much of the country, 'the burden of transport was borne by the cart, rather than the pack-horse or barge', and the Gough map of *c.* 1360 shows a network of trunk routes converging on London and penetrating into most of the extremities of the kingdom.[21] It could be assumed in 1252 that Northampton would be provisioned by cart with grain and salt meat, as well as with straw and cloth by pack-horse and with firewood and sea fish by boat. Carts also brought bread and grain to Southampton in *c.* 1300 and grain, char-coal, peat, brushwood and lead to Newcastle upon Tyne in 1327; and wool travelled by cart from Abbey Dore (Herefords.) to Windsor in 1216, from Vaudey abbey (Lincs.) to Boston in 1275, from

---

[20] C.T. Flower, ed., *Public Works in Medieval Law*, II, pp. xvi, xviii, 45, 208, 214, 271, 314; W.O. Ault, ed., *Court Rolls of the Abbey of Ramsey and the Honour of Clare*, p. 174; S.S. Walker, ed., *Court Rolls of the Manor of Wakefield, 1331–3*, p. 110.
[21] H.C.Darby, ed., *A New Historical Geography of England*, pp. 119, 174–5; also D.M. Stenton, 'Communications', in A.L. Poole, ed., *Medieval England*, I, p. 201 and D.L. Farmer, 'Marketing the produce of the countryside, 1200–1500', in *AHEW*, III, p. 352.

Basingwerk abbey (Flints.) to London in 1277, and from Combermere abbey (Cheshire) to Boston in 1283.[22]

The roads, as well as serving to move traffic by cart (especially as the faster horse-drawn cart replaced the ox-cart in the course of the thirteenth century), also provided routes for animals on the hoof, able to graze on the verges as they travelled. By the thirteenth century there was a regular cattle trade from Wales to markets at Gloucester and Newnham (Glos.); as early as 1209 Winchester manors in southern England got horses from Wales and sheep from Lincolnshire; and later in the century Merton College seems to have engaged in a 'long-distance trade in horses', which it bought at Winchcombe and Chipping Campden (Glos.) and sold far away in Kent. The college also bought horses at Roxburgh in Scotland in 1305–6, one of which ended up in Oxford; and Durham priory, in addition to its purchases at Corbridge fair, bought oxen at Roxburgh, Penrith and Kendal, and horses at Ripon.[23]

Indispensable as the roads were, however, the transportation of heavy and bulky goods, especially if they were also of relatively low value, for long distances by road could prove prohibitively expensive. In our period, as we shall see, and indeed up until the railway age, transport by water was normally far cheaper than transport overland. It was with good reason, therefore, that when the Earl Marshal bought at King's Lynn two millstones for his Cambridgeshire manor at Kennet, they travelled much of the way by water. They may well have reached King's Lynn from Tyneside by sea; and from Lynn they travelled to their final destination by river, except for the short distance to the banks of the Ouse at the start of their journey through the Fenland and the few miles from Soham to Kennet at its end. Road and river travel often complemented each other. Purchases by the bursar of Durham priory at Boston fair in 1302–3 went by boat to Lincoln, then by cart to Torksey, by boat again along the Trent and Yorkshire Ouse to Aldwark, near Boroughbridge, and thence by cart to Durham; and in the 1330s William de la Pole bought wool in Nottinghamshire, Swaledale and Lindsey and had it delivered to Hull by the combined use of boats, carts and pack-horses. Even

---

[22] P. Studer, ed., *Oak Book of Southampton*, p. 2; C.A.Markham and J.C.Cox, eds, *Records of the Borough of Northampton*, I, pp. 41–3; *CPR*, 1327–30, pp. 3–4; R.A. Donkin, *The Cistercians: Studies in the Geography of Medieval England and Wales*, Pontifical Institute of Medieval Studies, Studies and Texts, 38, Toronto, 1978, pp. 138–9.
[23] Farmer, 'Marketing the produce of the countryside', pp. 347–9, 353, 382; Merton College Muniments, 5977; N. Morimoto, *Monastic Economy and Medieval Markets: the Case of Durham Cathedral Priory*, pp. 276–99.

people might move from boat to horseback and back again. When the young scholars of King's Hall in Cambridge were invited to spend Christmas with Edward II at York in 1319, they travelled to Spalding by boat, then took horses to Boston, and completed their journey from Boston by boat once more.[24]

Great rivers like the Thames and Severn, and the network of waterways converging on the Wash and the Humber estuary, therefore, were integral parts of the medieval communications system; and even smaller streams, like the Lymne in Kent or the Welland in Northamptonshire, could be described as 'the king's highroad'. It was for this reason that there was so much concern to keep rivers clear of obstructions to navigation. A clause of Magna Carta, echoing roughly contemporary London charters, ordered the complete removal of fish-weirs from the Thames and the Medway, one of many similar injunctions which were less than effectively enforced. Long after 1215 commissioners were enquiring about the obstruction of the Severn, 'so that ships cannot pass as heretofore', and about the placing of nets in the Yorkshire Ouse and Derwent 'so that ships can scarce pass without danger'. Parliament had to intervene in an attempt to ensure 'common passage' for merchants along the Thames between London and Oxford; but in 1347 petitioners were still demanding that the 'four great rivers of England' (the Thames, Severn, Ouse and Trent) should be cleared of obstacles for the benefit of the kingdom and of the cities and good towns upon their banks.[25] Clearly there might be impediments to trade on inland waters, but at least on the main rivers they should not be exaggerated. There is nothing to suggest that the bursar of Durham priory with his spices from Boston, or the agents of William de la Pole with wool from Swaledale or Lindsey, travelled other than smoothly and did so for the most part by boat.

Much water-borne traffic hugged the coast as well as travelling along the rivers. One focus of this coastal trade was London. Wine was being shipped there from Sandwich and Portsmouth even in the early thirteenth century, and later coal came by sea from Tyneside,

---

[24] PRO SC 6/768/7; Farmer, 'Marketing the produce of the countryside', p. 353; E.B. Fryde, *Studies in Medieval Trade and Finance*, chpt. IX, pp. 17–18; D.M. Stenton, 'Communications', p. 205.
[25] Flower, ed., *Public Works in Medieval Law*, I, pp. xxvi, 311 and II, pp. 251–2; Magna Carta, c. 33; J.C. Holt, *Magna Carta*, Cambridge, 1965,pp. 49, 324–7; *CPR*, 1281–92, p. 459; *Rot. Parl.*, I, p. 475 and II, p. 169.

timber from Kent and Sussex and grain from King's Lynn.[26] At the latest by the 1280s, too, some grain leaving King's Lynn went north instead of south, and the port may already have been a distributive centre on a small scale for north-eastern coal: in 1277 a Gascon merchant thought it worthwhile to seize a Norwegian ship in the port of Newcastle, throw out its crew, and take it off to King's Lynn with a cargo of sea-coal.[27] The Scottish wars reinforced, as well as impeded at times, commercial contacts between south-east and north-east, for they called for supplies for armies in the north, making it in no way surprising that markets sprang up in Clee, Humberstone and other villages on the coast of Lincolnshire.[28] There was also an active coastal traffic along the south coast, again linked to London and with Southampton as one of its hubs. Southampton, of course, also had overland connections. It was Winchester's outport, the port from which much Berkshire and Gloucestershire wool was exported, and a market in which Oxford merchants could buy wine to supply Henry III at Woodstock. Its maritime connections were also extensive. By 1300 it was getting coal from Tyneside, fish from the east coast as well as from the South-West, cereals and iron from Kent and Sussex, ropes and sails from Bridport, marble from Purbeck, slate from Devon, and tin from Cornwall.[29] Most coastal trade, admittedly, had no great range: rather it was a matter for small boats plying locally from harbours which were often improvised. In 1234 the port of Wainfleet (Lincs.) accommodated cargoes of grain, salt and fish, but there was nothing elaborate about its facilities. 'If any house shall be situated so near the harbour that a ship . . . cannot conveniently anchor . . . then the sailors of the ship can freely ... bind their ropes about the posts of that house . . . without hindrance from anyone.'[30] This short-range local traffic, however, helped to nourish the developing longer-range coastal trade.

The availability of means of communication, then, is not in doubt. They included the rivers and fen dykes which contributed so much to the development of King's Lynn; the coastal waters upon which

[26] *Close R.*, 1227–31, p. 286; A.H. Thomas, ed., *Cal. of Early Mayor's Court Rolls, 1298–1307*, p. 192; *CCR*, 1288–96, p. 70; V. Parker, *The Making of King's Lynn*, pp. 10–11.

[27] *CPR*, 1281–92, p. 25; *Cal. Inq. Misc.*, I, no. 1140. Alien merchants exported some sea-coal from King's Lynn by the 1320s: D.M. Owen, ed., *The Making of King's Lynn*, pp. 351–9.

[28] *Rot. Parl.*, I, p. 412.

[29] *Rot. Hundr.*, I, pp. 18, 175, 177; *CLR*, 1251–56, p. 50; C. Platt, *Medieval Southampton*, pp. 82–3; Darby, ed., *New Historical Geography of England*, p. 175.

[30] D.M. Stenton, *English Justice, 1066–1215*, pp. 132–3.

London relied so heavily; and roads, including the salt-ways along which carts and pack-horses linked the Cheshire wiches and the Droitwich brine springs to many parts of northern and midland England. Salt, too, was not the only commodity to travel long distances overland. Around 1200 the canons of Waltham Holy Cross (Essex) sent 20 carts a year via Thetford to Norwich to buy herrings, a North Sea harvest which (provided it was smoked or salted) had a conspicuously extensive market. Beaulieu abbey in Hampshire, as we have seen, had a herring house in Great Yarmouth; before 1235 Abbot William Trumpington of St Albans also got a house to store herrings there 'to the inestimable utility and honour of the house of St Alban'; and even earlier carts belonging to Londoners, loaded with pickled herrings, were to be seen passing through Bury St Edmunds on their way home. Other foodstuffs might also travel far: in 1273–4 the reeve of Sevenhampton (Wilts.) paid the transport costs for venison, presumably salted, or smoked, coming from Holderness in East Yorkshire *en route* for Crewkerne (Somerset).[31]

Traffic, of course, might face many difficulties along these routes. Apart from neglect in maintaining them, encroachments on highways and the clogging of rivers, traders might face insecurity on their journeys and in markets, and coastal vessels were as likely as other ships to fall victim to pirates, who were often fellow Englishmen. For years the mariners of Yarmouth and the Cinque Ports conducted guerilla warfare with each other; and if they were something of a special case, in 1294, before Anglo-Scottish war might have provided justification, a merchant ship from Berwick-upon-Tweed was plundered by Norfolk fishermen and another was detained by the earl of Norfolk when it sought shelter from a storm at Harwich. Quarrels over jurisdiction were another cause of high-handed actions, leading Thomas and Maurice Berkeley to beat and ill-treat the burgesses of Bristol (or so it was alleged) within town and without, 'and contempts, injuries and damages of this sort do not cease . . . in all the fairs and markets of the surrounding district'. Even Lionel de Bradenham of Langenhoe became a plunderer as he grew older: in 1350 he was said to have laid siege to Colchester, exacted tribute from merchants trading at markets and fairs, and extorted money from the fishermen of the Colne estuary.[32] The dangers

[31] R.Ransford, ed., *Early Charters of Waltham Abbey*, nos. 600–1; H.T. Riley, ed., *Gesta Abbatum S. Albani*, I, pp. 289–90; H.E.Butler, ed., *Chronicle of Jocelin of Brakelond*, p. 76; Farr, ed., *Accounts and Surveys ... of Adam of Stratton*, p. 76.

[32] H. Rothwell, ed., *Chronicle of Walter of Guisborough*, p. 315; CCR, 1288–96, pp. 353–4; *Rot. Parl.*, I, p. 168; Britnell, 'Production for the market', p. 385.

which traders faced in a violent society help to explain why kings endeavoured to impose a special peace upon fairs and markets and on the roads leading to them. When, in 1121, Henry I invited the barons and burgesses of England to come to St Ethelbert's fair at Hereford, for instance, he promised them 'as good customs as in any fair in England and . . . the king's firm peace in going, in remaining there and in returning'.[33]

Financial exploitation could also operate in restraint of trade. The lords of markets and fairs were entitled to charge dues for leave to trade in them; towns taxed traders and trading to repair their streets, walls and quays; and tolls, like those the church of Durham levied on the Tyne or Abingdon abbey on the Thames, had to be paid on many strategic routes.[34] Once again, however, government intervention helped to prevent these imposts becoming too burdensome. The inhabitants of Dover had already been freed from payment of toll throughout England by 1066, and the Norman kings were soon extending this liberty to others.[35] In the thirteenth century the levels of tolls, and the institution of new ones, were subjected to increasingly strict government control. In other ways, too, the interests of traders were furthered: by the provision, for example, of more effective and expeditious means to secure payment of what was owed to them, a matter of perennial difficulty. The fact that the terms on which trade was conducted attracted governmental concern is, in itself, an indication of the importance of commerce (including the inland trade) in the everyday life of thirteenth-century England.

3. TRANSPORT COSTS

It remains to say something about the costs of transport. A universal feature of them, to begin with, is that they are a relative rather than an absolute matter, for their significance depends upon the value, as well as the bulk and weight, of the commodities carried. The respective costs of carting for ten miles a quarter of coal purchased for 3d. at the pithead and a quarter of wheat bought for 5s. at the farm gate might be very similar; but the final selling price of the coal might

[33] *Regesta*, II, no. 1267.
[34] *Ibid.*, no. 937; J. Raine, ed., *Historiae Dunelmensis Scriptores Tres*, Appx. p. xxxii.
[35] *Dd*, I, f. 1; *BBC, 1042–1216*, pp. 180–95.

need to be doubled to defray the costs of carriage, while that for the grain would be increased only by 5 per cent. If such costs might on occasion be prohibitively high, on the other hand, they did not have to be met in full by everyone. Many lords of manors, for relatively short-range movements of goods at least, could demand carrying services from their villeins for that purpose. In 1251 the bishop of Ely could call upon his tenants to drive back livestock bought at Bury St Edmunds fair, to transport by road or river grain that he had bought or was sending for sale, to go to Reach fair to get timber, to cart mill-stones, and to go to markets for necessary food supplies. A network of services linked the bishop's manors to each other and to market towns like Cambridge, Thetford, Bury St Edmunds, Norwich, Ipswich and Colchester, to the Huntingdonshire fair town of St Ives, to the port of King's Lynn, and in the case of the southernmost manors to the great market of London itself. In like manner, virgat-ers at Buckland (Glos.) owed carrying services every other week to Gloucester, Tewkesbury, Evesham, Chipping Campden, Clifford or Worcester; tenants of Bec abbey's English manors took grain for sale to neighbouring markets or market towns or sought the lord's food there; and the tenants of Holy Trinity, Caen, at Felstead owed carry-ing services to London, took wheat or oats by pack-horse to Maldon for sale, and went to Maldon or Colchester to fetch salt or to Horstead (Norfolk) to bring back herrings. The fellows of Merton College, Oxford, too inherited from earlier lords of Cuxham a right to call upon their tenants there to take corn to market at Henley and Wallingford.[36]

Short-range carrying services, therefore, often provided lords of manors with transport which called for little or no outlay on their part; and if tenants might be entitled to some expenses and allow-ances for longer journeys, again the net cost to their lord was often relatively small. On the Ely manor at Littleport, for example, those who performed 'long' services got allowances of food and could count their service against the total labour services they owed.[37] There can be no doubt that customary carrying services heavily subsi-dized the costs of marketing for many landlords; and royal powers to requisition transport as well as goods, and to impress those who manned it, may often reduce well below the economic level the

---

[36] E. Miller, *Abbey and Bishopric of Ely*, pp. 84–6; W.H. Hart, ed., *Historia et Cartularium Monasterii Gloucestriae*, Rolls Ser., 1865, II, p. 61; Chibnall, ed., *Select Documents of the English Lands of the Abbey of Bec, passim; idem*, ed., *Charters and Custumals of the Abbey of Holy Trinity, Caen*, pp. 90–1, 95; Harvey, ed., *Manorial Records of Cuxham*, pp. 607, 661.
[37] CUL EDR G.3.27, f. 12.

expenditure recorded for transporting supplies purveyed for armies and navies. Even lords who did not have villeins at their call, moreover, and others who farmed on some scale, often had full-time employees or equipment which could be used to transport goods bought or for sale at relatively little additional expense; and many peasant farmers were also in a position to provide their own transport, at least over a short distance. There were, in fact, large reserves of carts and of draught and pack animals in villages up and down the country which were not fully employed the year round in agricultural tasks, swelling the supply of available cartage and doubtless helping to keep its price down. Even as early as 1210–11 an estate as well provided as the bishop of Winchester's made use of hired transport on more than half its manors.[38] At the same time, what the economic cost of transport was is not easily determined from the available records given the power of landlords (or of the king in the case of supplies purveyed for armies) artificially to drive it down.

For this reason it is difficult at this time to establish with any confidence ratios between the cost of transport by the different means which were available; but what does seem to be clear is that transport by water was much cheaper than transport by road and that, of water-borne journeys, transport by sea was much cheaper than transport by river. A combination of transport by land with transport by water, therefore, could moderate the cost incurred, especially for goods of any value. The wool William de la Pole bought in Lindsey cost him just over £7 a sack when it was ready for export from Hull in 1337. Of that total £6 7s. 2d. represented the purchase price of the wool (with the agent's commission) in Lindsey. The balance of 13s. 0$^{1}/_{2}$d. (only 9 per cent of the total cost) was spent on transport, warehousing and packing, and the charges for warehousing and packing were more than double those for transport. It cost more, of course, to bring wool from Nottinghamshire and Swaledale to Hull, and more still to bring wool from the Cotswolds or West Midlands to the port of London; but even so, packing, warehousing and transport accounted only for about 14 per cent of the cost of Shropshire wool when it sailed from London.[39]

[38] M. Postan, in *CEcH*, II, pp. 151–2; Farmer, 'Marketing the produce of the countryside', pp. 350–1.
[39] C.C. Dyer, 'The consumer and the market in the later middle ages', *EcHR*, 2nd ser. XLII (1989), p. 309; J. Masschaele, 'Transport costs in medieval England', *ibid.*, XLVI (1993), p. 273; Fryde, *Studies in Medieval Trade and Finance*, chpt. IX, pp. 25–30.

Water transport, consequently, was preferred for most commodities whenever convenient, and it was essential to use it to the fullest extent for heavy or bulky goods. Millstones could be brought the 36 miles or so from London to Henley by river for about 2s. each, only about one sixth the cost per mile of bringing millstones overland from Wareham (Dorset) to Taunton in Somerset, even though it is equally clear that, although more expense was involved, the road system in central and southern England 'was adequate for carting heavy items like millstones'. The cost of carriage was also heavy in the case of building stone. At Exeter cathedral in the early fourteenth century transport accounted for 63 per cent of the cost on site of stone from Caen in Normandy; but also for at least as high a proportion of the cost of stone from Beer, Salcombe and Branscombe quarries, only twenty miles or so from Exeter as the crow flies, but which was brought most of the way by the longer sea and river route. The impact of the cheapest means of transport was even more dramatic in the case of a commodity with a value as low as coal. In 1364 a chaldron (i.e. approximately 28 cwt.) of coal, priced at 17d. at Winlaton on Tyne, cost over 3s. 6d. to ship to London, and in 1377 4s. was allowed for shipping costs. Yet if the coastal transport of coal to London raised its price by substantially more than 200 per cent, that from Boston to Exeter accounted only for about 6 per cent of the delivered cost of a more valuable commodity like lead for the cathedral, and a mere 3 per cent of the cost of iron brought 35 miles or so along the coast from Dartmouth and up the estuary of the Exe. By contrast, the carriage of horse-shoes and other iron articles by pack-horses around 40 miles from Lopen fair in Somerset to Exeter contributed some 7 per cent to their final cost even though the cathedral supplied the horses.[40]

Wine, although water carriage was preferred whenever possible, was another commodity sometimes sent for substantial distances overland, although as a luxury item the enhancement of its cost may have seemed to matter less to those who could afford it. On the Winchester estate in 1208–9 it cost 1s. 2d. to move a tun of wine the twelve miles between Southampton and Bishop's Waltham (Hants.), 4s. 6d. for the 36 miles between Bitterne and Burghclere at the

---

[40] Farmer, 'Marketing the produce of the countryside', pp. 252–3; *idem*, 'Millstones for medieval manors', p. 103; J.B.Blake, 'The medieval coal trade of north-east England', *North. Hist.*, II (1967), pp. 2–4; T.J. Taylor, 'The archaeology of the coal trade', *Proc. Archaeological Institute of Great Britain and Ireland*, I (1858), pp. 208–10; Erskine, ed., *Accounts of the Fabric of Exeter Cathedral*, I, pp. 9, 14, 16, 18, 96; II, pp. 221, 237, 262–5, 276.

opposite extremes of Hampshire, and 6s. for the 70 miles or so between Southampton and Witney (Oxon.). In the north, at a somewhat later date, transport costs for the fifteen miles between Newcastle and Durham ranged from 1s. 2d. to 2s. per tun (accounting for 2–3$\frac{1}{2}$ per cent of the cost of the wine). For other journeys, perhaps depending largely upon the extent to which boats could be used, the charges varied from 7d. per tun for the nineteen miles between Darlington and Durham (just over one per cent of the final cost), 7s. 2d. for the 72 miles between York and Durham (5 per cent), and 13s. 10d. for the 82 miles between Berwick and Durham (although that was in a year of war with the Scots at the end of the thirteenth century).[41]

Much of the traffic along England's roads, rivers and coastal waters, however, carried more every-day commodities than wine, of which grain was one of the most important. Most grain, of course, whether from manorial demesnes or peasant plots, was sold locally or in markets not more than ten miles from where it was grown. For such sales the widespread availability of labour services, or the use of farm carts and pack-horses, might result in transport costs which were very low; but even when vehicles and labour had to be hired there are some indications that this could be done at a cost of about 2d. per quarter to move grain for ten miles overland. That was a figure low enough, given the slightly higher levels of urban prices, to make it worthwhile for those with corn to sell to make relatively short journeys to the markets of towns like Colchester; and also to enable Colchester corn dealers to buy in bulk in the surrounding countryside with a reasonable prospect of profit even when they met the costs of transport themselves.[42]

The costs of transport over longer distances, and long-haul cartage in particular, were inevitably much higher and might raise the price of grain above competitive levels except in times of scarcity or when it was a matter of government purchases to supply the armed services. These costs once again, however, could be mitigated by the use of cheaper water transport to make a longer-range grain trade practicable. The 'common transit of ships and boats' along Fenland waterways, combined with access to the coastal routes to London and

[41] Hall, ed., *Pipe Roll of the Bishopric of Winchester, 1208–9*, pp. 2, 9, 18; Morimoto, *Monastic Economy and Medieval Markets*, pp. 371–6.
[42] Farmer, 'Marketing the produce of the countryside', pp. 363–5, 367–70; *idem*, 'Two Wiltshire manors and their markets', *AHR*, XXXVII (1989), pp. 5–7; H., Gough, ed., *Scotland in 1298*, pp. 1–5; R.H. Britnell, 'Colchester and the countryside in the fourteenth century' (Cambridge Univ. Ph.D. Dissertation, 1969), pp. 108–11.

the north, made King's Lynn the 'corn depot' for a wide and fertile region of eastern England; and the fact that grain could be moved relatively cheaply along the Thames made Henley one of London's most important sources of supply throughout the middle ages.[43] Transport costs, of course, were not the sole influence conditioning the development of the medieval grain trade. The growth of London in particular called for supplies from an ever greater distance; and by the early fourteenth century a group of cornmongers (*bladers*) controlled much of the city's grain trade and was well established in its civic hierarchy.[44] They brought to the business of provisioning London a degree of organization, a level of investment and a control of shipping which made their services indispensable to agricultural producers in the hinterlands of Henley, Great Yarmouth and King's Lynn. It is also likely that other towns of any considerable size were coming to depend upon grain supplies from an increasing distance, although we know much less about how those supplies were organized.

Much of England's inland trade continued undoubtedly to be short-range and to involve 'marketing in penny parcels'; but equally evident is an increase in the range of exchanges and in the volume of transactions in the three centuries which followed the Norman Conquest. To that extent there is perhaps justification for a verdict upon medieval communications less pessimistic than that sometimes given. J.F. Willard's conclusion over sixty years ago, and there is much to be said for it, was that 'the transportation of goods was to a high degree free of danger. On every stream there were boats; on every road there were carts and pack-horses. The most vivid impression is that of the large amount of movement along the roads and streams, and with it the lack of isolation of medieval towns and villages'.[45] The relatively high cost of overland transport might limit the range of trading, especially in the case of such rudimentary commodities as firewood, turves, coal, lime and marl; but the cost of many journeys could be much reduced where the use of sea or river transport was possible and, in any case, they tended in some measure to be kept down by the availability of carrying services for some marketing and by the large reserves of carts, draught animals and men

[43] W.H. Hart and P.A. Lyons, eds, *Cartularium Monasterii de Rameseia*, III, p. 144; N.S.B. Gras, *Evolution of the English Corn Market*, pp. 62–3; Farmer, 'Marketing the produce of the countryside', pp. 353, 371; R.H.Britnell, *Commercialisation of English Society*, pp. 86–8, 99.
[44] G.A.Williams, *Medieval London*, pp. 161–4.
[45] J.F. Willard, 'Inland transportation in England during the fourteenth century', *Speculum*, I (1926), pp. 361–74; cf. Postan, in *CEcH*, II, pp. 144–6, 155.

in English villages. The consequence was that, if carts and pack-horses could not carry cheap and heavy goods for any appreciable distance without raising their price excessively, they coped well enough with widely traded goods of higher value like wool, grain, salt, cloth and wine. To this extent improvements in the transport system made their contribution to the expansion of exchanges and the increased commercialization of English society which are features of the central middle ages.

4.   MARKETS AND MARKETING[46]

An indicator of a growing inland trade during this period was the proliferation of fairs and markets, even though we still cannot measure the volume of internal commerce at any particular point in time. The surviving records rarely provide quantitative statements about transactions in fairs and markets, and many commercial transactions in any case took place outside them. Informal trading was characteristic of every level of society; it may well have increased much more than formal exchanges in the early part of our period and it did not cease in later generations. Bargains were struck between villagers, of which we learn when they were not honoured, which related to many things: at Littleport, for example, to a boat, bundles of reeds, ewes which turned out to be afflicted with rot, a cow and a calf, eels, and ale sold by false measure. At Wakefield, too, men who were presumably cloth workers in a small way owed money for little parcels of wool, and at Houghton (Hunts.) two peasants owed small consignments of wool to a merchant. Very often it was arranged that payments due under these deals should be made by instalments, for to buy a horse or ox or cow represented a considerable outlay for a villager; and families which were short of cash or food might promise to deliver grain after the harvest for which payment had been made in advance, or to pay later for loans of grain made to them in time of need. The temptation to default on arrangements of this sort was doubtless greatest in hard times like the hungry years in the early fourteenth century. In 1317 one Yorkshire peasant still had 2s. outstanding on the purchase of a quarter of oats nearly two years earlier, and to make matters worse the vendor was demanding an

---

[46] What follows depends heavily upon R.H. Britnell, 'The proliferation of markets in England, 1200–1349', *EcHR*, 2nd ser. xxxiv (1981), pp. 209–21.

extra 5s. to bring the price up to the famine levels of those years. The informal market was full of pitfalls for those who were poor or improvident.[47]

It was also very common for much richer men to deal directly with merchants. Durham and Norwich priories, for instance, bought wine in the ports of Hull and Great Yarmouth, and Abbot Walter de Wenlok of Westminster had many and various dealings with Londoners: with John of Sawbridgeworth for poultry, William of Fulham for fish, John of Burford for wax and spices, and with 'divers merchants of London' for herrings, onions, garlic, a saddle cloth and a barrel of sturgeon. One Cahorsin immigrant into London, William Servat, is even to be encountered in the north selling wine to Durham priory.[48] Rich men also sold as well as bought directly. When the Earl Marshal's reeve at Kennet sold wheat and malt *in patria*, such sales did not necessarily take place in a formal market, and especially for wool many thirteenth-century sales were effected directly between magnates and merchants. Meaux abbey, on one occasion, sold 120 sacks of wool to merchants of Lucca for £800. Kirkstall abbey also contracted to sell its wool to Lucchese merchants, but Rievaulx dealt with Florentines and Pipewell with a group of Cahorsins.[49] Denizen merchants, too, struck similar bargains with sheep-owners. In 1289 Lawrence of Ludlow and his brothers owed money to Bruern abbey (Oxon.) for its wool; Reginald de Thunderle, an alien who had settled in London, bought up Westminster abbey's wool in 1294 from its collecting centre at Sutton-under-Brailes (Glos.); and a little later the Bec wool from Combe (Hants.) was bought by John of Wantage, who visited the manor to supervise its weighing and packing, just as the Cahorsins arranged to do in the case of the wool they bought from Pipewell.[50]

[47] Britnell, *Commercialisation of English Society*, pp. 10, 97–101; F.W.Maitland and W.P.Baildon, eds, *The Court Baron*, pp. 114, 119, 128, 132, 136, 139; J. Lister, ed., *Court Rolls of the Manor of Wakefield*, IV, pp. 68–9, 198, 202–3; Ault, ed., *Court Rolls of the Abbey of Ramsey*, pp. 34, 163, 230–1, 249, 267.
[48] James, *Studies in the Medieval Wine Trade*, p. 181; Harvey, ed., *Documents Illustrating the Rule of Walter de Wenlok*, pp. 108, 119, 121; Fowler, ed., *Account Rolls of Durham Abbey*, II, p. 494.
[49] PRO SC 6/768/22–3; E.A. Bond, ed., *Chronica Monasterii de Melsa*, II, p. 156; W.T. Lancaster and W.P. Baildon, eds, *Coucher Book of the Cistercian Abbey of Kirkstall*, no. 324; J.C. Atkinson, ed., *Cartularium Abbathiae de Rievalle*, pp. 409–11; *CCR*, 1288–96, pp. 192–5.
[50] *Ibid.*, pp. 42, 130; Harvey, ed., *Documents Illustrating the Rule of Walter de Wenlok*, pp. 64–5; Chibnall, ed., *Select Documents of the English Lands of the Abbey of Bec*, pp. 150, 156, 168–9.

Important merchants buying in bulk, of course, are most likely to leave traces in the records, but most trading was done by small traders in a small way of business. In 1276 the little town of Newnham-on-Severn (Glos.) evidently felt surrounded by unfair competitors: bakers and butchers had set up business in two neighbouring villages; at Little Dean 'a certain brother . . .. exercises all manner of trade except in cloth'; and in another village a tanner forestalled hides which should have come to Newnham market. So the tale of woe goes on, carrying the impression of widespread small-scale trading. The numerous rural 'merchants' and other traders who appear in the records convey a similar impression, including the 'certain merchant of Earith' (Hunts.) who bought up a Houghton villein's goods in 1307, or the cornmonger of Northfleet (Kent) who, to win pardon for the death of a woman, had to serve in the army in Scotland. Many country 'merchants', in fact, appear to have had very limited resources. Fifteen of them appear among the tax-payers in ten of the villages of Blackbourne hundred in Suffolk in 1283; but their taxable wealth tended to be lower than that of the average villager.[51]

The consumption habits of villagers and townsfolk, most of them poor or at best of very moderate means, required the services of petty traders, tinkers, chapmen and hucksters, many of them women, who retailed cheap goods from the roadside or from door-to-door. There was a widespread and continuous demand for goods like second-hand clothes, for crude, locally produced table ware made both of pottery and wood, for old brass cooking pots and pans (often much repaired), and for personal items such as belts, buckles, combs, purses and ornaments of low quality, so that sales of this sort (in addition to the trade in victuals) constituted a large part of the trade which took place in villages and small towns. In a poor society as little as possible was allowed to go to waste, and a significant portion of economic activity was devoted to recycling metals and textiles and anything else which could be salvaged. Archaeological evidence of these trades is already substantial and accumulating rapidly. In addition to the abundance of cheap pottery uncovered on sites in villages and small towns throughout England, a wide range of other downmarket items is being unearthed and catalogued. Recent excavations in the city of London, for example, have made clear the

---

[51] *Rot. Hundr.*, I, p. 182; Ault, ed., *Court Rolls of the Abbey of Ramsey*, p. 242; *CPR*, 1301–7, p. 33; E. Powell, ed., *A Suffolk Hundred in 1283, passim.*

popularity of shoddy, mass-produced articles in base metal.[52] Such goods were too inferior both in quality and value to give rise to gild organizations or gild regulation, although the trade in them was subject to some legal controls. Unfortunately the presentments by jurors of petty commercial offences have rarely survived, and the less exalted the trade the less likely are they to do so; but in one Norwich ward in 1312–13, in addition to dealers in grain, cheese, butter and eggs, and poulterers, butchers, brewers, cooks and chandlers, eleven sellers of second-hand clothes were accused of improper trading practices.[53]

If men and women of this sort traded only in a small way, they might still do so consistently. A handbook for keepers of manorial courts preserves a model charge against Thomas Fisher who, 'all this year, every day, hath ... sold fish in full market to his neighbours and to strangers, and to all alike fish and herring stinking and rotten and in all wise corrupt'.[54] It may be surprising that Thomas got customers, but it seems unlikely that his daily sales took place in a formal village market, for these were normally held on one day each week. On the other hand, a degree of certainty as to where business might be done was clearly to the interest both of traders and their customers. One central and public place which might conveniently serve for this purpose was the churchyard; and in 1299 the Walsoken (Norfolk) court leet decreed that no fisherman 'shall in future sell any fish outside the vill before they have brought their fish to the church for sale in case any from the vill wish to buy'. Even Northampton fair was held in All Saints churchyard until that use was banned after 1235; and as late as 1306 there was an informal market at Crosthwaite churchyard in Cumberland for grain, flour, peas, beans, flax, yarn, flesh and fish, which took away trade from nearby Cockermouth market. Informal gatherings of this sort might develop into formal markets; and there was an obvious advantage in holding them, until sabbatarian church legislation in the thirteenth century checked the practice, on Sundays when congregations might be turned into customers. This helps to explain why so many early

---

[52] D. Woodward, '"Swords into ploughshares": recycling in pre-industrial England', *EcHR*, XXXVIII (1985), pp. 175–91; G. Egan and F. Pritchard, eds, *Medieval Finds from Excavations in London: Dress Accessories*.
[53] On all these matters see R.H.Hilton, *Class Conflict and the Crisis of Feudalism*, pp. 194–204.
[54] Maitland and Baildon, eds, *The Court Baron*, p. 26.

formal markets were Sunday markets, including that which the Conqueror granted to Battle abbey.[55]

Important as informal trading was, however, a significant sign of the times was the proliferation of formal markets, i.e. markets chartered by the crown or recognized as having a prescriptive validity. Figures for markets authorized prior to 1349 have been established by R.H. Britnell for 21 of the English counties (just over half the area of the country) and are summarized in Table 3.1.[56] There is a good case for arguing that most of the markets entered under the 'sometime before 1349' heading were in fact established before 1200; but a growing momentum of market foundations in the period 1200–74 appears to be beyond question, even when every allowance is made for the crown's increased insistence that every market should have specific authorization, and for the fact that some grants of markets were abortive or only briefly effective. Although the number of new foundations fell away appreciably in the final quarter of the thirteenth century, and even more markedly in the 25 years before 1349, in the first quarter of the fourteenth century the rate was not all that much lower than it had been in 1200–74. All in all, on the eve of the Black Death England had in the region of three times as many licensed markets as in 1200, 'manifesting the optimism of an age of expansion'. Even though the degree of optimism

Table 3.1 Markets established in England before 1349

Region	No. of counties	Date of foundation of markets		
		Sometime before 1349	1200–74	1275–1349
Southern	3	48	35	15
East Midlands	5	43	43	28
West Midlands	4	41	81	36
East Anglia	3	92	131	63
Northern	5	73	102	78
South-West	1	32	33	29
Totals	21	329	425	249

[55] Ault, ed., *Court Rolls of the Abbey of Ramsey*, p. 179; *Close R.*, 1234–37, pp. 206–7; L.F. Salzman, *English Trade in the Middle Ages*, pp. 133–5; *Rot. Parl.*, I, p. 197; *Regesta*, I, no. 61 and II, no. 1348. For other early Sunday markets, *ibid.*, II, no. 92 and III, nos. 293, 384, 456, 597.

[56] Britnell, 'The proliferation of markets in England', esp. p. 210.

had varied from time to time and markets were somewhat unevenly spread, most people by that time had reasonably convenient access to a market and not infrequently to more than one.[57]

Many of the markets listed in Table 3.1 were in towns or places which were growing into towns, but even more were in villages. Northumberland had 22 markets outside Newcastle in 1349, a number in relation to its size that was below average; but, as well as those in little market towns like Alnwick, Morpeth, Corbridge and Haydon Bridge, there were also weekly markets at places without urban pretensions like Wark-on-Tweed, Chatton, Embleton, Elsdon, Netherwitton and Ovingham.[58] There were some village markets which had been established before the mid-twelfth century,[59] and doubtless there were even more places where informal trading was carried on as a matter of course in the churchyard or some other convenient place; but the multiplication of formally constituted markets during the ensuing two centuries is one visible sign of the extent and generality of the commercialization of English society which was achieved during those generations.

The precise character of the trade done in village markets is seldom documented in detail; but customary legal formulae, probably based on court proceedings in Edward I's reign, refer to a market 'held every week on Wednesdays, to which . . . all the people of the countryside used to come to sell and buy oxen and cows, sheep and other kinds of animals, wheat, rye and barley, etc., sendal, silk and other kinds of textiles'. This record is illuminating for the emphasis placed on the way in which markets in particular offered facilities for trading in agricultural produce and in the farmer's requirements. Information contained in pleadings before the Shropshire justices in 1256 about competition between the neighbouring markets of Hawkesbury (Glos.) and Sherston (Wilts.) is also of interest in this connection. Their tax assessments in 1334 suggest that both places were no more than villages and that Hawkesbury was a very small

---

[57] B.E. Coates, 'The origin and distribution of markets and fairs in medieval Derbyshire', *Derbyshire Arch. Jnl.*, LXXXV (1965), p. 101; Farmer, 'Marketing the produce of the countryside', pp. 329–31.

[58] For markets in 1293: C.M. Fraser, 'The pattern of trade in the north-east of England, 1265–1350', *North. Hist.*, IV (1969), p. 44, to which should be added fourteenth-century foundations at Haltwhistle and Haydon Bridge, and perhaps also at Tynemouth and South Shields: J. Hodgson, *History of Northumberland*, II (3), pp. 121, 376; *NCH*, VIII, pp. 75, 79. For the density of markets per 100 sq. miles in England generally, Farmer, 'Marketing the produce of the countryside', p. 331; in Northumberland it is doubtful if this was any higher than, or even as high as, in Co. Durham.

[59] E.g. *Regesta*, I, no. 477; II, nos. 925, 1576, 1664, 1666; III, nos. 118, 172, 710.

one; but in Henry III's time merchants were bringing goods for sale to their markets, the villagers themselves bought and sold grain, meat and other things there, and some merchants bought grain to supply the Bristol market some twenty miles away.[60] Weekly markets in villages and small towns, in other words, enabled small farmers and rural artisans to dispose of surplus produce (and it was perhaps there that lords of manors disposed of some of the goods they sold *in patria*); and they also made it possible for those who needed to buy food to do so, for all who required them to buy salt and fish, and for peasants and craftsmen to buy livestock or raw materials and perhaps the 'chapmen's wares' they had failed to get from hucksters. Some village markets, finally, were supply points for some of the foodstuffs and raw materials needed by towns – something which explains the presence of cornmongers engaged in provisioning Bristol at Hawkesbury and Sherston; and large towns might rely on small town markets for supplies, as Leicester seems to be doing when its merchants got some of their wool at Hinckley market.[61]

The obvious convenience of having market facilities close at hand does much to explain their proliferation and the highly localized character of much of the trade done in them; and landowners were not unwilling to satisfy this dictate of convenience and to procure charters for markets which might, after all, yield them revenue. It was this revenue which was at issue when markets were alleged to compete with each other. As early as 1202 Ely priory's market at Lakenheath, where meat and livestock and fish and grain and merchandise of diverse sorts were sold, was said by Abbot Samson to be detrimental to the abbey's fair at Bury St Edmunds 'in that the abbot loses his customs'; and the grievance about the abbot of Pershore's Hawkesbury market in 1256 was that 'the toll and stall-dues and other customary payments which should and are accustomed to be paid on goods bought in the market at Sherston' were being diverted to the abbot. In 1227 the bishop of Lincoln tried to protect himself from loss on these grounds by securing a promise from Henry III that no market established after Henry's coronation would continue if it damaged any market the bishop had possessed before that date; and later Bracton's view was that a market set up less than $6^2/3$ miles from another was a 'wrongful nuisance' which must be cast down, since that was the distance, while leaving reasonable time

[60] E. Shanks, ed., *Novae Narrationes*, Selden Soc., LXXX (1963) p. 87; A. Harding, ed., *Roll of the Shropshire Eyre of 1256*, pl. 403; R.E.Glasscock, ed., *The Lay Subsidy of 1334*, pp. 102, 344.
[61] Britnell, 'The proliferation of markets', p. 217; Farmer, 'Marketing the produce of the countryside', pp. 333–4; Bateson, ed., *Leicester Borough Records*, I, p. 271.

to do business, which might conveniently be travelled coming and returning in a day.[62] Despite the law's constraints, however, there were markets in Derbyshire in 1349 only a mile or so apart; Hawkesbury and Sherston, on the Wiltshire–Gloucestershire border, were less than five miles apart; and even in Northumberland Chatton was only four miles as the crow flies from Wooler, Alnmouth only four miles from Alnwick, and Corbridge only four miles from Hexham.

The multiplication of village markets was one reason for the reduction in the rate of market foundations after 1275, although markets did not cease to be established and the rate of foundations even picked up again in the first quarter of the fourteenth century. Some of these late established markets, which often had no long-term future and accommodated business on a very small scale, may have been a response to the needs of country folk with insufficient land to sustain themselves and their families: they were designed 'more to accommodate the poor than for profit'. On the other hand, when markets did little business, the reason might be that countrymen had found others ways of buying and selling which did not entail incurring market charges, or that they were using markets, even though they were rather further away, where prices were better or the range of goods was wider. The extensive range of market opportunities available by the fourteenth century was very considerable even for a small estate like Robert of Madingley's Cambridgeshire manor at Harston. There were exchanges with neighbouring villages (Wimpole, Barrington, Hauxton, Great Shelford and Fowlmere), and a good deal of buying and selling in Cambridge and at Barnwell fair just outside that town; but in addition calf and sheep skins were sold at Haverhill (Suffolk), sheep were bought at Hadstock (Essex), harness was bought at Ickleton fair (Cambs.), oats were sold at Saffron Walden (Essex), sheep skins were sold and sheep and cart wheels were bought at Royston (Herts.), cart wheels were also bought at Baldock (Herts.), and the manorial wool clip was sold to a chapman at Histon on the other side of Cambridge. Commercial openings for countryfolk by the second decade of the fourteenth century were clearly diversified, whether or not they were offered by formal fairs and markets.[63]

---

[62] Harding, ed., *Roll of the Shropshire Eyre of 1256*, pl. 403; *CRR*, II, p. 136; *Reg. Antiquissimum*, I, no. 229; S.E. Thorne, ed., *Bracton, De Legibus et Consuetudinibus Angliae*, III, p. 198.
[63] Britnell, 'The proliferation of markets', pp. 219–21; Farmer, 'Marketing the produce of the countryside', p. 338; BL Add. Roll 18522.

The multiplication of markets took place in towns as well as villages, and not merely because new towns were added to old. At Leicester, for instance, the original market was probably that held on Wednesdays at High Cross; but by the fourteenth century this was mainly a market for butter and eggs, and the more important Saturday market was in fact a series of distinct markets occupying all the south-east quarter of the town. At Lincoln, too, if the *Lay of Havelock the Dane* can be taken literally, servants from the castle and the Bail came down in early times to the High Bridge in order to buy meat and fish; but markets were later dispersed over the hill descending from the Bail to the river: a fish market just below the Bail, a corn market further downhill by St Cuthbert's church, and separate markets for poultry, cloth, skins and, by the river, for malt. At Ipswich there was a similar array of markets for different commodities: at Salisbury sellers of meat, vegetables, poultry, corn, cheese, fish, and of wool and yarn each occupied their specific part of the spacious market place; and at Winchester the market, which originally had occupied much of High Street, by the thirteenth century had spilled over into the side streets, with particular trades tending to concentrate in particular rows of shops, and there was a new market for grain, livestock and firewood in the north-western part of the cathedral cemetery where the royal palace had stood until it was destroyed in 1141.[64]

Increased provision for marketing in towns reflects their dependence upon a regular inflow of foodstuffs from their hinterlands, a dependence which increased as urban populations grew. At the same time town craftsmen needed raw materials like wool, yarn, skins, wood and iron; merchants in the larger towns were customers for commodities made in smaller towns (like the Coggeshall and Maldon cloth which found a market in Ipswich) or by country artisans; and town shops and workshops sold to visitors from the countryside as well as to fellow townsfolk. In these senses the existence and growth of towns depended fundamentally upon the inland trade; but most of them were also more than the focal points of a reciprocal trade between themselves and their hinterlands. They were, in addition, centres for a much longer-range distribution of goods. Thirteenth-century Ipswich could offer at its quay iron from Spain, Normandy and Cologne, steel and herrings and furs from the

---

[64] *VCH Leics.*, IV, pp. 46–8; J.W.F.Hill, *Medieval Lincoln*, pp. 153–4, 157, 175–6; T. Twiss, ed., *Black Book of the Admiralty*, II, pp. 184–204; K.H. Rogers, 'Salisbury', in M.D. Lobel, ed., *Historic Towns*, I, p. 6; Keene, *Survey*, I, pp. 330–2 and map on p. 336.

Baltic, Irish and Eastland timber, wine probably from Gascony, and spices from the Mediterranean and beyond. Some of these commodities, in turn, probably found their way from Ipswich to the inland market towns which sent their cloth to that port, and which acted as secondary centres of distribution.[65] In like manner Bristol merchants are found selling wine in Gloucester, Worcester and Hereford merchants found buying wine in Bristol, and Adam Feteplace of Oxford getting the wine with which he supplied the king at Woodstock in the port of Southampton. This increasingly extensive distributive network explains the diversity of goods which were available in Leicester in the early fourteenth century: not only wine, but pepper, ginger, almonds, rice, sugar, cumin, Paris candles, figs and raisins. Even Battle, though no more than 'a tolerably well situated market town', could provide the abbey with some wine (although more was likely to come from Winchelsea or Hastings), saffron, oil, beef and fish; and the Durham priory bursar was able to buy in Durham market, well before 1349, wine by the gallon, wax, saffron and a whole range of other spices, making less and less necessary the long journey to Boston fair which had earlier been required to procure these supplies.[66]

The inland trade also enabled goods to be gathered up to meet the demands of merchants from the greater towns and of exporters. Government enquiries in 1276 afford some glimpses of this process in the case of wool. Men from Newbury (Berks.) bought wool in the neighbourhood of that town for despatch to Southampton; Gloucestershire wool was also sent to Southampton (in some cases by Bristol merchants) as well as to Oxford; and Dover merchants and the agents of a London merchant collected wool for export in Kent and Essex respectively. Even in North Yorkshire Scarborough merchants bought wool in the countryside around their town, a Berwick merchant was alleged to have bought up a thousand sacks of wool, and York and Newcastle men were buying wool around Whitby and Richmond. Nor is it surprising to find that the port of London was a magnet for provincial exporters, including merchants from

[65] N.S.B. Gras, *Early History of the English Customs System*, pp. 159–63, for a list of customs, probably of Ipswich.
[66] *Close R.*, 1231–34, pp. 245, 247, 249; *CLR*, 1251–60, pp. 50, 388–9, 438; M. Bateson, ed., *Leicester Borough Records*, I, pp. 258–9, 263–5, 314, 326; Searle and Ross, eds, *Cellarers' Rolls of Battle Abbey*, p. 55; E. Searle, *Lordship and Community*, pp. 351–3; Fowler, ed., *Account Rolls of the Abbey of Durham*, II, p. 494; Morimoto, *Monastic Economy and Medieval Markets*, pp. 200–19.

Dunstable, Baldock, Ludlow and Winchester.[67] Other commodities were bulked for marketing in a similar manner. In the thirteenth century cheese from Minchinhampton was regularly sent to Cirencester for onward transmission to Henley and shipment down the Thames; King's Lynn, as we have seen, was a collecting centre for the grain surpluses of a wide hinterland; and Ipswich offered a market for cloth made in inland villages and market towns. In the South-West, too, the arrangements for taxing working tinners furthered a concentration of the trade in tin at Lostwithiel, Bodmin and Truro in Cornwall and at Chagford, Ashburton and Tavistock in Devon.[68]

An inland trading network linking districts and regions, therefore, became more extensive over time. Even at the relatively local level, in the areas centred on village markets and market towns, there are many signs of increased commercial activity; and the ripples of a longer-range commerce generated by the greater boroughs were superimposed on this pattern of local exchanges. Leicester men were not only to be found at relatively modest and not too distant markets like those at Rothwell (Northants.), Hinckley and Blackfordby; they also bought timber from Arden (Warks.), Cannock Chase and Needwood (Staffs.), they traded in Chester, Shrewsbury, Derby and Northampton, and they bought gloves in Coventry.[69] Metropolitan districts, those centred on the great ports especially, overlapped the hinterlands even of substantial boroughs. Bristol, for instance, supplied inland towns like Gloucester, Hereford and Worcester, and also provided outlets for their merchants; while Hull and York in combination, and also Southampton, played similar roles. Finally, almost certainly from the start, London was *sui generis*. Its size demanded that it should cast its net more widely for provisions and raw materials than any other town; as a centre of manufacture and an international port it was a market in which an exceptional variety of goods were to be found; and its merchants were familiar figures in places far from the capital. William Servat not only sold wine and sugar to Durham priory, but also bought some of its wool; and in 1276 Stephen of Cornhill was merely one of a number of Londoners who had bought up large consignments of Lincolnshire wool. Trade and merchants, and by no means least

---

[67] *Rot. Hundr.*, I, pp. 18, 108, 115, 118, 132–3, 162, 172, 175, 177, 207, 406, 416.

[68] E.M. Carus-Wilson, 'Evidences of industrial growth on some fifteenth-century manors', *EcHR*, 2nd ser. XII (1959), pp. 192–3; J. Hatcher, *English Tin Production and Trade before 1550*, pp. 76–7.

[69] Bateson, ed., *Leicester Borough Records*, I, pp. 25, 42–3, 114, 271, 280, 312, 321.

London merchants, were giving to England a measure of economic unity.[70]

5. FAIRS

Much of the inland trade, between the late twelfth and the early fourteenth centuries, was carried on at fairs as well as markets. A great deal of the business done at many fairs, indeed, was very similar to that done in local markets; but some fairs served for bulk sales and purchases and attracted customers from much greater distances than most markets were likely to do. At the end of the twelfth century it was a matter of routine for the chamberlain of Abingdon abbey to visit Winchcombe fair to buy cloth for the community, for the manor of Dumbleton (Glos.) had a standing obligation to find lodgings for him; and a century later Durham priory sent its wool for sale to Boston fair, and bought there cloth, furs, wax, a whole array of spices, tablecloths, linen, knives, parchment and gloves.[71] Many fair-goers, however, had more modest and ordinary requirements. One Cambridgeshire manorial lord in 1251–52 bought a cart at Barnwell fair and horse-shoes and the nails for them at St Ives fair; and early in the fourteenth century the things needed to maintain carts and ploughs on the Ramsey manor of Graveley were bought at St Ives and Stourbridge fairs.[72] Fairs, moreover, attracted townsmen as well as countryfolk. Leicester merchants were visiting Stamford fair as early as 1196 and St Giles's fair at Winchester by 1207; and thereafter they were frequent attenders at Boston, King's Lynn, St Ives and Northampton fairs.[73] How wide an appeal a fair might have is illustrated by those who did business at St Ives fair. Apart from merchants from Flanders, Brabant and elsewhere overseas, they included numerous villagers and their lords from Huntingdonshire, Cambridgeshire and other parts of eastern England, and traders from London, Stamford, Northampton, Oxford, Boston, Nottingham, Leicester, Norwich and St Albans. Occasionally, too,

[70] Fowler, ed., *Account Rolls of the Abbey of Durham*, II, p. 494; N. Morimoto, *Durham Cathedral Priory: the Economic History of an Ecclesiastical Estate in the Later Middle Ages*, p. 365; *Rot. Hundr.*, I, p. 385.

[71] J. Stevenson, ed., *Chronicon Monasterii de Abingdon*, II, p. 300; Fowler, ed., *Account Rolls of the Abbey of Durham*, II, pp. 492, 494–5.

[72] PRO SC 6/765/15, 767/13.

[73] Bateson, ed., *Leicester Borough Records*, I, pp. 14, 24, 29, 33, 80 etc.

there were men from even more distant places, among them Beverley, York, Scarborough, Chester and Winchester.[74]

There is much that is uncertain about the origins even of some of the most important fairs. Boston fair, for instance, certainly existed by 1135, but little more than that is known about its beginnings.[75] Even when the record is apparently clearer we cannot always be sure that it is complete. William Rufus in 1096 authorized the bishop and monks of the Old Minster to hold a fair 'at St Giles's church . . . situated on the eastern hill of Winchester' for three days each year (a period subsequently extended by Henry I and Stephen); but there is at least a possibility that there had been an earlier annual market or fair, mainly for the sale of agricultural produce, before 1096. At Westminster, too, there may have been a pre-existing fair long before it emerged in the documentary record in the reign of Henry III.[76] Whatever uncertainties there are about the origins of fairs, their owners, like the owners of markets, increasingly sought royal authorization for them; and, like markets, the number of fairs increased, at least until the latter part of the thirteenth century. Surviving charters suggest that almost forty of them had been authorized by the end of Stephen's reign, including some of the 'great fairs' of the future (Winchester, King's Lynn, St Ives and Bury St Edmunds), together with others with lesser prospects like those at Eynesbury (Hunts.), Bawsey (Norfolk), Tintinhull and Hamdon Hill (Somerset) and Woodkirk (Yorks.).[77]

By the early fourteenth century fairs were much more numerous. Even in Northumberland at least sixteen fairs were licensed: in old royal vills like Corbridge and Bamburgh, in little market towns like Alnwick and Norham, and in small and sometimes remote villages like Chatton and Elsdon.[78] Cambridgeshire, in a more developed region of England, was even better provided. Cambridge itself, as well as controlling Reach fair ten miles away in the fen at the interchange point between river and road traffic, had three fairs around

---

[74] E. Wedemeyer Moore, *Fairs of Medieval England*, pp. 77–84. On all matters relating to fairs we have depended heavily upon Dr Moore's book.

[75] The fair is mentioned in a charter to St Mary's abbey, York, which can be dated 1125–35: W. Farrer and C.T. Clay, eds, *Early Yorkshire Charters*, IV, p. 10, and cf. Hill, *Medieval Lincoln*, p. 315.

[76] *Regesta*, I, no. 377; II, no. 947; III, no. 952; M. Biddle, ed., *Winchester in the Early Middle Ages*, p. 287; G. Rosser, *Medieval Westminster, 1200–1540*, pp. 97–9.

[77] *Regesta*, II, nos. 762, 953, 1371, 1599; III, nos. 291, 591, 622.

[78] J. Raine, *History and Antiquities of North Durham*, 1852, p. 258; J. Hodgson, *History of Northumberland*, II(1), p. 87; M.R.G. Conzen, *Alnwick, Northumberland: a Study in Town-Plan Analysis*, p. 24; *NCH*, I, p. 125; X, pp. 34–6; XIV p. 208.

its own perimeter by 1215: Garlic fair, Midsummer or Barnwell fair, and Stourbridge fair. There were also one or more annual fairs licensed for 24 places in the county and the Isle of Ely, although some were in places so undistinguished that the grant of a fair may have been abortive (at Kingston and Brinkley, for example, nothing more is heard of a fair after the initial grant). Ely fair, on the other hand, which was granted to the bishop in the 1120s, flourished sufficiently to be regarded two centuries later as a threat to the abbot of Ramsey's fair at St Ives; and the fairs authorized for Linton in 1246 and for Barham in 1282 both lingered on until the 1870s. As we have seen, too, the manor of Harston in the early fourteenth century traded extensively at Midsummer fair outside Cambridge and at Royston fair just outside the county, as well as buying harness at the village fair at Ickleton.[79]

Landlords or towns were moved to seek grants of fairs for motives which were not least financial. Henry I, for instance, confirmed to the bishop of Norwich rights of jurisdiction in his fairs at Norwich, King's Lynn and Hoxne, and justice in the middle ages (as the saying went) produced great emolument; the bishop of Rochester, at the fair in his cathedral city, and the bishop of Lincoln at Stow fair were granted the tolls charged in them; and the payment made by traders for stalls at Great Bricett fair in Suffolk were conceded to the priory which had been founded in that village early in the twelfth century. The accounts of St Giles's fair at Winchester offer the most complete statement of the revenues which might accrue to the lords of fairs: they included rents for accommodation, tolls of one sort and another, payments for grazing draught and other animals, and profits from the fair courts, the gross total of which in 1238 and 1239 was just short of £164. Around 1200 gross returns from Boston and St Ives fairs, too, often reached £100 or more; and at Winchester the bishop's net income from the fair, after expenses had been deducted, was still running at that level down to the 1280s. Many fairs, of course, produced revenues of quite a different order. On the estate of the earl of Cornwall in 1296–97, the tolls of the market and fair at Howden (Yorks.) were farmed together for only £5, the farm of Oakham fair (Rutland) was £3 11s. 7d.; and the profits of Rockingham fair (Northampton) were a mere £2 1s. 11d. These, moreover, were by no means the least lucrative of the earl's fairs: fair

---

[79] RCHM (England), *Inventory of the Historical Monuments of the County of Cambridge*, II, pp. 85–6; *VCH Cambs.*, II, p. 87; III, pp. 91–3; V, p. 117; VI, pp. 96, 138; C.H. Cooper, *Annals of Cambridge*, I, p. 34; *Regesta*, II, no. 1620; H.G. Richardson and G.O. Sayles, eds, *Rotuli Parliamentorum Anglie hactenus Inediti*, pp. 91, 173; BL Add. Roll 18522.

tolls amounted only to 10s. at Bradninch (Devon), 5s. at Helstone-on-Trigg (Cornwall) and 3s. 5^1/$_2$d. at Lydford (Devon). Bec abbey's returns from Swyncombe fair (Oxon.), too, seldom exceeded 10s. and were usually less in the 1270s and 1280s, and Adam of Stratton's income from his fair at Stratton St Margaret was only about £1 10s. a year.[80]

The great variation in the profits lords got from their fairs carried an implication that their economic importance must similarly have varied greatly. They appear, in fact, to have operated on three different levels. First, there were the 'great fairs', the range of which was international and to which we must return. Secondly, there were regional fairs which attracted participants from considerable distances: they seem to have included Corbridge, Darlington and Bolton fairs in the north, and in the Cotswolds Chipping Campden and Winchcombe fairs (the Abingdon chamberlain travelled forty miles to this last fair). The agents of Exeter cathedral covered a similar distance to reach Lopen fair in Somerset, and the Cambridge fairs attracted customers from all over the county and beyond. Finally, many of the village fairs must have had a much more localized appeal: judging by the revenue they generated they must have been little more than neighbourhood events. Many of the village fairs and some of the regional fairs (like those at Corbridge, Northallerton, Bolton, Winchcombe and Chipping Campden) seem to have been particularly important as markets for livestock and markets at which agricultural requisites could be bought. It has been said, indeed, that since fairs played little part in the marketing of grain, 'agrarian producers made money at markets and spent it at fairs'. Certainly they offered opportunities for buying replacement livestock and manorial necessities, and for villagers to sell hides and dairy produce and perhaps even products of rural crafts; but they were also occasions to which merchants came, in numbers and variety depending upon the importance of the fair, 'with divers merchandises to buy and sell'. Fairs, therefore, offered to country-folk access to some of the luxuries, however modest in character, which the countryside around them could not supply. By the opening of the thirteenth century, indeed, it could be assumed that

---

[80] *Regesta*, II, no. 864, 868; III, no. 118; Farmer, 'Marketing the produce of the countryside', p. 346; Keene, *Survey*, II, p. 1124; L.M.Midgley, ed., *Ministers' Accounts of the Earldom of Cornwall, 1296–7*, I, p. 91; II, pp. 160, 170, 203, 213, 218, 230; Farr, ed., *Accounts and Surveys ... of Adam of Stratton*, pp. 38, 48, 58; M. Chibnall, ed., 'Computus rolls of the abbey of Bec (1272–1289)', in *Camden Miscellany*, XXIX, pp. 32, 61, 100, 124, 153; Moore, *Fairs of Medieval England*, pp. 12–18, 204–9.

villagers were likely to attend their local or regional fair, for rents for many holdings in North Yorkshire villages had to be paid at Richmond fair – and not only for places near to Richmond, but also for more distant tenements in Bellerby, Hessleton and Langthorne in Bedale over the hills in Wensleydale. In 1229, too, it was assumed that Newark fair would have a wide appeal: its establishment was to be publicly proclaimed by the sheriffs of Nottinghamshire, Leicestershire, Lincolnshire and Yorkshire.[81]

A few fairs, however, were of a different order of importance from those whose essential purpose was to service agricultural England. These were the fairs at Boston, Stamford, St Ives, King's Lynn and Winchester, and probably also those at Northampton, Bury St Edmunds and (from the mid-thirteenth century) Westminster. All, of course, served as local fairs for their own neighbourhoods; but over and above, like the contemporary fairs of Flanders and Champagne, they were international trading emporia. This did not imply any very elaborate setting. St Ives was no more than a little country town, set in a rural manor, which was temporarily turned into a major centre of commerce during the three or four weeks after Easter each year. To accommodate an influx of sellers and buyers the front rooms of houses in the town were requisitioned as places of trade, and villeins from Ramsey abbey's neighbouring manors were put to work building temporary wooden shops. To sustain visitors and their horses oats and fish were sold from boats as well as shops, there were stalls occupied by bakers, butchers and cooks, and provision was made for the sale of hay. At Bury St Edmunds, too, the abbey's sacrist in the twelfth century was empowered to let some houses, or their ground-floor front rooms, to merchants in fair-time; at Westminster there was only temporary provision for the fair in the abbey churchyard until about 1280; and at Winchester, while a grid of streets with permanent buildings had been laid out around St Giles's church outside the city walls, most of the houses seem only to have been occupied for part of the year and the open land surrounding them was used during fair-time for temporary stalls, for cart parks, and for tethering horses and other animals.[82]

---

[81] Farmer, 'Marketing the produce of the countryside', pp. 341–7; Maitland and Baildon, eds, *The Court Baron*, p. 64; Clay, ed., *Early Yorkshire Charters*, V, nos. 152, 184A, 196, 205, 248, 268 and pp. 81, 179; *Close R.*, 1227–31, p. 195.
[82] Moore, *Fairs of Medieval England*, pp. 13–14, 143–6, 229–30, 263–9; R.H.C. Davis, ed., *Kalendar of Abbot Samson*, pp. 77–9; Rosser, *Medieval Westminster*, pp. 100–1; Keene, *Survey*, II, p. 1092.

There continued, then, to be a degree of improvisation about even the 'great fairs', but by the thirteenth century they lasted far longer than the two or three days at most which were the rule at local fairs: Boston fair by the 1330s for a month, and Winchester fair for sixteen days beginning on 31 August (but with a tendency for merchants thereafter to go down into the city and to continue doing business until the end of September).[83] It was also characteristic of fairs that they were open for business to all comers and free from restrictions upon the activities of 'foreigners' which applied in most town markets.[1] Those who attended the 'great fairs', therefore, were very diverse: buyers and sellers from their immediate neighbourhoods, rich men or their agents from much further away, merchants from distant as well as nearer English towns, and merchants too from distant lands. As early as 1224 traders from Spain, Toulouse, Normandy, Flanders and the German Empire attended Winchester fair, and they found sponsors there among citizens of London, Southampton, Worcester, Lincoln, York and Oxford. The names of the streets and rows of the thirteenth-century fair site at Winchester tell a similar story, attesting the presence of merchants from Exeter, Cornwall, Leicester, Bristol, Nottingham and Ireland; and what was later known as the Drapery was called Ypres and Douai Street in 1261. At St Ives, too, there was a Frenchman's Row mainly occupied by Douai merchants, a stone hall housing merchants of Ypres, and rows of shops for the merchants of Lincoln, Beverley, Coventry and York.[85]

Merchants from many English towns, therefore, congregated as a matter of course at the great fairs. Leicester merchants in the 1270s, indeed, were so often absent from the town for this reason that, during the fair season, judicial sessions there were suspended. Certainly their presence is plentifully attested during the thirteenth century at Stamford, Boston, St Ives, King's Lynn, Northampton and Winchester fairs. Stephen de Stanham, a Lincoln merchant who played a large part in provisioning the parliament held in the city in 1301, usually attended two or three fairs each year; Norwich merchants had their own organization under their own alderman at Boston, King's Lynn and Yarmouth fairs; and Oxford merchants did business at St Ives, Winchester, Stamford and Northampton

[83] Biddle, ed., *Winchester in the Early Middle Ages*, p. 287; *Rot. Parl.*, I, p. 97; Moore, *Fairs of Medieval England*, pp. 15–17.
[84] *Ibid.*, pp. 93–4.
[85] *Ibid.*, pp. 150–2, 195, 208–13; *RLC*, I, p. 620; Keene, *Survey*, II, pp. 1096–1110.

fairs.[86] Londoners too, of course, were regular fair-goers. They dealt in wool, wine and cloth at Boston; London burellers went regularly enough to St Giles's fair at Winchester for their 'street' there to acquire the alternative name of Candlewick Street; a London tailor was already doing business at King's Lynn fair in 1239; and more Londoners went to St Ives fair than men from any other place. The arrangements made by Thomas Flory of London in 1320 suggest what a well-organized routine his fair-going followed. He bought in London a quantity of spices and dyestuffs, and also arranged for a further consignment to be delivered to him at King's Lynn; all this was in preparation for Bury St Edmunds fair, where Flory presumably intended to sell the merchandise he had brought together.[87]

Merchants from overseas, too, came to the 'great fairs'. Spaniards attended Winchester fair long after 1224 and also attended Boston fair, as did German, Flemish and Gascon merchants. Normans and later Brabanters were among the foreign traders coming to St Ives, and Montpellier as well as German merchants came to Westminster.[88] For much of the thirteenth century, however, merchants of Flanders (and of Douai and Ypres especially) were the most important group of foreign traders at the fairs. Their presence in the mid-century was noted at 'divers fairs in England', and at St Ives, Bury St Edmunds, Boston, Stamford, Northampton and Winchester most particularly.[89] Soon afterwards the Italians also made their appearance. A little cloth was bought from Florentines at Boston fair in 1269, and in 1277 we are told that merchants from Lucca were 'about to meet at Boston fair'. By that time, indeed, Lucca merchants were buying Meaux abbey's wool clip under contract and doing financial business with Isabella de Forz at Boston fair, and they also did business with St Swithin's priory at St Giles's fair at Winchester. By the late thirteenth century Italians were inevitably to

[86] Bateson, ed., *Leicester Borough Records*, I, pp. 29, 33, 79–80, 84–8, 94–6, 162–3; Moore, *Fairs of Medieval England*, p. 66; Hill, *Medieval Lincoln*, p. 239; W.Hudson and J.C. Tingey, eds, *Records of the City of Norwich*, I, pp. 260–1; *CLR*, 1245–51, p. 319; PRO C 47/3/29.
[87] *Rot. Hundr.*, I, p. 385; Keene, *Survey*, II, p. 1097; Moore, *Fairs of Medieval England*, pp. 67–8, 82; *CCR*, 1288–96, p. 302; H.M. Chew and M. Weinbaum, eds, *London Eyre of 1244*, pl. 131; H.M. Cam, ed., *Eyre of London, 14 Edward II*, pls. 242–3.
[88] W.R. Childs, *Anglo-Castilian Trade in the Later Middle Ages*, pp. 12, 14; *Close R.*, 1227–31, p. 367; James, *Studies in the Medieval Wine Trade*, pp. 73–4; Moore, *Fairs of Medieval England*, pp. 83, 210–14; Rosser, *Medieval Westminster*, p. 99.
[89] *CLR*, 1249–51, pp. 163, 273, 385; 1251–60, pp. 47, 128, 174, 192, 416, 438, 449; Keene, *Survey*, II, pp. 1116–19.

be found at the 'great fairs', and indeed anywhere else where business was done.[90]

The 'great fairs' had a variety of economic functions. They offered to the very rich, to begin with, opportunities for retail purchases on a grand scale. The large-scale buying by the monks of Durham in the late thirteenth century at Boston fair has already been noticed; in 1274 the earl of Gloucester owed £700, and in 1277 a further £225, to Flemish merchants for cloth and other goods bought, at least in part, at Stamford fair; and the earl's expenditure was insignificant compared with that of the king's household. In 1247 Henry III's agents bought cloth worth £1,572 from Ypres and Douai merchants at divers fairs; in 1231 they purchased 300 robes for members of his household staff and 300 tunics to be given as alms to the poor, in this case at Northampton fair; and in 1264–5 the king owed £80 to Beverley merchants alone for cloth they sold to him at St Ives fair. Many things other than woollen cloth were also on sale at fairs: speciality fabrics like silk and cloths of gold, spices and wax, horses and falcons, and furs in quantity (Henry III bought 25,000 squirrel skins at Boston and King's Lynn fairs in 1243). Boston fair, furthermore, was so important a source of royal wine supplies that the king's butler maintained a deputy there who made large annual purchases for the court.[91]

As well as being retail markets, for the rich especially, the 'great fairs' were wholesale markets from which goods filtered down to the local centres of economic life. Lincoln vintners and taverners, and York merchants bought wine at Boston fair for subsequent resale in their own cities; and it was at Boston that Leicester's stormy petrel, Jakemin de Leges, got the wine which he later retailed from his house in illegal measures. Boston fair was likewise the probable source of the spices and wax with which Robert Sharnford supplied the earl at Leicester in about 1270. Conversely, Leicester merchants on occasion bought wool at Boston fair, presumably as a raw material for the town's textile industry. The 'great fairs', in other words, served as links in a series of extended distributive chains which might stretch from the vineyards of Gascony to Jakemin de Leges's back door, or from some distant village sheep pasture to a weaver's

---

[90] Moore, *Fairs of Medieval England*, p. 26; *CPR*, 1272–81, pp. 131–2; R.W. Kaeuper, *Bankers to the Crown: the Riccardi of Lucca and Edward I*, pp. 23, 31, 37–8.
[91] Moore, *Fairs of Medieval England*, pp. 32–3, 40, 51–3; Morimoto, *Monastic Economy and Medieval Markets*, pp. 82–99, 135–7, 200–19; *CLR*, 1245–51, p. 163; *Close R.*, 1231–34, p. 1; PRO E 101/350/4; James, *Studies in the Medieval Wine Trade*, pp. 73–4.

workshop in some midland town (or even in Douai, Ghent or Ypres).[92]

English businessmen, however, were sellers as well as buyers at the 'great fairs'. Leicester merchants took cloth for sale to Boston fair,[93] as Oxford merchants did to the fairs at St Ives, Northampton, Stamford and Winchester, some of it perhaps for eventual export as well as to supply the home market; but English wool rather than English cloth was the commodity which attracted buyers for export in the thirteenth century. Much wool, of course, found its way overseas without recourse to fairs, but they did offer a convenient way of disposing of wool in bulk because numerous English and foreign merchants habitually visited them, and this is one reason why some sellers were willing to travel long distances to them. In the thirteenth century the Cistercian houses at Vaudey (Lincs.), Combermere (Cheshire), Fountains (Yorks.), Louth Park (Lincs.), Meaux (Yorks.) and Stanlow (Cheshire) all sold wool on occasion at Boston fair, and at Winchester fair wool was sold, not only in Wool Street and Wool Row, but in Exeter and Hereford Streets, names which are likely to indicate the wool's origin. Hereford wool dealers were also found at St Ives fair, and as late as the early fourteenth century up to 550 sacks of wool (perhaps 140,000 fleeces or rather more) were being sold each year even at Westminster fair. As institutions playing a major role in the distribution of wool during the twelfth and thirteenth centuries the fairs had a vital part in the commercialization of English medieval society.[94]

By the end of the thirteenth century, however, the 'great fairs' were losing ground. The bishop of Winchester's gross revenue from St Giles's fair, which had been £146 in 1189 and which had averaged £133 a year in the period 1238–62 and £117 in the 1280s, was down to £68 in the 1290s, to £53 in the 1320s and to £34 in the 1340s.[95] Lincoln merchants ceased to attend Winchester fair with any regularity in the 1290s, at about the same time as the servants of the archbishop of York gave up their visits to St Ives fair, the income of which had dwindled to about half what it had been in the 1250s. The 'distinctive cosmopolitanism' of Westminster fair, too, had disappeared by the early fourteenth century; the monks of Durham

[92] Bateson, ed., *Leicester Borough Records*, I, pp. 126–7, 180, 182, 207.
[93] *Ibid.*, pp. 80, 84–5, 95–6.
[94] Moore, *Fairs of Medieval England*, pp. 47–50; Donkin, *The Cistercians*, pp. 138–9, 191; Keene, *Survey*, II, p. 1116; Rosser, *Medieval Westminster*, p. 100.
[95] Keene, *Survey*, II, pp. 1124–5; for the bishop's net income from the fair, see Farmer, 'Marketing the produce of the countryside', p. 346.

bought more rarely at Boston fair; and even the king's officers were restricting their buying at fairs to St Ives and Boston. This decline of the 'great fairs', however, should not be taken to indicate a more general economic decline, and still less a backward step in England's commercial development. The decline of the fairs as international cloth markets had begun when the Flemish part in England's inland trade was undermined in the 1270s and became more complete in the first half of the fourteenth century as English textiles captured more of the market which had earlier been served by imports. In addition, English merchants (and those of Bristol, Southampton, Sandwich and London especially) became the principal importers of wine into England, so there was less need for the supplies which Gascons had brought to Boston; and the wool export trade was increasingly concentrated in certain staple towns and ports, where commercial facilities were available at all times, rather than in the temporary marts afforded by fairs. The growing share of England's trade in the hands of English merchants, in other words, helped to divert commerce from periodic fairs to towns in which trading was a continuous activity and resident merchants were better placed to determine the terms of trade.[96]

The great days of the 'great fairs', in brief, owed much to the dominant role played by alien merchants in many of the branches of English commerce. Down to the late thirteenth century, aliens were major purveyors of quality textiles and wine, and of such desirable commodities as spices, furs and even Baltic timber; and they were also important customers for English products, English wool particularly. As this dominance was modified, so was the role of the fairs in which they had done much of their business. The king, who earlier had shopped in divers fairs, could satisfy most of his needs in London by the 1320s: the establishment of the great wardrobe, his principal storehouse of supplies, in the capital from Edward I's reign was symptomatic of this new situation.[97] While fairs were losing their international role, however, many of them continued to be locally or regionally important. St Giles's fair at Winchester, for instance, survived as a centre for the inland trade of the west country, and Westminster fair, even though it had lost its earlier cosmopolitanism,

---

[96] Moore, *Fairs of Medieval England*, pp. 204–22; Rosser, *Medieval Westminster*, pp. 107–8; Morimoto, *Monastic Economy and Medieval Markets*, pp. 82–3, 92–9, 135–7, 200–19; Britnell, *Commercialisation of English Society*, p. 90.
[97] E.g. the predominance of royal cloth purchases in London in 1325–27: PRO E 101/381/9, 382/2; for the great wardrobe, see T.F. Tout, *Chapters in the Administrative History of Medieval England*, IV, Manchester, 1928, pp. 397–403.

was not necessarily diminished by the succeeding 'overwhelming preponderance of Londoners'.[98] Even fairs with a less distinguished past might retain great economic significance for their region. In 1589 a charter described Stourbridge fair at Cambridge as one which 'far surpassed the greatest and most celebrated fairs of all England' and for William Harrison it was 'not inferior to the greatest marts in Europe'; and even around 1800 Corbridge fair was still one of the most important livestock markets in northern England, with upwards of 100,000 black-faced sheep being offered for sale there each year, together with 'everything which is bred or of use in farming operations'. As had been the case at fairs at all times, 'every variety of booth or hut for refreshment or dissipation' was also to be found at Corbridge fair; and not surprisingly it continued to attract visitors from all over the north, including 'the Scotchman in his kilt and the Yorkshireman in his smock-frock'. Fairs like Stourbridge and Corbridge were still essential centres of the inland trade long after the international role of the 'great fairs' was a thing of the past.[99]

6.   MARKETS, FAIRS AND URBAN DEVELOPMENT

A network of exchanges progressing both in intensity and sophistication, therefore, was a basic feature of English economic development during the twelfth and thirteenth centuries. Measurement of that progress is difficult, because the further back we go the less complete is the available evidence; but some indication of its scale can perhaps be obtained by comparing certain features of the West Midland counties of Gloucestershire, Worcestershire and Warwickshire in 1086 and in *c.* 1300. Domesday listed in these counties a total of eight boroughs and three other places where there were markets. By the early fourteenth century, on the other hand, eighteen places in the region on occasion were taxed as boroughs and, in addition to the principal towns (Bristol, Cirencester, Gloucester, Worcester, Warwick and Coventry), some 80 places had licensed markets and some of them also fairs. When every allowance is made for omissions in the Domesday record the reality

[98]   Keene, *Survey*, II, p. 1121; Rosser, *Medieval Westminster*, pp. 107–8.
[99]   C.H.Cooper, *Annals of Cambridge*, II, p. 466; L. Withington, *Elizabethan England: from a Description of England by William Harrison*, Scott Library, London, n.d., p. 42; *NCH*, IV, p. 209 and X, pp. 135, 146–7.

of commercial expansion is clear. The places with markets, of course, varied greatly from mere villages like Snitterfield (Warks.) or Tortworth (Glos.) up to the salt town at Droitwich, the ancient borough of Winchcombe, and the new towns or quasi-towns at Stratford-upon-Avon, Chipping Campden and Northleach.[100] The English regions by 1300, therefore, were better equipped than they had been two centuries earlier to participate in the inland trade, and there were also influences breaking down regional exclusiveness. They included the great fairs, with their international dimension, and also developing ports like Bristol and Southampton through which West Midlanders found gateways to a wider world of commerce. Finally, of course, there were Londoners like John of Burford, who not only bought the bishop of Winchester's wool clip on occasion, but who exploited his connections with his native Cotswolds to link that corner of provincial England to the port of London and to Boston fair.[101]

Central to the efficiency of inland trading contacts was their diversity. Village markets and fairs were the groundwork of the developing distributive system and, while some grants of markets were ineffective and while only a few markets served other than mainly local customers, for some communities they represented the first step towards an ampler commerce and an ultimate urban future. Twelfth-century licences for the bishops of Lincoln to have a market and fair at Sleaford (Lincs.) probably furthered the development of 'New Sleaford', valued for taxation purposes in 1334 at £240, compared with the value of £85 placed on 'Old Sleaford'. At Northleach, too, the development of the active little market town of the late middle ages was initiated by the abbot of Gloucester securing permission to have a market and fair there in the 1220s; by 1235 Northleach had a borough court and by 1267 some 80 burgesses.[102]

The stages by which a village was transformed into an embryo town are seldom clearly discernible, but to that rule the history of

[100] H.C.Darby, *Domesday England*, pp. 364–70; R.H. Hilton, *A Medieval Society*, pp. 168–77; J.F. Willard, 'Taxation boroughs and parliamentary boroughs, 1294–1336' in J.G. Edwards *et al.*, eds, *Historical Essays in Honour of James Tait*, pp. 430–5.
[101] Farmer, 'Marketing the produce of the countryside', p. 400; Williams, *Medieval London*, pp. 143–4, 151.
[102] Beresford, *New Towns*, pp. 440–1; *Reg. Antiquissimum*, I, no. 183; D.M. Smith, ed., *English Episcopal Acta*, I: *Lincoln, 1067–1185*, British Academy, 1980, no. 116; *Regesta*, III, no. 476; Glasscock, ed., *Lay Subsidy of 1334*, p. 172; H.P.R. Finberg, *Gloucestershire Studies*, p. 66.

Stratford-upon-Avon is a partial exception.[103] Stratford in 1182, as it had been in 1086, was 'wholly rural in character'; but in 1196 the bishop of Worcester, presumably to take advantage of the manor's growing population and of agricultural expansion in the surrounding district, obtained from Richard I a charter authorizing a weekly market there. The next step was for the bishop formally to create a borough, laying out uniform burgage tenements to be held for uniform rents by burgage tenants, to whom he also conceded freedom from toll for ever. How successful the bishop's initiative had been is made clear by a survey in 1251–2 which distinguished the 'borough of Stratford', with 234 tenants, from 'Old Stratford' which had only 70 tenants. In 1182 there had been a mere 45 tenants in the undivided manor. There are some parallels to the making of a borough at Stratford at Morpeth in Northumberland, although at a rather later date and with rather less success. Morpeth castle had long been the centre of the Merlay barony when, in 1200, Roger de Merlay II got from King John licence for a market and fair at Morpeth, and at sometime during his long life (he held the barony from 1188 to 1239) he granted to his free burgesses there all their liberties and free customs, unfortunately without specifying what they were. The main development of the town, however, seems to have come under his son, Roger de Merlay III (1239–65), who laid out burgage plots on the other side of the river from the castle to be held for fixed and uniform rents, confirmed to their holders their customary market place, and (according to the Newminster cartulary) 'conferred on the men of Morpeth many liberties which they exercise to this day'. Roger III had no doubts about his own creative role, for in one charter he speaks of 'the new town of Morpeth which I have founded'.[104]

To get a grant of a market and fair for a place did not, of course, guarantee its development into a town. William de Say did so for his manor of Linton (Cambs.) in 1246, and in 1279 he had 80 tenants there, 35 of whom held burgages and at least some of them give the impression of being craftsmen or tradesmen. The market and fair, moreover, continued to be held, and there continued to be a few craftsmen (especially tanners) in the village; but we hear no more about burgage tenure in Linton after 1279 and it took no further

---

[103] Thanks to Sir William Dugdale, who preserved the substance of the town's lost twelfth-century foundation charter, and to E.M. Carus-Wilson, 'The first half century of the borough of Stratford-upon-Avon', *EcHR*, 2nd ser. XVIII (1965), pp. 46–63.
[104] J.T.Fowler, ed., *Chartularium Abbathiae de Novo Monasterio*, pp. 6–7, 272; Hodgson, *History of Northumberland*, II(2), pp. 480–3; Beresford, *New Towns*, pp. 472–3.

steps along the road to burghality.[105] What is important, however, is that the upgrading of many villages into market villages, and of some market villages into market towns, is one of the manifestations of the expansion of the inland trade during the twelfth and thirteenth centuries.

This expansion was not necessarily continuous. In some parts of the country it may have been interrupted by the political troubles of the mid-twelfth century, and at other times by civil disorders, or temporary famine, or war in the north or in the Welsh marches. The reduced rate of market foundations by the last quarter of the thirteenth century, too, perhaps suggests that England may have been approaching the point at which it had as many markets as it needed to satisfy its trading requirements. By that time, moreover, the continued proliferation of markets, most of which could never be anything but small affairs and local in their range, did not necessarily indicate continued economic development. The growth of country industry may have called for the establishment of some new markets, but the flurry of market foundations in the first quarter of the fourteenth century may also have owed a good deal to an increase in the number of countrymen with insufficient land for their sustenance who needed to buy what they could not grow, and to the drift away from demesne cultivation by landlords, leaving more land in the hands of smaller producers who were more likely to depend upon strictly local distributive services. As was the case with the 'great fairs', there was also a stage in England's commercial development when the trade done in some local markets was eroded by the expansion of alternative channels of distribution: the increased numbers and substance of English merchants and the greater sophistication of their trading networks were one of the influences at work, and so was the expanding influence of many boroughs and towns. Nor did these and other influences operating to these effects cease to do so after 1349, as is made clear by the fact that less than 40 per cent of the markets founded before that date survived into the sixteenth century. Part of the explanation of the collapse of so many of them doubtless lies in the decline of total marketing activity accompanying the population fall of the later middle ages and part, too, in the excessive optimism in the boom years of lords who, believing that growth would persist for ever, bought market charters for villages which had little chance of generating sufficient trade to support a market. It is noteworthy that the

---

[105] *VCH Cambs.*, VI, pp. 81, 96–7.

survival rate of markets originating before 1250 was much greater than those of later foundation, and that generally small town markets had much better chances of survival than village markets. Whereas half the village markets in the West Midlands and 60 per cent of those in Lincolnshire had disappeared by the sixteenth century, almost all the small town markets in both areas continued to exist.[106]

The pronounced slow-down of market foundations after 1325, and the demise of many markets subsequently, should not, however, lead us to underrate the magnitude or the significance of what had been achieved in this respect during the twelfth and thirteenth centuries. The development of the inland trade and the proliferation of markets during those centuries represented a crucial stage in the commercialization of English society. They were a condition for a period of urban growth, made possible because towns could cast their nets increasingly widely for food supplies, raw materials, customers for their products, even for necessary fuel. It also made feasible an increase of regional specialization which helped to make the most of the natural resources and conditions of different districts, and at the same time enlarged the range of employments available for a growing population. This progress of specialization was evident in the agricultural sector where more active and longer-range trade in grain and wool and even livestock permitted a greater concentration upon either arable or pastoral farming, wherever that was appropriate; but it could also be discerned in the increasingly diversified economic activities which exploited regional resources of every kind. Cloth-making areas were developing which took advantage of England's store of excellent wool, mining areas which found wider than local markets for metals and coal, woodland areas which provided metal workers with fuel, even North Sea fisheries which made sea fish an essential part of the diet of inland England. Like the medieval towns, these regional specializations, which the development of the internal trade during the central middle ages helped to foster, were an enduring economic achievement which continued, both after the Black Death and in the post-medieval generations, to provide much of the framework of England's domestic economy.[107]

[106] Britnell, 'The proliferation of markets', pp. 210, 219 (Tables 1 and 2); R.H. Hilton, 'Medieval market towns and simple commodity production', *Past and Present*, no. 109 (1985), pp. 9–11; A. Everitt, 'The marketing of agricultural produce', *AHEW*, IV, pp. 467–77.
[107] Britnell, *Commercialisation of English Society*, pp. 113–15, 123–4, 196.

CHAPTER FOUR
Overseas Trade

England's overseas trading was, as we have seen, already old when the Domesday Book was made. The tales that the Phoenicians regularly visited Cornwall for tin should perhaps be discounted, but the South-West's virtual monopoly of this essential constituent of bronze ensured that some tin was exported long before the arrival of the Romans in Britain; Anglo-Saxon men and women, too, desired the products of other lands – spices, exotic fruits, gold, furs and precious fabrics; and the profit to be got from satisfying these appetites of the rich induced Dark Age merchants to undertake long-distance trading over hostile oceans and continents. Yet, however lucrative these élite trades may have been for successful merchants, they were too small to sustain a frequent or regular traffic, for which a greater volume and wider range of commodities were necessary. These were achieved during the central middle ages. In England and elsewhere industries developed which depended upon imported raw materials, either because they were not available locally, or because their quality or price made them especially desirable. English tin and lead and wool, for example, were in demand overseas, and English cloth workers needed to import alum and a range of dyestuffs. The market for consumer goods also expanded and became more discriminating, so that England both imported and exported cloths of varying qualities, colours and functions; and, although there were English vineyards, a taste for the wines of Anjou and Gascony gave rise to a major international trade between these lands and England.

At the same time, demand in itself was insufficient to sustain overseas trading: it also depended upon a reasonable degree of political stability and of security for those who ventured abroad. If trade was to flourish, furthermore, an infrastructure of currency exchanges, credit, transport facilities, and wholesale and retail distribution was also needed. In these respects, of course, internal and external trades nourished each other. The sale or purchase of commodities in England might be the last or the first stage of a much longer-range movement of goods. Travelling merchants gathered up some commodities in ports or at fairs for despatch overseas, and also brought in others to add to the stream of native products which flowed into town or village market places and rich men's mansions. The generations after 1066 saw a progressive expansion both of the scale and the value of this external commerce, so that by the opening of the fourteenth century England was sending the fleeces of up to eight million sheep overseas each year and importing wine worth £60,000. The growth of overseas trade, of course, was hardly without interruption or set-back, but that the general trend was upwards seems beyond doubt even if particular sectors or interests intermittently lost ground. It is also undeniable that, despite the uncertainty of individual or sectional fortunes, England was increasingly integrated by ties of commerce into a wider western economy. The economic links which established close bonds between the regions of western Europe during the twelfth and thirteenth centuries were as notable an achievement on the part of merchants as were the ecclesiastical and cultural links that were forged by churchmen.

1. THE THIRTEENTH CENTURY AND BEFORE

(a) England's trade in c. 1230

The first opportunity to gain some sort of overall view, however sketchy, of England's medieval trade occurs in 1229–30 when Henry III determined that he would take advantage of the youth of Louis IX of France in order to recover the continental lands lost by King John. The preparations for that enterprise included the requisitioning of merchant ships to provide transport for an expeditionary force, and also the arrest of enemy alien merchants and their goods in English ports. It is the records generated by these measures which throw some light, however fitful, upon the character of England's overseas trade at that time.[1]

---

[1] Most of the arrests of ships are noted in *Close R.*, 1227–31, *passim*.

So far as the North-East was concerned, these records tell us little about the port of Newcastle, but they do make clear the fact that Hull was already an active centre of commerce. York, London and Hedon merchants traded through its port, as did merchants of Flanders, Ponthieu and Agen; and Hull was one of the ports through which the Templars exported wool produced on their estates. Hull's connections with Flanders appear to have been especially close, and its exports, in addition to wool, included hides and lead. Other east-coast ports, including Boston, King's Lynn and Yarmouth, exported substantial quantities of wool to Flanders. King's Lynn also had a close trade relationship with Norway, and Norwegians brought oil and timber to Grimsby, although Norwegian ships were arrested at Ipswich in 1230 because the men in them were 'completely unknown'. In addition to Flemings, Boston attracted shippers from the German Empire bringing cloth and wine, and like King's Lynn had conections with Holland and Normandy; King's Lynn also sup-plied the Scots with grain and wine and salt; and Yarmouth's commercial contacts extended to Lorraine, Cologne, Brabant and Normandy as well as Flanders. Its exports, as well as wool, included herrings and hides, and it imported wine, millstones, iron and steel.[2] Even Dunwich, already threatened by the sea, traded with Normandy and Poitou; and Ipswich and the Orwell ports, as well as exporting wool, sent hides overseas and were frequented by Dutch, Cologners, and Londoners in addition to the occasional Norwegian.

The records of 1229–30 unfortunately provide a very deficient pic-ture of London's trade. They show that Florentine and other Lombard merchants traded there; that wine came there from Gascony, and also from Sandwich or Portsmouth where it had first been landed; and that Spanish merchants arrived there in a Bayonne ship. A few roughly contemporary scraps of evidence can be added to this meagre information. A Nantes merchant shipped wine to London; in 1234 it was assumed that Cologne and other German merchants would trade there; in 1237 Henry III bought in London from French and Spanish merchants 6,000 rabbit skins which had come from southern France, Galicia and Majorca; and in the same year the Londoners made an agreement with the citizens of Amiens who imported into England woad, wine, garlic and onions. All this, however, hardly adds up to a total of London's commerce in *c.* 1230.[3]

---

[2] *Close R.*, 1231–34, pp. 242, 247, 532; 1234–37, p. 42; *CRR*, XIII, pp. 11, 472–4.
[3] *Close R.*, 1231–34, pp. 374, 453; 1234–37, p. 479; H.T. Riley, ed., *Munimenta Gildhallae Londoniensis*, II, pp. 64–6, 532–4.

Of other south-eastern ports Sandwich appears clearly to have been pre-eminent, followed by Winchelsea and then, a long way behind, by Romney, Seaford and Shoreham. Wine seems to have been the principal import, much of it from Gascony but with some from La Rochelle. The trade of these ports, however, had a considerable diversity. They attracted London, Winchester and Scottish merchants, together with shippers from Gascony, Normandy, Abbeville, Bruges, Nantes, Gravelines, Douai and La Rochelle; and they exported oats, hides and especially wool. There are also signs of a Spanish connection, for in 1228 a San Sebastian ship, with a cargo which included wine, yarn and civet skins, was plundered at Sandwich; and Italians, too, exported through Shoreham although the commodities concerned are not specified.

Overseas trade on the south coast was dominated by Southampton and Portsmouth, with wine once more (mainly from Gascony) as the principal import. On the other hand, the southern ports also had many contacts with Normandy, Flanders and Brabant, Cahorsin merchants exported wool from Southampton, and Southampton acted as the outport for the great international fair at Winchester. Information about the south-western and western ports is much scarcer. We hear of a Dunwich ship picking up Gascon wine at Helford (Cornwall); of a Ponthieu ship loaded with onions and garlic being arrested at Branksea Island (Dorset); of Bordeaux merchants taking wine to Haverfordwest (Pembroke); of Chester merchants in Ireland and Irish merchants in Chester. These notices, unfortunately, give no clear indication of the importance of Bristol's trade, although we do know that in 1234 a Bristol merchant imported wheat and oatmeal from Ireland, that Henry III informed Bristol when French merchants were again given safe-conduct to trade in England, and that wine was imported into Bristol. Henry III assumed in 1231 that 60 tuns of best Gascon wine could be procured for him there, and wine from Bristol supplied Hereford, Worcester and Gloucester as well as Walter de Beauchamp.[4]

It is clear, then, that many overseas merchants frequented English ports in the 1230s. Flemings were to be found everywhere from Hull to Portsmouth, and Normans occur hardly less frequently. Gascons, on the other hand, went mainly to Bristol and the south-coast ports, although they also visited Boston fair and traded wine for herrings at Yarmouth. Norwegian, Dutch, Brabant and German merchants, by

---

[4] *Close R.*, 1227–31, p. 131; 1231–34, pp. 12, 16, 172, 245, 247, 249, 455; 1234–37, p. 38.

contrast, went mainly to the east-coast ports, Cahorsins and Iberians to London and the southern and south-western ports. In these particular records denizen merchants are less visible than aliens, although we catch glimpses of York, Hedon and Beverley men exporting through Hull, of Stamford men exporting through King's Lynn, of Lynn merchants voyaging to Scotland and Norway, of a Sandwich ship exporting wool and lead from Boston, of a Winchester merchant exporting hides from Sandwich, of Chester and Bristol men doing business in Ireland, and of Londoners exporting wool and hides from Hull, Boston, Ipswich and Sandwich. Only very occasionally, however, can we learn much about individual English merchants who traded overseas; but Walter le Fleming of Southampton, a leading figure in that town during the forty years after 1211, owned several ships and traded in wine, wool, salt and cloth. He supplied the court and had close business associations with the keeper of the king's wines at Southampton. London, inevitably, had business men of a similar sort, including Andrew Bukerel, who exported hides (sometimes through Hull), who had agents in Dublin in 1220, and who traded in wool and in Anjou wine. Hugh Selby of York, too, had representatives in Anjou in 1235 and imported Anjou wine, and he also exported wool from Hull to Flanders. His trading may well have generated much of the wealth which made the Selby family one of the most enduring of the York civic dynasties.[5]

The records of 1229–30 permit no estimates to be made of the quantities of goods involved in England's overseas trade at that time, but they do provide indications of its general character. Among exports, wool seems to have had a clear pre-eminence in all the ports from Hull around to Southampton. Other outward cargoes included hides from Hull, Ipswich and Sandwich, lead from Hull and Boston, grain and salt from King's Lynn, oats from Sandwich and herrings from Yarmouth. About imports the records of 1229–30 are less informative. A consignment of honey from Bordeaux to Sandwich is hardly of great significance; the oil and timber which came from Norway to Grimsby were perhaps more important; but the superficial impression conveyed by these records is that the most prominent import was wine. That impression may well be misleading, but that wine imports were considerable is not in question. They came into Bristol, all the south-coast ports, and ports as far north as

[5] C. Platt, *Medieval Southampton*, p. 240; G.A. Williams, *Medieval London*, pp. 324–5; E. Miller, 'Rulers of thirteenth-century towns', *Thirteenth-Century England*, I (1986), pp. 134–6.

Yarmouth and Boston; the king bought wine from Gascon merchants in London and at King's Lynn fair; and Hugh Selby brought the vintages of Anjou to Hull and York. From the ports wine went on to a multitude of inland places, so that the court could expect to be able to buy supplies at Lincoln or Canterbury. Royal purchases also suggest that Gascon wine had gone far towards capturing the English market. In those years between 1226 and 1240 for which evidence is available, Gascony provided nearly 80 per cent of the wine the king bought, and by the late 1230s Anjou supplied only an insignificant amount.[6]

The records of the king's household reveal more clearly than those of 1229–30 how wide the range of imports was. Wax, almonds, rice, raisins, figs, ginger and cinnamon came into Southampton and Sandwich; large quantities of wax, presumably of Baltic provenance, was available at Boston fair; and a Londoner supplied Henry III with imported silk and Swedish merchants provided squirrel skins. The records of 1229–30 also tell us little about cloth imports save that six cogs from the German Empire brought cloth (perhaps picked up in Flanders) to Boston fair; but England's large exports of wool to Flanders suggest that there may have been some compensatory flow of Flemish cloth to England. The large consignments of robes with which the king's tailors supplied the royal household from Boston, Stamford and King's Lynn fairs may, at least in part, have been made from imported cloth; and certainly dyed cloth from Ypres and Ghent was bought for Henry III's sister at Bury St Edmund's fair in 1231, and in 1234 the king ordered 60 Arras cloths to be bought for him in London. The looms of Flanders were clearly already serving the English market.[7]

Much of England's trade in *c.* 1230, therefore, was aimed at satisfying the appetites of the rich – for rare fruits, spices, furs, wine, silks and other quality fabrics. Imports of this sort, indeed, are likely to have increased in volume as the incomes, especially of the English landowning classes, rose as settlement expanded. Not all imports, however, fell into the category of luxuries: many imports of timber, for example, hardly did so, and imports of woad and other dyestuffs provided necessary supplies for England's cloth workers. England's exports, too, were not lacking in diversity. Agricultural products were prominent among them: hides, grain and above all wool; but

[6] *CLR*, 1226–40, pp. 5, 49, 60, 63, 107, 119, 258, 273, 288; Y. Renouard, ed., *Bordeaux sous les rois d'Angleterre*, pp. 53–9.
[7] *CLR*, 1226–40, pp. 91, 139, 170–1, 264, 367, 482, 493; *Close R.*, 1227–31, p. 367; 1231–34, pp. 4–5, 381.

there were also some exports of lead and tin; and, as well as importing cloth, England also exported both quality and cheaper textiles to Mediterranean Europe and to the German lands.[8] Most of the basic features of England's trade as it would be in 1300, in fact, were already established; England was an integral part of a wider western economy; and English as well as alien merchants were contributing to that economy's development. The main commercial arteries, as they had been in 1066, were those which led to the Low Countries and northern France, and then via the Low Countries to Lorraine and Cologne, and perhaps via France to the fairs of Champagne. The traditional sea route to the north was also still being followed by merchants from King's Lynn and other east-coast ports, and also by Norwegians for whom King Haakon asked Henry III for protection against 'unjust vexation'. In the meantime horizons to the south had expanded. Bordeaux wines were coming to dominate the English market, and English ports and fairs were becoming familiar with Gascon merchants, with Spaniards from further south, and with Cahorsins who, as well as practising usury in England, brought in the wines of France and the luxuries of the Mediterranean. In 1234, too, Florentines were given safe-conduct to trade in England: within a generation Italian merchants would become a major interest in England's commerce.[9]

(b) English trade before 1230

If we go back before 1230 the details of commercial development are even less adequately documented, although many indirect indicators point to an expansion of trade over time. The increased commercial facilities offered by towns and fairs are likely to have been a response to a growth of external, as well as internal, transactions; English towns appear increasingly anxious to obtain rights to trade within the larger context of the Angevin empire as well as within England itself; trade sanctions came to be used more regularly as an adjunct of international diplomacy; and the long-term stability of the English currency perhaps suggests that bullion stocks were periodically replenished from favourable trade balances. There is a danger, admittedly, that because records become more plentiful as government activity increased they will create an illusion that

[8] P. Chorley, 'English cloth exports during the thirteenth and early fourteenth centuries', pp. 3–5.
[9] W.W. Shirley, ed., *Royal and Historical Letters of Henry III*, I, Rolls Ser., 1862, no. 193.

commerce was increasing; but this only makes more essential a review of such evidence as there is.

It shows, first, some continuities with the trade of pre-Conquest England. Contacts with Scandinavia persisted, for example, for Rufus gave protection to Norwegian merchants in England; Danes and Norwegians had a privileged position in London (Danes, like Englishmen, could go to fairs and markets anywhere in the land) in the reign of Henry I; an Icelandic saga tells of the 'very great crowd of men . . . from Norway' at Grimsby, and indeed a writ of Henry II's assumed their presence in that town. Anglo-Norman cultural influences were also strong in the Baltic kingdoms, where churches were dedicated to English saints and liturgical observances were shaped by those of England and France.[10] So far as the character of Anglo-Scandinavian trade was concerned, the saga account of the founding of Grimsby suggests that Scandinavians imported fish into England and English exchequer records suggest that, at least on occasion, the northern lands relied upon English exports of cereals.[11] This was a trade which persisted into the thirteenth century, for England and Norway made a commercial agreement in 1217, and commercial privileges were granted to the native merchants of Gotland although, with that island, they soon passed into the possession of German interlopers. The sale by the Danes of their London hall in the course of the twelfth century may point to a reduction of Scandinavian trading activity in the capital, but possibly this was balanced by increased business in the developing ports of Boston, Grimsby and King's Lynn. By the early thirteenth century, however, Germans were penetrating Scandinavia, and very soon merchants from Lübeck and other north German ports were following the Gotlanders to England, just as Englishmen joined traders from the Low Countries at the Scania herring fairs.[12]

---

[10] A.L. Poole, *From Domesday Book to Magna Carta*, p. 88; M. Bateson, 'A London municipal collection of the reign of John', *EHR*, XVII (1902), p. 499; Ballard, *BBC, 1042–1216*, p. 178; J.W.F. Hill, *Medieval Lincoln*, pp. 174–6; A.E. Christensen, 'Scandinavia and the advance of the Hanseatics', *Scandinavian EcHR*, V (1957), pp. 99–100.

[11] Hill, *Medieval Lincoln*, pp. 174–5; *Pipe Roll*, 32 Henry II, p. 68 and 4 John, pp. 104, 131.

[12] T. Rymer, ed., *Foedera*, I(1), revised edn, Rec. Comm., 1816-30,p. 149; Christensen, 'Scandinavia and the advance of the Hanseatics', pp. 103–4; *Close R.*, 1234–37, p. 426; K. Höhlbaum *et al.*, eds, *Hansisches Urkundenbuch*, I, no. 281; T.H. Lloyd, *England and the German Hanse, 1157–1611*, p. 17; P. Dollinger, *La Hanse (XIIe–XVIIe siècles)*, pp. 54–7.

In the twelfth century, however, mention of the 'German merchants' or 'men of the empire' mainly implied Rhinelanders, and Cologners above all. Henry of Huntingdon, early in the century, wrote of the extensive trade between England and neighbouring parts of Germany by way of the Rhine, and the exports from England seem to have included fish, meat, wool and tin.[13] The fullest account of this traffic is the so-called 'Law of the Lotharingians', possibly reflecting eleventh-century conditions, which also attests the export of wool, together with hides and lambskins, from England. In return the Lorrainers brought in goods from the Meuse region, from the Rhineland, and via Ratisbon from the Danube lands and eastern Europe: they included German wine, linen and coats of mail from Maintz, vessels of gold and silver, precious stones, textiles (some even from Constantinople), furs, pepper and cumin, wax and fustians, and the metalwork of the Meuse valley.[14] There is little evidence of English merchants being involved in this trade, but merchants from Tiel, Bremen and Antwerp were engaged in it. By the mid-twelfth century, however, there is no question about the primacy of the Cologners. We cannot be sure that the German ships which came to York in the 1120s or to Chester in *c.* 1200 were chartered by Cologne merchants; but a Norwich source of the mid-twelfth century does refer to a Cologne merchant in that city who imported wine and took away wool. Thereafter, too, the Cologners were unusually successful in attracting the patronage of English rulers. In 1157 Henry II took them and their gildhall, the existence of which probably implies that they had some sort of corporate organization, into his protection. He also encouraged their wine trade and, in 1175, emphasized his benevolence towards them, *quia homines et fideles mei sunt.* Richard I also endorsed the privileges enjoyed by the Cologners in 1194, their right to travel safely throughout the land, and their power to buy and sell freely in fairs and in London and in other places. These were promises which were reiterated by King John.[15]

---

[13] T. Arnold, ed., *Henry of Huntingdon. Historia Anglorum*, pp. 5–6; A. Joris, *La ville de Huy au moyen âge*, Paris, 1959, p. 235n.; J.Hatcher, *English Tin Production and Trade*, pp. 25–6.

[14] For the text, see Bateson, 'A London municipal collection of the reign of John', pp. 495–502, and also M. Weinbaum, *London unter Eduard I and II*, II, pp. 29–37; for the date, C.N.L. Brooke and G. Keir, *London, 800–1216*, p. 267 and Lloyd, *England and the German Hanse*, p. 13.

[15] N.E.S.A. Hamilton, ed., *William of Malmesbury, De Gestis Pontificum Anglorum*, p. 208; H.J. Hewitt, *Medieval Cheshire*, pp. 123–4; W.Hudson and J.C. Tingey, eds, *Records of the City of Norwich*, II, p. xi; Höhlbaum *et al.*, eds, *Hansisches Urkundenbuch*, I, nos. 25, 40; K. Wand, 'Die Englandpolitik der Stadt Köln und ihrer Erzbischöfe in 12. und 13. Jahrhundert', *Aus Mittelalter und Neuzeit: Festschrift G. Kallen*, pp. 77–84.

There is much to suggest, on the other hand, that twelfth-century England's closest commercial links were with its nearer neighbours across the North Sea – the Low Countries and northern France. Ties with Normandy are likely to have been strengthened by the Conquest and, though they came under strain in Stephen's reign, Henry of Anjou was taking steps to revive them even before he succeeded to the English throne. In 1150–51 he confirmed the freedom of members of the Rouen merchant gild from all duties in London except those on wine and porpoises, their right to go to markets throughout England, and their possession of Dowgate wharf in London. The mention of wine imports by Rouen merchants perhaps indicates a major source of England's wine supplies before the Angevin and Gascon connections shifted provision southward after 1154. The archaeological record at Southampton certainly suggests that, for much of the twelfth century, wine imports and some pottery came mainly from Normandy.[16]

There is also evidence in *c.* 1200 of a somewhat more northerly trade route along which woad for England's textile industry travelled from Picardy. In 1196–98 woad was being shipped to Lincolnshire, Ipswich and London, some of it by Flemings, some by merchants of Amiens who were to dominate the thirteenth-century woad trade, and some by Englishmen (a few years later these last included the Leicester notable, Henry Costein). The trade in woad was sufficiently important to have inspired one of John's experiments in commercial taxation. In the years 1210–14 there are scattered notices of receipts from an assize or custom on woad, although unfortunately they seem to be combined with the issues of some sort of taxation of the wine trade. They are recorded for the ports of Durham, Yorkshire, Lincolnshire, Norfolk, Suffolk, Essex, Kent, Sussex and Hampshire, together with the port of London (apparently the most important centre of these trades). The information is not such, however, as to enable us to attribute quantities to them.[17]

There is much to suggest, however, that the most important trading connection in *c.* 1200 was that linking England to the Low Countries and the adjacent parts of northern France, for which Richard I's and John's trade embargoes and safe-conducts for

[16] J.H. Round, ed. *Cal. Documents preserved in France illustrative of the History of Great Britain and Ireland, 918-1206,* 1899, nos. 109–10; Platt, *Medieval Southampton,* p. 21.
[17] *Pipe Roll,* 9 Richard I, pp. xxiii, 113, 166, 240; 10 Richard I, p. 182; 4 John, p. 40; 7 John, p. 34; 13 John, pp. 105, 196–7; 14 John, pp. 16, 42, 45–6; 16 John, pp. 37–8, 144; *Pat. R.,* 1216–25, p. 2; T.H. Lloyd, *Alien Merchants in England in the High Middle Ages,* pp. 73–9; M.Bateson, ed., *Records of the Borough of Leicester,* I, pp. 6, 11, 34–5, 39.

merchants of this region as diplomatic weapons in their wars with France offer indirect testimony.[18] It has not uncommonly been assumed, especially in the light of the later history of the English wool trade, that the mainstay of the commerce which took this route was the export of English wool to the textile towns of Flanders, and that these exports had grown steadily perhaps even from pre-Conquest times. These are assumptions which, in recent years, have been questioned on various grounds. Doubts have been raised, as we have seen, about how significant English exports of wool were before 1066. Secondly, the notion that in the twelfth century Flemish merchants trading to England, principally for wool, had formed a federal organization, the 'Flemish hanse of London', has been effectively demolished; indeed, whether that organization ever actually came into existence even in the thirteenth century now seems dubious. Finally, the question has been raised on general grounds whether, even at the end of the twelfth century, English wool exports were essential to the Flemish industry.[19] These are matters important enough to demand a review of the twelfth-century evidence, such as it is.

As we have seen, there may be some, mainly indirect, evidence for Flemish dependence upon supplies of English wool even in the eleventh century, but only in the twelfth century do a few pieces of direct information appear. There is, to begin with, the circumstantial account by a canon of Laon early in the century of merchants crossing from Wissant to England to buy wool, of how they carried money with them for that purpose, of their extensive travels in England to make their purchases, and of their Dover warehouse where they stored the wool until they were ready to return home. There is also a significant passage in the description of Britain with which Henry of Huntingdon (who died *c.* 1155) prefaced his *Historia Anglorum*. Most of it is copied more or less verbatim from Bede, but an addition explains how the export of fine wool from England was in part responsible for an inflow of silver in return.[20] These scraps of information suggest that, in the mid-twelfth century, England's wool

[18] Höhlbaum *et al.*, eds, *Hansisches Urkundenbuch*, I, no. 55; *RLP*, p. 98.
[19] For the 'Flemish hanse', see H. van Werveke, *Miscellanea Medievalia*, pp. 63–8, 92–3; E. Perroy, 'Le commerce anglo-flamand au XIIIᵉ siècle: la hanse flamande de Londres', *Revue Historique*, CCLII (1974); Lloyd, *Alien Merchants in England*, pp. 105–6 and *idem*, *The English Wool Trade*, pp. 23–4. For a sceptical view of twelfth-century wool exports to Flanders, A.R. Bridbury, *Medieval English Clothmaking*, p. ix.
[20] "De Miraculis S. Mariae Laudunensis', in J.P. Migne, ed., *Patrologia Latina*, 217 vols, Paris, 1844-55, CLVI, cols. 975–7; Arnold, ed., *Henry of Huntingdon , Historia Anglorum*, pp. 4–5

exports were a matter of common knowledge both at home and on the continent. In the first decade or so of Henry II's reign, too, there is more plentiful testimony to the activities of Flemish merchants in England, including men from the clothing towns of St Omer, Bruges, Ghent and Ypres. William Cade of St Omer was an active merchant and usurer in England as well as providing financial services to Henry II's government; and in 1155–58 Henry granted that the burgesses of St Omer might go to fairs and markets throughout England to buy and sell, although there is still too little precise information about what they bought and what they sold.[21]

Thereafter the surviving evidence is somewhat more informative. Flemish involvement in the revolt of Henry II's sons against their father in 1173 resulted in the confiscation of Flemish goods in England, revealing a Flemish presence in Yorkshire, Lincolnshire, Northamptonshire, Essex, Sussex, Hampshire and London. The goods of some Flemish merchants were also arrested in Somerset when they were on their way back from Ireland, and Worcester dyers were said to owe money to Flemings (perhaps for woad). The goods seized in Yorkshire, Essex and Sussex certainly included wool; but one Flemish ship taken in Essex was loaded with grain, it may have been for exporting grain to Flanders that a number of Cambridge burgesses were punished in 1176–77, and in the 1190s substantial quantities of grain were apparently shipped from eastern and south-eastern England (especially from King's Lynn and Dunwich) 'to the king's enemies in Flanders'.[22] In the 1190s, however, as well as grain we hear of wool owned by Flemings, of wool being sold to them, and of wool being exported to Flanders from Hull, Lincolnshire and London. The commerce between England and the Low Countries, which Richard I and John regulated for their diplomatic advantage, may well have included exports to Flanders of grain and other foodstuffs, but it also included exports of wool and the likelihood is that these were substantial. It is also likely that it was as wool merchants that citizens of St Omer were granted export licences in 1205 and the following years, and certainly in 1215 merchants from Ghent were buying wool in Gloucestershire.[23]

---

[21] R. Doehaerd, *L'expansion économique belge au moyen âge*, Brussels, 1946, p. 51; *CEcH*, III, pp. 451–2; L. Delisle and E. Berger, eds, *Recueil des actes de Henri II*, I, no. 71.

[22] *Pipe Roll*, 19 Henry II, pp. 13, 29, 50, 130, 165, 196; 20 Henry II, pp. 14, 54, 103, 131; 21 Henry II, p. 175; 23 Henry II, pp. 183–5; 10 Richard I, pp. 92–3, 137–8, 209, 258; F.W.Maitland, *Township and Borough*, p. 171.

[23] *Pipe Roll*, 10 Richard I, pp. 49–50, 182–3; Lloyd, *The English Wool Trade*, pp. 7–15; G. Espinas, *La draperie dans la Flandre française au moyen âge*, II, Paris, 1923, p. 52; *RLC*, I, pp. 209, 211.

The twelfth-century evidence, then, is less than conclusive and far less than complete; but the most plausible conclusion from it continues to be that England's most important commercial contacts were with the Low Countries, that certainly by the second half of the century English wool exports were a major component of Anglo-Flemish trade, and that Flemish dependence upon supplies of English wool had an early origin and had continued to grow through all or most of the century. The evidence, moreover, has an intrinsic bias: most of it relates to alien merchants and it may well understate the involvement of native merchants in wool-exporting. Clearly, denizens shipped grain to Flanders in the 1170s and the 1190s; English, as well as Amiens and Flemish, merchants imported woad into England; and one of the first mercantile success stories of the middle ages is about an Englishman – the Lincolnshire beachcomber turned pedlar and then overseas merchant who, before embracing a religious life which turned him into St Godric of Finchale, had made his fortune travelling the seas between England, Scotland, Denmark and Flanders. Perhaps, too, Gervase le Riche of Southampton, who died in *c.* 1196, owed his riches in part to overseas trade in wine, wool and grain as well as to the internal trade within this country. Unfortunately, however, the sources tell us all too little about the cargoes which Englishmen carried on the seas.[24]

A final question remains to be asked about the Anglo-Flemish trade: what cargoes came to England in return for the exports of wool, grain and possibly other foodstuffs like cheese and fish? The canon of Laon and Henry of Huntingdon suggest that, at least in the first half of the twelfth century, England's exports were paid for by an inflow of bullion or currency; and it has also been argued that increased bullion imports occasioned by a sharp upward trend of wool exports around 1200 may have contributed to the marked inflationary trend at that time.[25] It is clear, however, that goods as well as money came into England. Flemish merchants imported woad, and their goods arrested in the 1170s and 1190s also included silk and wine. Possibly, too, some of the cloth bought for the king at Winchester fair in the late twelfth century may have been of Flemish manufacture, for Flemish merchants would be prominent at that fair

[24] H. Pirenne, *Les villes et les institutions urbaines*, I, Paris and Brussels, 1939, pp. 366–7; *Pipe Roll*, 4 John, pp. xxi, 2, 11, 16, 95, 128–9, 143, 153, 210, 253; Platt, *Medieval Southampton*, pp. 39–40, 97, 241–2, 269–70.
[25] P.D.A. Harvey, 'The English trade in wool and cloth, 1150–1250', in M. Spallanzani, ed., *Produzione, commercio e consumo dei panni di lana nei secoli XII–XVII*, pp. 369–75; *idem*, 'The English inflation of 1180–1220', *PP*, no. 61 (1973), pp. 3–30.

early in the thirteenth century; and some of the cloth sold wholesale in London by foreign merchants early in John's reign may likewise have come from Flanders. Henry II's charter to the burgesses of St Omer suggests even more than that, for it empowered them to 'break up their bales without seeking permission'. The implication perhaps is that, as early as the 1150s, as well as importing cloth into England they were selling some of it retail.[26]

A few other branches of England's trade at the end of the twelfth century call for mention. In 1198, for instance, tin from south-west England, as well as going to Cologne, was being exported through La Rochelle by Bayonne merchants.[27] England, too, exported as well as imported cloth, for around 1200 English cloth was available in Genoa and from there it was sent on to Sicily and other Mediterranean destinations. Relatively few English merchants are likely to have been engaged in this trade, but some Londoners were living and trading in Genoa at this time. Thirteenth-century evidence suggests, however, that English cloth often reached Genoa through Provençal merchants (who in turn may have got it through Gascony or Cahors), or through Flemings who may have bought it at the Champagne fairs.[28] It would also seem likely, as was later to be the case, that some English cloth found its way to the markets of northern Europe, but this is a matter about which more information is needed.

Exports of cloth to Genoa, however, do make clear that twelfth-century English trade had a southern dimension, although the principal commodity concerned in it was wine. Under Henry II England mainly relied upon supplies of wine from Anjou and Poitou; and even in 1201 the king's wines at Southampton and Winchester, in addition to $284^1/_2$ tuns of unspecified provenance, consisted of 125 tuns from Poitou, 158 tuns from Anjou, and 150 tuns from Berry further inland. Wine, moreover, was not consumed exclusively by the court, for in this same year punishments for breaches of regulations governing the sale and price of wine were

---

[26] *Pipe Roll*, 18 Henry II, p. 86; 19 Henry II, p. 29; 20 Henry II, p. 103; 10 Richard I, p. 183; *RLC*, I, p. 145; M.Biddle, ed., *Winchester in the Early Middle Ages*, p. 286; W. Cunningham, *Growth of English Industry and Commerce*, I, pp. 616–17; Delisle and Berger, *Recueil des actes de Henri II*, I, no. 71.

[27] *Pipe Roll*, 10 Richard I, p. 182.

[28] R.L. Reynolds, 'The market for northern textiles in Genoa, 1179–1200', *Revue Belge de Philologie et d'Histoire*, VIII (1935), pp. 840–1; *idem*, 'Some English settlers in Genoa in the late twelfth century', *EcHR*, IV (1933), pp. 217–23; R. Doehaerd, *Relations commerciales entre Gênes, la Belgique et l'Outremont*, I, pp. 176–7; Carus-Wilson, *MMV*, pp. 211–15.

imposed in sixteen counties. Evidently, the import trade served an extensive market.[29] Very soon, on the other hand, the territory lost by King John pushed the sources of these imports still further south. In 1207 the royal household got some supplies from Gascony; later in the reign Hubert de Burgh 'borrowed' wine from a Bordeaux merchant to munition Dover castle; in 1226 £400 was still owed to Bordeaux merchants for wine supplied to King John; and in 1211 the bishop of Winchester bought Gascon wine in Southwark. The capture of La Rochelle, earlier the main port of departure of wine ships for England, by the French king in 1224 confirmed this south-ward drift. The consequences are reflected in royal wine purchases in 1226–29, when out of 857 tuns bought, 670 came from Gascony, 118 from Anjou, nine from 'France' and 60 from elsewhere (mainly Bergerac and Moissac). One advantage of the shift was that Gascon wines were rather cheaper than the wines of Anjou.[30]

Bordeaux merchants, then, were trading to England at the open-ing of the thirteenth century, and the Cahorsins may even have arrived before them. Cahors, situated at the junction of the north–south pilgrim route leading to Compostela and an east–west route linking the Atlantic to the Mediterranean, came to supply England with wines from inland France via Bordeaux, and also with spices and other southern luxuries via La Rochelle. A Cahorsin has been identified in England as early as 1205, in 1233 Henry III took Cahorsin merchants in England into his protection, and two years later he supported them when the citizens of Bordeaux tried to interfere with their commerce. In the meantime, other southern merchants were finding their way to England: a merchant from Navarre in 1217, and in 1223 merchants from Toulouse. In 1220, too, merchants from Bologna received protection from Henry III, and the evidence for Florentine trade with England goes back to 1224.[31]

England at the opening of the thirteenth century, therefore, was frequented by merchants of many lands, and to some at least of those lands Englishmen ventured in turn. There is no way, however, of establishing a confident measure of the trade they did. Even the

---

[29] Renouard, ed., *Bordeaux sous les rois d'Angleterre*, pp. 53–9; *Pipe Roll*, 21 Henry II, p. 16; 22 Henry II, p. 199; 23 Henry II, pp. 197–9; 4 John, pp. 82–3.
[30] *RLC*, I, p. 89; *CLR*, 1226–40, *passim*; N.R.Holt, ed., *Pipe Roll of the Bishopric of Winchester, 1210–11*, p. 154.
[31] Y. Renouard, 'Les Cahorsins, hommes d'affaires français du XIIIe siècle', *TRHS*, 5th ser. XI (1961), pp. 43–54; *Pat. R.*, 1216–25, pp. 54, 84, 248, 370, 384, 528; E. von Roon-Bassermann, 'Die ersten Florentiner Handelsgesellschaften in England', *VSWG*, XXXIX (1952), p. 103.

receipts from the customs duties instituted by King John, and recorded on the exchequer accounts drawn up at Michaelmas 1204, do not permit us to do that. They may have been the proceeds of 'a general levy on imports and exports' in the form of an *ad valorem* tax on their value; but we cannot be quite certain that this was so, or that all goods and all merchants were liable, or what period was covered by the record compiled in 1204. If the receipts, amounting to some £5,000, were from a general levy on trade at the rate of a fifteenth of its value, and if, as has been suggested they were for a period of 12–16 months, we would certainly not be encouraged to underrate the volume of England's trade at that time, for the sums paid into the exchequer suggest that it could have been worth as much as £55,000–£75,000. To put these figures into perspective we need to remember that *c.* £75,000 had been the annual value to their lords placed by the Domesday commisioners on all the land of England. Of course the weight which can be given to such calculations is limited, but they suggest the possibility that the specific records of twelfth-century commerce which have survived seriously underrate its importance.[32]

If the records of the 'fifteenth' are an uncertain guide to the volume of England's trade, they do identify many of the main centres of trade at that time. They suggest that London, which accounted for 17 per cent of its yield, was clearly England's leading port; but it was followed fairly closely by Boston (with 16 per cent of the receipts), Southampton (with 14 per cent), and Lincoln and King's Lynn (each with 13 per cent); and then at a distance by Hull (with 7 per cent), York (with 4 per cent) and Newcastle (with 3 per cent). The remaining 27 towns for which an account was rendered contributed only 13 per cent of the receipts from the tax between them. Among them Yarm, Hedon, Grimsby, Yarmouth, Winchelsea and Fowey seem to have been the most active. Once again we cannot be sure that these figures tell the whole story. There is no mention in the accounts of Chester and, perhaps more important, of Bristol; but two other points of interest do emerge from them. First, while Southampton's prominence may reflect the part it played in the southern (and especially the wine) trade, most of the ports which stand out are located on the east coast, again suggesting the importance of England's trade with the Low Countries, the Rhineland and Scandinavia. Secondly, of the eight most active ports, only London,

[32] Lloyd, *The English Wool Trade*, pp. 9–12 and Table 1; N.S.B. Gras, *Early English Customs System*, pp. 217–22; S. Painter, *The Reign of King John*, Baltimore, 1949, pp. 137–9.

Southampton, Lincoln and York were old towns, while Boston, King's Lynn, Hull and Newcastle were urban creations of the post-Conquest period. The commercial importance of this latter group in 1204 once again buttresses the conclusion that the twelfth century was a time when trade expanded.

(c)   The alien ascendancy, c. 1230–1303

This expansion of overseas trading continued in the thirteenth century, with foreign merchants probably contributing rather more to it than Englishmen, as indeed they may already have done in the twelfth century. Certainly, by 1230, alien merchants had a major stake in some branches of English commerce which one group or another of them was to retain for at least a couple of generations. The first of these dominant alien interests seems undoubtedly to have been the Flemings. Whatever the situation had been in the twelfth century, by the mid-thirteenth the Flemish textile industry was dependent upon supplies of English wool and England was an important market for its products. The growth of Anglo-Flemish trade was furthered by a settlement of disputes between England and Flanders in 1236, a period of peaceful relations with France after 1243, and the concession of commercial privileges to individual Flemish towns, including Ypres (1232, 1259), St Omer (1255), Ghent (1259) and Douai (1260).[33] There are many incidental notices of Flemish wool merchants in England between the 1230s and the 1270s – with cargoes of $205^1/_2$ sacks of wool at Yarmouth, 135 sacks at Beverley, 92 sacks at Winchelsea, 39 sacks at Hithe, seventeen sacks at Bedhampton (Hants.) and eight sacks at Portsmouth, as well as shipments at Tynemouth in the north-east and Bristol in the south-west in 1242 alone. Even in 1276, when the active Flemish trade had passed its peak, there were still merchants from Flanders and the adjacent regions in England. In Yorkshire they bought wool from religious houses at Scarborough; merchants of Liège, St Omer and Amiens exported wool from Essex; Amiens merchants exported wool from Oxfordshire via Bristol and the abbot of Tintern sold wool to Flemings each year; in Kent Flemish merchants went around buying up wool in small parcels; and in Lincolnshire merchants from Ypres, St Omer and elsewhere in Flanders bought wool in Louth and other places and exported from Lincoln, Boston, North

[33] Lloyd, *The English Wool Trade*, pp. 21–3.

Coates and Wainfleet. The part played by Flemings in the English wool trade is evident enough.[34]

A rising demand for English wool in Flanders and the adjacent textile regions perhaps helps to explain increased producer prices for wool in England in the 1230s and again in the 1260s.[35] At the same time, a flourishing import trade in Flemish textiles is no less evident. Purchases for the court suggest that it was dominated by the cloth merchants of Ypres and Douai. In 1247 Henry III owed nearly £1,600 to merchants of these two towns for cloth bought at divers English fairs; and records of cloth worth nearly £12,000 bought for the king between 1240 and 1269 show that more than 80 per cent of it by value was supplied by Ypres and Douai merchants. Deteriorating political relations with Flanders meant that the peak of Flemish trading relations with England was reached before 1270, but their eclipse was not immediate. Even at the end of the 1260s Nicholas de Lyons of Douai and his associates were still coming to St Ives and other fairs, and they still supplied the king with cloth worth nearly £1,000.[36] Nor did the Anglo-Flemish dispute of 1270–5 totally interrupt Flemish trade with England. In 1275–6 wool exporters from Hull included nine merchants from Ghent, three from Bruges, and one each from Douai and St Omer, and three of the Ghent merchants between them exported 350 sacks of wool, perhaps about 90,000 fleeces. The renewal of Anglo-French conflicts in the 1290s, however, opened an extended period of English pressure on Flanders and of intervention in commercial relations which resulted in a further reduction of Flemish participation in trade with England. At the opening of the fourteenth century there were very few Flemings among the 69 alien merchants who paid customs in the port of Hull; in 1303 Bruges, Ghent, Poperinghe and Ypres each had only a single merchant exporting from Boston; and at Bristol a solitary Ghent merchant put in an appearance in the period 1303–9. At Sandwich in 1303–5, on the other hand, thirteen Flemish merchants made use of the port and continued for the most part to export wool and grain and to import cloth; and a few individuals, too, still traded in these staples on a considerable scale. Andrew Brotherlamb of Ypres, for example, exported 124 sacks of wool from Boston in the

---

[34] *Close R.*, 1237–42, pp. 466, 473, 475, 478, 480; 1242–47, p. 77; *Rot. Hundr.*, I, pp. 113, 131–2, 134, 162–3, 176–7, 225, 328, 338, 370, 375, 385–6, 400.
[35] T.H. Lloyd, *The Movement of Wool Prices in Medieval England*, p. 69 (Fig. 4); D.L. Farmer, 'Prices and wages', in *AHEW*, II, pp. 754–7.
[36] *CLR*, 1245–51, p. 163; 1266–72, nos. 732, 914; E.Wedermeyer Moore, *Fairs of Medieval England*, p. 28.

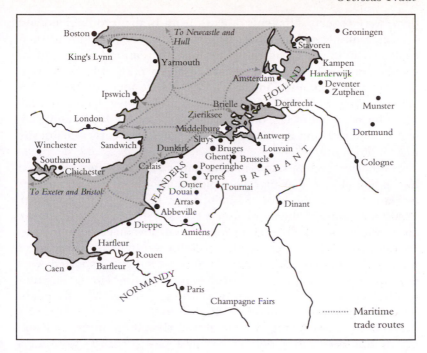

Map 4 (a) Principal points of commercial contact between England and Western Europe, *c.* 1300: The North Sea Trade

Sources: J. C. Davies, 'Wool Customs Accounts for Newcastle', AA, 4th ser. XXXII (1954); customs accounts printed by Gras, *Early English Customs System*; and T.H. Lloyd, *Alien Merchants in England in the High Middle Ages.*

second half of 1303 and 241 sacks from Hull in the three years beginning in 1304; and he also imported 173 cloths into Boston in 1303, 751 cloths into King's Lynn in 1303–5, and 30 cloths into London in 1308–9. By that time, all the same, among merchants of Flanders he was something of an exception.[37]

Where the Flemings lost ground, other aliens were ready to step into their place. Initially the English were not well placed to do so, since they faced the same difficulties in trading in Flanders as the Flemings faced in trading in England; but Brabançon merchants already had established English contacts. They received a surprisingly large number of licences to export wool in 1273, and from 1271

[37] Gras, *Early English Customs System*, pp. 224–44, 273–360; Lloyd, *Alien Merchants in England*, pp. 108, 111.

there were regular shipments of cloth from Brabant to England and notices multiply of Londoners who owed money for cloth to merchants of Louvain.[38] Thereafter we hear increasingly frequently of Brabançon merchants doing business in many parts of England: trafficking in Norfolk and Lincoln in 1293–94; resident in London in 1298; finding difficulties with the new currency legislation in 1299 when buying wool in Lincolnshire and the East Midlands; and trading at Sandwich and Boston and St Ives fair in the early years of the fourteenth century.[39]

Southern merchants, too, took advantage of the difficulties faced by the Flemings. Cahorsins had exported wool from England, either to Flanders or to the fairs of Champagne, fairly regularly since the 1230s; and some of them, including Poncius de Mora (buyer of the king's wines) and the Beraud brothers, took advantage of their court connections to secure export licences for substantial quantities of wool in the period 1271–74. In 1276, too, Poncius exported wool both from London and from Lincolnshire.[40] At times in the late thirteenth century it almost looked as though the Cahorsins might become the dominant interest in English trade, and as late as 1291 a group of them, including William Servat, viewed the future with sufficient confidence to undertake to buy Pipewell abbey's wool for a dozen years ahead. As well as exporting wool, moreover, men like Servat also imported wine, spices, silk and cloth; and Servat at least never failed to improve the shining hour. In 1305 he shipped wine to Aberdeen for the English occupying army, and called at Newcastle on the way back to pick up a cargo of coal; next year he collaborated with Italians in shipping wool from Hull. In the late thirteenth century, however, Edward I got less financial assistance from the Cahorsins than he had hoped, and by 1305 they seem to have been losing ground in England's commerce. William Servat, it is true, is something of an exception, becoming Edward II's 'dear merchant', but that was as a naturalized Englishman and alderman of London.

---

[38] *Close R.*, 1231–34, p. 251; *CPR*, 1232–47, p. 108; E. von Roon-Bassermann, 'Die Handelssperre Englands gegen Flandern 1270–74, und die lizenzierte englische Wollausfuhr', *VSWG*, L (1963), pp. 71–7; Lloyd, *The English Wool Trade*, pp. 48–9; Doehaerd, *L'expansion économique belge au moyen âge*, pp. 56–7; *CLB A*, pp. 4, 33.
[39] *Calendar of Chancery Warrants*, p. 38; *CCR*, 1288–96, p. 353; 1296–1302, pp. 257, 439; A.H. Thomas, ed., *Cal. Early Mayor's Court Rolls*, pp. 7–9.
[40] Lloyd, *The English Wool Trade*, pp. 46–7; Renouard, 'Les Cahorsins', pp. 57–8; *Rot. Hundr.*, I, pp. 385, 404.

Poncius de Mora's fortunes may have been more typical: by 1300 he was old and feeble and living in poverty.[41]

The Italians, on the other hand, attained their maximum influence on English economic affairs in the reign of Edward I. They figure most prominently in the records as 'bankers to the crown', especially the Riccardi of Lucca and later the Frescobaldi of Florence; but they also provided deposit services to landowners with large, scattered estates, and made advances to individuals and communities of every sort. In the early 1290s Lewes priory owed £2,800 to Italian merchants and the earl of Lincoln £360, but Hulne priory in Northumberland owed only £1 6s. 8d. and a certain parson a mere £1.[42] Even the largest private debt, of course was small when compared with what the king owed. Total loans by the Riccardi to Edward I in the period 1272–94 were of the order of £400,000, although regular repayments meant that at any given moment the king's debt was a mere fraction of that sum. Later, advances by the Frescobaldi in the period 1294–1310 averaged about £4,000 a year down to 1302 and £15,000 a year thereafter, and totalled around £155,000 when interest due is included.[43] In the meantime, of course, much smaller business continued to be done by Italian merchant-financiers. Sir William Howard got a loan of £13 6s. 8d. on the security of an alms dish and a silver cup; and the security Aymer de Valence put up for a loan consisted of a silver cup, a silver basin, four gold rings set with sapphires, and another ring set with a topaz. The financial business done by the Italians ranged from financing governments to lending to individuals and pawnbroking; and firms like the Mori and Spini of Florence had a house in London at which debtors might pay what they owed.[44]

[41] *CCR*, 1288–96, pp. 192–5; 1302–7, pp. 3, 8–9; *CPR*, 1301–7, p. 538; *CLB A*, pp. 6, 10–11, 37, 52; *Cal. Chancery Warrants*, pp. 156, 181; N.Morimoto, *Monastic Economy and Medieval Markets*, pp. 218, 371; F. Arens, 'Wilhelm Servat von Cahors als Kaufmann zu London (1273–1320)', *VSWG*, XI (1913), p. 482; PRO E 101/359/18; Thomas, ed., *Cal. Early Mayor's Court Rolls*, pp. 192–3; Lloyd, *Alien Merchants in England*, pp. 95, 188–9.

[42] See generally, R.W. Kaeuper, *Bankers to the Crown: the Riccardi of Lucca and Edward I*, and *idem*, 'The Frescobaldi of Florence and the English crown', in *Studies in Medieval and Renaissance History*, x (1973), pp. 45–95; and also E.B. Fryde and M.M. Fryde, 'Public credit with special reference to north-western Europe' in *CEcH*, III, pp. 454–8; N. Denholm-Young, *Seignorial Administration in England*, Oxford, 1937, pp. 60–6; *CCR*, 1288–96, pp. 126, 133, 186, 200.

[43] Kaeuper, *Bankers to the Crown*, pp. 129–31; *idem*, 'The Frescobaldi of Florence and the English crown', pp. 68–72. A. Sapori put the total Frescobaldi loans in the period 1298–1310 at £122,000: *Studi di Storia economica (secoli XIII–XIV–XV)*, Florence, 1955, p. 591.

[44] Thomas, ed., *Cal. Early Mayor's Court Rolls*, pp. 110, 129; PRO E 368/61, m. 32.

At the same time the Italians were able to become financiers because they earned profits as merchants and, from the start, it was part of their strength that they appeared in England not as isolated individuals but as the representatives of organized companies. They were not newcomers to this country in the reign of Edward I. Merchant groups with headquarters in Bologna, Florence and Siena were active in England by 1240; in the middle years of Henry III's reign merchants of Lucca and Genoa supplied the court with silks and cloths of gold; and the origins of the Riccardi company can possibly be traced back to Luke of Lucca and his partners who supplied Henry III's wardrobe in the 1250s.[45] Like the Cahorsins, too, but with greater effect, they seized the opportunity presented by Anglo-Flemish disputes in the 1270s to move into the export trade in wool on the grand scale. If they took full advantage of the export licences they received in 1273, and without taking account of large unlicensed exports by them (especially from Lincolnshire), they may then have been shipping about a quarter of the English wool which went overseas. It was not, of course, a trade in which they were without experience. Wool exports from the Holderness estates of Isabella de Forz were already in the hands of the Riccardi in the 1260s; and a neighbouring estate, that of Meaux abbey, also seems to have contracted with Lucca merchants for the sale of the abbey's wool from a flock of some 11,000 sheep.[46]

Italian merchants, moreover, continued to be wool merchants. In 1275–76 seven Italian companies exported 52 per cent of the wool leaving Hull that year; in 1293–96 Hugolino Gerarduci of Lucca was one of the largest exporters from Newcastle, although the fact that he seems to have married the daughter or widow of a local wool merchant may make him a special case;[47] and Italians frequently undertook to purchase monastic wool on a regular basis. Rievaulx entered into such an agreement with a Florentine company in 1280 and, in 1292, Kirkstall accepted a contract with the Betti of Lucca for a term of ten years. At the same time the Italians did not disdain

---

[45] E. von Roon-Bassermann, 'Die ersten Florentiner Handelsgesellschaften in England', p. 104; *Close R.*, 1227–31, pp. 212–13; 1237–42, p. 239; 1254–56, p. 54; *CLR*, 1245–51, p. 118; 1251–60, pp. 14, 148; Kaeuper, *Bankers to the Crown*, pp. 4–6.

[46] A. Schaube, 'Die Wollausfuhr Englands vom Jahre 1273', *VSWG*, VIII (1908), p. 68; *Rot. Hundr.*, I, pp. 328, 353, 385–6, 396; Denholm-Young, *Seignorial Administration in England*, p. 60; E.A. Bond, ed., *Chronica Monasterii de Melsa*, II, p. 156.

[47] Gras, *Early English Customs System*, pp. 225–44; J.C. Davies, 'Wool customs accounts for Newcastle upon Tyne in the reign of Edward I', *AA*, 4th ser. XXXII (1954), p. 254; C.M. Fraser, ed., *The Northumberland Lay Subsidy Roll of 1296*, p. 44; Kaeuper, *Bankers to the Crown*, pp. 42–3.

smaller consignments: in Yorkshire they were under contract to receive two sacks from Birdsall in the East Riding, two and a half sacks from Micklethwaite in the West Riding, and seven sacks from Sir John Bulmer of Ryedale in the North Riding. They also ranged widely in their trading, buying wool in Hertfordshire as well as Yorkshire, and shipping from southern ports like Southampton and Shoreham as well as from harbours in Lincolnshire and the North-East.[48] What total shipments from England by Italians were at the end of the thirteenth century cannot be established with any confidence, but clearly they were considerable. In the years 1294–97 the Frescobaldi alone exported some 1,400 sacks of wool; and ten Florentine and Lucchese firms operating in England when Edward I requisitioned their wool in 1294 held, or were owed under contract, about 2,700 sacks. This was probably well below the amount they would usually have handled in a year, since some of their shipments seem already to have been despatched; even so it represented 10 per cent or so of English wool exports at that time.[49]

The destination of the wool the Italians exported is even more difficult to determine. It is doubtful if much of it went overland to Italy; and, although some was shipped to the Mediterranean from London or Sandwich by Genoese and Majorcan galleys as early as the 1280s, substantial and regular shipments to Italy only began in the early fourteenth century.[50] Italian wool exports from England, in other words, probably mainly went across the North Sea to the Low Countries as one line only of a far more diversified Italian commerce. In Edward I's later years Italians were still importing silks and cloths of gold into England, but those brought by Genoese merchants in 1303 arrived via Wissant, possibly suggesting that they came from the Champagne fairs or from the entrepôts of the Low Countries rather than from Italy direct; and cloth sold to the king's wardrobe in 1301 by the Frescobaldi, or imported into Sandwich by Italians in 1304–05, may well have come from Flanders or Brabant. What the Sandwich customs accounts do make abundantly clear, however, is the variety of the Italian trade with England. They exported hides as well as wool; they re-exported mercery, figs and raisins; and they imported, as well as cloth and luxury fabrics, alum, almonds, sugar, licorice, figs, mercery, groceries, leather, iron, yarn,

---

[48] J.C. Atkinson, ed., *Cartularium Abbathiae de Rievalle*, pp. 409–11; W.T. Lancaster and W.P. Baildon, eds, *Coucher Book of the Cistercian Abbey of Kirkstall*, no. 324; PRO E 368/61, mm. 26, 29, 30d; Kaeuper, *Bankers to the Crown*, p. 43.

[49] *Ibid.*, pp. 44–5; Fryde, *Studies*, chapt. XIV, p. 294.

[50] Fryde, *Studies*, chapt. XIV, p. 295.

and also horses of considerable value. The earl of Lincoln, too, got a sword from an Italian merchant for which he paid the fairly high price of 53s. 4d. Perhaps it was made in Milan, a city with a reputation for the manufacture of arms and armour.[51]

In 1300, then, many Italians were active in England and in that year Edward I ordered his officials to cease troubling an array of companies for currency offences – the Amanati of Pistoia; the Pulci and Rembertini, the Cerchi Neri, the Cerchi Bianchi, the Mori, and the Bardi from Florence; and the Ballardi from Lucca. By this time, too, the Frescobaldi of Florence were emerging as the crown's principal bankers and a member of the Florentine Spini company was in the Tower for unspecified misdeeds at Boston. A London tallage in 1304 attests the presence of some dozen Italian companies as well as individual Italian merchants among those living in the city. Such groups, of course, were likely to be unpopular as aliens, and the fact that their financial services to the crown won them special commercial privileges made their unpopularity all the greater. Tales were told of them by a London jury which lost nothing in the telling. They raped the wives, daughters and servants of the good men of the city; they raised uproars in the city by abusing, beating and wounding all who opposed them; and on a Saturday evening at the hour of vespers, as they sat at supper in their lodgings and talked of the war between France and England, they magnified and praised the king of France, but called the king of England 'a wretched and captive king'.[52]

Italians were not the only alien merchants resident in London in 1304. There were also a fair number of Gascons, especially in Vintry ward, and of Germans, mainly in Dowgate ward. The Gascon presence reflected the continuing dominance of the English market by Gascon wines; for, except when war interrupted the trade, England in *c*.1300 took about a quarter of the 80,000 tuns of wine exported annually from Bordeaux.[53] By that time English merchants had a considerable stake in this trade; earlier Flemish merchants had sometimes brought Gascon wine to England when they came for wool; and in 1293 Italian merchants, and merchants from Bayonne,

[51] *CCR*, 1302–7, pp. 34, 337, 360; PRO E 101/359/18 and DL 29/1/2; Gras, *Early English Customs System*, pp. 302–46.
[52] *CCR*, 1296–1302, pp. 353–4, 360; Lloyd, *Alien Merchants in England*, pp. 229–31; Thomas, ed., *Cal. Early Mayor's Court Rolls*, pp. 115–17.
[53] Renouard, ed., *Bordeaux sous les rois d'Angleterre*, p. 255; M.K. James, *Studies in the Medieval Wine Trade*, pp. 9–10.

Map 4 (b) Principal points of commercial contact between England and Western Europe, *c.* 1300: The Northern and Southern trades

Sources: J. C. Davies, 'Wool Customs Accounts for Newcastle', AA, 4th ser. XXXII (1954); customs accounts printed by Gras, *Early English Customs System*; and T. H. Lloyd, *Alien Merchants in England in the High Middle Ages.*

Toulouse, Cahors and the Iberian peninsula, all shipped wine from Gascony to England. For most of the thirteenth century, however, the trade was dominated by the merchants of Bordeaux who, as well as supplying London, frequented the ports of Southampton, Ipswich, Sandwich, Hull, Bristol and Boston, and who at Boston fair furnished wine for Lincoln vintners, York merchants, and customers from as far away as Cumberland.[54] Gascon merchants, in fact, were almost as ubiquitous as the Italians, although they were especially active in London where they were consistently supported by Edward I against endeavours by the Londoners to curtail their rights of residence and their freedom to trade. They were also much more than wine merchants, for they were associated with other merchants from south-western Europe in a much more general commerce. Trading debts enrolled in London in Edward I's reign show Gascon, Provençal and Spanish merchants importing into England leather, spices, wool, yarn, and the skins of goats and rabbits; Gascon and Portuguese shipments into Bristol in the early fourteenth century included figs, raisins, oil, almonds, pepper, sugar, rice, saffron, wax, leather and pomegranates; and at about the same time Bordeaux merchants imported alum, licorice, almonds, dates, honey, figs and rice into Sandwich, to which Spanish importers added iron, quicksilver, nutmeg, yarn, leather and wool, and Provençal merchants spices of diverse sorts. The luxuries and some of the raw materials of Mediterranean Europe were being made directly available to English ports.[55]

The English exports which helped to pay for imports of wine and southern products appear mainly to have been grain, fish and tin. Wheat was shipped to Gascony from time to time from Sandwich, the Isle of Wight and Bristol; and the sea and land routes from south-west England through south-west France to the Mediterranean were among the main arteries of the tin trade. Bayonne merchants as early as 1198 bought up more than a quarter of the current output of the Stannaries, and continued during the ensuing century to export tin from Lostwithiel and grain and fish from a number of ports in south-western England. Gascon exports from this part of England at the end of the century still included tin and perhaps some meat and dairy produce, together with herrings from Yarmouth and grain, cloth, hides and a little lead from Bristol. Whether these exports were valuable enough to balance the cost of

---

[54] *Ibid.*, pp. 73–4; *Close R.*, 1227–31, pp. 306–7; *CCR*, 1288–96, pp. 321, 355, 362; *CLB A*, pp. 40–1, 47, 52, 92, 99.
[55] Gras, *Early English Customs System*, pp. 267–73, 302–60.

importing wine and southern goods the evidence is insufficient to determine.[56]

By 1300, too, long-term changes had taken place in England's northern trade. First, the merchants of the north German towns, under the leadership of Lübeck, had turned the Baltic into a Hanseatic lake. They dominated trade with Gotland and Scania, had outposts in the eastern Baltic in new towns like Riga and Reval, and had established trading posts in inland Russia like Novgorod. They had also developed a flourishing trade from towns along the southern shores of the Baltic with their hinterlands in Mecklenburg, Pomerania and Prussia, and they had virtually subjected to their control the Norwegian port of Bergen. A consequence was, so far as England was concerned, that even though Norwegian ships still called at Newcastle and King's Lynn in the early fourteenth century, traders from Scandinavia ceased to be the force they had been earlier in English economic life.[57] Secondly, the old primacy of Cologne and the Rhinelanders in Anglo-German trade was progressively undermined. The merchants headed by the Cologners were still the only recognized association of 'merchants of the kingdom of Germany' in England in 1260; but well before that time they had been joined in English ports by shippers from north Germany. Bremen merchants were granted safe-conduct in England in 1213, and Bremen and Hamburg ships were coming there in 1223–24; in 1226 Lübeck merchants trading to England got imperial protection against the Cologners; and Henry III gave safe conduct to Brunswick merchants in 1230 and conferred privileges (although less extensive than those enjoyed by the merchants of Cologne) upon the Lübeck merchants in 1238.[58]

In 1266–67, moreover, Henry III granted to these 'Eastland' merchants that, like the Cologners, they might have their own organization (their 'hanses') in England. The headquarters of this organization was perhaps originally at King's Lynn; and the expansion of the Eastland trade with England during the second half of

---

[56] *Ibid.*, pp. 346–60; Lloyd, *Alien Merchants in England*, p. 92; Renouard, ed., *Bordeaux sous les rois d'Angleterre*, p. 260; *Close R.*, 1237–42, p. 398; *CPR*, 1292–1301, pp. 292, 326; *CCR*, 1296–1302, p. 3; J.Hatcher, *English Tin Production and Trade*, pp. 22–3.

[57] *Cal. Inq. Misc.*, I, no. 1965; Gras, *Early English Customs System*, pp. 380, 383, 387, 391–2; Lloyd, *England and the German Hanse*, pp. 4–5.

[58] K. Kunze, 'Die ersten Jahrhundert der deutschen Hanse in England', *Hansische Geschichtsblätter*, VI (1889), pp. 129–35; Christensen, 'Scandinavia and the advance of the Hanseatics', pp. 105–17; Dollinger, *La Hanse*, pp. 57–8; Lloyd, *England and the German Hanse*, pp. 16–20; Höhlbaum *et al.*, eds, *Hansisches Urkundenbuch*, I, nos. 237, 552.

the thirteenth century, indeed, or even for rather longer, may have been principally with the east-coast ports.[59] Some Eastlanders, however, soon found their way to London, including John de Brilond from Lübeck who supplied Henry III's court with furs and wax, imported cloth from Flanders, and was exporting wool by 1271. He was still described as a 'merchant of Almain' in 1272, but by 1277 he had been naturalized as a merchant of London.[60] The 'merchants of the hanse of Germany then living in the city' who came to an agreement with the London authorities in 1282 included at least one Hamburg man; and a single association under Lübeck's leadership, representing all German merchants, came into being in London, with merchants from the other maritime towns establishing themselves in other buildings around the old Cologne gildhall. The Eastlanders continued to maintain important trading stations at Boston and King's Lynn, and were also active in the ports of Newcastle, Scarborough, Hull and Ravenser; but London was emerging as the political centre for all Germans trading to England and as the headquarters from which they dealt with the English government.[61]

The German trade around 1300, therefore, represented a fusion of two commercial currents: the traditional trade with the Rhineland on the one hand, and, on the other, the newer Eastland trade which brought to England goods of which the cargoes of some Lübeck ships arrested in northern ports in the 1290s were not untypical. They consisted mainly of timber, herrings, stockfish, hides, furs, butter, tallow, flax (with some linen and canvas), iron, steel, and a few rarities like falcons and otter skins. The two currents can be seen converging at Boston in 1303. At least 52 German merchants were trading there that year, twenty of them Eastlanders from Lübeck and other northern towns. The latter brought to England the sylvan products of the Baltic region (timber, furs, wax) together with steel, hawks and large shipments of fish, and took back beans, malt, salt and cloth. These Eastlanders were joined at Boston by merchants from Cologne, Lorraine and Holland who brought swords, helmets, cooking pots and a good deal of miscellaneous merchandise (although imports of Rhine wine seem to have all but succumbed to

[59] *Ibid.*, I, nos. 633, 636; Kunze, 'Die ersten Jahrhundert der deutschen Hanse in England', pp. 135–6; Lloyd, *England and the German Hanse*, pp. 37–9.

[60] *CLR*, 1251–60, p. 37; 1260–67, p. 190; 1267–72, no. 198; *CPR*, 1266–72, pp. 86–7, 195, 310, 524, 553, 593, 689; *Calendar of Chancery Rolls (Various)*, pp. 8, 14.

[61] Lloyd, *Alien Merchants in England*, pp. 132–4; *idem*, *England and the German Hanse*, pp. 6, 21; H.T.Riley, ed., *Liber Albus*, Rolls Ser., 1859, pp. 485–6; *CCR*, 1288–96, pp. 407–8, 411.

Gascon competition), and they exported from England butter, salt, wheat and lead as well as broadcloths and worsteds.[62]

Before 1303, however, the Germans had also moved into the carrying trade across the North Sea. In 1298 the Londoners were complaining that they were wholesalers of *avoirdupois* (miscellaneous spices and groceries, probably picked up in the Low Countries), dealers in cloth which may well have come from Flanders or Brabant, and woolmen. Their role as wool exporters may have been in part a compensation for the relatively narrow range of English commodities which attracted the Eastlanders at a time when their imports into England were expanding: exporting English wool to the Low Countries was a way of sending their trade balance overseas. The Anglo-Flemish disputes of the 1270s were an opportunity for the Germans, like the Italians, to move into the wool trade on some scale, and in 1275 they exported about 17 per cent of the wool sent overseas from Hull. The German share of England's wool trade increased still further in the 1290s when that of the Flemings was further narrowed and the position of the great Italian companies was seriously weakened. In the early fourteenth century Hanseatic merchants handled up to 57 per cent of wool exports from Hull, and had a substantial stake in the wool trade from Boston and even from London.[63]

It is, of course, misleading to look at England's trade in the reign of Edward I mainly from the angle of those parts of it which were the responsibility of alien merchants, and in due course we must assess the contribution of denizens to it; but during this reign an expanding range of foreign traders was involved, probably in unprecedented numbers, in almost every branch of English commerce and enjoyed a greater degree of government patronage than ever before. The alien trade, therefore, was not untypical of England's trade as a whole, and clearly had contributed very significantly to the expansion of English commerce during the thirteenth century. That expansion did not detract from the primacy of the trading artery across the North Sea from England to the Low Countries, the Rhineland and northern France; on the contrary, that had been enhanced as the textile industries of this area became increasingly dependent upon supplies of English wool, making it

---

[62] J.C. Davies, 'Shipping and trade in Newcastle upon Tyne, 1294–6', *AA*, 4th ser., XXXI (1953), pp. 188–9, 202–4; Gras, *Early English Customs System*, pp. 273–302.
[63] Thomas, ed., *Cal. Early Mayor's Court Rolls*, pp. 7–9; Lloyd, *The English Wool Trade*, pp. 65–6, 141–3; *idem, Alien Merchants in England*, p. 156; *idem, England and the German Hanse*, pp. 42–5.

possible for England in turn to absorb more of the products of those industries, Rhineland manufactures, and the great variety of commodities that were available in the entrepôt towns of the Low Countries. Even though Scandinavian merchants came more rarely to England by 1300, Dutch and north Germans were more regular visitors. They brought to England furs and fish and the forest products of the Baltic; and at least at Boston in 1303 English cloth was a prominent return cargo. In the meantime a southern trade had developed contemporaneously, mainly to Gascony, Provence and Iberia, providing England mainly with wine and Mediterranean luxuries, but also with Spanish iron and leather and with woad from Languedoc. These southern regions also provided markets for English cloth by the opening of the fourteenth century, and for grain, for herrings from Yarmouth, and for salt, iron, meat and even 'sea-coal' from Southampton. Like some branches of the northern trade, this southern trade was in great measure a thirteenth-century enlargement of the range of England's overseas commerce.[64]

2.   CHANGES IN ENGLAND'S COMMERCE, *C.* 1303–48

(a)   Customs duties and the measurement of English trade

The duties imposed upon wool exports from 1275, and upon all alien exports and imports from 1303, for the first time provide data enabling some branches of English trade to be measured. The picture, of course, is still incomplete. English merchants, except when exporting wool and importing wine, traded duty-free, so that much of their share of England's commerce is not recorded by this evidence. To get an impression of what their share was, therefore, it is best to start with wool exports. Total exports, leaving aside the troubled war years in the 1290s, seem to have increased from an annual average of about 26,000 sacks in the period 1279–89 to 29,000 sacks in 1299–1304 and to 41,000 sacks in 1304–9.[65] The shares of aliens and denizens in the trade, however, can only be confidently established in the last of these periods, when aliens were responsible for 45 per cent of the total, although the figure varied

---

[64] Gras, *Early English Customs System*, pp. 360–73.
[65] Calculated from E.M. Carus-Wilson and O. Coleman, *England's Export Trade, 1275–1547.*

greatly from port to port and was as high as 64 per cent at Hull. Even so, denizen shipments accounting for 36 per cent of the exports from Hull look significantly higher than they had been earlier. Their share in 1274–75 had apparently only been 4 per cent and in the range 12–28 per cent in 1291–92.[66]

There was, of course, nothing new in the fact that Englishmen were exporting wool in the reign of Edward I: York merchants like Hugh Selby and Southampton merchants like Walter and James le Flemyng had done so in the 1220s, as had Londoners like Richard *Crassus* through south-coast ports.[67] It is not until 1273, however, that we get any indication of how much they may have exported. In that year the trade was subject to licences and those granted to English merchants were for about 35 per cent of the permitted exports.[68] This may well be more wool than denizens had been exporting before 1273, since they may have been (like Italian and German merchants) seeking to take over trade previously in Flemish hands; and it cannot be determined how fully they took advantage of their licences. All the same, if a 35 per cent share of the wool trade indicates English ambitions in 1273, they had gained a good deal of ground by 1304–9. Then, denizens handled 55 per cent of wool exports which were larger than at any time in the past.

If English merchants advanced, during the last quarter of the thirteenth century, from being a minority to a majority interest in the North Sea wool trade, the indications are that their share in other branches of England's overseas trade may have been smaller. They were responsible only for about a quarter of wine imports; they do not appear to have had any significant stake in other branches of the southern trade; they were hardly known in the Mediterranean and do not appear to have played a major role in the Baltic. Alien merchants, in other words, dominated the northern and southern trades; while in the trade across the North Sea, although there are clear signs of English advances as wool exporters by the opening decade of the fourteenth century, it is very difficult to gain any clear impression of their activity in other branches of commerce. The cargoes of some English ships pirated in the North Sea in the years 1301–3 may possibly offer some pointers, although the information unfortunately relates only to fourteen ships going out and six ships coming in, most of them on the Brabant route, and the components

---

[66] Lloyd, *The English Wool Trade*, pp. 64–5.
[67] *Pat. R.*, 1216–25, pp. 451, 463, 472; *RLC*, II, p. 16.
[68] Schaube, 'Die Wollausfuhr Englands vom Jahre 1273', p. 68.

of the cargoes are not always clearly distinguished. The clear implications of these piracies is, nonetheless, that wool was the principal export carried, possibly accounting for 70 per cent of the value of the cargoes going out. The only other significant export was cloth, although there was also a little tin and lead, some grain and cheese, a consignment of re-exported wine from Winchelsea, and £56 in cash. The smaller sample of imported cargoes was even more conspicuously dominated by a single commodity, cloth accounting for 81 per cent of their value. In addition, there was one fairly large consignment of salt fish, another of metal, some re-exported northern goods like fish oil and timber, some rabbit skins, and £43 in cash. If cloth was both imported and exported, moreover, the Brabançon cloth brought in by six ships was worth considerably more than the English cloth which thirteen ships took overseas.[69]

There remain, therefore, large gaps in our knowledge of England's overseas trade in the opening years of the fourteenth century. The customs records, however, provide data enabling the volume, and more tentatively the value, of wool exports, wine imports, and both the imports and the exports by alien merchants to be calculated, however approximately – a sufficiently large part of the total range of English commerce at that time to make worthwhile an attempt to complete the picture. This has been done in Table 4.1 for the years 1304–9 by calculating the imports and exports of English merchants (other than of wine and wool) roughly in accordance with the composition of the cargoes pirated in the North Sea in 1301–3. Obviously the result can be no more than an approximation and the possibilities of error are immense. As we have seen, alien cloth shipments out of England may have been rather larger than the customs accounts seem to suggest; the English imports falling into the hands of pirates in 1301–3 may have been highly untypical; and any attempt to place a value on the various branches of trade raises every sort of difficulty. For general merchandise carried by alien merchants the customs valuations have been accepted; while for other goods an average price had to be adopted for commodities which must have varied in value according to their quality and the state of the market.[70]

---

[69] G.P. Cuttino, *English Diplomatic Administration, 1259–1339*, pp. 212–20.
[70] Figures for alien trade have been calculated from data in Lloyd, *Alien Merchants in England*, appendix. 1. Italicized figures in the quantities column are estimates, as are all the values except those for alien shipments of general merchandise, for which customs valuations have been used.

Table 4.1 Estimates of England's overseas trade, 1304–9 (averages per annum)[71]

	Alien trade		Denizen trade		Totals	
	Quantity	Value (£)	Quantity	Value (£)	Quantity	Value (£)
Imports						
Cloths	11,684	46,736	*6,000*	24,000	*17,684*	70,736
Wax (cwts)	1,805	5,415	–	–	1,805	5,415
Wine (tuns)	*15,000*	45,000	*5,000*	15,000	*20,000*	60,000
General merchandise	–	55,125	–	6,000	–	61,125
	–	152,276	–	45,000	–	197,276
Exports						
Wool (sacks)	18,508	115,675	22,802	142,513	41,310	258,188
Hides (lasts)	117	2,340	included in general merchandise		117	2,340
Cloths	379	1,516	*3,500*	14,000	3,879	15,516
General merchandise	–	14,935	–	11,000	–	25,935
	–	134,466	–	167,513	–	301,979

If the figures so established can be allowed any validity they suggest, first, that wool enjoyed absolute primacy among England's exports which, when exports of hides, grain, fish and metals like lead and tin are brought into account, were predominantly of primary products. Secondly, the cost of cloth and wine imports, together with that of spices, rare fruits, silks, furs and many of the manufactured goods entered under general merchandise, points to the 'luxury' character of much of the inward trade. Thirdly, with wool exports

---

[71] For wax a wholesale price has been calculated from current retail prices; hides have been valued at about £20 per last (cf. Carus-Wilson and Coleman, *England's Export Trade*, p. 1 note); and wool has been valued at £6 5s. per sack: rather less than the value of wool in the hands of Italian merchants in 1294, but about the figure placed by the exchequer on the 8,000 sacks to be purveyed in August 1297 (Lloyd, *Movement of Wool Prices in Medieval England*, Table 5; M. Prestwich, ed., *Documents illustrating the Crisis of 1297–98 in England*, Camden 4th ser. xxiv (1980), no. 97). It is impossible to establish an average value for a commodity varying so greatly in quality as cloth did; but to obtain a possible indication of the value of cloth entering into international trade we have used an average of the cost of royal purchases in the years 1301–2 and 1325–26 (PRO E 101/359/18, 381/9). For wine £3 per tun seems to have been a normal price in the period before the outbreak of the Hundred Years' War (James, *Studies in the Medieval Wine Trade*, chapt. 1).

running at a very high level in the early fourteenth century, it looks as though the net balance of trade may have been very much in England's favour and that it had possibly been positive even in the 1270s. That may have helped to explain the availability of bullion supplies to support the remarkably stable English currency. Finally, despite recent advances by English merchants as wool exporters, alien merchants still dominated England's overseas trade as a whole. They must have done so still more markedly before the surge of wool exports, seemingly English led, in the first decade of the fourteenth century.

The figures also prompt a few further, no less tentative, observations. First, if indeed England's overseas trade in 1304–9 had an annual value of around £500,000, in part this reflected the effects of thirteenth-century inflation. Wine prices had perhaps doubled since 1226–40 and wool prices in the early fourteenth century were about two and a half times their level in the second decade of the thirteenth century.[72] Even so, the figures suggest that the value of England's overseas trade may have increased at least threefold in real terms between 1203–4 and the early fourteenth century, and it may already have doubled (or more than doubled) by Edward I's early years. Once again, the indications are that the thirteenth century witnessed a notable expansion of England's commerce. Secondly, there also appear to have been some notable shifts in the fortunes of English ports so far as these can be measured by the proportion by value of alien imports and exports and of denizen wine imports and wool exports (between them accounting for four-fifths of the value of English trade) which they handled at the beginning of the fourteenth century. By this criterion, Boston and the Lincolnshire ports handled about 22 per cent of England's overseas trade, Hull and the Yorkshire ports about 12 per cent, Southampton and the ports of Hampshire and Dorset about $8^1/_2$ per cent; but London, with 36 per cent, was well ahead. Sandwich, Yarmouth, Newcastle, Ipswich and King's Lynn, each with 3–5 per cent, were very much in a second division.[73] By comparison with the situation in 1203–4 Boston, Southampton and King's Lynn had perhaps more or less maintained their shares; Hull, Sandwich, Yarmouth and Ipswich may have gained a little ground; but the salient feature is the advance of the port of London. The capital by 1300, in fact, was coming to occupy a

[72] For wine prices in the early thirteenth century, *CLR*, 1226–40, *passim* for royal purchases; for wool prices, Farmer, 'Prices and Wages', in *AHEW*, II, p. 757.
[73] Figures for the individual ports have been calculated for the annual average value of their alien trade in 1303–11, wool exports in 1304–9 and wine imports in 1300–1.

unique place in English economic life; and, particularly when the activities of London merchants in provincial ports is also taken into account, the expansion of London's trade must have contributed notably to the growth of England's commerce during the thirteenth century.

(b) The advance of the English

Commercial expansion did not continue without interruption after the surge at the opening of the century. If the combined value of the alien trade, wine imports and wool exports is again taken to be indicative, this hardly averaged £300,000 a year around 1330 compared with £436,000 twenty-five years earlier. The comparison, admittedly, takes no account of price changes, of possible defects in the administration of the customs system which prompted the reforms of 1331,[74] or of an increased share by denizens of trades other than those in wool and wine. While it is impossible to put a figure on the total value of England's trade in *c.* 1330, it does seem clear that, in the six years between 1326 and 1333 for which information is reasonably complete, the alien trade had fallen in value to about half what it had been worth in 1304–9. Alien cloth imports into England, it is true, were something of an exception to this general trend, for they were still running at about 90 per cent of their earlier level in *c.* 1330 despite a temporary check caused by restrictions on the wearing of foreign fabrics in 1326.[75] A more pronounced downturn of alien cloth imports soon set in, however, for in 1333–36 they averaged only 7,800 cloths a year compared with 10,500 cloths annually in 1326–33. While there may have been some compensatory increase of imports by denizens, from 1336 onwards disruption occasioned by war drastically reduced all cloth imports into England, and alien imports were down to about 2,000 cloths a year by the late 1330s. It is clear, nonetheless, that the reasons for this collapse were mainly political rather than economic; for in the 1350s, despite the dislocation of markets by plague in 1348–50, alien imports increased once more to around 4,000–5,000 cloths a year.[76]

[74] R.L. Baker, 'The English customs service, 1307–43', *Trans. American Philosophical Society*, LI (1961), pp. 30–1; Lloyd, *The English Wool Trade*, pp. 123–4.

[75] Lloyd, *Alien Merchants in England*, Appx. 1; A.R. Bridbury, *Medieval English Clothmaking*, pp. 39, 45.

[76] H.L. Gray, 'Production and export of English woollens in the fourteenth century', pp. 14, 19; Carus-Wilson, *MMV*, p. 242 note.

Purchases for the king's household in 1324–26 illustrate the continuing importance of imported textiles and alien importers. Most of these purchases were of cloths of Malines, Louvain, Douai and Ghent; and in 1324–25 more than half of them by value were bought from foreign merchants, and more than two-thirds of them in 1325–26. There were, of course, English importers too: there is a record of five Exeter merchants loading a ship in Flanders with cloth and other goods to be brought to England, and it was assumed in 1317 that the Londoner, Simon Swanland, might be expected to import up to 2,000 cloths. Simon, admittedly, was a 'king's merchant' who became mayor of London and rich enough to be knighted; but it looks as though English merchants in the 1320s could supply up to a third or even more of the imported textiles bought for the king.[77] If this reflected anything like their share of cloth imports, the English market may still have absorbed 16,000 foreign cloths yearly in the period 1326–33, nearly 12,000 cloths in 1333–36 and, after a fall to about 3,000 cloths in the late 1330s, still some 7,500 cloths in the 1350s. The conquest of the home market by native textiles was neither sudden nor without set-backs, and was an achievement of the second, rather than the first, half of the fourteenth century.

The fortunes of the wool trade are easier to chart. Shipments varied widely from year to year, often for reasons that were political or diplomatic, but the long-term trends are clear enough. Exports retreated from the average of over 40,000 sacks a year in 1304–9 to a level slightly above that in the peace-time years of Edward I's reign, averaging 30,000 sacks or rather less annually in the period 1311–36. They were pushed below 25,000 sacks a year by war between 1337 and 1342, but after an interval in which customs records are lacking, they had recovered by the 1350s to average 33,000 sacks a year. These over-all figures, however, mask one important change which was taking place. In the decade before the opening of the French war in 1336 English merchants shipped almost as much wool overseas as they had been doing in the boom years at the beginning of the century, but the quantity exported by alien merchants had been more than halved. In 1326–36, therefore, English merchants controlled almost three-quarters of the trade, compared with 55 per cent in 1304–9. Edward III's need in war-time for financial support

---

[77] PRO E 101/380/14, 381/9; *CCR*, 1313–18, p. 496; 1327–30, p. 534; Lloyd, *Alien Merchants in England*, p. 112; E. Ekwall, *Studies on the Population of Medieval London*, p. 291; Williams, *Medieval London*, pp. 131–2.

from English merchants was to confirm their growing dominance of England's wool trade.

North Sea commerce, therefore, saw both continuity and change during the first half of the fourteenth century. Although the English share of this trade was growing, relatively at least, it also continued to engage the Italian companies and the merchants of the German Hanse, together with rising commercial interests like the Brabanters and the Dutch. The waters of the North Sea, in fact, were still very much international waters, and it was characteristic enough that in the 1320s payments were made by the Scali company of Florence at Lincoln in England of sums due to German merchants in satisfaction of bonds entered into at Antwerp in Brabant.[78] In general, however, the Italian stake in the North Sea wool trade seems to have been a declining one as their interests were increasngly diverted to direct shipments of wool to Italy. Furthermore, the possibility that the Germans might step into the place the Italians had occupied as wool exporters to the Low Countries, which had seemed not unlikely at the beginning of the century, failed to materialize. For this trade the principal German base had been Hull, where in the first decade of the century they controlled some 40 per cent of wool exports (about the same share as denizens); but by 1323–29 English merchants were responsible for 67 per cent of the wool exported from Hull and for 88 per cent of it by 1329–36.[79]

There were, of course, other shippers involved in other lines of commerce in the North Sea region. The Dutch brought salt, grain, onions, millstones, Rhine wine and herrings to King's Lynn, and herrings also to Scarborough; and it was assumed that Dutch traders would be likely to be found at Newcastle, Ravenser Odd, Boston and Great Yarmouth. Exports of grain from England to Holland and Zeeland, too, were licensed in the 1330s, and ale was exported to Holland during the first half of the fourteenth century, mostly from King's Lynn, but occasionally from Boston; and the merchants of Brabant carried some of the cloth which was imported into England. There was also a diversified Anglo-Norman trade. Caen merchants traded to Sandwich and Barfleur ships to Portsmouth and Lymington; one Norman merchant brought millstones to Ipswich and another wine to Southampton; and a Londoner sent salt and other merchandise worth £460 to Normandy in a Boston ship. It is further likely that the trade in woad from Picardy expanded as

[78] *CCR*, 1327–30, p. 223.
[79] Lloyd, *The English Wool Trade*, pp. 128–9; W.R. Childs, *The Trade and Shipping of Hull, 1300–1500*, p. 8.

English cloth output increased, engaging some English merchants, but most of all the merchants of Amiens. The latter are found in most of the ports of southern and eastern England, and the trade may account for the presence of Picards even in such northern towns as Newcastle, Beverley and Pontefract. This commerce inevitably suffered severely when war with France broke out in the 1330s, but until then it had almost certainly been growing.[80]

The Gascon wine trade, the best documented branch of England's southern trade, was likewise badly affected by the French war. In 1300 England had been Gascony's best customer for wine, and even in the early 1330s was taking almost as much Gascon wine as at the start of the century at a price which, in England, was scarcely higher than it had been a generation earlier. From 1336, however, war hit the Bordelais hard and drove up freight prices between Bordeaux and London, so that in 1350–51 imports of Gascon wine were about half what they had been in *c.* 1300 and a permanent rise had taken place in the wholesale and retail price of wine. In the meantime there had also been important changes in the character of the trade. Early in the century aliens (mostly Gascons) were responsible for about three-quarters of the wine imports into England; but their share fell to about one third in the early 1330s and to a quarter by 1350. Denizen imports, on the other hand, by the 1330s were about two or three times what they had been at the beginning of the century and, despite war and plague, they were still above that level in 1350.[81] This change was not merely a result of war. English merchants, and especially the Londoners, had worked tirelessly against the privileges the Gascons had won from Edward I, and by no means without success. In 1310 Gascon exemption from civic taxation in London was withdrawn; in 1315 a Gascon's wine stock was confiscated for doing business with another alien to the prejudice of the franchise of the city; and in 1323–24 an additional toll of 2s. per tun was imposed on wine unloaded in London by merchant vintners of Aquitaine. Not surprisingly, the Gascons petitioned parliament in 1334 pointing to the grievances they suffered at the hands of the Londoners, the men of Bristol and others. The result was said to be that many who had come to England with their merchandise in the past had now gone to other countries, and many

---

[80] Gras, *Early English Customs System*, pp. 374–92; *CCR*, 1327–30, pp. 43, 49, 62, 69, 86, 175–6, 203–4, 236, 301, 306–7, 321–2, 337, 340–1, 428; N.J.M. Kerling, *Commercial Relations of Holland and Zeeland with England*, pp. 104–5, 110–11, 213, 216–17; Lloyd, *Alien Merchants in England*, pp. 78–83.

[81] James, *Studies in the Medieval Wine Trade*, pp. 9–22, 141–3.

who had come to England this year did not intend to do so in the future.[82]

England, of course, got wine from elsewhere – La Rochelle, for example, and the Rhineland; but Gascony remained the main source of supply. Wine imports flowed through almost every English port. Even Chester shipped some wine from Gascony; but London as usual was pre-eminent, handling about a quarter of England's wine trade in 1350 as it had done at the start of the century. In 1350 London was followed fairly closely by Sandwich and Bristol (Bristol's share of the trade had increased notably since 1300); there were considerable wine shipments into Southampton and the south-western ports; and in the north-east Hull appears to have been moving into the place formerly occupied by Boston. It was to Hull that the monks of Durham sent in 1347–48 for some of the wine their house required.[83]

The ships plying between England and Gascony also continued to carry goods other than wine. Bayonne merchants especially brought Iberian products to England and Bordeaux was something of an entrepôt for Mediterranean commodities. England in turn, although the thirteenth-century tin trade seems to have been much diminished, still supplied Gascony with grain, Yarmouth herrings, hides and lead; and an Exeter merchant in 1328 sent to Bordeaux a cargo which also included money and cloth.[84] The money may indicate that the Anglo-Gascon wine trade remained a deficit trade, while the cloth he exported possibly suggests that while alien cloth exports of English cloth were falling there may have been a compensatory increase of denizen cloth exports. It is impossible to attribute a figure to this latter trade until it became liable to duties in 1347, but on the eve of the Black Death English merchants shipped some 90 per cent of the broadcloths exported, together with virtually all the worsteds going out from Yarmouth. During the first half of the fourteenth century, therefore, an expanding market overseas for English cloth may have been compatible with shrinking exports by foreign merchants. Certainly Bristol cloth exporters had become a numerous and important interest. There were more than seventy of them

---

[82] *CLB D*, p. 226; *CLB E*, p. 45; A.H. Thomas, ed., *Cal. Plea and Memoranda Rolls of London*, I, p. 3; *Rot. Parl.*, II p. 74.
[83] *CCR*, 1327–30, pp. 61–2, 141–2, 301–2, 371, 458, 466–7; Gras, *Early English Customs System*, pp. 383, 386, 390; H.J. Hewitt, *Medieval Cheshire*, pp. 130–5; James, *Studies in the Medieval Wine Trade*, p. 98; Morimoto, *Monastic Economy and Medieval Markets*, p. 376.
[84] Lloyd, *Alien Merchants in England*, pp. 92–3; Hatcher, *English Tin Production and Trade*, p. 91; *CCR*, 1327–30, p. 243.

in 1348–50, about half of whom at some time during these years served on the city's council of forty-eight, and nine of whom had held or would in the future hold the office of mayor. Many probably would have described themselves as 'merchants and drapers' as one of their number, Walter Derby, did when he made his will. His testament, however, was not only concerned with property and money and ships, but also included bequests to wine-drawers and labourers on the quay. At Bristol wine importing and cloth exporting seem to be two sides of the same business.[85]

Gascony, moreover, was only one of the destinations to which cloth went from England in the 1340s. Cloth was taken from London by ships from Dordrecht and Sluys, from Sandwich by a Sluys ship, from King's Lynn by a Middleburg ship, from Yarmouth by ships from Dunkirk, Brill, Middleburg and Hamburg. Ships would not necessarily deliver their cargoes at their ports of origin, but clearly there was a significant trade in English cloth by this time across the North Sea. The customs accounts, moreover, present an incomplete picture of it, because the German Hanse refused to pay the new duties on cloth, so that the scale of Hanseatic cloth exports cannot be established until the late 1350s at the earliest. The refusal of the Hansards to pay the duties, on the other hand, does not suggest that their involvement in the trade was an insignificant one. The 4,423 broadcloths exported in 1347–48 shown in the customs accounts, which in any case need to be increased by 10 per cent or so to take account of worsted exports, must therefore be regarded as a minimum figure, and one which showed some effects of the war-time dislocation of European trade. What the 'normal' value of exports may have been it is impossible to determine, but one estimate puts it at more like 6,000 broadcloths annually.[86]

The detailed course of England's cloth export trade during the first half of the fourteenth is difficult to reconstruct mainly because, until 1347, it is impossible to put a figure on the denizen share of it. It does seem, however, that by the fourteenth century there are few traces of English cloth in northern Italian markets and it had virtually disappeared from the markets of southern Italy and the Levant. In compensation, on the other hand, exports to Gascony were

[85] For the cloth customs in 1348–50, Gras, *Early English Customs System*, pp. 414–34 and Carus-Wilson and Coleman, *England's Export Trade*, p. 75, with some minor amendments in Bridbury, *Medieval English Clothmaking*, p. 188; for Walter Derby, T.P. Wadley, ed., *Notes . . . of the Wills contained in the Great Orphan Book and the Book of Wills in . . . Bristol*, Bristol, 1886, no. 23.
[86] Carus-Wilson and Coleman, *England's Export Trade*, pp. 12–13, 75–8; Carus-Wilson, *MMV*, pp. 244–5.

increasing, and so quite probably were those by Hanseatic merchants (who were already shipping cloth from Boston in 1303).[87] If total alien exports of cloth fell between the early years of the century and the 1330s, moreover, what is known about the history of cloth manufacture in England during that period suggests that denizen exports of cloth from England may have grown slowly down to 1336, perhaps with the export of worsteds leading the way. That increase possibly continued after the outbreak of the French war, since interruptions in the supply of English wool to continental manufacturers and heavy English duties on their raw materials gave the English industry a competitive edge. The fact that Bruges in 1346 procured a ban on imports of English cloth into Flanders suggests that the effects of that advantage were being felt.[88] An expansion of English exports was resumed in the 1350s despite the devastation of Gascony by contending armies and the dislocation of all markets by the Black Death. They totalled 5,444 cloths according to the customs accounts in 1355–56, even though the German Hanse continued to refuse to pay the cloth duties, and denizens were responsible for 83 per cent of the exports. If Hanseatic exports could be measured, the total figure would doubtless be a little higher and the denizen share of it a little lower; but that English merchants were principally responsible for a renewed expansion of English cloth exports after the doldrums of the thirteenth century seems certain.[89]

English merchants, of course, were engaged in other trades besides those in wine and wool and cloth. Yarmouth and Southampton merchants traded with Normany; Londoners and others imported salt from Poitou, although normally salt exports exceeded imports. It is true, on the other hand, that English merchants were only very ocasionally mentioned in Italy, and the number of them visiting Spain increased markedly only after 1350.[90] They were perhaps a little more prominent in northern waters, for King's Lynn merchants took grain to Norway and brought back fish; a Newcastle ship which took on a cargo of herrings and other merchandise was plundered at Copenhagen in 1329; and Yarmouth and Norwich merchants in 1333 loaded a Yarmouth ship with cloth and other goods, intending to take them to Hamburg. Englishmen were

---

[87] Chorley, 'English cloth exports in the thirteenth and early fourteenth centuries', pp. 5–9.
[88] Carus-Wilson, *MMV*, p. 244 note.
[89] *Ibid.*, pp. 245–7; Carus-Wilson and Coleman, *England's Export Trade*, pp. 75–6.
[90] *CCR*, 1327–30, pp. 175, 203–4, 298; *Rot. Parl.*, II, p. 82; A.R. Bridbury, *England and the Salt Trade in the Later Middle Ages*, pp. 29–31, 45–6; W.R. Childs, *Anglo-Castilian Trade in the Later Middle Ages*, pp. 31–2, 128.

already staking a claim in Hanseatic waters, but as yet they had scarcely established a significant presence there and they had scarcely penetrated the Baltic. The advance of the English during the first half of the fourteenth century, if the Bordeaux wine run is excepted, was achieved above all along the trade routes of the North Sea.[91]

Despite the changes which were taking place in the generation or two before 1349, moreover, there was also a good deal of continuity, and not least in the role of alien merchants in England's commerce. The Italian stake in it owed a good deal to the fact that they continued to act as bankers to the crown and got commercial privileges in return. For a time under Edward II Antonio Pessagno of Genoa assumed that role almost single-handed, but concurrently and subsequently down to the early years of the Hundred Years' War it passed to the Bardi and Peruzzi of Florence. As well as providing financial services these Italians supplied spices, cloth and other goods to the court (Pessagno even providing half the provisions for the English army defeated at Bannockburn); and they continued to engage in the wool and other trades across the North Sea. Some of that wool may have then been sent overland, as Venetian decrees of 1333 and 1356 envisage, from Flanders to Italy; although it is more likely that most of it went to the cloth industries of the Low Countries. On the other hand, English wool undoubtedly reached Italy by other routes. That suggested by Pegolotti was by ship from London to Gascony, and thence by pack-horse to Montpellier and Aigues-Mortes where it was loaded into galleys for Italy.[92] Some wool also went directly to Italy via the Straits of Gibraltar, a sea route apparently pioneered by the Genoese who sent ships regularly to Flanders from 1298. These ships soon began to call at English ports: it was probably a Genoese galley that brought spices to London in 1303, and Genoese ships and merchants (including Antonio Pessagno as early as 1306–7) exported wool from England. In 1324 a quite incidental notice refers to eleven Genoese galleys, loaded with 4,000 sacks of wool, putting into Falmouth harbour.[93] By the 1330s, moreover, Venice also sent eight

[91] *CCR*, 1327–30, p. 537; 1333–7, pp. 125, 667; Lloyd, *England and the German Hanse*, pp. 48–9.

[92] N. Fryde, 'Antonio Pessagno of Genoa, king's merchant of Edward II of England', *Studi in memoria di Frederigo Melis*, pp. 159–78; E.B. and M.M. Fryde, in *CEcH*, III, pp. 458–9; *CCR*, 1327–30, p. 120; *Calendar of State Papers (Venetian)*, I, nos. 23, 32; R.S. Lopez and I.W. Raymond, eds, *Medieval Trade in the Mediterranean World*, New York, 1955, pp. 252–4.

[93] W. Stubbs, ed., *Chronicles of the Reigns of Edward I and Edward II*, I, p. 130; L.F. Salzman, *English Trade in the Middle Ages*, p. 418; P. Chaplais, ed., *The War of St Sardos (1323–1325)*, Camden 3rd ser. LXXXVII, nos. 45–6; and see generally Fryde, *Studies*, chapt. XIV, pp. 292–303.

or nine galleys a year to Flanders, and some Venetians came to England; although one ship which brought sugar to England, and then loaded a cargo of wool at Boston, apparently did so with the intention of taking it to Flanders. Anglo-Venetian relations, on the other hand, were not always smooth. A visit by Venice's 'Flanders galleys' to Southampton in 1319 led to an anti-Italian riot there, and Edward III's attempt to secure naval assistance from Venice was conspicuously unsuccessful. Regular voyages to England by Venetian galleys, in fact, had to await the 1390s.[94]

The closest commercial relations in the second quarter of the fourteenth century, in any case, seem to have been with the Florentines. The Bardi and the Peruzzi, the principal royal bankers, exported substantial quantities of English tin to Italy via Bruges, and they shipped wool both to the Low Countries and to Italy by sea, getting a licence in 1339 to export 8,000 sacks of wool to Italy and in fact exporting at least 7,365 sacks for which they had to round up Castilian, Catalan and Majorcan vessels as transport. That they were able to do so points to the continuing trade links between England and the lands of the western Mediterranean, to which there is also testimony in notices of 'drogges' 'spicerie'and Seville olive oil brought to England by merchants of Montpellier and Spain.[95] Down to the early 1340s, however, the Italians were the dominant group of Mediterranean merchants active in England; and, if the range and value of the exotic commodities they brought to this country were much less than they would be in the fifteenth century, their involvement in England's overseas trade was by no means restricted to Anglo-Mediterranean exchanges.[96] In the 1340s, on the other hand, the bankruptcy of the Bardi and Peruzzi, Genoese flirtations with France, and Venetian hesitation at undertaking the Flanders run in war-time combined to end for the time being, and in certain respects definitively, Italian participation in the traditional commerce across the North Sea. Maritime contacts between Italy and north-western Europe continued, although not without some interruptions; but in this branch of overseas trade English merchants played little part.

[94] F.C. Lane, *Venice and History*, Baltimore, 1973, pp. 209, 213; *Calendar of State Papers (Venetian)*, I, no. 11; A.A. Ruddock, *Italian Merchants and Shipping in Southampton*, pp. 24–9, 39–41.

[95] *Ibid.*, pp. 29–32; Hatcher, *English Tin Production and Trade*, pp. 93–6; *CCR, 1327–30*, pp. 113–14; Thomas, ed., *Cal. Plea and Memoranda Rolls of London*, I, p. 149.

[96] On the relatively low value of Italian imports in the period 1322–44, cf. G.A. Holmes, 'Florentine merchants in England, 1346–1436', *EcHR*, 2nd ser. XIII (1960), p. 199.

In the meantime much of the basic character of England's trade with the German north remained unchanged, both the move of Hanseatic merchants into large-scale wool exporting from England in the early part of the century, and that of Tidemann Limberg of Dortmund into the provision of financial services to the crown in the 1340s, proving to be short-lived. Among the Hanseatic merchants trading to England, on the other hand, Eastlanders from the north German ports continued to increase in importance and, consequently, so did imports of Baltic products (grain, timber, wax, furs and fish from the northern seas, commodities which accounted for two-thirds by value of the cargoes coming into King's Lynn in 1324–25).[97] Return shipments by German merchants still included some wool for the Low Countries, grain and other food for the Scandinavian countries, salt for the Baltic fisheries, and perhaps to a growing extent English woollens and worsteds. In this trade English merchants played only a restricted role, and this at a time when the rights and privileges of Hanseatic traders in England were being consolidated. The court, which the alderman of the German Hanse was holding in London as early as 1282, was asserted in 1302 to be entitled to entertain all pleas between German merchants and Englishmen; and in 1309 it was claimed that half of each jury in cases which involved German merchants should consist of their countrymen. There was, of course, much resistance to such claims, especially on the part of the Londoners; but the competence of the alderman of the Hanse to settle in his court pleas of debt and contract between Germans in London, and to reclaim from the city courts pleas in which Germans were involved, were liberties formally asserted before the king's justices in 1321.[98]

The Hansards, at the same time, were laying claim to fiscal privileges. In 1317, when the duties imposed on alien commerce in 1303 were temporarily in abeyance, they secured a promise that 'the king and his heirs will not place any new undue custom on their goods and merchandise, saving to the king and his heirs their old prises'. The Hansards made the most of that promise. When the 1303 duties were reimposed in 1322, they argued that they should be exempt from them; and, although their argument did not prevail initially, in

---

[97] Dollinger, *La Hanse*, pp. 212–14; Gras, *Early English Customs System*, pp. 374–92.

[98] Riley, ed., *Liber Albus*, pp. 485–8; Höhlbaum *et al.*, eds, *Hansisches Urkundenbuch*, I, no. 902; II, nos. 27, 375; Thomas, ed., *Cal. Early Mayor's Court Rolls*, p. 140; K. Kunze, ed., *Hanseakten aus England*, no. 40; *PQW*, p. 455; H.M. Cam, ed., *Eyre of London, 14 Edward II*, II, p. 184.

the 1340s they secured exemption both from the export duties on cloth imposed by Edward I in 1303 and from those imposed by Edward III in 1347. By the middle of the fourteenth century, therefore, the Hansards had established important concessionary rights in England, and especially in London, and fiscal liberties, especially in respect of cloth exports, which were of significant help to them in playing the important part they did in English commerce during the late middle ages and into the sixteenth century.[99]

3. THE RISE OF AN ENGLISH MERCHANT CLASS

(a) Merchants

Merchants from other lands occupied a large place in England's overseas trade between the eleventh and the fourteenth centuries, and continued to do so for long after 1349; but the century or so before the Black Death was also a vital period in the evolution of a native merchant class. There had, of course, as near as makes no matter, always been merchants, but the word or its equivalents were used to describe men engaged in economic activities which differed greatly in scale and character. *Mercatores* might be anything from overseas adventurers to petty dealers in the most local of markets. Ælfric's merchant, or the Anglo-Saxon merchant who throve to thegn-right, or St Godric before he abandoned commerce for a hermitage, were men who crossed the sea and took their profit from the international trade of their day. On the other hand, the Canterbury merchant, 'whom in our tongue we call a monger', conveyed to a thegn by King Æthelwulf in 839, was obviously a dependant and, as a trader, his activities are likely to have been of the same restricted sort as those of many village and even town *mercatores* and hucksters later. Nor was trading restricted to *mercatores*. In the 1230s some ecclesiastical landlords arranged for the export of wool grown on their lands; in 1276 the constable of Bolingbroke was said to have bought up wool *per patriam* which he sold for export through Wainfleet; and various abbeys, Cistercian abbeys especially, in like manner acted as 'middlemen between exporters and small farmers'.[100]

[99] *Calendar of Charter Rolls*, 6 vols, 1903-27, III, p. 371; *Rot. Parl.*, II, pp. 46–7; Lloyd, *England and the German Hanse*, pp. 26–32.
[100] W.J. Urry, *Canterbury under the Angevin Kings*, pp. 105, 148; *Pat. R.*, 1216–25, pp. 449, 451, 471; *Rot. Hundr.*, I, pp. 115, 304, 390; E.E. Power, *The Wool Trade in Medieval English History*, pp. 44–5.

Dabbling in trade from time to time, however, or dealing in a modest range of basic commodities in local markets, did not make a man a merchant in any true sense or provide the basis for the development of a 'community' or class of merchants playing a distinctive economic role. By the reign of Edward III, on the other hand, the word merchant was increasingly reserved for men trading regularly on a significant scale as wholesalers rather than, or in addition to, as retailers. Further, the making of a merchant class demanded that the interests of those who composed it should transcend the parochial. Initially the majority of *mercatores* were rooted in a particular town or village, finding in that centre and its hinterland supplies of, and customers for, the goods in which they traded. Town merchants, too, had a natural desire to become the sole intermediaries between their town and its hinterland, on the one hand, and the wider world on the other. This was a basic strand in the policies of early medieval towns, allowing little room for a community of interests between town merchants and their counterparts in other places. Merchants of any particular town, therefore, sought their natural allies in other groups within their own community and neighbourhood: municipal associations dominated by traders, exemplified by the *gilda mercatoria*, are characteristic of this phase in the evolution of a merchant class. By the fourteenth century, on the other hand, while towns continued to look jealously upon interlopers (whether denizens or aliens) into what they regarded as their own market areas, there was also a growing awareness of an 'estate of merchants' to which substantial traders belonged, whatever their local ties. That estate, moreover, was capable of being represented and taking corporate action when individuals of different communities were brought together and reached decisions on behalf of 'the community of merchants of the realm'.[101]

Details about individuals also indicate the changes which were taking place. William Acastre, for instance, a York merchant active in the 1330s and 1340s, was mainly associated with other York men and much of his trade was in Yorkshire wool exported through Hull. Over and above, however, he helped to finance the Londoners, Walter Chiriton and his fellows, in their management of the king's financial affairs in the late 1340s, he figures repeatedly in agreements concluded in London, in 1347 he got a licence to export 1,500 sacks of wool through Boston and earlier he had been a

---

[101] E.g. *CCR*, 1341–43, p. 553 (July 1342).

member of a syndicate buying wool in Lancashire as well as in Yorkshire. He was in no way an outstanding merchant, but clearly his range of action was more than a local one. It was appropriate, therefore, that in March 1340 he should be summoned to an assembly, reputedly of 'all the great merchants of England', to speak with the king in person.[102]

(b)   The early stages

The surviving evidence tells us relatively little about the origins of an 'estate of merchants', for urban records are biased towards the recording of titles to property and royal concern about minting probably gives moneyers an undue prominence. The Canterbury sources, for instance, suggest that there was a twelfth-century elite 'dwelling in stone houses' and including many moneyers and goldsmiths; and in London, too, there were moneyers among the early aldermen and the sources suggest that the leading citizens were more concerned with real property than with trade.[103] Yet townsmen, or some of them, were traders even though it is seldom possible to learn much about them as individuals. Burgess-merchants of Newcastle upon Tyne, for example, had the sole right in Henry I's reign to buy wool and hides in the town or its hinterland: at Lincoln early in Henry II's reign the retail trade in cloth was restricted to members of the city's gild merchant; and at Bristol late in the same reign foreign merchants could only buy wool, hides and grain from burgesses. These rules possibly suggest that the main concern of twelfth-century English merchants was the inland trade in their own neighbourhood; but some of them also ventured overseas, for the men of Oxford and the Cinque Ports were exempted from tolls throughout England and Normandy, an exemption also extending in the case of the citizens of York to Aquitaine, Anjou and Poitou.[104] By the early thirteenth century there are occasional records of individuals, like Adam Flur of York, James le Flemyng of Southampton, and Richard *Crassus* and other Londoners exporting wool and sometimes hides and cheese, and as we have seen there

[102] Fryde, *Studies*, chapt. XI, pp. 5, 17; *CPR*, 1340–43, p. 435; *Report from the Lords' Committees ... touching the Dignity of a Peer*, Appendix. to 1st Report, no. 1, part 2, p. 514; *Rot. Parl.*, II, p. 108; G. Unwin, ed., *Finance and Trade under Edward III*, p. 202.
[103] Urry, *Canterbury under the Angevin Kings*, pp. 172, 174–6; Reynolds, *Introduction*, p. 78; Brooke and Keir, *London, 800–1216*, pp. 41, 210–11.
[104] *BBC, 1042–1216*, pp. 180–90, 209–14.

were Londoners resident and trading in Genoa. Merchant adventurers may not have been very numerous at this time, but that they existed there can be no doubt.[105]

The development of a body of English merchants is somewhat clearer during the thirteenth century, partly because the evidence becomes fuller, but also because this was an age of economic expansion, of intensified commercial relationships between the countries of western Europe, and probably also of more sophisticated consumption habits, especially on the part of the upper and middling ranges of English society. It was a time when the fortunes of English merchants depended, at least in part, upon the role they played in the wool export trade, the import and export of cloth, and the import of wine and other luxuries. On the other hand, there were also profits to be made from bulking wool for sale at fairs or in the ports, and from the distributive trades in wine, fine textiles, spices and other exotic consumer goods. It is possible, indeed, that in the thirteenth century this internal trade was the prime source of English mercantile wealth, a fact which would help to explain the early prominence of rich merchants in London. Londoners, after all, had the double advantage of having the court market, as well as a large city, on their doorsteps. It has been suggested that 'great merchants and royal purveyors' are first discernible there in significant numbers under Richard I and John, and that their subsequent fortunes owed much to Henry III's taste for fine things and good living. Drapers, vintners, pepperers, mercers and goldsmiths were prominent in London life throughout the century. They were not necessarily themselves importers, but at least they engaged in the lucrative work of distributing what importers brought in. Edward I transferred much of the court patronage to Italians and Gascons, but this shift lasted only for a generation or two, and Londoners never ceased to profit from being purveyors to the court.[106]

The Londoners who played that part were characteristically versatile. In the 1250s, for instance, Adam de Basing provided for Henry III gold-wrought altar cloths, copes of violet, orphreys and red samite, tunics and dalmatics and such like things of beauty; but he also supplied wax from Rouen, he was involved in the grain and hides trade with Ireland, he provided the silver dishes the queen gave to Simon de Montfort in 1242, and he bought grain from

---

[105] *Pat. R.*, 1216–25, pp. 461, 463, 472; *RLC*, II, p. 16; Reynolds, *Introduction*, p. 77.
[106] S. Reynolds, 'The rulers of London in the twelfth century', *History*, LVII (1972), pp. 349–50; Williams, *Medieval London*, pp. 59–73.

Hertfordshire during the 1258 dearth. The scale of his business cannot be determined, but some of the bills he presented to the king were considerable – one for nearly £300 in 1251 and another for over £200 in 1252, for example.[107] The interests of Londoners, too, often spilled over into the export trades. Royal favour secured for Adam de Basing all the wool of the bishop of Winchester's estate in 1244; and Londoners, including some resident aliens, got licences which may have enabled them to handle a ninth of England's wool exports in 1271–74, and a third of the wool exported by denizens. While English merchants at this time were still a minority interest in the wool trade, Londoners were clearly well ahead of exporters from any other English town. The evidence also shows that, while many London merchants engaged in the wool trade from time to time, often in only a modest way, a few of them were deeply committed to it. Adam de Basing's nephew, Thomas, in 1273 exported 124 sacks of wool (although he had a licence for 204 sacks), Wolmar of Essex exported 151$\frac{1}{2}$ sacks, and William Box, a member of another well known city dynasty, exported 303 sacks.[108]

As well as Londoners, however, provincial merchants from a wide range of towns got licences to export some two-thirds of the wool authorized to be sent overseas by Englishmen in 1273. The main provincial towns appear to have been Winchester, Southampton, Andover and Sandwich in the south, Bristol and Shrewsbury in the west, Dunstable in the home counties, and King's Lynn and Newcastle in the east. Some of the business done by English exporters at this time, of course, may represent a move into the vacuum created by a ban on Flemings trading in England, but what is significant is that there were provincial merchants capable of exploiting this opportunity, some of them on a scale which suggests that they were not newcomers to the trade. Bernard de Hampton of Southampton in partnership with John le Long of Bristol got a licence to export 200 sacks of wool in 1273; William Fisher and John Duraunt of Dunstable, jointly and severally, had licences for 720 sacks (and in fact exported 734); and seven Shrewsbury merchants shipped 493$\frac{1}{2}$ sacks. One of these Shrewsbury merchants was Nicholas of Ludlow, and he was certainly not without experience, for 330 sacks of his wool, worth over £1,800, had been confiscated in Flanders in 1270. It was not, therefore, inappropriate that Nicholas

---

[107] *Ibid.*, pp. 72–3, 323–4; *CLR*, 1251–60, pp. 1, 39.
[108] The 1273 licences are in *CPR*, 1272–81, pp. 13–39; and see Lloyd, *The English Wool Trade*, pp. 50–9.

should be chosen, together with Thomas de Basing of London, to go to Flanders in 1276 to negotiate for money owed to English merchants.[109] Men like these, moreover, had wide-ranging commercial contacts. The debtors of Nicholas of Ludlow's son Lawrence, for instance, included in 1289–93 Bruern abbey in Oxfordshire, Adam de Elmerugge in Worcestershire, Edmund Mortimer in Shropshire, Roger Mortimer in Shropshire and Staffordshire, and the earl of Arundel. Not every debt, of course, necessarily had a commercial origin; but perhaps enough of them had in Lawrence of Ludlow's case to have made it reasonable to suppose that he had sufficient influence with England's wool merchants to win their agreement to Edward I's demand for higher export duties in 1294.[110]

Provincial merchants, however, like their London contemporaries, were seldom specialists. Richard de la Haye and Thomas Carliol of Newcastle, for instance, who got licences to export wool in 1273, also dealt in cloth (possibly imported); and Simon Draper of Winchester, who exported 60 sacks of wool bought from the bishop's estate in 1273, was a cloth merchant and a wine merchant besides.[111] Peter Appleby of York, without in any way being an outstanding figure, had at least as many interests. As well as exporting wool through Hull, he sold cloth to Robert Greystoke on credit and furs to Sir William Barton of Oswaldkirk, and the cargo of a ship of his coming into the Tyne included wine.[112] Some provincial merchants, too, were purveyors to the court. Henry III bought cloth from York merchants in London and at Boston and St Ives fairs; William Brand and Henry Gupil of Lincoln supplied him with scarlets and other fabrics; and Oxford merchants sold cloth for his use at divers fairs. Over and above a number of Oxford notables provided wine for the court, and Bristol and Southampton importers were frequently called upon to supplement the stocks of wine the king obtained in London.[113] The versatility of the provincial merchants who served these varied markets in the later part of the thirteenth century was not something totally novel. In the early decades of the century Hugh Selby of York had shipped wool to Flanders and imported

[109] *Ibid.*, pp. 51–6.
[110] *Ibid.*, p. 76; *CCR*, 1288–96, pp. 41–2, 111, 119–20, 139, 316.
[111] W. Page, ed., *Three Early Assize Rolls for Northumberland*, p. 394; Lloyd, *The English Wool Trade*, p. 53; Keene, *Survey*, II, p. 1218.
[112] *Catalogue of Ancient Deeds*, IV, no. A6264; PRO JI 1/1055, m. 45d; PRO E 122/55/2; *Rot. Parl.*, I, p. 28.
[113] *Close R.*, 1237–42, p. 203; 1251–53, pp. 146, 272; 1253–54, p. 57; 1254–56, pp. 269, 278; *CLR*, 1245–51, p. 321; 1251–60, pp. 50, 220, 366, 388–9, 438; 1260–67, pp. 146, 206, 221, 280; 1267–72, no. 1363; PRO E 101/350/4, C 47/3/29.

wine from Anjou (which on occasion he sold to Henry III); and his contemporary, Walter le Flemyng of Southampton, traded in wine and wool and salt and cloth, and had commercial ties with Flanders, Anjou, Poitou and Gascony.[114] Versatility, however, was a still more notable characteristic of the Londoners, and by no means least of the Cahorsin immigrant who became an alderman of London, William Servat. He was exporting wool as early as 1273 and as late as 1306, and he was a member of the syndicate which contracted to buy Pipewell abbey's wool for a term of thirteen years. He was also a ship-owner; he provided many things for the king's household, including wax, wine, cloth and spices, for some of which he sent his servant to Provence; he supplied Londoners with spices and silks and, at the other end of the kingdom, the monks of Durham with wine and sugar (as well as buying some of their wool).[115]

What became increasingly evident during the thirteenth century was the existence of English merchants who, whether or not they traded overseas (as many of them did), ranged far beyond their home neighbourhoods in the business they did. William Servat and Peter Appleby obviously did so; and so did many London wool merchants around 1300, when Reginald Thunderle bought Westminster abbey's Gloucestershire wool, Martin Box the Sussex wool of the earl of Warenne, and William Combemartin Bardney abbey's Lincolnshire wool. Combemartin, indeed, in the year beginnning at Michaelmas 1312, exported 438 sacks of wool, worth perhaps £2,750; and his commercial range was almost national in its scope. He shipped wool from Boston and Southampton as well as from London; he was the Londoners' warden at Boston fair; and the queen rewarded him for his financial services with a grant of the wardship of a Somerset heir. The horizons even of provincial merchants, moreover, were expanding. William Doncaster of Chester in the early fourteenth century, for instance, leased lead mines in North Wales and marketed the lead from them, supplied the king with horseshoes, sent to Gascony for wine and to Ireland for grain, and exported wool through Ipswich.[116]

[114] Miller, 'Rulers of thirteenth-century towns', p. 134; Platt, *Medieval Southampton*, pp. 70–1, 240.
[115] Arens, 'Wilhelm Servat von Cahors', *passim*; *CPR*, 1272–81, p. 37; 1301–7, p. 538; *CCR*, 1288–96, pp. 192–5; 1302–7, pp. 3, 8–9; *Cal. Docs. Scot.*, II, no. 453; *Calendar of Chancery Warrants*, I, p. 181; *CLB A*, pp. 31, 37; Morimoto, *Monastic Economy and Medieval Markets*, pp. 218, 371.
[116] B.F.Harvey, ed., *Documents Illustrating the Rule of Walter de Wenlok, Abbot of Westminster*, pp. 64–5; *CLB B*, p. 58; Lloyd, *The English Wool Trade*, pp. 130–3; Williams, *Medieval London*, p. 151; *CCR*, 1302–7, p. 322; *CPR*, 1301–7, p. 372; H.J. Hewitt, *Cheshire under the Three Edwards*, pp. 38–9, 46–7, 73.

As the range of trading became longer collaboration between merchants of different places became more common, and some lesser traders were drawn into a measure of participation in long-range trade. This is clearest in the thirteenth-century wool trade, and most particularly in the role of the Londoners in it. The capital's immediate hinterland was not a region of large sheep flocks producing high-quality wool. London wool merchants, therefore, had to seek sources of supply up-country and establish a network of contacts with middleman suppliers in the provinces. In the 1270s James de Troys of London exported wool from Yarmouth and King's Lynn, James Dorkyng exported from Essex, another Londoner bought wool in Rutland and sold it at Boston, and various others (including Thomas de Basing) dealt in Lincolnshire wool. Conversely, provincial merchants brought wool to London for sale or export, including William Fisher and John Duraunt of Dunstable, Nicholas of Ludlow and his sons from Shrewsbury, John de Kyndecote from Leicester, and others from Baldock, Watford, Brackley, Oxford, Ludlow and Winchester. Even some Lincolnshire wool reached St Omer via London, and Northampton merchants exported to Rouen through London as well as through Southampton.[117]

A wide-ranging provincial trade was also evident which did not necessarily have London connections. An Andover merchant in the 1270s, in partnership with a Dorchester man, bought wool for export at, among other places, Tewkesbury in Gloucestershire, Burford and Faringdon in Oxfordshire, Silchester in Hampshire, and Salisbury and Lacock in Wiltshire; the Shrewsbury merchant, Nicholas of Ludlow, bought Gloucestershire wool at Lechlade for export through Southampton, and also purchased large quantities of Lincolnshire and Northamptonshire wool; and Newcastle merchants bought wool in the Richmond and Whitby districts of north Yorkshire. Thomas Carliol of Newcastle collaborated as a wool exporter not only with some of his fellow-citizens, but also with Thomas de Basing of London. Consortia such as these, transcending the limits of locality, together with the increasingly dense network of contacts between merchants within regions, represent a significant stage in the evolution of an English merchant class.[118]

[117] *CCR*, 1272–79, p. 86; *Rot. Hundr.*, i, pp. 162, 371, 385, 394, 402, 404–23; ii, pp. 2, 15, 52.
[118] *Ibid.*, i, pp. 132–3, 177, 385; ii, p. 13; *CPR*, 1272–81, pp. 32–3; Lloyd, *The English Wool Trade*, p. 53.

(c)   The demands of the crown and the evolution of an estate of merchants, 1275–1336

The limitations of English commercial enterprise in the thirteenth century, all the same, need constantly to be kept in mind. Denizens are quite likely to have shipped less wool than Flemings under Henry III; English merchants responded relatively slowly to opportunities presented by the contraction of Flemish trading after 1270; and under Edward I, if native merchants shipped rather more of England's wool, in overseas trade generally they may have lost some ground to Italians, Gascons and eventually Germans.[119] Nevertheless, in the course of the century and whoever the carriers may have been, England's overseas and inland trades had expanded notably; and by the opening decades of the fourteenth century the economic foundations existed for a definitive emergence of an English merchant class. The boom in wool exports with which that century began was apparently English led; and even when the level of wool exports fell from that high point the English share of them was permanently increased. Native merchants, too, dominated a growing export trade in English textiles, they became the principal importers of Gascon wine, and they may also have increased their stake in some other branches of commerce.

The wool trade provides much evidence of this denizen advance. To begin with, the scale of the operations undertaken by individuals was growing. William Combemartin's export of 438 sacks of wool in the year 1312–13 was nearly half as much again as any Londoner exported in 1273. Nor was large-scale exporting exclusive to Londoners. Over the period 1298–1315 three Beverley and one Pontefract merchant each exported through Hull more than 1,000 sacks of wool; members of the Chesterton family exported on a comparable scale through Boston; and, even at Newcastle, Richard Embleton exported 133 sacks in 1308 alone (by comparison, the export licences received by the three largest Newcastle exporters in 1273 had been for fourteen sacks between them). Denizen shipments also increased in aggregate. In 1273 English merchants were authorized to export 8,100 sacks, worth perhaps £50,000; but their annual exports in 1331–35 averaged 24,000 sacks, and the 10,700 sacks they delivered to Dordrecht in 1337–38 were valued at £114,000.[120]

---

[119] *Ibid.*, pp. 40–59; Williams, *Medieval London*, pp. 106–48.
[120] Williams, *Medieval London*, p. 151; Lloyd, *The English Wool Trade*, pp. 51, 57–8, 129, 131, 136, 149; E.B. Fryde, *William de la Pole*, pp. 79, 84–5.

An indication of the growing resources of which English merchants disposed is afforded by the fact that a group of them, with Londoners prominent, 'committed themselves to the tricky business of loan finance' on a hitherto unprecedented scale. The debtors of the London draper, John Pulteney, for example, were to be found in almost every county in southern and midland England; and by 1338 the king, too, owed him £1,106 for wool seized at Dordrecht, £200 for a cash loan and £221 for wine supplied on credit.[121] Increasingly, indeed, they were called upon to render commercial or financial services to the king. They were asked more and more frequently, for example, to extend their traditional role of supplying the court to provisioning new-style armies and navies mobilized for the Scottish and French wars. In York all sorts of men turned their hand to this task, some of whom found the opportunity sufficiently profitable to establish their families among the fourteenth-century rulers of the city. In Newcastle, too, Richard Embleton sent his ships and servants overseas to get victuals for the town garrison on a number of occasions; and, somewhat later, the Melchebourne brothers of King's Lynn, two of Edward III's financiers in the 1340s, had fitted out ships for the king during the preceding decade, delivered 2,000 quarters of wheat and 1,000 quarters of oats costing some £950 to Berwick in 1336, and had requisitioned supplies for the fleet in 1341. Their experience in large-scale operations was gained largely in the crown's service.[122]

The utility of merchants to the crown, however, went much further than such services. Their trade was also exploited to the king's advantage; and to this end they had to be consulted or persuaded from time to time, thus thrusting something like a national organization upon them. The point of departure was the grant by the magnates of the realm of export duties on wool, woolfells and hides 'at the request of the communities of merchants of all England', a request which the borough representatives summoned to this 'general parliament' in 1275 may have been cajoled into making.[123] The 'ancient custom' thus established in 1275 was soon augmented. Alien merchants were persuaded to accept additional duties on both exports and imports in 1303, cloth exports by both

---

[121] *CPR*, 1338–40, p. 125; *CCR*, 1337–39, p. 364; PRO C 135/95/11.
[122] PRO E 122/55/5–6, 10, 22; PRO JI 1/1117, m. 8; *VCH City of York*, p. 100; *CPR*, 1313–17, pp. 281, 542; 1321–24, pp. 207, 231; 1330–34, p. 32; 1340–43, p. 252; *CCR*, 1337–39, pp. 196, 209.
[123] Gras, *Early English Customs System*, pp. 223–4.

aliens and denizens were subjected to duties in 1347, and in every financial crisis between 1294 and 1349 the rates of duty fixed in 1275 were augmented by 'evil imposts' (*maltotes*). Quite apart from these charges, the wool trade and wool traders were exploited in a diversity of ways. Wool was requisitioned for the king, taxes were levied in wool, government wool-trading ventures were undertaken, and the resources of wool merchants were raided for loans and advances. Such expedients made periodic consultations with merchants a necessity.

Most of the methods of exploiting trade and traders for the king's benefit were devised initially by Edward I. When war broke out with France in 1294, he may have intended originally to requisition the kingdom's wool for a state trading venture, but a consortium of merchants headed by Lawrence of Ludlow persuaded him to abandon that plan in exchange for their agreement to steeply increased customs duties on wool exports, fixed eventually at six times the 1275 level, and also an undertaking that the merchants, to meet the king's expenses overseas, would lend him a part of their trading profits. Higher duties, the *maltote*, were the principal advantage which the king got from this bargain, for they raised the average annual revenue from the wool custom from £11,600 in 1290–94 to about £33,000 in 1294–97. Edward also tried to persuade merchants to direct their trade to a fixed overseas market (first Dordrecht, then Antwerp, and finally Bruges), both to reward allies and to make it easier for him to manage and profit from commercial operations. In 1297, however, Edward reverted to plans for requisitioning wool for state trading ventures, only for these to bring to a head a revolt by the English baronage, which brought to an abrupt and unsuccessful end wool exporting by the state and also, for the time being, swept away the *maltote*.[124]

It was a further consequence of the baronial revolt of 1297 that the king's freedom to levy direct taxes was curtailed, making him all the more likely in the future to look to taxes on trade for additional revenue. In 1303 Edward I got alien merchants to accept higher customs both on their imports and exports; and then he convoked an assembly of merchants from 42 English towns, alleging somewhat disingenuously his understanding that denizens, too, were willing to

---

[124] Lloyd, *The English Wool Trade*, pp. 16–17, 39–40, 62, 78–9, 91; E. Miller, 'War, taxation and the English economy in the late thirteenth and early fourteenth centuries', in J.M. Winter, ed., *War and Economic Development*, p. 14 (where the revenue from the *maltote* is somewhat overestimated); W.M. Ormrod, 'The crown and the English economy, 1290–1348', in B.M.S. Campbell, ed., *Before the Black Death*, pp. 170–3.

grant him these enhanced duties. About many of the men who gathered at York in response to the king's summons not a great deal is known. Clearly, however, some of them were men of influence in their own communities: John Spicer served as mayor of York (as his son did after him); Richard Spicer was the son of one mayor of York and married the widow of another; Alexander fitzMartin was to serve as mayor of Lincoln; and John Taverner served as mayor of Bristol at least three times. There were also experienced businessmen among those who came to York: Peter Graper and Richard Embleton of Newcastle, wool merchants on some scale; Ralph Gegg, a Scarborough merchant who commissioned North Sea fishing boats; and Stephen Stanham of Lincoln who helped to provision the army in Flanders in 1297 and the court during the Lincoln parliament in 1303, and who also delivered lampreys to Edward I at Stirling in 1304. If there was a good deal of diversity in the composition of this assembly, its decision was clear and apparently unanimous: it in no way assented to 'an increase in the *maltote*'.[125]

The gathering at York in 1303 indicates that an English 'estate of merchants' was taking shape, that this 'estate' could be consulted through its representatives, and that its acquiescence was not something which could be taken for granted. Contemporaneously, 'the merchants of the realm of England' were establishing an organization on the other side of the North Sea which had sufficient corporate cohesion to secure commercial privileges from the Duke of Brabant in 1305 and to have an elected head described as their mayor, and which made Antwerp a preferential market, especially for English wool. An overseas staple market, however, became compulsory in 1313, when strained relations between England and Flanders resulted in all wool exports being directed to St Omer, outside Flemish territory. The management of this St Omer market was vested in the 'mayor of the merchants of our realm', who was soon to be known as the 'mayor of the wool staple'. The first holder of that office was yet again a Shrewsbury man, Richard de Stury.[126] These staple arrangements persisted almost to the end of Edward II's reign, although the location of the staple market varied from time to time. Naturally they provoked much debate in merchant assemblies called

---

[125] F. Palgrave, ed., *Parliamentary Writs*, I, pp. 134–5; for Gegg, *CCR*, 1302–7, pp. 46–7; and for Stanham, Hill, *Medieval Lincoln*, pp. 239, 323; W.S. Thomson, ed., *A Lincolnshire Assize Roll for 1298*, pp. 188, 261; *Cal. Docs. Scot.*, II, no. 1568.
[126] Lloyd, *The English Wool Trade*, pp. 102–7; T.F. Tout, *The Place of Edward II in English History*, pp. 220–3.

to regulate them; for many foreign merchants were strongly opposed to overseas staple markets (the Italians in 1320 even appealing to Magna Carta's prohibition of restraints on the freedom of trade), but so were many English 'burgesses, merchants and others who principally trade within our kingdom and not in foreign parts'.[127] These interests favoured home staples (i.e. designated English markets to which all wool should be brought for sale and to which all potential exporters would have access), to which even the Londoners had been converted by 1326. Debate continued, however, until 1328 when parliament abolished all staples. Home staples were briefly revived in 1333–34, but then, in 1336, the outbreak of war with France radically transformed the conditions under which trade was conducted.

The first third of the fourteenth century, then, saw a significant stage in the evolution of an English merchant class. English merchants won a growing share of the country's overseas trade, enlarging their resources in the process; and they showed themselves capable of devising forms of organization enabling them to pursue more effectively their common interests. Of course the king used the associations they established to his own advantage; but that did not prevent merchants from acting independently of all authority. In 1332, for instance, some English merchants in Bruges 'ordained a certain staple contrary to the statute lately ordained in parliament'.[128] These particular rebels did not include Londoners or Lincolnshire men; but in their number were some merchants of substance (Thomas Holme and Adam Tyrewit from Beverley, Henry Belton of York, Jordan de Shepeye of Coventry and Robert Inkpenne of Winchester); and the towns represented included, in addition to Beverley, York, Coventry and Winchester, such centres as Norwich, Newark, Northampton, Warwick, Ipswich, St Albans, Salisbury, Ludlow, Abingdon and Berkhamsted. Merchants at home, too, found a common voice in the consultative assemblies of merchants and burgesses which the king convened with increasing regularity. In this respect, the fact that mercantile interests acquired increasingly organized forms was something in part imposed on them from above, but as early as 1303 English merchants had demonstrated that assemblies convoked by authority were not of necessity docile.

---

[127] *Ibid.*, pp. 227, 232.
[128] *CCR*, 1330–33, pp. 466–7 and Lloyd's comments, *The English Wool Trade*, pp. 120–1.

(d) Edward III and the financing of the Hundred Years' War, 1336–49

The fiscal expedients adopted by Edward III in the early years of the war with France were a futher influence in the development of an 'estate of merchants'. Increases in the taxation of trade and the manipulation of the wool trade to the king's financial and diplomatic advantage were central to his policies, and for the first time English merchants were treated as 'a serious source of credit for the crown'.[129] The higher taxes on trade fell mainly upon wool exports, and they were manifestly productive even though they never produced as much revenue as the king felt he needed. Receipts cannot accurately be calculated for most of the years between 1336 and 1349, but the customs revenue, which had averaged about £14,750 a year in the period 1317–36, was £65,000 in the year 1338–39, was 'farmed' for £50,000 in 1345 (and must have yielded more in order to leave some profit for the farmers), and was to average £87,500 in the years 1351–62.[130] The increase in the export duties on wool, in other words, was a permanent one and it was, moreover, only a part of the demands Edward III made of merchants. He sought 'not merely a tax on wool, but a share in the profits from its sale, together with the anticipation of both by loans'. To these ends, he had to 'construct a monopoly of the wool trade with a group of merchants who could make advances to the crown', by using 'prerogative pre-emption, an embargo placed on exports for a specified period, and the restriction of sale to a designated staple'.[131] There were many permutations of these courses of action, but all were basic to the ways in which Edward III sought to raise money for war.

The first outline of these policies emerged from discussions between the king, merchant assemblies and parliament in 1336–37. Export duties were increased and monopoly rights to export wool were conferred on a syndicate of some 99 merchants, together with powers to pre-empt 30,000 sacks of wool to be delivered to Dordrecht in Holland. The king was to get half the profits made by the merchants from the sale of this wool, and also a loan from them of £200,000 repayable from the customs. The managers of the scheme were William de la Pole of Hull and Reginald de Conduit of London, and in addition to the initial members of the syndicate some 200 other merchants were drawn into it, if only as suppliers of

---

[129] Fryde, *Studies*, chapt. XII, p. 18.
[130] Ormrod, 'The crown and the English economy', pp. 171–3.
[131] G.L. Harriss, *King, Parliament and Public Finance in Medieval England*, pp. 435–6.

the principals. In the event, however, only about one-third of the planned 30,000 sacks of wool had reached Dordrecht by the early months of 1338; and, when the merchants refused additional demands upon them, royal agents took over the 10,700 sacks which had arrived, paying for them only a small first instalment of their value. In the meantime Edward continued in his attempts to raise revenue from England's wool: first he sought to raise as a loan the 20,000 sacks of wool the merchants had failed to deliver to Dordrecht, and then a tax in wool from the country at large, but with results which were disappointing. He was compelled, therefore to rely heavily on advances from merchants, including in 1338–39 loans of £126,000 from the Bardi and Peruzzi and of £111,000 from William de la Pole. Not only were the king's debts piling up, but he had to make concessions to merchants to get loans which undermined his plans for managing the wool trade.[132]

The king continued in his endeavours to mobilize stocks of wool for his schemes down to 1342, empanelling merchant syndicates to give them effect and to sell them through a compulsory staple, now at Bruges, to prevent wool being smuggled overseas with a consequent loss of customs revenue. The compulsory staple had the further advantage that exporters were conveniently available at an overseas centre to provide financial services for the king. If these policies seldom produced as much money for the king as was hoped, they did give rise to many dissatisfactions: among wool producers whose prices were driven down by them, and among many merchants whose markets were disrupted to the advantage of a privileged minority of their own number who collaborated with the king in giving effect to them. By 1343 even 'the king's liege merchants' were calling for home staples in order that 'the wool of the kingdom might be of better price'.[133] Such grievances were given an edge by the fact that few of the merchants whose wool had been seized at Dordrecht five years before had yet received much in the way of recompense.

A settlement in the summer of 1343 was designed to assuage these tensions. Edward III managed to secure the continuance of the wool customs at the levels to which they had climbed in war-time; but in order to do so he had to promise that some part of the duties which merchants incurred in future could be offset against what the king owed them for Dordrecht wool. By this time, moreover, since the

---

[132] Fryde, *William de la Pole*, pp. 2, 30–1, 78 note, 79, 122.
[133] *Rot. Parl.*, II, p. 143.

Bardi and Peruzzi had been ruined largely by the demands the king had made upon them and his failure to meet his liabilities, he had to turn more definitively to Englishmen as sources of credit. In 1343 management of the customs was vested in a syndicate of 34 merchants, headed by Thomas Melchbourne of King's Lynn (but with William de la Pole in the background), which undertook to make regular advances to meet the recurrent expenses of government. The arrangement, however, soon took on a more monopolistic appearance. In 1344 21 of the 34 members of the 1343 syndicate withdrew, and it was this smaller group which in 1345 undertook to 'farm' the customs for an annual payment of £50,000. The rump of the Melchbourne syndicate was succeeded by similar monopolistic groups, headed first by John Wesenham of King's Lynn, and then in 1346 by two Londoners, Thomas Swanlond and Walter Chiriton. The rewards the farmers of the customs hoped to secure were any duties which might be collected over and above the fixed payment they owed to the king, together with opportunities to profit from monopolistic privileges as wool exporters which were the fruits of royal favour; but in practice their gains were apt to be offset by the requirement to make substantial loans to the king. The Chiriton syndicate, for example, had to advance at least £55,000 to Edward III between September 1346 and October 1347. Most syndicate members, moreover, were not outstandingly wealthy. To lend on anything like the scale the king demanded, therefore, they had to borrow from others and, to secure these loans, to hand over to their creditors some of the rewards which came to them as bankers to the crown. In this way the circle enjoying access to monopoly privileges was somewhat enlarged; but the principal members of the syndicates were liable to come under pressure simultaneously from the king and from their own creditors, and might well be in no position to satisfy both or even either. It is not altogether surprising that Chiriton and Swanlond, like other crown bankers before them, ended in bankruptcy, and beyond that spent two years in gaol and had to forfeit all their property.[134]

(e)   *'The community of merchants of England', 1336–49*

'The community of merchants of England', as it was called in 1343,[135] had to play many parts and assume many obligations in the

---

[134] Fryde, *Studies*, chapt. X, pp. 1–17; Lloyd, *The English Wool Trade*, pp. 194–7.
[135] *CCR*, 1343–46, p. 217.

early years of the Hundred Years' War, as a few details relating to one individual indicate. The York merchant, Henry Goldbeter, was well enough regarded locally to have served as the city's bailiff in 1333, but in the war years he played a part on a somewhat larger stage. In 1343, Henry and four partners were still owed £1,400 for wool delivered to Dordrecht in 1338; he went on to be a member of syndicates which consisted mainly of York men, but also included Hugh Ulseby of London and Thomas Colle of Shrewsbury, and which undertook to buy up wool for the king in Yorkshire, Lancashire, Westmorland, Cumberland, Lincolnshire, Shropshire and Gloucestershire. If this commission had been fully carried out the cost would have been £32,500 for the wool, with a further £7,750 due for customs when it was exported. One syndicate to which Henry belonged also undertook in 1340 to pay £1,400 on the king's behalf to the duke of Brabant; and in 1341, in association with Ulseby once more together with Walter Prest of Melton Mowbray, he was empowered to export 1,220 sacks of the king's wool through Hull, Boston and London, for which customs charges alone would have been £3,050. The range of Henry's operations, in other words, became national rather than regional, the scale of his business had become larger than that which took him to Dordrecht in 1338, and he was clearly equipped by experience to be a representative of the 'community of merchants of England' when it negotiated with the king in 1343.[136]

The 'community of merchants' in this context, of course, consisted principally of wool merchants, for the good reason that it was the wool trade which Edward III mainly exploited, with the result that wool merchants figure much more prominently in the public records than any other traders. In this respect the records present a picture of the merchant class in the mid-fourteenth century which is distorted and incomplete. While wool was by far England's dominant export commodity, and while most merchants of any substance at least dabbled in the wool trade from time to time, few specialized in it to the exclusion of other exports; and many leading exporters were also engaged in the import trades and in the distribution to the home market of goods produced both in England and overseas. Nevertheless, as a guide to the personnel and the main bases of the English merchant class in the mid-century, there is much to be

---

[136] *CCR*, 1341–43, pp. 257–8; *CPR*, 1338–40, p. 542; 1340–43, pp. 268, 277; *Rot. Parl.*, II, pp. 120–1.

learned from the lists of merchants who received bonds for wool delivered at Dordrecht in 1338, of those who attended the merchant assemblies convoked by Edward III between 1336 and 1342, and of those who were members of the commercial and financial syndicates formed between 1336 and 1349.[137]

The first impression conveyed by this evidence is that wool merchants were markedly less important in the southern counties than they had been in 1273, and that the share of the wool trade for which Londoners and merchants from East Anglia and the home counties were responsible had been much reduced. By contrast, exporters from the North-East, the East Midlands, and probably the West Midlands appear to have gained in importance. Some of these impressions may be, at least in part, misleading. In the southern counties, for example, a good deal of wool had been diverted into direct shipments to Italy in Italian galleys, and the sack of Southampton by the French in 1338 disrupted trade there for some time.[138] On the other hand, only Winchester seems to have merchants exporting wool on some scale, including Robert Inkpenne and Thomas Palmer. Both had Dordrecht bonds for over £500; both ranged widely, for Inkpenne bought wool in Dorset and Palmer in Sussex, Hampshire, Somerset, Wiltshire and Surrey; both acted as English agents for merchants of Bruges and Ypres; and Palmer exported through London, Sandwich and Chichester as well as through Southampton.[139]

Any impression of a loss of ground by London merchants, however, is perhaps much more misleading. There can, in fact, be no question about the dominant position which the Londoners occupied in the English merchant class as a whole. They engaged in almost every line of business, many of them on a very large scale, and they often had a stake in provincial commerce as well as in trade done in the capital. Wool exporting, admittedly, was seldom the primary trade of London merchants, but more Londoners than merchants from any other English town sent wool to Dordrecht in 1338; and while many of their shipments were small, the vintner,

---

[137] For amounts of wool expected to be delivered, and actually delivered, at Dordrecht, Lloyd, *The English Wool Trade*, p. 177; Dordrecht bonds enrolled, *CCR, 1337–9*, pp. 424–35; summonses to assemblies of merchants, *Reports from the Lords' Committees . . . touching the Dignity of a Peer*, Appendix to 1st Report, no. 1, part 2, pp. 458–60, 463–4, 474, 477–8, 491–2, 510–15, 548–50. Members of wool syndicates are entered on the close and patent rolls.

[138] Fryde, *Studies*, chapt. XIV, pp. 301–2; Platt, *Medieval Southampton*, pp. 92–107; *CPR, 1338–40*, p. 288.

[139] *CCR, 1341–43*, p. 259; *CPR, 1340–43*; p. 199; Keene, *Survey*, II, pp. 1271, 1313.

Reginald de Conduit, got a bond for £950 and the pepperer, John de Grantham, one for £584. Various Londoners in the ensuing decade, too, like Hugh de Ulseby and Walter Chiriton, played their part in Edward III's commercial and financial schemes. Others preferred to remain in the background without necessarily being unimportant. The vintner, Henry Picard, for example was only an occasional wool exporter, but he was one of the financiers behind Chiriton and his wealth was still legendary in Tudor times; and the draper John Pulteney, who had grown rich by trading in wool and wine as well as cloth, also avoided the limelight in the 1340s, although he also financed Chiriton and accumulated much property in town and country. Ultimately, he 'lived in a mansion vacated by the Earl of Norfolk, endowed . . . seven priests to sing in a new chapel for his soul, and bequeathed ruby and diamond rings to his friends, the bishop of London and the Earl of Huntingdon'. By that time, however, like Henry Picard he had been knighted and was climbing out of the merchant class.[140]

Outside London, Dunstable merchants seem to have lost their thirteenth-century importance in the wool trade, and there was no more than a scatter of exporters in the small towns of the home counties. Further west the mid-century evidence tells us little about Bristol merchants as wool exporters, although they were clearly active in many other branches of commerce; and in the Cotswolds only a few merchants from Stow-on-the-Wold were even modestly prominent. One reason may be that Londoners controlled the export of much Cotswold wool: certainly two-thirds of the wool sent to Dordrecht by the London vintner, John of Oxford, was bought at Northleach, Burford and Thame.[141] In Norfolk, Suffolk and Essex only Norwich and King's Lynn had many exporters; but the King's Lynn shippers included Thomas Melchbourne and John Wesenham, and among those from Norwich was William But who got a Dordrecht bond for £317, was a representative of the 'community of merchants of England' in negotiations with the king in 1343, and later was one of the merchants who took over the management of the customs.[142]

---

[140] Fryde, *Studies*, chapt. X, pp. 5–6, 15; Unwin, ed., *Finance and Trade under Edward III*, pp. 14, 180, 295–6; Williams, *Medieval London*, p. 151; *CPR*, 1338–40, p. 83; *CCR*, 1346–49, pp. 36, 174, 247; PRO C 135/95/13; R.R. Sharpe, ed., *Cal. of Wills proved . . . in the Court of Husting, London, 1258–1688*, I, pp. 609–11.

[141] *CCR*, 1343–46, p. 152; Fryde, *William de la Pole*, p. 78.

[142] *CCR*, 1339–41, pp. 46–7; 1343–46, pp. 145, 217, 266–7, 622.

It was assumed, on the other hand, that about 70 per cent of the wool that would be sent to Dordrecht in 1337–38 would come from northern England and from the East and West Midlands. Wool exporters, in fact, were not very numerous in the West Midlands, but there were a few of them in most towns of the region and seven Shrewsbury merchants delivered wool to Dordrecht, among them Thomas Colle who got a bond for £469 and continued to export wool on some scale during the ensuing decade.[143] Northern England, and the East Midlands together with Lincolnshire, however, each sent more merchants to Dordrecht than any other English region. There were small numbers of wool merchants from small northern towns like Appleby and Darlington, but 20–30 each from Beverley, York and Newcastle. Most individual shipments in 1337–38 were relatively modest, excepting those of William de la Pole, who virtually monopolized shipments by Hull men and got a Dordrecht bond for £2,240, and of a few York merchants like Henry Belton, who got a bond for £1,668. Some of these northern merchants continued to be involved in Edward III's schemes to manipulate the wool trade, even Richard Galeway and two other Newcastle merchants undertaking to buy up for him 500 sacks of Northumbrian wool. York merchants, however, were by far the most prominent northerners in this connection. Henry Goldbeter, for example, was a central figure in many syndicates which provided finance for the king and got options on wool for export in return; and his kinsman, John Goldbeter, was one of those who provided financial backing for Chiriton as 'farmer' of the customs. John Goldbeter even survived the perils of involvement in Edward III's affairs to become, in 1361, 'governor of the king's merchants in the parts of Flanders'.[144]

The most important group of merchants shipping wool to Dordrecht, on the other hand, were undoubtedly those from Lincolnshire and the East Midlands. The main wool towns were Lincoln, Barton-on-Humber, Boston, Coventry, Newark and Nottingham, but there were also merchants of substance in smaller places like Market Harborough, Stamford and Melton Mowbray. The scale on which many merchants from this region operated is notable. Eight of them got Dordrecht bonds for between £500 and £1,000; Hugh Cokheved of Barton-on-Humber, Jordan de Shepeye of Coventry, and William Amyas and Robert de Bothale of Nottingham each had bonds for between £1,000 and £2,000; and

---

[143] *CCR*, 1343–46, p. 141.
[144] *CCR*, 1339–41, p. 520; Fryde, *Studies*, chapt. XI, pp. 3–27.

Roger de Wellesthorpe of Grantham, Walter Prest of Melton Mowbray and Henry de Tydeswell of Stamford received bonds for over £2,000. A number of these merchants, too, continued to be prominent in commerce and finance. Roger de Wellesthorpe, Walter Prest, Henry de Tydeswell, Hugh Cokheved and William Amyas were members of the syndicate which undertook to 'farm' the customs in 1343, and remained members of the smaller group to which that syndicate had been reduced by 1344.[145]

It is clear, nonetheless, that not all the wool merchants shipped to Dordrecht was necessarily owned by them. Much of the 463 sacks of wool delivered there by Henry de Tydeswell of Stamford was shipped by him as an agent for other merchants, or had perhaps been bought from them on credit. The same was true of other merchants who took wool to Dordrecht. A good deal of the cargo of Robert Dalderby of Lincoln belonged to fellow citizens and to a lady of Newark, and sub-contractors provided much of William de la Pole's cargoes. They included Thomas Gouk of Boston and merchants from York, Hull and Lincoln, and also William Bargayn of Tickhill whose contribution to Pole's shipments included a consignment from a Retford merchant. It has indeed been suggested that ten lesser agents may have stood behind each of the 250 exporters to Dordrecht, representatives of 'a hundred boroughs and market towns'.[146] Henry Tydeswell's Dordrecht wool reflected the common interest of merchants from a considerable district, for it had been supplied by merchants from Lincoln, Boston, Saxilby, Grantham and Uppingham; and William de la Pole's shipments were drawn from an even wider area. The wool trade, in other words, could be an influence bringing merchants together.

Edward III's war-time policies reinforced this commercial influence, for he needed to mobilize groups of merchants to buy up and export quite large quantities of wool, and to advance him large sums of money. Many syndicates formed for such purposes were locally based; but in 1339 Walter Prest of Melton Mowbray, Robert Pynson and Thomas Gouk of Boston, Henry Tydeswell of Stamford and Robert Dalderby of Lincoln combined to export 500 sacks of wool to Antwerp; and in 1340 Thomas Colle and another Shrewsbury man joined forces with merchants from Much Wenlock and Stafford to buy 800 sacks of Shropshire and Staffordshire wool. Some individuals were drawn into many associations. Walter Prest of

---

[145] *CCR*, 1343–46, pp. 266–7; *CPR*, 1343–45, p. 340.
[146] *CCR*, 1339–41, pp. 45–6, 50, 52, 361–2; Fryde, *Studies*, chapt. IX, p. 9 note; Unwin, ed., *Finance and Trade under Edward III*, p. 192.

Melton Mowbray exported some wool belonging to his fellow towns-folk to Dordrecht; in 1340 and 1341 he was a partner of Hugh Cokheved of Barton-on-Humber in exporting Rutland and Leicestershire wool; and in 1341 he also collaborated with a Market Harborough, a Bracknell and a London merchant to export Northamptonshire wool, and with Hugh Ulseby of London and Henry Goldbeter of York to buy wool reserved for the king. Perhaps the fact that Walter was a small-town man made a varied range of associations the more necessary.[147]

The ordinary routines of trading also brought merchants together. Collaboration enabled capital to be pooled and, given the hazards of the sea, there was good sense, especially in war-time, in not entrusting too much cargo to any one ship. Any particular ship, therefore, was likely to carry the goods of several merchants, so that when Walter Prest despatched wool from London to the Low Countries in 1344, the ship also carried cargo belonging to three Londoners and to merchants from Shrewsbury, Bridgnorth and Stow-on-the-Wold.[148] To assemble wool for export, moreover, often demanded the collaboration of exporters and various local mer-chants, and export merchants overseas might need some sort of organization in order to pursue their common interests. Finally, since most wool merchants were not narrow specialists, they were brought into necessary association with merchants whose concerns were principally with other branches of commerce. William Durham of Darlington, which was hardly one of the outstanding centres of trade in England, was the main purchaser of Durham priory's wool in the period 1333–40, but he also bought grain from the monks and supplied them with cloth, sugar, spices, wine and oxen. For such a man the wide range of business contacts which a 'community of mer-chants of England' made possible was indispensable.[149]

The king's policies and the king's needs helped to give this com-munity of merchants some degree of formality. Edward III found it necessary to re-establish staple markets for wool overseas where his need for money was most acute, and also to organize commercial associations to export the wool raised for his use, to sell it in foreign markets to his best advantage, and to allow the proceeds to be

---

[147] *CCR*, 1337–39, p. 606; 1339–41, pp. 57–8; 1341–43, p. 258; *Rot. Parl.*, II, pp. 120–1; *CPR*, 1340–43, pp. 103, 271.
[148] *CCR*, 1343–46, p. 404.
[149] Morimoto, *Durham Cathedral Priory*, pp. 230, 237–8, 267; *idem*, *Monastic Economy and Medieval Markets*, pp. 92, 96–8, 126, 195, 200–10, 218, 295, 373.

regarded as a fund from which he might borrow. The development of a staple company to play these various parts, therefore, reflected initially in the main the interests of the crown. A tendency for the organized group of wool exporters to become a monopolistic association dominated by the wealthier sections of the merchant class was perhaps inevitable. To meet his financial needs the king needed to control all or most of the wool trade, and the merchants he mobilized to manage it needed substantial wealth because the rate of profit accruing to wool exporters was too low to make it easy for them to pay the high export duties which the government continued to demand. To secure reasonable returns, therefore, merchants either needed to trade on a large scale or to do so on privileged terms; and trading privileges were only likely to be enjoyed by those who contributed significantly to the king's financial requirements. The embryo Staple Company, in consequence, was emerging as an association in which rich merchants had the ruling voice.[150]

At the same time, these war-time developments also undermined the solidarity of the English merchant class. By 1340–41 the handling of loans and taxes in wool for the king was for the most part in the hands of a ring of no more than 40 merchants who were often rewarded by being allowed to export wool on their own account even when all shipments other than of the king's wool were banned. In 1340, for example, Walter Prest and Hugh Cokheved were permitted to export 100 sacks of their 'own' wool from Yorkshire as well as 600 sacks of the king's wool from Leicestershire and Rutland.[151] By that time, indeed, some merchants were so deeply involved in the king's business that they were 'virtually commercial civil servants'. Hugh de Ulseby, who in the autumn of 1341 was appointed with Walter Prest and others to sell the king's wool in Flanders, was in a very literal sense a 'king's merchant'. He got his start in life in the service of William de la Pole's brother, Richard, who was the king's butler; but he supplied some of the wool Hugh Cokheved took to Dordrecht and continued to have interests in the wool trade. He was, however, soon drawn back into the king's service. In 1339–40 he was the king's butler and undertook the payment of the king's debts overseas; in 1341, with Henry Goldbeter, Thomas Colle and Walter Prest, he contracted to buy large consignments of the king's wool;

---

[150] Fryde, *Studies*, chapt. VII, pp. 1171–2 and chapt. IX, pp. 14–15; Lloyd, *The English Wool Trade*, pp. 171–2.
[151] *CCR*, 1339–41, pp. 537–8.

and he was one of the king's proctors who procured the deliverance of the king's great crown and various jewels which Edward III had pawned overseas. It is hardly surprising that he was appointed mayor of the staple in August 1341.[152]

Despite the hostility aroused by the privileged access to the wool trade of a narrow ring of 'king's merchants', Edward III managed to preserve the staple system which was central to his management of trade, just as he managed to preserve high levels of export duties. The compulsory character of the staple was intensified, indeed, by the decision of a merchant assembly in 1342 that anyone exporting elsewhere than to the designated staple market or without paying customs should be 'expelled from the communion of the merchants in the realm so that no merchant, whether denizen or alien, shall communicate with him'.[153] On the other hand, the king was compelled to allow somewhat more open access to the wool trade, and Melchebourne's syndicate of 34 merchants, which took over management of the customs in 1343, was possibly representative of English wool exporters generally; but any prospects that a radical change of direction was contemplated are less likely if, as has been suggested, William de la Pole played a leading part in devising the scheme for 'farming' the customs adopted in that year.[154] Melchebourne, too, was an unlikely person to seek basic policy changes, for he was as much a commercial civil servant as Ulseby. He had long served the king in East Anglia and the adjacent areas as a collector of customs, a deputy butler, a deputy admiral, a purveyor of victuals and of naval equipment, an arrayer of soldiers and of mariners, and a collector of royal wool.

Not surprisingly, therefore, monopolistic tendencies soon reasserted themselves. The 34 merchants who in 1343 undertook to manage the customs were soon reduced to a dozen or so, who were succeeded in this role by a series of short-lived syndicates which often included in their membership such indispensable figures as Walter Prest and Hugh de Ulseby.[155] From the king's point of view these were essentially financial arrangements, to provide him with current revenue and access to credit; but they had a wider significance since, to ensure that the 'king's merchants' disposed of the resources

---

[152] *CPR*, 1330–34, p. 434; 1334–38, p. 55; 1338–40, pp. 210–11, 401; 1340–43, pp. 31, 44, 272, 277, 296; 1343–45, p. 57; *CCR*, 1339–41, pp. 51–2; 1341–43, pp. 258, 296, 431, 458, 563.
[153] Unwin, ed., *Finance and Trade under Edward III*, pp. 208–10.
[154] Lloyd, *The English Wool Trade*, pp. 194–7; Fryde, *Studies*, chapt. X, pp. 9–11.
[155] *CCR*, 1343–46, pp. 574–5; 1346–49, pp. 72–4, 170, 197, 248–9, 451, 482.

they needed to make advances to the king, they were empowered to export wool on beneficial terms. The 'farm' of the customs, therefore, 'became the starting point of a whole series of arrangements that gave the farmers fairly complete control over the entire wool trade', guaranteed by periodic bans on exports other than those by the king's financiers or by their creditors whom they allowed to share their privileges. One merchant syndicate in April 1347, for instance, in return for a promise of regular payments to the king, was allowed to buy up a forced loan to the crown of 20,000 sacks of wool at favourable prices. To secure their market, all other exports of wool were banned for a year, although the syndicate was allowed to license exports by other merchants provided they agreed to pay additional duties. Such policies inevitably generated resentments and tended to drive down producer prices for wool. The commons in 1348 were speaking both for the growers and for merchants outside the ranks of the monopolists when they denounced the restraints and the heavy charges on trade as an 'outrageous grievance' and demanded that the passage of wool should be open to all.[156]

Even so, as we have seen, the privileges enjoyed by the financiers did not save some of them, like Chiriton and his associates, from bankruptcy and even gaol after fighting a losing battle to satisfy at the same time the king and their own creditors. John de Wesenham perhaps was fortunate in being supplanted very quickly as principal farmer of the customs, so that he was free to take up a second career as the king's butler, a wine importer, and an exporter of grain and cloth. In the end he was even to command a fleet, so becoming once more 'a royal official pure and simple'.[157]

(f)   The outcome

The events of the first dozen years of the Hundred Years' War have been discussed in some detail because they marked an important stage in the development of an English merchant class. From 1336 onwards merchants played a political and administrative role in the country at large more consistently than at any time in the past; they provided resources for Edward III on a scale previously matched

---

[156] Fryde, *Studies*, chapt. X, p. 7; *CCR*, 1346–49, pp. 290–1; *Rot. Parl.*, II, p. 201.
[157] Wesenham's career would repay more detailed study; for some glimpses, see Unwin, ed., *Finance and Trade under Edward III*, pp. 264, 296; Harriss, *King, Parliament and Public Finance*, pp. 358–9, 457, 464; Gras, *Early English Customs System*, pp. 414–15; *idem*, *Evolution of the English Corn Market*, p. 173.

only by the great Italian companies (William de la Pole's loans in 1338–39, for example, were without precedent for an English merchant and were only made possible by the fact that he, in turn, could rely upon advances from many other English merchants);[158] and from 1339 onwards English government finance came to depend principally upon the services of English merchant financiers. Their ability to play that part was often artificially buttressed by the grant of monopolistic privileges, the profits from which could be diverted into loans for the king; but it also reflected the economic advance of English merchants in the generation or two before 1336, and the network of commercial connections which so many of them had established both within and beyond their own neighbourhoods.

Edward III's exploitation of trade, on the other hand, in many respects checked the development of England's merchant class. War, trade embargoes and privateering interrupted commerce; the margins of traders were narrowed by steeply increased duties; and taxes or forced loans in wool diverted much of England's most important export commodity into the hands of monopolists who could be compelled to use much of their gains to provide credits for the king.[159] Not only did high taxes on trade become permanent, in brief, but a good deal of available commercial capital was drained off into loans to the government. A certain degree of compulsion, not surprisingly, was needed to enforce the king's policies. In 1347, for instance, on top of a forced loan in wool from the 'community of the realm', Edward III sought supplementary loans from many individual merchants. How insistently he did so is illustrated by the case of Thomas Carter of Worcester. He 'did not care to come' when he was called to appear before the council at Westminster to discuss 'things touching the war ... and the defence ... of England' (i.e. a loan), so the sheriff of Worcestershire was told to arrest his person or property. The threat was sufficient, for soon afterwards the sheriff was told no further action was necessary since Thomas had made a loan. New advances, too, might be the only way to secure settlement of old debts, as a group of Newcastle merchants, who had loaned £4,000 to the king, discovered in 1340. A promise to repay the original debt from the customs was cancelled with £1,900 still owing; and in order to secure a new assignment for the balance they had to advance a further 2,000 marks to the king. The result was that the king owed

---

[158] Fryde, *William de la Pole*, pp. 2, 30–1, 122.
[159] Ormrod, 'The crown and the English economy', pp. 176–81.

them £3,233 6s. 8d., not all that much less than he had done originally. Pressure to heap loan upon loan was applied even more
heavily upon financiers like Melchebourne, Chiriton and Swanlond
in the 1340s; not surprisingly, for them, the outcome was often
disaster.[160]

More important than the plundering of a few wealthy individuals
by the king, however, is the fact that important amounts of commercial capital were either permanently diverted from economic
investment or sterilized for prolonged periods. It is impossible to put
a figure on the amounts, but indicative in this respect is a statement
drawn up in 1343, five years after the king had seized the wool
belonging to a broad cross-section of English merchants at
Dordrecht, stating how much of it had been paid for and for how
much payment was still outstanding.[161] In round figures, it shows
that merchants who had been owed £77,000 on their Dordrecht
bonds, had only recovered about £10,000. The £67,000 of commercial capital frozen by the Dordrecht seizures and for five or more
years thereafter was equivalent to almost a quarter of the value of
England's total wool exports on the eve of the war. We cannot,
moreover, be certain that the 1343 list was a comprehensive statement of Dordrecht debts still outstanding, and those debts in any
case did not exhaust the king's debts to merchants. Thomas Palmer
of Winchester in 1340, as well as having an unredeemed Dordrecht
bond for £320, was owed £300 for wool he had loaned to the king
and £7 for the cost of transporting it from Winchester to London.[162]
When the cash advances the king demanded from merchants and
the high level of duties on trade are taken into account, the total
amount of commercial capital which was either drained away or
immobilized will not be set too low.

A few individuals, of course, did emerge relatively successfully
from these difficult years. Despite many tribulations William de la
Pole was one – partly, perhaps, because he was more skilful and
unscrupulous than most of his contemporaries, partly because he
found safer fields of investment than commerce in war-time, and
partly because he managed to extricate himself from the role of
crown banker before it was too late. As early as 1339 William professed himself wearied 'with labour and diverse vexations under the

---

[160] Unwin, ed., *Finance and Trade under Edward III*, pp. 218–20; *CPR*, 1338–40,
pp. 324–5, 385, 541; *CCR*, 1339–41, pp. 134, 414; 1341–43, pp. 16–17; 1346–49,
pp. 360–1, 363, 390–2.
[161] *CCR*, 1343–46, pp. 138–56.
[162] *CCR*, 1339–41, p. 544.

burden of the king's service', and got a promise that he would 'henceforth enjoy his own fireside at his pleasure'. The result perhaps taught him not to put too much trust in the word of princes; for by December 1340 he was in gaol for alleged irregularities as the king's banker. By that time, however, he had recovered about four-fifths of the enormous advances he had made to the king, and he had built up a considerable estate in Hull and in the English countryside. He returned briefly to the king's financial service in 1343; but by then he had so much capital tied up in land, or in private loans which often in the end led to the acquisition of more land, that he was able more or less to withdraw from dealings with the government. That did not save him from further persecution by the king in the 1350s; and, while in the end he got a comprehensive pardon, it was at the cost of relinquishing all claim to money which the king still owed him. By that time, however, he had accumulated sufficient landed property to provide the platform from which his son advanced to an earldom.[163]

Other participants in Edward III's financial affairs suffered for their alleged misdemeanours, including even John Pulteney who was arrested as a 'fraudulent minister' in 1340 and imprisoned first in the Tower and then in Somerton castle. The ingenuity of exchequer officials in pursuing any course which promised gain to the king was not less damaging. Reginald de Conduit, the London merchant who helped William de la Pole to organize the Dordrecht scheme, was still being pursued in 1343 over the detail of his accounts for the disposal of the king's wool there. Even Edward III admitted that the exchequer's proceedings in this case were 'too harsh', that in consequence Conduit's 'estate is much depressed', and that he had been impoverished beyond his fault.[164] There were others who were similarly or more seriously impoverished. Henry Belton of York, who died in 1340, got a Dordrecht bond for £1,668; six years after his wool had been taken, his executors had recovered less than £200 of what the king owed him, and were unable to export enough wool to recover the balance from allowances against customs duties. Thomas de Wodeley of Abingdon, who was owed £274 for Dordrecht wool, 'on account of his poverty' found himself in a similar situation, although he lived to experience it personally. So, like Henry Belton's executors, he sold his Dordrecht bond, probably at a substantial

---

[163] Fryde, *William de la Pole*, pp. 86, 102, 133, 212; R. Horrox, *The de la Poles of Hull*, pp. 18, 21, 25–7.
[164] *CCR*, 1341–43, pp. 111, 498, 584; 1343–46, pp. 152, 409; 650; *CPR*, 1340–43, pp. 110–11, 307, 405–6; H.T. Riley, ed., *Chronicles of Old London*, pp. 283–4.

discount since sales of these bonds often yielded no more than 2s. or 2s. 6d. in the pound.[165] Doubtless a small circle of financiers who bought up the bonds profited from such transactions, but a good deal of the capital of English wool merchants was permanently lost and the profits of financiers, too, were often swallowed up in meeting the demands of the king. One consequence was that, thereafter, English merchants were less willing to act as bankers to the crown. They still remembered, thirty years later, what had happened to Pole and Chiriton and others who, 'for such transactions made with the king in his great need and for very little gain, have since been impeached for this cause . . . and in the end some of them utterly destroyed'.[166]

This was not the only consequence of Edward III's financial policies. His reliance upon a small circle of merchant-financiers, endowed with monopolistic privileges and in a position to buy up the king's debts to their fellow merchants at a heavy discount, was a deeply divisive influence upon the 'estate of merchants'. It ranged against the monopolists those merchants who were excluded from the inner circle, up-country merchants, and merchants whose capital had been plundered by the king. It has even been supposed that, in the end, the commons in parliament and dissident merchants took advantage of these discontents to force upon the king the Ordinance of the Staple of 1353 which banned Englishmen, Irishmen and Welshmen from exporting wool altogether.[167] It seems, however, that this ordinance, drafted by the king's council, was designed as might be expected to secure the king's advantage: by confining the wool trade to aliens, who paid customs at higher rates than denizens, the king's revenue would be enhanced.[168] Even so, there are many indications by the later 1340s of an 'incurable division of interests' within the estate of merchants, reducing its coherence which had promised during much of the first half of the fourteenth century to make it a social group with national political potentialities.[169]

Nonetheless, an English merchant class, the leading members of which had interests which were more than local or sectional, was by this time a permanent feature of the country's economic life. In the

---

[165] *CCR*, 1337–39, p. 430; 1343–46, p. 402; Fryde, *Studies*, chapt. X, p. 8.
[166] Power, *The Wool Trade in English Medieval History*, p. 119 (the date is 1382).
[167] E.g. by Fryde, *Studies*, chapt. X, pp. 16–17 and Unwin, ed., *Finance and Trade under Edward III*, pp. xxiii–iv.
[168] Lloyd, *The English Wool Trade*, pp. 205–7; W. Ormrod, 'The English crown and the customs, 1349–63', *EcHR*, 2nd ser. XL (1987), pp. 27–9.
[169] Unwin, ed., *Finance and Trade under Edward III*, pp. 219–20.

1340s even a merchant of middling importance, Thomas de Berewick of Pocklington, had contacts well beyond his own neighbourhood, for he could find as his pledges a merchant of Hull, a merchant of Lincoln, a merchant of Boston and a merchant of Norwich.[170] By 1357, moreover, English merchants were again exporting English wool; and their return to the trade was quickly followed by the revival of an overseas staple and the re-emergence of a dominant group of wealthy exporters to service it. In this respect the early years of the Hundred Years' War had another importance, as a point of transition from the much more open trade of earlier days to the regulated commerce characteristic of the later middle ages. At the same time, these years also perpetuated a fiscal regime based in no small measure upon the heavy taxation of wool exports, which in the long run contributed to a decline in wool exports and a growth of the much more lightly taxed exports of English cloth.[171] This unforeseen consequence of fiscal expediency created new employment prospects in England itself and represented a shift, however modest, from England's role as an exporter mainly of primary commodities towards becoming an exporter of industrial products. Finally, while the 'community of merchants', which in the early years of Edward III and even before had acted at times as an estate of the realm, became in certain respects more fragmented, its members found other ways to advance their interests. The incipient organization of a Staple company, as well as being a harbinger of the more regulated trade of the future, enabled the voices of wool merchants to be heard more clearly; and the petitioning process being developed by the commons in parliament made it possible for every vested interest to secure a hearing. Already under Edward III the merchants of the realm were learning how to take advantage of it.[172]

[170] *CCR*, 1343–46, p. 123.
[171] Fryde, *William de la Pole*, p. 231.
[172] As Helen Cam pointed out long ago: 'The legislators of medieval England', in E.B. Fryde and E. Miller, eds, *Historical Studies of the English Parliament*, I, pp. 190–1.

CHAPTER FIVE

Medieval English Towns

Towns and town growth were integral components of the agrarian, commercial and industrial development of England between the Conquest and the Black Death. Some of the roles which towns played in the inland and overseas trades, in processing and manufacture, and in the provision of services contributing to specialization and expansion, have already been surveyed; but in this and the following chapter we turn to an examination of towns and townsfolk in their own right, not only for their economic importance, but for the ecclesiastical, governmental, educational and cultural functions they performed. These generations, as we shall see, not only saw the growth of larger towns and the foundation of more towns, something which was perhaps inevitable in a period when England's population, production and trade expanded notably; but also, in all likelihood an increase of the urban sector of English society which was relative as well as absolute.

The distinctiveness of urban communities in medieval European society has often been emphasized. This might be a matter of physical fact. Many larger towns were walled, contributing to their 'compact silhouettes . . . with densely packed buildings capped by the towers of churches and castles rising above the countryside around them'; indeed, the walls of Winchester were even depicted on the town's seal as a 'powerful symbol' of the city's 'urban identity'.[1] In varying degrees, too, towns were distinctive for their relative density of settlement in landscapes still for the most part fairly lightly peopled; and they also differed qualitatively from most

[1] E. Ennen, *Die europäische Stadt des Mittelalters*, Gottingen, 1972, p. 11; Keene, *Survey*, I, p. 31 note.

villages in that a majority of their inhabitants got their living from manufacture, food processing and trade rather than from agriculture. Their populations, consequently, were apt to be more heterogeneous than village populations; and many towns also developed certain characteristic institutional features. Townsfolk enjoyed a freedom of person and property denied to many villagers, as well possibly as a measure of administrative autonomy; and town life might generate distinctive attitudes, both because townsmen engaged in different ways in making a living from those of most villagers, but also because town communities were in great part creations of the more mobile elements in medieval society. They had, therefore, to develop institutions in which people who had abandoned their traditional attachments could put down roots.[2]

These characteristics which distinguished towns from villages are easy enough to discern in those larger communities which may justly be regarded as 'non-feudal islands in the feudal seas'; but the size of places that were clearly urban must not be set too high. Even in the seventeenth century the threshold between centres which had developed 'a specialist non-agricultural economic function', with the occupational structures that went with it, on the one hand, and simple market towns on the other, has been put at no more than 2,000 inhabitants.[3] At the same time, it would be misleading to regard even the larger medieval towns as alien bodies essentially antagonistic to the feudal agrarian order within which they developed. As we shall see, a high proportion of townsfolk were recent immigrants from the countryside, many of whom doubtless retained some rural ties; by no means all residents in towns relinquished all interest in crops or livestock; and from many points of view the urban economy was an integral part, and even the creation, of the medieval agrarian society dominated by the lords of the land. It was not only that lordship played a major role within towns: town markets enabled peasants to turn their surpluses into cash with which to pay seignorial dues and for necessities their land could not produce, and allowed those with ampler means to obtain desirable goods, sometimes brought by merchants from far away.[4]

---

[2] R. Holt and G. Rosser, eds, *The English Medieval Town, 1200–1540*, pp. 3–4; R.H. Hilton, 'Small town society in England before the Black Death', in *ibid.*, p. 75; J. Le Goff, ed., *Histoire de la France urbaine*, II, pp. 9–12.

[3] M.M. Postan, *The Medieval Economy and Society*, p. 212; N.R. Goose, 'In search of the urban variable: towns in the English economy, 1500–1650', *EcHR*, 2nd ser. XXXIX (1986), p. 169.

[4] R.H. Hilton, *Class Conflict and the Crisis of Feudalism*, pp. 179–80.

The intermingling of rural and urban features in medieval communities, and of trade and industry with agriculture, makes a workable definition of what constituted a town frustratingly elusive, especially at the lower end of the scale. Yet it is precisely at this level that the problem of definition assumes the greatest significance, for the contribution of small towns, and of villages with some urban characteristics, to the economic life of medieval England was very great. Small market towns were by far the most numerous group of medieval English towns: there were probably more than 500 of them by the early fourteenth century. Their variety inevitably raises problems of classification; some inhabitants were less clearly engaged in properly 'urban' activities than others; and villages as well as towns had craftsmen or even 'merchants', sometimes in numbers which ultimately transformed their character. Conversely, many market towns are perhaps more properly viewed as natural extensions of the rural economy which provided their setting, performing merely those rudimentary secondary functions which made possible the routines of agriculture and enabled rural settlements to be sustained. Any classification of towns, therefore, demands a good deal of empiricism; but that does not mean that an attempt to identify and classify the urban communities of the middle ages is an enquiry not worth undertaking. It is one which may perhaps begin with an endeavour to isolate some of their external and institutional characteristics.

1.   SOME FEATURES OF MEDIEVAL ENGLISH TOWNS

A first characteristic was that most towns were very close to the rural world in which they were set. That closeness, which has even been described as 'the penetration of towns by the country', was in part a matter of people: town populations depended upon rural immigration, a subject which must be discussed in greater detail in due course. In addition, however, many towns had suburbs and rural outskirts, and often islands of cultivation even within their boundaries, which contributed to their food supplies.[5] The town fields attached to many Domesday boroughs have already been noticed; and even within the walls of medieval Winchester, except in the very centre,

[5] In general, Le Goff, ed., *Histoire de la France urbaine*, II, pp. 197–200.

open ground occupied more space than buildings. There, too, gardens were valued as a source of vegetables; at least in the twelfth century grain was grown in suburban fields and closes; and there were vineyards in the southern suburb around the church of All Saints in the Vines. A town as large as York also had its periphery of gardens, closes and pasture 'strays', and the countryside pressed close upon twelfth-century London. There was farmland in Clerkenwell, Stoke Newington, Wanstead and Stepney; in the 1140s Geoffrey de Mandeville appropriated land in Smithfield to make a vineyard; and a century later beef cattle were fattened for the London market at Edmonton.[6] How indispensable such assets might appear to townsfolk is suggested by a plea in 1330 from Retford (Notts.) for special fiscal consideration because to that 'town pertains no manner of commodity like land, meadow and pasture', compelling its inhabitants to 'live entirely of their merchandise'.[7]

Meadow and pasture were perhaps the most essential of these 'commodities', both for fattening livestock for town butchers and to provide hay and grazing for cows and draught animals. Horses and oxen are found even in town centres: at Winchester they were often installed in backyards, and one citizen met his death trying to separate a mare and two stallions fighting in his kitchen. Still more commonly, towns acquired suburban pasture rights for cattle, horses and even sheep, and within the town limits poultry, and more particularly pigs, were seemingly ubiquitous. The assumption that burgesses would have pigs is hardly surprising in such partially urbanized places as Abbot's Bromley (Staffs.), Salford, Bolton and Manchester (Lancs.), or Knutsford (Cheshire); but the presence of pigs in London is perhaps somewhat more unexpected. Yet pig-styes were built in the city against walls belonging to neighbours and over the course of the Walbrook, and straying pigs trespassed, in the company of dogs, poultry and children, in the garden of the Austin friars in the parish of All Hallows, London Wall.[8]

Agriculture and stock-rearing, however, were far from being the main sources of livelihood of most townsfolk in most towns. Towns were primarily manufacturing and trading centres, attracting an inflow of the goods they required to meet their own needs,

---

[6] Keene, *Survey*, I, pp. 151–2; *VCH City of York*, p. 498; W.O. Hassall, ed., *Cartulary of St Mary, Clerkenwell*, Camden 3rd ser. LXXI (1949), nos. 39, 56, 83, 87; *Regesta*, III, no. 507; H.M. Chew and M. Weinbaum, eds, *The London Eyre of 1244*, pl. 192.

[7] *Rot. Parl.*, II, p. 42.

[8] Keene, *Survey*, I, pp. 153–4; *BBC 1216–1307*, pp. 70–5, 77–8, 83; H.M. Chew and W. Kellaway, eds, *The London Assize of Nuisance*, nos. 63, 263, 281, 382–3.

distributing goods produced by their craftsmen or brought in by merchants to their own inhabitants and to customers in their hinterlands, and perhaps also serving as collecting points for goods destined for more distant markets. Winchester, for example, assembled wool for export not only from neighbouring manors, but also from Wiltshire, the South West, the Welsh Marches and counties on the Middle Thames.[9] These economic functions, as we shall see, governed the diversified occupational structure of medieval English towns, a feature present even at an embryonic stage in the development of towns which never became particularly large or successful. There is some indication, for instance, of the occupations of around one-third of the inhabitants in the first decade of the twelfth century of the little town growing up at the gates of Battle abbey in Sussex. Its residents included some agricultural workers and abbey servants; but there were also provision traders and food processors (cooks, a miller, bakers, a brewer), metal and leather workers (a cordwainer, smiths, cobblers, a shoemaker, a goldsmith, a bellfounder), and also carpenters, a weaver and a mysterious *purgator*. The new town of Baldock (Herts.) in 1189 displays similar features: among its inhabitants were a mercer and a merchant, cooks and a vintner, tanners and shoemakers and a saddler, smiths and ironmongers and a goldsmith, tailors, masons, a clerk, a carter and a falconer.[10]

The basic characteristics of urban communities are also reflected in the role which town markets played as foci of town growth. At Winchester the main markets were in fact the streets, particularly the High Street, so that trading was concentrated where population was densest; at Bury St Edmunds the Anglo-Saxon borough and its post-Conquest extension were both centred on markets (that at the abbey gates on Angel Hill, and the 'great market' in the new borough); at Norwich another 'great market' was at the heart of the westward expansion of the city after its older core in Tombland was partially cleared to accommodate the castle and cathedral; and the new Norman borough at Northampton developed around the market in All Saints churchyard. Market facilities, in fact, were so basic to a town's existence that it is logical to trace the urban beginnings of Tavistock back to grants of a market and fair there in the period

---

[9] Keene, *Survey*, I, pp. 292–3.
[10] E. Searle, ed., *Chronicle of Battle Abbey*, pp. 52–9; B.A. Lees, ed., *Records of the Templars in England in the Twelfth Century*, pp. 65–9; M.W. Beresford, *New Towns of the Middle Ages*, pp. 432–3, 492–3.

1105–16, even though it was not until later in the century that a borough was formally created.[11]

Medieval, and sometimes even modern, street names, too, may preserve the memory of how medieval townsmen made their living. Market places, for example, were often divided into specialized areas, or were 'colonized' as permanent shops encroached on what had been open spaces occupied by temporary stalls. At Salisbury Oatmeal Row, Butchers' Row and Ox Row seem to have been intakes from the market place, and at Newcastle the market place by the castle and St Nicholas's church was divided into a number of distinct markets which were ultimately stabilized as separate 'streets'. On the north was the big (barley) market; on the west the groat (meal), wood and iron markets; and on the east the meat, cloth and fish markets. There was also some colonization of the central market area, creating Skinnergate at its upper end, Spurriergate in the middle and Saddlergate at the lower end. This localization of particular markets reflected a more general (although by no means a universal) tendency for particular crafts to be concentrated in particular lanes and streets. This might arise from their particular needs: fullers and tanners, for instance, needed easy access to a plentiful water supply; but the inclination of crafts to cling together is much commoner than such convenience would explain. It leaves its mark in Ironmonger, Cordwainer, Wheeler, Smiths' and Cooks' Rows in Salisbury, and thirteenth-century Oxford had recognized occupational quarters for drapers, cordwainers, skinners, cobblers, butchers, spicers, goldsmiths, mercers, vintners, cooks, cutlers and armourers.[12]

Towns, including even quite small towns, might have residents who were not traders or craftsmen. In the northern castle-town of Alnwick the burgesses lived in close proximity to Alnwick abbey's tenants in Canongate and to the lodgings of castlemen and suitors to the court of the barony in Bailiffgate.[13] In large towns the diversity of their inhabitants was likely to be even greater. York, as the capital of the northern province of the English church, accommodated an archbishop and his entourage from time to time, the minster church and its staff, and many visitors on church business. In addition St

[11] Keene, *Survey*, I, pp. 330–1; M.W. Beresford and J.K.S. St Joseph, *Medieval England: an Aerial Survey*, pp. 215–17; C. Stephenson, *Borough and Town*, pp. 198–200; J. Steane, *The Northamptonshire Landscape*, pp. 140–2; H.P.R. Finberg, *Tavistock Abbey: a Study in the Social and Economic History of Devon*, Cambridge, 1951, pp. 197–204.
[12] *VCH Wilts*, VI, pp. 85–6; R.J. Charleton, *History of Newcastle on Tyne*, pp. 173–9; *VCH Oxon.*, IV, pp. 26–8.
[13] M.R.G. Conzen, *Alnwick, Northumberland*, pp. 21–3, 44–6.

Mary's abbey lay close to the city walls; by the thirteenth century a nunnery, two priories and various friaries had also been established in or near the city; there was also a need for hospitals, of which St Leonard's was the largest; and also for schools, which included one asssociated with St Leonard's hospital in addition to the ancient grammar school kept by the minster.[14] The city, furthermore, was the headquarters of the sheriff of Yorkshire, the location of the county gaol, and the place where the county court sat and the king's justices held their sessions. Periodically, too, in the age of the Scottish wars from 1296 onwards, the offices of government occupied the castle and other York premises, turning the city into the northern capital of the kingdom; and during major recoinages the king's and archbishop's mints in York were among the sources of England's currency.

If York was exceptional among provincial towns, it was not unique. Every county had its county town upon which local administration was centred; many towns periodically accommodated the king's travelling justices; parish churches multiplied within town walls; and there were schools at an early date in many places, including Dunstable, Huntingdon and Gloucester. Many of the older towns lived in close proximity to an abbey or a bishop's seat, often located in an enclave within them, and in the thirteenth century these older establishments were reinforced (the English province of the Franciscans alone had 49 houses by 1256). Down to the twelfth century, too, new urban mints were still being licensed, although the number of minting places began to fall in Henry I's reign. Many things, therefore, as well as a desire to sell country produce or buy urban goods, drew people into town, including legal or administrative obligations, or a need to exchange coin which had ceased to be current, or social considerations (Winchester even staged a tournament in the cathedral cemetery in 1343); and diocesan occasions, or the fact that a town church possessed precious relics, might be no less influential. Such visits might persuade countrymen to invest in town property in order to ensure that they had a lodging or accommodation; and even if the primary purpose of coming to town was not economic, the fact that they did so might well turn out to be good for business.[15]

---

[14] A. Raine, *Medieval York*, pp. 32, 116; P.H. Cullum, *Cremetts and Corrodies: Care of the Poor and Sick at St Leonard's Hospital, York, in the Middle Ages*, Borthwick Papers, 79 (1991), pp. 5–10.
[15] *Regesta*, II, nos. 1659, 1827, 1936; D. Knowles, *The Religious Orders in England*, I, Cambridge, 1948, p. 135; Keene, *Survey*, I, pp. 194–5, 397–8.

Some of the basic characteristics of medieval English towns are most evident in London, especially when, in association with its suburban town of Westminster, it became the acknowledged capital of the kingdom. Politics, law and administration brought some of the wealthiest men in England to London with increasing regularity, and the convenience of these visitors became a dominant consideration. In 1310 tailors and skinners were forbidden, on pain of imprisonment, to scour furs in the highways and even some by-ways of the city except by night, 'lest the nobility and others be inconvenienced while passing'. A number of great men, too, found it advantageous to obtain a house in London for their visits, including Henry Lacy, earl of Lincoln. In 1285 he bought the house lately vacated by the Black Friars in St Andrew's parish, Holborn, later better known as Lincoln's Inn and for the fact that it was 'replenished with gentlemen studious in the common laws'. London's development as a capital, in other words, also favoured its development as a place where many luxury commodities were obtainable; but its many visitors, the attendants they brought with them, and the city's own rapidly expanding population also created a burgeoning demand for more mundane goods and services. In 1309 there were said to be 354 taverns and 1,334 brewers in London; and in the next year the bread baked in the city was supplemented by that brought in by women bakers from Stratford.[16]

While English medieval towns were small compared to modern cities or to many medieval towns in Flanders or Italy, they were still areas of relatively dense settlement. That density was least marked in small towns and in new towns, especially at an early stage of their development. Burgages in the new borough of Eynsham in 1215 ranged in size from a quarter acre to a whole acre; acre building plots are also mentioned at Newborough (Staffs.), Ormskirk, Salford and Bolton (Lancs.), and Chard (Somerset); those at New Salisbury in 1225 were each perhaps 635 square yards; and, while Edward I allowed for 600 houses on a site of $87^1/_2$ acres at New Winchelsea, the twelfth-century earls of Aumale set aside 320 acres for their port-town at Hedon, 60 acres more than the area enclosed by the medieval walls of York.[17]Even in many new towns, however, the

[16] *CLB, D*, pp. 215, 233, 242; W.J. Thoms, ed., *Survey of London Written in the Year 1598 by John Stow*, 1842, p. 164; W. Stubbs, ed., *Chronicles of the Reigns of Edward I and Edward II*, I, p. 267.
[17] H.E. Salter, ed., *Eynsham Cartulary*, I, p. 60; *BBC 1216–1307*, pp. 47–8, 51, 53, 55, 62; Beresford and St Joseph, *Medieval England*, pp. 219–20, 238–41; J.R. Boyle, *Early History of Hedon*, pp. 7–8.

density of settlement often increased with the passage of time, and a much more intensive use of space was usual in most older towns. Burgages were made to accommodate more than a single habitation; buildings were pushed below ground into cellars and upwards into solars, and the latter often projected over the narrow streets and lanes separating houses. In London, it was said in 1193, 'all sorts of men crowd together . . . from every country'; and it was asserted a century later that 'buildings in the city of London are so close together that in many places there is no vacant land, and some may occupy a neighbour's walls where they have no right at all'. Nor was London unique in this respect. It has been calculated that, at Winchester in *c.* 1300, a population of 10,000–12,000 was accommodated in the area within the walls at an overall density of 53.5 persons per acre, a figure rising to 90 persons or more in the High Street and its environs. Similarly, in the central areas of York, it has been estimated that the density of population in St Sampson's parish in 1377 was double the density of London's population as a whole, and two thousand times the density of population in York's surrounding countryside.[18] This was a feature of medieval towns which was vividly illustrated by H.E. Salter's remarkable reconstruction of the topography of Oxford. Travelling only a short distance along the north side of High Street from Carfax, a number of tenements are encountered with frontages of 7–16 feet; one with a frontage of 25 feet accommodated two messuages and four stalls; one with a frontage of $17^1/_2$ feet contained a house and two shops; and another with a frontage of 36 feet was occupied by five shops with a house behind. It was characteristic of medieval towns that many people were crowded into little space.[19]

2.   A PERIOD OF URBAN GROWTH, 1086–1348

The crowding of people in towns is one indicator of the fact that, between the late eleventh and early fourteenth centuries, the urban growth which had been evident from the late ninth century onwards had continued and had probably accelerated in Norman and Angevin England. This does not mean that it is possible to count

[18] J.T. Appleby, ed., *Chronicle of Richard of Devizes*, pp. 65–6; M. Bateson, ed., *Borough Customs*, I, pp. 247–8; Keene, *Survey*, I, pp. 368–70.
[19] H.E. Salter, *Survey of Oxford*, I, pp. 99 et seq.

heads, however ingeniously information designed for quite different purposes is manipulated. London's population in the early fourteenth century, for example, has been the subject of estimates ranging from not far short of 40,000 up to one of around 80,000. At the very best such figures can only be regarded as probabilities, as must similar figures for other town population or the estimate that London's population doubled between 1200 and 1340.[20] On the other hand, it is possible to document town growth during this period even though it cannot be precisely measured. In many places an expansion of the urban area is evident, there was much suburban growth outside town limits, and within towns vacant spaces were filled with habitations and spaces already inhabited were more intensively used. The topographical history of English towns may well provide a more satisfactory picture of the stages of urban growth than attempts to deduce population figures from recalcitrant documents. Furthermore, new towns were added in these generations to those inherited from the Anglo-Saxon past. England, in other words, had more towns in 1300, as well as many larger towns, than it had possessed in 1086. Not every town foundation was a successful enterprise, of course, and not every established town grew consistently. The growth of Winchester, for example, virtually ceased after the damage it sustained during Stephen's reign and it was no longer a regular royal residence. By contrast, Southampton only experienced the beginning of its building boom in the late twelfth century, perhaps reflecting the developing commercial contacts of its port with Poitou and Gascony.[21]

(a)   The expansion of urban settlements

In many places the growth of towns was manifest in the expansion of the main urban area. The early fourteenth-century walls of Newcastle upon Tyne, for example, enclosed a site extending along the routes leading to the main exits from the town (West Gate, Newgate, Pilgrim Street Gate) and starting from its primary nucleus around the bridgehead, the castle, St Nicholas's church and the market place; but, in addition, their line was diverted to take in the township of Pandon absorbed into Newcastle in 1298. The urban area of

---

[20] E. Ekwall, ed., *Two London Subsidy Rolls*, pp. 71–81; G.A. Williams, *Medieval London*, pp. 315–17; Holt and Rosser, eds, *The English Medieval Town*, p. 6.
[21] M. Biddle, ed., *Winchester in the Early Middle Ages*, pp. 470–508; C. Platt, *Medieval Southampton*, pp. 39–51.

Bristol grew to take in land around the Old Market outside the castle, around St James's priory, and across the Avon in Redcliffe. It may have been an exaggeration to say that Bristol, in the mid-twelfth century, was 'the richest city of all the region, receiving merchandise . . . from lands near and far'; but that description would have fitted the facts well a century later, by which time the various growth points had been ringed by new defences, and there was a new bridge to Redcliffe and a new harbour for ships frequenting the port. At Norwich, too, the walls completed in 1343, together with the river, enclosed an area a square mile in extent containing more than 50 parish churches and a built-up area roughly the same as it would be in the late eighteenth century.[22]

Expansion was not solely a matter of colonizing empty spaces within a town's perimeter, for there was also suburban development. The 'French borough' which developed between the Old English borough and the new Norman castle at Nottingham after the Conquest, or the 'new borough' growing outside the older urban nucleus at Northampton in 1086, were both originally suburban communities, although they were soon absorbed into larger borough areas. Similarly, the 'French borough' at Norwich eventually became the heart of the medieval city and its fortifications were extended to enclose suburban developments on every side, including some 'beyond the water' across the River Wensum; while Pandon, on the eve of its absorption into Newcastle, looks like an industrial suburb as well as a place of residence for Newcastle businessmen. Suburban settlement, in brief, was often a first stage in the expansion of the properly urban area.[23]

Much expansion, on the other hand, was never absorbed into the area delimited by town walls. By the thirteenth century a suburb had grown up outside the 'new borough' at Northampton along the Market Harborough road; at Oxford there were suburbs outside the north gate in Broad Street and St Giles's Street, to the west around St Thomas's church, and outside the south gate along Grandpont; and there was similar extra-mural growth at York outside Walmgate

[22] *NCH*, XIII, p. 271; J. Nolan *et al.*, 'The medieval town defences of Newcastle upon Tyne', *AA*, 5th ser. XVII (1989), pp. 29, 32; C.D. Ross, 'Bristol in the middle ages', in C.M. MacInnes and W.F. Whitthard, *Bristol and its Adjoining Counties*, pp. 182–7; K.R. Potter, ed., *Gesta Stephani*, pp. 37–8; E. Rutledge, 'Immigration and population growth in early fourteenth-century Norwich', *Urban History YB*, 1988, pp. 16–17.
[23] M.W. Barley and I.F. Straw, 'Nottingham', in M.D. Lobel, ed., *Atlas of Historic Towns*, I, pp. 2–3; Steane, *The Northamptonshire Landscape*, pp. 140–6; Stephenson, *Borough and Town*, p. 199; C.M. Fraser, ed., *The Northumberland Lay Subsidy Roll for 1296*, pp. 76–7.

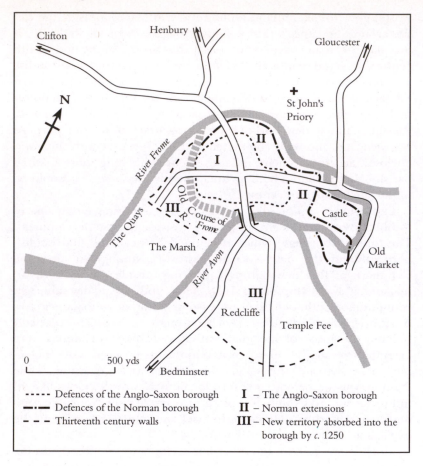

Clifton

Henbury

Gloucester

N

✠ St John's Priory

River Frome

II

I

The Quays

Old Course of R. Frome

III

II

Castle

The Marsh

River Avon

Old Market

III

Redcliffe

Temple Fee

0   500 yds

Bedminster

```
----- Defences of the Anglo-Saxon borough
-·-·- Defences of the Norman borough
- - - Thirteenth century walls
```

I – The Anglo-Saxon borough
II – Norman extensions
III – New territory absorbed into the borough by *c.* 1250

Map 5   The expansion of Bristol, c. 1066–1250

Sources: C.D. Ross, 'Bristol in the Middle Ages'; *English City: The Growth and Future of Bristol*, published by J.S. Fry and Sons Ltd, 1945; and M.D. Lobel, ed., *Atlas of Historic Towns*, II, pp. 3–7.

and Micklegate bars, at Lincoln outside Eastgate and in Newland and Newport, at Chester outside the east and north gates and across the river in Handbridge, and outside the various exits from Worcester and Gloucester. Some suburban developments were especially important, including those along the Strand and in Holborn, and perhaps Westminster, outside the city of London. At Canterbury extra-mural suburbs were more populous in Thomas Becket's time than they were to be in 1800; and at Winchester, which retained the Roman walls as its boundary, the suburban area in the late twelfth century was almost twice as large as the walled town, and, in 1148, contained 37 per cent of the properties listed in a survey of the city compiled in that year.[24] Suburbs, in fact, were 'the growing edges of the town', and often expanded into open sites where livestock could be marketed or where accommodation could be provided for the crowds of traders flocking to fairs like those held at Winchester or Northampton.[25]

The most significant increase of living space in medieval towns, however, was often achieved less by an extension of their boundaries and by suburban settlements, than by increasingly intensive use of land within the walls. This was especially true of older towns, where the spacious burgages of early days were 'split up, sublet and built over by houses, shops, inns, workshops and stables'; although some crowding was often evident even in newer towns. In the thirteenth century half-burgages were very common in the Herefordshire towns of Bromyard, Ledbury and Ross-on-Wye; at High Wycombe shops and houses encroached on the market place or were built behind or beside the 'head houses' on the twelfth-century burgage plots; and about a third of burgages laid out at Stratford-upon-Avon in the 1190s had been subdivided by the 1250s.[26] Space was even more at a premium in an old town like Winchester. Many cottages and shops, with a workroom or retail outlet on the ground floor and living space on the floor above, were very small. In the early fourteenth century some of them in the High Street had an average frontage of only 8 feet, and others in 1337 averaged only 5 feet in width and between 7 and 21 feet in depth. A century or more earlier, street frontages in the Cheapside area of London were already minutely divided and linked to the rear parts of the tenements within which they were set by a network of alleys and narrow lanes, some of which were also being developed. The frontages of the streets and many of the lanes were occupied by rows of shops, with larger structures

---

[24] *VCH Oxon.*, IV, pp. 23–6; J.F.W. Hill, *Medieval Lincoln*, pp. 117–18, 157, 169; H.J. Hewitt, *Medieval Cheshire*, p. 124; R.H. Hilton, *A Medieval Society*, pp. 185–7; *VCH City of York*, p. 53; W.J. Urry, *Canterbury under the Angevin Kings*, pp. 28, 185–9; Biddle, ed., *Winchester in the Early Middle Ages*, pp. 470–508.
[25] D.J. Keene, 'Suburban growth', in Holt and Rosser, eds, *The English Medieval Town*, pp. 98–9, 110, 114.
[26] Hilton, *Class Conflict and the Crisis of Feudalism*, pp. 166–7; A.T. Bannister, ed., 'A transcript of the Red Book', in *Camden Miscellany*, XV, pp. 9–18; L.J. Ashford, *History of High Wycombe*, pp. 10–16; 25–6; E.M. Carus-Wilson, 'The first half century of the borough of Stratford-upon-Avon', pp. 58–9.

called 'selds' behind them, in which a number of individuals owned or rented space for the sale or storage of goods. Many of the shops once again were very small: eight of them in Ironmongery Lane in *c.* 1220 had a combined frontage of 23 yards and a combined area of 106 yards. Nor did buildings jostle each other only on the ground. One Londoner complained in 1340 that a neighbour had built out the upper storey of his house so that it projected beyond the gutter in the middle of the lane between their houses.[27]

This is not to say that the urban area was anywhere totally built up. There were still more or less empty spaces in early fourteenth-century Winchester, confined though that city was within its Roman walls; and some town land was lost, as well as gained, for burgess occupation: to build castles in the years after 1066, to provide extensive precincts for religious establishments, and in due course to furnish sites for colleges and university buildings at Oxford and Cambridge. There was also empty land which remained undeveloped until a late date: the large sites given to Franciscans and Dominicans at Gloucester in the thirteenth century, with no indication that houses had to be demolished to accommodate the friars, or 'the divers void places in the town which might be approved' mentioned at Colchester in the 1320s. The intensification of urban settlement is not in question, but it did not involve the invasion of every open space.[28]

(b) New towns

Urban expansion also took the form of founding new towns, many of them an outcome of royal or seignorial initiative, although seldom in such romantic circumstances as those which attended the birth of the town of Woodstock (Oxon.). The town, it was claimed in 1279,

> was first established in the time of Henry [II], King of England, in the following manner. At the time the aforementioned king often stayed at his manor of Woodstock for love of a certain lady called Rosamund. And there was then a vacant plot outside the park of the manor and, because the king's men dwelt too far from his said manor, the king . . . granted . . . divers parcels of land from that vacant plot to divers men to build houses thereon . . . and fixed for these plots the rents recorded below, and gave to the men who dwelt therein a market

[27] Keene, *Survey*, I, p. 162; 'A report to the SSRC on a social and economic study of medieval London directed by D.J. Keene in 1979–83' (we are grateful to the ESRC and to Dr Keene for permission to quote from this report); Chew and Kellaway, eds, *The London Assize of Nuisance*, no. 358.
[28] *Rot. Parl.*, I, p. 397; M.D. Lobel and J. Tann, 'Gloucester', in Lobel, ed., *Atlas of Historic Towns*, I, pp. 7–8.

on Tuesday each week, from which market the tolls would be collected by the king's bailiff.

By 1279 there were 137 houses at Woodstock, the occupants of which included men whose names suggest that they were dyers, tailors, turners, an ironmonger, a baker, a carpenter, a slater, a smith, a parchmentmaker, a mason, a tanner, a weaver, a vintner, a thatcher, a plumber, a wimplemaker and a potter. The fact that Woodstock adjoined a royal residence obviously favoured its development, and Henry II gave it the start which launched many new towns: a site, standard building plots at more or less standard rents, and a market and market place.[29]

Not all new towns were as deliberately planted as Woodstock was, but whatever the manner of their foundation their development depended in part on the advantages offered by their location. Woodstock's turners in 1279 suggest that there was a local market for wooden utensils and available supplies of timber from which to make them; the growth of Tavistock owed a good deal to the fact that it was well placed to offer marketing services to Dartmoor tinners; and Cotswold and East Anglian wool and cloth towns had the advantage of being set in sheep country. Access to the harvest of the sea, too, might promote urban growth. Scarborough already had a herring-house 'under the cliff' in the early thirteenth century, some rents there were paid in herrings and the town's church got tithes from fishermen. The indications are that the growth of the town, reflected in the progressive increase of its annual payments to the king between 1163 and 1201, and in the substantial contributions it made towards Richard I's ransom in 1195 and a tallage of towns in 1201, owed much to fish. Even in the early fifteenth century fish tithes still brought in up to £80 a year to Scarborough church.[30]

A town's location might be advantageous in many other ways: if it was sited at a point where traffic was concentrated at a river crossing, for example, like Newcastle upon Tyne or Chelmsford, or where important routes intersected like Dunstable (although when Henry I established a borough there it was said to lie in wooded country that was full of thieves).[31] Proximity to an abbey or castle, as well as to a royal residence like Woodstock, might stimulate urban development, for a body of customers was conveniently to hand. The growth of

---

[29] *Rot. Hundr.*, II, p. 839; Beresford, *New Towns*, p. 478.
[30] *EYC*, I, pp. 284–8; P. Heath, 'North Sea fishing in the fifteenth century', *North. Hist.*, III (1968), pp. 11–12.
[31] *VCH Beds.*, III, pp. 355–6; *Mon. Angl.*, VI(1), pp. 239–40.

Westminster was directly related to the fact that it lay at the gates of the abbey and the palace; Winchcombe and Battle were geared to providing services for the abbeys beside which they grew up, although both also became modest local market centres; and in the early twelfth century, near the abbey at Burton-on-Trent, there were little groups of men taking their names from a craft, many of whom had little in the way of land.[32] Urban development in association with castles is, if anything, still commoner, especially in the generation or two which followed the Conquest. In the north, Newcastle upon Tyne and Alnwick both originated as castle towns, and Richmond (Yorks.) was 'planned as a new town around the . . . castle' which the earls of Richmond began to build in 1071 as the centre of their Yorkshire lordship. Towns of this type, moreover, were not only to be found in the remoter regions. At Wisbech (Cambs.) the main focus of urban development was the 'new market' by the castle; and before 1147 Bishop Alexander of Lincoln built castles with associated urban foundations at Sleaford (Lincs.) and Banbury (Oxon.).[33]

Many of these towns were deliberate seignorial creations. Deliberation is clearest when, as at Leeds in 1207, a borough was 'planted on a site distinct from that of the village', or when, as at Eynsham (Oxon.), the abbot and convent in 1215 assigned parcels of their demesne land lying outside the vill to establish the new borough there. At Eynsham the abbey also decreed that the building plots were to be held for fixed money rents without additional services, that they were to be freely alienable, and that those who held them should be free to devise their goods and chattels by will. These steps, in the abbey's view, were 'for the utility and advancement of our house': they would, in other words, enhance the value of the abbey's property and the revenue it could draw from it.[34] To found a borough, in other words, was a device of estate management, as it was in the view of the bishop of Bath and Wells when in 1235 he turned the vill of Chard (Somerset) into a borough 'because we desire the improvement of our manor'. Much earlier the lords of

---

[32] A.G. Rosser, *Medieval Westminster*, pp. 119–22; Hilton, *Class Conflict and the Crisis of Feudalism*, pp. 19–20; E. Searle, *Lordship and Community*, pp. 69–83; C.G.O. Bridgeman, ed., 'Early Burton abbey twelfth-century surveys', pp. 212–15.

[33] Beresford, *New Towns*, pp. 466, 517–18; R. Fieldhouse and B. Jennings, *History of Richmond and Swaledale*, pp. 11–12; P.D.A. Harvey, 'Banbury', in Lobel, ed., *Atlas of Historic Towns*, I, p. 2; *VCH Cambs.*, IV, p. 240.

[34] J. Le Patourel, ed., *Documents relating to the Manor and Borough of Leeds*, pp. xii–xiii, xix; Salter, ed., *Eynsham Cartulary*, I, pp. 60–1.

Tutbury, who had founded Newborough (Staffs.) and 'caused it to grow', were anticipating in the 1150s that it could be caused to grow still further, with a consequent increase of the revenue they might expect from the rents of houses, the issues of the fair and the tolls paid in the town.[35] How much urban growth depended upon seignorial initiatives, of course, doubtless varies greatly. At Higham Ferrars (Northants.) the castle may simply have been a natural magnet for settlers who saw the chance of making a living by supplying it, for the village seems to have been above the average size when its 88 original burgesses were enfranchised in 1251. In any case, it is probably unwise to differentiate too sharply between deliberately 'planted' towns and towns growing naturally in a period of increasing population, greater wealth and more active commerce. Seignorial initiative and natural growth were in no sense mutually exclusive. The little town of Halesowen (Worcs.) may have owed its origin to thirteenth-century initiatives on the part of the abbot of Halesowen, its manorial lord, but as the town grew it needed food processors, retailers and craftsmen to supply the needs of its inhabitants and of its surrounding rural area. Once established, towns developed their own independent momentum.[36]

The part played by landlords in the foundation of new towns illustrates once again the extent to which urban development was an integral feature of a society dominated by the lords of the land. Landowners of every rank played their part in it, including the king, whose lordship over so many of the older boroughs in any case endowed him with an exceptional influence in English urban history. Even Henry II, sometimes portrayed as no great friend of towns, was a founder of new towns at Woodstock, High Wycombe and perhaps at Market Harborough. Other lords were even more prominent in this respect, and in the West Midlands the relative contributions of different groups of landowners to urban development have been determined. In Gloucestershire, Warwickshire and Worcestershire 4 per cent of towns owed their foundation to bishops, 32 per cent to monasteries, 51 per cent to barons and 13 per cent to lesser lords. These precise proportions would not apply everywhere, but in aggregate the importance of seignorial patronage in urban development was clearly very great.[37]

[35] *BBC 1216–1307*, p. 3; A. Saltman, ed., *Cartulary of Tutbury Priory*, nos. 52, 71.
[36] Steane, *Northamptonshire Landscape*, pp. 154–6; Beresford, *New Towns*, p. 105; *BBC 1216–1307*, p. 142; Hilton, 'Small town society in England before the Black Death', pp. 76–9.
[37] Hilton, *Class Conflict and the Crisis of Feudalism*, pp. 196–7; W.G. Hoskins, *Provincial England*, 1963, pp. 57–60.

Some medieval new towns were conspicuously successful. The castle borough which grew up on the northern bank of the lower Tyne at Newcastle between 1080 and 1135 was a busy port and trading centre with its own body of customs before the end of Henry I's reign. Its growth continued, moreover, and by the 1330s its contribution to the king's taxes was not much smaller than that of the ancient city of York. King's Lynn, too, which developed on a site where salt had been sold before there was any sign of a town, found a patron in its lord, the bishop of Norwich, and got the king's endorsement of an open-door policy to visiting merchants, from wherever they might come. By 1203 the taxes levied on trade by King John suggest that the business done in the port of King's Lynn could bear comparison with that done by the merchants of Lincoln. Boston had also flourished notably by that date, and it continued to do so, both as a port and fair town, throughout the thirteenth century. In the 1280s, together with its associated Lincolnshire ports, it handled over a third of England's wool exports. By the early fourteenth century, admittedly, Boston had relinquished primacy to London both in wool exporting and in the volume of alien commerce which it handled, but in 1334 the value of the taxable goods of its inhabitants ranked Boston behind only London, Bristol, York and Newcastle among English towns. Yet Boston, too, had been a new town. There is no certain trace of it in the Lincolnshire Domesday, but the fact that subsequently it grew so notably probably owed something to the patronage of its lords, the earls of Richmond.[38]

As well as successes, of course, there were failures. Even old towns did not necessarily grow. Buckingham, for instance, had been a borough in 1086, but it cut no great figure then or later, and in 1334 it was taxed at the 'rural' rate and paid no more than many a village did. At that date, too, Old Sarum, deserted by the bishop for the new town of Salisbury a century before, was well on its way to becoming the classic 'rotten borough', and despite being assessed at the higher 'urban' rate it paid even less tax than Buckingham.[39] Some founders of new towns were also excessively optimistic. The Staffordshire

---

[38] E. Miller, 'Rulers of thirteenth-century towns: the cases of York and Newcastle upon Tyne', p. 129; D.M. Owen, ed., *The Making of King's Lynn*, pp. 7–12; T.H. Lloyd, *The English Wool Trade*, p. 12; *BBC 1042–1216*, p. 197; Beresford and St Joseph, *Medieval England*, pp. 217–19. In comparing towns in the taxation records, since not all towns were taxed at the same rate, we have used the assessed value of their taxable goods rather than the amount of tax they paid; for Boston's tax in 1334, see R.E. Glasscock, *The Lay Subsidy of 1334*, p. 169.

[39] *Ibid.*, pp. 16, 333.

foundation by the Ferrars family at Newborough, although there were still tenanted burgages there in the fourteenth century, did not have a long-term urban future: today it 'straggles along a country road and has nothing burghal remaining in its appearance'; Newtown, established by the bishops of Winchester in Burghclere (Hants.), has disappeared totally; and the failure of Warenmouth (Northumberland) was equally complete. It was 'caused to be built' by William Heron 'in the common pasture of the vill of Bamburgh' in the mid-thirteenth century; the king was persuaded to endow it by charter with all the liberties King John had conferred on Newcastle, and there were still burgages there in 1330. By the sixteenth century, however, no such place was known and subsequently its very location has been debated. In fact it never amounted to much, for in 1296 it could muster only three taxpayers, fewer than nearby agricultural communities like Adderstone and Mousen, and what chance it had of surviving was destroyed when it was 'burned completely' by the Scots in 1328.[40]

Most new towns of the twelfth and thirteenth centuries, however, did survive, although few became international trading centres like Boston or King's Lynn. The majority were in the literal sense market towns offering an outlet for the surpluses of a limited agricultural hinterland and access to some of the services, the industrial products, and perhaps the commodities of longer-range trade their rural neighbours needed. Halesowen was not untypical in this respect, even though admittedly at the lower end of the scale of urban achievement. The chronology of deliberate new town foundations during these generations probably reflects accurately enough the general course of urban development: their number was increasing throughout the twelfth century, reached a peak in the period *c.* 1170–1230, tailed off after *c.* 1250, and was very small after 1300. Taken in conjunction with the fact that some towns in the early fourteenth century were perhaps less welcoming to immigrants than previously, the implication may be that by that time England may have had a sufficiency of urban equipment, just as it seems to have had a sufficiency of markets.[41] Such a view, however, may involve taking too narrow a view of urban development. If the establishment of new market towns was petering out by 1300, the expansion during the next generation or two of semi-rural communities geared less to

---

[40] Beresford, *New Towns*, pp. 445, 475, 487–8; *NCH*, I, 194–6.
[41] Beresford, *New Towns*, pp. 327–38; A.B. Hibbert, 'The economic policies of towns', in *CEcH*, III, pp. 198–200.

marketing than to manufacture may have been the most significant sign of the times. In the textile villages of East Anglia, the south and the west, and in the metal-working centres of south Yorkshire and the West Midlands, some foundations of the industrial towns of the future were being laid. The foundation of market towns during the twelfth and thirteenth centuries had continued a line of development which had its origins long before the Norman Conquest and which contributed notably to the commercialization of England's medieval economy; but some of the new economic centres which came clearly into view during the early fourteenth century were probably the most original manifestations of economic advance during the central middle ages.

(c)   The extent and significance of urban growth

While the evidence available to us continues to preclude an accurate calculation of urban populations at any point during our period, recent archaeological and topographical studies have provided somewhat firmer bases for estimating what some of them may have been. Such estimates inevitably remain speculative, but one result has been suggestions that some of the leading English towns may have been considerably larger than had previously been supposed. London in *c.* 1300, for example, may have had around 80,000 citizens and Norwich in 1333 in the region of 25,000 inhabitants, in each case about double earlier estimates. At the same time, even if these revisions are acceptable, London would still be far ahead of all other English towns and smaller than many leading continental cities; and Norwich would have been smaller than Rouen and two or three other French provincial towns, and than Ghent and Bruges in Flanders. The contrast with northern Italy is even more marked. There may only have been four or five English towns with populations of 10,000 or more, but in northern Italy there were as many as thirty-five.[42]

The size of a few large towns, however, is not the only yardstick for measuring the extent of urbanization. In the early fourteenth century there may have been nearly twenty provincial towns with populations in excess of 5,000 compared with only four in the late eleventh century; and by *c.* 1300 there may also have been fifty

---

[42] Holt and Rosser, eds, *The English Medieval Town*, p. 6; Le Goff, ed., *Histoire de la France urbaine*, II, pp. 190–1; Rutledge, 'Immigration and population growth in early fourteenth-century Norwich', p. 27; R.H. Britnell, 'The towns of England and northern Italy in the early fourteenth century', *EcHR*, 2nd ser. XLIV (1991), pp. 21–4.

market towns with populations in the 2,000–5,000 range. In addition, a crucial contribution to England's commercial development was made by the very large number of smaller market towns with populations below, and often far below, 2,000 inhabitants (it is doubtful, for example, whether the town founded at Thornbury (Glos.) in the thirteenth century housed more than 500 people).[43] The spread of small market towns as well as the growth of larger towns, contributed to England's economic expansion during the central middle ages and to the increased commercialization of English society. Compared with the tally of 111 Domesday boroughs, there were probably more than 500 places with some urban characteristics in 1300. The results were apparent on the maps of every part of the country. In an old settled county like Hampshire, three Domesday boroughs (Winchester, Southampton and Twynham) had been joined by nineteen others, even though admittedly not all of the newcomers were destined to be urban successes. In 1086, likewise, Oxford was the only borough in Oxfordshire, while in neighbouring Gloucestershire there were boroughs at Gloucester, Bristol and Winchcombe, and some signs of urban development at Tewkesbury and Berkeley. In Gloucestershire Stow-on-the-Wold, Cirencester, Dursley, Newnham, Chipping Campden, Wotton-under-Edge, Chipping Sodbury, Northleach, Lechlade, Thornbury and Tetbury had been added to the county's list of towns by 1270; and the new towns of Oxfordshire included Banbury, Chipping Norton, Charlbury, Woodstock, Burford, Witney and Eynsham. The accessibility of urban markets and of urban goods and services had obviously been greatly expanded.[44]

The significance of urban development was probably even greater in some of the more peripheral parts of the country. In Northumberland, for instance, there may have been some proto-urban development before the Conquest in some of the principal royal vills (Corbridge, Bamburgh, perhaps Newburn), but it is doubtful whether it amounted to very much. This urban desert, however, was substantially transformed during the ensuing generations. The growth of Newcastle gave the North-East a major port and one of the larger English towns by the fourteenth century. While Warenmouth failed comprehensively and Newcastle frustrated attempts to develop North Shields as a port, small ports at Newbiggin and Alnmouth had

[43] R.H. Hilton, 'Towns in English medieval society', in Holt and Rosser, eds, *English Medieval Town* p. 22; *idem, Class Conflict and the Crisis of Feudalism*, pp. 179–80.
[44] Beresford, *New Towns*, pp. 230–1; H.P.R. Finberg, *Gloucestershire Studies*, pp. 65–7; K. Rodwell, ed., *Historic towns of Oxfordshire*, map on p. 16.

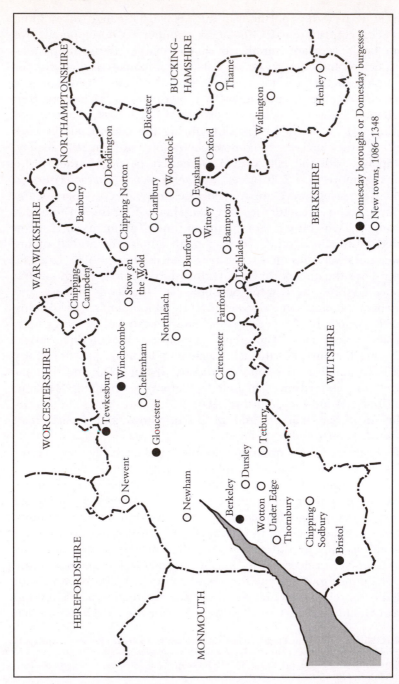

Map 6 Progress of urbanization: Oxfordshire and Gloucestershire, 1086–1348

Sources: K. Rodwell, *Historic Towns in Oxfordshire*; H.P.R. Finberg, *Gloucestershire Studies*.

rather more success, at least until the latter was destroyed by the Scots in 1336. Of the old royal vills, urban development soon faded from the picture at Newburn and was very limited at Bamburgh and Rothbury, but it was more in evidence at Corbridge. Hexham, too, may have developed up to a point in the shadow of the abbey church and some of the castle towns had a measure of success. Even though Mitford was never more than a hamlet and there was little that was urban about the 'borough' of Warkworth, Wooler, Alnwick and Morpeth became market towns for Glendale, north Northumberland and central Northumberland respectively; and a similar role was played by Norham in the Tweed valley, by Corbridge in Tynedale and by Newcastle for the lands along the lower Tyne. So far as Northumbrian villages were concerned the accessibility of urban services had been totally transformed.[45]

Those services, as we have already pointed out, were many and various. Towns were markets for rural produce, and in some cases enabled villagers to reach customers well outside their immediate district. The river port of Henley-on-Thames, for example, although it was still treated as a manor by the earl of Cornwall in 1296, was already taking on an urban character arising from its role as a collecting centre for grain to be shipped down-river to London. Countrymen, moreover, bought as well as sold in towns, encouraging diversification in the things in which townsmen traded and the things they made. Urbanization, especially in the peripheral areas, helped to make the English economy in 1300 much more uniform than it had been two centuries earlier; and at every level it was much more geared to exchanges. In this connection it is a relevant fact that by the opening of the fourteenth century few people were more than a day's journey from a town, and in many instances from more towns than one.[46]

An impression of how accessible urban services had become can be got from manorial accounts like those for the Oxfordshire village of Cuxham in the period 1276–1359. Without taking account of his dealings at fairs, the reeve of Cuxham did business in a number of towns. Most of the manor's grain went to Henley for sale; livestock was bought at Thame and Abingdon; iron, too, was purchased at

---

[45] *NCH*, II, pp. 473–6; VIII, pp. 285–93; X, pp. 28–9; J. Hodgson, *History of Northumberland*, II(2), pp. 213–17; E. Miller, 'Medieval new towns', *North. Hist.* III (1968), pp. 192–7.
[46] L.M. Midgley, ed., *Ministers' Accounts of the Earldom of Cornwall, 1296–1297*, pp. 91–5; D.L. Farmer, 'Marketing the produce of the countryside 1200–1500', in *AHEW*, III, p. 371; Holt and Rosser, eds, *The English Medieval Town*, p. 6.

Abingdon, hay and seed corn at Wallingford, and a millstone, apple seedlings and a bronze jar at Oxford. On occasion the reeve went even further afield: to Reading for iron and a horse, and to Southampton to get Spanish iron and a millstone.[47] This web of contacts between country places and town markets was a condition for the increasingly commercial character of English rural society, provided a wider range of market choices for the countryman both as a seller and a buyer, and probably involved improvements in the quality of life of medieval society at many levels. At the same time, the growth of towns offered to some countryfolk alternative opportunities of employment and settlement to those available in crowded villages.

The difficulty of quantifying the scale of urbanization during the central middle ages must, however, again be stressed. On the other hand, the simultaneous growth of established towns, the founding of new towns, and the assumption by many previously wholly agricultural communities of some urban characteristics make it plausible to suggest that urban populations increased at a somewhat faster rate than the rural population during the two centuries or so after 1086, and that by the opening of the fourteenth century at least 10 per cent of English men and women were townsfolk.[48] Admittedly, by that time, there were also some signs that towns were becoming less welcoming to immigrants than in earlier days, and increasing evidence of rural overcrowding possibly suggests that urban growth was no longer capable of keeping pace with the growth of England's population as a whole. Viewed solely in quantitative terms, therefore, the progress of urbanization had obvious limits and inadequacies.

This purely quantitative yardstick, however, provides an insufficient measure by itself of the contribution urbanization made to England's development in a period during which the country's population perhaps increased threefold. Towns, by expanding facilities for trade and, in the language of the economist, reducing transaction costs, encouraged specialization in other sectors of economic life; and, as demand grew for the services which towns could provide, so did specialization within towns themselves, involving

[47] P.D.A. Harvey, ed., *Manorial Records of Cuxham, Oxfordshire, passim.*

[48] This estimate is necessarily based on a good deal of guesswork; but if there were 550 small market towns with an average of 750 inhabitants, giving a total of 400,000, together with a further 300,000 people in towns with populations of 2,000 or more, this would be roughly 10 per cent of a total population, which was possibly around 6 millions. On all this see R.H. Britnell, *Commercialisation of English Society*, p. 115, who suggests, however, that possibly as much as 15 per cent of England's population lived in urban settlements by the early fourteenth century.

some economies of scale. An increase of a town's trade, or of the output of its industries, did not necessarily require a proportionate increase of its inhabitants. At the same time, the benefit derived by local communities from convenient facilities for selling rural produce and for purchasing non-agricultural commodities could be out of all proportion to the size of the town which provided them. And, of course, those benefits did not derive from towns alone, for, as we have seen, rural fairs and markets were an integral part of the trading network, there was much buying and selling outside formal markets, many villages were bases for some sort of industrial activity, and most mining, smelting and quarrying were necessarily rural activities Urbanization was a part only, although a very important part, of the economic expansion which characterized the central middle ages.

3.   BOROUGHS AND TOWNS

So far we have used the words town or borough more or less indifferently to describe the urban communities of medieval England. This conforms well enough with the indifference with which words like *villa* and *burgus* were employed in contemporary sources, but it is time to look somewhat more closely at the terms we use. The word town, in our usage, carries with it the connotation of a community distinctive in its economic character and function, and in particular of one with a range of non-agricultural occupations differentiating it from rural villages. At the same time, towns also tended to be distinctive social units, and this 'separateness of urban society' often found political, administrative and legal expression, something appropriately indicated by describing them as boroughs. As we have seen, many boroughs by 1086 were communities clearly distinguishable from the rural context in which they had developed, although as yet they 'were not . . . officially places of particular individual or corporate liberty'.[49] In the generations which followed, however, the political, administrative and legal separateness of many town communities was notably extended, enlarging and adding detail to the concept of what a borough should be. Inevitably, on the other hand, there was much variation from place to place in the scope and pace of such developments, so that it may be helpful to look at some of

[49] S. Reynolds, *Introduction*, pp. viii–x, 94–7.

the extremes between which they took place.

(a) Extreme cases: Clare and London

The little Suffolk market town (as it is today) of Clare may be taken as one extreme. It had a market before 1066 and there were burgesses there in 1086, although at that time it was simply described as a manor, and in the early thirteenth century the market was 'the market of the lord, the earl of Clare'. By 1262, however, the town which provided the earl's castle with supplies and services was territorially distinct from the manor, its affairs were regulated by a separate borough court, and it had a fair as well as a market. On the other hand, its separateness was probably still very far from complete, although it had been extended by 1325 when the burgesses were managing the market in return for a fixed annual payment; and in 1331 the town bailiffs (until then simple seignorial officials) were said to be elected 'by all the burgesses of the borough of Clare'. Even so Clare had not proceeded far along the road towards urban emancipation: it never seems to have had a gild merchant, it had no mayor or common seal in the middle ages, and the lord's steward continued to preside over the borough court. Clare remained, in fact, essentially an adjunct of the castle, a situation which the frequent visits to the castle of Elizabeth de Burgh, a co-heiress of the last Clare earl of Gloucester, helped to perpetuate down to her death in 1360.[50]

London was obviously at the opposite extreme from this little Suffolk borough. Already the greatest English town in King William's day, the taxes it paid suggest that its pre-eminence steadily increased. Under Henry I its geld was half as much again as that of its nearest rival, Winchester; under Henry II the aids it paid averaged three times those paid by the second city, York; and by 1334 it paid five times as much towards a lay subsidy as the most heavily taxed provincial town, which was now Bristol.[51] London may also have been exceptional from an early date in another way. Most Domesday towns were under the administrative control of the officers of the shire in which they lay; but London, possibly even from before 1066,

[50] G.A. Thornton, 'A study in the history of Clare, Suffolk', *TRHS*, 4th ser. XI (1928), pp. 85–105; C. Harper-Bill and R. Mortimer, eds, *Stoke-by-Clare Cartulary*, no. 234.
[51] Stephenson, *Borough and Town*, app. V and VI; H.C. Darby, ed., *New Historical Geography of England*, pp. 134, 181–2.
[52] C.N.L. Brooke and G. Keir, *London 800–1216: the Shaping of a City*, p. 197. What follows relies heavily on this work, and also on S. Reynolds, 'The rulers of London in the twelfth century', *History*, LVII (1972), pp. 337–57.

was associated with the county of Middlesex under a common authority, and the evidence points to 'the key importance of the city itself as a centre of power'.[52] The city, all the same, had not gone far towards achieving municipal self-determination. The sheriffs of early twelfth-century London, whose responsibilities also included Middlesex, and the local justiciars with whom they were sometimes associated, were royal officers whose duty it was to safeguard the king's interests and to give effect to his commands – duties in which they often had the backing of other royal servants like the constables of the Tower and even the king's moneyers.[53] Nor were the early sheriffs and justiciars, where something can be learned about them, representative citizens. Roger nephew of Hubert was indeed a Londoner by birth and Hugh Buckland was a canon of St Paul's, but the former was founder of the Cornhill dynasty of professional royal officials and the latter was one of Henry I's leading administrators. Others were still less closely identified with the citizens, including the Essex barons Ralph Baynard and Aubrey de Vere, the Hertfordshire baron Roger de Valognes, and perhaps the first Geoffrey de Mandeville, lord of High Easter in Essex. The common task of these bureaucrats and barons was to preserve the king's lordship over England's principal city, to give reality to his power there, and to ensure that his revenue due from it was collected. Like many other local communities London compounded for much of this revenue by paying a fixed annual 'farm', apparently standing at somewhat over £500 in 1129–30. In twelfth-century terms that was a sum large enough to be well worth safeguarding.

Although the king's lordship was paramount, other lords had interests in Norman London. Castle Baynard and Montfichet castle were private fortresses on the city's western edge; and the city was also 'bristling with sokes', enclaves of private property over which their proprietors had administrative and judicial authority. These sokes were in many hands, including those of the queen, the lord of the honour of Mortain, the earl of Gloucester, some private citizens, and of course many ecclesiastics. Henry I restored authority over the soke of Cripplegate to the church of St Martin-le-Grand; in the abbot of Westiminster's soke merchants paid dues to the abbot and its inhabitants owed no suit to the city courts; and the inhabitants of the bishop of London's soke were exempt from all external jurisdic-

[53] Reynolds, 'The rulers of London', p. 340.

tion unless the bishop's court denied them justice. This honeycomb of immunities fragmented the administrative integrity of the city in much the same way as feudal lordships and feudal liberties fragmented the administrative unity of twelfth-century shires.[54]

There were, however, some unifying influences in Norman London and some institutions which gave Londoners a voice of their own. The city had its own assembly (the folkmoot) and its own court (the husting) well before 1066, although little is known about them; and the citizens enjoyed their own customs, those laws of which they had been worthy in the Confessor's time and which the Conqueror confirmed.[55] By 1127, too, the city had been divided into wards, each headed by an alderman; and most aldermen were English and presumably citizens. The wards provided a framework for organizing the defence of the city and for its general administration; each had its own court; and the aldermen may already have been developing into an elite group in the city. From these bases, moreover, the citizens may have tried from time to time to assert a greater control over their own affairs. A charter late in the reign of Henry I, if it could be taken at its face value, might represent a significant step in that direction. In addition to some particular concessions and confirmations, it professed to grant to the citizens in perpetuity a right to 'appoint from among themselves' whoever they wished to be their sheriff and justiciar, and also to hold the city for a farm over £200 less than what appears to have been the twelfth-century norm. Taken literally, these provisions would have reduced significantly the financial obligations of the citizens to the king and, still more important, advanced their capacity to manage their own affairs.[56]

The authenticity of this charter, however, is no longer unquestioned, although in 1129–30 the citizens seem successfully to have offered Henry I money to have a sheriff of their own choice, the known sheriffs and justiciars at this period do appear to have been more often native Londoners, and the succession struggle after 1135 may have encouraged new assertiveness in the city. At the start of Stephen's reign the 'better born' Londoners, alleged that it was the city's peculiar privilege to have a say in the choice of a successor to a dead king; and possibly they formed themselves into a sworn associa-

---

[54] Brooke and Keir, *London 800–1216*, pp. 105, 156; *Regesta*, II, nos. 556, 1249–50, 1824; III, no. 927; F.M. Stenton, 'Norman London', in D.M. Stenton, ed., *Preparatory to Anglo-Saxon England*, pp. 33–5.

[55] *EHD*, II, p. 945.

[56] For the text, W. Stubbs, ed., *Select Charters*, p. 129, translated in *EHD*, II, pp. 945–6; it is dated probably 1130 in *Regesta*, II, no. 1645.

tion (a 'commune') which Stephen may have recognized to get their support, sealing the bargain by 'an oath taken on both sides'. The commune, on the other hand, availed the Londoners little. Both Stephen and his rival, Henry I's daughter Matilda, recognized Geoffrey de Mandeville's claim to be sheriff of London and Middlesex by inheritance and to hold the city for the reduced farm of £300 a year specified in Henry I's supposed charter to the city. Matilda went further, promising Geoffrey to make no agreement with the Londoners, 'for they are his mortal enemies'.[57]

For much of the rest of the twelfth century little is known in detail about the government of London, although there are some signs that the citizens were making some quiet advances towards greater self-determination. Although the annual farm the city paid in Henry II's early years was back to the £522 it had paid under Henry I, most of the sheriffs after 1154 seem to have been Londoners, they were sometimes nominated by the city, the citizens took corporate responsibility for levying some of the taxes Henry demanded from them, and it is 'reasonable to guess that a decision-making body was beginning to develop within the husting and that the aldermen were the chief decision makers'.[58] Developments under Richard I were more dramatic. A sworn commune was again set up, probably early in 1189, which once again negotiated a reduction of the city's farm to £300 and secured explicit endorsement of the right of the citizens to nominate the city's sheriffs. At the latest by 1193 there was also a 'mayor of the city of London', a new officer envisaged as 'the city's own representative, its leading magistrate . . . set between the government of the city and the kingdom'. Inevitably there was some reluctance to accept all the city's demands; but, in Richard I's absence, Count John and the magnates apparently formally recognized the commune in 1191; King John in 1199 acknowledged that the sheriffdom of London and Middlesex should belong to the citizens for ever for an annual farm of £300; and finally, in 1215, he allowed that they 'may elect for themselves a mayor of themselves every year'. The mayoralty by 1215 had existed for a couple of decades or more and, while King John's charter ordained that the

[57] C.N.L. Brooke and G. Keir, 'Henry I's charter for the city of London', *Jnl. of the Society of Archivists*, IV (1973), pp. 558–78; M. McKisack, 'London and the succession to the crown during the middle ages', in R.W. Hunt, W.A. Pantin and R.W. Southern, eds, *Studies in Medieval History presented to Frederick Maurice Powicke*, Oxford, 1948 pp. 78–9; K.R. Potter, ed., *Gesta Stephani*, pp. 5–6; *Regesta*, III, nos. 275–6; William of Malmesbury, *Historia Novella*, ed., K.R. Potter, Medieval Texts, 1955, p. 54.
[58] Reynolds, 'The rulers of London', pp. 343–5.

mayor should be faithful to the king, he was also to be 'discreet and fit for the government of the city'. From that time forward he was the unquestioned head of the city's government, and by 1220 a mayor's court existed which ultimately took over much of the juris-diction traditionally exercised by the husting court.[59]

The king's lordship over London, of course, did not disappear. The mayor-elect had to appear before the king or his justiciar to swear fealty; and the king continued to tax the city, to oversee its administration and, when maladministration or failure to do justice was demonstrated, he had the power to resume direct rule. The new dispensation, moreover, did not necessarily reflect the aspirations of every Londoner. In the 1190s the grievances of the poorer citizens were voiced by the 'popular demagogue' William fitzOsbert, creating a threat to public order which had to be ended by smoking William out of the church of St Mary-le-Bow. In fact, 'for reign by sheriffs under royal control the city had exchanged a tight oligarchy of established citizens'. The events of the late twelfth century con-firmed the growing dominance within the city of a narrow circle of substantial families which more or less monopolized the office of alderman, and of which London's first mayor, Henry fitzAilwin, was a typical member. Probably the son and grandson of an alderman, he had himself served long in that office before becoming mayor in *c.* 1190. Nor should too much be made of the provision in John's charter for annual mayoral elections. FitzAilwin apparently contin-ued in office until his death in 1212; and later Serlo the Mercer was mayor in 1214 and for five years beginning in 1217, Richard Renger for five years beginning in 1222, and Andrew Bukerel for seven years beginning in 1231. London certainly saw no democratic revolution at the close of the twelfth century, for the mayoralty was the preserve of a small circle and it was decreed that the council of twenty-five, sworn to advise the mayor from 1200 onwards, should consist of the 'most discreet men of the city'.[60] The emancipation of the city from day-to-day royal controls and from authority exercised by royal ser-vants, on the other hand, and its capacity to manage its own affairs through its own officers, did make significant progress at that time in directions in which, so far as they were able, other towns would

[59] Brooke and Keir, *London 800–1216*, p. 236; *BBC 1042–1216*, pp. 220, 247; Stubbs, *Select Charters*, p. 311.
[60] A. Lane Poole, *From Domesday Book to Magna Carta*, p. 443; Brooke and Keir, *London 800–1216*, p. 248; H.T. Riley, trans., *Chronicles of Old London*, pp. 1–6.

follow.

(b)   Towns and their lords

The context in which progress towards self-determination took place was the fact that all towns initially were subject to lordship. In 1066 the most important manifestation of that fact had been the overriding lordship possessed by the king over most of the boroughs and cities of the kingdom. Some of their lordship kings granted away before and after 1086, and their authority was much less direct in the case of many of the new towns which appeared during the twelfth and thirteenth centuries; but they continued to exercise special powers in most of the oldest, and very often the largest, English urban communities. The king's lordship was, to begin with, a source of profit. As the principal landowner in most of these older boroughs he was entitled to rents and other charges paid by tenants; and, in addition, to an income from penalties imposed by borough courts, tolls on trade and traders, the profits of local mints, and perhaps other traditional payments. These revenues were usually consolidated into a fixed annual sum, the borough 'farm', for payment of which the county sheriff was usually primarily responsible. Sheriffs, of course, might sub-allot financial responsibility to a subordinate, a reeve or portreeve, so that at Rochester we hear of the 'issues of the reeveship' and the 'dues . . . pertaining to the reeve of the city'; but generally speaking in early Norman England the towns were integrated into a pattern of royal administration in which the sheriffs were the key officers.[61]

The administrative system, moreover, was not only concerned with collecting the king's revenue. Sheriffs and their subordinates were expected to ensure locally that the king's peace and justice prevailed and that the sources of the king's revenue were duly safeguarded. The sheriff of Oxfordshire and the reeves of Oxford, therefore, presided in the Oxford portmoot as well as accounting for the city's farm.[62] On the whole, however, at this stage financial obligations leave the clearest imprint in the records, and it is clear that those obligations were by no means static. In the Conqueror's time, as we have seen, some borough farms rose substantially, leaving a sense of grievance like that reflected in the Domesday entry for

---

[61] *Regesta*, II, nos. 936, 1867; Stephenson, *Borough and Town*, p. 110; J. Tait, *Medieval English Borough*, pp. 140–52.
[62] H.E. Salter, ed., *Cartulary of Oseney Abbey*, I, p. 82; II, pp. 5–6, 8, 395.

Wallingford, telling us that the borough's value had increased from £30 to £60, '*and yet* it pays £80 for farm'. The upward movement of borough farms seems to have been much less marked during the twelfth century; but they were increasingly supplemented by lump sum payments for privileges and pardons, payments by gilds, an increasing range of judicial penalties imposed by royal justices, and periodic direct royal taxes (*dona*, aids, tallages which after Henry I's reign took the place of the geld). These last imposts were levied irregularly, but they could be very lucrative. London on five occasions during Henry II's reign paid around 1,000 marks; York on at least one occasion paid nearly as much; and Norwich, with an annual farm of just over £100, paid over £44 as a *donum* in 1158–59. The king profited in various ways from town growth and, partly in consequence, his agents were apt to intervene in more and more areas of burghal life.[63]

In the older towns, however, the king was seldom the only lord. In Domesday England what Maitland called 'tenurial heterogeneity', an intermingling of royal and private lordship, was characteristic of nearly all of them.[64] Some lords exercised authority over relatively compact portions of urban territory, as was the case in the London sokes and the ecclesiastical enclaves in numerous medieval towns. One of the 'shires' into which York was divided in 1086 was so fully the archbishop's that he took 'full custom' from it (i.e. all the revenues which elsewhere went to the king); and he held a court at the Minster door for his tenants in the city. The church of Lincoln was perhaps seeking recognition of a similar immunity when it persuaded Henry II to order an enquiry into what liberties the bishop enjoyed in his land and burgages in Lincoln in Henry I's time.[65] Laymen, too, had comparable privileges. Early twelfth-century Leicester, according to Orderic, had four masters: the king, the bishop of Lincoln, the earl of Huntingdon and Ivo fitzHugh; private courts were held in Oxford by Geoffrey de Clinton as well as Abingdon abbey and St Frideswide's priory; and in Winchester, where St Swithun's priory retained manorial jurisdiction in one large

---

[63] *Dd*, I, f. 56; Tait, *Medieval English Borough*, pp. 152, 184; Stephenson, *Borough and Town*, App. IV.

[64] F.W. Maitland, *Domesday Book and Beyond*, p. 182.

[65] *VCH City of York*, pp. 20, 38; *Reg. Antiquissimum*, I, no. 175.

[66] M. Chibnall, ed., *The Ecclesiastical History of Orderic Vitalis*, VI, p. 18; Salter, ed., *Cartulary of Oseney Abbey*, I, p. 425; J. Stevenson, ed., *Chronicon Monasterii de Abingdon*, II, pp. 165, 248; M.D. Lobel, 'Notes on the history of medieval Oxford', *Oxoniensia*, III (1938), p. 94; *Regesta*, II, no. 1516; Biddle, ed., *Winchester in the Early Middle Ages*, pp. 66, 340–1; Keene, *Survey*, I, p. 72.

city tenement until the sixteenth century, early twelfth-century surveys suggest that 'the pattern of jurisdiction ... was ... as that of landownership'.[66]

Private lordship, of course, was not restricted to enclaves in royal towns, for the king granted some royal towns to subjects and a very high proportion of the new towns founded during the twelfth and thirteenth centuries were established by private lords. Some magnates came to be the lords of many towns. The earl of Cornwall in 1296, for example, was lord of burgesses at Newport (Essex), Wilton (Wilts.), Ilchester (Somerset), Chichester (Sussex), Berkhamsted (Herts.), Oakham (Rutland), in the 'new borough' at Glatton (Hunts.), at Boroughbridge (Yorks.), Bradninch and Lydford (Devon), and at Tintagel, Helston-in-Kerrier, Saltash, Launceston and Lydford (Cornwall). Lords of towns drew revenue from their urban lordship just as the king did from royal boroughs. In some cases the sources of revenue in private boroughs, like those in the king's boroughs, were 'farmed' for a fixed annual sum, but very often this was not the case. At Wallingford in 1296 borough rents were accounted for separately, and at Boroughbridge the earl's officers accounted for £83 16s. 11$^{1}/_{4}$d. from the town, and from bridge tolls, the issues of the market and fisheries, stallage, and the profits from mills. Direct and detailed accounting was very common in small boroughs especially: the income its lord got from Burford (Oxon.), for example, was never farmed during the thirteenth and fourteenth centuries; and such revenues, as well as the items listed at Boroughbridge, might also include the profits of the jurisdiction exercised in a borough. When the Norman kings granted the city of Bath to the bishops, the grant included 'all pleas and laws and judgements' and was made explicitly 'for the augmentation of the see'.[67]

There was, of course, a tendency for the payments which townsmen made, like many of those made by manorial tenants, to become fixed at customary levels. Borough farms tended to become stabilized at the latest by the late twelfth or early thirteenth centuries; and the chief rents which holders of town property paid to the king or other lord became immutable at an early date. What the king got was only a penny or two pence per house in an old town like Cambridge in the thirteenth century, when towns of later founda-

---

[67] Midgley, ed., *Ministers' Accounts of the Earldom of Cornwall, 1296–1297, passim*; R.H. Gretton, *Burford Records*, pp. 16–18; *Regesta*, I, no. 326; II, nos. 573, 988.

tion might command a standard rent of 12d. per burgage; although even in the latter places custom was likely to give fixity to the burgess's outgoings and the fall in the value of money to erode the real value of their property to urban landowners.[68] Not surprisingly, therefore, some lords of towns sought to develop powers to tax their boroughs similar to those the king enjoyed in royal towns; the bishop of Salisbury, for example, securing in 1217 a right to levy a 'reasonable aid' from the citizens of 'new Salisbury' whenever the king tallaged his domains.[69] Where lords retained more direct control of their towns they were likely in the twelfth and thirteenth centuries to be in a position to draw enhanced returns from property rents, court profits and other sources of revenue, in the process touching the lives and interests of the townsfolk at many points. Leicester under the earls of Leicester and later of Lancaster, for instance, was slow to secure right of self-determination and other liberties. Its inhabitants were not wholly free of labour services until the earl abolished them in *c.* 1200; they had to grind their corn at the earl's mill and bake their bread in his oven, and, in Stephen's reign, the earl had not hesitated to grant certain burgesses to the church of Lincoln in recompense for injuries done to it. Much later, under Edward II, the town had frequently to provide troops for the earl; after 1330 Earl Henry of Lancaster, with his sight failing, spent much time in Leicester castle and presents to him, and to his son on his succession, were heavy charges on the town. The earl also retained powers to requisition grain and meat in the town at prices determined by himself, together with horses and carts to provide the carriage he needed.[70]

The lords of towns also needed administrative resources in order to exercise their rights. In a royal borough like Winchester under Henry II, the king relied on the city's reeves, under the supervision of the sheriff of Hampshire, to see to the holding of the city courts, the collection of the various items of royal revenue, and perhaps the enforcement of the customary rules governing the lives of the citizens.[71] While by the end of the twelfth century many of the larger towns were acquiring varying rights of self-government, in many

---

[68] *BBC 1216–1307*, pp. 44–60; Hilton, *Class Conflict and the Crisis of Feudalism*, pp. 167–8; Maitland, *Township and Borough*, p. 70; Keene, *Survey*, I, p. 196.
[69] *Rot. Parl.*, I, pp. 174–5.
[70] *VCH Leics*, IV, p. 9; *Reg. Antiquissimum*, II, no. 324; J. Nichols, *History and Antiquities of the County of Leicester*, I(1), 1795, app. p. 15; M. Bateson, ed., *Records of the Borough of Leicester*, I, pp. 296, 302, 320–1, 328–33, 340; II, pp. xx–xxi.
[71] Keene, *Survey*, I, pp. 68–9.

smaller places and in seignorial boroughs in particular, the direct exercise of authority by the lord continued to be common and to make it necessary for them to have agents on the spot. This was true in our period at Clare and Burford; at Alnwick the bailiff of the borough was clearly the lord's servant; at Sheffield in 1297 the court was held by the lord's bailiffs 'as hitherto has been accustomed'; and at Reading in 1254 the abbey or its bailiffs were entitled to plead 'all pleas pertaining to the town'. In such circumstances townsfolk might easily be aggrieved by the heavy hand of their lord or his agents: certainly, the burgesses of Leicester, to judge by their complaints in 1322, had no doubt that the rule of Thomas of Lancaster over them was oppressive, extortionate and unmindful of their interests.[72] The burden of lordship was one good reason for townsfolk to seek to achieve municipal liberties.

The battle to do so between towns and their lords was often hardest when the lord of a town was an ecclesiastic, and particularly a monastic corporation, the rights of which were most likely to be recorded and carefully preserved. The bishops of Salisbury, for example, do not seem during the thirteenth century to have used their powers under the 1227 charter to tax their cathedral city; but they did not forget them and tried in 1305 to levy a tax. The citizens, 'grown wanton with fatness', resisted and ultimately the bishop surrendered his right to tax them, but only on condition that his lordship over the city was confirmed.[73] Other ecclesiastical lords were much less accommodating. The abbot of Halesowen kept the inhabitants of the little town he founded there under the strictest controls, rigorously enforcing payment by the burgesses of marriage fines and other charges which were a mark of servile status. It is not surprising that they cursed and defamed him, or that one burgess hanged a dog in the abbey's pillory. The burgesses of Dunstable, too, said they would rather go to hell than pay the taxes the priory imposed on them and they opened negotiations with a neighbouring landowner for a new site where they might live toll-free, and managed in the end to buy remission from some of their obligations; and at Bury St Edmunds in 1327 there was a full-scale rising against the abbey which was brutally suppressed. The townsfolk of Cirencester also had many complaints against their monastic lord in 1342: the abbot, they said, had got hold of their borough charter

---

[72] *BBC 1216–1307*, pp. 197–8; *Cal. Inq. Misc.*, II, no. 548.
[73] *Rot. Parl.*, I, pp. 175–6; K.H. Rogers, 'Salisbury', in Lobel, ed., *Atlas of Historic Towns*, I, p. 7.

and burned it, had suppressed their borough court in 1308, and had bought up so many burgages that the town had been transformed into a mere appendage of the abbey's manor. There may have been less justification for these allegations than has sometimes been assumed; but in any event the town failed to substantiate them and gained nothing from them. Cirencester's burghal aspirations were decisively blocked.[74]

4. MUNICIPAL DEVELOPMENT

The urban communities of Norman England, therefore, were part of a territorial order dominated by a class of landlords of whom the king was the greatest. Some of these communities already had certain distinctive characteristics in 1066. London had its own 'laws' which the Conqueror confirmed and Chester had 'laws' that were set out in Domesday Book. Many towns, too, had their own portreeves, although they were likely to be the agents of the local sheriff; some perhaps had aldermen in charge of the wards into which they were divided or lawmen who were guardians of a town's customs; and many towns had a borough court, although as part of the system of public tribunals which the monarchy had instituted. Some seeds of municipal development existed in these features of Domesday boroughs, for they were part of an institutional framework which in due time passed into the control of the townsfolk; but for that to happen required concessions from the king and other territorial lords under whose seignorial authority the Domesday boroughs and others of later foundation developed.

(a)   *The gild merchant*

Associations called gilds merchant played an important part in this process of municipal development. By the thirteenth century the right to establish such a gild was a privilege often conferred as a mat-

---

[74] Hilton, *Class Conflict and the Crisis of Feudalism*, pp. 201–2; *VCH Beds.*, III, pp. 357–8; H.R. Luard, ed., *Annales Monastici*, III, pp. 122–4; N.M. Trenholme, *English Monastic Boroughs*, p. 15; M.D. Lobel, *The Borough of Bury St Edmunds*, pp. 143–5; Finberg, *Gloucestershire Studies*, pp. 74–9 (which now needs to be read in conjunction with C.D. Ross, ed., *Cartulary of Cirencester Abbey*, I, pp. xxxvi–xl, 123–4, 126, 140).

ter of routine on newly enfranchised boroughs; and indeed, at Ipswich at the very beginning of the century, in giving effect to John's borough charter, the establishment of a gild merchant and of borough institutions proceeded simultaneously.[75] In the twelfth century, by contrast, gilds merchant seem to have come into existence with little in the way of authorization, at least until long after the event. Henry I, for instance, granted exemption from toll to 'my burgesses of Wilton of the *gilda mercatoria*', a gild of which there is no previous mention; and York's gild merchant, first explicitly authorized by Henry II, can be shown to have existed in Henry I's time. Henry II's confirmation of gilds merchant at Lincoln and Wallingford, too, stated that they went back to the Confessor's day, the Leicester gild was said early in the twelfth century to have been in existence under the first two Norman kings, and both Chichester and Lewes were alleged to have had gilds merchant in the Conqueror's reign. It would, of course, be rash in every case to take such allegations literally, but they do suggest that when gilds are first mentioned in these places they were already of respectable antiquity. Certainly when Henry II confirmed Oxford's gild merchant in 1156 his charter implied that it had existed in Henry I's reign; and in fact there is a record of the gild in action in 1147 and charters to Burford suggest that it may go back at least to *c.* 1100.[76] In these early days, therefore, it is difficult to determine how and when gilds merchant began; and indeed, even in the thirteenth century membership rolls of the Shrewsbury gild go back to 1210 even though the gild apparently did not receive royal licence until 1227. Gilds merchant, in other words, probably originally grew out of a latent capacity in the still small urban communities to band together in order to determine what action might be necessary when some circumstance demanded it, a capacity which achieved a greater degree of organization as time went on, although even then in a form of association as 'unselfconscious . . . as the committee is today'.[77] In 1147, for instance, 'the citizens of Oxford of the commune of the

---

[75] G.H. Martin, *Early Court Rolls of the Borough of Ipswich*, University of Leicester Department of Local History, Occasional Papers, no. 5 (1954), p. 13. The record of 1200 is in C. Gross, *The Gild Merchant*, II, pp. 115–22, and is translated in C. Stephenson and F.G. Marcham, *Sources of English Constitutional History*, pp. 96–101.

[76] *Regesta*, II, no. 1275; III, no. 181; *VCH City of York*, pp. 31–2; Hill, *Medieval Lincoln*, p. 186; Gross, *The Gild Merchant*, II, pp. 28–9, 181; *VCH Leics.*, IV, p. 33; C.T. Clay, ed., *EYC*, VIII, no. 50; Stubbs, *Select Charters*, pp. 198–9; Salter, ed., *Cartulary of Oseney Abbey*, IV, pp. 86–7; R.B. Patterson, ed., *Earldom of Gloucester Charters*, nos. 42–3.

[77] G.H. Martin, 'The English borough in the thirteenth century', *TRHS*, 5th ser. XIII (1963), pp. 126, 135.

city and of the gild merchant' conveyed the 'island' of Medley to Osney abbey by common assent in the borough court (*portmanmoot*). The citizens' commune, however, was not very developed at that time. It had no common seal to authenticate its decision; and, so far as is known, the gild merchant had not yet received royal confirmation, its alderman was apparently a baron who was castellan of the king's castle, and its powers were uncertain since the sheriff of Oxfordshire at once intervened to undo what the citizens had ordained. Yet in 1147 a gild merchant may have existed for a generation or more, and there are earlier hints concerning the capacity of the citizens to act in concert. Domesday tells us that they held pasture outside the walls in common (*communiter*) and, in the mid-eleventh century, the reeve and all the citizens had collectively witnessed a lease. While it cannot be assumed that the gild merchant was in being as early as this, a capacity to act *communiter*, of which the gild was later a manifestation, seems clearly to be present.[78]

In the twelfth century, when gilds merchant appear with growing frequency in the records, the information about them is seldom as precise as might be desired; but one assumption which is sometimes made appears to be that the gild's membership was roughly identical with the body of citizens or burgesses of a town. Glanville, late in the century, appears to take that identity for granted when he writes of the villein becoming free after residing in a town for a year and a day, 'so that he is admitted as a citizen into their commune, that is to say their gild'.[79] Gild members at Shrewsbury in the first two decades of the thirteenth century, certainly, were so numerous that they must have included almost every householder (some of them women), and they embraced a range of occupations from vintners, mercers and goldsmiths to bakers, carpenters and Henry the harp-player. The Leicester gild at the end of the twelfth century had a similar membership; the citizens of Oxford in 1147 and 1191 described themselves as being of the commune of the city and gild merchant, and in 1191 no less than 63 of them witnessed a record of decisions they had reached; and the common seal of Gloucester about the same time carried the inscription 'seal of the burgesses of the gild

[78] Salter, ed., *Cartulary of Oseney Abbey*, IV, pp. 86–7; R.H.C. Davis, 'An Oxford charter of 1191 and the beginnings of municipal freedom', *Oxoniensia*, XXXIII (1968), pp. 57–61; *Dd*, I, f. 154; *VCH Oxon.*, IV, p. 48; H.E. Salter, *Medieval Oxford*, pp. 26, 34–5.
[79] G.D.G. Hall, ed., *Tractatus de Legibus et Consuetudinibus Regni Anglie qui Glanvilla vocatur*, p. 58.
[80] W. Cunningham, 'The gild merchant of Shrewsbury', *TRHS*, NS IX (1895), pp. 99–117; Gross, *The Gild Merchant*, II, pp. 137–8; Davis, 'An Oxford charter of 1191', pp. 53–4; Poole, *Domesday Book to Magna Carta*, p. 72; Tait, *Medieval English Borough*, p. 229.

merchant of Gloucester'. In these times, in brief, the burgesses and the gild merchant appear nearly, if not quite, 'two aspects of the same body'.[80]

This did not necessarily mean that gild membership included every townsman or consisted of townsfolk only. Some town dwellers were doubtless at all times too lowly to be considered suitable or too poor to contemplate assuming the obligations which membership entailed; and, at least in some towns as we have seen, certain craftsmen (mainly textile workers) were deliberately excluded from the ranks of burgesses and gildsmen alike. Further, while at Leicester in the 1240s gild members were required to reside in the town, the Shrewsbury gild during the first half of the thirteenth century admitted large numbers of outsiders, and Lincoln's gild merchant was authorized by Henry II in 1157 to consist of 'the men of the city and other merchants of the county'.[81] When gild merchants admitted outside members, their openness probably strengthened the ties between towns and their hinterland; but in addition, since town growth depended heavily upon immigration, a 'foreigner' buying his way into a town's gild might have taken the first step towards becoming a permanent resident. The gild merchant in early days, in other words, might be an open door to burgesship.

Evidence relating to the purposes which early gilds merchant were designed to serve is fragmentary in the extreme; but where they enrolled a high proportion of a town's inhabitants (including many who were clearly artisans) they were hardly gilds of merchants in any strict sense, and where they also admitted 'foreigners' it is difficult to regard them as merely exponents of urban xenophobia. Burgesses and some dwellers in a town's hinterland, on the other hand, might have this in common: they dealt in the town's market place, had an interest in finding in the town essential facilities for trade, and were concerned that trade was carried on there within a known and consistent framework of regulations. Gilds merchant might offer a means of expressing these concerns, and perhaps of framing and even of enforcing desirable rules for trading. This may be what Archbishop Thurstan of York meant when he granted to his burgesses of Beverley in 1122 their 'hanse-house ... to consider their statutes ... to the amendment of the town'. Henry I had earlier expressed this right as having 'their gild merchant with their pleas',

---

[81] Bateson, ed., *Records of the Borough of Leicester*, I, pp. 63–4, 72; C.H. Drinkwater, 'The merchant gild of Shrewsbury: seven rolls of the thirteenth century:', *Trans. Shropshire Arch. Soc.*, NS XII (1900), pp. 229–82; *BBC 1042–1216*, p. 204.

suggesting that the gild had powers to see that its 'statutes' were obeyed. Such a concession did not necessarily infringe any vital interest of a town's lord: on the contrary, Archbishop Thurstan seems to have thought it would increase Beverley's prosperity and so the town's value to him.[82]

To bring such an organization into existence may at first have called for little formality, but as written titles to rights and privileges assumed growing importance it became increasingly desirable for townsmen to secure explicit recognition of their gild. Henry II's confirmation of the gild merchant at Wallingford in 1156 recognized that it had long been in existence, and the king also acknowledged that it had taken the burgesses at least one short step along the way to self-determination. They were to have their gild 'with all its customs and laws freely, so that no reeve or justice of mine will meddle concerning that gild, but only their own alderman and minister', who was clearly distinguished from the reeve of the borough. At least in certain matters the burgesses of Wallingford controlled their own affairs.[83]

Some lords long after the mid-twelfth century, of course, were unwilling to allow the gild or its officers much in the way of autonomy. At Reading in 1254 the abbot insisted upon his right to choose the warden of the gild merchant, although he did allow that the warden should be a burgess of the gild with whom the burgesses were content. The warden, too, took an oath to the abbot as well as to his fellow gildsmen, and the abbot or his bailiff presided in the court held in the gildhall.[84] At Leicester, on the other hand, although the earl made some rules binding on gildsmen and the earl's steward on occasion attended gild meetings, the officers and council of the gild merchant from an early date were chosen by the gildsmen from their own number. The exceptional documentation preserved by the Leicester gild from the late twelfth century onwards, moreover, provides unusual insights into the role played by a gild merchant operating under the constraints of lordship. It enabled its members, for example, to recover debts owed to them by fellow gildsmen; it enforced regulations against cloth 'dishonestly' made, wool deceitfully dyed, the mixing of bad wool with good, or cloth defectively fulled; it gave effect to rules giving gildsmen a privileged position in the town's trade; and it laid down regulations for

---

[82] *Regesta*, II, nos. 1137, 1332.
[83] Gross, *The Gild Merchant*, II, pp. 244–5.
[84] *Ibid.*, pp. 202–4; *BBC 1216–1307*, p. 281; *VCH Berks.*, III, pp. 344–5; C.F. Slade, 'Reading', in Lobel, ed., *Atlas of Historic Towns*, I, pp. 3–4.

Leicester men trading in the great fairs. It was the town's chamber of commerce and marketing authority, with powers both of regulation and enforcement. It was also the defender of the community's solidarity, and when Henry Houghil declared at a gild meeting that he cared no more for the mayor than for a straw, he was fined two tuns of wine. The gild also controlled the only revenue belonging unconditionally to the burgesses, for it received entry fees paid by its members and could levy loans or taxes from them. The possession of funds strengthened the gild's hand in negotiations with the town's lord, enabling it to buy out charges like pontage and gavelpenny or to secure a change in the rules governing succession to real property.[85]

The fact that a gild merchant could serve the interests of its members was not necessarily something which disadvantaged a town's lord. The burgesses of Beverley under Henry I had their gild to which the archbishop of York granted the market tolls of the town in return for an annual payment of £12. It was no doubt advantageous for the burgesses to secure the banishment of the archbishop's financial agents from the market place, where their presence gave many opportunities for extortion; but it was also convenient from the archbishop's point of view to receive a fixed payment each year instead of having to collect a multiplicity of small sums, and probably the gild was the obvious body to arrange for their collection. The gild merchant, in other word, could be a useful piece of fiscal machinery for a town's lord. It was in order that 'stranger merchants' trading in Lincoln should be rated to all the customs of the town that Henry II ordered them to be members of Lincoln's gild merchant; and perhaps for similar reasons Henry II ordered members of the Wallingford gild who ceased to live in that town to continue paying contributions to the gild so long as they traded in Wallingford market.[86]

The fact that gild members paid charges reflected an assumption that membership conferred advantages, which in some places are clearly defined: at Worcester an exclusive right to trade in the city and suburb, at Leicester to trade wholesale or retail in the borough, at Chester to buy or sell any merchandise coming to the city by land

[85] *VCH Leics.*, IV, pp. 14–16; Bateson, ed., *Records of the Borough of Leicester*, I, pp. 65–107; Martin, 'The English borough in the thirteenth century', pp. 133–4..
[86] *Regesta*, II, no. 1332; Hill, *Medieval Lincoln*, pp. 185–6; Gross, *The Gild Merchant*, II, pp. 244–5.
[87] *Ibid.*, pp. 40, 272–3; Bateson, *Records of the Borough of Leicester*, I, p. xxviii; *CRR*, XI, pl. 2055.

or sea, at High Wycombe to retail woollen or linen cloth or dyes-tuffs.[87] The monopolistic character of the gildsman's rights have often been stressed unduly. It was, after all, not unreasonable that those who bore the cost of creating favourable conditions for trading should enjoy some advantage in using them; and the gild's monopoly was a very open one, embracing craftsmen as well as merchants, and often non-burgesses as well as burgesses. On the whole, too, the early gilds merchant seem to have welcomed recruits, making them a posi-tive influence in urban development. Not every lord, of course, saw them in this favourable light. Some, as we shall see, feared them as conspiracies; and Alan Basset in 1224 quashed the gild merchant at High Wycombe because he believed the town was likely to be 'improved' by allowing any merchant to trade there who wished to do so. In many twelfth-century towns, however, gilds merchant enabled townsfolk, while they were still subject to wide-ranging seig-norial authority, to exercise a measure of self-determination, especially in regard to those central aspects of urban life, trading and marketing. For certain purposes, therefore, lords dealt with their burgesses not as individuals but as organized associations with their own officers: to this extent, in many places, the gild merchant may still be regarded as the 'nucleus of the municipality'.[88]

This was not, on the other hand, a stage of municipal develop-ment through which all towns necessarily passed: London (and apparently Colchester and Northampton) never had such gilds, and Ipswich secured a gild merchant and municipal government simul-taneously in 1200. So long as towns were subject to seignorial control, however, gilds merchant gave to burgesses some powers of organizing their own affairs, and the means of negotiating with their lords and of raising money for their own purposes. This explains why so many town charters were granted to 'my citizens of the gild merchant', 'my citizens who are of the gild merchant', or 'all my bur-gesses who are in the gild merchant'.[89] The gild was the 'nucleus of the municipality', in other words, in that it was a dynamic force in the urban community rather than because later municipal institu-tions developed from it directly. The progress of municipal self-government after 1200, moreover, made the gild less essential as an instrument of civic initiative. At York it virtually disappeared from the scene; at Bedford and eventually at Southampton it more or less fused with the institutions of the borough; or it narrowed into a

[88] Stephenson, *Borough and Town*, pp. 150–1, 171–2.
[89] Gross, *The Gild Merchant*, II, pp. 47, 202, 251–2, 351.

socio-religious fraternity, like the Corpus Christi gild at Ipswich, or into a rich man's club as at Oxford, where the 'lesser commune' in 1257 clearly regarded it as an instrument of extortion. The same may have been true at King's Lynn, where membership of the 'great gild' was necessary for those who wished to trade in the town, but where the gild's chief characteristic was the 'lavish funerals and soul masses' for its members and the large number of chaplains it eventually employed. At Southampton, too, while gild members had a privileged position in the town's trade in *c.* 1300, they could also expect succour if they fell into poverty and, in the end, a suitable funeral, their fellow gildsmen watching and burning candles by their bodies and carrying them to their graves.[90]

Where gilds merchant continued in their twelfth-century role after 1200, the reason was likely to be failure on the part of urban communities to achieve a significant degree of municipal self-government. This was to some extent the case, as we have seen, at Leicester; and at Totnes (Devon) William de la Zouche's seignorial authority was intrusive enough to give rise to contentions between the burgesses and their lord as late as 1304. The Totnes burgesses found a means of giving voice to their interests through a gild merchant, which they probably owed to a grant by King John, but which they were claiming in 1255 to have had 'time out of mind'. The numbers admitted to the gild during the fifteen years or so after 1260 suggest that a high proportion of burgesses found a place in it, and, as well as merchants, some were clearly craftsmen and others 'strangers'. Gildsmen enjoyed exemption from toll in the town, but the gild also exercised some rights of jurisdiction in commercial matters, giving the town as a business community some powers of self-regulation.[91] A gild merchant as a means of expression for burgess interests was also found in some monastic boroughs where lordship was perpetuated and sometimes felt to be oppressive. At Bury St Edmunds a gild emerged, obscurely and perhaps surreptitiously, in the course of attempts by the burgesses to win concessions from the abbey in the late twelfth century, and was still central to the town's struggle for greater liberty a century later. In 1292 the gildsmen were accused of appointing an alderman without the abbey's consent, of raising a common fund for their own purposes, and of entertaining pleas between gildsmen which should have gone to the

---

[90] *Ibid.*, I, pp. 161–3; *PQW*, pp. 17–18; *VCH Beds.*, III, p. 17; Owen, ed., *The Making of King's Lynn*, p. 61; *Cal. Inq. Misc.*, I, no. 238; Platt, *Medieval Southampton*, pp. 20, 54; P. Studer, ed., *Oak Book of Southampton*, I, pp. 28, 34–6.
[91] Gross, *The Gild Merchant*, II, pp. 235–40.

abbey's courts; in 1304 the abbot totally rejected the right of the burgesses to have either a gild or an alderman; and in 1327 this prolonged conflict culminated in a violent revolt during which the townsmen extracted a charter from the abbey proclaiming that 'the community of the town of St Edmund shall have a perpetual alderman, commune and common seal and gild merchant'. Needless to say the revolt was crushed and every concession cancelled.[92]

(b)   The emergence of municipalities

Other townsfolk fared better than the burgesses of Bury St Edmunds, and by the thirteenth century most of the more important urban communities had achieved a significant degree of municipal self-government. But, as the history of Oxford shows, 'most towns became corporate bodies by a very gradual process'.[93] Oxford's later municipal constitution embodied elements which originated as expressions of the king's lordship over that town: a portreeve by the mid-eleventh century, who probably represented the king and sheriff in the city's administration; a fixed annual 'farm' as a composition for the various payments the city owed to the king by 1066; and in all probability a separate borough court, since that court in the twelfth century had the Old English name of 'portmanmoot'. Oxford's gild merchant, in existence by 1100 or soon after, was perhaps to a greater extent an instrument of the citizens, for in 1147 it seems to have given their consent to certain transactions in the portmanmoot; but if that was so, we cannot make too much of the initiative it permitted them. As we have seen, the sheriff of Oxfordshire quashed the decisions taken on that occasion and the gild's alderman appears to have been a local baron. A further short step forward, however, may have been taken in *c.* 1155 when a charter was secured from Henry II endorsing those rights the citizens were said to have enjoyed under Henry I. These included their gild merchant, the members of which should have sole right to trade in the city, exemption from tolls throughout England and Normandy, certain customs the citizens had in common with Londoners, and freedom from being impleaded in any tribunal outside the city. This last provision might ensure that their affairs were governed by customary rules compatible with urban ways of life.[94]

---

[92] Lobel, *The Borough of Bury St Edmunds*, pp. 16, 73–4, 120–3, 133–4, 137–45.
[93] Davis, 'An Oxford charter of 1191', p. 56.
[94] *VCH Oxon.*, IV, pp. 48–50, 58; Stubbs, *Select Charters*, pp. 198–9.

What part the gild merchant played in securing these rights and Henry II's endorsement of them cannot be determined, although it is at least likely that the gild raised the £78 Oxford paid for Henry's charter. By 1191, however, a document by which 'the citizens of Oxford of the community of the city and of the gild merchant' regulated certain pasture rights indicates significant progress since 1147 and 1155. It has been described as a 'public declaration of their communal existence' on the part of the citizens.[95] It was attested by 63 members of the gild merchant; it shows that there were now two reeves and two gild aldermen, all of them citizens; it was sealed with the city's common seal; and other roughly contemporary evidence suggests that the reeves were acting independently as presidents of the portmanmoot rather than as assistants of the sheriff. Then, in 1199, John empowered the citizens themselves to collect the revenues which made up the city's farm and account for them to the sheriff, and also to elect their own reeve, thus removing the suggestion that he was the sheriff's underling. Finally, in 1257, the citizens were allowed to account directly at the exchequer for their farm, putting an end to the sheriff's residual control over their finances. A possible indication of the source of the initiative underlying developments around the turn of the century may be the apparently dominant role in Oxford played by two successive aldermen of the gild merchant, John Kepeharm and his son Lawrence. By 1205, moreover, Lawrence Kepeharm had taken the title of mayor, perhaps indicating his appreciation that he was the chief officer of a municipality and not merely of a gild merchant.[96]

Municipal development along lines which were well marked at Oxford by 1200, was often accompanied by internal unification as well as revised relationships with external lordship. At Oxford, indeed, private courts had disappeared by the thirteenth century apart from the fair court held by St Frideswide's priory; and the coalescence of the various growth points at Bristol was probably furthered by Henry III's encouragement of participation by the inhabitants of the suburb of Redcliffe in the improvement of the port and his decree that they should answer before the king's justices as and where the burgesses of Bristol did. At Lincoln, too, the inhabitants of the castle Baile were made liable to taxes imposed on the city 'because they are of the gild merchant with the men dwell-

---

[95] By Davis, 'An Oxford charter of 1191', p. 63.
[96] *BBC 1042–1216*, p. 225; *VCH Oxon*, IV, p. 58.

ing in the city', and it was ruled in 1284 that the English and French boroughs at Nottingham should have a common mayor even though, 'because of the diversity of customs', each was still to have its own bailiff.[97] Unification in many places came slowly and often incompletely. At York the large possessions of the Minster and St Mary's abbey continued to be 'spangled and embroidered ... with great privileges'. The suburb of Bootham, dominated by St Mary's, was even declared a free borough from which the city authorities were excluded in 1275; and they did not recover control there until 1354, and then not totally. The time when London had been a 'complex of sokes' also left its mark in the archaic liberties claimed by St Paul's and other churches in 1321; at Leicester men from the bishop of Lincoln's fee were excluded from the gild merchant and borough office until the 1270s; and the city officers at Winchester had no authority or right to levy civic taxes in the bishop's suburban liberty.[98]

Even partial unification, of course, was not achieved everywhere. Durham, for example, achieved little by way of either unity or emancipation. It continued to be a cluster of five 'boroughs' grouped around the castle and cathedral, each borough having its own lord, courts, officials and 'miniature administration'. So far as there was any central authority it resided in the seignorial courts of the bishop and the prior. The citizens, therefore, had limited scope for displaying initiative, and their lords showed little enthusiasm for granting them liberties which would have enabled them to do so. Prior Bertram in *c.* 1200 did grant to the inhabitants of the 'new borough' of Elvet exemption from certain exactions and various tenurial privileges, but he reserved the authority of his court over them, his power to insist that they should grind their corn at his mill, and control over any market or fair which they might acquire in the future. An earlier charter of Bishop Puiset's for the bishop's borough is positively misleading in granting to it the customs enjoyed by Newcastle. Durham never developed as Newcastle did, never achieved municipal unity in medieval times, never even had a gild merchant. This

[97] *VCH Oxon*, IV, pp. 52–6; N.D. Harding, ed., *Bristol Charters, 1155–1373*, pp. 18, 22; *Close R.*, 1242–47, p. 422; W.H. Stevenson, ed., *Records of Nottingham*, I, p. 58.
[98] T. Widdrington, *Analecta Eboracensia*, ed. C. Caine, 1897, p. 219; *VCH City of York*, pp. 38–40, 68–9; H.M. Cam, ed., *The Eyre of London, 14 Edward II*, I, pp. 112. 115, 191–4; E. Smirke, 'Winchester in the thirteenth century', *Arch. Jnl.*, IX (1850), p. 374.
[99] M.M. Bonney, *Lordship and the Urban Community: Durham and its Overlords*, pp. 41–9, 199–205; W. Greenwell, ed., *Feodarium Prioratus Dunelmensis*, Surtees Soc., LVIII (1872), p. 199 note; M. Hope Dodds, 'The bishop's boroughs', *AA*, 3rd ser. XII (1915), pp. 90–1; C.M. Fraser, *A History of Anthony Bek, Bishop of Durham, 1283–1311*, Oxford, 1957, p. 86.

was perhaps only to be expected of a place the ecclesiastical lords of which were headed by a bishop whose authority between Tyne and Tees was claimed to be a regality.[99]

The degrees of self-determination towns achieved, therefore, varied greatly and it usually took time to achieve very much. For much of the twelfth century even relatively developed urban centres seldom went far towards self-determination, though their distinctive character was increasingly recognized. They commonly had their own courts which generated and preserved customary laws appropriate to the ways of life of urban communities, and a right to compound for the dues they owed to the king or other lord by a fixed annual payment, a 'farm'. The significance of such things must not, on the other hand, be exaggerated. After all manors, too, had their courts, their own customs, and reeves who might owe a 'farm'. The portreeve, furthermore, in origin was an agent of the town's lord (or of the sheriff in the case of royal boroughs); his duty was first and foremost to raise from a town what it owed to its lord and master; and the fact that a 'farm' was agreed between a town and its lord did not mean that it was immutable. In addition to the steep increases the Conqueror made in the farms of royal boroughs, those paid by Bedford, Cambridge, Derby, Lincoln, Northampton and Norwich were higher under Henry II or Richard I than in 1086.[100] It is true that some farms fell rather than rose over this period, but it was also a time when the king was devising new ways of taxing the resources of townsfolk, and it is unlikely that other lords failed to follow the royal example.

Even during the twelfth century, nonetheless, municipal progress was being made. A gild merchant appeared in many towns, representing at that time 'the active communal principal in the English borough'; and gilds merchant were probably often responsible for securing liberties which made boroughs in many respects privileged communities. Some of their privileges recognized the interests of townsfolk as traders, like exemptions from toll within a county (Beverley in *c.* 1130), or throughout England (London in 1131), or throughout 'my whole land of England and Normandy, Aquitaine and Anjou' (Wallingford in 1156). Even commoner was a recognition that urban ways of making a living demanded special personal and tenurial conditions. Tenurial freedom, the right to buy town property as a means of holding capital, to sell it to raise money for current business requirements, and to devise it by will to provide for the next

---

[100] For a table of borough farms, Tait, *Medieval English Borough*, p. 184.

generation or for the salvation of the testator's soul, was enjoyed by
townsfolk even in places where municipal development had not
gone far. At Bury St Edmunds even early in the twelfth century a
burgess could sell his patrimony 'without any leave from a reeve, a
wife, or sons or any kinsman'; and Prior Bertram of Durham, hardly
generous in such matters, at least allowed that the Elvet burgesses
should hold their property *iure hereditario*.[101]

Much of the freedom implied by burgage tenure in the twelfth
century may well, at least in the older towns, have had earlier roots;
but townsmen in town courts continued to have some power to
shape rules governing town property in ways which met their needs,
and the rules which applied in older towns were extended to new
ones by royal or seignorial concessions. Newcastle burgesses under
Henry I were free to sell their land; in the mid-twelfth century the
earl of Cornwall granted that his burgesses at Bradninch (Devon)
might hold their burgages *hereditario* for ever at fixed rents; and burgesses at Hedon in Henry II's time held their burgages freely like the
burgesses of York and Lincoln. Later, around the turn of the century, the bishop of Worcester granted to his new burgesses at
Stratford-upon-Avon 'the inheritance of their burgages'; at
Lostwithiel (Cornwall) Robert de Cardinan's burgesses held their
property for fixed rents, in inheritance and with powers of alienation;
and at Eynsham burgages likewise owed standard rents and could be
sold or devised by will. More and more the rules of tenure appropriate
to town property became a matter of common assumption.[102]

More and more it also came to be assumed that town air made
men free. The sort of personal unfreedom characterizing much of
rural England was not easily compatible with full-time engagement
in trade or manufacture; for unfreedom could mean that a man's
lord could make pre-emptive calls upon his labour or his goods, that
his freedom of movement was restricted, and that his capital was subject to arbitrary raids. As early as Henry I's reign, however, the rule
at Newcastle was that, 'if a villein comes to reside in the borough,
and shall remain a burgess in the borough for a year and a day, he
shall thereafter remain there'; and before the century's end

[101] *Ibid.*, pp. 230–1; *BBC 1042–1216*, pp. 180–94; D.C. Douglas, ed., *Feudal Documents from the Abbey of Bury St Edmunds*, p. 114; Greenwell, ed., *Feodarium Prioratus Dunelmensis*, p. 190 note.
[102] *BBC 1042–1216*, pp. 38–9, 41, 45–6, 48, 64, 66, 68, 74, 76; Carus-Wilson, 'The first half century of the borough of Stratford-upon-Avon', pp. 48–50.
[103] *EHD*, II, p. 971; Hall, ed., *Tractatus de Legibus et Consuetudinibus Regni Anglie*, p. 58; and cf. the rule in a collection of *c.* 1210: R.S. Hoyt, *The Royal Demesne in English Constitutional History*, Ithaca, NY, 1950, pp. 187–8.

Glanville attributed general currency to the principle that, if a villein dwelt peacably as a burgess in a privileged town for a year and a day, 'he is thereby freed from villeinage'.[103] By the thirteenth century the royal courts were enforcing this rule, for instance against a Wiltshire lord who tried to reclaim as a villein a man who for ten years had been a free burgess of Salisbury. By 1251 the presumption that townsmen would be free men was so strong that the earl of Derby's first step towards realizing his intention to turn Higham Ferrers into a borough was to enfranchise his tenants there, 'so that we and our heirs shall not be able henceforth to have or exact any servitude from them or from any of their issue'.[104]

If the personal and tenurial rights that were appropriate to burgesses became widely accepted even during the twelfth century, their powers to manage the affairs of their communities were apt to be much more restricted. In particular, most towns continued to be subject to the financial control of the king or other lord. Leaving aside the exceptional case of London, the citizens of Lincoln appear to have been pioneers when, in 1130, they secured the right 'to hold the city of the king in chief' – i.e. to assume the responsibility themselves for collecting and accounting for the revenues which the city owed to the king. It was a privilege which Lincoln retained, although not without cost: the city paid a substantial sum down to Henry I in 1130 and had to accept increases in its annual farm both in 1130 and in 1156. Northampton likewise negotiated a similar concession from Henry II in 1184–85, again accepting an enhanced farm and paying 200 marks down; and Cambridge in the same year tried to obtain a like privilege. In the latter case, however, the burgesses clearly committed the town to paying more than it could raise, and Cambridge soon reverted to the sheriff's control. Most towns, in fact, down to the end of Henry II's reign, continued to be under effective royal or seignorial authority.[105]

Townsfolk may have chafed at the leading strings in which they were kept, and this may explain why in some places they may have formed themselves into sworn associations ('communes'); but of these little is known except for that established by the Londoners under Richard I.[106] A need for money to finance their wars on the part of Richard and John, in any case, was more effective in extend-

[104] M.T. Clanchy, ed., *Civil Pleas of the Wiltshire Eyre, 1249*, pl. 467; *BBC 1216–1307*, p. 142.
[105] Tait, *Medieval English Borough*, pp. 156–7, 175–6; Hill, *Medieval Lincoln*, pp. 183–5; C.A. Markham and J.C. Cox, eds, *Records of the Borough of Northampton*, I, p. 21.
[106] Reynolds, *Introduction*, pp. 106–7.

ing urban liberties, since rights could be sold to townsmen for hard cash. Even so, what was conceded was often surrendered grudgingly. Cambridge, for example, early in John's reign again offered money to have the right for the burgesses themselves to farm their town, and in fact they were allowed to do so; but the charter John gave to them in 1201 makes no mention of this concession. Only in 1207 did a further charter grant the borough to the burgesses in perpetuity, allow them to account for the farm directly to the exchequer and permit them 'to make of themselves a reeve, whom they will and when they will', to act as their accounting officer. Newcastle, too, in 1201 experienced the limits of John's generosity. He responded favourably at first to that town's request to be allowed to farm the borough revenues, promising cash down for this right and to increase the farm from £50 to £60. The king, however, soon restored the authority of the sheriff of Northumberland, and the burgesses of Newcastle had to wait until 1214 to be allowed to farm their borough, and then for an annual farm of £100. If the king gained financially, however, the burgesses received assurances that they would no longer be answerable either to the sheriff of Northumberland or to the constable of the castle.[107]

About two dozen towns had assumed responsibility for raising and accounting for the revenues they owed to the king by 1216, and perhaps double that number by 1308.[108] Those that had done so were also empowered, explicity or tacitly, to choose from their own inhabitants a reeve or other officer to be responsible for payment of the farm, so that he became the agent of the townsfolk rather than of the king or sheriff. The implications of direct accountability were spelled out when the burgesses of Ilchester (Somerset) in 1204 were allowed to farm their town in perpetuity: they were to account at the exchequer by their own hands, 'so that the sheriff shall not in future intermeddle therein'.[109]At the same time this sort of concession had more than a merely financial significance, since town reeves were more than merely financial officers. At Oxford, for example, the reeves had long played a central part in the borough court, and their thirteenth-century successors, now called bailiffs, presided over one of the main city courts. As the sheriff's power in towns was whittled away, moreover, reeves or bailiffs became the channel of communi-

[107] *VCH Cambs.*, III, pp. 31–2; F.W. Maitland and M. Bateson, eds, *Charters of the Borough of Cambridge*, pp. 4–8; J. Brand, *History and Antiquities ... of Newcastle upon Tyne*, II, pp. 132–6.
[108] Reynolds, *Introduction*, p. 110.
[109] *BBC 1042–1216*, p. 229.

cation between towns and an increasingly interventionist central government, assuming responsibility for seeing that royal commands were obeyed and royal writs duly returned – a responsibility needing specific authorization from the 1250s. In these respects the bailiffs of privileged boroughs, including some which were not royal boroughs, continued to be royal agents, but with the difference that they were townsfolk chosen by their fellow townsfolk. Like the knights and lawful men of the shires, burgesses in Angevin England were saddled with many duties, and to the extent that they achieved significant self-governing powers they were 'obliged . . . to answer directly to the crown for all those functions which [they] had taken over from the sheriff'.[110]

The stages of municipal development in the twelfth and even the thirteenth centuries can seldom be established in detail, for town charters often confirm pre-existing privileges rather than create them, and rights were frequently acquired by quiet usurpation or tacit administrative arrangements with their lords or their local agents. At least one town charter, however, did have a constitutive effect. In 1200 King John granted that the burgesses of Ipswich might hold their town in perpetuity for an annual farm payable at the exchequer by reeves chosen by themselves, that they might also choose four coroners for the town, that they might enjoy freedom from toll and other charges, that they might have a gild merchant, that their property in the borough would be protected by the custom of the borough, and that they would be subject only to the jurisdiction of the borough court. What is unusual is that Ipswich preserved a record of the steps taken to give effect to the king's charter. Four general meetings of the townsfolk were held between 29 June and 12 October 1200. At the first, two 'good and faithful men' were elected to be reeves and four to be coroners, and it was also agreed that twelve 'chief portmen' should be appointed, 'as there are in other free boroughs in England', to assist in the government of the town and in doing justice. The portmen were duly chosen at the second meeting of the town and swore to maintain the liberties and free customs of the town, while the body of burgesses took an oath to be 'obedient, attentive, agreeable and helpful with their body and with goods'. Thereafter, the bailiffs, coroners and portmen determined how the farm would be collected and paid, appointed two beadles to make arrests and keep prisoners, and decided to have a common

---

[110] M.T. Clanchy, 'The franchise of return of writs', *TRHS*, 5th ser. XVII (1967), p. 66; W.L. Warren, *The Governance of Norman and Angevin England*, 1987, pp. 218–19.

seal made, to appoint an alderman for the gild merchant with four associates, and to proclaim the borough's new status throughout Norfolk and Suffolk. These decisions were endorsed by a third general meeting and, at a fourth, the new common seal was displayed, the alderman of the gild and his associates were chosen 'by the common counsel of the townspeople', and arrangements were made for other 'people of the town' to come before the alderman and his associates 'in order to put themselves in the gild' and pay the necessary fee. In this way the privileges conferred by the king's charter were, in a few crowded weeks, elaborated into a civic constitution.[111]

This unique record from Ipswich calls for a few additional comments. It is unlikely that the real initiative for the proceedings there in 1200 came from the 'good and lawful men of the town' who assembled at the meetings in the churchyard of St Mary Tower. They came together as a traditional, even an archaic communal assembly, 'no ordinary court but the folkmote . . ., one that may even have been only a memory, revived for a great occasion'.[112] The true source of initiative is likely to have been some smaller group, and perhaps the names of those chosen to be the town's officers, portmen and gild officials may offer a hint to their identity. The presence of the good and lawful men, on the other hand, was more than mere antiquarian decoration. They constituted in the literal sense the community of the town, capable of choosing who would have authority over it and of swearing collectively to maintain the town and its government. They manifested the growing capacity of towns by that time to take corporate action, not merely for specific and limited ends like those served by the gild merchant, but to achieve a more general control over their own affairs. One symbol of a town's capacity to act as an independent community, as the burgesses of Ipswich made clear, was the possession of a common seal to authenticate corporate acts. Town seals appear in a number of places around 1200, and the legend on Oxford's (which was in use by 1191) makes clear what its significance was. It was the 'common seal of all the citizens of the city of Oxford'.[113]

---

[111] Gross, *The Gild Merchant*, II, pp. 115–22; Martin, *Court Rolls of the Borough of Ipswich*, pp. 8–9, 13, 23.
[112] *Ibid.*, pp. 23–4.
[113] *VCH Oxon.*, IV, p. 340; Davis, 'An Oxford charter of 1191', pp. 54–6.

(c)   The mayoralty

By the thirteenth century, therefore, many towns had significantly extended their capacity to manage their own affairs. They may have been influenced to one degree or another by the communal movements in towns on the other side of the Channel, although it is also likely that similar circumstances bred similar aspirations.[114] Whatever the influences at work, English burgesses, as well as sometimes organizing themselves as sworn associations, in a number of towns were 'symbolizing their new unity of administration by setting up an entirely new officer, the mayor, with a council . . . to act with him on behalf of the community'. The word mayor is a French word, and may indicate some cross-Channel inspiration; but the important thing is that the mayor was 'a purely urban official who symbolised the town's unity'. The office spread rapidly after the Londoners established it in *c.* 1190; and by 1216 there were mayors at, among other places, Winchester, Exeter, Lincoln, Barnstaple, Oxford, York, Northampton, Beverley, Bristol, Grimsby and Newcastle upon Tyne. In 1234 the bishop of Norwich, having earlier excommunicated the burgesses of King's Lynn for having 'created a mayor among themselves', grudgingly allowed that the 'burgesses and their heirs shall henceforth elect and create a mayor for themselves, whomsoever they wish, out of their own number'. The representative character of the mayoralty could hardly be better illustrated.[115]

   The office had appeared in many further towns by the mid-fourteenth century, although not before 1345 at Coventry, in face of the prior's reluctance to accept it, and later still in some important towns (including Norwich, Colchester and apparently Canterbury). A wide range of royal and seignorial boroughs, on the other hand, had acquired mayors by 1349: among others Cambridge and Bedford, Nottingham and Carlisle, Chester and in due course Preston and Macclesfield.[116] Even the bishop of Durham in 1230 allowed that his burgesses at Hartlepool might have a mayor and a gild merchant 'as other burgesses best and most honourably have in the boroughs of our lord the king'; and in *c.* 1272 the earl of Lincoln empowered his burgesses at Congleton (Cheshire) to elect a mayor. In places like Congleton, of course, it is wise not to make too much of the mayor's office: he had, along with the catchpoll and ale-tast-

---

[114] R.H. Hilton, *English and French Towns in Feudal Society: a Comparative Study,* pp. 127–34.
[115] Tait, *Medieval English Borough*, pp. 234–6, 291; *BBC 1216–1307*, pp. 362–3.
[116] Reynolds, *Introduction*, pp. 109, 114; Urry, *Canterbury under the Angevin Kings*, pp. 87–8.

ers, to swear before the earl's bailiff to serve the earl (as well as the borough community) faithfully; and just like the mayors of small Gloucestershire boroughs like Berkeley and Wotton-under-Edge, he may have been 'essentially nothing more than a collector of urban dues'. It was another matter in the great towns, and above all in London where the mayor became 'the personification of the city'. 'All courts were considered to be held by his warrant' and 'all officials derived their authority from him'; even the sheriffs, although their office was older than the mayor's, were, by the fourteenth century, the 'eyes of the mayor'. The office was recognized as conferring on the mayor an exceptional dignity, and the town devised ceremonial to make that manifest.[117]

5. TOWN GOVERNMENTS

It cannot be claimed that, in the early fourteenth century, there was any common pattern of government in English towns, for at one end of the scale there was a scarcely modified manorialism and at the other a substantial degree of autonomy. At the same time, those towns where municipal autonomy was most extensive are of special interest. They included most of the towns which had developed furthest economically, and their institutions reflected urban aspirations most fully and contemporary perceptions of how those aspirations might best be satisfied. Their governmental systems, however, like most medieval systems of government, did have one common characteristic: they tended to lack those divisions of function which mark more recent patterns of government. Medieval urban institutions were usually, at one and the same time, judicial and deliberative and executive; and officials, who at one moment sat in judgement, at others were general administrators or bearers of financial responsibility. Even the buildings which housed town administration had to be flexible in use. At Worcester the citizens built a great hall called Booth Hall, where 'the pleas of the aforesaid city are held and where the prison of the city is'; but it also served as a place for Hereford

---

[117] *BBC 1216–1307*, pp. lvii, 360–6; *VCH Cambs.*, III, p. 38; Gross, *The Gild Merchant*, II, pp. 18, 38, 44, 171, 195; Finberg, *Gloucestershire Studies*, p. 72; Williams, *Medieval London*, pp. 29–30. The list of towns with mayors, of course, makes no pretence of completeness.
[118] M.S. Arnold, ed., *Select Cases of Trespass in the King's Courts*, I, Selden Soc., C (1985), p. 116.

merchants to set out for sale the hides which they brought to market in Worcester.[118]

(a) Some patterns of municipal government

The institutions of towns which had acquired a reasonable degree of autonomy differed in detail, but they also had a good deal in common. Their common features were sometimes a result of the deliberate borrowing of customs and liberties. Royal charters on occasion conferred more or less identical privileges upon more than one place (John's charter for Gloucester in 1200, for example, is almost identical with Richard I's for Winchester in 1190), and the liberties enjoyed by one place might be transferred in whole or in part to another. John, before his accession, gave Bristol certain rights copied from those possessed by London; and, in 1204, he allowed the bishop of Norwich to choose whatever borough in England he liked to provide a model for the liberties he was minded to confer on King's Lynn. The bishop, in fact, chose those of Oxford, but Oxford's customs, as we have seen, were not unique. In 1156 Henry II had recognized that some customs it shared with London, and as late as the fourteenth century the citizens of Oxford might appeal to the Londoners to settle doubts about how a particular liberty should be interpreted. Not every borrowing of this sort was effective: Norham, for example, was hardly sufficiently developed as an urban community to sustain 'all the liberties and free customs . . . which Newcastle has' granted to it by the bishop of Durham; but borrowings of liberties helped to create some of the family resemblances between boroughs.[119]

At the same time, towns enjoying a measure of autonomy could shape their own institutions in their own ways, and both resemblances and differences are perhaps best illustrated by a few specific instances. At Oxford in 1285 the principal city officers were the mayor, two bailiffs, four electors (more commonly called aldermen), and eight jurats or counsellors. The mayor's office appeared early in the thirteenth century, and its holder, who headed the city's government, was elected annually, although re-election was common. The bailiffs, descendants of the twelfth-century portreeves, were responsible for raising the borough farm and paying it to the exchequer, but

[119] W.H. Stevenson, ed., *Cal. of the Records . . . of Gloucester*, pp. 6–9; *BBC 1042–1216*, pp. 13, 32, 52; Stephenson, *Borough and Town*, pp. 127–8, 133–5, 140–3; A.H. Thomas, ed., *Cal. of Plea and Memoranda Rolls . . . of London, 1323–64*, p. 52.

they were also the mayor's principal administrative aides, and the four aldermen by 1279 were clearly in charge of the wards into which the city was divided. Much of the time of these officers was taken up by their duties in the city's courts. The main court, descended from the ancient portmanmoot, dealt with police matters and much property litigation, and was normally under the presidency of the bailiffs, but by the late thirteenth century it was tending to divide into two: the bailiffs' court and a husting court, in which the aldermen sat as well as the bailiffs and which dealt with pleas initiated by writ. By Edward I's reign there was also a mayor's court, which dealt with offences against market and craft regulations and with much small debt litigation.[120]

In the background of Oxford's formal institutions, there was doubtless much informal consultation between the mayor, aldermen and jurats. The role of this inner circle in determining the personnel and the policy of the city government is illustrated by complaints from some humbler citizens, the 'lesser commune' as they called themselves, in 1257. The jurats, they alleged, chose the bailiffs from their own ranks; and the mayor and jurats had imposed a common charge on ale-wives, compelled working craftsmen to pay for membership of the gild merchant, and made regulations for cloth-making and the marketing of sea-fish. By order of the mayor and jurats, too, the bailiffs forcibly entered the house of the leader of the 'lesser commune' and prevented him from carrying on his business. The jurats clearly acted as a sort of town council and, with the mayor and aldermen, as the directorate of an oligarchy.[121]

The Winchester usages of *c.* 1275 provide glimpses of the constitution of another ancient city. They tell us little about the *burghmote*, the general assembly of the citizens, perhaps because by this time its role was scarcely more than a formal one, although it did have a part to play in the election of the mayor and bailiffs. Winchester had the familiar officers: a mayor, elected annually by the jurats and the body of citizens, called the commune, to be 'the principal sustainer of the franchise'; 24 jurats, chosen from the wisest and most trustworthy of the city to aid and counsel the mayor; and two bailiffs, responsible as the old reeves had been for payment of the city farm due to the king, also for 'doing right to all the community', who were chosen by the 'commune' in the *burghmote* from four names

---

[120] J.E. Thorold Rogers, ed., *Oxford City Documents . . . 1268–1665*, p. 223; *VCH Oxon.*, IV, pp. 58–62, 336–7; *Rot. Hundr.*, II, p. 796; Salter, *Medieval Oxford*, pp. 51–3.
[121] *Cal. Inq. Misc.*, I, no. 238.

proposed by the mayor and jurats. Winchester also had its own coroners (as Oxford did) and aldermen in charge of the wards into which the city was divided, although the latter do not seem to have been, as they were at Oxford, the mayor's counsellors. At Winchester, too, a single mayor's and bailiffs' court seems to have served all the city's jurisdictional needs, save that eventually it held special sessions (called *piepowder* courts) to deal with mercantile cases.[122]

The basic pattern of municipal government at Oxford and Winchester is repeated in most of the larger boroughs of thirteenth-century England. Usually (but not quite universally) urban administrations headed by a mayor, assisted by a bailiff or bailiffs, were responsible for raising and accounting for the town farm, for much of the justice done in town courts, and for a range of administrative duties which grew wider as Angevin government heaped new tasks upon the officers of local communities. Many towns, too, had aldermen in charge of the subdivisions of their territory; 57 towns by 1300 had their own coroners;[123] and usually a small circle of counsellors provided backing for the town officers. The constitution devised for Ipswich in 1200 can perhaps be regarded as an early version of this scheme, while London's thirteenth-century government represented a developed form of it. By then London's oldest court, the folkmoot, had decayed, but the surviving husting court had developed a number of offshoots (including the sheriffs' and the mayor's courts), and the ward courts continued to deal with much of the city's police business. The centre of the stage, however, belonged to the mayor and to the aldermen, the mayor's principal advisers. For particular purposes the mayor might consult more widely, usually with groups of better and more discreet citizens chosen by the wards; but as yet these steps towards establishing a 'common council' seem to have been purely *ad hoc*. Power in London remained firmly in the hands of the mayor and aldermen, with the sheriffs as their principal aides. The aldermen, by the mid-thirteenth century, were elected by the *probi homines* of the 24 wards, usually for life; and it was from this small circle that mayors were invariably chosen, and many sheriffs were also drawn from it or joined it after their period of

---

[122] J.S. Furley, ed., *Ancient Usages of the City of Winchester*, pp. 8–12, 19–20, 26–9; Keene, *Survey*, I, pp. 75, 81–4.
[123] R.F. Hunnisett, *The Medieval Coroner*, Cambridge, 1961, p. 138.
[124] Reynolds, *Introduction*, pp. 119–23; Williams, *Medieval London*, pp. 28–35.

office. The 'aldermanic court, with its senior member the mayor' may indeed fairly be described as 'the sovereign council of the city'.[124]

(b)   Civic responsibilities and civic officials

Towns which acquired a substantial degree of autonomy were not relieved of financial obligations to their lords: on the contrary, where burgesses were allowed to 'farm' their borough responsibility for raising the fixed annual payment was placed firmly upon them. It was prudent to designate specific sources of revenue to meet this recurrent charge and 'particulars from which the farm of the city ought to be raised' were put on record at Canterbury in *c.* 1234, which included rents from some properties, charges for market stalls, proceeds from the city courts, and income from the king's mill and meadow land. Court profits were also assigned to this purpose at York in the 1290s, together with some city rents, tolls on trade, some issues of fairs, and charges levied on wool belonging to non-citizens entering or leaving the city. At Lincoln charges for market stalls and fines on delinquent victuallers helped to defray the farm, and at Newcastle the most important contribution came from the profits of the port and its coal trade in particular.[125]

The financial responsibilities of town governments were not ended when they had paid the farm. The lords of towns from time to time made further demands of them, and the townsfolk themselves had urgent needs calling for expenditure. Civic buildings had to be erected or repaired; markets had to be provided; roads, walls, bridges and quays had to be kept up; general taxes or fincancial penalties imposed by the crown had to be met; ships had to be built or troops provided and equipped for the king (or at Leicester for the earl of Lancaster); increasingly numerous civic officials were owed wages or expenses; and visitors, including the king's judges, needed to be sweetened by entertainments and presents. Towns, from time to time, were allowed to levy special local taxes for some of these purposes: pavage for road-works, murage for work on town walls, and so forth. From the start, indeed, 'free boroughs' must have needed to raise revenue for municipal purposes. At Hull in 1321–24 the town's income came from three main sources: rents of property

[125] Urry, *Canterbury under the Angevin Kings*, pp. 43, 443–4; PRO SC 6/1088/13; *VCH City of York*, p. 35; Hill, *Medieval Lincoln*, pp. 214–16; A.J. Lilburn, 'The pipe rolls of Edward I', *AA*, 4th ser. XXXVI (1958), pp. 286–9.

belonging to the town (not yet a very significant item), fees paid by those becoming burgesses, and taxes ('tallages') assessed on the town's inhabitants, as well as from murage and pavage charges on traders. Later evidence suggests that York's city government relied on similar sources of revenue, except for 'tallages', but augmented by charges for using the crane on the quay, penalties for trade offences, and charges on non-citizens doing business in the city.[126] At Leicester, perhaps because the townsfolk had rather less control over their own affairs, taxes assessed by the town authorities were raised frequently and for many purposes: to pay fines incurred by the town, to discharge the debts of the community, to meet expenses of civic delegations, to buy presents for the earl, to maintain the North Bridge, to bribe juries, to purchase a town charter, to raise troops for the king. These impositions were so frequent, indeed, that it is hardly surprising that Henry Sturdy abused the tallage assessors or that Richard Gerin broke the seal on the tallage collector's warrant.[127]

Financial responsibilities, moreover, were merely one of the obligations which privileged municipalities had to assume. They also had to manage a wide range of economic activities, to give their citizens and visitors access to justice, and to carry out the numerous delegated duties imposed by the king's government upon local communities. These responsibilities in turn conditioned the administrative development of privileged boroughs. York, for example, by Edward I's time not only had a common fund, but chamberlains in charge of it; and chamberlains' accounts have survived from, or are known once to have existed in, a number of other towns (including King's Lynn, Oxford, Cambridge, Exeter and Winchester) in the first half of the fourteenth century or soon afterwards.[128] Chamberlains and their accounts, furthermore, are indicative of a general trend, especially in the larger boroughs, towards more elaborate record-keeping, a proliferation of officialdom, and an advance of bureaucracy. The first signs of this trend were perhaps the keeping of records by gilds merchant, which go back to 1196 at Leicester and to 1209 at Shrewbury; but, as urban autonomy was enlarged, it was manifested by every branch of municipal administration. There is a

---

[126] R. Horrox, ed., *Select Rentals and Accounts of Medieval Hull*, pp. 53–5; R.B. Dobson, ed., *York City Chamberlains' Account Rolls, 1396–1500*, passim.
[127] Bateson, ed., *Records of the Borough of Leicester*, I, pp. 126–315 for the period 1267–1324.
[128] Dobson, ed., *York City Chamberlains' Account Rolls*, pp. xvii–xix.

Northampton custumal from about the end of the twelfth century; Wallingford tax and borough court rolls from the 1220s, Shrewsbury account rolls from 1256, rolls from Cambridge borough court produced before the king's justice in 1261 – in brief, 'a substantial body of working documents' of which only chance survivals have been preserved. Town government, like every other branch of medieval government, was based more and more upon written record.[129]

A government so based called for a growing staff of officials, some of them in the strict sense professionals. Even in 1200, at Ipswich, in addition to the elected borough officers, four men to help the bailiffs to collect revenue were considered necessary, together with two beadles to make arrests and a keeper of the town gaol. Municipal officers of this sort continued to become more numerous and, at least in the larger towns, two new principal officers eventually made their appearance. A chief legal officer, the recorder, only did so in the fourteenth century or later; but as record-keeping increased, in addition to clerks employed intermittently in their administration, a number of towns from the thirteenth century onwards appointed a common or town clerk to head their secretariat. Ipswich had done so by 1272, for the clerk decamped with some of the town records; Newcastle seems to have had a veritable dynasty of common clerks following each other in office during much of the century; and at Oxford the title of town clerk was first used in *c.* 1252.[130]

As might be expected, the multiplication of professional officials was most in evidence in London where, by the opening of the fourteenth century, an administrative élite had been added to the city's ruling circle. It was headed by the common clerk, the serjeant at law and (at the latest from 1304) the recorder – representatives of those legal and clerical professions, the importance of which was growing at every level of government. These principal officers, and the mayor, sheriffs, chamberlain and aldermen, were supported by a troop of serjeants, clerks, bailiffs, gaolers and other subordinates; and by Edward III's early years official salaries accounted for about two-thirds of the chamberlain's normal annual expenditure. In addition to full-time officers, moreover, the city retained an array of lawyers on a part-time basis as pleaders for the community. A list of them from Edward II's reign includes William Herle (later Chief

[129] Martin, 'The English borough in the thirteenth century', pp. 123–44; M.T. Clanchy, *From Memory to Written Record*, 1979, esp. p. 74.
[130] Martin, 'The English borough in the thirteenth century', pp. 139, 142–3; *VCH Oxon.*, IV, p. 61.
[131] Williams, *Medieval London*, pp. 91–105; *CLB, D*, pp. 314–15; Cam, ed., *The Eyre of London, 14 Edward II*, I, pp. xxxviii–xlvii.

Justice of Common Pleas), Edmund Passelewe (King's Serjeant and later Baron of the Exchequer), another King's Serjeant in Gilbert de Toudeby, and at least two others who served as Justices of Assize. London not only offered employment to lawyers, but to lawyers of distinction.[131]

(c) Oligarchical tendencies

The part played in municipal government by professional, bureaucratic and salaried men, however, must not be exaggerated. For the typical mayor, reeve, bailiff or chamberlain, office was a responsibility rather than a source of income; and the men elected into urban offices had much in common with those 'loyal and substantial men' who were the 'king's maids-of-all-work' in the thirteenth-century shires. In the eyes of contemporaries the ideal civic officer came from the ranks of the *probi homines*, honourable men, more discreet men, better men in the terminology of that time; for 'such participation by the body of respectable and solid citizens would equally avoid corruption, domination by cliques, and the disorders of mob rule'.[132] This was a view reinforced by practical considerations. Office called for much expenditure of time and energy, with much inevitable diversion from the business of making a living. That was something which only the more substantial townsfolk could easily afford. The intrinsic influences making for oligarchy in municipal government were very strong.

The operation of those influences was evident from the start. The ruling circle installed in Ipswich in 1200 was a tight little group. When the burgesses filled the offices of twelve portmen, two bailiffs, four coroners, three keepers of the borough seal, an alderman of the gild merchant and his four associates – 26 posts in all – twelve burgesses proved to be sufficient to do so. Two men combined the offices of portman, bailiff, coroner and keeper of the seal, and six of the other portmen were each appointed to one or two additional offices. The ruling group at Oxford in the mid-thirteenth century had a similar close-knit appearance. Of the 32 'magnate' burgesses about whom the 'lesser commune' complained in 1257, nine at some time served as mayor, ten as bailiff, and at least two others were

---

[132] H.M. Cam, *Liberties and Communities in Medieval England*, pp. 28, 35; Reynolds, *Introduction*, p. 176.
[133] Gross, *The Gild Merchant*, II, pp. 116–21; *Cal. Inq. Misc.*, I, no. 238; C.M. Fraser, 'Medieval trading restrictions in the North-East', *AA*, 4th ser. XXXIX (1961), pp. 147–60; Miller, 'Rulers of thirteenth-century towns', pp. 130–2.

members of office-holding families. The list included more than two-thirds of the bailiffs in the period 1245–70, and only two mayors in that period do not figure in it. A similar list of the 'rich' burgesses of Newcastle in 1305 is rather longer and some of those named in it may not have been conspicuously wealthy; but again it includes nearly three quarters of the bailiffs in the period 1295–1315 and of the mayors in those years only Richard Embleton is missing.[133]

The concentration of municipal authority in a few, relatively wealthy hands need not be regarded as a sinister conspiracy of the rich against the poor. Town governments and town officers, of course, were perfectly capable of abuses of power, and rich men were equally capable of using control of the levers of power for their own advantage. Sometimes they did so to an extent that undermined the solidarity of urban communities, and sometimes they may have clung to power for the sake of exercising power. Too tight an oligarchy might also breed resentment as may have been the case at Winchester in the decade or so before 1275.[134] At the same time, the prominence of wealthy, or relatively wealthy, men in the governing circles of medieval towns principally reflected the practical facts that such men commanded respect and were in a position where they could afford to serve the community. No doubt there were always some men of modest means who wished to undertake public service and some rich men with no taste for office, but in the main the assumption that municipal authority should be in the hands of men who were *majores* was accepted both as necessary and desirable.

It must also be kept in mind in this connection that, while mayors, bailiffs and counsellors were 'elected', the process by which this was done bore little resemblance to modern democratic procedures. At Ipswich in 1200 the reeves and coroners were said to have been unanimously chosen by the common consent of the whole town; but the twelve chief portmen were 'elected' from the ranks of 'the better, more discreet and more influential men' of the town by four men from each parish nominated by the bailiffs and coroners. At Cambridge in 1344 the election of the town's government was even more roundabout. The mayor and other officers on the one hand, and the 'commonalty' or body of burgesses on the other, each chose one 'approved and lawful burgess'. These two chose twelve more 'approved and lawful men' and the twelve chose a further six, the

---

[134] Keene, *Survey*, I, pp. 78–9.
[135] C.H. Cooper, *Annals of Cambridge*, I, p. 96.

resulting eighteen elected the mayor and other officers and counsellors for the ensuing year. There was a great variety of electoral processes used in medieval towns, but most favoured the claims to office of 'approved and lawful men' who were, in the words of the Cambridge ordinance of 1344, 'fit and sufficient for the government of the town' and none was incompatible with tendencies towards oligarchy.[135]

(d)   The limits of medieval municipal development

In discussing municipal development emphasis has necessarily been placed upon towns, most of them royal towns, which became 'free boroughs' with substantial powers to manage their own affairs. Such towns, however, were a minority of the communities which may reasonably be regarded as urban in the early fourteenth century. They did not include some towns of respectable antiquity which were subject to ecclesiastical lordship, or even some county towns with secular lords. Leicester, for example, gained burghal liberties late and piecemeal, and in Warwick the borough revenues were still being collected by the earl's officials in the fifteenth century. Smaller boroughs, too, many of which had come into existence on the estates of private lords in the twelfth and thirteenth centuries, often continued to accept, without many signs of distress, the restraints of seignorial authority. At Alnwick in 1289 and 1342 burgage rents and the profits of the borough court were among the assets of the town's lord, as were tolls, customs and stallage charges in the market and fair in 1342, and the lord's bailiff presided over the borough court. The lord's presence was equally visible in many other places. At Banbury the bishop of Lincoln's bailiff presided in the portmanmoot; Stratford-upon-Avon and Evesham lacked the 'simple but basic autonomy' of being able to exclude outside collectors of rents and tolls; at Thaxted, the administrative separation of the borough from the manor in which it had developed gave the burgesses few real powers of self-government; and Lavenham 'administratively ... remained a large manorialized village', with its day-to-day affairs controlled by six 'headboroughs' appointed by the town's lord.[136]

Towns which failed to become 'free boroughs' in the fullest sense

[136] Hilton, *A Medieval Society*, p. 220; PRO C 133/54/7; C. Hartshorne, *Feudal and Military Antiquities of Northumberland*, 1858, App. pp. cxxiv–v; Harvey, 'Banbury', in Lobel, ed., *Atlas of Historic Towns*, I, pp. 5–6; K.C. Newton, *Thaxted in the Fourteenth Century*, p. 22; D. Dymond and A. Betterton, *Lavenham*, p. 5.

might still acquire some of the rights which 'free boroughs' enjoyed. The townsfolk of Bury St Edmunds, for all the suffocating authority exercised by the abbey, held their property by burgage tenure, sought to defend the jurisdiction of their portmanmoot which administered the custom of the borough, and despite the abolition of their gild merchant in 1327 found a new way of making their influence felt in the Candlemas gild which had its own elected aldermen. Alnwick, too, though it was never more than a small market town, probably had a gild merchant and certainly had burgage tenure, a borough seal and a borough court; and Macclesfield, even though in the fourteenth century the earl of Chester's bailiffs exercised a general oversight in the town and the tenants of the earldom had to grind their corn at the earl's mill and bake their bread in his oven, had been granted a charter in 1261 allowing property there to be held by burgage tenure, a gild merchant, a portmoot with sole jurisdiction over the townsfolk, and the right of the latter to choose their own reeve or bailiff subject only to the advice and assent of the earl's officers. These liberties were deemed sufficient to make Macclesfield a 'free borough', and Macclesfield's government was still based upon this charter in the mid-fourteenth century save that, by that time, the town also had a mayor. The office had probably developed from the headship of the gild merchant.[137]

A charter, of course, did not absolutely guarantee the uninterrupted enjoyment of urban franchises. Those of Dunwich were withdrawn in 1272 because of discords among the burgesses; and in 1324–25 they were being more insidiously undermined, for by then the sea had eroded more than a third of the town. The burgesses, therefore, asked the king to resume the liberties he had granted to the town, a request they repeated in 1347.[138] It must also be remembered, however, that self-governing privileges, like any other franchise in Angevin England, entailed responsibilities as well as rights, and the monarchy particularly insisted that in royal chartered boroughs power was exercised lawfully and properly and obligations were fulfilled to the letter. Failure to carry out these responsibilities,

---

[137] Lobel, *The Borough of Bury St Edmunds*, pp. 106–9, 147–8; R.S. Gottfried, *Bury St Edmunds and the Urban Crisis, 1290–1539*, pp. 180–8; G. Tate, *History of the Borough, Castle and Barony of Alnwick*, 2nd edn, 2 vols, Alnwick, 1866–9, *passim*; *BBC 1216–1307*, pp. 3, 47, 76, 87, 124, 153, 218, 266, 280, 354; H.J. Hewitt, *Cheshire under the Three Edwards*, pp. 69–70; P.H.W. Booth, *Financial Administration of the Lordship and County of Chester, 1272–1377*, Chetham Soc., 3rd ser. XXVIII (1981), pp. 98–9, 113.

[138] *CPR*, 1272–81, pp. 2, 4–5; *Rot. Parl.*, I, p. 426; II, pp. 210–11.

at least under Henry III and Edward I, was likely to mean that chartered privileges would be withdrawn and direct royal rule would be resumed. Oxford lost its liberties in 1247 for a time because the king's brother-in-law's baker was murdered in the city, and so did London and Lincoln in the 1260s because of their citizens' involvement in the baronial rebellion against Henry III. Norwich suffered a similar punishment in 1272 when a quarrel between the town and the clergy resulted in the bishop's palace and the priory being set on fire; and in 1274 Edward I took Winchester into his hand, and suspended the election of mayors and bailiffs, because of the internal discords in the city.[139]

Edward I, in fact, appeared to use the suspension of liberties with some regularity to impose discipline upon urban England. He did so when towns failed to pay, or pay promptly what they owed at the exchequer. In 1290 those which suffered on this ground included Ipswich, Norwich, York, Lincoln, Canterbury, Nottingham, Northampton and Gloucester; and York was again in the king's hand for the five years beginning in 1292, and Newcastle for a similar period, for a like reason. Liberties were also withdrawn for other defaults. London was taken into the king's hand between 1285 and 1298 because of the prevalence of feuds and disorders in the city and the insubordination of the city's rulers when called upon to answer for them, although for much of the time the normal course of the city's government was little interrupted save for the fact that the mayor was replaced by a warden nominated by the king. Earlier, in 1280, York's franchises had been resumed because the citizens had tampered with a royal charter, and those of Southampton were withdrawn in 1290 because of a violent assault on a royal official. As well as temporarily losing its liberties, Southampton had to pay a substantial fine and its farm was increased by £20 yearly.[140]

It is not surprising, therefore, that towns were apprehensive about the security of their franchises, as the customary steps the Londoners took when it was known that the king's justices were about to descend upon the city would seem to indicate:

First ... the magnates and more discreet men of the same city ... are

[139] *Close R.*, 1247–51, pp. 4, 26; Williams, *Medieval London*, pp. 234–42; Hill, *Medieval Lincoln*, p. 210; Luard, ed., *Annales Monastici*, IV, pp. 249–51; *CPR*, 1272–81, pp. 1, 60.
[140] PRO E 368/61, mm. 9d, 10d, 14–15, 18, 41d, 45d; *Rot. Parl.*, I, p. 58; *VCH City of York*, pp. 34–5; Lilburne, 'The pipe rolls of Edward I', *AA*, 4th ser. XXXIII (1955), pp. 166–7; F.M. Powicke, *The Thirteenth Century*, Oxford, 1953, pp. 626–8.
[141] Cam, ed., *The Eyre of London, 14 Edward II*, I, p. 5.

accustomed to assemble in a . . . suitable place to pacify the angers, grudges and discords which have . . . arisen in the city. So that when peace and friendship have been re-established among them they may be one man and one people in will and assent for the preservation intact of themselves, their customs and their liberties. And if by chance anyone should happen to trouble the city and disquiet the citizens, this man should be considered by all to be hostile and a public enemy, and both he and his heirs should for ever lose. . . the liberties of the city. For it is intolerable that because of such an one the lord king should take the city and its liberties into his hand, to the hardship and hurt of the whole people.[141]

This record, made in 1321, suggests that the Londoners had not forgotten what had happened in 1285. In fact, however, after about 1300, the suspension of borough liberties ceased, at least until the reign of Richard II, to be a common resort of the king's government. Royal powers of control were exercised for the most part through administrative routines, and possibly in any case with greater moderation than they had been in the reign of Edward I.

6. ENGLISH TOWNS IN THE EARLY FOURTEENTH CENTURY

The period between the Domesday inquest and the Black Death is one of great importance in English urban history. It is beyond doubt that, by the first half of the fourteenth century, there were many more towns, many more places with at least some urban characteristics, and many more people engaged in urban occupations than there had been in Domesday England. By Edward III's succession, indeed, the proportion of the population living in towns was almost certainly higher than ever before, and the list of urban centres which served the needs of pre-industrial England was nearing completion. Those centres were distinguished from rural communities both by the fact that more of their inhabitants were engaged in non-agricultural occupations and by the fact that they had developed distinctive forms of organization which marked them off from neighbouring agricultural villages. There was, admittedly, no absolutely uniform pattern to which every borough, or village being turned into a borough, had to conform: rather, there was a scale of urban privilege, stretching from a few simple and restricted burgess rights to comprehensive powers of local government which, in the case of some of the larger towns, conferred virtual autonomy under the king.

The scope of urban liberties and privileges, and how quickly they were obtained depended upon the respective bargaining strengths of lords and their burgesses; but the process by which they were acquired often had little resemblance to a struggle between irreconcilable interests. On the contrary, compromise usually followed from an appreciation of mutual advantage, with townsmen gaining the freedoms they cherished and their lords financial benefit from conceding them. A common tendency of these centuries, in every area of society, was for lords to commute into money payments their rights to control dependants and to demand personal services from them. Their relations with their urban dependants were no exception to that tendency. On the other hand, important though financial gain may have been to impecunious kings and barons in times of war or political conflict, other motives might shape the attitudes of lords to their towns. Medieval England was a customary society in which rights and perquisites often had a value that was far greater than their current market price. Ecclesiastical landlords in particular frequently regarded themselves as temporary trustees of the endowments of eternal institutions, and they were apt to resist temptations to secure short-term gains to the detriment of long-term rights. This attitude does much to explain the slowness with which many monastic boroughs freed themselves from oppressive lordship and the incompleteness of the liberties they gained.

Because they were the outcome of individual bargains in circumstances which varied from place to place, the privileges won by towns also varied; but for all their variety their object was to safeguard some of the basic needs of urban life. Personal and tenurial freedom were all but essential for full-time traders and craftsmen; and so were access to market facilities, restraints on the capacity of their lord arbitrarily to raid their resources, and a voice in shaping a town's laws and customs in ways which suited the occupational needs of its inhabitants. These basic requirements might be met without too much elaboration: at Birmingham in the second quarter of the fourteenth century, for example, by establishing a regular market, allowing a privileged group among the lord's tenants to hold by burgage tenure, and instituting for that privileged group a borough court separate from the court of the manor. These provisions seem to have satisfied the needs of a place which, although it lacked a borough charter and much in the way of borough organization, appears

[142] R. Holt, *The Early History of the Town of Birmingham*, pp. 5–9.

to have been, from the taxes it paid, the third largest Warwickshire town.[142] At the opposite end of the scale of privilege were towns which enjoyed an extensive degree of municipal autonomy, with many more lying somewhere between these extremes. What is clear, however, is that the citizens of Bristol in 1344 were in no doubt that rules which townsfolk were enabled to fashion for themselves and the franchises they succeeded in winning were advantageous to businessmen. 'The customs and ordinances in use from old time' at Bristol, they said, together with the liberties Edward III had granted or ratified by his charter, were designed to ensure that 'his merchants of this town may the better and more fully exercise their trade'.[143]

The multiplication of urban centres, and the establishment of their organization and privileges, were largely complete by the early decades of the fourteenth century. The growth of industrial villages into small towns, especially in the clothing areas, did continue during the later middle ages; and a few places did secure some accretion of liberties within the scale which by then was familiar. Macclesfield got the right to have a mayor; the burgesses of Bury St Edmunds discovered ways of exercising some initiative in face of the abbey's lordship; and Leicester at last achieved full autonomy as a free borough when its lord, the earl of Lancaster, became king of England in 1399. Among innovations of the late middle ages, one or two of the larger towns were granted county status; but the main advance was the acquisition by many towns of formal rights of incorporation, starting with Edward III's grant in 1345 that the men of Coventry, 'their heirs and successors, shall in future have a community among themselves'. The recognition of the urban group as a perpetual corporation may or may not, as Thomas Madox thought, have 'fitted the townsmen for a stricter union among themselves, for a more orderly and steady government, and for a more advantageous course of commerce'; but certainly it made it easier for town governments to acquire and hold civic property, the revenue from which gave added stability to their finances.[144] In the last resort, however, incorporation merely rounded off a process of definition which, by the opening of the fourteenth century, had made towns distinctive local government areas, as well as distinctive social and economic communities, in an England that was still overwhelmingly rural. It was not

[143] F.B. Bickley, ed., *Little Red Book of Bristol*, I, pp. 27–8.
[144] M. Weinbaum, *The Incorporation of Boroughs*, pp. 8–9, 48–50, 56–7; T. Madox, *Firma Burgi, or an Historical Essay concerning the Cities and Boroughs of England*, 1726, p. 295.

CHAPTER SIX
Medieval Townsfolk

The responsibilities resting upon urban groups which acquired rights to manage their own affairs helped to mould towns into communities, if only because their inhabitants could be called upon to answer collectively for the ways in which they fulfilled the obligations which responsibility entailed. At the same time towns were also communities in a more positive sense in that their inhabitants, or at least those of them who fully accepted the common burdens which responsibility also involved, enjoyed common privileges. The word *pares* ('peers', with the implication of equality), often used in Norwich as a synonym for 'citizens', although it has been interpreted otherwise, is perhaps to be understood in this sense.[1] The privileges enjoyed might include political rights to participate in a town's municipal government, and special advantages when engaged in its trade; but also a right to be governed by laws and customs that were appropriate to urban ways of making a living. Even in the twelfth century, a knight's son came of age when he was twenty-one and the son of a free peasant when he was fifteen, but the son of a burgess was of age when he could count money carefully, measure cloth and 'otherwise do his father's business'.[2] The distinctive skills a burgess needed to make his way in the world are here put pragmatically enough, but evidently they were different skills from those needed by soldier-landlords or by agricultural tenants. The character of burgess communities, therefore, and the rules by which they operated were different from those prevailing in the communities of rural England.

---

[1] W. Hudson, ed., *Leet Jurisdiction in Norwich*, pp. lxxxv–viii, 48.
[2] Glanville, quoted by M. Chibnall, *Anglo-Norman England, 1066–1166*, pp. 182–3.

1. TOWNS AND THEIR INHABITANTS

(a) The occupational structures of urban communities

The distinctive feature of towns was that the majority of their inhabitants got their living from manufacture, food-processing and trade, with the result that, even in small market towns, the range of occupations was likely to be much greater than in villages. Where, in rural communities, the diversification of economic activity passed a certain point, those communities may properly be said to have become urban. This had happened at Thaxted by the mid-fourteenth century, for a town of 90 houses and 36 shops had grown up by the manor house, and was happening, perhaps rather more slowly, at Clare where, during the thirteenth century, there were 'merchants', tanners, quilters, a mason, a spicer, a saucer, a saddler and a tailor among its inhabitants.[3] Economic diversification, of course, was most conspicuous in London, by far the largest English town, a major port, a centre of international trade, and a developing capital city in which rich men from many parts of the country could expect to find manufactured or made-up products of high quality. The range of occupations in London, therefore, and the numbers engaged in them were correspondingly large. Even in the twelfth century, when no more than the occasional craftsman was likely to figure in the witness lists of rural charters, one London charter was attested by two felters, a cook, a carpenter, a baker, a smith, two merchants, a porter and a lime-burner.[4]

A more comprehensive indication of the occupations of Londoners towards the close of our period is afforded by information about the crafts of some taxpayers and by craft surnames contained in the London lay subsidy roll of 1332. This evidence suggests that Londoners engaged in more than a hundred distinct occupations, and that the number employed in some crafts was very large. Brewers, bakers, chandlers and butchers were certainly very numerous, reflecting London's size as a body of consumers; but the market was also large enough to support many specialist trades – a pie-baker, a herring carter, makers of arrows or mirrors or lace or cushions, a pewterer, a haymonger, a timbermonger, a madderman

---

[3] R.H. Hilton, 'Small town society in England before the Black Death', in R. Holt and G. Rosser, eds, *The English Medieval Town, 1200-1500,* p. 75; K.C. Newton, *Thaxted in the Fourteenth Century,* p. 20; S.H.A. Hervey, ed., *Suffolk in 1327,* pp. 203–4; C. Harper-Bill and R. Mortimer, eds, *Stoke-by-Clare Cartulary,* nos. 187, 226–8, 234, 592.
[4] R. Ransford, ed., *Early Charters of the Augustinian Canons of Waltham Abbey,* no. 560.

(although one dealer in this particular dyestuff was a woman). A very similar impression of occupational diversity is conveyed by the enrolments of the 900 or so Londoners who became freemen of the city by redemption or who entered upon or completed apprenticeships in the years 1309–12.[5] In sum these sources suggest that, while London did not specialize in manufacture, it had a range of crafts that was exceptional in England at that time, it was generously equipped with general merchants and provision traders, and some of the latter (vintners, fishmongers, bladers and pepperers) were diversifying into general trade. London may have had somewhat fewer organized crafts than there had been in Paris in the late thirteenth century; but the number of occupations in which Paris gildsmen were engaged, around 101–128 of them, was not all that different from those in which Londoners found employment a generation later.[6]

Because London was so exceptional, however, the occupational character of English towns is perhaps better illustrated in communities which were smaller than the capital. To this end occupational information has been assembled for 421 citizens of Winchester in the period 1300–39, 717 citizens of Norwich in the years between 1285 and 1311, and nearly 2,000 entrants into the freedom of the city of York in the years 1307–49; it is summarized in Table 6.1. For no city is the material complete. That for Winchester relates only to a relatively small sample of individuals whose occupations can be identified with some confidence;[7] that for Norwich is drawn from parties to property transactions in the city;[8] and at York the freemen's register does not consistently give occupational particulars, the entries for some years are missing, and those whose 'title to the franchise rested on birth or patrimony' find no place in it.[9] Even so, the samples of Winchester and Norwich citizens were engaged in some seventy and sixty occupations respectively and the York citizens in nearly one hundred. Occupational diversity was certainly in no way peculiar to London.

---

[5] The 1332 London subsidy roll is analysed in G.Unwin, ed., *Finance and Trade under Edward III*, pp. 35–92; and the enrolments of 1309–12 are in *CLB D*, pp. 75–179. By this time, of course, a craft surname might indicate an ancestor's occupation rather than that of the man currently known by it.

[6] R.H. Hilton, *English and French Towns in Feudal Society*, pp. 66–7.

[7] The figures are reclassified from material in Keene, *Survey*, I, p. 250 and Table 26.

[8] S. Kelly *et al.*, *Men of Property: an Analysis of the Norwich Enrolled Deeds, 1285–1311*, pp. 13–30.

[9] *VCH City of York*, pp. 114–16; R.B. Dobson, 'Admissions to the freedom of the city of York in the later middle ages', *EcHR*, 2nd ser. XXVI (1973), pp. 7–11.

Table 6.1 The occupations of some citizens of Winchester, Norwich and York

Occupational group	Occupational sub-groups	Number			Per cent		
		Y	W	N	Y	W	N
Trade	Food trades (butchers, bakers, brewers, vintners, millers, etc.)	448	88	130			
	Traders in textiles and textile requirements (drapers, woad-dealers, etc.)	34	26	80			
	Traders in hides and skins (skinners etc.)	69	20	34			
	General traders (merchants, mercers, chapman, etc.)	233	73	97			
		784	207	341	40	49	47
Manufacture	Textiles	96	66	64			
	Clothing (tailors, hosiers, hatters, etc.)	138	17	52			
	Leather and leather goods	352	38	140			
	Metal crafts	263	17	60			
	Miscellaneous (bowyers, shipwrights, coopers, potters, etc.)	110	5	11			
		959	143	327	49	34	46
Services	Transport (shipmen, mariners, porters, etc.)	87	11	4			
	Building	70	21	35			
	Professions (doctors, clerks, lawyers, etc.)	39	26	7			
	Miscellaneous (barbers, etc.)	12	13	3			
		208	71	49	11	17	7

Y = York freemen (1307–19); W = Winchester citizens (1300–39);
N = Norwich citizens (1285–1311)

Clearly, to the extent that the occupational structures of these major provincial cities were reflected accurately in these sources, they were in no way identical. The proportion of manufacturing craftsmen seems to be larger at Norwich and York than it was at Winchester; Norwich had relatively fewer citizens engaged in service occupations than York or Winchester; but at Norwich traders in textiles (linens as well as woollens) and in materials required by the textile industry were relatively an important group even though textile craftsmen there were relatively less numerous than they were at Winchester and York. Probably the Norwich traders in cloth and textile requisites were principally engaged in servicing, not the industry of their town, but the cloth and linen industries of the villages and small towns of the county. The comparatively numerous merchants and general traders at Winchester, too, perhaps reflected the importance of that city's markets and fair as collecting centres for exports going through Southampton and for distributing goods imported through the same port. Among manufacturing crafts, cloth workers were relatively numerous in Winchester and the leather trades in York and Norwich. The broad similarity of the occupational structures of these three cities, however, is perhaps more impressive than the differences between them, and in one respect is very striking. In each, provision traders (most of them traders in foodstuffs, but also in a few other necessities like candles) accounted for 20–25 per cent of the samples analyzed. At Norwich the records of the city courts also suggest that in the early fourteenth century there were some 250–300 delinquent brewers there (many, of course, only brewing part-time), and that sellers of 'victuals and other items in the budgets of the poor', and perhaps of those who were not so poor, were similarly very numerous.[10] This prominence of provision traders, especially when taken in conjunction with the large numbers of other craftsmen, like tailors or shoemakers or potters, fashioning goods for common consumption, underlines the fact that a high proportion of urban populations was principally engaged in satisfying the day-to-day needs of their fellow townsfolk.

York, Winchester and Norwich were large towns by medieval English standards, but similar occupation structures are evident in towns of medium size. Much information about occupations and occupational surnames is contained in membership rolls of gilds merchant, charter witness lists, court rolls and tax returns as well as from registers of freemen; and a review of some of these sources for

[10] R.H. Hilton, *Class Conflict and the Crisis of Feudalism*, pp. 198, 209–11.

Newark (*c.* 1175), Canterbury (1153–1206), Oxford (1160–1330), Shrewsbury (1232–68), Exeter (1286–1348), Cambridge (1298–*c.* 1320), Colchester (1301), and Leicester (1300–49), despite differences in time and the diversity of the sources, does suggest a fair degree of consistency.[11] About two-fifths of the inhabitants of these provincial towns, the evidence implies, were traders – retailers of provisions, general merchants in a large or small way, or dealers in skins, hides, textiles and the requirements of the textile industry; but nearer 50 per cent were employed in a very diversified range of manufacturing crafts, and about 12 per cent were providers of services (including transport and building).

Again, of course, there were variations between towns. Oxford and Cambridge, for instance, seem to have had an above average complement of provision traders, probably reflecting demand from the university populations developing within their bounds; and at Exeter dealers in hides and skins were exceptionally numerous, perhaps not surprising given the 'cattle husbandry' already evident in its region in 1086.[12] Textile workers were relatively numerous in twelfth-century Newark and Colchester in 1301; but at Colchester the leather trades were more prominent than cloth working, and tanners than weavers, as was also the case at Exeter and Leicester. Industrial specialization, however, was never at the expense of a wide spread of small-scale manufacture to meet the consumption needs of towns themselves and of their hinterlands, however willing towns were to make the most of local resources, like the hides of Devonshire or Leicestershire cattle or the fleeces of Lincolnshire sheep.

Considerable occupational diversity was also to be found even in the still more numerous towns with populations below *c.* 2,000 persons. Linton (Cambs.), although it never fully realized the urban promise it was showing in 1279, at that date had inhabitants engaged in fifteen or more crafts, thirteenth-century High Wycombe in twenty

---

[11] Sources: M.W. Barley, ed., *Documents relating to the Manor and Soke of Newark on Trent;* Thoroton Soc. Rec. Ser., XVI (1956); S.R. Wigram, ed., *Cartulary of the Monastery of St Frideswide,* I, Oxford Hist. Soc., XXVIII (1895),and N. Denholm-Young, ed., *Cartulary of the Medieval Archives of Christ Church* (Oxford), Oxford Hist. Soc., XCII (1931); W.J. Urry, *Canterbury under the Angevin Kings,* pp. 221–382; C.H. Drinkwater, ed., 'The merchants' gild of Shrewsbury', *Shropshire Arch. and NH Soc. Trans.,* 2nd ser. XII (1900), pp. 234–69; M.M. Rowe and A.M. Jackson, eds, *Exeter Freemen, 1266–1967,* pp. 1–29; M. Bateson, ed., *Cambridge Gild Records,* pp. 1–24, 129–34, 151–7 and PRO E 179/242/76 (Cambridge); *Rot. Parl.,* I, pp. 243–65 (Colchester); H. Hartopp, ed., *Register of the Freemen of Leicester, 1196–1770,* pp. 25–40.
[12] R. Trow-Smith, *A History of British Livestock Husbandry to 1700,* 1957, p. 73.

or more, and fourteenth-century Thame (Oxon.) in at least twenty five; while Highworth (Wilts.), although in 1334 it paid less tax than the average neighbouring village, had inhabitants employed in two dozen occupations. In this respect Highworth was comparable to little West Midland towns like Halesowen or Thornbury, with their petty traders dealing in local commodities, their craftsmen and craftswomen producing mainly for local consumption, and their provision traders and food processors – many families being involved in more than one of these occupations. As elsewhere, brewing especially was seldom a full-time occupation, for it required only 'the resources of a household kitchen' and was often women's work. To produce a sufficient supply of a beverage as indispensable as ale, however, needed many hands. At Highworth in the 1270s thirty one individuals on average were presented annually for breaches of the assize of ale. This is a small number compared with the hundred or so brewers presented each year at Colchester in 1336–46, or the 290 presented in six of the Norwich leets in 1298–9; but the borough of Highworth had only 61 tenants when it was surveyed in 1262. Most of these Highworth brewers appear only sporadically in the portmoot rolls, but a few did so with greater regularity. Even in brewing, and in a place as small as Highworth, there were some tendencies towards specialization.[13]

Small towns were likely to be closer to their rural settings than larger urban communities, but they existed primarily, nonetheless, to fulfil urban functions and their inhabitants were engaged principally in urban (and not agricultural) occupations. These modest centres provided markets in which the local peasantry could sell their small surpluses and buy basic manufactured necessities; and they were consequently the homes of petty traders, small-scale craftsmen, and food distributors and processors who served both their fellow townsfolk and the inhabitants of their neighbourhood.[14] Larger towns, too, were in part local market centres, and in any case needed the range of consumption goods and the services of the sorts of traders, craftsmen and food processors found in smaller towns. This helps to explain the common characteristics of occupational structures in English medieval towns of all sorts, even though the

[13] On small towns generally, see Hilton, *Class Conflict and the Crisis of Feudalism*, pp. 175–86, 196–204; *idem*, 'Small town society in England before the Black Death', pp. 71–96; and *idem*, *English and French Towns in Feudal Society*, pp. 53–9. For Highworth, R.B. Pugh, ed., *Court Rolls of the Wiltshire manors of Adam de Stratton*, pp. 111–63.
[14] Hilton, *English and French Towns in Feudal Society*, p. 55.

products of York or Lincoln cloth workers reached markets not dreamed of by Halesowen weavers, and merchants of Bristol or Norwich dealt with very different customers and did business of a very different order than the traders of Thornbury or Highworth.

(b)   Recruitment

Town records of the central middle ages, as well as telling us something about urban occupations, also point to another characteristic of town populations. The first entries in York's register of freemen list 36 men who 'entered the liberty of the city of York' in 1271–2. The crafts of some of them are stated, but we are told, in addition, that a cordwainer, Thomas, was 'of Fulford', a baker, James, was 'of Pickering', a skinner, Robert, was 'of Clifton', and so on.[15] Place-name surnames of this type were extremely common in every sort of town, and clearly imply that a high percentage of townsfolk, or their ancestors, had at some time been incomers. In part this inflow was demanded by the growth of urban populations between Domesday and the early fourteenth century; but in addition townsfolk belonged to the most mobile element in medieval populations, and they moved out of as well as into particular urban communities, and possibly, too, high death rates and an 'endemic deficit of births' may have made it impossible for urban communities to maintain, let alone to increase, their populations by natural generation. Even so modest a place as High Wycombe was the home of a 'fluid society into which new blood was repeatedly introduced'.[16]

To determine a rate of immigration is another matter. An apparently promising source, like the York freemen's register, before the fifteenth century ignores entrants who succeeded their fathers as citizens, and at King's Lynn sons of burgesses and apprentices were sometimes listed (and sometimes not) among those who took up the freedom of the town. In London in the later middle ages the number of those who acquired 'freedom by birth' was apparently quite low; at Leicester in 1298–1327 only 9 per cent of the entrants to the gild merchant were sons taking over their fathers' seats, although a further 20 per cent appear to have been born in Leicester, leaving 71 per cent as apparent incomers; and at Exeter, where citizens might succeed fathers, grandfathers, uncles, brothers and other

---

[15] F. Collins, ed., *Register of the Freemen of the City of York*, I, p. 1.
[16] K.F. Helleiner, 'New light on the history of urban populations', *Jnl. of Econ. Hist.*, XVIII (1958), pp. 58–61; Keene, *Survey*, I, pp. 399–400; L.J. Ashford, *History of High Wycombe*, p. 36.

relatives in the franchise, the proportion which did so was again only about 29 per cent.[17] The admission of citizens or burgesses, of course, is an imperfect measure of immigration into towns, since this information refers principally to those elements in town populations which possessed, or which were in the process of establishing, a permanent and secure urban base. It is likely to be much less informative about those who drifted into towns from an over-populated countryside, including a significant number of women, without skills or a niche in urban society. Such immigrants filled the ranks of the numerous casual workers in medieval towns and, if they were women, of the petty retailers described as hucksters, the spinsters and alewives, the laundresses and nurses, and the dressmakers and sellers of bread for bakers.[18]

Not every immigrant into a town, of course, lacked skills. Some had learned a trade in another town or as a village craftsman, and becoming a servant of an established burgess might enable them to become established in their turn. For those needing to acquire skills service as an apprentice with a burgess might be a way into a town community. In fourteenth-century Bristol, indeed, to have been a servant or apprentice were regarded as the normal avenues to burgessship, the entrant's master being required to testify to his good repute.[19] Service and apprenticeship also channelled immigration into towns, for masters with country connections or business contacts might exploit them to recruit servants or apprentices. A London mercer whose origins were in Foulsham (Norfolk) took a Norfolk lad from Aylsham as his apprentice; and a London ironmonger, born in one of the Cambridgeshire Abingtons, found an apprentice in his native village. Some of these immigrants, of course, came from towns rather than villages: Aylsham, indeed, by the fourteenth century must be regarded as a town, and as early as 1185 the new town of Baldock had attracted settlers from London, Cambridge and Hertford. Leicester, too, recruited Londoners and settlers from a number of other towns, including Chester and Tiverton and Dublin. London, most of all, drew its citizens from far and wide. Reginald of Cambridge, in the thirteenth century, belongs to a migrant family

[17] A.H. Thomas, Ed., *Cal. of Plea and Memoranda Rolls of the City of London, 1364–81*, pp. xxviii–xxx; M. Bateson, ed., *Records of the Borough of Leicester*, I, pp. 354–7; Rowe and Jackson, eds, *Exeter Freemen*, pp. xiv, 1–11; M. Kowaleski, 'The commercial dominance of a medieval provincial oligarchy', in R. Holt and G. Rosser, eds, *The English Medieval Town*, pp. 186–7.
[18] Hilton, 'Small town society in England before the Black Death', p. 83; Keene, *Survey*, I, p. 390.
[19] F.B. Bickley, ed., *Little Red Book of Bristol*, I, pp. 37–8.

which flourished as goldsmiths and married into the aldermanic class; and later Robert Chaucer came to London from Ipswich, although he may have been brought there by prospects of employment in the customs service rather than in the wine trade. This, too, was the start of a success story, although of a different sort. Robert's son John and his grandson Geoffrey also found employment in the customs service, John was also a London vintner, but Geoffrey in addition was one of England's greatest poets.[20]

Some of the immigrants into medieval towns were foreigners in the modern sense of that word. We have already encountered William Servat from Cahors, an 'outstanding alderman-pepperer' in early fourteenth-century London; much earlier the Barbeflets (presumably from Barfleur in Normandy) were well established in late twelfth-century Southampton and sold wine in the adjacent counties; in the period 1272–1348 at least 27 aliens became freemen of York, including incomers from Italy, France, Germany, Flanders and Brabant; and families originating in Germany, Norway, Spain and St Omer were entrenched in King's Lynn, John *de Hispania* serving as mayor in the late thirteenth century and Lambert of St Omer in 1313.[21] Overseas immigrants were inevitably more numerous in major ports and trading centres. It was a common requirement in the port towns that stranger merchants had to be 'hosted' in the households of burgesses, which encouraged the formation of close relationships, sometimes leading to marriages and settlement. One Lucca merchant, for example, married the daughter of Bernard le Moigne, a leading Southampton merchant; and another, Hugh Gerardino, married Isolda of Pandon, a Newcastle widow, and soon joined his wife in the ranks of Newcastle's burgesses, taxpayers and wool exporters.[22] Not all alien incomers, of course, were merchants. The citizens of fourteenth-century York were reinforced before 1349 by a French tanner, by metal workers from France and Germany, and by a doctor from Cambrai as well as by immigrant textile workers coming mainly from the Low Countries.

---

[20] E. Ekwall, *Studies on the Population of Medieval London*, pp. 20–2, 36, 93, 97–8; B.A. Lees, ed., *Records of the Templars in England in the Twelfth Century*, pp. 65–9; C.J. Billson, *Medieval Leicester*, p. 145.
[21] C.A.F. Meekings, ed., *Crown Pleas of the Wiltshire Eyre, 1249*, pp. 126–8; Collins, ed., *Register of the Freemen of the City of York*, I, pp. 1–41; H. Ingleby, ed., *Red Register of King's Lynn*, I, pp. 1, 13, 18, 21–2, 50; D.M. Owen, ed., *The Making of King's Lynn*, pp. 202–3.
[22] C. Platt, *Medieval Southampton*, pp. 69–70, 252; J.C. Davies, 'The wool customs accounts for Newcastle upon Tyne in the reign of Edward I', *AA*, 4th ser. XXXII (1954), pp. 247, 253–5; C.M. Fraser, ed., *Northumberland Lay Subsidy Roll for 1296*, pp. 44–5.

It is abundantly clear, however, that most incomers to towns came from the English countryside. A few came from families of some substance. Among Newcastle's more notable citizens around 1300, the Actons were descended from a younger son of the lord of a manor and the Grapers from a gentry family in Colwell which seems to have fallen on hard times; and at Leicester the Wigstons were apparently descended from a free peasant family holding considerable property in Wigston Magna which they left for the county town in the 1340s.[23] Most immigrants, on the other hand, appear to have been of peasant stock of no great distinction. The relative freedom of the peasantry of eastern England possibly favoured early and vigorous urban development in that part of the country; but generally, even in the twelfth century, residence in a town and acceptance into its community became one of the villein's 'bolt-holes to freedom'.[24] Enfranchised villeins, therefore, as well as free peasants, contributed to the growth of urban populations during the twelfth and thirteenth centuries, although by the fourteenth century some towns were less willing than they had been in the past to accept immigrants of villein birth. At Norwich in *c*. 1340 it was ordained, 'because all who are received as citizens (*in parem civitatis*) should be free and the serf of no-one, let good enquiry be made before they are received'; and Bristol regulations about the same time rejected as a potential freeman anyone 'if he be not of free condition'. Rules like this perhaps reflected some slackening of the pace of urban growth, but unfree immigrants continued to find their way into towns and perhaps particularly into small towns. To the abbot of Halesowen the unfreedom of some incomers to that little market town might even seem to offer advantages. He was enabled to levy a fine from a certain Juliana who, being of unfree origin, had allowed herself to be deflowered; and in 1308 a dyer had to agree to pay the abbot two capons at Christmas in recognition of his servility.[25]

Because so many townsfolk had country origins, whatever the standing of their ancestors had been, they frequently also had rural ties which survived their migration. Some retained contacts with country kinsfolk, like the London girdler who left money by his will to the poor members of his family at Dullingham (Cambs.); others,

[23] E. Miller, 'Rulers of thirteenth-century towns', pp. 136–7; W.G. Hoskins, *The Midland Peasant: the Economic and Social History of a Leicestershire Village*, 1957, p. 37.
[24] The phrase is A.L. Poole's, *Obligations of Society in the Twelfth and Thirteenth Centuries*, pp. 28–30.
[25] Hudson, ed., *Leet Jurisdiction in Norwich*, pp. lxxxvii–viii; Bickley, ed., *Little Red Book of Bristol*, I, pp. 36–7; Hilton, *Class Conflict and the Crisis of Feudalism*, pp. 200–2; *idem*, 'Small town society in England before the Black Death', pp. 81–4.

like the Wigstons of Leicester, at least for the time continued to hold property in their native village; and others again bought up property in a familiar area or displayed a regard for rural churches. Roger Horsham, a London alderman, sheriff and mercer who took his name from a Norfolk village, purchased land in East Anglia and made his will at Runhale (Norfolk), leaving bequests to Thetford and Walsingham priories. Paradoxically, immigrants who were most successful in their new urban environment were perhaps most likely to be in a position to show how much they cherished their rural roots.[26]

An indication of the range of immigration into towns is furnished by place-name surnames, which are much commoner in towns than in villages (two or three times as common in Nottingham, for instance). These names suggest that towns frequently attracted immigrants over relatively short distances. The population of twelfth-century Canterbury, for example, included a couple of Danes, a couple of Germans, an Irishman and perhaps a Scot, as well as occasional-name incomers from Sandwich or Rochester; but most of its citizens were recruited from the more or less adjacent countryside – Robert from Thanet, William from Chartham, Henry from Shelford and so forth. In small towns especially most immigrants had not travelled far. At Needham Market in Suffolk in 1251 one had come from Barking, two miles away, one from Stonham, four miles away, and another from Bures probably also came from within the county. Similarly, most of the population of Halesowen in the late thirteenth century had originated within five miles of the town, and most of that of Stratford-upon-Avon in the 1250s within a radius of eight miles – roughly the area from which Stratford market drew its customers. The pull of a town market, indeed, probably did much to determine patterns of migration.[27]

In general, therefore, the larger a town was, and the consequent range of its market influence, the greater was the extent of its catchment area. In *c.* 1300, for example, nearly 70 per cent of the places from which the inhabitants of Leicester and Norwich took their names were within a radius of twenty miles; but this proportion was only 51 per cent at York and 21 per cent in London. There were

26 Ekwall, *Studies on the Population of Medieval London*, pp. 3, 66.
27 P. McClure, 'Patterns of migration in the middle ages: the evidence of English place-name surnames', *EcHR*, 2nd ser. XXXII (1979), p. 174; Urry, *Canterbury under the Angevin Kings*, pp. 171, 250–9, 441; Gonville and Caius Coll, Cambridge, Ms. 485/489, ff. 334–4d; Hilton, *Class Conflict and the Crisis of Feudalism*, pp. 199–200; E.M. Carus-Wilson, 'The first half-century of the borough of Stratford-upon-Avon', pp. 53–4.

other influences which helped to determine the range from which towns recruited. One seems to have been the rate at which a town was growing (York's catchment area increased significantly when the city was expanding particularly rapidly in the 1360s); and the special character of some places needs to be taken into account. London's very large 'magnetic field' and the fairly uniform pull the city exercised over a radius of 60 miles or more are doubtless largely to be explained in terms of the city's exceptional size and character; but it is more surprising to find that Westminster, a suburban settlement with a population not much above 2,000 in 1300, attracted immigrants from almost as wide an area. Westminster's developing importance as a royal residence and seat of government, and the contacts created by Westminster abbey's possession of manors along the middle Thames and further west, may help to explain its attractiveness to immigrants. Winchester's catchment area, too, seems to have been more like London's than Leicester's, perhaps a consequence of the fact that it accommodated a royal residence and an international fair. It may be significant that its area of recruitment appears to be contracting by the second quarter of the fourteenth century when the visits of the court to the city were rarer and St Giles's fair was in full decline.[28] A new town under vigorous patronage might attract immigrants over unusually long distances, as New Winchelsea may have done when Edward I granted settlers there exceptionally favourable terms; and so might a port providing outlets for an extensive hinterland. It may be for this reason that only about one-third of the King's Lynn gildsmen in the late thirteenth and early fourteenth centuries seem to have originated within twenty miles of that town.[29]

The available evidence cannot tell us what proportion of the inhabitants of a given town at any given moment were recent immigrants, but it does suggest that many of them were either themselves incomers or the descendants of incomers. While some of them kept contact with their kinsfolk and places of origin, as immigrants into towns they are likely to have lacked much of the support individuals can draw from their kindred and a familiar neighbourhood. This may help to explain the importance in urban society of 'artificial' associations: burgess households embracing apprentices and servants

---

[28] McClure, 'Patterns of migration in the middle ages', pp. 174–82; A.G. Rosser, *Medieval Westminster*, pp. 168–9, 182–90; Keene, *Survey*, I, pp. 375–9.
[29] M.W. Beresford, *New Towns of the Middle Ages*, pp. 194, 497–8; Owen, ed., *The Making of King's Lynn*, pp. 295–313.

as well as family members in our narrower sense, or fraternities which saw their members through hard times and decently buried in the end, or gilds uniting those who belonged to them for religious observance or to manage the market or to regulate a particular trade or craft. The fact that towns were in great measure creations of the mobile element in medieval society made such associations an essential part of the fabric of medieval urban life.

(c)   The distribution of wealth in urban communities

It has been persuasively argued that 'a sense of community was . . . of the essence of medieval urban society',[30] but that did not imply any equality of wealth or standing among town residents. On the contrary, towns were marked by conspicuous inequalities. Admittedly it is seldom, if ever, possible to view any urban community as a whole, for usually the surviving evidence relates only to part of it – to those who were citizens, burgesses, gildsmen or masters. Even taxation records, the most useful source of comparative information about the wealth of individuals, have a variety of deficiencies. Substantial, but varying, proportions of townsfolk were too poor to be taxed and consequently do not appear in the tax returns; most taxes were assessed on the value attributed to the taxpayer's goods and chattels (though some goods were exempt), and not on his income or profits; and the bases of taxation were not consistent from tax to tax and, for the same tax, almost certainly from place to place. All the same, taxation records do offer some information, however imperfect it is, about the relative economic standing at least among townsfolk with sufficient resources to make them liable to pay taxes. The most revealing of these records are those which itemize and value the goods of individuals, and such a return for Bridport in 1319 makes it clear that a townsman's goods might not be very valuable.

> The richest man owned one cow, two hogs, two brass platters, some hides and a little furniture, the total value of his possessions amounting to £4 8s. A respectable innkeeper was assessed for two hogs, two beds, two table cloths, two hand napkins, one horse, one brass pot and one platter, a few wooden vessels and a little malt.[31]

---

[30] A.G. Rosser, 'The essence of medieval communities: the vill of Westminster, 1200–1540', *TRHS*, 5th ser. XXXIV (1984), pp. 111–12.
[31] *VCH Dorset*, II, p. 241.

A similar return from Colchester in 1301 relates to a somewhat more developed urban community. The occupations of 146 of the town's taxpayers are stated or can reasonably be inferred: 87 of these (about 60 per cent) had goods valued at under £1, and a further 28 (about 19 per cent) had goods worth between £1 and £2. The goods of only 25 taxpayers (17 per cent) were valued at between £2 and £5, and those of a mere six (three tanners, two butchers and a mercer) at £5 or more. Relative affluence was not closely related to a man's trade, for nine out of twelve merchants, four out of nine butchers and five out of thirteen tanners had goods valued at less than £1. There does, however, appear to be some connection between a taxpayer's wealth and the diversity of his enterprise. Henry Persun, for example, with goods worth rather more than £5, looks as though he combined butchering with a bit of farming, dealing in a little cloth, and occasional brewing.[32]

Part of a similar assessment for King's Lynn in *c.* 1285–90 has also survived, although clearly it relates to a community differing greatly from Colchester and was drawn up by taxors working to very different instructions, for gradations of wealth were much steeper. Nearly a quarter of the 43 taxpayers listed had goods valued at less than £1 and more than half at under £5; but 37 per cent of them had goods worth between £5 and £100, and a small elite of four taxpayers had goods valued at £100–£250. These very rich men were merchants with fingers in many pies. Simon Leverington dealt in herrings, charcoal and timber; Reginald Taverner in herrings and wool; Hugh le Moygne in wool and woad; and (richest of all) the shipowner, Philip Bek, in herrings, dried fish, Poitou salt, wax, timber and wine. These assessments seem to reflect real differences in standards of living, for the value of household goods, fuel and clothing contributed only 2s. 10d. to a total assessment of just over £3 in the case of a cooper, but £18 to Philip Bek's total of £246.[33]

Detailed assessments like those for Colchester and King's Lynn survive only rarely, and usually we must be content with a simple list of names and of the total value of the goods each owned or the amount of tax each owed. What such lists can tell us may be illustrated by the assessments to the twentieth of 1327 for Bury St Edmunds, Ipswich, Chichester, Scarborough, Yarm, York, Stafford, Huntingdon, Godmanchester, Cambridge, Derby, Chesterfield,

[32] *Rot. Parl.*, I, pp. 243–65.
[33] Owen, ed., *The Making of King's Lynn*, pp. 234–49 (the details do not appear to be totally trustworthy).

Ludlow, Shrewsbury, Leicester and Market Harborough.[34] The pro-portion of taxpayers with goods valued at less than £5 only fell below 70 per cent at Yarm; the corresponding figure at Bury St Edmunds, Chichester and Derby was 70–79 per cent, at Stafford, Scarborough, Shrewsbury, Leicester and Market Harborough 80–89 per cent, at Cambridge, Ipswich, York, Huntingdon, Ludlow and Chesterfield 90–99 per cent, and at Godmanchester all taxpayers. Taxpayers with goods valued in the £5–£10 range, therefore, were many fewer, and those with goods worth £10–£50 were fewer still. Only Ipswich had two merchants with goods valued at more than £50. These figures are broadly comparable with those for taxpayers with goods worth less than £5 in 1332 at Southampton (72 per cent), Exeter (81 per cent) and Winchester (94 per cent).[35] Despite the probability of widespread under-assessment, the implication is that most townsfolk, including the typical urban craftsman and retail trader, had modest possessions and that the relatively wealthy were a fairly small minor-ity; a distribution of wealth which underlay the marked tendencies towards urban oligarchy which are so often evident.

Who the men of wealth were doubtless varied from town to town in some degree. The relatively high proportion of taxpayers in 1332 at Southampton with goods worth over £10 probably reflected the fact that it was an international port and a base for many mercantile entrepreneurs, who stood out all the more because much of the town's population consisted of labourers servicing ships who were too poor to be taxed. At York in 1327 most of those with goods val-ued at £10 or above were engaged in the wool trade or in supplying northern armies or the court; but some craftsmen appear to have had goods worth £5–£10. At Shrewsbury, too, some of the taxpayers with the highest assessments in 1327 (including Thomas Colle, Robert Weston, John Lynleye, Hugh Dunfowe and Richard Hulton) were prominent wool exporters, as were William Orleton of Ludlow, Thomas Reigner of Market Harborough, Robert Selyman of Stafford and John Wentlond of Huntingdon. Some dealers in cloth and wine and groceries and in grain and other foodstuffs, especially to supply London, the court, royal armies and navies, and the larger provincial towns, were also among those with above average wealth. Among Londoners paying tax at a high rate in 1332 were two bladers (i.e.

---

[34] These and other published subsidy rolls are listed in E.B. Graves, ed., *Bibliography of English History to 1485*, Oxford, 1975, pp. 484–91, except for J.A. Raftis and M.P. Horgan, eds, *Early Huntingdonshire Lay Subsidy Rolls*, which was published more recent-ly.
[35] Keene, *Survey*, I, pp. 414–15.

corn merchants), a fishmonger, and Nicholas Crane, the first butcher to become an alderman of the city.[36]

Levels of taxation, of course, were only one of the indicators of the wealth of townsfolk. Most of them, even those in relatively easy circumstances, lived in conditions which to modern eyes were almost impossibly cramped. The poorest of them had to 'crowd their families into single rooms in alley tenements', which might also have to serve as workshops; shops and selds for the sale of their products were commonly minute; and even rather better-off families were often content with a single bedroom, although there might be separate sleeping quarters for servants and apprentices. Really rich men, on the other hand, lived much more grandly, as William Servat did in his Bucklersbury mansion in London early in the fourteenth century, or John Pulteney later in his great house in St Lawrence's parish which was subsequently bought by the Black Prince, or Richard Lyons in the 1370s in a house in Royal Street which had a hall, a parlour, a principal chamber (or bedroom), a second and third chamber, a chapel, a chapman's chamber, a pantry and buttery, and a kitchen and larder.[37] There were parallels, although probably on a smaller scale, to these great London houses in the stone houses so self-consciously mentioned in York and Norwich charters in the years around 1200, in the 'great stone tenement' in Southampton in which Richard Southwick lived at the end of the thirteenth century, and in the large houses in Winchester set in spacious sites (that occupied by the Devenish family was more than an acre in extent). Richard Southwick of Southampton, moreover, not only lived in a grand house; his possessions included pewter, imported glass, and the best pottery that Spain and south-west France could supply.[38]

Winchester illustrates yet another characteristic of medieval English towns: absence of that 'zoning of wealth' which has become the rule in more recent times, so that rich and poor were 'strikingly intermingled'.[39] In medieval towns, furthermore, people with scant resources were very numerous. They might include new immigrants who, at least initially, like incomers at Norwich in the early fourteenth

---

[36] G.A. Williams, *Medieval London*, p. 161.

[37] S. Thrupp, *Merchant Class of Medieval London*, pp. 130–4; R.R. Sharpe, ed., *Cal. of Wills proved . . . in the Court of Husting, London*, I, pp. 609–11; A.R. Myers, 'The wealth of Richard Lyons', in T.A. Sandquist and M.R. Powicke, eds, *Essays in Medieval History presented to Bertie Wilkinson*, pp. 307–29.

[38] Platt, *Medieval Southampton*, pp. 103–4; Keene, *Survey*, I, p. 159.

[39] Keene, *Survey*, I, pp. 419–23.

century, simply 'increased the number of the urban poor'; and, as Gregory King discovered in the late seventeenth century, servants and labouring people had to be classed among the poor, since their incomes were small and uncertain. Much of the manual labour in towns was engaged on a casual basis when it was needed. How common this was in the building trades we have already seen; in the twelfth century *The Lay of Havelock the Dane* speaks of porters waiting to be hired on the High Bridge at Lincoln, and a coroner's inquest heard in 1305 about those who 'stood at the cross in Bedford in order to be hired'.[40] Men and women at this level were apt to leave a mark in the records only if they were involved in crime or met an untimely death. A servant, who aided in killing and robbing a Jew and his wife, characteristically was a 'stranger', not in a tithing and possessing no chattels; and a man who murdered his woman companion was likewise a 'stranger' from the marches of Wales and similarly possessionless. In London, too, those fortunate enough to pick up casual employment often did so in jobs which were arduous and dangerous as well as offering scant reward. They included the unfortunate porter who fell from a ship into the Thames when he was unloading coal and was drowned, or another who dropped dead when carrying a load of cheese along Bread Street, and yet another who fell on the pavement when carrying a load of fish and was crushed by the weight.[41]

Despite their difficulty in earning an adequate living, servants and labourers were by no means at the bottom of the urban pile. Langland was to list, among the unfortunates who 'cannot provide for themselves and . . . should be supported by Holy Church', some of those who were: the old and infirm, expectant mothers who can no longer work, the blind, the bedridden and disabled, the victims of robbery or fire or flood or unjust litigation, and men and women burdened with many children whose meagre earnings were swallowed up by the cost of feeding and clothing them and paying rent. Others are revealed in the twelfth-century Canterbury records, like the 'poor, blind, unlettered' lady who features in one of the miracles at Becket's tomb, or the beggars who gave Lodderelane outside Newingate its name; and others again by the London chronicler who tells us that in 1322 the press of the poor waiting for alms at

---

[40] E. Rutledge, 'Immigration and population growth in early fourteenth-century Norwich', *Urban History YB*, 1988, p. 28; J.W.F. Hill, *Medieval Lincoln*, pp. 175–6; R.F. Hunnisett, ed., *Bedfordshire Coroners' Rolls*, no. 268.
[41] H.M. Chew and M. Weinbaum, eds, *The London Eyre of 1244*, pll. 40, 106, 110, 130, 139.

the Blackfriars' gate was so great that 55 men and boys were smothered.[42]

The poor or relatively poor, then, were of various sorts. Some started poor, like two London glovers allowed to become freemen in 1309 at a reduced rate *quia pauper*, and others descended into poverty through ill fortune, or sickness, or old age, or like Reginald Conduit, one-time mayor of London, by providing financial services to Edward III which resulted in the 'miserable depression of his estate'.[43] Again, while not every servant was poor (a wealthy widow's maid in King's Lynn in the 1280s had goods worth £2 and her servant goods valued at £18), the graduated poll tax for that town in 1379 recognized social realities when servants and labourers, together with those engaged in ill-rewarded occupations, such as spinners, tapsters and some sailors, were assessed at the lowest rate of contribution. The remuneration of many employees, moreover, was strictly controlled. The wages of wool-packers (who were often women) in thirteenth-century Leicester, for instance, were fixed, and they were forbidden to work for 'strangers' or in places outside the town; and the York bucklemakers could not pick and choose from which of the city's girdlers to accept employment. They had to take whatever work was offered.[44]

Social differences in medieval towns, therefore, were far wider than those separating 'magnate burgesses' from rank and file craftsmen and petty traders. It is impossible to set a figure on how numerous the poor or relatively poor were, for no source encompasses all of the truly indigent; but there is much to suggest that such a figure would not have to be set too low. In 1377, for example, about one-third of those liable for the poll tax in the four central parishes of York were servants; and in the much smaller Suffolk town of Stowmarket in 1379 10 per cent of the taxpayers were labourers and their wives and a further 20 per cent were servants.[45] These proportions cannot necessarily be transferred to a time two or three generations earlier, before the heavy plague mortalities during the

---

[42] D. Pearsall, ed., *Piers Plowman by William Langland: an Edition of the C Text*, 1978, IX, lines 70–97, 175–86; Urry, *Canterbury under the Angevin Kings*, pp. 173–4; W. Stubbs, ed., *Chronicles of the Reigns of Edward I and Edward II*, I, p. 304.

[43] *CLB D*, p. 36; *CCR, 1341–43*, p. 584.

[44] Owen, ed., *The Making of King's Lynn*, pp. 221–32, 244–6; Bateson, ed., *Records of the Borough of Leicester*, I, pp. 185–6, 190, 216, 226; M. Sellars, ed., *York Memorandum Book*, I, p. 181.

[45] J.I. Leggett, 'The 1377 poll tax return for the city of York', *Yorks. Arch. Jnl.*, XLIII (1971), pp. 131–9; E. Powell, *The Rising in East Anglia in 1381*, Cambridge, 1896, pp. 89–91.

third quarter of the fourteenth century, but evidence from Bristol in the first quarter of the century perhaps points in the same direction. In 1313 some 916 inhabitants of that town contributed to a tallage there, compared with only 347 assessed for the lay subsidy in 1327; and at least 430 of the 1313 tallage-payers appear to have had possessions of too small value to have made them liable to the 1327 lay subsidy. Those who were relatively poor seem to have been a large part of Bristol's population. At about the same time, too, the poor deserving charity were as numerous as taxpayers in London, for Robert of Lincoln's will in 1300 left one penny each to 2,000 poor persons, which was almost identical to the number of heads of households in the city assessed to pay the taxes of 1319 and 1332.[46]

(d)   The ruling circles in English towns

Since the leading figures in urban communities were normally men who were relatively wealthy, what information can be got about the ruling circles in medieval towns also provides insights into the sources of above average riches for townsfolk as well as about the character of the dominant elements in urban society. These groups, in most towns of any size, had certain common features.[47] First, those with their hands on the levers of power were relatively few, although as towns gained increased powers of self-government more individuals were called upon intermittently to perform some task or to fill some minor office. The principal civic officers, however, town councillors and later the representatives of towns in parliament, tended to be drawn from a much smaller circle. At Oxford in 1285, for instance, there were some fifteen people in the main seats of power: Nicholas Kingston, the mayor, two bailiffs, eight jurats and four aldermen. This inner circle had many oligarchical features. Nicholas Kingston was mayor some fifteen times; one of the bailiffs served at least eight times; nine of the jurats and aldermen also served as bailiff, some of them more than once; and a few of the group were willing to serve in minor offices like those of coroner or

[46] E.A. Fuller, 'The tallage of 6 Edward II and the Bristol rebellion', *Trans. Bristol and Gloucestershire Arch. Soc.*, XIX (1894–5), p. 202; E.M. Veale, 'Craftsmen and the economy of London in the fourteenth century', in Holt and Rosser, eds, *The English Medieval Town*, pp. 123–4.
[47] For what follows, Miller, 'Rulers of thirteenth-century towns', pp. 128–41; *idem*, 'English town patricians, c. 1200–1350', in A. Guarducci, ed., *Gerarchie Economiche e Gerarchie Sociali, secolo XII–XVIII*, pp. 217–40.

constable of the peace.[48] It was likewise characteristic of this circle that it included some names which recur over the generations. The great-grandfather of Henry Owen, an alderman in 1285, had been reeve of Oxford in *c.* 1200, and Henry's grandfather was the city's bailiff probably in the 1220s. This dynastic tendency, together with the propensity of some leading figures to accept office repeatedly, had the result that nine-tenths of the known mayors of Oxford in the period 1226–1300 were supplied by a dozen families; and these same families, together with three others, also provided nearly three-quarters of the bailiffs. Dynastic characteristics were reinforced by marriage alliances between dynasties. Henry Owen, for instance, married his three daughters (he left no son) into office-holding families, and he himself married a bailiff's daughter, an alliance which made him the brother-in-law of Nicholas Kingston who served so often as mayor. Family relationships, of course, can divide as well as unify, but on the whole they are likely to have strengthened the coherence of Oxford's ruling group.

Finally, some of its members were clearly among the wealthier inhabitants of Oxford at that time. One or two may have been craftsmen, but Henry Owen and Nicholas Kingston were apparently large-scale wine merchants, and either Henry Gamage or his father was also engaged in that trade. Owen and Kingston, furthermore, put out work to country weavers and doubtless marketed the cloth they made; there were other cloth merchants in the group, and Philip de Eu was a wool exporter.[49] Oxford's ruling group in the 1280s, in brief, consisted mainly of merchants, although many of them also had considerable amounts of real property. In 1279 Nicholas Kingston had city property in seven Oxford parishes, as well as a country estate at Norton; Henry Owen had a score of messuages and shops, together with a right to rents totalling £6 a year; and even Ralph le Plomer, a lesser member of this inner circle although he was a cloth merchant, had three properties in St Aldate's parish and another in St Michael's South.[50] The acquisition of property helped to stabilize Oxford's ruling elite; passed on to sons and heirs it

---

[48] J.E. Thorold Rogers, ed., *Oxford City Documents . . . 1268–1665*, pp. 166, 176, 194, 223; H.E. Salter, ed., *Medieval Archives of the University of Oxford*, II, p. 142.
[49] *CLR*, 1245–51, p. 229; 1251–60, pp. 50, 388, 473; *Close R.*, 1254–56, p. 106; 1256–59, p. 74; Thorold Rogers, ed., *Oxford City Documents*, pp. 207–8; Jenkinson and Fermoy, eds, *Select Cases in the Exchequer of Pleas*, Selden Soc., XLVIII (1932), pl. 134; *CPR*, 1266–72, pp. 691–2.
[50] R. Graham, ed., 'Description of Oxford . . . 1279', in *Oxford Hist. Soc. Collectanea*, IV (1905); *Rot. Hundr.*, II, p. 693.

reinforced the dynastic tendencies already noticed; and even when no sons survived (as happened to both Nicholas Kingston and Henry Owen) daughters might take it to husbands whose place among Oxford's ruling families was thereby strengthened.

Ruling groups in other thirteenth-century towns were very similar to Oxford's. First they were apt to be small: that of Southampton in the first half of the century consisted of about a dozen families bound together in an 'intricate web of cross allegiances fostered by office, expanded by trade and confirmed by intermarriage'. Further, members of each group held office repeatedly. At Leicester, Henry Rodington was mayor for thirteen consecutive years in the mid-century, and even in the fourteenth century, over a period of thirty years, John Alsy was mayor ten times, and John Burton and William Cloune each served thirteen times as bailiff. Dynastic tendencies were also evident enough. The Dunning family provided Cambridge with its first mayor early in the thirteenth century; his son served as bailiff and his grandson was seven times mayor; and there were still Dunnings holding office in the fourteenth century.[51] Some dynasties were even longer lived. Hugh Selby was mayor of York, perhaps the city's first, in 1217; many of his descendants held city offices in the course of the thirteenth and fourteenth centuries; and one of them was still serving as alderman in 1416. There were similar, although perhaps not quite such enduring, lines elsewhere: the Holm family at Lincoln, Flemings and Isembards at Southampton, or Scotts and Carliols at Newcastle (two families which between them provided that town with mayors in at least 55 of the years between the 1240s and 1330s).

Finally, as at Oxford, office-holders in other towns of any size were normally drawn from the wealthier townsfolk and were very frequently merchants. Walter Fleming, for example, who so often held office in Southampton in the first half of the thirteenth century traded in wine, wool, salt and cloth;[52] and Hugh Selby of York, who himself was probably descended from an established family of wine and grain merchants, shipped wool to Flanders and wine from Anjou. Later in the century Thomas Carliol of Newcastle also exported wool (some of it in association with a Londoner), which he bought up as far afield as North Yorkshire. The profits of commerce, of course, might be put out in loans or used to acquire real property.

---

[51] Platt, *Medieval Southampton*, p. 59; Hartopp, ed., *Register of the Freemen of Leicester*, passim; F.W. Maitland, *Township and Borough*, pp. 134–6, 164–6.
[52] Platt, *Medieval Southampton*, pp. 62, 240.

Walter Fleming of Southampton, for instance, not only bought real estate there, but also in Chichester, Portsmouth and Winchester (some of it, perhaps, with the intention of providing benefactions for local religious institutions). Hugh Selby, on the other hand, accumulated property both in York and the neighbouring country-side to which his immediate descendants added, providing a base for the family which made it unnecessary for some of them to incur the risks that commerce entailed.

Close-knit as these urban elites were, however, it was by no means impossible for men of enterprise to break into them. Richard Embleton seems to have been a first-generation immigrant into Newcastle from a Northumbrian village, who began to export wool in a small way in the mid-1290s; but, within a decade, he was by far Newcastle's greatest merchant, and in the early decades of the four-teenth century he was mayor no less than 22 times. Like Hugh Selby, too, he acquired much property; he was able to assign Newcastle rents totalling £10 a year to found a chantry for his soul, and he also had land in a score of Northumberland and Durham villages. It was this estate, as well as continuing commercial ventures conducted mainly through agents, which enabled him in his later years to spend so much time upon Newcastle's administration and on other admin-istrative duties in the north. On the other hand, unlike Hugh Selby, he did not leave a son to succeed him, so he founded no dynasty.

The type of ruling group to be found at Oxford or York or Newcastle in the thirteenth century cannot necessarily be assumed to have existed in twelfth-century towns. The evidence is neither plenti-ful nor clear in its implications; but, such as it is, it suggests that, at least in the ancient boroughs, wealth may have been concentrated in a traditional property-holding class which provided the principal sui-tors to borough courts and office-holders like portreeves, supervisors of castle works, and the like. Some members of this class may also have supplied the households of the king or other lords with neces-sary commodities, but perhaps more as 'palace merchants' of a type familiar since the early middle ages than as commercial entrepren-eurs. The Cornhill family in London may have been men of this sort. Its earliest known member, Roger nephew of Hubert, was a reeve of London in the early twelfth century and was granted the manor of Chalk (Kent) by Henry I; and when Roger died in *c.* 1130 he was suc-ceeded in what was clearly a considerable estate by his son Gervase. Gervase consolidated the family's fortunes, in part probably by money-lending, but still more by service to the king. He was the local justiciar in London under Stephen, and under Henry II was sheriff of the city more than once and served in other London contexts. His activity, however, was not restricted to London, for he was also sheriff of Kent and Surrey, and he had property in several counties as well as in London. There is, however, 'no evidence that Gervase dealt in anything but land and money or that his ancestors were even as "mercantile" as that'. His two sons continued in his tradition. Henry served as sheriff of London, and both acted as businessmen for Henry II and John respectively, but as professional crown servants rather than as independent merchants.[53]

Other London notables were of the same type as the Cornhills, although the available evidence being what it is they appear most prominently as speculators in property. Reiner fitzBerengar, for instance, sheriff of London early in Henry II's reign, had both town and country property and, like a gentleman, authenticated documents with an equestrian seal. His son, Richard, was also sheriff of London in 1187–89, and was a close associate of the king's butler in provisioning the court, an accumulator of property in the city, a tenant by knight service at Shenley (Herts.), and the patron of that village's church.[54] There were similar figures in some provincial towns. As we have seen, early in the century, Canterbury's portreeve, William Cauvel, belonged to a family with 'more affinities with the country knights than with their fellow citizens', and the alderman of Oxford's gild merchant in 1147 appears to have been a local baron. At Cambridge, too, the Dunning who gave its name to one of the city's most enduring families had sufficient property there to confer 50 acres in the town fields upon Barnwell priory; one of his sons lived in the stone manor house in the town later called the School of Pythagoras; and the latter's son in turn was alderman of the gild merchant and probably Cambridge's first mayor. He also had land in half a dozen Cambridgeshire villages and possesed an equestrian seal, as did his contemporary, Baldwin Blancgernun, member of a family which under Henry II had supplied someone to supervise work on Huntingdon castle. There were other men of property in Cambridge, including Osbert Domesman who left to a son who became prior of Barnwell, 140 acres in the town fields and many

---

[53] S. Reynolds, 'The rulers of London in the twelfth century', pp. 346–7 and for the 'few traces of their mercantile interests', C.N.L. Brooke and G. Keir, *London 800–1216*, p. 41; for the Cornhill family, S. Painter, *The Reign of King John*, Baltimore, 1949, pp. 80–1, 88, 137; J.H. Round, *Geoffrey de Mandeville*, pp. 304–12; J.E.A. Jolliffe, *Angevin Kingship*, 1955, pp. 289–93.

[54] H. Hall, ed., *Red Book of the Exchequer*, 3 vols, Rolls Ser., 1896, p. 303; L.C. Loyd and D.M. Stenton, eds, *Sir Christopher Hatton's Books of Seals*, Oxford, 1950, nos. 82, 158, 429; W. Page, *London: its Early Development*, pp. 245–6.

messuages in the town. Osbert's surname possibly suggests that he was a hereditary lawman; but whether or not that was so there is nothing to connect him, any more than there is to connect the Dunnings and Blancgernuns, with any trade or craft.[55]

There are tantalizing glimpses of comparable figures in other twelfth-century towns. Roger Baard, who supervised the rebuilding of Newcastle castle late in the century, and arranged for lead to be sent to continental monasteries as gifts from the king, was descended from a Yorkshire gentry family and himself had land in Jesmond; the reeves of Winchester early in the century may have been very like the king's thegns who held office in Alfred's time;[56] and later in the century there were influential York citizens with much property, but no indication of any engagement in trade. William Tickhill and his son-in-law, Hugh fitzLefwin, for example, were close associates of the great Yorkshire baron, Roger Mowbray. Two of Roger's charters were drawn up in William Tickhill's house in York; both William and Hugh witnessed Roger's charters; and Roger gave to William (perhaps in return for a crusading loan) the manor of Askham Richard by a charter in which he refers to William as his friend. Hugh, however, explicitly describes himself as a citizen of York and he was certainly involved in its affairs, for he was a keeper of the exchange associated with the York mint; and Hugh's brother, Gerard, appears to have had a long association with the mint in York. Hugh eventually succeeded his father-in-law as lord of Askham Richard, and he was addressed by Roger Mowbray as one of the 'men holding his demesnes in England'. Men like this might be citizens, but their interests and associations made them part of those seignorial classes which ruled Norman and early Angevin England.[57]

By 1200 or soon after there are signs that urban élites were changing. Even before 1200 the reeves of Winchester were being drawn from the ranks of 'commercial citizens' and one of them appears to have been a vintner; York's earliest known mayor, Hugh Selby, was a wool and wine merchant; and an exporter of hides, Simon

---

[55] J.M. Gray, *School of Pythagoras*, Cambridge Antiquarian Soc., Quarto Pubns, NS IV (1932), pp. 2–4; H.M. Cam, *Liberties and Communities in Medieval England*, pp. 23–4; *Pipe Roll*, 20 Henry II, p. 63; J.W. Clark, ed., *Ecclesie de Bernewelle Liber Memorandorum*, pp. 65, 98.

[56] F.W. Dendy, 'An account of Jesmond', *AA*, 3rd ser. I (1904), pp. 33–5; J. Hodgson, *History of Northumberland*, III(3), p. 23; M. Biddle, ed., *Winchester in the Early Middle Ages*, p. 447.

[57] *Pipe Roll*, 12 Henry II, p. 49; 21 Henry II, pp. 179–80; 31 Henry II, p. 76; 10 John, p. 158; W. Farrer and C.T. Clay, eds, *Early Yorkshire Charters*, I, nos. 147, 208; D.E. Greenway, ed., *Charters of the Honour of Mowbray*, nos. 126–7, 308, 315, 347.

Curlevache, became alderman of the gild merchant at Leicester.[58] Businessmen were taking over, in part because the king and other lords of towns were more and more willing to exercise their lordship indirectly, leaving much of the routine of local government to towns-folk themselves. This responsibility was increasingly shouldered by a town's own élite rather than by functionaries closely linked to men of power in the English countryside. The development of these new urban élites, of course, was conditioned by the expansive forces at work in the medieval economy. A more and more sophisticated royal court, and great men's households, the purchasing power of which was enhanced by the high level of seignorial incomes, offered expanding markets; there was growing demand in every locality as population levels rose towards their maximum; and both internal and external exchanges increased in range and intensity. Business opportunities were being significantly expanded at a time when rising prices may well have increased the margins of profit which entrepreneurs could earn.

Men engaged in the more lucrative trades and occupations, therefore, came to play the leading roles, at least in the larger towns, although the character of these ruling groups inevitably varied from place to place.[59] That which dominated London by the end of our period was shaped by the fact that the city was very large, making provisioning it big business, that it was a major international port with something like a national market, and that it was becoming a capital which for that reason regularly attracted many wealthy visitors. A high proportion of London's wealthier citizens, therefore, were engaged in luxury trades or crafts (as goldsmiths, mercers, spicers or vintners, for example), but others were employed in the large-scale provision trades and yet others in England's most rewarding line of commerce, the wool and cloth trades with the Low Countries. Consequently, lists of leading Londoners summoned before the king in 1328, of the citizens who paid the most taxes in 1332, and of the principal contributors to London's loan to Edward III in 1340, have very similar appearances. They included pepperers (spicers or grocers), drapers, fishmongers, vintners, woolmongers, goldsmiths, and mercers, together with the occasional butcher, blader (corn merchant) and corder, these last belonging to the craft

[58] Biddle, ed., *Winchester in the Early Middle Ages*, pp. 424, 448; *VCH Leics.*, IV, pp. 41–2; Bateson, ed., *Records of the Borough of Leicester*, I, pp. 6, 11, 34–5.
[59] For what follows, see Williams, *Medieval London*; Platt, *Medieval Southampton*; and the articles, cited above p. 342, note 47.

which distributed much of the increasing imports of Hanseatic goods into London. The dominant role of merchants in London is clear enough.[60]

It was the same in other towns. Thirteenth-century mayors of York and Oxford included wine merchants who supplied the court and, even at Chester, William Doncaster imported wine from Gascony as well as dealing in wool and grain and dabbling in Welsh mining. Again, at York, among prominent citizens who contravened civic regulations in 1301 there were a number of provision merchants, including taverners, who were often wine merchants in addition and who had wives who brewed ale. One, who was later to be mayor, was also a fishmonger.[61] At Oxford in the mid-thirteenth century a whole group of the town's *majores* organized and financed cloth-making in the surrounding countryside; and both John Verdennel of York and William Brand of Lincoln supplied cloth for Henry III's court.[62] By the fourteenth century wool exporters were an increasingly prominent element in the ruling circles of many towns; but at Bristol a new generation of English cloth exporters had emerged, and there were influential groups of lead merchants at Derby and of tin merchants at Bodmin and Lostwithiel. Meanwhile, at Newcastle upon Tyne, Nicholas Scott, a member of one of that port's oldest dynasties, anticipated its future in 1341 when he sent a ship to Flanders laden with coal as well as hides.

The prominence of merchants in urban élites in the generation or two before 1349 was obviously related to the advance of native commercial interests in the same period, which quickened the rate at which ruling families in towns received infusions of new blood. At York, the Langton family, which for three generations provided the city with a succession of mayors between 1297 and 1356, had made money as wool exporters before becoming property-owning rentiers; and of the five mayors who alternated with the Langtons in the 1330s and 1340s, all of them new men, three were large-scale wool merchants and a fourth was active in the internal wool trade.[63] The Selbys, too, were helped to survive among York's leading families by once again becoming traders in wool and groceries; at Southampton a dominant group of merchant magnates consisted mainly of new

---

[60] Thomas, ed., *Cal. of Plea and Memoranda Rolls of London, 1322–64*, p. 74; Unwin, ed., *Finance and Trade under Edward III*, pp. 61–92; *CLB F*, pp. 46–9.
[61] A.W. Hopkins, ed., *Select Rolls of the Chester City Courts*, pp. lxvi–vii; *CCR, 1296–1302*, p. 439; 1302–7, p. 160; M. Prestwich, ed., *York Civic Ordinances, 1301*, pp. 22–8.
[62] *CLR*, 1251–60, pp. 174, 220, 366; 1260–67, p. 146.
[63] E.B. Fryde, *Studies in Medieval Trade and Finance*, chpt. XI; *CPR, 1348–50*, p. 129.

men who became rich as shipowners and traders in wine and victuals; and at Newcastle the long reign of Scott and Carliol reached its term as new generations of wool merchants, first Actons and Grapers, and then Richard Embleton, the Galloways and John Denton moved into positions of power. Even at Oxford new names came to the fore – Worminghall, Dukelinton, Burcestre and Cary; and William Burcestre at least exported wool through London.[64]

Even in towns of some size, of course, the ruling groups were similar rather than identical; and the variations between them have been illustrated in the West Midlands in *c.* 1300. Bristol, as a great port, was dominated by merchants; Gloucester had a smaller mercantile élite which drew more of its income from property; Coventry merchants as yet had less influence over the government of their town than the merchants of Bristol and Gloucester; and at Worcester there seems to have been less correspondence than elsewhere between office-holding and wealth as measured by taxation.[65] Such differences become even more marked when we turn to smaller towns. Colchester at the opening of the fourteenth century, for example, possessed municipal institutions which were still rudimentary; and only about one in three of the town's bailiffs can be shown to have been engaged in trade or industry, although almost all of them held property and some of them agricultural property. In this respect 'the community of the borough merged into the community of the shire' and fourteenth-century Colchester may still have been more like a twelfth-century town than those places where municipal development had proceeded further.[66]

Even smaller places than Colchester, however, had their own élites. The little West Midland towns at Thornbury and Halesowen were both closely controlled by their lords; but each had its little ring of notables supplying most of the jurors and town officers, and acting as mediators between the burgesses and their lords. At Thornbury it was composed of butchers, graziers, grain and malt dealers, innkeepers and victualling retailers; and Halesowen's élite, which provided jurors, bailiffs, ale-tasters and other officials, consisted of men of a similar sort. There are glimpses of a comparable group at the end of the thirteenth century in the portmoot rolls of Adam de Stratton's little borough at Highworth. They included John Evingham (perhaps a baker, for the bread he made was periodically

---

[64] C.M. Fraser, 'The life and death of John Denton', *AA*, 4th ser. XXXVII (1959), pp. 305–7; *CCR*, 1327–30, p. 284; *VCH Oxon.*, IV, pp. 67–8.
[65] R.H. Hilton, *A Medieval Society*, pp. 202–4.
[66] R.H. Britnell, *Growth and Decline in Colchester*, pp. 16–17, 24–34.

adjudged to be unsatisfactory), and also Robert Magge, who was presented as a delinquent brewer 22 times between 1275 and 1287.[67] Men like this, of course, had no great wealth and were small fry when compared with Hugh Selby or Richard Embleton, to say nothing of the great merchants of London; but they, too, even though under strict seignorial controls, were rulers of their own small towns.

About these small-town figures we will never know much, but some of their counterparts in larger towns are rather more knowable. Many of them, as well as being successful businessmen or the descendants of successful businessmen, were clearly also substantial property owners. At Winchester outstanding fourteenth-century citizens like Roger Inkpenne and John Devenish had rent incomes from city property of around £30 a year, at a time when most citizens had at best a single property. It was rarer even for members of the city's ruling group to have rural holdings, although the thirteenth-century wool merchant, Simon Draper, acquired three manors in Hampshire; but he was on his way to becoming sheriff of the county and a knight.[68] At Exeter, too, few citizens had country property, perhaps a reflection of the limited resources of a provincial élite; and at Cambridge even town property may have been relatively unimportant as a source of income for most townsfolk. A tallage levied there in 1312–13 was charged both on rents and on the value of men's chattels. Only 17 per cent of the 513 taxpayers were assessed on rents alone, many of them religious houses or outsiders like Sir Giles of Trumpington with property in the town or its fields. A further 21 per cent of the taxpayers were assessed both on rents and chattels, and this group included members of some of the town's leading families like the Dunnings and the Semans. Nearly two-thirds of the tallage payers, however, 320 in all, were assessed solely on their goods, and presumably relied principally on a trade or craft, and not on property, for their income.[69]

For some wealthy townsfolk, nonetheless, property ownership was clearly important as a source of income. Henry Owen, one of the Oxford 'magnates' of the mid-thirteenth century, was a many-sided businessman, but he also had an interest in some forty city properties; and some townsmen acquired country estates, even if few of

---

[67] Hilton, *Class Conflict and the Crisis of Feudalism*, pp. 177, 183, 202; *idem*, 'Small town society in England before the Black Death', pp. 71–96; R.B. Pugh, ed., *Court Rolls of the Wiltshire Manors of Adam de Stratton*, pp. 111–63.
[68] Keene, *Survey*, I, pp. 218, 231; II, p. 1218.
[69] Kowaleski, 'The commercial dominance of a provincial oligarchy', p. 212; PRO E 179/242/76.

them could match the Londoner, John Pultney, who possessed thirteen manors in seven counties and the patronage of a Leicestershire church. These holdings of property might represent deliberate investment to secure income or store capital, or were perhaps a by-product of money-lending when land had been offered as security for loans that were not repaid. Some urban families accumulated sufficient property to live entirely or mainly as rentiers, as the Selbys and Langtons seem to have done in York; but, for the leading towns-folk, business and property-ownership were more commonly co-ordinate rather than alternative sources of income, although their relative importance might change over a man's lifetime. The cycle reflected in Richard Embleton's career, with the emphasis in later years upon civic office and property accumulation, was not untypical.

For that cycle there were good practical reasons. Civic offices might be time-consuming, and those assuming them, except for the relatively few people with substantial amounts of inherited property, were likely to have needed time to establish themselves before they did so. In the case of twenty three mayors and bailiffs of Leicester in the late thirteenth and early fourteenth centuries, on average sixteen years elapsed between their admission to the gild merchant and becoming a bailiff, twenty years before they served as mayor and thirty-six years before they appeared in the records for the last time. This suggests that civic office was likely to be a matter for men of middle age, beginning perhaps in their late thirties when even burgesses who were incomers might have had time to acquire enough property to supplement whatever income from business was compatible with the tenure of office. Beyond the years of public service property might also provide a pension fund, as it did for Thomas Carliol of Newcastle, who arranged for his manor of Swarland to provide him with an annuity of £50 in his old age; and, in the still longer term, it might support a family's continuing prominence in a town, whether or not that prominence was reflected in the tenure of town office.[70]

The ruling classes of England's medieval towns of any size were drawn principally from the ranks of successful businessmen, although they might also include representatives of what may perhaps be called a class of property-owning bourgeois-gentlemen, many of whom ultimately drifted back to the countryside from which they or their ancestors may originally have come. At York, early in

[70] Hartopp, ed., *Register of the Freemen of Leicester*; Miller, 'Rulers of thirteenth-century towns', pp. 135–6.

the thirteenth century, the Fairfaxes and Clarevaus withdrew to Walton and Croft; in the mid-century the descendants of Gace de Chaumont retired to the manor of Colton in the Ainsty; and later the Basy family became lords of Bilbrough, the Louths lords of East Ness, the Sampsons lords of Appleton Roebuck. In the end even the Langtons abandoned the city and established themselves at Farnley. This was the classic form of medieval social promotion whereby a bourgeois was turned into a gentleman. At the same time, even the acquisition of country estates did not automatically lead wealthy townsfolk to abandon their town. The Langtons did not cease their involvement in York's affairs until long after they had begun to obtain rural property, and the Selbys did not do so even after holding agricultural land for several generations. At Newcastle, too, Carliols still served as mayor in the third generation after they got the manor of Swarland. Once again the social gap between townsfolk and countryfolk appears not excessively wide.

(e) Indications of social distinctions

Social differences within towns, however, were as marked as those to be found in the English countryside. There were, as we have seen, great differences of wealth between small circles of *majores* and the majority of burgesses, the great mass of craftsmen and retail traders; and there was no less of a gulf between the latter and the crowd of servants, casual labourers and plain poor. In London, moreover, there were many signs of a social structure which was becoming more hierarchical, as some crafts became the employees of other crafts, and as some occupations demanding limited skills employed many who had never been apprenticed or men, who in effect, were permanent journeymen. Similar tendencies were not absent in other places and were one of the consequences of the intensification of economic activity and the expansion of markets.[71]

There were outward and visible signs of these urban social disparities in the ways in which townsfolk lived. It has been calculated, for example, that in Winchester most of the houses of citizens of middling rank measured about $16^1/2 \times 23$–36 feet. Such houses could be subdivided to accommodate poorer families, some of whom also occupied cottages on sites no larger than 10 feet × 10 feet; while by contrast, the site of the Devenish family mansion, although a good deal of it was garden, measured 246 feet × 361 feet. Even without

[71] Williams, *Medieval London*, pp. 176–95.

taking account of the grand houses of rich Londoners, there were wealthy townsfolk elsewhere with houses which stood out from those of their neighbours. Hugh Selby's son John had a house in York which, unusually in the thirteenth century, had its own name (Munsorel); the house in Oxford which became the nucleus of the Mitre Inn was acquired early in the fourteenth century by Philip Worminghall, a member of one of that town's richest families; and the Cambridge house, later known as the School of Pythagoras, which Merton College, Oxford, got from Richard Dunning in 1271, seems to have consisted of a hall measuring *c.* 60 feet × 20 feet built over an undercroft, with an added 'solar wing' on two floors and measuring *c.* 20 feet × 10 feet.[72] Another indication of the wealth of those who had occupied it was the fact that the School of Pythagoras was a stone house. Characteristically, around 1200, Hugh fitzLefwin had a stone house on the Coney Street–Stonegate corner in York, and there were some thirty stone houses in Canterbury, mostly owned by merchants or financiers. Such houses were inevitably more costly to build than the usual timber-framed town house, but they had the advantage of being less combustible at a time when most towns were ravaged by fires from time to time.[73]

Wealthier townsfolk were also distinguished, of course, by the quantity and value of their personal possessions, although these are seldom listed in full in surviving records. A fragmentary and damaged tax assessment for a few York parishes in 1319, however, does include a valuation of the goods of Nicholas Fleming, mayor of York, who died that year fighting against the Scots at Myton-on-Swale. Unfortunately much of it is illegible, but Nicholas's possessions included a good riding horse, various pieces of plate, and two relatively expensive gowns belonging to his wife. What is significant, however, is that the total value of his taxable goods was greater than the value of all the goods of all the other taxpayers in St Helen's parish, Stonegate, put together, and that they were worth more than thirty times what the goods of a glasswright, and more than sixteen times what the goods of a plumber, were worth. The will of a leading fourteenth-century Oxford man conveys a similar impression. William Burcestre bequeathed, among other things, four robes (one

[72] Keene, *Survey*, I, pp. 155–9, 162, 175–7; Muniments of the Dean and Chapter of York, Vicars' Cartulary, ff. 8–9; H.E. Salter, *Survey of Oxford*, I, p. 115; RCHM, *Inventory of the Historical Monuments of the City of Cambridge*, II, pp. 377–9.
[73] Farrer and Clay, eds, *Early Yorkshire Charters*, I, nos. 242, 246–7; Urry, *Canterbury under the Angevin Kings*, pp. 193–4.

to his personal chaplain), silver plate engraved with his coat of arms, a couple of dozen silver spoons, and various books of romance.[74]

There is much to suggest, in fact, that in their ways of life the urban rich often resembled the landowners of the surrounding countryside more than the craftsmen among whom they lived. The conclusion of one of the few systematic attempts to investigate this question is clear: they 'behaved like aristocratic consumers in that, after spending a good proportion of their income on food, . . . their other main areas of expenditure were building and textiles. . . . They also displayed and stored their wealth by buying silver plate and jewels'.[75] These common ways of life help to explain why town *majores* seem to move easily in the company of their landowning contemporaries, so that Roger Mowbray could call William Tickhill of York his friend, Richard Embleton of Newcastle could be appointed to survey Thomas of Lancaster's Northumbrian lands and to take charge of Dunstanburgh castle, and Nicholas Scott of Newcastle could serve both as mayor of Newcastle and sheriff of Northumberland. And, of course, Richard Embleton, like Nicholas Fleming of York, died in battle with the Scots. Nor were these simply instances of northern eccentricity. William Burcestre of Oxford was also much in demand for government business. He enquired into obstructions to navigation in the Thames, into an attack on an Oxfordshire manor, into poaching at Bolney, into misdemeanours by the king's purveyors in Oxfordshire and Berkshire. A butcher spoke slightingly of William's record as mayor of Oxford, but Edward III seems to have thought better of him.[76]

It is also significant that, by the thirteenth century, some townsmen were knighted, like Thomas Carliol of Newcastle because he had enough land to support him in that rank or like John Sampson of York in the 1290s for service to the king (including military service).[77] A knighthood might, of course, mark a stage in a bourgeois family's withdrawal from town to country; but the fact that a number of families made that transfer with apparent smoothness perhaps owed something to the close association of the wealthier townsfolk and their landowning neighbours in running the affairs of local communities. By the reign of Edward II, moreover, that association

---

[74] PRO E 179/242/95; *VCH Oxon.*, IV, p. 69.
[75] C. Dyer, *Standards of Living in the Later Middle Ages*, chpt. 7 and esp. p. 205.
[76] Miller, 'English town patricians', p. 229; *CPR*, 1324–27, p. 114; 1327–30, pp. 156, 209, 215; 1330–34, p. 542; 1338–40, p. 283; *VCH Oxon.*, IV, p. 40.
[77] F. Palgrave, ed., *Parliamentary Writs*, I, p. 216; Miller, 'Rulers of thirteenth-century towns', pp. 137–8.

had ceased to be merely local. A treatise, apparently written in that reign, included the granting of taxes to the king among the things which ought to be done by the three 'grades' of parliament: 'the proctors of the clergy, the knights of the shires, and the citizens and burgesses, who represent all the community of England'. Before long the clerical proctors would withdraw from parliaments, and it took time for the knights and burgesses to come together in a house of commons which could speak for all the secular communities of England. Their collaboration in parliament grew out of their local collaboration, underlining once more the fact that the class distinction which mattered in medieval England was not that between bourgeois and countryman.[78]

2. THE LIMITS OF URBAN SOLIDARITY

(a) Townsfolk and their rulers

As was the case in any sort of community there were limits to the solidarity of medieval urban communities. To begin with, because power in most towns was in relatively few hands, potential sources of tension existed even though those who exercised power conferred benefits upon their fellow townsfolk by paving streets, bringing in drinking water, building quays and markets, developing waterways and founding hospitals.[79] Oligarchical tendencies, on the other hand, were seemingly inescapable; and although urban oligarchies were relatively open to new wealth, they might appear insufficiently open to those who were on the outside. There might, therefore, be some battles for power within the ranks of the relatively wealthy. In some cases, too, ruling élites used their political authority to further sectional economic interests: to reinforce mercantile control over the manufacturing crafts in the textile industry in the twelfth and thirteenth centuries, or to impose strict controls upon those who worked for wages. The detailed list of charges which porters in Southampton might legitimately make, promulgated in *c.* 1300, was characteristic in this respect. It covered the moving of almost every

[78] We have accepted the provenance and dating of the *Modus* suggested by N. Pronay and J. Taylor, *Parliamentary Texts of the later Middle Ages*, p. 113, although there are dissenting voices: see G.O. Sayles, *Scripta Diversa*, 1982, pp. 331–60. Our view of early parliaments relies heavily upon the work of Helen Cam: see esp. E.B. Fryde and E. Miller, eds, *Historical Studies of the English Parliament*, I, pp. 9, 263–79.

[79] Cf. J.F. Lemarignier, *La France Médiévale: Institutions et Société*, Paris, 1970, p. 304.

sort of commodity, and the penalty for breach of the regulations was imprisonment for a day and a night and, more seriously, a ban on the offender acting as a porter for a year and a day. Prolonged unemployment for an ill-paid casual worker was a punishment of real severity.[80]

Civic dissensions more commonly arose, not out of class antagonisms, but from the fact that town governments exercised a wide range of powers which might affect the interests of particular individuals or groups.[81] Town governments, for example, had extensive rights of economic regulation to defend common interests: to prevent a merchant cornering the supply of hides coming into Norwich by 'privily leading merchants by signs to his house'; or to prevent townsfolk using out-of-town facilities like country fulling mills or entering into partnerships with 'strangers' as distinct from fellow townsfolk. It was similarly culpable for a Leicester burgess to stand a couple of servants outside the east gate of the town on Saturdays to intercept wool-fells coming in by road before they reached the market.[82] Because virtually every town dweller was from one point of view a consumer, however, victuallers attracted the maximum attention from town governments. Consumers buying for their own use often had a prior right to buy goods brought into town up to a certain hour, and town retailers who 'heightened the market' by intercepting goods on their way into town were punished, as was John Kyng of Colchester who bought up fish 'in the market and in secret houses' and sold them 'dearer to the people than if they [had] remained in the merchants' hands'. Such regulations governed a great diversity of goods, including whelks and oysters, dairy produce and 'any other kind of victual'; and in addition town courts enforced price regulations based on national legislation for bread, ale and wine.[83]

Civic authorities were concerned with quality as well as price – that leather was sufficiently tanned, that meat was not 'putrid' or 'measled', that fish was not 'stinking', and that provisions in general were 'wholesome and clean'. They also tried to ensure that goods were sold by recognizable measures, so they were concerned that

[80] P. Studer, ed., *Oak Book of Southampton*, I, pp. 70–4.

[81] S. Reynolds, *Introduction*, pp. 136–8.

[82] Hudson, ed., *Leet Jurisdiction in Norwich*, p. 48; Bateson, *Records of the Borough of Leicester*, I, pp. 91–3, 102, 168, 308, 347.

[83] Hudson, ed., *Leet Jurisdiction in Norwich*, pp. 2–3, 5, 9, 12–14; Studer, ed., *Oak Book of Southampton*, I, pp. 64–70; Bateson, ed., *Records of the Borough of Leicester*, I, pp. 180–1; I.H. Jeayes, ed., *Court Rolls of the Borough of Colchester*, I, pp. 3–4, 19, 147; Ingleby, ed., *Red Register of King's Lynn*, I, p. 46; *Cal. Inq. Misc.*, I, no. 1243.

cloth was in 'length and width according to the ancient assize', and about the size of the loaf of bread and the capacity of the gallon of ale. The 'malignity of bakers' attracted particular attention, for they were prone 'to make loaves that are false as well as to the dough as to the weight thereof'; and the servants of out-of-town bakers selling bread in London were punishable in the same way as their masters would have been if it had been possible to bring them to book. Inevitably some of those who were punished under these many regulations felt resentment. One London baker, when he came home after being dragged through the streets on a hurdle because his bread was false, took a bone and threw it at a tabor-player and broke his tabor through the middle.[84]

Resentment might also arise from the duty of the town authorities to safeguard the community's solidarity and to act as guardians of law and order. A Colchester burgess was expelled from the town in 1334 for failing to give backing to a fellow townsman, although subsequently the delinquent was allowed to compound with a fine, most of which was pardoned; and at Southampton a principal duty of the alderman of the gild merchant was to bring peace to burgesses between whom strife had arisen, 'so that good peace and unity may be kept among the *prudhommes* of the town'. On the other hand, at Leicester in 1277, because 'crowds make riots, batteries and burglaries in the town', justice was ordered to be done on their bodies or, if they were 'obstinate doers of such outrages', they were to be banished from the town. Even draconian punishments, however, did not always bring amendment. The daughter of a Leicester gildsman had been pilloried once and twice compelled to abjure the town before, in 1264, she was sentenced to have an ear cut off and had to abjure the town yet again. This time it was on condition that, if she returned, she would bring upon herself the 'judgement which is not to be written', although its severity is not to be doubted.[85]

If those who incurred punishment were likely to have a sense of grievance, a more generalized source of dissension was probably the suspicion that a narrow ring of rich men used their authority to feather their own nests and to place undue burdens on their fellow

[84] Jeayes, ed., *Court Rolls of the Borough of Colchester,* I, pp. 29, 140; Studer, *Oak Book of Southampton,* I, pp. 50–2; J.S. Furley, ed., *Ancient Usages of the City of Winchester,* pp. 28, 34; H.T. Riley, trans. and ed., *Memorials of London and London Life,* pp. 180–2; A.H. Thomas, ed., *Cal. of Early Mayor's Court Rolls . . . 1298–1307,* p. 67.
[85] Jeayes, ed., *Court Rolls of the Borough of Colchester,* I, p. 133; Studer, ed., *Oak Book of Southampton,* I, pp. 60–2; Bateson, ed., *Records of the Borough of Leicester,* I, pp. 103–4, 160.

townsfolk. At King's Lynn in 1305, for example, it was alleged that tallages had been levied without the unanimous consent of the community, poor men and men of modest means had been forced to pay great sums in the form of common fines, and much of the proceeds from these charges had been converted to use of the town's rulers.[86] Similar complaints were voiced in many towns. In the 1250s the 'burgesses of the lesser commune' at Oxford also alleged that they were tallaged at double the rate at which the *majores* paid and that, on one occasion, the latter had levied money from them to buy wine for the city dignitaries at a party which ended in fisticuffs. There were similar grumbles about Lincoln's ruling élite in the late thirteenth century and when, in 1350, the middling and common folk established a Corpus Christi gild no mayor or bailiff was to be admitted to it unless he was found to be of humble, good and honest conversation. Similar tensions between *majores* and *minores*, or between the wealthy, office-holding minority and the mass of burgesses, surfaced in many other places, including Grimsby in 1258, Northampton in 1276, Gloucester in 1290, and Cambridge in 1291 where it was alleged that the rich levied manifold tallages from the poor without reasonable cause.[87]

Fiscal grievances of this sort sometimes led to criticism of the oligarchical character of these governments. At Oxford in 1257 the lesser commune complained that the jurats chose the town's bailiffs from their own number; and an intensification of oligarchy at Winchester in the 1260s and 1270s resulted in sharper internal conflicts and the insistence in the usages drawn up in *c.* 1275 upon the annual character of the mayor's office and a carefully defined electoral process for the appointment of the bailiffs.[88] Internal disputes, however, were often between ins and outs rather than between rich and poor, and were probably intensified in the late thirteenth and early fourteenth centuries when the expansion of denizen commerce bred an assertive new-rich class in many towns. Conflict, in other words, was between men of wealth, although no doubt the factions sought what allies they could get among other groups in their town. At Bristol under Edward II, the little ring of leading burgesses which controlled the town was challenged 'by other leading burgesses backed up by the mass of the townsfolk'. In disputes at

---

[86] Hist. Mss. Comm., *11th Report*, Appx. III, p. 187.
[87] *Cal. Inq. Misc.*, I, no. 238; Platt, *The English Medieval Town*, p. 118; Hill, *Medieval Lincoln*, pp. 211–13, 298, 300–1, 402–5; *CPR*, 1281–92, pp. 404, 457; *BBC 1216–1307*, pp. 38–9; *Rot. Hundr.*, II, pp. 2–3; *Rot. Parl.*, I, p. 47.
[88] Furley, ed., *Ancient Usages of the City of Winchester*, p. 26; Keene, *Survey*, I, pp. 78–9.

Southampton and Ipswich, too, men of substance were active on both sides; and at York, in the early fourteenth century, the factions had leaders drawn from the better off, but with followings of more modest citizens. At Newcastle in the 1340s the concern of the lesser burgesses to prevent the town's revenues being fraudulently converted by those in office was given an edge by competition for power among leading wool merchants which ended with John Denton, one of the most ruthless of the merchants, being arrested on a charge of having betrayed the town to the Scots twenty years earlier and, being allowed a diet so restricted in prison, he was soon dead.[89]

In London, too, there were similar troubles. In 1241 it was alleged that the mayor 'laid his hand heavily on the poorer citizens and secretly laid up money for himself', and fraud on the part of the holders of city offices was alleged by the 'middling and lower orders' in 1258 and 1275–6. From this time forward to break the control exercised by the oligarchs and the power of the aldermanic class became 'permanent aspirations of the popular movement in the city', with the developing crafts playing an important part in attempts to achieve these ends.[90] Edward I's confiscation of the city's liberties in the period 1285–99 also made its contribution to the development of the anti-oligarchic movement by breaking the continuity of the control of London's government by the old patrician families; but popular suspicion of the aldermanic class remained strong, as an old clothes dealer demonstrated in 1307 when he derided the mayor and aldermen riding past by neighing like a horse. Oligarchy, however, remained in place and, in 1315, Edward II confirmed the right of the aldermen and 'other of the more discreet and powerful citizens' to elect the mayor and sheriffs at a time when some of the common people and plebeians, by conspiracy among themselves and 'holding clandestine meetings in private', had tried to intrude into these electoral processes. Edward II's political troubles weakened royal control over the city, and made it easier for the 'community' to enlarge its influence and for factions to contend for power with each other. In 1320 Robert Kelsey was toppled from his aldermanry by the 'commune' who blamed him for the heavy taxes it had to bear, and who were also moved to rancour by malevolent rivals of his; and a faction led by the mercer, William

[89] E.A. Fuller, 'The tallage of 6 Edward II and the Bristol rebellion', pp. 174–5; C. Platt, *The English Medieval Town*, p. 119; *idem, Medieval Southampton*, p. 241; Miller, 'Rulers of thirteenth-century towns', pp. 131–2; Fraser, 'The life and death of John Denton', pp. 303–25.
[90] For this whole question, Williams, *Medieval London*, chpts. VII–XII, esp. p. 227.

Hackforth, was said to have bound itself by mutual oaths to maintain false plaints, and to have dominated the elections of mayors, sheriffs and other officers.[91] Doubtless there had always been jockeying for advantage within the city's ruling groups, but in these years the part played by the 'commonalty' in London's government was steadily enlarged, laying the foundations for the regime in the later middle ages when control was shared between the aldermanic court and the common council and access to the freedom of the city was channelled through the crafts. These developments were built into the settlement which followed the revolutionary upsurge in London in 1326–27, and which was endorsed by the charter given to the city by the young Edward III's government in 1327.

(b)   Craft gilds and town governments

The character of London's ruling class, of course, was not totally transformed in Edward II's reign, and continued to consist of a relatively small circle of rich men, many of them merchants. On the other hand, the turn-over of its personnel was henceforth somewhat more rapid and the range of its recruitment was widened as the crafts came to control more effectively access to the business life of the city. The influence exercised by the crafts was also increasing elsewhere. An abortive attempt to revise Newcastle's constitution in 1342 envisaged handing over control of the personnel and conduct of the town's government to its twelve 'misteries'; and in 1369 it was ordained that Norwich's officers and aldermen were to be elected by 'the good and best men of the misteries of the city'.[92] Except in London the formal organization of the various trades in craft gilds was largely a phenomenon of the fourteenth and fifteenth centuries, and therefore in great measure falls outside the limits of the present study; but many of the craft organizations of the late middle ages had earlier roots, and in any case they belong to forms of organization with many manifestations in the medieval west. For centuries voluntary groups had come together for a diversity of common purposes: as simple fraternities, or social clubs (Walter Map called them 'drinkeries'), as gilds merchant, as sworn urban communes, perhaps as associations to keep the peace in a disordered age or to enforce

---

[91] Thomas, ed., *Cal. of Early Mayor's Court Rolls . . . 1298–1307*, p. 261; *CLB D*, pp. 25–6; H.M. Cam, ed., *The Eyre of London, 14 Edward II*, pp. 42, 47; Williams, *Medieval London*, pp. 267, 272, 281–2.
[92] R. Welford, *History of Newcastle and Gateshead*, I, pp. 114–16; J. Tait, *Medieval English Borough*, p. 317.

the truce of God.[93] Our concern, however, is specifically with those associations which brought together men united by the ways in which they made their living. They might have some of the attributes of fraternities or social clubs, but their essential character was that they were 'crafts' or 'misteries', bodies of men engaged in a specific *ministerium* or *métier*, a trade or calling, for which they had a special skill.

Craft gilds, so defined, appeared early. In London, during the twelfth century, there were gilds of bakers, weavers, pepperers, cloth workers, butchers, goldsmiths and saddlers. A number of them, in the late twelfth century, were described as 'adulterine', i.e. as having no royal or municipal warrant for their existence, but some of them did have such authorization even at that time. They included groups, especially of weavers and fullers, who obtained royal authority for an association to defend their sectional interests. In this sense many of the early craft gilds were spontaneous associations designed to defend the economic interests of their members, their formation perhaps being favoured by the tendency for some occupations to be concentrated in particular locations. They were by no means restricted to textile workers, for York's 'adulterine' gilds in 1180 included associations of glovers, skinners, saddlers and hosiers.[94] Some gilds, on the other hand, look like deliberate creations in order to provide instruments for the seignorial control of particular areas of the urban economy. When Abbot Hugh allowed the bakers of Bury St Edmunds, sometime before 1180, to have a gild (for which he nominated a hereditary alderman), he did so in order that their *ministerium* should be conducted 'to the profit of the church and of all the town of St Edmunds'. After all, Bury's daily bread was not something which could be left to chance.[95]

It was a common characteristic of these early gilds that their members had a monopoly of their craft within a town (or, in the case of some weavers' gilds, within a town and its region), and that they were headed by their own officer – a hereditary alderman in the case of the Bury bakers or a seneschal in the case of the Oxford

---

[93] Reynolds, *Introduction*, pp. 83–4; E. Coornaert, 'Les ghildes médiévales (Vᵉ–XIVᵉ siècles)', *Revue Historique*, CXCIX (1948), pp. 22–55, 208–43.
[94] G. Unwin, *Gilds and Companies of London*, pp. 35–8, 42, 48, 53; *Pipe Roll*, 26 Henry II, pp. 71–2, 153–4.
[95] For these early gilds generally, G. Mickwitz, *Die Kartelfunktionen der Zünfte*, pp. 137–54; for Bury, M.D. Lobel, *The Borough of Bury St Edmunds*, p. 52 and D.C. Douglas, ed., *Feudal Documents from the Abbey of Bury St Edmunds*, p. 149.

cordwainers.[96] Some of them, too, may have exercised a measure of private jurisdiction over their members, as the London weavers and fishmongers claimed to do in 1321, and we also hear about the 'customs of the hallmoot' of the London bakers early in the thirteenth century: indeed, some means of enforcing craft regulations would appear to be indispensable for fulfilling the purposes for which these gilds came into existence.[97] Powers and privileges, on the other hand, did not come gratis for gildsmen. Gilds authorized by royal charter commonly owed an annual payment at the exchequer, and the Winchester fullers in Richard I's reign also had to pay off by instalments a charge for the renewal of their privileges.[98] Jurisdiction over the Bury St Edmunds bakers, too, could be expected to yield profits in the form of penalties imposed on them, which were shared equally between the gild and the abbey's sacrist.

The evidence for continuing craft development in the thirteenth and early fourteenth centuries, almost inevitably, is fullest for London. There, the fishmongers were themselves enforcing their craft regulations in their own hallmoot which they claimed went back to a time beyond memory. In the time of troubles between 1263 and 1272 a whole array of London crafts thrust themselves into view and secured, at least temporarily, authorization of their existence and 'statutes'. The 1271 ordinances of the cordwainers, indeed, showed 'all the leading features of that organization, which a century later had become common to all the handicrafts of London, already fully developed'.[99] The development of the crafts continued under Edward I's stricter controls, and late in his reign we find carpenters holding a 'parliament' at Mile End in 1299 and the cordwainers securing a reissue of their charter in 1301. With Edward's heavy hand removed, London's self-government restored, and England's commercial expansion so notably focused on London, craft formation was more vigorous still in the early fourteenth century. In 1328 twenty-five London misteries were empowered to elect their own officers, and a high proportion of the 51 crafts which, fifty years later, elected the city's common council probably had some form of organization. The crafts, by then, provided a pattern for London life, craft membership was the avenue to

---

[96] H.E. Salter, ed., *Cartulary of Oseney Abbey*, II, p. 10.
[97] Unwin, *Gilds and Companies of London*, pp. 35–7, 44.
[98] *VCH Hants.*, v, pp. 476–7.
[99] Unwin, *Gilds and Companies of London*, pp. 83–4; Williams, *Medieval London*, pp. 167, 172–3, 222–30, 244.

citizenship, and the organized crafts were the substructure of the city's constitution.[100]

By that time, too, there were similar developments elsewhere. By 1349, at York, as well as a weavers' gild there were gilds of butchers and pinners, and probably of drapers and vintners; and in 1307 the city had approved a set of ordinances 'at the asking of the girdlers and riveters and all that belong to that craft'. At Oxford, likewise, as well as the ancient gilds of the weavers and cordwainers, the butchers, tailors, barbers and perhaps the mercers and goldsmiths may have developed some sort of organization; at Leicester after about 1279 the supervision of weaving, fulling and dyeing may have been taken over from the gild merchant by the individual crafts; at Lincoln ordinances were drawn up by the fullers, tailors and tilers between 1297 and 1328; and at Bristol between 1339 and 1347 the fishmongers promulgated ordinances 'provided of their own common assent', the tailors had sufficient organization to present their grievances to the mayor, ordinances of the weavers 'in use of old' were reissued, and new ordinances were made in consultation with the fullers. At about the same time the twelve misteries of Newcastle (cloth merchants, mercers, skinners, tailors, saddlers, corn merchants, bakers, tanners, cordwainers, butchers, smiths and fullers) were listed for the first time; but they failed in their attempt to become a controlling influence in the town when, in 1345, the rights of 'reputable and discreet burgesses' were restored.[101]

Craft gilds inevitably were most in evidence in towns in which economic activities were highly differentiated and the various occupation groups were large enough. In Cambridge, for example, unlike Oxford, they leave no trace, and when in the fourteenth century the skinners founded a gild associated with St Benet's church there is no sign that it regulated their craft or that its membership was restricted to skinners.[102] Nor was the establishment of craft gilds always welcomed by town governments. At Leicester in the 1260s and 1270s the ruling gild merchant tried to prevent the town's weavers from making regulations independently and the fullers from holding

[100] *Ibid.*, p. 265; Veale, 'Craftsmen and the economy of London in the fourteenth century', pp. 125–6, 130; Unwin, *Gilds and Companies of London*, pp. 87–8; *CLB E*, pp. 232–4.

[101] *VCH City of York*, pp. 92, 96; Sellars, ed., *York Memorandum Book*, I, pp. 180–1; *VCH Oxon.*, IV, pp. 312–27; H.E. Salter, *Medieval Oxford*, pp. 62–3; Bateson, ed., *Records of the Borough of Leicester*, I, pp. xxxiv–v; L. Toulmin Smith, ed., *English Gilds*, pp. 179–88; Bickley, *Little Red Book of Bristol*, II, pp. 1–14, 23–4, 26; J. Brand, *History and Antiquities of . . . Newcastle upon Tyne*, II, pp. 157–62.

[102] M. Bateson, ed., *Cambridge Gild Records*, pp. ix, xi–xii, 82–91.

their own assemblies; and at Norwich the city's acceptance of craft gilds was grudging in the extreme. A charter was obtained from Henry III forbidding the establishment of gilds which were detrimental to the city, a ban repeated in 1285; and when gilds were authorized in 1286, they still needed the city's licence, the city appointed the gild officers, and those officers reported to the city authorities. A vigilant eye, moreover, continued to be kept upon the crafts. In 1287–88 and 1291 the alderman of the tanners' gild was accused of usurping powers belonging to the city's bailiffs; in 1292–93 the cobblers, saddlers and fullers were all said to have gilds 'hurtful to the lord king'; and in 1299–1300 the chandlers were alleged to have made a price-fixing agreement among themselves. In Norwich, as in many other places, the gilds were eventually integrated into the city's late medieval constitution, but that process took time.[103]

The history of the Norwich gilds makes it clear that tensions between the crafts and the city authorities might be political as well as economic. The gilds, in effect, were self-regulating immunities, at least for certain purposes, within urban communities; and they naturally sought to extend their powers of self-regulation to the advantage of their members. For this reason there were always potential grounds for conflict between crafts and municipal authorities seeking to impose unitary controls upon urban groups. Such conflicts were particularly likely to arise in the case of those gilds which had external authorization in the form of a royal charter. At Oxford, the city had accused the cordwainers' gild of usurping jurisdiction over its members in 1280, but after the gild had secured a confirmation of its twelfth-century charters in 1319 it was the city authorities that were rebuked for failing to observe their terms. At Winchester, on the other hand, perhaps because the fullers and weavers found difficulty in meeting their financial obligations to the king, the farms which they had owed at the exchequer were transferred to the city in 1205, with an inevitable increase of the city's control over the gilds.[104] The battle between the city of London and the London weavers was much more protracted. In 1201–2 the city offered an annual payment to the king higher than that paid by the gild for its suppression, but the weavers beat off that attack by

---

[103] Bateson, ed., *Records of the Borough of Leicester*, I, pp. 106, 168; E. Lipson, *Economic History of England*, I, pp. 373–4; *BBC 1216–1307*, p. 283; W. Hudson and J.C. Tingey, eds, *Records of Norwich*, I, p. 192; Hudson, ed., *Leet Jurisdiction in Norwich*, pp. lxxxviii–ix, 13, 39, 42–3, 52.

[104] *VCH Oxon.*, IV, pp. 313, 316; Keene, *Survey*, I, p. 296.

accepting an increased farm. Even so, in 1221, they deemed it wise to deposit their charter in the exchequer for safe-keeping. They secured a confirmation of this charter in 1243, but in 1252 they had to seek Henry III's support in the face of molestation by the mayor.[105] The battle had intensified by the end of the century. In 1300 the weavers were arraigned before the mayor because, among other things, they annually chose their own bailiffs to preside over their own court, and they made ordinances on their own authority to the prejudice of the community of London. In the face of these charges the weavers admitted that on some points they had failed to observe rightful usages and customs; and they had to accept a new set of ordinances drawn up by a committee on which the gild's representatives were in a minority, and to agree that offences against these ordinances would be punished by the mayor and aldermen, and that in the future the gild's bailiffs would be sworn before the mayor. The new dispensation was still in operation in 1310.[106]

Not every London weaver, however, accepted the surrender of 1300. As early as 1301 some of them were refusing to obey certain of the new ordinances, and in 1303 the gild got a confirmation of Henry II's charter which was the warrant for its liberties. Those liberties were again called in question when the king's justices visited London in 1321, and the weavers were accused of confederation and conspiracy. A jury empanelled to pronounce upon these charges declared in favour of many of the weavers' customary rights, but also declared that, some thirty years earlier, they had adopted rules which were 'for their own profit and to the common detriment of the people'.[107] Clearly, in all this, while the city authorities were anxious to bring the weavers to heel, more than constitutional issues were involved. The attack on the weavers in 1300 was mounted by 'certain burellers', i.e. members of the mercantile craft which put out work to weavers and fullers. The burellers' complaints were that the weavers' controls over manufacturing standards were both excessive and ineffective; and that they raised manufacturing costs by fixing unduly high charges for their services, reducing the numbers of looms in operation, restricting hours of work, and ordaining a long Christmas holiday lasting until the beginning of February. The

---

[105] Unwin, *Gilds and Companies of London*, pp. 45–6; Mickwitz, *Die Kartelfunktionen der Zünfte*, p. 139; H.T. Riley, ed., *Liber Custumarum*, I, p. 48; *Close R.*, 1251–3, pp. 206–7.
[106] Thomas, ed., *Cal. of Early Mayor's Court Rolls . . . 1298–1307*, pp. 53–5; Riley, ed., *Liber Custumarum*, I, pp. 121–6; *CLB C*, p. 56; *CLB D*, p. 237.
[107] Thomas, ed., *Cal. of Early Mayor's Court Rolls . . . 1298–1307*, pp. 106–7; Riley, ed., *Liber Custumarum*, I, pp. 416–24.

jurors in 1321 agreed that these actions were detrimental to the people. To get their way the weavers could withdraw their labour, a weapon which was effective because their charter gave them a monopoly of their craft in London and Southwark. The ordinances of 1300 tried to ban use of this strike weapon, but the jurors in 1321 supported the weavers' contention that all weavers in London must belong to their gild. By 1336, however, this custom was being ignored and burellers, with their servants and apprentices, were undertaking weaving without being members of the gild. A city ordinance gave its blessing to the situation, declaring it to be lawful for all freemen of the city to weave and sell cloth at their will.[108]

In London and elsewhere, therefore, a mixture of considerations governed the relations between crafts and town governments. In the capital, in the case of the victualling gilds, the independent gild courts of the fishmongers and bakers were no more welcomed than the court of the weavers' gild; and there was a general suspicion that the monopolies claimed by these gilds for their members were likely to result in their customers paying more. It is hardly surprising, therefore, that conflicts between the city and the victualling gilds were a permanent theme in London's history.[109] The city, too, from the time of the earliest gild ordinances showed a concern for the quality of goods which gildsmen produced, responding to the interests both of consumers and of mercantile groups. Thus the London saddlers got the mayor's backing for regulations to prevent defects in the work joiners did for them and from which many great damages 'accrued day by day to the great lords and people of the land'. For like reasons night work was banned in many trades, for as the spurriers said in 1345 'no man can work so neatly by night as by day'; and to preserve the repute of their craft there were occasions when the aid of the city's courts was sought to enforce gild regulations, as when 30 cordwainers were presented in the mayor's court in 1298 for fraudulent work. Regulation of the charges a craftsman might make were likewise designed to benefit customers or commercial entrepreneurs, as when prices were set for the work curriers did for skinners in 1300, or when coopers were denied the right in 1298 arbitrarily to raise the charge they made for fitting hoops to casks. It was also an abuse, and to the detriment of those who employed them, when the carpenters were found to have used intimidation to prevent men accepting lower wages than the craft had fixed; and

[108] *CLB E*, pp. 291–6.
[109] Unwin, *Gilds and Companies of London*, pp. 35–42.

worse still when, in 1299, the 'parliament of carpenters' bound those present by corporal oath not to observe ordinances made by the mayor and aldermen for their craft and their wages. This was rebellion as well as conspiracy.[110]

The problems arising from the development of craft gilds in provincial towns were similar to those which appeared in London. The crafts invaded areas of authority claimed by town governments and diverted revenue from civic chests. These were the charges levelled at the Oxford cordwainers' gild in 1315: the gild's court encroached on the mayor's jurisdiction, it laid down customs for the craft, and it took the fines for infringements of those customs. Gild policies, moreover, might be contrary to the interests of customers, the Oxford cordwainers also being charged by the university with inflating the price of shoes by restricting the numbers entering their craft; specification of what manufacturing craftsmen like the Winchester weavers might be paid for their work may have had the advantage both of consumers and of merchants in view; and the purposes of the detailed regulations for cloth making enacted by the mayor and council of Bristol in 1346 were clearly put. They were 'the preservation of the good fame of the same' and 'the profit which they shall take on the sale of their cloth'. The profit in view was primarily that of Bristol cloth merchants.[111]

By the mid-fourteenth century in the larger towns the crafts were part of the fabric of urban life and had largely been subordinated to the municipal authorities acting as the guardians of the interests of merchants, of consumers and of the community at large. These authorities used the crafts 'as a sort of municipal police ... determining the distribution of labour, the length of the working day, the remuneration of labour, and various matters of production technology'.[112] For the most part, municipalities domesticated the gilds, wherever they existed, just as they had absorbed most of the sokes and other enclaves which had breached the unity of their territories. Gild ordinances needed the sanction of the town authorities, gild officers had to be presented to and sworn before the officers of the municipality, and the penalties gildsmen incurred for breaches

[110] Riley, ed., *Liber Custumarum,* I, pp. 78–81, 94; Thomas, ed., *Cal. of Early Mayor's Court Rolls . . . 1298–1307,* pp. 1–2, 4–5, 25, 52; H.T. Riley, ed., *Memorials of London and London Life,* p. 226; Thomas, *Cal. of Plea and Memoranda Rolls of the City of London, 1323–64,* p. 108.

[111] H.E. Salter, *Medieval Oxford,* pp. 61–2; Furley, ed., *Ancient Usages of the City of Winchester,* pp. 29, 31; Bickley, ed., *Little Red Book of Bristol,* II, pp. 2–3, 40.

[112] Holt and Rosser, eds, *The English Medieval Town,* pp. 9–10; R.H. Hilton, 'Towns in English medieval society' in *ibid.,* p. 25.

of the rules of their craft might find their way in part into municipal coffers. The crafts had become, in other words, 'organs of deputed authority'.[113] The fact that municipalities depended upon the crafts as executive instruments increased their influence, but they were no longer immunities like the gilds which kings had chartered in the twelfth century. They were an integral part of civic constitutions.

(c) Craft gilds and their members

Craft gilds, at the same time, were something more than instruments of the municipalities. They were also spontaneous confederations of master craftsmen engaged in specific branches of trade or manufacture for the defence of their common interests and the rewards their craft brought them. To these ends gildsmen, too, needed to defend the good repute of their craft and its products, so that quality regulations served their interests as well as the interests of merchants and consumers; and they were willing to accept that, for the achievement of a gild's purposes, financial contributions might be necessary. In addition to entry fees these might take the form of recurrent contributions, either for specific purposes or as regular subscriptions. At the end of the thirteenth century, for instance, every London smith paid a farthing a week to the gild, which had a special box in which to keep this revenue safely.[114]

What the gild members got in return were common privileges, usually including a monopoly of a craft or trade for the gildsmen, a 'closed shop'. The lorimers' ordinances as early as 1260 prescribed that no 'stranger' was to engage in that craft in London unless he had paid his dues to the city and the gild and undertaken to observe the gild's ordinances; and the London mercers achieved a similar objective in 1341 when 'foreigns' from Norfolk were forbidden to retail silk kerchiefs, thread, 'Aylshams' and linen stuff in the city. Again, of the earliest ordinances of the London pewterers, approved by the mayor and aldermen in 1348, the first stipulated the alloys and methods of manufacture to be used, and the second decreed that 'no person shall intermeddle with the trade aforesaid if he be not sworn before the good folks of the trade'.[115] These twin rules restricting those allowed to practise the craft and controlling the

---

[113] Unwin, *Gilds and Companies of London*, pp. 52–3.
[114] Thomas, ed., *Cal. of Early Mayor's Court Rolls . . . 1298–1307*, pp. 33–4.
[115] Thomas, ed., *Cal. of Plea and Memoranda Rolls of the City of London, 1323–64*, pp. 134–5; Riley, ed., *Liber Custumarum*, I, pp. 78–9; J. Hatcher and T.C. Barker, *History of British Pewter*, pp. 145–6.

quality of its output were mutually reinforcing. Insistence upon using good materials and upon high manufacturing standards made it easier to identify and seize substandard wares, and insistence that master craftsmen must possess high levels of skills effectively limited the right to operate a workshop.

Craft monopolies, of course, could be used restrictively as well as to defend the gildsmen's legitimate interests, and how gild policies looked could depend upon the perspective from which they were viewed. The London weavers in the early fourteenth century, like the Oxford cordwainers and the Norwich shoemakers, were accused of restricting entry to their crafts, by charging high entrance fees, and thus conspiring to raise the cost of their services by limiting output and competition. The ordinances of the London lorimers in 1260, on the other hand, like those of the York girdlers in 1307, included rules for the admission of suitably qualified 'strangers' into their craft which suggest that this was a normal occurrence; and the growing control of municipal authorities over the crafts probably helped to keep doors open in the interests of consumers and merchants. Again, while London masons and carpenters may well have feared for their living standards when faced by an invasion of 'foreigns' or workmen employed by the king, it did not justify them in the eyes of the city government in threatening to beat up those working for the king for less than the current London rates.[116] Nor should it be assumed that the rights and privileges to which gilds laid claim could always be exercised effectively. Often, as in the case of the London pewterers, the enforcement of gild regulations was at the discretion of the city council; the restrictive policies of the London weavers were ultimately broken by the joint endeavours of the city government and the merchant burellers; and the monopoly which Henry II had granted to the Lincoln weavers' gild had to all intents collapsed by 1348 because the city government stood idly by while citizens hired weavers, who were not members of the gild, to work cloths for sale.[117] Furthermore, crafts which used cheap and easily obtainable raw materials, which needed little capital equipment, and which required relatively low levels of skill, might find it almost impossible, even when they had the backing of municipal authorities, to stamp out illicit competition.

Other groups, in addition to master craftsmen, were encompassed by craft gilds, if only in the role of subordinates. There were, to

---

[116] Thomas, ed., *Cal. of Plea and Memoranda Rolls of the City of London, 1323–64*, p. 108; idem, ed., *Cal. of Early Mayor's Court Rolls . . . 1298–1307*, p. 251.
[117] *Ibid.*, p. 213; Hilton, *Class Conflict and the Crisis of Feudalism*, p. 206.

begin with, servants or journeymen. Some of them served one master only and might live in his house, and were thus 'assimilated to the family'.[118] The number of servants retained by a single master was usually quite small, although London cordwainers in 1271 were each allowed to have eight; but Bristol shoemakers in 1364 were limited to a single 'covenant-hyne'. Such employees may often have been recruited from the ranks of a master's apprentices and may in some cases have been working off obligations incurred during the term of their apprenticeship. The Bristol shoemaker, however, as well as having his 'covenant-hyne', could put out work to independent journeymen without restriction, provided that he did not pay them more than the piece-work rates prescribed by the gild. This latter type of journeymen might be trained men unable to set up on their own account, or 'strangers' allowed to work on making a payment to the gild funds, or members of a subordinate craft (like the York bucklemakers who were 'common servants' to the city's girdlers). In some industrial crafts, indeed, master craftsmen may have given an increasing share of their time to entrepreneurial, managerial and marketing tasks, leaving more of the manual tasks to journeymen.[119]

These tendencies were most evident in London where, by the end of the thirteenth century, there was a class of employees whose condition was sufficiently permanent for them to seek to form organizations of their own. A cooper in 1298, for instance, arraigned a number of others of that trade, who must have been working as employees or piece-workers, for conspiring to raise the charges for making hoops, with the result that the defendants ended in gaol. A few years later a confederation of journeymen cordwainers accused their masters of having lowered their wages; and in 1304 a 'confederacy of journeymen skinners' had a box for storing their common fund.[120] In brief, although rarely as yet, some of the servants of gild masters were 'gelding together' to defend their own interests and standards of living, a first stage in the development of the organized yeomanry which became a feature of the London crafts in late medieval and early modern times.

Master craftsmen were likely to have apprentices as well as servants, although apprenticeship was not of necessity associated with

---

[118] L.F. Salzman, *English Industries in the Middle Ages*, pp. 255–6; Bickley, ed., *Little Red Book of Bristol*, II, pp. 41–4.

[119] Sellars, ed., *York Memorandum Book*, I, p. 181.

[120] Riley, ed., *Liber Custumarum*, I, p. 84; Thomas, ed., *Cal. of Early Mayor's Court Rolls . . . 1298–1307*, pp. 1–2, 16, 148–9, 154.

craft gilds. In the twelfth century, long before the Norwich crafts existed, the future St William of Norwich was apprenticed to a skinner at the age of eight, and notices of the institution became more numerous from the early thirteenth century onwards. By 1307 the ordinances of the York girdlers required masters of the craft to have served an apprenticeship either in that city or elsewhere.[121] The number of apprentices a master might have varied considerably. The York girdlers were allowed only one, and the London skinners and lorimers perhaps kept the number down by prescribing high premiums; but the London weavers allowed apprentices to be taken on 'for such a sum as can be agreed between the master and the apprentice', and many London merchants and craftsmen in the early fourteenth century had more than one apprentice. A Coleman Street chandler of no great wealth had four apprentices registered on the same day in 1310.[122]

Apprenticeship was primarily a course of technical education which enabled a young man to acquire the skills necessary for the practice of a craft and to maintain its good repute – one good reason why apprenticeship was something required and regulated by gilds. There was much variation in the rules governing how long an apprenticeship should last. Four years were prescribed by the York girdlers in 1307, six years by a Norwich spicer in 1291, and ten years by the London lorimers in 1260 and spurriers in 1300. In the capital there was still much diversity in March 1310, when terms were for thirteen years (one instance), twelve years (one instance), ten years (five instances), eight years (eight instances) and seven years (nine instances). It was not until later that a seven-year term became the London standard and spread from London to the rest of England.[123]

One of the earliest surviving apprenticeship indentures is that between a Norwich spicer and a Yarmouth lad in 1291. The spicer undertook to teach the apprentice his craft in buying, selling and so forth, but more than a merely technical education was envisaged. The apprentice was diligently to obey his master, he was in no way to damage his master or cause or incite contention among neighbours

---

[121] Hudson and Tingey, eds, *Records of Norwich*, II, pp. xi–xii; Sellars, ed., *York Memorandum Book*, I, p. 181.
[122] Lipson, *Economic History of England*, I, p. 318; Riley, ed., *Liber Custumarum*, I, p. 125; E. Ekwall, ed., *Two Early London Subsidy Rolls*, pp. 75–7; *CLB D*, p. 119.
[123] Hudson and Tingey, eds, *Records of Norwich*, I, p. 245; Riley, ed., *Liber Custumarum*, I, pp. 78–9; Thomas, ed., *Cal. of Early Mayor's Court Rolls ... 1298–1307*, p. 52; *CLB D*, pp. 109–13; Lipson, *Economic History of England*, I, p. 315.

or merchants to his master's disadvantage. Training, in other words, was designed to produce a good citizen as well as a good craftsman, and a 'malicious'apprentice could be regarded as having broken the compact under which his master had accepted him. The apprentice or his family usually paid a premium, in advance or periodically during his term, for 'teaching and sustenance', and the apprentice was absorbed into his master's family. The Norwich spicer promised to provide for his apprentice's food, drink, clothing, linen and shoes, and during the last four years of his term an appropriate surcoat or tunic. In London the master's obligations were matters of legal requirement, for a father sued a master who had failed to feed, clothe and instruct his son (although it turned out that the youth had been frightened by a beating his master had given him for certain misdemeanours and had run away). A master, in fact, stood to his apprentice *in loco parentis* where justifiable chastisement was concerned, although excessive harshness was not permissible. In that case, the Norwich indenture provided that the apprentice might leave his master and an appropriate portion of his premium would be refunded.[124]

To an increasing extent, therefore, more and more townsfolk, whether as masters or journeymen or apprentices, were absorbed into federations of small groupings, each focused on a master's house or workshop; and their prime association was with the craft group rather than with the larger body of burgesses in general. At the same time, for their members, the crafts were something more than economic groupings and agencies of economic control. The London lorimers in 1260 had an alms box to which entrants into the gild contributed and from which the wardens gave relief to members who fell into poverty; and the farthing a week contributed by London's master smiths provided a fund to keep a taper burning in honour of the Virgin and to relieve members of the gild in need. In like manner, the London carpenters provided sick brothers and sisters of the gild with 2d. a day; the white tawyers paid 1d. a day to old or sick members and to the widows of members as long as they did not remarry; and the London goldsmiths in 1341 founded an almshouse, and the York mercers a generation later a hospital, for the poor, aged and sick of their crafts. These charitable activities of the gilds were closely bound up with their religious affiliations, of which there is much evidence. The London weavers' gild assembled

---

[124] Hudson and Tingey, eds, *Records of Norwich*, I, pp. 245–7; Thomas, ed., *Cal. of Early Mayor's Court Rolls . . . 1298–1307*, pp. 170, 190; *CLB A*, p. 5.

annually on St Edmund's day in the church of St Nicholas Acon; the Lincoln weavers' gild was constituted in the name of the Holy Cross; the central church of the London fishmongers in the 1290s was St Magnus's where one of its fraternities was based; and late in the thirteenth century it was a painters' fraternity, associated with St Giles's, Cripplegate, which procured a grant of craft ordinances for the London painters. Religious fraternities were as essential manifestations of the life of the crafts as were their economic functions, and in many cases preceded their formal organization as misteries.[125]

The craft gilds, therefore, have many aspects: as trade associations, groups organized around a cult, agencies for technical education, and charitable and social clubs. They merge into, and sometimes they emerge from, the many similar types of association found in medieval towns. There were cult gilds which had nothing to do with a particular craft, like the numerous Corpus Christi gilds of the later middle ages; technical education through apprenticeship might exist outside a craft framework, as in twelfth-century Norwich or in Cambridge later; there were gilds representing social groups which were not craft groups, like St Michael's gild at Lincoln with a membership drawn from 'common and middling men'; and there were social and charitable gilds that were not associated with a mistery, like St Katherine's gild at Norwich, founded in 1307 as a burial club, a charitable club and a dining club, and which had its livery of a special hood. Urban life, in fact, was honeycombed by fraternities and similar associations. The distinctive quality of the craft gilds was that they added to the charitable, social and cult objectives of all such associations the particular aim of furthering the interests of their members as participants in a particular branch of trade or manufacture.[126]

The appearance of craft gilds, therefore, depended upon the development on some scale of specific branches of economic activity. It is not surprising that they emerged first in the textile, and to a lesser extent the leather, industries which were already employing large groups of specialist craftsmen in the twelfth century, or that they developed precociously in London, by far England's largest town. The fact, however, that by the fourteenth century the crafts were becoming a normal feature of most towns of any size reflects

[125] Riley, ed., *Liber Custumarum*, I, pp. 78–9, 122; Thomas, ed., *Cal. of Early Mayor's Court Rolls . . . 1298–1307*, pp. 33–4; Lipson, *Economic History of England*, I, pp. 343–4; Unwin, *Gilds and Companies of London*, pp. 93–7.
[126] Toulmin Smith, ed., *English Gilds*, pp. 19–21, 178.

the intensification of urban life, and the division of labour which accompanied it. Organization and association became characteristics of economic life at many levels and for many purposes. As the role of commercial capital expanded in expanding markets and in organizing industrial production to serve them, groups of merchants came together to secure their interests; and manufacturing craftsmen and provision traders formed defensive associations in face of the merchant oligarchs who dominated gilds merchant and town councils, of mercantile groups which controlled the producer's access to markets, and of municipal authorities which gave expression to the consumer's distrust of suppliers of basic necessities like bread and ale and meat. Finally, at least in London, where in some crafts journeymen were developing into something like a permanent class of employees, they too in some cases sought, by association, to defend their living standards.

In these respects many of the forces making for association came from below, from those involved in particular branches of economic activity; but there were also 'forces of formulation' operating from above. Gilds merchant and municipalities might impose a measure of organization upon trades in order to control them. This was especially true of the victualling trades. In London the bakers' and fishmongers' courts were instruments to regulate trades which were regarded as public services, and misteries developed out of the groups of craftsmen subject to these courts; and it was to establish a comparable regulatory authority that the abbot instituted a gild of bakers, under the watchful eye of the sacrist, at Bury St Edmunds. More commonly still, town governments adapted to their own ends gilds which developed spontaneously from ties generated by a common occupation, a common neighbourhood, and common religious observance. By the early fourteenth century even the gilds which had been authorized by royal charter in earlier days, where they survived, had been brought under municipal control. By 1350 in many towns gild membership was the avenue to citizenship, and the emerging common councils of towns in some measure 'represented' the crafts, but the price the latter paid was their subordination to the municipal authorities. The control they exercised over their members became a responsibility for which they were held accountable, their existence required civic licence, their ordinances needed civic endorsement and the civic authorities shared in enforcing them. Within towns the crafts were clearly 'organs of deputed authority', subordinate agencies which were supervised in the control they exercised over their art or mistery.

(d)   Parishes

The gilds or fraternities which attracted the allegiance of many townsfolk were often based in one of the parish churches which, by the thirteenth century, had partitioned town territories between them; and these churches might also, in their own right, command the allegiance of the inhabitants of urban neighbourhoods.[127] Many parish churches, it is true, had originally been private foundations by families or individuals with a stake in the urban community. Some were established by outside landowners with town property, like John the Baptist's church in Oxford sited in the *curia* owned by one of the coheirs of Miles of Gloucester's barony; others by leading townsmen like the Cambridge Blancgernuns, proprietors of All Saints church by the castle until they gave it to Barnwell priory; others by families of hereditary priests, like St Denys's in Walmgate, York, built in the patrimony of one such cleric; and some, perhaps, by groups of pious laymen building churches for their own use and supporting the priests who served them.[128] In the older and larger towns most of these foundations, and the boundaries of the parishes centred on them, were established by around 1200; and by the mid-thirteenth century patronage of a high proportion of urban parish churches had passed to religious establishments. Most of them also had another characteristic, however much it was modified by later population growth and liturgical changes: they were usually very small. The most striking feature of Winchester churches in the thirteenth century was 'their apparent poverty'; and an eighteenth-century description of the church of St Peter-le-Bailey at Oxford perhaps recalls its original character – it was 'a very old little church and odd'. The urban parochial pattern generally was that found in London around 1200: 'groups small and large – but never very large – of neighbours gathered around a small church', which their forbears had built, in which they worshipped, and to which they paid dues.[129]

The smallness of parishes and parish churches, their relative intimacy, were perhaps strengths of parochial communities as neighbourhood associations. The value placed by parishioners upon

---

[127] In what follows we have relied upon material in *VCH City of York*, pp. 365–403; *VCH Cambs.*, III, pp. 123–32; and *VCH Oxon.*, IV, pp. 369–412. The assessment of Cambridge parishes in 1254 is in Clark, ed., *Ecclesie de Bernewelle Liber Memorandorum*, p. 192.

[128] For foundations of churches by 'groups of neighbours', Brooke and Keir, *London 800–1216*, pp. 131–3.

[129] *Ibid.*, p. 134; Keene, *Survey*, I, p. 119; *VCH Oxon.*, IV, p. 403.

the spiritual services provided by churches and their pastors is not something which can be measured and, beyond doubt, at times they resented the contributions the parish church demanded of them. At the same time, the parish church might be a source of mundane support as well as of spiritual sustenance. Pastoral care, in the eyes of Bishop Grosseteste of Lincoln in 1250, included 'the feeding of the hungry, . . . giving drink to the thirsty, . . . clothing the naked, . . . visiting the sick and prisoners'. All these were aspects of a duty of 'hospitality' required of parish priests like other clergy.[130]

While the smallness of parishes, backed by the solidarity conferred by neighbourliness, underpinned their coherence, their smallness also limited their available resources to dispense 'hospitality'. In Cambridge in 1254 the average value of town parishes, as assessed for papal taxation, was about £2 15s., less than the £3 6s. 8d. laid down in 1222 as the income a vicar needed to 'keep hospitality according to the measure of his resources'.[131] In 1291 the value of most York benefices was higher, but by that time the value of money had fallen and only St Mary's Bishophill Junior and St Olave's in Marygate were conspicuously wealthy. In the case of these two churches the reason for their affluence was that they received substantial amounts of tithe revenue from agricultural land outside the city. At Cambridge in 1254 there was a similar contrast between town parishes and country parishes in the neighbouring villages like Fulbourn. The country livings were worth around £20 each, about seven times as much as town benefices. Further, because so many urban churches were appropriated or owed an annual pension to a bishop, chapter, monastery, college or some other ecclesiastical establishment, the resources available to a resident parson from which to dispense 'hospitality' might be a good deal less than the nominal worth of the benefice.

Even if incumbents, therefore, observed synodal statutes to be 'as hospitable to the poor as their resources allow', what they could do depended upon the share of parochial revenue which had not been diverted to other purposes. Within these limitations most of them probably did what they could for the small groups of townsfolk of which they found themselves in charge. It needs to be kept in mind that we are more likely to hear of those who failed in this respect than about the many others who 'carried on according to the traditions which they had inherited and were generally accepted by the

---

[130] B. Tierney, *Medieval Poor Law*, esp. pp. 68, 97–101.
[131] *Ibid.*, p. 93.

people'.[132] Parishes, moreover, provided a framework for directing charitable gifts and bequests from private individuals to those in need; and voluntary associations were commonly based in parish churches, including craft gilds, fraternities and religious gilds which have been described as fulfilling in towns the role of 'corporate families'.[133] In Cambridge there were eight of the latter in 1389, attached to Great St Mary's (3), Holy Trinity (2), St Andrew's, St Benet's and St Botolph's respectively, each with sufficiently formal organization to have written statutes. They were essentially lay organizations (one of them banned priests from serving as gild officers on the ground that clerks ought not to be involved in secular business), although two of them undertook, 'while fortune smiles on us', to support chaplains. Apart from St Katherine's gild in St Benet's church, however, which seems to have had some sort of connection with the town's skinners, their membership was not restricted to a specific craft or even to the parish of the church in which the gild was based. The coherence of these associations derived from an organization in which all were equally participants (the new entrant into the Holy Trinity gild in St Botolph's church kissed all the brethren as a sign of their fraternity); from common religious observances; from the help the gild would offer those who fell into poverty or misfortune; and perhaps not least from the sure knowledge that the gildsman who died would be buried suitably attended, that masses and prayers would be said for his soul, and that he would be commemorated in perpetuity.[134]

The parochial contribution to the cohesion of urban life may also have included the ways in which the church accommodated itself to the social hierarchies of medieval towns. The twelfth-century canons of St Paul's cathedral differed little from, and indeed were often recruited from, well-off city families; a younger son of Hugh Selby, the early thirteenth-century mayor of York, became a canon of York minster; and London's religious houses provided 'vocations for numerous citizens' and its nunneries 'homes for the daughters of well-to-do citizens'.[135] The contribution parish churches made in this respect was doubtless more modest, but it was governed by the absence of any marked segregation of classes in medieval towns.

---

[132] M. Rubin, *Charity and Community in Medieval Cambridge*, pp. 239–40; J.R.H. Moorman, *Church Life in England in the Thirteenth Century*, Cambridge, 1945, pp. 152–3.
[133] By G. le Bras, cited Rubin, *Charity and Community in Medieval Cambridge*, p. 252.
[134] The 1389 ordinances are in Bateson, ed., *Cambridge Gild Records*, pp. 63–128.
[135] Brooke and Keir, *London 800–1216*, pp. 328–9, 341–3, 358–9; J.H. Round, *The Commune of London*, p. 102; J. Raine, ed., *The Register of Walter Gray*, Surtees Soc., LVI (1872), p. 261 note.

Some relatively wealthy families were likely to be found in most parishes, whose standing in parish congregations was likely to be commensurate with their wealth. This was often demonstrated most conspicuously by the ceremonial attending their funerals, by the number of poor who were recipients of their charity on the day they were buried, and from the thirteenth century onwards by chantries in their parish church to celebrate for their souls in the after-life. In York Andrew Bolingbroke and Henry Belton were commemorated in this fashion in All Saints, Pavement, the Langtons in Holy Trinity, King's Court, Robert Meek in St Crux's, Nicholas Seizevaus in St Martin's, Coney Street, Richard Basy in St Mary's Bishophill Senior, Robert Verdenel in St Saviour's, and Nicholas Fleming in St Wilfrid's. At Oxford, too, there was a chantry for William Burcestre in All Saints', for John Dukelinton in St Aldate's and for Robert Worminghall in St Peter's-le-Bailey. The men commemorated in this way had often been citizens of wealth and influence in their time, and the memory of their eminence could be remarkably enduring. At York, almost two centuries after 'old Hugh Selby's' death, his fifteenth-century descendants still nominated the chaplain to serve his chantry in St William's chapel on Ouse bridge.

(e) Aliens and Jews

Parish congregations, crafts and fraternities provided many of the mechanisms enabling the largely mobile and often immigrant populations of medieval English towns to be absorbed into urban communities. Even individual immigrants from overseas were sometimes assimilated remarkably readily, whether they were commercial magnates like London's Cahorsin alderman, William Servat, or the cloth workers from the Low Countries or the metal workers from Germany who settled in York and elsewhere. The result might be that some townsmen, for a time, were of uncertain standing. Cristin le Alebrewere may have been a case in point: he was certified by the mayor of King's Lynn to be a burgess of that town, but a London inquest declared him to be a burgess of Ypres.[136] Perhaps he was in the process of migrating, and he may well have settled into King's Lynn with no great difficulty. Most aliens coming to England, however, did so with the intention of trading and not of migrating, but trading might involve residence for shorter or longer periods in English towns the inhabitants of which were accustomed to regard

---

[136] *CLB D*, p. 249.

trade within their town, or trade between that town and its hinterland, to be the preserve of its burgesses. Alien residents, therefore,
might find their freedom of action strictly limited. In London the
traditional rules were that they should be lodged with citizens who
would supervise what they did, that they should not have houses or
associations of their own, and that their stay should be limited to 40
days. The fact was, however, that in Edward I's time Italians,
Provençals, Cahorsins and Gascons did possess their own houses in
London, the Germans did have the Steelyard as their London headquarters and bases in King's Lynn and elsewhere, Italian companies
and the German Hanse gave their members increasingly effective
instruments for the protection of their interests, and at
Southampton in order to keep up property values no attempt was
made to prevent merchant strangers from renting their own houses.
Even so lessees of houses in Southampton were not allowed to use
them for trading in goods belonging to others; and the limits applying to alien residents in London perhaps persuaded the Hansards to
claim in 1342 that, in view of the payment they made annually to the
city and their responsibility for the repair of Bishopsgate, they
should be treated not as strangers but as denizens.[137]

To ask that much was to seek the impossible, but in London and a
number of port towns especially a resident alien presence continued
to be a feature of urban life despite the fact that by the fourteenth
century the part played by foreign merchants in England's internal
trade was significantly reduced. That this was so owed something to
the fact that foreign traders, and those from southern Europe in
particular, advanced loans and could be accused by the defenders of
local monopolies of being usurers. As early as 1235 Matthew Paris
called the Cahorsins a 'horrible nuisance' because they cloaked
usury under a show of trade; in 1244 the only Christian usurers in
London were said to be Italian merchants; and in 1251 the
Cahorsins, who were building themselves 'palaces' in London, were
described as heretics and traitors because they practised usury while
professing to be Christians.[138] Alien merchants, and the Italians in
particular, found a counterpoise to attacks of this sort in royal support in return for the advances they were compelled or persuaded to
make to the royal exchequer. That support went so far, especially

---

[137] M. Weinbaum, *London unter Eduard I und II*, pp. 55–6, 160; Studer, ed., *Oak Book of
Southampton*, I, p. 50; Thomas, ed., *Cal. of Plea and Memoranda Rolls of the City of London,
1323–64*, pp. 151–2.
[138] Chew and Weinbaum, eds, *The London Eyre of 1244*, pl. 327; H.R. Luard, ed.,
Matthew Paris, Chronica Majora, III, pp. 328–32; V, pp 245–6.

under Edward I, as registering the debts due to them from private borrowers on the chancery rolls and affording assistance to them in recovering what they were owed. Until the time, in fact, when Edward III's exploitation of his Italian bankers ruined them, alien merchants continued to be an important source of private as well as public credit; and, because interest rates were high, that fact helped to generate anti-foreign sentiments which could be enlisted in the defence of local commercial interests. That it might also introduce an element of unease into the relations between resident aliens and native townsmen was likely enough.

The same was true of the relations of townsfolk with one other group established in many English towns during the two centuries after the Norman Conquest – the Jews. Because usury was 'forbidden by the canon law, yet indispensable for the exigencies of everyday life', the Jews as non-Christians were even less inhibited than their Christian neighbours in satisfying demands for credit.[139] At the same time ecclesiastical prohibitions of usury restricted the availability of credit and raised the cost of borrowing, especially since the capital resources at the disposal of Jews were almost certainly quite inadequate to meet potential demand. Furthermore, the heavy financial demands made by the king upon the Jews were a constant drain on those resources which helped to maintain their interest rates at an artificially high level. Their unpopularity arose, therefore, not only from the fact that they loaned money at interest, or even that the narrow range of economic activities in which they were allowed to engage forced them into an excessive concentration upon money-lending, but also that the rates of interest they needed to charge meant that borrowers from Jews included a disproportionate number who were desperate or extravagant, and many who, to get a loan, had to pledge their inheritances. The resentments of debtors, of course, was given an edge, and could seek an excuse, in the distinctiveness of the customs, language and religion of the Jews, and might even find a veneer of respectability in the anti-semitic legislation and propaganda of the western church.

Until Edward I's reign, however, there was a Jewish element, and often an element of considerable importance, in the life of many English towns. That this was so was a direct consequence of the Norman Conquest, for English Jewry originated as an offshoot of the Rouen community and remained closely associated with it until the

---

[139] C. Roth, *History of the Jews in England*, p. 105. What follows depends heavily upon this work and upon H.G. Richardson, *English Jewry under the Angevin Kings*.

381

loss of Normandy early in the thirteenth century. Some incomers, of course, came from elsewhere – from other parts of France, the Rhineland, Spain and Italy, even perhaps from Russia; but essentially English Jewry was part of the Anglo-Norman society fashioned by the Conqueror and his successors. Jews were established initially under royal protection in London's Old Jewry and only began to settle outside the capital in Stephen's reign, when they are to be found in Norwich, Oxford, Cambridge and Winchester. Under Henry II there were little communities as far west as Gloucester and Exeter, as far north as Lincoln and York, and even in smaller places like Thetford and Bungay. The number of them probably reached a maximum in the later decades of the twelfth century, when their further dispersal was checked by the anti-Jewish pogroms of 1190 and the intensified financial exploitation initiated by Richard I and John. In the early years of Henry III the principal Jewish settlements were in London, Bristol, Cambridge, Canterbury, Colchester, Exeter, Gloucester, Hereford, Lincoln, Northampton, Norwich, Nottingham, Oxford, Stamford, Winchester, Worcester and York; but the King's Lynn community was exterminated by the pogrom of 1190 and in 1234 Newcastle was empowered permanently to exclude Jews from the town. The total number of communities in the thirteenth century can seldom have exceeded twenty. They were to be found in most of England's principal towns, but the numbers of their inhabitants were relatively small. On the eve of the expulsion of the Jews from England in 1290 an estimate that they numbered 2,500–3,000 seems if anything to be on the high side; and, if they may have been somewhat more numerous earlier, even the London community probably never exceeded a few hundreds and most others a hundred or so.[140]

While the Jews were minority groups in English towns, they were distinguished more sharply from their neighbours than other urban incomers. Each urban community, by royal privilege, had a measure of autonomy. Many matters, like those relating to matrimony or the rights of widows, they could settle themselves according to Talmudic law; Jewish custom regulated many issues relating to property, and even in the king's courts criminal cases involving Jews might be determined by purely Jewish juries; and each community had its own officers (bailiffs, treasurers, ritual butchers and masters of the Jewish law). Whereas this was a degree of distinctiveness not all that much greater than Hanseatic residents in English towns enjoyed, and while

[140] Keene, *Survey*, I, pp. 385–6; Richardson, *English Jewry under the Angevin Kings*, pp. 8–19, p. 216 and note; Roth, *History of the Jews in England*, p. 82; J. Brand, *History and Antiquities of . . . Newcastle upon Tyne*, II, p. 140.

it was doubtless resented by town governments like any other immunity, it was more important still that Jewish communities were also distinctive religious groups, each focused on a synagogue or synagogues which were communal meeting places as well as places of worship. It was this religious separatism which made the Jews targets of ecclesiastical hostility, and the ecclesiastical establishment was peculiarly equipped to make them victims of a propaganda which was notably effective.

In many respects, on the other hand, the differences between Jews and their urban neighbours should not be exaggerated. Some Jews, too, were small-scale traders, vintners, fishmongers, cheesemongers and cloth pedlars; Jewish pawnbrokers sometimes refurbished unredeemed jewellry, plate or clothing for sale; and there were Jewish goldsmiths and physicians. Even the great Jewish financiers, like Aaron of Lincoln in the twelfth century, might be drawn into commerce when their advances were secured on growing crops. When he died the debts owed to him included wheat and cartloads of hay; and a similarly outstanding figure in Henry III's time, Aaron of York, seems to have gone further and to have been on occasion an importer of wine.[141] At the same time, the conventional picture of Jews in medieval England principally as moneylenders is by no means without foundation. As they themselves pointed out to Edward I, when he allowed that they might engage in trade or handicrafts, they could not travel as safely as Christians could or expect to get paid if they allowed their customers credit.[142] The increasingly hostile environment in which Jews found themselves by the thirteenth century, combined with their own socio-religious separatism, made it hard for Jews and Christians to do business on equal terms and compelled medieval Jewry to concentrate on the business of moneylending.

Their engagement in that business was at many levels. Much lending was on a small scale, like the loan to a Babraham peasant who had to sell a couple of acres of his land to repay it, or similar advances to craftsmen, small traders and Oxford undergraduates. The debtors of Aaron of Lincoln, when he died in 1191, were altogether more diverse. They included parish priests and canons of Lincoln, fellow Jews from York and Stamford and Lincoln, prominent burgesses from York and Lincoln, substantial country gentlemen, and

---

[141] *Pipe Roll,* 3 Richard I, pp. 17–24; Richardson, *English Jewry under the Angevin Kings,* pp. 68, 248; Roth, *History of the Jews in England,* p. 114 and note.
[142] G.O. Sayles, ed., *Select Cases in the Court of King's Bench under Edward I,* III, Selden Soc., LVIII (1939), pp. xxxii, civ.

men and women of rank – among them the earl of Chester, Adam de Brus, the count of Brittany and his wife, the archbishop of Canterbury, and the king of Scots (who owed him £2,776).[143] In the next century Aaron of York had a similar variety of debtors, among them John Balliol's scholars at Oxford, Saffron Walden abbey, knights serving Henry III in Gascony in the 1240s, and some landowners of substance. Even great landowning monasteries might have recourse to Jewish loans. In the thirteenth century Fountains abbey was heavily indebted to a York Jew and, late in the twelfth century, the abbot of St Albans 'owed much to Christians, but more still to Jews'.[144]

Jewish moneylending, therefore, was something likely to touch members of every class, so that it is important to establish what the consequences of borrowing might be. First, it involved the payment of interest at rates varying according to the creditworthiness of the borrower, but very commonly 1d. or 2d. per £ per week (or $21^2/_3$ or $43^1/_3$ per cent per annum), with the higher of these rates becoming something of a norm. The debtor who failed to repay a loan quickly, therefore, found his indebtedness increasing very rapidly. Secondly, while many debts were doubtless secured on chattels, many others, whether they were owed by a Babraham peasant or by a landowner of substance, were either secured on land or could only be repaid by the alienation of land. Borrowing, therefore, could lead to shifts in the ownership of property although, because Jews seldom took actual possession of land, between Christians rather than between Christian and Jew. William Fossard's debts to Aaron of Lincoln, for example, totalled some £1,200 secured on his lands in East Yorkshire; but Meaux abbey stepped in to buy up these debts at a discount and to settle them William conveyed to the monks the manor of Wharram Percy.[145] There was some justification, therefore, for the view expressed in1258 that the Jews were partners of the barons and monasteries in the latter getting their hands on the property of lesser landowners.

This, of course, was not quite the whole truth. Monasteries and barons, too, borrowed from Jews, and those who benefited from the market in encumbered estates included wealthy Londoners, royal

---

[143] St John's Coll., Cambridge, Muniments, Drawer XXV/11; *Pipe Roll*, 3 Richard I, pp. 17–24; Hill, *Medieval Lincoln*, pp. 218–20.

[144] *CPR*, 1247–58, pp. 41, 59, 343; 1266–72, p. 446; *Close R.*, 1234–37, p. 299; 1242–47, pp. 15, 17, 30, 396; H. Jenkinson, ed., *Cal. Plea Rolls of the Exchequer of the Jews*, III, Jewish Historical Soc. of England, 1929, pp. 18–20, 99, 198; H.T. Riley, ed., *Gesta Abbatum Monasterii S. Albani*, I, pp. 183, 193–4.

[145] Richardson, *English Jewry under the Angevin Kings*, pp. 70, 83–9; J.C. Holt, ed., *The Northerners*, Oxford, 1992, pp. 166–7.

officials like Adam de Stratton or Walter de Merton (and so ultimately Merton College, Oxford), and 'new men' of the local
ministerial class like the Braybrookes in Northamptonshire whose
acquisitions were largely at the expense of indebted baronial families
like the Leydets and the Foliots.[146] Men of every sort, however, borrowed and very often from Jews; and borrowing could lead to losses
of land from which they lived and which determined their status.
This sharpened for many resentment directed against Jews, the
depth of which sometimes emerges even in formal documents. A
charter of Henry II's tells how Roger de Wancy pledged his manor of
Stanstead (Herts.) to a London Jew, and by the time his son Michael
succeeded his father interest charges had doubled the amount that
was owed. Michael, therefore, implored the king, for the love of
God, to pay the debt for him, promising in return to give half
Stanstead to whatever religious house the king might nominate. The
king did pay the debt and Michael did relinquish half of Stanstead
'lest I should lose the whole of the said manor on account of the usuries which grow day by day'. The ultimate beneficiary was the abbey
of Waltham Holy Cross and the change of ownership is indicated by
the fact that the portion of Stanstead Michael de Wancy alienated
became Stanstead Abbots; but what is perhaps most significant is the
bitterness implicit in these documents.[147]

The situation which generated this bitterness was, in no small
degree, of governmental contrivance. The Jews were sometimes
described as 'serfs of the king's chamber', and the so-called 'laws of
Edward the Confessor' claimed in the twelfth century that they and
all their chattels belonged to the king.[148] From Richard I's and
John's times at the latest this royal lordship over the Jews was turned
into remorseless exploitation. The assets, at least of wealthy Jews,
often passed to the crown when they died; and their heirs in the thirteenth century had to pay a relief which might be as high as 5,000 or
even 10,000 marks at a time when the relief paid by an earl's heir was
£100. The Jews, too, like serfs, were subject to arbitrary taxes; and in
this respect the tallage levied by John in 1210, and the barbarous
methods of collecting it, was a turning point in the plundering of
the Jews even though the amount the king hoped to raise by it was

---

[146] P. Elman, 'Economic causes of the expulsion of the Jews in 1290', *EcHR*, VII
(1937), pp. 149–50; C. Roth, 'Oxford starrs', *Oxoniensia*, XXII (1957), pp. 63–7;
Richardson, *English Jewry under the Angevin Kings*, pp. 100–2, 270–80.
[147] BL Harleian Ms. 391, ff. 40, 77, 85; Ransford, ed., *Early Charters of the Augustinian
Canons of Waltham Abbey*, nos. 354–6.

unduly optimistic.[149] The average contribution of Jewish tallages to the exchequer, however, was about £2,000 a year in the period 1221–31 and nearly £5,000 a year in 1233–57; and under Edward I, despite the erosion of Jewish resources, the figure still averaged £1,600 a year down to the expulsion. By contrast, in years of unprecedented fiscal pressure between 1290 and 1307, parliamentary taxation of the whole of English secular society yielded on average only £20,000 a year.

The effects of this policy of expoitation were predictable enough. On the one hand Jewish moneylenders were driven to keep interest rates as high as they were able to, further angering those who had to pay them; and on the other the Jewish communities were progressively impoverished, making them a less profitable asset to the king, who for this reason had a declining interest in resisting demands for anti-Jewish measures. The freedom of the Jews to ask for security for loans in the form of land was progressively curtailed; and the Statute of Jewry in 1275 forbade them to lend at interest at all. Compensatory permission for them to engage in trade and crafts, lease land for tillage, and freely traffic in 'lawful goods and merchandises' meant little, for by this time it was simply impossible for Jews to trade on equal terms with Christians. Most were reduced to clandestine usury, a punishable offence, or to clipping the currency which was likely to lead to the scaffold. Meantime, the Statute of Jewry added an annual poll tax to their burdens: the statute, indeed, merely completed their impoverishment.[150]

This was the background of Edward I's decision in 1290 to order that 'these enemies of the cross of Christ and blasphemers of the Christian faith', who impoverished Catholic folk by their usuries and compelled many of them thereby to sell their lands and possessions, should for ever depart.[151] The king's motives were undoubtedly mixed. That he was responding to anti-semitic pressure, especially from the magnates, seems clear. Such pressure, on the other hand, was nothing new, but there were perhaps a number of reasons for his capitulating to it on this occasion. As one chronicler points out, a precedent he may have had in mind was his expulsion of the Jews from his Gascon domains and his seizure of their goods in 1289. Apart from that, his advisers were doubtless aware of the

---

[149] Richardson, *English Jewry under the Angevin Kings*, p. 166; and for what follows, Roth, *History of the Jews in England*, p. 273 and Elman, 'Economic causes of the expulsion of the Jews in 1290', pp. 153–4.

[150] Roth, *History of the Jews in England*, p. 66; *CCR*, 1272–9, p. 577.

[151] H.R. Luard, ed., *Annales Monastici*, IV, pp. 326–7.

impoverishment of the Jews in England and the fact that they were making a decreasing contribution to the crown's increasing demands for revenue. Edward I's debts in 1290, moreover, were enormous, far beyond anything he could have raised from English Jewry; but capitulation to the anti-semitic demands of the English landed classes won for him assent to the most productive lay subsidy of his reign. Chroniclers are clear that it was conceded to him by the 'people' in thanksgiving for the expulsion of the Jews.[152]

It has been necessary to deal at some length with the situation of the Jews in the twelfth and thirteenth centuries, for clearly their situation was a unique one. Even so, in considering them among the groups inhabiting English towns, there are reasons for not exaggerating excessively the divide separating Jew and Christian. In early days a Jewish scholar could engage the abbot of Westminster in amicable debate on matters of religion in an atmosphere reminiscent of Toledo rather than London, and there were other contacts which clearly were not unfriendly. In Henry II's time the Cornhill family in London were involved in financial deals with Aaron of Lincoln aimed at developing property near the modern Mansion House, and Jews and Christians met socially as well as to do business. We hear of them drinking together, of 'a certain Jew ... journeying towards Shrewsbury with the archdeacon of that place', of a Hereford Jew in 1286 inviting his Christian friends to his daughter's wedding (although the bishop of Hereford was scandalized), and of Jews and Christians being jointly indicted for hunting a deer through the streets of Colchester. The possibilities of co-existence clearly were present, and at Winchester the Jews seem to have especially good relations with some of the leading citizens as they found common interests in the wool trade, where Jewish contacts and financial services could prove useful.[153]

The character of Jewish urban settlements perhaps tells a similar story. It was common for them to be concentrated in a given street or streets: at Oxford there was a Jewish quarter on both sides of St Aldate's Street; at Cambridge the modern All Saints Passage was Jews' Street in 1219, although there were also Jews and a synagogue in the Guildhall area; and at Norwich most Jewish families lived

[152] H. Rothwell, ed., *Chronicle of Walter of Guisborough*, pp. 226–7; H. Maxwell, trans., *Chronicle of Lanercost, 1272–1346*, Glasgow, 1913, pp. 58–9; H.R. Luard, ed., *Flores Historiarum*, III, pp. 70–1, 84; H.T. Riley, ed., *Willelmi Rishanger Chronica et Annales*, Rolls Ser., 1865, p. 118.

[153] J. Armitage Robinson, *Gilbert Crispin, Abbot of Westminster*, Cambridge, 1911, pp. 60–7; Richardson, *English Jewry under the Angevin Kings*, pp. 47–8; Roth, *History of the Jews in England*, pp. 119–20, 279; Keene, *Survey*, I, p. 386.

within a radius of 100 yards of the synagogue near the Haymarket. This sort of concentration, however, is not found everywhere: at York, for instance, Jews seem to have been widely dispersed through the city; and even where there was concentration it did not amount to something akin to the ghettoes which developed in some modern European towns. In Cambridge and Norwich, for instance, while there were Jewish quarters, Jews and Christians lived there side by side, properties passed back and forward between them, and some Jews lived elsewhere, including some of the wealthiest Jewish families of Norwich. At Cambridge, too, in 1277 Joce son of Samuel was permitted to live in what was then the suburban village of Chesterton, 'so that he might have access to Cambridge to ply his merchandise there and to repair the houses he has in the town'. If members of the Jewish communities in English towns tended to live close to each other, it was not so much that they were compelled to do so, but rather (like the Germans and other alien groups in thirteenth-century London) 'for safety, for religious observance, and for social and intellectual companionship'. The tendency for Jews to live apart was doubtless strengthened by their religious distinctiveness; but their segregation was never so extreme as to cut them off from possibilities of social intercourse with their Christian neighbours.[154]

One reason why those possibilities were ultimately unrealized was a growing anti-semitism in both rural society and urban communities of which the first general manifestation was the pogroms which in 1190 spread from London to most of the other eastern towns in which Jews were settled. The ringleaders in these attacks, as is clear at York and Lincoln, were drawn both from the ranks of the citizens and of country landowners (some of them crusaders); and that to massacre the Jews was part of an effort to write off debts was evident at York, where the pogrom culminated in a bonfire of the records of loans made by Jews.[155] Such attacks, which became more frequent from that time forward, were also encouraged by the increasingly organized anti-Jewish teaching of the western church. It was in England that the death of a skinner's apprentice at Norwich in 1144 gave rise to the first accusation of a ritual murder by Jews in medieval Europe. The supposed victim was buried in Norwich cathedral and venerated as a saint, the prototype of a number of other alleged child martyrs in other towns. In the thirteenth century, especially, the church did much both to stimulate and to justify anti-semitism,

---

[154] *VCH Oxon.*, IV, p. 37; *VCH City of York*, p. 48; *VCH Cambs.*, III, p. 95; D.V. Lipman, *Jews of Medieval Norwich*, pp. 16, 136–7, 141; Keene, *Survey*, I, p. 385.
[155] *VCH City of York*, p. 47.

beginning with Archbishop Stephen Langton's determination to give effect to the legislation directed against the Jews by the Lateran Council of 1215.

Given these circumstances the situation of Jews in English urban communities became increasingly difficult. Even in Winchester, where relations between Jews and leading townsfolk had been reasonably good, there was a groundswell of antagonism among the lesser citizens which was sometimes manifested in attacks on Jews.[156] In this atmosphere it was also easier to secure the enactment of a whole range of discriminatory anti-Jewish measures. England was the first western country to make Jews wear a special badge, partly for the reason that otherwise they might not be recognized as such and Christians might unwittingly be seduced by them. Jews were also banned from employing Christian servants, obliged to pay tithes to the priest of the parish in which they lived, and forbidden to deposit goods for safety in Christian churches. Had the church got its way, Christians who sold foodstuffs to the Jews would even have been liable to excommunication. The church's teaching, in brief, fostered a pervasive anti-Jewish sentiment, and gave an ideological edge to the resentments of debtors and a specious justification to government policies which were discriminatory at best and often barbarous. All this made the day-to-day living of Jews in communion with their Christian neighbours increasingly difficult and, in the end, gave to their final expulsion in 1290, which robbed English society of any further Jewish contribution until the seventeenth century, the appearance of a Christian act for which Edward I won praise from his contemporaries.

3.   THE QUALITY OF URBAN LIFE

As Frederic William Maitland said long ago, in the England of the twelfth and thirteenth centuries there were 'some mighty forces making . . . for communalism of a certain sort'; for men were 'drilled and regimented into communities' to serve the ends of government, with the consequence that 'communities were far more often the bearers of duties than of rights'. Yet, of these communities, boroughs, and in some degree many other towns which did not achieve the full range of borough franchises, differed from the rest in

---

[156] Cf. Keene, *Survey*, I, p. 387.

'attaining the degree and kind of organization which we call corporate'. At the same time, the texture of the urban community was 'unusually heterogeneous', and continued to be so even though the heterogeneity of urban societies altered with the passage of time and accommodated to an unusual extent voluntary associations like gilds and fraternities.[157] The community aspects of urban life endowed towns with a measure of solidarity which was compatible with levels of participation which varied considerably between individuals and groups. But the complex texture of urban communities also gave rise to tensions as well as solidarity – between a town's ruling group and the body of its inhabitants, between mercantile entrepreneurs and craftsmen, between masters on the one hand and servants, journeymen and apprentices on the other, between those with a stake in the town and those who were 'outsiders' or who were at least marginal to its society (the poor, aliens, the Jews). This form of heterogeneity contributed to the high levels of violence evident in medieval towns. Some of it, as at Winchester, was 'associated with drinking, gambling and prostitution', but much of it took place 'within the unstable population of strangers in the city, and between strangers of all types and the more well-established inhabitants'.[158]

Many other things influenced the quality of medieval urban life as well as the rootlessness of many of those who drifted into towns in a period of rural over-population. Many townsfolk lived and died in absolute or relative poverty, death-rates were high, and the low levels of life expectancy were only slightly modified by the blood-letting and other medical services available from barber-surgeons. It is true that expectations of life may have been somewhat better between the eleventh and early fourteenth centuries than they were to be after 1348, when endemic plague was added to the causes of mortality; but even in these earlier times immigrants seem to have been necessary to maintain, let alone to enlarge, urban populations.[159] Again, people seem to have lived in conditions which were almost impossibly congested – as in London's Fishingwharf Lane, leading down to the Thames, which was too narrow for carts to turn in it and which in any case was too crowded with stalls; and both domestic and working accommodation was minimal. A few rich men might enjoy spacious living; but even where open spaces were by no means lacking or burgages were of relatively generous dimensions, the housing space of most individuals was often cramped. Houses, too, were apt

[157] F. Pollock and F.W. Maitland, *History of English Law*, I, pp. 635, 637–9, 688.
[158] Keene, *Survey*, I, p. 395.
[159] *Ibid.*, pp. 400–1.

to be huddled together, something which often made for strained relations between neighbours. We have seen how dense occupation was in streets like Winchester's High Street, but even in a place as small as Alnwick, where burgage plots extended back from the streets to a depth of up to 580 feet or more, the houses, probably mostly 'small single-storey thatched buildings', occupied only 18–20 feet of this depth and had frontages of 14–32 feet. Proximity, almost inevitably, bred quarrels. It is therefore not surprising to find a widow in the London parish of St Botolph's, Billingsgate, complaining that a neighbour had piled up firewood so high against her window that she was deprived of a view, light and fresh air; and a Friday Street parson alleging that water from a potter's house next door flooded his churchyard and that the potter's tenants threw filth and refuse from the windows of the house on to land consecrated to God.[160]

Maintaining even the most elementary sanitary standards was a still more intractable problem. In Southampton in *c.* 1300 it proved necessary to ordain that no butcher or cook was to throw into the street any matter whereby the town became more dirty, filthy or corrupt; London tawyers were forbidden in 1311 to flay dead horses in the city or its suburb; and in medieval Winchester there is archaeological confirmation of the impression conveyed by the records that there were heaps of refuse in every street and numerous dung-hills, especially near markets, inns and places where people congregated. Pollution of water-supplies was a special problem, since they depended heavily upon open water-courses which were also used for washing and scouring clothes (including babies' napkins), for depositing woad-waste by dyers or entrails and blood by butchers, and for soaking sheepskins or hides in the course of tanning. No less eternal were the problems posed by the waste products of human beings: by privies which discharged into water-courses, or those built so close to a neighbour's property that it was invaded by sewage, or plumbed into some convenient gutter which eventually became blocked and neighbours were greatly inconvenienced by the stench therefrom. It is perhaps hardly surprising that such sanitary matters were among the commonest nuisance provoking complaint in medieval London.[161]

---

[160] M.R.G. Conzen, *Alnwick, Northumberland*, pp. 52–4; H.M. Chew and W. Kellaway, eds, *The London Assize of Nuisance*, nos. 81, 312, 396.

[161] *Ibid.*, nos. 2, 165, 200, 214; Studer, ed., *The Oak Book of Southampton*, I, p. 52; *CLB D*, p. 258; Keene, *Survey*, I, pp. 53, 64.

There is not, however, a single verdict to be passed upon the quality of medieval English urban life. There are moments when we are reminded of conditions in some of the third-world towns of our own day: apart from a good deal of casual violence and from the fires which were inescapable when wood and thatch were principal building materials, there was also 'filth running in open ditches in the streets, fly-blown meat and stinking fish, contaminated and adulterated ale, polluted well-water, unspeakable privies'.[162] Such things in some measure affected townsfolk of every class and contributed to the high levels of urban mortality; but the poor, and there were many of them, had their own special disabilities. As Langland put it, in urging mayors and other officers of town, 'be sure that you punish all fraudulent tradesmen, the brewers, the bakers, the butchers and the cooks. . . . For these are the men who do most harm to the poor, poisoning them with adulterated food at extortionate prices. They grow rich . . . by robbing the bellies of the poor'.[163] Some contemporary observers, however, were rather less critical. Thomas Becket's clerk, perhaps remembering the London he had known around the middle of the twelfth century, did so with affection. He recalled the healthiness of the city's air, its 126 parish churches in addition to the 13 larger conventual churches, a River Thames which was full of fish, the polished manners of the citizens, the horse market at Smithfield, and the port to which merchants from every nation under heaven brought their cargoes. Even London's cooks got a favourable mention, for they were capable of supplying dishes of the highest quality, of relieving the hunger of the many travellers coming to or leaving the city, and of providing a take-away service for citizens upon whom visitors descended unexpectedly. And his final memory was of London's sports, 'for it is not fitting that a city should be merely useful and serious-minded, unless it also be pleasant and cheerful'.[164]

---

[162] Holt and Rosser, eds, *The English Medieval Town*, p. 15.
[163] William Langland, *Piers the Ploughman*, trans. J.F. Goodridge, Harmondsworth, 1966, p. 47.
[164] *EHD*, II, pp. 956–62; and see D. Knowles's comment, *Thomas Becket*, 1970, pp. 5–6.

CHAPTER SEVEN
England under the Three Edwards, 1272–1348

1. THE ECONOMIC AND SOCIAL BACKGROUND, 1086–1300

Towards the close of the fourteenth century, looking eastwards one May morning from the Malvern hills, Langland's dreamer saw a 'fair field full of folk, ... all manner of men, the mean and the rich, working and wandering, as the world asketh'.[1] Had he been viewing this scene at the beginning rather than the end of the century, before the mortality occasioned by plagues from the mid-century onwards, the field would have been fuller still. Any attempt to put a figure on England's population at any time during the middle ages, of course, entails the risk 'of errors on a truly heroic scale'. Estimates for the years around 1300 have ranged from as low as 3.7 millions to as high as 7 millions or above. Perhaps the most judicious statements of current thinking would suggest a total of 6 millions or rather more.[2]

If England did support a population of around 6 millions in *c.* 1300, that figure prompts two immediate comments. First, it is very substantially higher than any assigned to the population of Domesday England. The suggestion that it totalled 1.5 millions or even less in 1086 is probably to put it too low, for the incompleteness of Domesday as a record of people has become increasingly evident; but that it was fewer than 3 millions, and possibly no more than

---

[1] W.W. Skeat, ed., *William Langland, The Vision of William concerning Piers the Plowman*, p. 1.
[2] M. Postan, 'Medieval society in its prime: England', in *CEcH*, I, pp. 561–2; H.E. Hallam, in *AHEW*, II, p. 536; R.M. Smith, 'Demographic developments in rural England, 1300–48', in B.M.S. Campbell, ed., *Before the Black Death*, pp. 48–9.

somewhat over 2 millions, are perhaps figures which carry as much conviction as the evidence allows.[3] Such computations suggest, in turn, a rate of population increase between 1086 and *c.* 1300 that approached threefold, which is in no way incompatible with a great deal of indirect evidence, and especially the expansion of rural settlements, the growth of old towns and the foundations of new ones, and indications of a shrinkage over the long term of the amount of land per head available to English villagers. Secondly, if England did indeed support 6 millions or more inhabitants in 1300, this was perhaps more than it would have again for the next 450 years.[4] Economic expansion on many fronts must have been needed to sustain as many people as there were in Edward I's England, and if that expansion had begun long before the Normans came it was continued through the Norman and Angevin centuries.[5]

(a) People and resources

The growth of population was both a condition and a cause of economic expansion, for more people represented more potential producers and, at the same time, more consumers with needs to be satisfied. In the countryside, consequently, settlements multiplied and also became larger, until in the Lincolnshire fenland townships like Moulton and Whaplode were assessed for taxes at much the same level as the borough of Stamford. Wherever possible arable acreages were increased, but so was the extent of land which could be used more appropriately for other purposes. Drainage works and sea-defences enabled fens and salt-marshes to be reclaimed; and in the uplands, where even sheltered valleys gave only modest arable returns, there was grazing at least in the summer months for growing numbers of sheep and cattle. Both multiplied in Devon and Cornwall during the twelfth and thirteenth centuries despite the fact that the wool of these counties was too coarse to attract foreign buyers; in the North large numbers of sheep grazed the Pennine moors

---

[3] H.C. Darby, *Domesday England*, pp. 88–91; S. Harvey, 'Domesday England', in *AHEW*, II, pp. 46–9; H.R. Loyn, *Anglo-Saxon England and the Norman Conquest*, p. 349; R.H. Britnell, *The Commercialisation of English Society*, pp. 5–6; J. Hatcher, *Plague, Population and the English Economy 1348-1530*, p. 68.

[4] E.A. Wrigley and R.S. Schofield, *The Population History of England, 1541–1871: a Reconstruction*, pp. 208–9; D.M. Palliser, 'Tawney's century: brave new world or Malthusian trap?', *EcHR*, 2nd ser. XXXV (1982), pp. 341–3.

[5] In what follows we have tried to draw together some of our conclusions in the first, as well as the present, volume of this work, modified in some instances by publications since 1978 when the first volume appeared.

as well as the pastures of the Vale of Pickering, the Wolds and Holderness; there was large-scale cattle farming in Swaledale and Wensleydale and Blackburnshire as well as at Otterburn in Northumberland; and the earl of Arundel's lands in the Welsh marches supported more than 5,000 sheep in 1349.[6] Intensified and diversified exploitation of all types of terrain enabled aggregate agricultural output to be increased and rural England to support more people, including some who were not primarily agricultural producers as well as many more who were.

Rural expansion both reflected and helped to give rise to increasing demands for consumer goods of every sort – not only foodstuffs, but also manufactured goods and the commodities (like fuels, minerals, wood, textiles and leather) required to produce them. Self-supply, of course, continued to be a basic objective of peasant producers, while even great lords relied to one degree or another upon demesne produce for supplying their households and many townsfolk supplemented their diet with what they could grow in gardens or on suburban fields. These survivals of subsistence cultivation, however, were compatible with an increased market orientation even in the countryside. Great estates have been likened to 'federated grain factories' producing for the market, and most of them also accommodated commercial sheep or cattle farms, and perhaps commercial pig farms like that of Isabella de Forz at Cockermouth where pannage pigs from Derwentfells were fattened and turned into bacon. Numerous lesser landlords, too, managed their land in at least as businesslike a fashion; while peasants were both drawn into marketing some of their produce by the increased availability of commercial opportunities, or were compelled to do so to meet demands made upon them by their lords, which were more and more levied in cash rather than in kind or service.[7]

The number of buyers in the market, as well as sellers, was also increasing. It has been estimated that by 1300, even in rural England, 60 per cent of the million or so households depended for their livelihood upon small or even minuscule holdings, so that they might need to buy food to satisfy at least some of their needs; and far more people than in 1086 lived in communities which had to procure a significant part of their food supplies from outside their own neighbourhoods. This was true, for example, of some of the mining areas, of some forested districts, and above all of many towns. By

[6] *AHEW*, ii, pp. 395–8, 409–10, 486.
[7] *Ibid.*, pp. 408–9.

1300 there were not only many more towns than there had been in 1086, but also more towns which were relatively large. It is no more possible to make an accurate count of townsfolk in the reign of Edward I than it is to put a number on any other section of the community, but one estimate suggests that around 15 per cent of the population, perhaps almost a million people, lived in centres with pronounced urban characteristics.[8] Town growth, moreover, was merely the clearest manifestation of the commercialization of England's economy. The multiplication of village markets and regional fairs must also be taken into account, together with improved communications by land and water, which together offered better marketing facilities even to small producers and reduced their transaction costs in taking advantage of them.

Government action and policies, at least in part, may have reinforced these economic trends. In the first place, the Norman and Angevin kings continued to insist, as their Anglo-Saxon predecessors had done, that there should be one money current in the land and that this should be royal money. Increasingly minting was concentrated at the royal mint in London, although there was a substantial output from the Canterbury mint down to the early fourteenth century and even under Edward I various provincial mints were temporarily re-opened to assist with major recoinages. Strict royal control over the currency was thus preserved, a monopoly power which appears to have been exercised with considerable responsibility. As well as maintaining the standard of the coinage (something rare enough in the Europe of that day), there appears to have been a concern to provide coin in sufficient quantities and of appropriate types for the needs of a society becoming increasingly commercialized at every level.[9] It is no easier to estimate the value of the coin in circulation during the middle ages than to put a figure on England's population; but current opinion seems to be that it may have been no more than £25,000–£37,500 in the Conqueror's reign, that it had increased by 1205 (and especially dramatically in the late twelfth century) to about £250,000, that it continued to grow intermittently during the thirteenth century to £600,000 or rather more by Edward

---

[8] C.C. Dyer, *Standards of Living in the Middle Ages*, pp. 126–7; M.W. Beresford, *New Towns of the Middle Ages*, table on p. 330; Britnell, *Commercialisation of English Society*, p. 115.
[9] J. Craig, *The Mint*, pp. 55–8. Once again, on matters relating to money and the money supply we are grateful for advice and information from N.J. Mayhew and Pamela Nightingale.

I's reign, and that it expanded dramatically at the opening of the fourteenth century to reach £1,100,000 by Edward II's reign.[10]

The implication of such estimates is that the supply of money increased substantially faster than was demanded by rising population and inflation. If the population of England approximately trebled between the later eleventh century and Edward II's reign then the amount of money per head of population may have grown around tenfold, from perhaps 4d. to 40d. The consequence of such an increase was, of course, moderated by inflation, but far from completely: the conclusion that has been drawn from admittedly sparse data, is that the century after the Conquest was a period of price stability, while a possible fourfold increase took place between the mid-twelfth and the early fourteenth centuries.[11] As well as probably helping to push up prices at times, the increased volume of coins in circulation provided progressively for the needs of more people, and also enabled them to engage in an expanding range of cash transactions. Furthermore, in addition to enlarging the money supply the coins which were issued had a greater diversity. Down to the thirteenth century the only pieces minted were silver pennies, coins that were too valuable for small transactions. That problem was mitigated in part by the long-term rise of prices, but it was also exacerbated by an increasing volume of small sales and purchases. For that reason, from 1279, half pence and farthings as well as pence were minted, although for long the complaint was that not enough of them were issued. Edward I also minted a 4d. groat for use in larger transactions, although the coin had no great success until Edward III revived it in 1351, soon after he had instituted an English gold currency, with an eye especially to the needs of merchants engaged in international trade.[12]

These monetary policies were merely one manifestation of a growing government intervention in economic affairs. Kings, as we have seen, were generally willing (especially when they could draw a profit

---

[10] N.J. Mayhew, 'Money and prices in England from Henry II to Edward III', *AHR*, xxxv (1987), pp. 121–33; *idem*, 'Numismatic evidence and falling prices in the fourteenth century', *EcHR*, 2nd ser. xxvii (1974), p. 7. Not all commentators agree that there was a steep bout of inflation, perhaps associated with a marked increase in the money supply, at the end of the twelfth century: see A.R. Bridbury, *The English Economy from Bede to the Reformation*, p. 164 and J.L. Bolton, 'Inflation, economics and politics in thirteenth-century England', *Thirteenth-Century England*, IV (1992), pp. 5–6.
[11] D.L. Farmer, 'Prices and wages', in *AHEW*, II, pp. 716–17, 734, 748, 778.
[12] Craig, *The Mint*, pp. 45–6, 65–7; and for revised figures for the output of the London and Canterbury mints, C.E. Challis, *A New History of the Royal Mint*, pp. 675–80.

from it) to act as patrons of urban development and emancipation, to license fairs and markets, and to offer protection to merchants, both alien and denizen. They also made the licensing of new internal tolls a regalian power which they exercised sparingly; in the interests of consumers they established machinery to control the prices and quality of basic commodities like bread, ale and wine; and, in the last resort, the internal peace they did their best to keep was good for business.[13] Further, because many transactions were not accompanied by immediate payment, government initiatives to safeguard the interests of creditors had considerable economic significance. Even in the twelfth century Glanville preserves the text of a writ which would bring before the king's court a party to a contract of sale who had not fully paid what he owed, and ensure that payment was made. From John's reign the machinery of the exchequer was put at the disposal of creditors to the same end, and in the late thirteenth century many debts were enrolled in the records of chancery, which meant that payment could be automatically exacted if a debtor failed to meet his obligations. Finally, in 1283–85, Edward I introduced procedures for registering debts at local registries together with more effective and expeditious ways of enforcing credit agreements. Not every debt, of course, was a trading debt, and in early days perhaps most of them were not; but Edward I's legislation does appear to have merchants, and perhaps particularly alien merchants, especially in mind.[14]

It may also have favoured economic advance that, for much of our period, royal taxation was at a relatively low level. Other authorities, of course, had powers to tax those who were subject to them (manorial lords and municipalities, for instance, and ultimately the papacy), but the king's taxative capacity increased only slowly. The Norman kings inherited a right to levy a general land tax (the geld) and developed various feudal taxes (aids, scutages, the right to take over tenancies-in-chief during minorities or in default of heirs and the estates of most bishops and many abbeys during vacancies); and they continued to draw a mixture of seignorial charges and administrative profits from the English counties and many boroughs. This rag-bag of assets invited improvised government financing and the exploitation of administrative process for financial profit with the

---

[13] E. Miller, 'The economic policies of governments', in *CEcH*, III, pp. 306–13.
[14] G.D.G. Hall, ed., *Tractatus de Legibus et Consuetudinibus Regni Anglie qui Glanvill vocatur*, pp. 116–17, 129; Pollock and Maitland, *History of English Law*, II, pp. 203–16; M.M. Postan, *Medieval Trade and Finance*, pp. 1–27; T.F.T. Plucknett, *Legislation of Edward I*, pp. 136–50.

danger, since so many of these taxative powers were feudal in character, that their exercise would excite opposition from some of the most powerful interests in the land. Henry I seems still to have levied the geld regularly and in 1130 it accounted for about one-tenth of the receipts of his exchequer; but after 1162 Henry II seems to have concluded that it was an impolitic form of taxation, and relied instead upon scutages, feudal aids, and tallages or 'gifts' from local communities (especially boroughs and royal estates) to supplement normal crown income from the counties, from feudal lordship and from administration. These supplementary resources perhaps brought in on average not much more than £1,200 a year, about half what the Danegeld had been worth to Henry I in 1130.[15] Thereafter Richard I and John not only exploited every fiscal right more rigorously than ever before, but were fertile in new fiscal experiments, including those forms of taxing the English Jewish community which by the middle years of Henry III's reign were producing about three times as much supplementary revenue as Henry II had been able to raise from all sources, and which virtually destroyed the viability of the Jewish community in England.[16] Only under Edward I, between 1275 and 1290, were the foundations of a new fiscal system laid. Two lay subsidies, levies of a proportion of the value of the goods and chattels of all but the poorest, showed how, at least from time to time, very large sums could be raised; and from 1275 export duties on wool and hides provided an additional regular revenue which averaged nearly £9,600 a year down to 1290. In that period the supplementary crown income raised by Edward I, mainly from these two sources, amounted on average to about £18,000 per year, well above anything Henry III had managed; and it was from lay subsidies and customs, together with income taxes from churchmen, that still larger sums were raised from 1290 onwards.[17]

The increases of government income, however they were achieved, had important consequences. More officials could be paid regular salaries in cash, something indispensable for the growth of a

---

[15] J.A. Green, 'The last century of danegeld', *EHR*, XCVI (1981), pp. 241–58; J.H. Ramsay, *History of the Revenues of the Kings of England*, I, pp. 64–196. For much of the twelfth and thirteenth centuries, for want of better, we have used material provided by Ramsay with all the reservations made necessary by its unsatisfactory character.

[16] *Ibid.*, I, pp. 295–327; S.K. Mitchell, *Studies in Taxation under John and Henry III*, New Haven, 1914, pp. 220–87; C. Roth, *History of the Jews in England*, p. 273.

[17] Ramsay, *History of the Revenues of the Kings of England*, II, pp. 1–34; R.W. Kaeuper, *Bankers to the Crown: the Riccardi of Lucca and Edward I*, p. 169; M.C. Prestwich, *War, Politics and Finance under Edward I*, pp. 178–203; H.S. Deighton, 'Clerical taxes by consent, 1279–1301', *EHR*, LXVIII (1972), pp. 161–92.

professional administrative service, with all that meant for the power of the state; and the crown was enabled to hire more and more men for an expanding range of purposes, from soldiers and sailors to carters and building workers and even silver miners, whose wages were a further call upon the small change which Edward I's mints turned out.[18] Down to the late thirteenth century, however, royal taxation in England remained relatively light. Indeed, the most effective instruments of direct taxation may have been the king's courts. The cash penalties ('amercements') which they imposed were, by the thirteenth century, being 'inflicted right and left', and 'most men in England must have expected to be amerced at least once a year'. Even in Henry II's time, in 1172 and 1187, they brought in about £1,500 a year.[19]

Relatively light taxation was probably a favourable condition for economic expansion, but a more positive influence was England's increasing absorption into the international economy of the day, which diversified the inflows of imports and the openings for exports and stimulated the internal commerce required to supply exporters and to distribute imports. Much of the expansion of overseas trade was achieved by alien merchants, but Englishmen were involved in it from the start and were especially concerned to monopolize the inland trade so far as possible. By 1300, moreover, the English stake in overseas trade was a growing one even though English merchants had to share the maritime trade routes with Germans, Dutchmen, Brabançons, Cahorsins, Gascons and Italians. By the opening of the fourteenth century, indeed, the English merchant class had sufficient maturity roundly to refuse in 1303 to pay the enhanced customs duties Edward I had negotiated with alien traders. In the next few years, too, English merchants took the lead in a booming export trade in English wool, and enough of them were operating on a sufficient scale to make English commercial capital a significant item among the country's economic assets.

General economic expansion, therefore, enabled England by 1300 to support a population probably larger than it would be under the Tudors and the Stuarts. Admittedly, as the thirteenth century wore on, a growing proportion of that population could be expected to secure no more than a bare subsistence, and in great measure throughout the central middle ages increases in the volume of

[18] Bolton, 'Inflation, economics and politics in thirteenth-century England', pp. 7–10.
[19] Pollock and Maitland, *History of English Law*, II, p. 513; Ramsay, *History of the Revenues of the Kings of England*, I, p. 195.

production simply reflected the growth in the number of producers. On the other hand, as we have seen, there were some improvements contributing to increased productive capacity, not least those in England's commercial infrastructure. The growth of towns, old and new, the multiplication of fairs and markets, and the slow increase of horses for haulage which made market transactions speedier and widened their range, were powerful stimuli to agriculture as well as to trade and industry.[20] As local marketing facilities became better in virtually every part of the realm, the produce of farms could be sold conveniently even by small producers, and a wider range of consumer goods were available for purchase so that farmers were encouraged to produce more to procure the means to purchase them. Aggregate production, too, was increased not only by a massive expansion of the acreage devoted to agriculture, but by a more intensive use of this enhanced acreage. Commercialization also permitted more land to be used for purposes for which it was best suited, whether that was raising animals rather than crops or one type of grain or animal in preference to others. Even regions with inferior soils, so long as they had access to markets, were economically viable when diversification was combined with specialization: by raising rabbits and sheep and growing fine malting barley on the thin sandy soils of the Norfolk and Suffolk Brecklands; or fattening pigs, making charcoal, cutting timber and firewood, mining and working iron, and making a little glass and pottery on the unrewarding clays of the Forest of Dean.[21]

Technological improvements also contributed to increased production. During the central middle ages wheel-thrown pottery and a better control of its firing became general; there were some advances in the methods of mining and smelting; water-power came to be used for fulling cloth and a few other purposes as well as, in combination with wind-power, for corn milling; and by the early fourteenth century the spinning wheel was beginning to take the place of the distaff; and the horizontal treadle-loom was increasing the output of weavers. In the countryside, meantime, improvements in livestock management, at least in the case of some demesne flocks and herds, had the potential of achieving higher dairy yields and heavier fleeces; and there was some enclosure of arable, and possibly some successful conversion of a two-field to a three-field rotational

---

[20] J. Langdon, *Horses, Oxen and Technological Innovation*, pp. 268–72.
[21] M. Bailey, *A Marginal Economy?*, pp. 115–42; J. Birrell, 'Peasant craftsmen in the medieval forest', *AHR*, XVII (1969), pp. 91–107.

system in open fields (although whether that by itself increased output is more problematical).[22] In some parts of the country, too, particularly in east Norfolk and in Kent and Sussex, demesne yields were certainly improved by heavier seeding, assiduous weeding of the growing crops, the introduction of nitrogenous plants into the rotational cycle, and a reduction of the area fallowed each year.[23] These agricultural methods, however, required 'massive labour inputs' and could only be envisaged because real wages were low. Significant as the structural and technological advances we have noted were in contributing to the increase of production needed to support a growing population, they fell far short of representing the decisive transformation of the economy which would have been required to postpone indefinitely the adverse consequences of the progressive reduction in the amount of land per head available to the rural majority of Englishmen.

(b) The attitudes and institutions of a traditional society

There were other influences, too, which limited the scope of economic expansion in the twelfth and thirteenth centuries, including inherited attitudes and institutions. Even in the early fourteenth century, for instance, England remained a traditional agrarian society in which power, including many powers of economic direction, was vested in its landlords – the secular baronage, the bishops, religious houses large and small, and those smaller lay landlords who may, however anachronistically, be described as gentry. Some of these landlords, especially from the thirteenth century onwards, tried to increase output from their estates with the sale of some of their demesne produce as a prime objective; and most of them, as surviving manorial accounts show, displayed a 'calculating carefulness with money and stores that can be regarded as one of the characteristics of a commercial frame of mind'.[24] The landlords of the central

[22] K. Biddick, *The other Economy: Pastoral Husbandry on a Medieval Estate*, pp. 81–115; M.J. Stephenson, 'Wool yields in the medieval economy', *EcHR*, 2nd ser. XLI (1988), pp. 368–91; H.S.A. Fox, 'The alleged transformation from two-field to three-field systems in medieval England', *EcHR*, 2nd ser. XXXIX (1986), pp. 526–48.

[23] P.F. Brandon, 'Cereal yields on the Sussex estates of Battle abbey during the later middle ages', *EcHR*, 2nd ser. XXV (1972), pp. 403–20; *idem*, 'Farming techniques: south-eastern England', in *AHEW*, II, pp. 318–25; B.M.S. Campbell, 'Agricultural progress in medieval England: some evidence from eastern Norfolk', *EcHR*, 2nd ser. XXXVI (1983), pp. 26–46; *idem*, 'Population pressure, inheritance and the land market in a fourteenth-century peasant community', in R.M. Smith, ed., *Land, Kinship and Life Cycle*, p. 90.

[24] Britnell, *Commercialisation of English Society*, pp. 115–17.

middle ages, all the same, were not necessarily businessmen and were certainly not businessmen exclusively. Men of religion were sometimes precisely that, including Robert Grosseteste, bishop of Lincoln, even though he was capable of drawing up rules (no doubt with much professional advice) on how to 'guard and govern lands and household' for the countess of Lincoln.[25] Bishops, too, had dioceses as well as estates to manage; many of them were political figures or served as ministers of the crown; and abbots had parts to play in the affairs of their order. Earls and barons, in turn, were centres of webs of patronage, they were the king's 'natural' counsellors, and they often commanded his armies. In company with some of the bishops, moreover, they brought King John to heel in 1215, humiliated Henry III in 1258, forced Edward I to capitulate in 1297, and dethroned (and eventually murdered) Edward II in 1327. Lesser landowners also had many preoccupations even though, like Lionel Bradenham of Langenhoe in Essex, they might be perfectly competent at playing the markets for the produce of their land. Many tasks were heaped upon men of this standing. Some served local bishops or barons in various ways and many were dragooned into serving, as sheriffs and in other offices, as the king's 'maids of all work in the shires'. While the Angevin regime of local 'self-government at the king's command' entailed much public work for lesser landowners, their traditional military obligations did not disappear. Those with sufficient income for the purpose were required to equip themselves as knights; Edward I on occasion conscripted them for service against the Scots; and later Sir John Bekering both went to sea in Edward III's navy and fought on land at Crécy. Like their betters, small landowners might find that concentration upon the business of estate-management was liable to much interruption.[26]

The business of estate-management, furthermore, had intrinsic problems. The estates of the greater landlords were not constructed according to dictates of economic convenience or efficiency, for most of them were random collections of lands: fruits of the piecemeal character of the Norman settlement, of royal or seignorial patronage, of marriage settlements, and in the case of ecclesiastical estates of the unpredictable generosity of benefactors. The problems

---

[25] D. Oschinsky, ed., *Walter of Henley and other Treatises on Estate Management and Accounting*, pp. 192, 388–9.
[26] R.H. Britnell, 'Production for the market on a small fourteenth-century estate', pp. 380–7; H.M. Cam, *Liberties and Communities in Medieval England*, esp. pp. 27–48; Prestwich, *War, Politics and Finance under Edward I*, pp. 83–91; M. Bassett, *Knights of the Shire for Bedfordshire during the Middle Ages*, Beds. Hist. Rec. Soc., xxix (1949), pp. 14–15.

these chance accumulations of territories posed might be mitigated by the thirteenth century by the fact that their owners could hire skilled administrators to run their estates, but these administrators in turn were apt to require closer supervision than they commonly received. Smaller estates, too, often had similar disadvantages of structure, and their fortunes were more likely to depend upon the interests and capacities of their lords since the cost of skilled administrators was beyond their resources. The chief financial officer of a landowning Cambridgeshire judge in the early fourteenth century was his chaplain, and another chaplain was in charge of one of his principal properties. Such agents at least were literate and presumably numerate; but so far as estate-management went, as was the case of those in charge of knightly estates in Sussex at about this time, many of the necessary skills they had to teach themselves, or were 'learned from others as they went along'.[27]

When these circumstances are taken into account, the entrepreneurial achievements of many large landlords deserve rather better than the 'sluggish and indifferent' label which has been attached to them.[28] The income which the bishop of Ely drew from his estate in the 1290s, about 40 per cent of it from the sale of agricultural produce, was perhaps three times what it had been in 1171; the income of the bishop of Worcester likewise increased threefold between 1165 and 1299; and, if the abbots of Westminster and archbishops of Canterbury only managed to double their receipts over a similar period, at least the archbishops increased the proportion of them derived from agricultural produce from 49 per cent in 1206 to 63 per cent in the 1290s.[29] At the same time, while landlords might have at least limited success in increasing the revenues they drew from their estates, their patterns of expenditure were determined by their social position rather than by commercial criteria. The first

---

[27] BL Add. Roll 18522; N. Saul, *Scenes from Provincial Life*, pp. 100–4.

[28] By Bridbury, *The English Economy from Bede to the Reformation*, pp. 20, 122.

[29] E. Miller, *Abbey and Bishopric of Ely*, pp. 81–2, 94–5; C. Dyer, *Lords and Peasants in a Changing Society*, p. 53; B.F. Harvey, *Westminster Abbey and its Estates in the Middle Ages*, p. 63; F.R.H. Du Boulay, *The Lordship of Canterbury*, pp. 243–5. Bridbury's verdict upon the archbishop of Canterbury (*The English Economy from Bede to the Reformation*, p. 20) as one of the 'dismal financial failures' among medieval landlords is less than securely grounded in that he compares Domesday manorial values, which Bridbury himself regards as misleading statements of manorial revenues, and the figures we have for the archbishop's net revenue in 1273–4. This in any case, as Du Boulay makes clear, was a bad year, and it was also one in which some of the archbishop's most important manors were missing from the record. Not surprisingly, therefore, the archbishop's recorded revenue in 1273–4 was 20 per cent below its average for the century and 33 per cent below what it would be in the 1290s.

calls upon the profits generated by great agricultural estates were household and personal consumption, political and religious activities, building castles, abbeys and cathedrals, and retaining knights and fighting wars. Expenditure by the landowning gentry was probably similar in character, if smaller in amount, to that of the magnates. In either case investment in the assets which produced their receipts had a low priority and seldom exceeded 5 per cent of gross income. Such a figure may not have been wholly inappropriate so far as seignorial demesnes were concerned, but the fact that landlords invested not at all in the holdings and stock of their tenants, most of whom were smallholders with small resources, meant that the predominant sector of the medieval rural economy was starved of capital.[30]

A positive entrepreneurial spirit was also restrained by traditional institutions and attitudes among the mass of villagers who, in 1279, occupied about two-thirds of the land of England.[31] Most were small family farmers with holdings tending on average to become smaller as village populations grew and the reserves of reclaimable land became scarcer. As in all peasant societies, the prime objective of these farmers was to produce food for themselves, using family labour for this purpose whenever possible; but they were neither able nor willing to limit their enterprise to this subsistence purpose, and they made in fact a major contribution to the increases both of agricultural output and of the trade in agricultural produce. That they did so was in part a consequence of the fact that peasant tenants had to pay to their lords rents and other charges (and these more and more frequently in cash); the more substantial among them were called upon more and more frequently to pay taxes to the king; and they needed to secure the means to purchase essential commodities which their holdings could not produce. The fact that such outgoings were unavoidable compelled peasants to market a proportion of their produce.

On the other hand, by no means all peasant marketing was the result of compulsion; for the desire to work for gain, to trade and to accumulate was also innate. Improved marketing facilities, therefore, were an advantage for the peasantry as well as for their lords; and peasants, too, had access if they needed it, to the reserves of cheap

---

[30] For consumption, Dyer, *Standards of Living in the Later Middle Ages*, pp. 49–85; and investment, R.H. Hilton, *The English Peasantry in the Later Middle Ages*, pp. 184–90, and M.M. Postan, 'Investment in medieval agriculture', *Jnl. of Economic History*, XXVII (1967), pp. 576–87.
[31] E.A. Kosminsky, *Studies in the Agrarian History of England*, p. 100.

labour in overcrowded villages in order to supplement that available in their own families. That labour was in plentiful supply, combined with the fact that many peasant holdings were too small to give full employment to a family, may help to explain why some tenants seem to have been willing to deploy lavish labour inputs in order to augment the productivity of their land. Here, a desire for gain was reinforced by the fact that peasant holdings provided much of the subsistence of the families living on them; and in a situation in which rural population was growing, involving some reduction in the average amount of land available per head, the balance between people and resources became an increasingly delicate one. If evidence from seignorial demesnes can be taken as typical (and we have no other), in order to avert a rise in wheat prices, in the early thirteenth century a yield of 3.3 times the amount of seed sown was sufficient; but that figure had increased to 3.5-fold later in the century and to nearly fourfold by the early fourteenth century. Scarcity, in other words, was a growing possibility and, for the small farmer, the experience of hunger might be added to the incentives to maintain, or if possible to improve, the productivity of his farm.[32]

There were many circumstances which might limit his capacity to do so. The various open-field regimes characteristic of much of England meant that a large part of the arable land both of lords and tenants was dispersed and intermingled, making necessary a degree of uniformity in routines of cultivation. In addition, there were extensive 'common' rights, guaranteed by custom, not only over pastures but also over the arable fields when they were not under growing crops. This framework restricted the freedom of individuals to exercise initiative; and, at a time when a growing population intensified the demand for land, reinforced a regime of small farms and even tended to make them smaller. In such circumstances attempts to break away from traditional patterns of farming became more rather than less difficult. Even when early enclosures of the open fields occur, as they do in east Devon in the thirteenth century, they took the form of 'diminutive closes', the result of 'hedging small bundles of strips rather than the consolidation of larger blocks which could have been possible under less competitive conditions'.[33] Peasant farmers, moreover, as well as being members of village groups, were also subject to constraints as manorial, and often servile, tenants. They were generally successful in invoking custom to

[32] Farmer, 'Prices and wages', in *AHEW*, II, p. 738.
[33] H.S.A. Fox, 'The chronology of enclosure and economic development in medieval Devon', *EcHR*, 2nd ser. XXVIII (1975), pp. 192–6.

limit the ability of their lords arbitrarily to increase the demands made upon them;[34] but in aggregate those demands made significant inroads into their incomes, their capital, and even into the time they could devote to their own holdings, involving some inevitable reduction of their potential contribution to the economic development of medieval England.

A positive entrepreneurial spirit was much diluted in the towns as well as in the countryside. The typical townsman was a small shop-keeper, or an artisan who was literally a handicraftsman, carrying on a family business from a domestic working base, and representing a scale of production and exchange which was narrowly local in its horizons. Much of the industry located in the countryside rather than in towns was similar in both organization and scale. Except in the larger towns it was often prudent to avoid too much specialization, so that some involvement in agriculture or horticulture might continue, or in other cases the employment of a range of skills. Many urban merchants, too, had horizons that were little, if at all, wider than those of craftsmen and shopkeepers; and the most successful among them were liable to be drawn into assuming local administrative tasks, which multiplied in the boroughs as they did in the shires. Active trading, therefore, was often a young man's occupation soon abandoned, at least in part; and the money a merchant made by trade was frequently diverted into investment in property, including agricultural property, both to further social promotion and as provision for the merchant's dependants and for his own old age. This regular outflow of capital from commerce, and from the industrial activities which commerce might nourish, limited the rate of capital accumulation and the scale of commercial and industrial development.

There can be no doubt that trading activity centred upon towns increased notably during the twelfth and thirteenth centuries, but its expansion had to face a variety of limiting influences. Each town tried to secure for its inhabitants a monpolistic position in its own neighbourhood and to bar 'foreigners' (from elsewhere in England as well as from other lands) from much of the trade within its walls and in what was regarded as its hinterland. Some twelfth-century towns succeeded in getting charters which put outsiders at a disadvantage, and doubtless that was Lincoln's objective later when it levied punitive charges on traders from Grimsby and Louth.[35] Town

---

[34] M.M. Postan and J. Hatcher, 'Population and class relations in feudal society', *PP*, no. 78 (1978), pp. 32–6.

[35] C. Gross, *The Gild Merchant*, II, pp. 146–7.

governments, therefore, strictly controlled their market places in the interests of their own burgesses; and craft gilds likewise discriminated against 'strangers' when they claimed monopolies of production and imposed restrictions on dealings with non-gildsmen. As the craft gilds developed, moreover, they tended to insist upon the common interests of their members at the expense of individual enterprise, controls which by Edward I's reign were being set down in writing even outside London. In this respect the cloth working gilds were precocious, and surviving ordinances show the weavers of Northampton, Leicester, Winchester and Bristol, as well as London, from 1250 onwards being subjected to rules governing the quality of their work, their hours of employment and their rates of pay.[36] Some of these regulations may have been imposed upon weavers by merchants in the interests of merchants' profits; but gild rules supporting common interests even at the expense of individual initiative represented something of a norm, and breaches of them might involve penalties of some severity. The rules of the York girdlers in 1307 prescribed when a craftsman might work, from whom he might buy the materials he needed, and to whom he might sell his product; and also that if he was 'rebel or do the contrary' he would incur penalties to the city and its officers totalling 14s. 4d. This was a sum which, at that time, would have taken a building craftsman fifty days to earn. Since it is unlikely that York girdlers were much, if at all, more affluent than building workers, 'rebellion' against the rules of girdler-craft was not something to be contemplated lightly.[37]

Protectionist attitudes and restrictive policies, of course, were no absolute barrier to urban and industrial development; and, in any case, the emergence of a growing class of native merchants with horizons wider than their own town and its hinterland, and the activities of alien merchants operating under royal patronage and protection wherever there was business to be done, helped to offset some of the introspective responses of medieval townsfolk. There were, however, other influences narrowing the scope for development. First, as the proportion of smallholders and landless in rural communities increased and as the long-term growth of England's population slowed down, the modest resources of which the peasant majority

---

[36] These regulations are listed in M.H.M. Hulton, 'The urban weavers of medieval England', University of Birmingham Ph.D. thesis, 1990, Appx. 1(a).

[37] M. Sellers, ed., *York Memorandum Book*, I, pp. 180–1; E.H. Phelps-Brown and S.V. Hopkins, 'Seven centuries of building wages', in E.M. Carus-Wilson, ed., *Essays in Economic History*, II, p. 177.

disposed set limits to the demand for consumption goods, the commerce which provided such goods, and the growth of the urban communities in which many of these goods were produced. Secondly, the disproportionate share of the national income received by the landlord class, with its tradition of conspicuous consumption, gave to those townsfolk who catered for its needs an undue prominence and earning capacity, and also contributed to the 'underdeveloped' character of much of England's overseas trade. Although imports included 'considerable quantities of raw materials and basic foodstuffs',[38] manufactured and luxury products also loomed large and were paid for principally by exports of primary products. Indeed, if England enjoyed a favourable trade balance at the opening of the fourteenth century, this was due essentially to massive wool exports, which in part paid for imports of textiles often made from English wool.

The consequences of these basic characteristics of the medieval economy were by no means all of them adverse. The export market had required the fleeces of 5–7 million sheep by the mid-thirteenth century,[39] and possibly of as many as 10 millions in the last years of Edward I's reign. While many exporters were aliens, the wool trade also attracted a growing number of English merchants and accounted for much of the growth of their capital resources; a build-up of sheep flocks must have taken place, and a few sheep may have helped some peasant smallholders to survive despite the squeezing of their arable acres; and for some landlords sheep-farming was clearly big business and augmented still further their disproportionate wealth. At the same time, however, the availability of a booming export market for wool encouraged a spread of specialist stock-farming in areas where that might be the best use to which the land could be put.

2. ENGLAND BEFORE THE BLACK DEATH: FORCES OF CHANGE, *C.* 1300–48

By the last years of Edward I's reign many of the expansive influences which shaped England's economic development during the central middle ages were petering out; but, during the half century

---

[38] Bolton, 'Inflation, economics and politics in thirteenth-century England', p. 12.
[39] This is Bridbury's estimate, *The English Economy from Bede to the Reformation*, p. 12.

or so preceding the Black Death, changes were also at work which are important in their own right and for the part they played in shaping the society of late medieval and early modern England. The England to which plague came in 1348–49 was not the same as the England of 1300. Some of the differences which had emerged had roots going back to earlier times than 1300, but the fact that those differences existed conditioned the way in which the country weathered the demographic shock which the coming of plague initiated.

(a)   Some industrial trends

It became increasingly apparent in the early fourteenth century that economic expansion was no longer to be achieved principally by multiplying markets, and by enlarging old towns and founding new ones, each of them the focus of exchanges for a surrounding hinterland. Specialist producing areas were emerging, which relied upon merchants for access to distant and sometimes export markets. There was, of course, nothing new about industrial production aimed at distant markets. The textile industry of the great eastern towns had done so even in the twelfth century, and long before 1300 so had the tin miners of the South-West, the lead miners of the Peak District and Alston Moor, and the potters of Scarborough. During the first half of the fourteenth century, however, there do appear to have been significant increases of industrial activity, much of it aimed at wider than local markets and located in the countryside where surplus labour was likely to be available and regulation less intrusive. These developments are evident, not only in the tin-mining districts of the South-West and the lead-mining districts of the North, but also in many of the places where iron was mined and worked (including West Yorkshire and the Weald), or where coal was dug and, in the case of Tyneside, exported to other parts of England and across the North Sea. They also appear in cloth making, where a new wave of expansion had begun before 1349 in the villages and small towns of East Anglia, West Yorkshire, the Cotswolds, Wiltshire and Somerset, and a measure of recovery was manifested in some of the older urban centres in which the industry had been in retreat during much of the thirteenth century. By 1349 native products had captured parts of the home market which had been supplied by imported fabrics in 1300, and they were also making a slowly growing contribution to exports. The signs of this growth of cloth making is perhaps to be seen in the relatively high tax assessments of some villages and small towns in 1334: in Norfolk of Worstead and North Walsham, in Suffolk of Clare and Lavenham, in Wiltshire of Pewsey, Bradford on Avon and Steeple Ashton, in Gloucestershire of Lechlade and Fairford and Wotton under Edge, in Somerset of Bruton and Frome and Mells. In Yorkshire, too, cloth making as well as metal working may explain the high assessments of Sheffield and Rotherham, where certainly drapers and cloth workers were to be found in 1379.[40]

These industrial trends of the early fourteenth century were still of modest importance, but they represent the early phase of developments which ultimately would give England's economy a new shape. First, they reflected a more decisive shift in some places and regions towards more specialized patterns of production both for some goods of general consumption and some of the materials used in their manufacture, allowing some economies of scale and favouring some development of skills. Secondly, so long as skilled labour was available or could be trained, there was no reason for these developing industrial centres to accept the constraints of the local and limited markets which had been the context in which much of medieval urban manufacture had developed. Thirdly, where scarce materials were readily to hand, or fiscal influences, as in the case of cloth-making, gave English producers a marked advantage over their foreign competitors, export as well as home markets were well within the range of English manufacturers, an influence helping to modify the 'colonial' character of England's medieval commerce. There were elements of promise in England's pre-plague economy, even if their realization as yet had not proceeded very far.

(b)   The role of merchants

An expansion of the outlets for some industrial projects, however, depended upon merchants, and more particularly upon the development of an English merchant class, in the sense of a body of traders whose interests were not narrowly local, but extended into regional or even into international exchanges. Such men had existed, of course, long before the fourteenth century, but it was in that century that an 'estate of merchants' emerged, uniting merchants of substance from many parts of England and endowing them with a capacity for concerted action. Its emergence reflected the fact that by that time there were more English merchants than there had

[40] R.E. Glasscock, ed., *The Lay Subsidy of 1334*, pp. 95, 100, 202, 262, 268–9, 291, 338, 348, 393; for the poll tax returns from the West Riding in 1379, *Yorks. Arch. Jnl.*, v (1877–8), pp. 25–7, 40–4.

been earlier operating in a larger way of business and winning a growing share of England's overseas trade. Individually and collectively, therefore, English merchants disposed of substantially increased resources. This was a circumstance not entirely without disadvantages. With the beginning of the Hundred Years' War, 'indirect taxation on overseas trade became the very centre-piece of royal finance',[41] and Edward III over and above siphoned off a good deal of England's commercial capital. English merchants, for the first time, became bankers to the crown in a major way, a diversion of capital from trading which, for instance in William de la Pole's case, competed with the more traditional propensity of merchants to invest trading gains in real property with an eye to social promotion.

Commercial capital, nevertheless, became increasingly indispensable to the workings of the English economy at every level. Merchants linked consumers to producers and producers to markets locally, regionally and even internationally. William Durham of Darlington, for example, was hardly a merchant of great renown, but he exported northern wool to the Low Countries and he must have dealt in many markets nearer home in order to dispose of the grain he bought from Durham priory and to procure the livestock and other commodities with which he supplied the monks of Durham. The services of merchants, in other words, were basically important for those improvements which derived from regional specialization. The viability of Suffolk's Breckland economy, for instance, depended on the services of merchants in places like Thetford and Bury St Edmunds for access to the major regional market at Norwich, to the cloth making areas of southern Suffolk and north Essex and, via King's Lynn and Yarmouth, to the coastal and overseas trades of the North Sea. The same trade routes and commercial contacts also enabled Breckland to obtain supplies of wheat, which its poor soils grew badly, and of the salt fish which were the harvest of the sea.[42]

The specialization manifested in Breckland is to be seen in other parts of the country which were ill-suited to the predominantly cereal husbandry of midland England. In the far South-West, for instance, the fact that much of the land was not well adapted to growing grain was offset by plentiful supplies of pasture and a regime of long recuperative leys, making this a mixed farming region sustained by convertible husbandry and large numbers of livestock, cattle in particular. Parts of northern England, too, were

[41] W.M. Ormrod, 'The crown and the English economy, 1290–1348', in Campbell, ed., *Before the Black Death*, p. 173.
[42] Bailey, *A Marginal Economy?*, pp. 148–58.

almost exclusively cattle country: parts of the Lancashire slopes of the Pennines, Arkengarthdale and the upper reaches of Swaledale and Wensleydale in Yorkshire, and moorland shielings like those at Tarset in Northumberland. Specialization in sheep farming was even commoner and in the chalk downs of southern England, apart from supplying much wool for sale, sheep provided the manure which made corn crops better than they might otherwise have been. It was this combination which made thirteenth-century Wiltshire 'a great wheat and sheep county'. Areas like the Forest of Dean, too, exploited their strengths: abundant grazing, timber resources, and deposits of coal and iron; and many places around the coast supplemented farming with salt-boiling and fishing.[43]

The instances of specialization indicate the degree of commercialization which took place in England during the central middle ages, although this is not something which we should exaggerate. The resources at the disposal of peasant farmers, and even of manorial officers, tended to favour small sales of agricultural produce over short distances. Even on the eve of the Black Death corn merchants were rare outside London and some of the eastern ports; and, if wool was grown almost exclusively as a cash crop, many peasants had few or no sheep. As for cereal crops, it has been estimated that sales of bread grains possibly represented no more than 20–30 per cent of the amounts harvested.[44] Seignorial demesnes, on the other hand, did market most of their wool, a fair amount of their grain, and not inconsiderable numbers of surplus or culled livestock; peasant farmers were compelled to sell some of their produce in order to meet essential cash outgoings; remote stock farms in the Lancashire Pennines or North Tynedale were dependent upon the availablity of commercial facilities like those on offer at Bolton and Corbridge fairs; and in South-West Yorkshire by 1379 'merchants of beasts' were prominent in many of the villages of the region.

Industrial producers had no less need for commercial services, and not least those of them supplying markets at any distance. That

[43] J. Hatcher, 'A diversified economy: late medieval Cornwall', *EcHR*, 2nd ser. XXII (1969), pp. 212–14; *AHEW*, II, pp. 256–7, 362, 387–98; Birrell, 'Peasant craftsmen in the medieval forest', *AHR*, XVII (1969), p. 106; Britnell, *Commercialisation of English Society*, pp. 113–15; and also M. Bailey's important theoretical discussion of these matters, 'The concept of the margin in the medieval English economy', *EcHR*, 2nd ser. XLII (1989), pp. 10–13.

[44] For sheep, M.M. Postan, *Essays on Medieval Agriculture and the General Problems of the Medieval Economy*, pp. 214–48; and for cereals and the grain trade, Britnell, *Commercialisation of English Society*, pp. 83, 86, 120–3, and *idem*, *Growth and Decline in Colchester*, p. 39.

need had been evident in the organization of England's first major industry, the cloth industry of the twelfth century; and was no less a requirement for the revived and expanded native textile industry during the first half of the fourteenth century. The fact that so much of that expansion took place in villages and small towns made the merchant's contribution the more indispensable. Thus, by 1315, worsteds and aylshams made in the Norfolk countryside were being sold to traders in Norwich, and soon found outlets to maritime trade routes through King's Lynn and Yarmouth. By 1327, too, London mercers provided virtually all the worsteds bought by the royal household; and, when cloth export figures become available in 1347, Londoners were also exporting some worsteds, although that trade they had to share with East Anglian and Hanseatic merchants.[45] Derbyshire and Swaledale miners, likewise, needed merchants to deliver the lead they produced to Hull (where alien merchants bought some of it for export), or to King's Lynn, or to Boston fair where the Keeper of the Fabric at Exeter cathedral was among their customers. Before 1349, too, Newcastle merchants like Hugh Hawkin and Hugh Sadlingstones were shipping Tyneside coal to Yarmouth, and doubtless also to Hull and King's Lynn as well as London, where by 1330 the officials who measured the amounts of coal landed were numerous enough to have formed themselves into a fraternity. Meantime, at the other end of the country, in order to reach their eventual markets, Cornish tinners relied on commercial services provided by Londoners and alien merchants as well as by local merchants and master tinners.[46]

The Cornish tin industry also demonstrates, as we have seen, that merchants might provide more than merely distributive services. By 1300 much of the tin mining there was being financed by a relatively small group of master tinners, whose advances enabled working tinners to operate until they had tin available for sale; and the master tinners, in turn, relied for some of their capital upon advances by London and alien merchants against future deliveries of tin. In this industry, in other words, commercial capital contributed to

[45] E. Lipson, *Economic History of England*, I, pp. 489–90; *Rot. Parl.*, I, p. 292; G.A. Williams, *Medieval London*, pp. 136–9. Export figures at this time are less than trustworthy: E.M. Carus-Wilson and O. Coleman, *England's Export Trade, 1275–1547*, pp. 199–201.

[46] W.R. Childs, *The Trade and Shipping of Hull, 1300-1500* p. 12; E. Wedermeyer Moore, *Fairs of Medieval England*, p. 52; A.M. Erskine, ed., *Accounts of the Fabric of Exeter Cathedral, 1279–1353*, pp. 19, 35, 50, 61; J.B. Blake, 'The medieval coal trade of north-east England', *North. Hist.*, II (1967) pp. 10–14; J. Hatcher, *History of the British Coal Industry*, I, pp. 24–5; *idem, English Tin Production and Trade*, pp. 49–52.

production as well as distribution. This may well also have been the case in the textile industry from an early date. Even in the twelfth century fullers and weavers often appear to have been in a position of dependence in relation to cloth merchants; in the thirteenth century Leicester merchants were putting out work to manufacturing craftsmen and Oxford merchants provided looms for country weavers; in 1300 hiring out looms to London artisans, previously banned, was finally allowed; and in the mid-fourteenth century Lincoln citizens were hiring weavers to make cloth for sale and Bristol merchants had set up looms and employed cloth workers in their houses.[47] Merchants, of course, were not alone in providing some of the capital resources required by an expanding economy. Landowners did so, too, when they financed the construction of corn or fulling mills, or provided forges to be leased out to iron workers as the earls of Cornwall did in Knaresborough Forest.[48] It was, however, the financial and distributive services offered by merchants on a regular basis which was most effective in making possible the measure of development evident in a number of branches of industry in the first half of the fourteenth century.

At the same time, the economic tendencies in the generation or two preceding the Black Death had a longer-term significance. Economic diversification and specialization continued after 1349, including a measure of industrialization in some regions, leaving a mark in some of the changes in the geographical distribution of wealth between 1334 and the early sixteenth century revealed by tax assessments. The industrializing West Riding of Yorkshire, for example, seems to have become relatively wealthier, and the agricultural East Riding relatively poorer, over that period; and the most significant increases in wealth, in addition to those in the south-eastern area around London, seem to have been in Cornwall, Devon and Somerset together with Worcestershire, Dorset and Gloucestershire. In these counties it is reasonable to connect growing wealth with mining or cloth making, an impression strengthened when we look at districts smaller than counties. Taxable capacity increased notably, for instance, in the textile areas of southern Suffolk, north Essex, and around Norwich and Beccles; and similar increases in the districts around Leicester and Northampton are perhaps to be associated with expanding leather industries. Growing wealth during the late middle ages, in other words, might owe as much or more to

[47] Above, chpt. 2; Lipson, *Economic History of England*, I, pp. 468–9, 480.
[48] L.M. Midgley, ed., *Ministers' Accounts of the Earldom of Cornwall, 1296–1297*, II, pp. 187–8.

industrial development as to the fortunes of agriculture, thus pro-
longing into later times those tendencies towards economic
diversification and specialization which became evident in England
in the generations before 1349.[49]

(c) Political society

Changes in society and politics in these generations inevitably had
economic implications, although in their nature these changes were
often not perceptible immediately. England continued to be ruled
by a traditional monarchy, even if under Edward II the king's person
was treated with something well short of reverence, and by a traditional landowning nobility and landowning prelacy with their
wide-ranging powers of patronage. The grip of nobility and prelates
upon so many of the levers of power was recognized and accepted by
Edward III as was indicated by the part which bishops played in his
administration, by the leading roles which many noblemen took in
his wars, and by the king's patronage of tournaments and his foundation of the Order of the Garter.[50] By Edward III's time, however,
other social groups had established claims to the exercise of a measure of influence at least at a local level. A class of lesser landowners
had crystallized out of the often undistinguished ranks of the
Norman *milites*; for knighthood was recognized to be a title of honour which required an income of £20, £30 or even £40 a year from
land to sustain it. For landlords with resources of this order knighthood became an obligatory status; and if it carried with it enhanced
status, those with the title of knight or who were deemed eligible for
it were liable, as well as to the traditional military obligations of their
order, to 'attendant civil duties'. They came to form, in other words,
the administrative cadres of their shires, an obligation investing
them with a measure of recognized authority, at least in their own
neighbourhoods.[51] In the boroughs, too, little groups of 'rich
burgesses' or *optimates* undertook a similar range of public responsibilities, and a few of them with sufficient property were likewise
accorded the title of knight.

[49] R.S. Schofield, 'The geographical distribution of wealth in England, 1334–1649',
EcHR, 2nd ser. XVIII (1965), pp. 483–510; H.C. Darby *et al.*, 'The changing geographical distribution of wealth in England, 1086–1334–1525', *Jnl. of Historical Geography*, V
(1979) pp. 247–62; *AHEW*, III, pp. 27–9, 52, 150–1.
[50] On this 'new chivalry', see M. McKisack, *The Fourteenth Century*, Oxford, 1959,
pp. 250–5.
[51] S.P.J. Harvey, 'The knight and the knight's fee in England,' *PP*, no. 49 (1970),
pp. 1–43; M.R. Powicke, *Military Obligations in Medieval England*, pp. 75–9, 105–9.

These particular social and administrative developments had a mainly local significance, but by the end of the thirteenth century they also began to leave their mark upon national political structure. That this was so owed much to the fact that, from Edward I's reign onwards, the fiscal demands of the crown came increasingly to be satisfied from direct taxes upon the population of the country at large and from duties on England's overseas trade. There was a strongly held view that, if free men were to be subjected to common imposts, the concurrence of those called upon to pay them was requisite, and governments in any case might conclude that such concurrence might be the most likely course to enhance the productivity of these imposts. This was one powerful influence which, by the reign of Edward III, had gone far towards transforming a feudal assembly of king, barons and prelates assembled to deal with 'common business' into a parliament, which increasingly regularly also included representatives of the 'communities', the shires and boroughs which provided the framework of local government. Those who represented these 'communities' in parliament, moreover, were for the most part men of the same sort, or indeed often the same men, as those who exercised power in local administration. And it was these men who came for the communities to parliaments who in the 1320s were described by the *Modus tenendi parliamentum*, by contrast with the magnates who represented only themselves, as representing 'the whole community of England'.[52]

This developing political structure achieved confirmation in consequence of the repeated and extraordinary fiscal demands which Edward III made upon his subjects after the outbreak of war with France in the 1330s. The 'commons' became established as a regular part of the structure of parliaments and, if only because they were regularly present, the role they played in parliaments was slowly and hesitantly enlarged. They became the channel of communication between the localities and the centre, in particular as petitioners in parliament on behalf of individuals, of special interest groups, and of their local communities. However limited the pressure they could bring to bear, they enabled the many and often discordant voices of the 'community of the realm' to be heard, however faintly, in the highest councils of the land, widening the range of influences which determined government actions and shaped government policies.

---

[52] N. Pronay and J. Taylor, eds, *Parliamentary Texts of the Later Middle Ages*, pp. 38–9, 77, 89–90.

3.   ENGLAND BEFORE THE BLACK DEATH: ECONOMIC PROBLEMS, *C.* 1300–48

During the half-century before 1349, therefore, many of the economic and social characteristics of late medieval and early modern times were taking shape in England, but these were also generations during which some of the underlying deficiencies of the medieval economy became acutely manifest. In many populous parts of the country, even including agriculturally advanced districts like northeastern Norfolk, the majority of peasant farmers 'were compressed into a single class of impoverished smallholders', many of them with less land than is commonly assumed to be essential for a family's subsistence. They were helped to survive by exploitation of a flexible land-market and, so we must suppose, by the peasant's capacity to make the most of what land he had, even if the cost was backbreaking labour. They may, too, have been able to earn a little supplementary income from casual employment as wage-labourers; but the lives of smallholders must inevitably have been hard and any failure of crops inevitably caused widespread distress.[53] Certainly there is no question about the severity of the consequences of the series of disastrous harvests from 1315 to 1317, when the London and St Paul's annals record 'dire famine and mortality', with wheat prices soaring and many poor folk dying of want and wretchedness. Manorial records offer some support to the chroniclers, for they show average producer prices for wheat in those years were about three times, and prices for barley and oats were more than double, the prices obtained during the first decade of the century. There was also concurrently heavy mortality of plough oxen and sheep as well as of people, followed by further livestock epidemics in the 1320s. Livestock prices, therefore, were also high during this period, substantially raising the capital cost of restocking to make good losses. The troubles of farmers, in the view of a canon of Bridlington, were greater and lasted longer than ever before had been the case.[54]

[53] Campbell, 'Population pressure, inheritance and the land market in a fourteenth-century peasant community', pp. 102–7, 118.
[54] W. Stubbs, ed., *Chronicles of the Reigns of Edward I and Edward II*, I, pp. 236, 238, 278–9; II, p. 48; Farmer, 'Prices and wages', in *AHEW*, II, pp. 704, 747–8; I. Kershaw, 'The great famine and agrarian crisis in England, 1315–22', *PP*, no. 59 (1973), pp. 1–50.

(a)   The population trend

The way in which contemporaries regarded those years clearly had much justification, even though the deaths of people as a consequence of dearth and of livestock from 'murrain' (the word used for almost any animal disease) were by no means without precedent. Some modern commentators, however, go much further than contemporary chroniclers when they argue that the famine years of the early fourteenth century constitute an economic turning point, in that those years made it evident that soil exhaustion and a growing scarcity of suitable new land to colonise, in combination, were making it progressively more difficult for England's fields to support the country's swollen population. The years of crisis mortality in 1315–17, therefore, were more than a short-term misfortune or an example of the recurrent experience of food-shortage characteristic of all pre-industrial societies; for they were followed by decades during which death rates were kept above their level in the early 1290s. As a consequence, although other influences may have contributed to the fact, 'evidence of the population ceasing to expand, or even starting to decline, begin to accumulate in the first half of the fourteenth century'.[55]

The fact is, however, that the evidence available is of varying quality and does not all point in the same direction. Direct demographic evidence, like that contained in tithing lists and similar records listing all males aged twelve or more, is anything but plentiful and, such as it is, it is less than unanimous. On the bishop of Winchester's great manor of Taunton, for example, it suggests that the rate of population growth was already slowing down in the late thirteenth century, but also that, after losses amounting to some 10 per cent in the period 1311–19, there was then a slow resumption of growth down to the 1330s when the evidence runs out. Similar listings from a number of manors in central Essex, on the other hand, suggest population losses of around 15 per cent during the famine years, but that these were followed by continuing contraction by almost one-third before 1348.[56] At the same time, since direct information of this sort is rarely available, investigators have sought instead to derive a picture of village populations from the information about

[55] M.M. Postan, *Essays on Medieval Agriculture and the General Problems of the Medieval Economy*, esp. pp. 159–62; *idem, The Medieval Economy and Society*, pp. 33–5.
[56] J.Z. Titow, 'Some evidence of thirteenth-century population increase', *EcHR*, 2nd ser. XIV (1961), pp. 218–24; L.R. Poos, 'The rural population of Essex in the later middle ages', *EcHR*, 2nd ser. XXXVIII (1985), pp. 515–30.

individuals and families preserved in manorial documents, and court rolls in particular. This is a proceeding calling for many approximations, and once again the resulting population trends which emerge are often contradictory. At Halesowen in Worcestershire, after the losses of the famine years, population seems to have grown again in the period 1321–49, although the rate of growth was less than it had been in the late thirteenth century. In some Huntingdonshire manors, on the other hand, the number of inhabitants appears to have been falling consistently from the second decade of the fourteenth century, or from even earlier, until 1349; but on some Norfolk estates, with very high densities of settlement, population growth was apparently continuous right down to the coming of plague.[57]

Clearly, then, there remain many uncertainties in our picture of the demographic tendencies at work in the generation before the Black Death. That the leaden skies and heavy rains of the years 1315–17 revealed how 'calamity-sensitive' England then was is not in doubt, but it is much more difficult to answer with any confidence the question of how the population trend in England was affected by the famines and murrains of those years. Indeed, it may well be that there is no single categorical answer to that question that would be valid for England as a whole. In some places, in the generation before 1349, the long-term rise of population may have been halted or even reversed, but this does not seem to have been universal, for some of the direct demographic evidence makes it clear that there were some areas where the upward trend was apparently resumed after 1317. The continuance of assarting in the Welsh marches, in parts of Lancashire and the West Riding, and in Cornwall and Devon perhaps also suggests that the impetus may in part have come from continuing population growth in those areas.[58] At the same time, even where economic and demographic resilience were most evident, the poorer peasantry most particularly were frequently driven to raise money in years of insufficient harvests by selling plots of land in the hopes of being able to replace them in better years. Needless to say, that hope was not always realized, and the result in the long term was that small and sub-economic holdings multiplied. The small man's problem has been succinctly summed up: 'a market economy and a subsistence level of production – this could be seen as a

---

[57] Smith, 'Demographic developments in rural England, 1300–48', pp. 37–47; *AHEW*, III, pp. 1–2.
[58] *AHEW*, II, pp. 242–5, 254–5, 265–7.

most unfortunate combination, and those who lived with it lived dangerously'.[59]

(b) The rural economy in the second quarter of the fourteenth century

The fortunes of countrymen, of course, were influenced by other things than the circumstances which governed the levels of population. As we have seen, agricultural improvements and industrial developments might help to sustain high or even rising numbers of people, while equally, extraneous influences might work in the opposite direction. These included Scottish raids in the north, a possible tendency for livestock diseases to appear more frequently and to become more severe, and climatic deterioration and a rise of sea levels forcing cultivation downhill in upland areas, causing increasing coastal erosion in eastern England, and inundating low-lying land along the coasts and the estuaries of the Humber and the rivers flowing into the Wash.[60] Such things had a mainly local or regional impact, but some more general adverse influences seem to have been at work as the immediate effects of the famine years faded into the background. When Edward III in 1341, for example, levied a tax in the form of a ninth of the value of the grain, wool and lambs produced that year, the collectors had to face a barrage of protests about the difficulties rural communities had in meeting the king's expectations. Livestock diseases had left many sheep dead or 'putrid' or sick, and much land had fallen out of cultivation, not only because in some cases the soil was poor and sterile or because the weather had been inclement, but because tenants were 'impotent' and because prices were low. Certainly in some parts of the country there had been a significant contraction of the area under crops, and especially in the North Riding of Yorkshire, Shropshire, Sussex, and in a group of counties to the north and west of London stretching from Cambridgeshire to Oxfordshire.[61]

---

[59] B. Harvey, 'Introduction: the "crisis" of the early fourteenth century', in Campbell, ed., *Before the Black Death*, pp. 14–15.

[60] *AHEW*, II, pp. 258–9; III, pp. 35–6, 43; M. Mate, 'The agrarian economy of southeast England before the Black Death', in Campbell, ed., *Before the Black Death*, pp. 91–3; M. Bailey, '*Per impetum maris*; natural disaster and economic decline in eastern England', in *ibid.*, pp. 184–208.

[61] A.R.H. Baker, 'Evidence in the *Nonarum Inquisitiones* for contracting arable land in England during the early fourteenth century', *EcHR*, 2nd ser. XIX (1966), pp. 518–32. The areas of substantial arable contraction may be more widespread than is stated here, since some of the returns are missing or inadequate.

Harder times for country folk were not made more bearable by the fact that, at least from 1336 onwards, they were more heavily taxed. Taxation, admittedly, was much lower in the period 1300–36 than it had been in the 1290s, a decade during which Edward I had raised £450,000 or more in taxes. The average annual weight of taxation receded to about £38,000 during the first and second decades of the fourteenth century and to about £26,000 in the third. Even this last figure, however, was substantially higher than Edward I's tax revenue before 1290, and fiscal burdens soared once more in the early days of the Hundred Years' War. In the period 1336–42 Edward III, in addition to borrowing heavily from merchants, raised a total of some £665,000 in taxes and requisitioned large amounts of supplies for the forces for which payment was often made, if at all, long in arrears. Requisitioning clearly had direct economic implications, and so had a good deal of the taxation of these years. Duties on trade, and on wool exports especially, were steeply increased; some taxes were taken in wool; changes in the method of assessing direct taxes tended to increase the share of them falling upon poorer folk; and even a poet noticed that the burden taxes represented was enhanced by the fact that they were levied year after year, leaving no interval for the poor man in particular to reassemble resources.[62]

It was the more unfortunate that this piling up of fiscal burdens coincided, as taxpayers complained in 1341, with price trends which were distinctly unfavourable to agricultural producers (see Table 7.1). By the 1330s the grain prices secured by farmers were not only well below those ruling in the famine years in 1315–17, but also below those they got earlier in the first decade of the century; and enhanced wool duties, together with Edward III's manipulation of the wool trade for fiscal and diplomatic purposes, together largely account for the fact that the fall in the price the wool producer could expect was even heavier. The impact of falling prices for the agricultural producer was made all the greater by the fact that agricultural wages preserved a large part of the gains they had made in the era of high prices in the second and third decades of the century. Falling agricultural prices must have adversely affected lords and more substantial peasants alike, and seignorial demesnes

[62] Ormrod, 'The crown and the English economy, 1290–1348', pp. 176–82; J.R. Maddicott, 'The English peasantry and the demands of the crown, 1294–1341', in T.H. Aston, ed., *Landlords, Peasants and Politics in Medieval England*, pp. 285–359; E. Miller, 'War, taxation and the English economy in the late thirteenth and early fourteenth centuries', p. 26.

Table 7.1 Agricultural prices and wages in the early fourteenth century
(decennial averages: 1300–1310 = 100)[63]

Decade	Agricultural prices			Agricultural wages			Cost of basket of consumables
	Wheat	Barley	Wool	Threshing	Reaping & binding	Mowing & spreading	
1310–20	148	143	100	102	122	110	133
1320–30	128	119	109	111	117	117	115
1330–40	98	99	74	112	113	112	96
1340–47	91	91	73	114	108	100	87

especially were likely to have found both prices and wages operating
to their disadvantage.

It seems reasonable to suppose that many features that have been
noticed in rural England in the second quarter of the fourteenth
century were related to these economic circumstances. The retreat
of the frontiers of cultivation evident in 1341, for instance, may at
least in part be attributable to the fact that, with prices falling much
more sharply than wages, it became less economic to cultivate some
of the poorer soils or to defend reclaimed land by expensive sea-
defences or fen drains. Landlords, too, were increasingly willing to
jettison demesne acres. On the 26 largest Winchester manors the
average area under crops, which had already begun to contract in
the last quarter of the thirteenth century, did so more markedly
thereafter, shrinking by 1,427 acres in 1300–24 and by a further
1,439 acres in 1325–49. By the second quarter of the fourteenth century, in other words, the bishops of Winchester cultivated only about
two-thirds of the land they had cropped for much of the thirteenth
century. At the same time, because livestock prices stood up much
better than prices for grain and wool, the cost of replacing flocks
and herds thinned by disease was relatively high; and, at least in
south-east England, some of the relatively high-cost methods of raising agricultural productivity had to be given up as too expensive.
Nor could peasant willingness to take up, at almost any price, lands
their lords abandoned be taken for granted. At Downham-in-the-Isle
in 1321–22 the bishop of Ely sowed only 112 acres of his demesne,
the remaining 348 acres being let to tenants; but as a result of unusually heavy (although unexplained) mortality by 1327–28 he could let

---

[63] Calculated from Farmer, 'Prices and wages', *AHEW*, II, pp. 734, 757, 768, 778.

only 250–70 acres and, even more significantly, the rents which demesne lettings brought in fell even more heavily, by about a half.[64]

It remains difficult to envisage these problems of rural England in the 1330s and 1340s as reflections essentially of a downturn of population after the famine years earlier in the century. Such a view is not easily compatible with the fact that the marked fall in producer prices during these decades was accompanied by a 'gentle retreat' of wage rates, a combination suggesting that changes in the money supply may have been an influence of some importance.[65] This is a matter to which more attention has been directed in recent years than in the past.[66] Earlier in the century, Edward I's government in that king's last years had produced bountiful supplies of coin which helped to keep prices high into his son's reign. That this was possible probably depended upon a steady influx of bullion generated by England's favourable trade balance at that time. That balance, however, became less favourable as wool exports fell back from their early fourteenth-century peak; and it hardly seems likely to be a coincidence that, in the second decade of the century, mint output was much lower than in the first, and that it fell still lower in the period 1320–43. By the 1330s, indeed, the average number of coins issued each year by the two principal mints at London and Canterbury was worth little over £1,000.[67] If the estimate that, in the thirteenth century, a mint output in each decade of coin worth £250,000 was required to replace lost, worn-out and hoarded money is a valid one, the output of coins in the 1330s was far less than was needed in order to maintain the money supply; and some calculations envisage the value of coin in circulation as having fallen by around a half, from £1,100,000 in the first decade of the century to around £500,000 in the 1340s.[68] If estimates of the money supply are inevitably

---

[65] Bridbury, *The English economy from Bede to the Reformation*, pp. 154–79; Farmer, 'Prices and wages', in *AHEW*, II, pp. 723–5, 751–4.
[66] Bolton, 'Inflation, economics and politics in thirteenth-century England', pp. 1–14; Mayhew, 'Money and prices in England from Henry II to Edward III', pp. 121–32; *idem*, 'Numismatic evidence and falling prices in the fourteenth century', *EcHR*, 2nd ser. XXVII (1974), pp. 1–15; M. Prestwich, 'Currency and the economy of early fourteenth-century England', in N.J. Mayhew, ed., *Edwardian Monetary Affairs (1279–1344)*, pp. 45–58; *idem*, 'Edward I's monetary policies and their consequences', *EcHR*, 2nd ser. XXII (1969), pp. 406–16; M.E. Mate; 'High prices in early fourteenth-century England: causes and consequences', *EcHR*, 2nd ser. XXVIII (1975), pp. 1–16.
[67] Challis, *A New History of the Royal Mint*, pp. 674–80.
[68] Mayhew, 'Money and prices in England from Henry II to Edward III', p. 125 and *idem*, 'Numismatic evidence and falling prices in the fourteenth century', pp. 7–8. He estimates the value of the currency in circulation in the 1340s at between £433,000 and £586,000.

debatable, there is a strong case for supposing that its reduction in these decades may have been sharp enough to exert a strong downward pressure on prices, and probably also on economic activity in general. Certainly contemporaries thought that this was so when they alleged that 'for lack of money in men's pockets' markets were virtually idle.[69]

However severe the deflationary impact of falling money supply may have been, it was clearly something capable of being remedied by the resumption of a minting programme more adequate for the country's needs. Edward III's monetary policies from 1343 onwards look like an attempt to do precisely that, so that the economic effects of scarce money were essentially short-term. From 1343 a reduction of the silver content of the coinage took account of rising bullion values and enabled more coins to be struck from a given bullion stock; mint output was increased; and a gold currency (designed mainly as a medium for international payments by merchants) was added, at first not very successfully, to the basic silver currency. Although fiscal policies, which raided the small margins of many with small resources and depressed producer prices for wool, remained in place, there are some signs, at least in southern England, that the monetary reforms of 1343–44 may have provided some stimulus for economic activity. Wool prices do appear to have improved somewhat and grain prices in 1346 and 1347 were unusually high for the period, and lords and peasants in the South-East resumed marling their land and rebuilding their stocks of cattle and sheep. At the same time, however, the weight which can be placed upon these indications of rural recovery cannot be set too high. They come principally from the south-eastern counties, and therefore from that part of the country favourably placed for provisioning London's burgeoning market and also the market across the Channel to which access was opened up by England's capture of Calais.[70]

[69] Miller, 'War, taxation and the English economy in the late thirteenth and early fourteenth centuries', p. 26.
[70] Mate, 'The agrarian economy of south-east England before the Black Death', pp. 104–7; statistical appendix to Farmer, 'Prices and wages', in *AHEW*, II, pp. 787–810; Mayhew, 'Money and prices in England from Henry II to Edward III', pp. 128–9.

4.   CRISIS OR EQUILIBRIUM?

What the outcome of the situation developing in the late 1340s might have been, had it been allowed to work itself out in its own way, is something we simply cannot determine, for at the end of 1348 its context was transformed by the coming of plague. For that reason, any final judgement upon the medieval economy at the stage it had reached in the early fourteenth century is not something which can be based on certainties. This is a matter which has been much discussed in recent years.[71] In the view of some commentators, well before 1349 England was already in the grip of a long-term crisis which was to dominate the later middle ages. Its background, it is argued, was increasing over-population, shrinking agricultural productivity in a countryside which had been and was being over-exploited, and deepening peasant poverty which had grown worse as peasant numbers had risen and as a consequence of the toll levied by landlords upon poor men's productive efforts. These conditions were merely confirmed by the unwillingness of landlords, the one class with the resources to do so, to undertake agricultural investment on anything like an adequate scale. These influences in combination not only set limits to the general development of the economy, well before 1349 they had also checked and finally reversed the long-term growth of England's population. In this respect the agrarian crisis of 1315–22, with its succession of bad harvests and livestock mortalities, marked the point at which long-term economic contraction took over from long-term economic expansion.

As we have seen, however, this view of an early fourteenth-century crisis raises many difficulties. In the first place, the demographic information available to us makes it difficult to give a categorical answer to the question whether the centuries-long growth of population had been checked, and if so how decisively, before 1349. Scrutiny of what evidence there is seems to point to some places where the number of inhabitants may already have been falling in 1300 and continued to do so, to others where numbers continued to rise despite interruption during the famine years in 1315–17, and yet others again where their population may have reached something of a plateau at around this time. Not all the evidence upon which these views are based is beyond questioning, and in any case there is no

---

[71] Interpretations of England's economy in the late middle ages are discussed by N. Hybel, *Crisis and Change: the Concept of Crisis in the light of Agrarian Structural Reorganization in Late Medieval England* (pp. 256–76 for the early fourteenth century).

426

way of striking a balance between the different demographic experiences of different places. If we do seek to establish a national aggregate, one implication of the conflicting indications may be that, apart from the crisis mortality of 1315–17, the size of the movement of England's population level during the first half of the fourteenth-century was not very substantial. In that event the behaviour of population may have resembled that in the second half of the seventeenth century when, after a century and more of rapid growth, it meandered gently upwards and downwards for more than fifty years. On this question, as on so many others, much work remains to be done.

What is clear, however, is that, whether or not population during the first half of the fourteenth century fell somewhat from its level in *c.* 1300, it remained large by the standards of pre-industrial times. The demand for land in villages, in consequence, continued to be high and peasant tenants remained acutely vulnerable to fluctuations in harvest yields and in agricultural prices. In the face of that vulnerability, too, they were easily tempted into raising the wind by selling plots of land, a course which favoured the break-up of tenements and the formation of more and more uneconomic holdings. We have already encountered the 'impoverished smallholders' of the densely settled villages in north-east Norfolk, but even in regions where there was far more scope for colonization, like the far South-West of England, the splintering of holdings can be observed.[72] Yet, after the shock waves caused by the harvest failures and livestock epidemics in the period 1315–22 had subsided, the ability of smallholders to survive was at least as striking as their poverty, and even in the crowded villages of Norfolk 'no major subsistence crisis ever materialized'.[73]

One of the reasons for this was the fact that there were favourable as well as adverse influences at work in the 1330s and 1340s. Some land had passed, and continued to pass, from seignorial demesnes into the hands of the peasantry, countering in some measure the tendency for the average amount of land available per head to fall as population had increased; and some peasants, too, as well as some landlords were learning to use what land they had more productively. There are also some signs of increased industrial activity, a

[72] Campbell, 'Population pressure, inheritance and the land market in a fourteenth-century peasant community', pp. 102–7; J. Hatcher, *Rural Economy and Society in the Duchy of Cornwall*, pp. 99–100.
[73] Campbell, 'Population pressure, inheritance and the land market in a fourteenth-century peasant community', p. 107.

good deal of it in country places. English cloth workers, sheltered by the heavy duties on exports of English wool on which their foreign competitors relied, were capturing some parts of the home market from foreign importers and exporting a small, but still growing amount of English cloth. The production of tin, too, rose strongly to new peaks; and in parts of the West Riding of Yorkshire, for example, the activities of small-scale coal miners and iron smelters (as well as of textile workers) crop up with great frequency in the manor court rolls. English merchants, furthermore, were successful in securing for themselves a growing share of England's trade, fitting them for the first time for the role of bankers to the crown, capable of financing a major war. That role, of course, involved a diversion of much commercial capital often into non-economic purposes, but the fact that they were able to undertake it is one measure of the advances which had been made by the English merchant class by the mid-fourteenth century.

At the same time, whether the promising ingredients of the economy prior to the Black Death were potentially strong enough both to resolve the numerous short-term problems afflicting Edward III's England, and to relieve the stresses arising from the adverse ratio between land and people, must be open to doubt, particularly given existing levels of technology and the existing structure of society. The overwhelming majority continued to be villagers, and because as yet export industries had not developed far, rural poverty meant that employment prospects that would offer alternatives to those in agriculture were severely restricted. The poorer peasantry had little to spend on manufactured goods or non-essentials, and the number of more substantial peasant farmers disposing of considerable purchasing power was very low compared with later times. The fall in the price of food in the 1330s and 1340s, moreover, while it made easier the lives of the landless and cottagers, also had the effect of reducing the incomes of those villagers with produce to sell; and low producer prices combined with other adverse influences to depress the cash surpluses, and hence the purchasing power, of owners of estates.[74] It may likewise be no coincidence that there are some signs of the movement of urban expansion, which had been so marked a feature of the twelfth and thirteenth centuries, reaching its term about this time.

[74] R.H. Hilton, 'A crisis of feudalism', in T.H. Aston and C.H.E. Philpin, eds, *The Brenner Debate: Agrarian Class Structure and Economic Development in Pre-Industrial Europe*, pp. 129–30.

Many of these things were probably regarded by contemporaries as no more than the inevitable imperfections of the human condition; but some grievances were recognized for what they were and there was no hesitation in attributing responsibility for them. It was recognized that an inadequate money supply pushed down producer prices, that fiscal policies imposed unheard-of burdens on the poor, that the king's foreign policies diverted too much of the nation's resources into supporting war and diplomacy, channelled wool and grain into state trading ventures or army supply rather than the market, and sterilized a good deal of the commercial capital which merchants had been accumulating. Such things generated strongly felt grievances at the time; and, if the complainants made the most of them, this is not to say that they were imaginary.

What the eventual outcome of this mix of enduring deficiencies, temporary adversities and promising new developments, left to itself, might have been for England's economy and society in the longer term is a question which cannot be answered. The fact is that the mix as it was in the early decades of Edward III's reign was not allowed to work itself out. In late 1348 the most deadly pestilence in recorded history reached England's shores, having scythed westwards and northwards across Europe from the east, leaving devastation in its wake. The coming of plague had consequences of a different order from those attending the famine years of the second decade of the fourteenth century. The Black Death of 1348–49 affected the whole of the country, and it was much more lethal than anything previously experienced, for estimates of the death rate it occasioned range up to 45 per cent. Furthermore, the plague of 1348–49 was not an isolated incident: it was followed by successive waves of epidemics, which were more or less general, more or less lethal, and doubtless of a variety of sorts. Their cumulative effect, however, was that, before the fifteenth century closed, England's population had been reduced to a level little, if at all, above what it had been when Domesday Book was compiled, and perhaps only a third of what it had been at its peak in *c.* 1300. Demographic attrition on so massive a scale inevitably had social and economic consequences of the first importance. It is for this reason that the coming of plague marked a turning point in a way that the famine years earlier in the century did not.

Select Bibliography

The list of books and articles which follows is not intended as a comprehensive bibliography of the subjects discussed in this book or even to include every work to which we have made reference. The object is to provide an indication of some of the further reading which students might find helpful and details of those works we have cited most frequently or which are especially important for the topics with which they are concerned. For a more comprehensive and systematic bibliography, see C. Gross, *A Bibliography of English History to 1485*, ed. E.B. Graves, Oxford, 1975; and since that volume was compiled *The Economic History Review* provides annual lists of publications on economic and social history. In the lists which follow the place of publication is London unless it is stated to be elsewhere. The bibliography is divided up as follows:

1.   PRINTED PRIMARY SOURCES

1.   Public records etc.
2.   Chronicles, biographies and literary sources
3.   Estate records, accounts and court rolls
4.   Town records
5.   Records of commerce
6.   Legal treatises and legal records

2. SECONDARY WORKS

1. General and regional studies of medieval society and the medieval economy
2. Domesday England and its background
3. Population and the distribution of wealth
4. Agriculture and its markets
5. Industry and manufacture
6. Internal trade
7. Overseas trade
8. Towns and townsfolk
9. Money and money supply
10. The English economy and society on the eve of the Black Death

1. PRINTED PRIMARY SOURCES

(a) Public records etc.

Brown, W., ed., *Yorkshire Lay Subsidy, being a Ninth collected in 25 Edward I, 1297.* YAS Rec. Ser., XVI (1894).

Calendar of Chancery Rolls, Various. 1912.

Calendar of Chancery Warrants. 1927.

Calendar of Charter Rolls. 6 vols, 1903-27.

Calendar of Close Rolls, 1272–1485. 45 vols, 1892–1954.

Calendar of Documents relating to Scotland, 1108–1509, ed. J. Bain, 4 vols, Edinburgh, 1881–88.

Calendars of Inquisitions, Miscellaneous, Henry III– . 1916– ,in progress.

Calendar of Liberate Rolls, 1226–72. 6 vols, 1917–64.

Calendar of Patent Rolls, 1232–1509. 52 vols, 1891–1916.

Calendar of State Papers (Venetian), I. 1864.

Catalogue of Ancient Deeds in the Public Record Office. 6 vols, 1890–1915.

Close Rolls, 1227–72. 14 vols, 1902–38.

Crowley, D.A., ed., *The Wiltshire Tax List of 1332.* Wilts. Rec. Soc., XLV (1989).

Curia Regis Rolls preserved in the PRO. 1922– , in progress.

Davis, H.W.C. *et al.,* eds, *Regesta Regum Anglo-Normannorum,* 1066–1154. 3 vols. I, 1066–1100, ed. H.W.C. Davis; II, 1100–35, eds C. Johnson and H.A. Cronne; III, 1134–54, eds H.A. Cronne and R.H.C. Davis. Oxford, 1913–68.

Delisle, L. and Berger, E., *Recueil des actes de Henri II concernant les provinces Françaises et les affaires de France.* 3 vols, Paris, 1916–27.

Douglas, D.C., general ed., *English Historical Documents.* I, *c.* 500–1042, ed. D. Whitelock; II, 1042–1189, ed. D.C. Douglas and G.W. Greenaway; III, 1189–1327, ed. H. Rothwell; IV, 1327–1485, ed. A.R. Myers. 1953–75.

Farley, A., ed., *Domesday Book seu Liber Censualis.* 2 vols, 1783. Text, with facing translation, now available in 40 county vols, general ed. J. Morris, Chichester, 1975–86.

Farrer, W., ed., *Lancashire Inquests, Extents and Feudal Aids.* 3 vols, Lancs. and Cheshire Rec. Soc., XLVIII, LIV, LXX (1903–15).

Finberg, H.P.R., ed., *The Early Charters of the West Midlands.* Leicester, 1961.

Finberg, H.P.R., ed., *The Early Charters of Wessex.* Leicester, 1964.

Foster, C.W. and Longley, T., eds, *The Lincolnshire Domesday and the Lindsey Survey.* Lincoln Rec. Soc., XIX (1924).

Fraser, C.M., ed., *The Northumberland Lay Subsidy Roll of 1296.* Society of Antiquaries of Newcastle upon Tyne, Rec. Ser., I (1968).

Gaydon, A.T., ed., *The Taxation of 1297: a translation of the Local Rolls of Assessment.* Beds. Historical Rec. Soc., XXXIX (1959).

Glasscock, R.E., ed., *The Lay Subsidy of 1334.* BARSEH, NS. II (1975).

Gough, H., ed., *Scotland in 1298: Documents relating to the Campaign of King Edward the First in that Year.* Paisley, 1888.

Hardy, T.D., ed., *Rotuli Litterarum Clausarum in Turri Londinensi Asservati.* 2 vols, Rec. Comm., 1833–44.

Hardy, T.D., ed., *Rotuli Litterarum Patentium in Turri Londinensi Asservati, 1201–1216.* Rec. Comm., 1835.

Hardy, T.D., ed., *Rotuli de Liberate, Misis et Praestitis, regnante Johanne.* Rec. Comm., 1844.

Harmer, F.E., ed., *Anglo-Saxon Writs.* Manchester, 1952.

Hervey, S.H.A., ed., *Suffolk in 1327: being a Subsidy Return.* Suffolk Green Books, no. IX. Woodbridge, 1906.

Illingworth, W. and Caley, J., eds, *Rotuli Hundredorum.* 2 vols, Rec. Comm., 1812–18.

Illingworth, W. and Caley, J., eds, *Placita de Quo Warranto.* Rec. Comm., 1818.

Palgrave, F., ed., *Parliamentary Writs and Writs of Military Summons.* 4 vols, Rec. Comm., 1827–34.

Patent Rolls, 1216–32. 2 vols, 1901–3.

Pipe Rolls. Pubns. of the Pipe Roll Soc., 1884–   , in progress.

Powell, E., *A Suffolk Hundred in the Year 1283.* Cambridge, 1910.

Pronay, N. and Taylor, J., eds, *Parliamentary Texts of the Later Middle Ages*. Oxford, 1980.

Raftis, J.A. and Horgan, M.P., eds, *Early Huntingdonshire Lay Subsidy Rolls*. Pontifical Institute of Medieval Studies, Toronto, 1976.

Reports from the Lords' Committees . . . for all Matters touching the Dignity of a Peer. 5 vols, 1820–29.

Richardson, H.G. and Sayles, G.O., eds, *Rotuli Parliamentorum Anglie hactenus Inediti*. Camden 3rd ser. LI (1935).

Robertson, A.J., ed., *Anglo-Saxon Charters*. Cambridge, 1939.

Rotuli Parliamentorum. 6 vols, 1783.

Stephenson, C. and Marcham, F.G., eds, *Sources of English Constitutional History*. New York, 1937.

Stubbs, W., ed., *Select Charters and other Illustrations of English Constitutional History from the Earliest Times to the Reign of Edward I*. 9th edn, revised by H.W.C. Davis. Oxford, 1929.

Twiss, T., ed., *Black Book of the Admiralty*. 4 vols, Rolls Ser., 1871–76.

Whitelock, D., ed., *Anglo-Saxon Wills*. Cambridge, 1930.

(b)   Chronicles, biographies and literary sources

Appleby, J.T., ed., *Chronicle of Richard of Devizes*. Med. Texts, 1963.

Arnold, T., ed., *Henry of Huntingdon, Historia Anglorum*. Rolls Ser., 1879.

Bond, E.A., ed., *Chronica Monasterii de Melsa, ab anno 1150 usque ad annum 1506*. 3 vols, Rolls Ser., 1866–68.

Butler, H.E., ed., *Chronicle of Jocelin of Brakelond*. Med. Texts, 1949.

Chibnall, M., ed., *The Ecclesiastical History of Orderic Vitalis*. 6 vols, Med. Texts, 1968–80.

Garmonsway, G.N., trans., *The Anglo-Saxon Chronicle*. 1953.

Hamilton, N.E.S.A., ed., *William of Malmesbury, De Gestis Pontificum Anglorum*. Rolls Ser., 1870.

Luard, H.R., ed., *Annales Monastici*. 5 vols, Rolls Ser., 1864–69.

Luard, H.R., ed., *Matthew Paris, Chronica Majora*. 7 vols, Rolls Ser., 1872–84.

Luard, H.R., ed., *Flores Historiarum*. 3 vols, Rolls Ser., 1890.

Potter, K.R., ed., *Gesta Stephani*. Med. Texts, 1955.

Riley, H.T., ed., *Gesta Abbatum S. Albani*. 3 vols, Rolls Ser., 1867–69.

Rothwell, H., ed., *The Chronicle of Walter of Guisborough*. Camden 3rd ser. LXXXIX (1957).

Searle, E., ed., *The Chronicle of Battle Abbey*. Med. Texts, 1980.

Skeat, W.W., ed., *William Langland, The Vision of William concerning Piers the Plowman*. Oxford, 1869.

Stubbs, W., ed., *Chronicles of the Reigns of Edward I and Edward II.* 2 vols, Rolls Ser., 1882–83.

(c)   Estate records, accounts and court rolls

Amphlett, J. and Hamilton, S.G., eds, *Court Rolls of the Manor of Hales, 1270–1307,* 2 vols, Worcs. Hist. Soc., 1910–12.

Atkinson, J.C., ed., *Cartularium Abbathiae de Rievalle.* Surtees Soc., LXXXIII (1889).

Ault, W.O., ed., *Court Rolls of the Abbey of Ramsey and the Honour of Clare.* Yale Historical Pubns., IX. New Haven, 1928.

Austin, D., ed., *Boldon Book: Northumberland and Durham.* Chichester, 1982.

Ballard, A., ed., *An Eleventh-Century Inquisition from St Augustine's, Canterbury.* BARSEH, IV (1920).

Bannister, A.T., ed., 'A transcript of the Red Book, a detailed account of the Hereford bishopric estates in the thirteenth century', *Camden Miscellany,* XV. Camden 3rd ser. XLI (1929).

Blackley, F.D. and Hermansen, G., eds, *The Household Book of Queen Isabella of England for the fifth Regnal Year of Edward II, 8 July 1311 to 7 July 1312.* University. of Alberta Classical and Historical Studies, I, Edmonton, 1971.

Blake, E.O., ed., *Liber Eliensis.* Camden 3rd ser. XCII (1962).

Bridgeman, C.G.O., ed., *The Burton abbey twelfth-century surveys,* William Salt Arch. Soc. Collections, 3rd ser. XLI (1916).

Brown, W., ed., *Cartularium Prioratus de Gyseburne.* 2 vols, Surtees Soc. LXXXVI and LXXXIX (1889–94).

Chapman, F.R., ed., *Sacrist Rolls of Ely (1291–1360).* 2 vols, Cambridge, 1907.

Chibnall, M., ed., *Select Documents of the English Lands of the Abbey of Bec.* Camden 3rd ser. LXXIII (1951).

Chibnall, M., ed., *Charters and Custumals of the Abbey of Holy Trinity, Caen.* BARSEH, NS V (1982).

Chibnall, M., ed., 'Computus rolls of the English lands of the abbey of Bec (1272–1289)', *Camden Miscellany,* XXIX. Camden 4th ser. XXXIV (1987).

Clark, J.W., ed., *Ecclesie de Bernewelle Liber Memorandorum.* Cambridge, 1907.

Colvin, H.M., ed., *Building Accounts of Henry III.* Oxford, 1971.

Davis, R.H.C., ed., *Kalendar of Abbot Samson of Bury St Edmunds and related Documents.* Camden 3rd ser. LXXXIV (1954).

Douglas, D.C., ed., *Feudal Documents from the Abbey of Bury St Edmunds.* BARSEH, VIII (1932).

Douglas, D.C., ed., *The Domesday Monachorum of Christ Church, Canterbury.* 1944.

Erskine, A.M., ed., *Accounts of the Fabric of Exeter Cathedral, 1279–1353.* 2 vols, Devon and Cornwall Rec. Soc., NS XXIV, XXVI (1981–83).

Farr, M.W., ed., *Accounts and Surveys of the Wiltshire Lands of Adam de Stratton.* Wilts. Rec. Ser., XIV (1959).

Farrer, W. and Clay, C. T., eds, *Early Yorkshire Charters.* 12 vols, YAS Rec. Soc., Extra Ser., 1914–65.

Foster, C.W. and Major, K., eds, *Registrum Antiquissimum of the Cathedral Church of Lincoln.* 10 vols, Lincoln Record. Soc., 1931–73.

Fowler, J.T., ed., *Chartularium Abbathiae de Novo Monasterio.* Surtees Soc., LXVI (1878).

Fowler, J.T., ed., *Account Rolls of the Abbey of Durham.* 3 vols, Surtees Soc., XCIX–C, CIII (1898–1901).

Greenway, D.E., ed., *Charters of the Honour of Mowbray, 1107–91.* BARSEH, NS I (1972).

Greenwell, W., ed., *Boldon Book: a Survey of the Possessions of the See of Durham . . . in the year 1183.* Surtees Soc., XXV (1852).

Habberjam, M., O'Regan, M. and Hale, B., eds, *Court Rolls of the Manor of Wakefield, 1350–1352.* YAS Wakefield Court Rolls Ser., VI (1987).

Hall, H., ed., *Pipe Roll of the Bishopric of Winchester . . . 1208–9.* 1903.

Harper-Bill, C. and Mortimer, R., eds, *Stoke-by-Clare Cartulary.* 3 vols, Suffolk Rec. Soc., IV–VI (1982–84).

Hart, W.H. and Lyons, P.A., eds, *Cartularium Monasterii de Rameseia.* 3 vols, Rolls Ser., 1884–94.

Harvey, B.F., ed., *Documents illustrating the Rule of Walter de Wenlok, Abbot of Westminster, 1283–1307.* Camden 4th ser. II (1965).

Harvey, P.D.A., ed., *Manorial Records of Cuxham, Oxfordshire, c. 1200–1359.* Hist. Mss. Comm., JP 23 (1976).

Hassall, W.O., ed., *Cartulary of St Mary Clerkenwell.* Camden 3rd ser., LXXI (1949).

Hockey, S.F., ed., *The Account Book of Beaulieu Abbey.* Camden 4th ser. XVI (1975).

Holt, N.R., ed., *The Pipe Roll of the Bishopric of Winchester, 1210–1211.* Manchester, 1964.

Jewell, H.M., ed., *Court Rolls of the Manor of Wakefield, September 1348 to September 1350.* YAS Wakefield Court Roll Ser., II (1981).

Lancaster, W.T. and Baildon, W.P., eds, *Coucher Book of the Cistercian Abbey of Kirkstall.* Thoresby Soc., VIII (1904).

Lees, B.A., ed., *Records of the Templars in England in the Twelfth Century.* BARSEH, IX (1935).

Lister, J., ed., *Court Rolls of the Manor of Wakefield*, III–IV (1313–17). YAS Rec. Ser., LVII (1917), LXXVIII (1930).

Maitland, F.W. and Baildon, W.P., eds, *The Court Baron.* Selden Soc., IV (1891).

Midgley, L.M., ed., *Ministers' Accounts of the Earldom of Cornwall, 1296–1297.* 2 vols, Camden 3rd ser. LXVI (1942), LXVIII (1945).

Oschinsky, D., ed., *Walter of Henley and other Treatises on Estate Management and Accounting.* Oxford, 1971.

Patterson, R.B., ed., *Earldom of Gloucester Charters: the Charters and Scribes of the Earls and Countesses of Gloucester to A.D. 1217.* Oxford, 1973.

Pugh, R.B., ed., *Court Rolls of the Wiltshire Manors of Adam de Stratton.* Wilts. Rec. Ser., XXIV (1970).

Raine, J., ed., *Historiae Dunelmensis Scriptores Tres.* Surtees Soc., IX (1839).

Ransford, R., ed., *The Early Charters of the Augustinian Canons of Waltham Abbey, Essex, 1062–1230.* Woodbridge, 1989.

Ross, C.D., ed., *Cartulary of Cirencester Abbey.* 2 vols, Oxford, 1964.

Salter, H.E., ed., *Eynsham Cartulary.* 2 vols, Oxford Hist. Soc., XLIX (1907), LI (1908).

Salter, H.E., ed., *Cartulary of Oseney Abbey.* 6 vols, Oxford Hist. Soc., LXXXIX–XCI, XCVII–VIII, CI (1928–36).

Saltman, A., ed., *Cartulary of Tutbury Priory.* Hist. Mss. Comm., JP 2, 1962.

Searle, E. and Ross, B., eds, *The Cellarers' Rolls of Battle Abbey, 1275–1513.* Sussex Rec. Soc., LXV (1967).

Stenton, F.M., ed., *Documents illustrative of the Social and Economic History of the Danelaw.* BARSEH, V (1920).

Stevenson, J., ed., *Chronicon Monasterii de Abingdon.* 2 vols, Roll Ser., 1858.

Walker, S.S., ed., *Court Rolls of the Manor of Wakefield, 1331–3.* YAS Wakefield Court Rolls Ser., III (1983).

(d)   Town records

Ballard, A., ed., *British Borough Charters, 1042–1216.* Cambridge, 1913.

Ballard, A. and Tait, J., eds, *British Borough Charters, 1216–1307.* Cambridge, 1923.

Bateson, M., ed., *Records of the Borough of Leicester.* 3 vols, 1899–1905.

Bateson, M., 'A London municipal collection of the reign of John', *EHR*, XVII (1902).

Bateson, M., ed., *Cambridge Gild Records*. Cambridge Antiquarian Soc., Octavo Ser., XXXIX (1903).

Bateson, M., ed., *Borough Customs*. 2 vols, Selden Soc., XVIII (1904), XXI (1906).

Bickley, F.B., ed., *The Little Red Book of Bristol*. 2 vols, Bristol, 1900.

Chew, H.M. and Kellaway, W., eds, *The London Assize of Nuisance, 1301–1431*. London Rec. Soc., X (1973).

Collins, F., ed., *Register of the Freemen of the City of York*. 2 vols, Surtees Soc., XCVI (1897), CII (1900).

Cooper, C.H., *Annals of Cambridge*. 4 vols, Cambridge, 1832–42.

Dobson, R.B., ed., *York City Chamberlains' Account Rolls, 1396–1500*. Surtees Soc., CXCII (1980).

Drinkwater, C.H., 'The merchants' gild of Shrewsbury', *Trans. Shropshire Arch. and NH Soc.*, 2nd ser. II (1890), VIII (1896) XII(1900); 3rd ser. I–III (1901–3).

Ekwall, E., *Two Early London Subsidy Rolls (for 1292 and 1319)*. 1951.

Fuller, E.A., 'The tallage of 6 Edward II and the Bristol rebellion', *Trans. Bristol and Glos. Arch. Soc.*, XIX (1894–95).

Furley, J.S., ed., *Ancient Usages of the City of Winchester*. Oxford, 1927.

Graham, R., 'A description of Oxford from the hundred rolls of Oxfordshire, A.D. 1279', *Oxford Hist. Soc. Collectanea*, IV. Oxford Hist. Soc., XLVII (1905).

Gretton, R.H., *The Burford Records: a Study in Minor Town Government*. Oxford, 1920.

Harding, N.D., ed., *Bristol Charters, 1155–1373*. Bristol Rec. Soc., I (1930).

Hartopp, H., ed., *Register of the Freemen of Leicester, 1196–1770*. Leicester, 1927.

Hopkins, A.W., ed., *Select Rolls of the Chester City Court: late thirteenth and early fourteenth Centuries*. Chetham Soc., 3rd ser. II (1950).

Horrox, R., ed., *Select Rentals and Accounts of Medieval Hull, 1293–1528*. YAS Rec. Ser., CXLI (1981).

Hudson, W., ed., *Leet Jurisdiction in Norwich during the thirteenth and fourteenth Centuries*. Selden Soc., V (1892).

Hudson, W. and Tingey, J.C., eds, *Records of the City of Norwich*. 2 vols, 1910.

Ingleby, H., ed., *Red Register of King's Lynn*. 2 vols, King's Lynn, 1919–22.

Jeayes, I.H., ed., *Court Rolls of the Borough of Colchester*, I (1310–1352). Colchester, 1921.

Leach, A.F., ed., *Beverley Town Documents*. Selden Soc., XIV (1900).

Leggett, J.I., 'The 1377 poll tax for the city of York', *YAJ*, XLIII (1971).

Le Patourel, J., ed., *Documents relating to the Manor and Borough of Leeds, 1066–1400*. Thoresby Soc., XLV (1957).

Maitland, F.W. and Bateson, M., eds, *Cambridge Borough Charters (Henry I–1685)*. Cambridge, 1901.

Markham, C.A. and Cox, J.C., eds, *Records of the Borough of Northampton*. 2 vols, Northampton, 1898.

Owen, D.M., ed., *The Making of King's Lynn: a Documentary History*. BARSEH, NS IX (1984).

Powell, E., 'The taxation of Ipswich for the Welsh War of 1282', *Proc. Suffolk Institute of Archaeology*, XII (1906).

Prestwich, M., *York Civic Ordinances, 1301*. Borthwick Papers, XLIX, York, 1976.

Riley, H.T., ed., *Liber Custumarum*, vol. II (in two parts) of Riley, ed., *Munimenta Gildhallae Londoniensis*, Rolls Ser., 1860.

Riley, H.T., ed., *Chronicles of Old London*, 1863.

Riley, H.T., trans. and ed., *Memorials of London and London Life in the XIIIth, XIVth and XVth Centuries*, 1868.

Rogers, J.E. Thorold, ed., *Oxford City Documents, Financial and Judicial, 1268–1665*. Oxford Hist. Soc., XVIII (1891).

Rowe, M.M. and Jackson, A.M., eds, *Exeter Freemen, 1266–1967*. Devon and Cornwall Rec. Soc., extra ser., I (1973).

Salter, H.E., ed., *Medieval Archives of the University of Oxford*. 2 vols., Oxford Hist. Soc., LXX and LXXIII (1920–21).

Sellars, M., ed., *York Memorandum Book*. 2 vols, Surtees Soc, CXX, CXXV (1912–15).

Sharpe, R.R., ed., *Cal. of Wills proved and enrolled in the Court of Husting, London, 1258–1688*. 2 vols, 1889–90.

Sharpe, R.R., ed., *Cal. of Letter Books of the City of London (A–L)*. 11 vols, 1889–1912.

Stevenson, W.H., ed., *Records of the Borough of Nottingham: Extracts from the Archives of the Corporation (1155–1702)*. 5 vols, 1882–1900.

Stevenson, W.H., ed., *Cal. of the Records of the Corporation of Gloucester*. Gloucester, 1893.

Studer, P., ed., *The Oak Book of Southampton*. 3 vols, Southampton Rec. Soc., 1910–11.

Thomas, A.H., ed., *Cal. of Early Mayor's Court Rolls preserved among the Archives of the City of London . . .. 1298–1307*. Cambridge, 1924.

Thomas, A.H., ed., *Cal. of Plea and Memoranda Rolls preserved among the Archives of the Corporation of the City of London at the Guildhall*, vols I–IV. Cambridge, 1926–43.

Toulmin Smith, L., ed., *English Gilds: the Original Ordinances of more than one hundred Early English Gilds.* Early English Text Soc., 1870.

Varley, J., ed., *A Middlewich Chartulary.* 2 vols, Chetham Soc., CV, CVIII (1941–44).

(e)   *Records of commerce*

Carus-Wilson, E.M., ed., *The Overseas Trade of Bristol in the Later Middle Ages.* Bristol Rec. Soc., VII (1937).

Carus-Wilson, E.M. and Coleman, O., *England's Export Trade, 1275–1547.* Oxford, 1963.

Davies, J.C., 'The wool customs accounts for Newcastle upon Tyne for the reign of Edward I', *AA*, 4th ser. XXXII (1954).

Gras, N.S.B., *The Early English Customs System.* Harvard Economic Studies, XVIII. Cambridge, Mass., 1918.

Höhlbaum, M. *et al.,* eds, *Hansisches Urkundenbuch.* 10 vols, Halle, 1876–1907.

Kunze, K., ed., *Hanseakten aus England, 1275–1412.* Halle, 1891.

Lopez, R.S. and Raymond, I.W., eds, *Medieval Trade in the Mediterranean World.* New York, 1955.

(f)   *Legal records and treatises*

Cam. H.M., ed., *The Eyre of London, 14 Edward II, A.D. 1321.* Selden Soc., LXXXV–VI (1968–69).

Chew, H.M. and Weinbaum, M., eds, *The London Eyre of 1244.* London Rec. Soc., VI (1970).

Clanchy, M.T., ed., *Civil Pleas of the Wiltshire Eyre, 1249.* Wilts. Rec. Soc., XXVI (1971).

Clanchy, M.T., ed., *The Roll and Writ File of the Berkshire Eyre of 1248.* Selden Soc., XC (1973).

Flower, C.T., ed., *Public Works in Medieval Law.* 2 vols, Selden Soc., XXXI (1915), XL (1925).

Hall, G.D.G, ed., *Tractatus de Legibus et Consuetudinibus Regni Anglie qui Glanvill vocatur.* Med. Texts, 1965.

Harding, A., ed., *The Roll of the Shropshire Eyre of 1256.* Selden Soc., XCVI (1981).

Hunnisett, R.F., ed., *Bedfordshire Coroners' Rolls.* Beds. Hist. Rec. Soc., XLI (1961).

Meekings, C.A.F., ed., *Crown Pleas of the Wiltshire Eyre, 1249.* Wilts, Rec. Soc., XVI (1961).

Page, W., ed., *Three early Assize Rolls for the County of Northumberland.* Surtees Soc., LXXXVIII (1891).

Robertson, A.J., ed., *Laws of the Kings of England from Edmund to Henry I.* Cambridge, 1925.

Summerson, H., ed., *Crown Pleas of the Devon Eyre of 1238.* Devon and Cornwall Rec. Soc., NS XXVIII (1985).

Thomson, W.S., ed., *A Lincolnshire Assize Roll for 1298.* Lincs. Rec. Soc., XXXVI (1944).

Thorne, S.E., ed., *Bracton de Legibus et Consuetudinibus Angliae*, vols I–IV. Cambridge, Mass., 1968–77.

van Caenegem, R.C., ed., *English Lawsuits from William I to Richard I.* 2 vols, Selden Soc., CVI–VII (1990–91).

2.   SECONDARY WORKS

(a)   General and regional studies of medieval English society and the medieval economy

Ashley, W.J., *An Introduction to English Economic History and Theory.* 2nd edn, 2 vols, 1892–93.

Aston, T.H., ed., *Landlords, Peasants and Politics in Medieval England.* Cambridge, 1987.

Bailey, M., 'The concept of the margin in the medieval English economy', *EcHR*, 2nd ser. XLII (1989).

Bateson, E., Hinds, A. B., Hodgson, J. C., Craster, H. H. E., Vickers, K. H. and Dodds, M. H., eds, *A History of Northumberland.* 15 vols, Newcastle upon Tyne, 1893–1940.

Beresford, M.W. and St Joseph, J.K.S., *Medieval England: an Aerial Survey.* Cambridge, 2nd edn, 1979.

Bolton, J.L., *The Medieval English Economy, 1150–1500.* 1980.

Bridbury, A.R., *The English Economy from Bede to the Reformation.* Woodbridge, 1992.

Britnell, R.H., 'England and Northern Italy in the early fourteenth century: the economic contrasts', *TRHS*, 5th ser. XXXIX (1989).

Britnell, R.H., *The Commercialisation of English Society, 1100–1500.* Cambridge, 1993.

Cam. H.M., *Liberties and Communities in Medieval England: Collected Studies in Local Administration and Topography.* Cambridge, 1944.

Carus-Wilson, E.M., *Medieval Merchant Venturers.* 2nd edn, 1967.

Carus-Wilson, E.M., ed., *Essays in Economic History*, vols I–II (1954–62).

Chibnall, M., *Anglo-Norman England, 1066–1166.* Oxford, 1986.

Cunningham, W., *Growth of English Industry and Commerce,* I. 5th edn, Cambridge, 1915.

Darby, H.C., ed., *A New Historical Geography of England.* Cambridge, 1973.

Dyer, C.C., *Standards of Living in the Later Middle Ages: Social Change in England, c. 1200–1520.* Cambridge, 1989.

Dyer, C.C., 'The consumer and the market in the later middle ages', *EcHR,* 2nd ser. XLII (1989).

Faull, M.L. and Moorhouse, S.A., eds, *West Yorkshire: an Archaeological Survey to A.D. 1500.* 4 vols, West Yorkshire County Council: Wakefield, 1981.

Fieldhouse, R. and Jennings, B., *A History of Richmond and Swaledale.* Chichester, 1978.

Finberg, H.P.R., *Gloucestershire Studies.* Leicester, 1958.

Finberg, H.P.R. and Thirsk, J., general eds, *Agrarian History of England and Wales.* I(ii), A.D. 43–1042, ed. H.P.R. Finberg; II, 1042–1350, ed. H.E. Hallam; III, 1348–1500, ed. E. Miller; IV, 1500–1640 ed. J. Thirsk. Cambridge, 1967–91.

Fryde, E.B., *Studies in Medieval Trade and Finance.* 1983.

Fryde, E.B. and Miller, E., eds, *Historical Studies of the English Parliament.* 2 vols, Cambridge, 1970.

Hatcher, J., *Rural Economy and Society in the Duchy of Cornwall, 1300–1500.* Cambridge, 1970.

Hewitt, H.J., *Medieval Cheshire: an Economic and Social History of Cheshire in the Reigns of the Three Edwards.* Chetham Soc., NS LXXXVIII (1929).

Hewitt, H.J., *Cheshire under the Three Edwards.* Chester, 1967.

Hilton, R.H., *A Medieval Society: the West Midlands at the end of the Thirteenth Century.* 1966.

Hilton, R.H., *The English Peasantry in the Later Middle Ages.* Oxford, 1975.

Hilton, R.H., *Class Conflict and the Crisis of Feudalism: Essays in Medieval Social History.* 1985.

Hodgson, J., *A History of Northumberland.* 3 vols in 7 parts. Newcastle upon Tyne, 1820–58.

Hoskins, W.G., *Devon.* 1954.

Hybel, N., *Crisis or Change: the Concept of Crisis in the light of Agrarian Structural Reorganization in late Medieval England.* Aarhus, 1989.

Lipson, E., *Economic History of England.* I. Revised edn, 1945.

Painter, S., *Studies in the History of the English Feudal Barony.* Johns Hopkins University Studies, Baltimore, 1943.

Pollard, S., and Crossley, A.E., *The Wealth of England, 1085–1966.* 1968.

Pollock, F., and Maitland, F.W., *History of English Law before the time of Edward I.* 2nd edn, 2 vols, Cambridge, 1923.

Poole, A.L., *Obligations of Society in the Twelfth and Thirteenth Centuries.* Oxford, 1946.

Poole, A.L., *From Domesday Book to Magna Carta.* Oxford, 1955.

Poole, A.L., ed., *Medieval England.* Revised edn, 2 vols, Oxford, 1958.

Postan, M.M., *Medieval Economy and Society: an Economic History of Britain in the Middle Ages.* 1972.

Postan, M.M., *Essays on Medieval Agriculture and General Problems of the Medieval Economy.* Cambridge, 1973.

Postan, M.M., *Medieval Trade and Finance.* Cambridge, 1973.

Postan, M.M., ed., *Cambridge Economic History of Europe*, I, *The Agrarian Life of the Middle Ages.* 2nd edn, Cambridge, 1966.

Postan, M.M. and Miller, E., eds, *Cambridge Economic History of Europe*, II, *Trade and Industry in the Middle Ages.* 2nd edn, Cambridge, 1987.

Postan, M.M., Rich, E.E. and Miller, E., eds, *Cambridge Economic History of Europe*, III, *Economic Organization and Policies in the Middle Ages.* Cambridge, 1965.

Sawyer, P.H., ed., *Medieval Settlement: Continuity and Change.* 1976.

Smith, R.M., ed., *Land, Kinship and Life-Cycle.* Cambridge Studies in Population, Economy and Society in Past Time, I, Cambridge, 1984.

Steane, J., *The Northamptonshire Landscape.* 1974.

Stenton, D.M., *English Justice between the Norman Conquest and the Great Charter, 1066–1215.* American Philosophical Soc., Philadelphia, 1964.

Stenton, D.M., ed., *Preparatory to Anglo-Saxon England: being the Collected Papers of Frank Merry Stenton.* Oxford, 1970.

Tout, T.F., *The Place of the Reign of Edward II in English History.* 2nd edn, Manchester, 1936.

Victoria History of the Counties of England. In progress, 1900– .

Willard, J.F., *Parliamentary Taxes on Personal Property, 1290–1334: a Study in Medieval English Financial Administration.* Medieval Academy of America, Cambridge, Mass., 1934.

(b) Domesday England and its background

Addyman, P.V., 'Late Saxon settlements in the St Neots area', *PCAS*, LXIV (1973).

Barker, P., 'The origins of Worcester', *Trans. Worcs. Arch. Soc.*, 3rd ser. II (1968–69).

Barlow, F., *Edward the Confessor*. 1970.

Biddle, M., and Hill, D., 'Late Saxon planned towns', *Antiquaries Jnl.*, LI (1971).

Campbell, J., 'Observations on English government from the tenth to the twelfth centuries', *TRHS*, 5th ser. XXV (1975).

Carter, A., 'The Anglo-Saxon origins of Norwich', *Anglo-Saxon England*, VII (1978).

Carver, M.O.H., 'Early Shrewsbury: an archaeological definition', *Trans. Shropshire Arch. and NH Soc.*, LIX (1969–74).

Carver, M.O.H., ed., 'Medieval Worcester: an archaeological framework', *Trans. Worcs. Arch. Soc.*, 3rd ser. VII (1980).

Darby, H.C. *et al*, *The Domesday Geography of England*. 5 vols. (*Eastern England, Midland England, South-east England, Northern England*, and *South-west England*), Cambridge, 1952–67.

Darby, H.C., *Domesday England*. Cambridge, 1977.

Davidson, B.K., 'The late Saxon town of Thetford', *Med. Arch.*, XI (1967).

Doehaerd, R., *Le haut moyen âge occidental: économies et sociétés*, Paris, 1971.

Dolley, R.H.M., ed., *Anglo-Saxon Coins: Studies presented to F.M. Stenton on the occasion of his 80th Birthday*. 1961.

Dornier, A., ed., *Mercian Studies*. Leicester, 1977.

Ellis, H., *General Introduction to Domesday Book*. 2 vols, Rec. Comm., 1833.

Gillingham, J., 'Levels of danegeld and heregeld in the early eleventh century', *EHR*, CIV (1989) and cf. ibid., CV (1990).

Green, J.A., 'The last century of danegeld', *EHR*, XCVI (1981).

Grierson, P., 'England and Flanders before the Norman Conquest', *TRHS*, 4th ser. XXIII (1941).

Grierson, P., 'Commerce in the Dark Ages: a critique of the evidence', *TRHS*, 5th ser. IX (1959).

Grierson, P., 'The volume of Anglo-Saxon coinage', *EcHR*, 2nd ser. XX (1967).

Harvey, S.P.J., 'Domesday Book and Anglo-Norman governance', *TRHS*, 5th ser. XXV (1975).

Harvey, S.P.J., 'Recent Domesday Studies', *EHR*, XCV (1980).

Haslam, J., ed., *Anglo-Saxon Towns in Southern England*. Chichester, 1984.

Haslam, J., 'The development and topography of Saxon Cambridge', *PCAS*, LXXII (1984).

Hodges, R., *The Anglo-Saxon Achievement*. 1989.

Hodges, R. and Hobley, B., eds, *The Rebirth of Towns in the West, A.D. 700–1050*. CBA Research Report, no. 68 (1988).

Holdsworth, P., 'Saxon Southampton: a new review', *Med. Arch.*, XX (1976).

Holt, J.C., ed., *Domesday Studies*. Woodbridge, 1987.

Hooke, D., ed., *Anglo-Saxon Settlements*. Oxford, 1988.

Hurst, J.G., 'Saxo-Norman pottery in East Anglia', *PCAS*, XLIX (1956) and LI (1958).

Keen, L., '*Illa mercimonia que dicitur Hamwih*: a study in early medieval urban development', *Archaeologia Atlantica*, I (1975).

Latouche, R., *Les origines de l'économie occidentale (IVᵉ–XIᵉ siècle)*. Paris, 1956.

Lawson, M.K., 'Levels of taxation in the reigns of Æthelred II and Cnut', *EHR*, civ(1989) and cf. ibid., CV (1990).

Lewis, A.R., *The Northern Seas: Shipping and Commerce in Northern Europe, A.D. 300–1100*. Princeton, 1958.

Lopez, R.S., 'An aristocracy of money in the early middle ages', *Speculum*, XXVIII (1953).

Loyn, H.R., *Anglo-Saxon England and the Norman Conquest*. 2nd edn, 1991.

MacDonald, J. and Snooks, G.D., 'Were the tax assessments of Domesday England artificial? The case of Essex', *EcHR*, 2nd ser. XXXVIII (1985).

Maitland, F.W., *Domesday Book and Beyond*. Cambridge, 1921.

Metcalf, D.M., 'How large was the Anglo-Saxon currency?', *EcHR*, 2nd ser. XVIII (1965).

Nightingale, P., 'Some London moneyers and reflections on the organization of English mints in the eleventh century', *Numismatic Chronicle*, CXLII (1982).

Nightingale, P., 'The evolution of weight standards and the creation of new monetary and commercial links in northern Europe from the tenth century to the twelfth century', *EcHR*, 2nd ser. XXXVIII (1985).

Radley, J., 'Economic aspects of Anglo-Danish York', *Med. Arch.*, XV (1971).

Round, J.H., *Feudal England: Historical Studies on the XIth and XIIth centuries*. 1909.

Sawyer, P.H., 'The wealth of England in the eleventh century', *TRHS*, 5th ser. XV (1965).

Sawyer, P.H., *From Roman Britain to Norman England*. 1978.

Stenton, F.M., *Anglo-Saxon England*. 3rd edn, Oxford, 1971.

Vinogradoff, P., *English Society in the Eleventh Century*. Oxford, 1908.
Wilson, D.M., ed., *The Archaeology of Anglo-Saxon England*. Cambridge, 1976.

(c)   Population and the distribution of wealth

Darby, H.C., Glassock R. E., Sheail, J. and Versey, G. R., 'The changing geographical distribution of wealth in England: 1086–1334–1525', *Jnl. of Historical Geography*, V (1979).
Hadwin, J.F., 'The medieval lay subsidies and economic history', *EcHR*, 2nd ser. XXXVI (1983).
Hatcher, J., *Plague, Population and the English Economy, 1348–1530*. 1977.
Poos, L.R., 'The rural population of Essex in the later middle ages', *EcHR*, 2nd ser. XXXVIII (1985).
Razi, Z., *Life, Marriage and Death in a Medieval Parish: Economy, Society and Demography in Halesowen, 1270–1400*. Cambridge, 1980.
Russell, J.C., *British Medieval Population*. Albuquerque, 1948.
Schofield, R.S., 'The geographical distribution of wealth in England, 1334–1649', *EcHR*, 2nd ser. XVIII (1965).
Titow, J.Z., 'Some evidence of the thirteenth-century population increase', *EcHR*, 2nd ser. XIV (1961).
Wrigley, E.A. and Schofield, R.S., *The Population History of England, 1541–1871: a Reconstruction*. 1981.

(d)   Agriculture and its markets

Bailey, M., *A Marginal Economy? East Anglian Breckland in the Later Middle Ages*. Cambridge, 1989.
Britnell, R.H., 'Production for the market on a small fourteenth-century estate', *EcHR*, 2nd ser. XIX (1966).
Britnell, R.H., 'Minor landlords in England and medieval agrarian capitalism', *PP*, no. 89 (1980).
Campbell, B.M.S., 'Agricultural progress in medieval England: some evidence from eastern Norfolk', *EcHR*, 2nd ser. XXXVI (1983).
Du Boulay, F.R.H., *The Lordship of Canterbury: an Essay on Medieval Society*. 1966.
Dyer, C., *Lords and Peasants in a Changing Society: the Estates of the Bishopric of Worcester, 680–1540*. Cambridge, 1980.
Farmer, D.L., 'Two Wiltshire manors and their markets', *AHR*, XXXVII (1989).
Gras, N.S.B., *The Evolution of the English Corn Market*. Harvard Economic Studies, XIII. Cambridge, Mass., 1915.

Harvey, B.F., *Westminster Abbey and its Estates in the Middle Ages.* Oxford, 1977.

Harvey, P.D.A., *A Medieval Oxfordshire Village: Cuxham, 1240–1400.* Oxford, 1965.

Kosminsky, E.A., *Studies in the Agrarian History of England in the Thirteenth Century,* trans. R. Kisch. Oxford, 1956.

Lloyd, T.H., *The Movement of Wool Prices in Medieval England. EcHR* Supplement, no. 6 (1973).

Miller, E., *The Abbey and Bishopric of Ely.* Cambridge, 1951.

Morimoto, N., *Durham Cathedral Priory: the Economic History of an Ecclesiastical Estate in the Later Middle Ages.* Kyoto, 1977.

Rogers, J.E. Thorold, *A History of Agriculture and Prices in England, 1259–1793.* 7 vols, Oxford, 1866–1902.

Searle, E., *Lordship and Community: Battle Abbey and its Banlieu, 1066–1538.* Toronto, 1974.

(e) Industry and manufacture

Basing, P., *Trades and Crafts in Medieval Manuscripts.* British Library, 1990.

Berry, E.K., 'Droitwich and its salt industry, 1215–1700', *University of Birmingham Historical Jnl.,* VI (1957–58).

Birrell, J.R., 'Peasant craftsmen in the medieval forest', *AHR,* XVII (1969).

Birrell, J.R., 'Common rights in the medieval forest', *PP,* no. 117 (1987).

Blake, J.B., 'The medieval coal trade of north-east England', *North. Hist.,* II (1967).

Blanchard, I.S.W., 'Derbyshire lead production, 1195–1505', *Derbyshire Arch. Jnl.,* XCI (1974).

Bridbury, A.R., *Medieval English Clothmaking.* 1982.

Carus-Wilson, E.M., 'The woollen industry before 1550', *VCH Wilts.,* IV (1959).

Carus-Wilson, E.M., 'Evidences of industrial growth on some fifteenth-century manors', *EcHR,* 2nd ser. XII (1959).

Clarkson, L.A., 'The organization of the English leather industry in the late sixteenth and seventeenth centuries', *EcHR,* 2nd ser. XIII (1960).

Dymond, D. and Betterton, A., *Lavenham: 700 Years of Textile Making.* Woodbridge, 1982.

Galloway, R.L., *Annals of Mining and the Coal Trade.* 2 vols, 1898.

Gervers, M., 'The textile industry in Essex in the late twelfth and thirteenth centuries: a study based on occupational names in charter sources', *Essex Archaeology and History*, XX (1989).

Gough, J.W., *The Mines of Mendip*. Oxford, 1930.

Gray, H.L., 'The production and export of English woollens in the fourteenth century', *EHR*, XXXIX (1924).

Hallam, H.E., 'Salt-making in the Lincolnshire Fenland in the middle ages', *Reports and Papers of the Lincs. Architectural and Arch. Soc.*, NS VIII (1959–60).

Hatcher, J., *English Tin Production and Trade before 1550*. Oxford, 1973.

Hatcher, J., *History of the British Coal Industry*, I: *Before 1700*. Oxford, 1993.

Hatcher, J. and Barker, T.C., *A History of British Pewter*. 1974.

Heaton, H., *The Yorkshire Woollen and Worsted Industries*. Oxford, 1920.

Holt, R.A., *The Mills of Medieval England*. Oxford, 1988.

Hunt, T.J., 'Some notes on the cloth trade in Taunton in the thirteenth century', *Proc. Somerset Arch. and NH Soc.*, CI–II (1956–7).

Langdon, J., 'Water-mills and windmills in the West Midlands', *EcHR*, 2nd ser. XLIV (1991).

Le Patourel, H.E.J., 'Documentary evidence and the medieval pottery industry', *Med. Arch.*, XII (1968).

Lewis, G.R., *The Stannaries: a Study of the English Tin Miner*. Harvard Economic Studies, III Cambridge, Mass., 1907.

Lipson, E., *History of the Woollen and Worsted Industries*. 1921.

Lloyd, T.H., 'Some costs of cloth manufacturing in thirteenth-century England', *Textile History*, I (1968–70).

McCarthy, M.R. and Brooks, C.M., *Medieval Pottery in Britain, A.D. 800–1600*. Leicester, 1988.

Miller, E., 'The fortunes of the English textile industry in the thirteenth century', *EcHR*, 2nd ser. XVIII (1965).

Pahl, J., 'The rope and net industry of Bridport', *Proc. Dorset NH and Arch. Soc.*, LXXXII (1960).

Phelps Brown, E.H. and Hopkins, S.V., 'Seven centuries of building wages', in E.M. Carus-Wilson, ed., *Essays in Economic History*, II (1962).

Rudkin, E.H. and Owen, D.M., 'The medieval salt industry in the Lindsey marshland', *Reports and Papers of the Lincs. Architectural and Arch. Soc.*, NS VIII (1959–60).

Salzman, L.F., *English Industries in the Middle Ages*. Oxford, 1923.

Salzman, L.F., 'Mines and Stannaries', in J.F. Willard, W.A. Morris and W.H. Dunham, eds, *The English Government at Work, 1327–1336*, III. Medieval Academy of America, Cambridge, Mass., 1950.

Salzman, L.F., *Building in England down to 1540.* Revised edn, Oxford, 1967.

Schubert, H.R., *History of the British Iron and Steel Industry from c. 450 B.C. to A.D. 1775.* 1957.

Straker, E., *Wealden Iron.* 1931.

Swanson, H., *Building Craftsmen in Late Medieval York.* Borthwick Paper no. 63, York, 1983.

Swanson, H., *Medieval Artisans: an Urban Class in Late Medieval England.* Oxford, 1989.

Walton, P.,'Textiles, Cordage and Raw Fibre from 16–22 Coppergate' in P.V.Addyman, ed., *Archaeology of York,* XVII (5): *The Small Finds.* Council for British Archaeology, 1989.

White, L., *Medieval Technology and Social Change.* 1962.

Whitney, K.P., 'The woodland economy of Kent', *AHR,* XXXVIII (1990).

Woodger, A., 'The eclipse of the burel weaver: some technological developments in the thirteenth century', *Textile History,* XII (1981).

(f)   Internal trade

Britnell, R.H., 'The proliferation of markets in England, 1200–1349', *EcHR,* 2nd ser. XXXIV (1981).

Coates, B.E., 'The origin and distribution of markets and fairs in medieval Derbyshire', *Derbyshire Arch. Jnl,* LXXXV (1965).

Egan, G. and Pritchard, F., eds, *Medieval Finds from Excavations in London: Dress Accessories.* 1992.

Farmer, D.L., 'Millstones for medieval manors', *AHR,* XL (1992).

Fraser, C.M., 'The pattern of trade in the north-east of England, 1266–1350', *North. Hist.,* IV (1969).

Langdon, J., *Horses, Oxen and Technological Innovation: the Use of Draught Animals in English Farming from 1066 to 1500.* Cambridge, 1986.

Masschaele, J., 'Transport costs in medieval England', *EcHR,* 2nd ser. XLVI (1993).

Moore, E. Wedermeyer, *The Fairs of Medieval England.* Toronto, 1985.

Morimoto, N., *Monastic Economy and Medieval Markets: the case of Durham Cathedral Priory.* Seto, 1983.

Willard, J.F., 'Inland transport in England in the fourteenth century', *Speculum,* I (1926).

(g) Overseas trade

Arens, F., 'Wilhelm Servat von Cahors als Kaufmann zu London (1273–1320)', *VSWG*, XI (1913).

Baker, R.L., 'The English customs service, 1307–1343', *Trans. American Philosophical Soc.*, LI (1961).

Bridbury, A.R., *England and the Salt Trade in the Later Middle Ages.* Oxford, 1955.

Childs, W.R., *Anglo-Castilian Trade in the Later Middle Ages.* Manchester, 1978.

Childs, W.R., *The Trade and Shipping of Hull, 1300–1500.* East Yorks. Local Hist. Soc., no. 43, 1990.

Chorley, P., 'The cloth exports of Flanders and northern France during the thirteenth century: a luxury trade?', *EcHR*, 2nd ser. XL (1987).

Chorley, P., 'English cloth exports during the thirteenth and early fourteenth centuries: the continental evidence', *Historical Research*, LXI (1988).

Christensen, A.E., 'Scandinavia and the advance of the Hanseatics', *Scandinavian EcHR*, V (1957).

Cuttino, G.P., *English Diplomatic Administration, 1259–1339.* 2nd edn, Oxford, 1971.

Davies, J.C., 'Shipping and trade in Newcastle upon Tyne, 1294–6', *AA*, 4th ser. XXXI (1953).

Doehaerd, R., *Les relations commerciales entre Gênes, la Belgique et l'Outremont, d'après les archives notariales génoises aux XIIIᵉ et XIVᵉ siècles.* 3 vols, Brussels, 1941.

Dollinger, P., *La Hanse (XIIᵉ–XVIIᵉ siècles).* Paris, 1964. English trans. by D.S. Ault and S.H. Steinberg, *The German Hansa*, 1970.

Fryde, E.B., *William de la Pole, Merchant and King's Banker.* 1988.

Harvey, P.D.A., 'The English trade in wool and cloth', in M. Spallanzani, ed., *Produzione, commercio e consumo dei panni di lana nei secoli XII–XVII.* Prato, 1976.

Holmes, G.A., 'Florentine merchants in England, 1346–1436', *EcHR*, 2nd ser. XIII (1960).

Horrox, R., *The De La Poles of Hull.* East Yorks.Local Hist. Soc., no. 38, 1983.

James, M.K., *Studies in the Medieval Wine Trade*, ed. E.M. Veale. Oxford, 1971.

Kaeuper, R.W., *Bankers to the Crown: the Riccardi of Lucca and Edward I.* Princeton, 1973.

Kaeuper, R.W., 'The Frescobaldi of Florence and the English crown', *Studies in Medieval and Renaissance Hist.*, x (1973).

Kerling, N.J.M., *Commercial Relations of Hollland and Zeeland with England from the late Thirteenth Century to the Close of the Middle Ages.* Leiden, 1954.

Lane, F.C., *Venice and History.* Baltimore, 1973.

Lloyd, T.H., *The English Wool Trade in the Middle Ages.* Cambridge, 1977.

Lloyd, T.H., *Alien Merchants in England in the High Middle Ages.* Brighton, 1982.

Lloyd, T.H., *England and the German Hanse, 1157–1611: a Study of their Trade and Commercial Diplomacy.* Cambridge, 1991.

Perroy, E., 'Le commerce anglo-flamand au XIIIe siècle: la hanse flamande de Londres', *Revue Historique*, CCLII (1974).

Power, E.E., *The Wool Trade in English Medieval History.* Oxford, 1941.

Renouard, Y., 'Les Cahorsins, hommes d'affaires français du XIIIe siècle', *TRHS*, 5th ser. XI(1961).

Renouard, Y., ed., *Bordeaux sous les rois d'Angleterre.* Bordeaux, 1965.

Reynolds, R.L., 'Some English settlers in Genoa in the late twelfth century', *EcHR*, IV (1933).

Reynolds, R.L., 'The market for northern textiles in Genoa, 1179–1200', *Revue Belge de Philologie et d'Histoire*, VIII (1935).

Ruddock, A.A., *Italian Merchants and Shipping in Southampton, 1270–1600.* Southampton, 1951.

Salzman, L.F., *English Trade in the Middle Ages.* Oxford, 1931.

Schaube, A., 'Die Wollausfuhr Englands vom Jahre 1273', *VSWG*, VIII (1908).

Sturler, J. de, *Relations politiques et échanges commerciaux entre le duché de Brabant et l'Angleterre au moyen âge.* Paris, 1936.

Unwin, G., ed., *Finance and Trade under Edward III.* Manchester, 1918.

van Werveke, H., *Miscellanea Medievalia: Verspreide Opstellen over Economische en Sociale Geschiedenis van de Middeleeuwen.* Ghent, 1968.

Veale, E.M., *The English Fur Trade in the Later Middle Ages.* Oxford, 1966.

von Roon-Bassermann, E., 'Die ersten Florentiner Handelsgesellschaften in England', *VSWG*, XXXIX (1952).

von Roon-Bassermann, E., 'Die Handelssperre Englands gegen Flandern, 1270–1274, und die Lizenzierte englische Wollausfuhr', *VSWG*, L (1963).

(h)   Towns and townsfolk

Ashford, L.J., *History of High Wycombe from its Origins to 1880*. 1960.

Beresford, M.W., *New Towns of the Middle Ages: Town Plantation in England, Wales and Gascony*. 1967.

Beresford, M.W. and Jones, G.R.J., *Leeds and its Region*. Leeds, 1967.

Biddle, M., ed., *Winchester in the Early Middle Ages: an edition and discussion of the Winton Domesday*. Winchester Studies, I, Oxford, 1976.

Billson, C.J., *Medieval Leicester*. Leicester, 1920.

Bonney, M.M., *Lordship and the Urban Community: Durham and its Overlords, 1250–1540*. Cambridge, 1990.

Boyle, J.R., *The Early History of the Town and Port of Hedon*. Hull, 1895.

Brand, J., *History and Antiquities of the Town and County of Newcastle upon Tyne*. 2 vols, 1789.

Britnell, R.H., *Growth and Decline in Colchester, 1300–1525*. Cambridge, 1986.

Britnell, R.H., 'The towns of England and northern Italy in the early fourteenth century', *EcHR*, 2nd ser. XLIV (1991).

Brooke, C.N.L. and Keir, G., 'Henry I's charter for the city of London', *Jnl. of the Society of Archivists*, IV (1973).

Brooke, C.N.L. and Keir, G., *London 800–1216: the Shaping of a City*. 1975.

Carus-Wilson, E.M., 'The first half century of the borough of Stratford-upon-Avon', *EcHR*, 2nd ser. XVIII (1965).

Charleton, R.J., *History of Newcastle-on-Tyne*. Newcastle upon Tyne, n.d.

Clanchy, M.T., 'The franchise of return of writs', *TRHS*, 5th ser. XVII (1967).

Conzen, M.R.G., *Alnwick, Northumberland: a Study in Town-Plan Analysis*. Institute of British Geographers Pubns., 27 (1960).

Cunningham, W., 'The gild merchant of Shrewsbury', *TRHS*, NS IX (1895).

Davis, R.H.C., 'An Oxford charter of 1191 and the beginnings of municipal freedom', *Oxoniensia*, XXXIII (1968).

Davis, R.H.C., *The Early History of Coventry*. Dugdale Soc. Occasional Papers, 24 (1976).

Dobson, R.B., 'Admissions to the freedom of the city of York in the later middle ages', *EcHR*, 2nd ser. XXVI (1973).

Dodds, M. Hope, 'The bishop's boroughs (Durham)', *AA*, 3rd ser. XII (1915).

Ekwall, E., *Studies on the Population of Medieval London*. Stockholm, 1956.

Elman, P., 'Economic causes of the expulsion of the Jews in 1290', *EcHR*, VII (1937).

Fraser, C.M., 'The life and death of John Denton', *AA*, 4th ser. XXXVII (1959).

Fraser, C.M., 'Medieval trading restrictions in the North-East', *AA*, 4th ser. XXXIX (1961).

Gottfried, R.S., *Bury St Edmunds and the Urban Crisis, 1290–1539.* Princeton, 1982.

Gross, C., *The Gild Merchant.* 2 vols, Oxford, 1890.

Hill, J.W.F., *Medieval Lincoln.* Cambridge, 1948.

Hilton, R.H., 'Medieval market towns and simple commodity production', *PP*, no. 109 (1985).

Hilton, R.H., *English and French Towns in Feudal Society: a Comparative Study.* Cambridge, 1992.

Holt, R., *The Early History of the Town of Birmingham.* Dugdale Soc. Occasional Papers, 30 (1985).

Holt, R. and Rosser, G., eds, *The English Medieval Town: a Reader in English Urban History, 1200–1540.* 1990.

Keene, D., *A Survey of Medieval Winchester.* Winchester Studies, II, 2 vols, Oxford, 1985.

Kelly, S., Rutledge, E. and Tillyard, M., *Men of Property: an Analysis of the Norwich Enrolled Deeds, 1285–1311.* Norwich, 1983.

Le Goff, J., ed., *Histoire de la France urbaine*, II: *la ville médiévale des Carolingiens à la Renaissance.* Paris, 1980.

Lipman, D.V., *The Jews of Medieval Norwich.* 1967.

Lobel, M.D., *The Borough of Bury St Edmunds: a Study in the Government and Development of a Monastic Town.* Oxford, 1935.

Lobel, M.D., ed., *Atlas of Historic Towns*, I–II, 1969–74.

McClure, P., 'Patterns of migration in the late middle ages: the evidence of English place-name surnames', *EcHR*, 2nd ser. XXXII (1979).

Maitland, F.W., *Township and Borough.* Cambridge, 1898.

Martin, G.H., *Early Court Rolls of the Borough of Ipswich.* Leicester, 1954.

Mickwitz, G., *Die Kartelfunktionen der Zünfte.* Helsingfors, 1936.

Miller, E., 'Medieval York', *VCH City of York*, 1961.

Miller, E., 'Medieval new towns', *North. Hist.*, III (1968).

Miller, E., 'Rulers of thirteenth-century towns: the cases of York and Newcastle upon Tyne', *Thirteenth-Century England*, I (1986).

Miller, E., 'English town patricians, *c.* 1200–1350', in A. Guarducci, ed., *Gerarchie Economiche e Gerarchie Sociali, secolo XII–XVIII.* Instituto Internazionale di Storia Economica 'F. Datini', Florence, 1990.

Myers, A.R., 'The wealth of Richard Lyons', in T.A. Sandquist and M.R. Powicke, eds, *Essays in Medieval History presented to Bertie Wilkinson.* Toronto, 1969.

Newton, K.C., *Thaxted in the Fourteenth Century.* Essex Record Office, Chelmsford, 1960.

Nolan, J. and others, 'The medieval town defences of Newcastle upon Tyne', *AA*, 5th ser. XVII (1989).

Owen, D.M., 'Bishop's Lynn: the first century of a new town', *Proc. Battle Conference on Anglo-Norman Studies*, II (1980).

Page, W., *London: its Origin and Early Development.* 1923.

Parker, V., *The Making of King's Lynn.* Chichester, 1971.

Platt, C., *Medieval Southampton: the Port and Trading Community, A.D. 1000–1600.* 1973.

Platt, C., *The English Medieval Town.* 1976.

Raine, A., *Medieval York: a Topographical Survey based on the Original Sources.* 1955.

Reddaway, T.F. and Walker, L.E.M., *The Early History of the Goldsmiths' Company, 1327–1509.* 1975.

Reynolds, S., 'The rulers of London in the twelfth century', *History*, LVII (1972).

Reynolds, S., *An Introduction to the History of English Medieval Towns.* Oxford, 1977.

Richardson, H.G., *English Jewry under the Angevin Kings.* 1960.

Rodwell, K., *Historic Towns in Oxfordshire: a Survey of the New County.* Oxford, 1975.

Rogers, A., ed., *The Making of Stamford.* 1965.

Ross, C.D., 'Bristol in the middle ages', in C.M. MacInnes and W.F. Whittard, eds, *Bristol and its Adjoining Counties.* Bristol, 1955.

Rosser, A.G., 'The essence of medieval urban communities: the vill of Westminster, 1200–1540', *TRHS*, 5th ser. XXXIV (1984).

Rosser, A.G., *Medieval Westminster, 1200–1540.* Oxford, 1989.

Roth, C., *A History of the Jews in England.* 3rd edn, Oxford, 1964.

Round, J.H., *Geoffrey de Mandeville: a Study of the Anarchy.* 1892.

Round, J.H., *The Commune of London and Other Studies.* 1899.

Rubin, M., *Charity and Community in Medieval Cambridge.* Cambridge, 1987.

Rutledge, E., 'Immigration and population growth in early fourteenth-century Norwich: evidence from the tithing roll', *Urban History YB*, 1988.

Salter, H.E., *Medieval Oxford.* Oxford Hist. Soc., c (1936).

Salter, H.E., *Survey of Oxford*, 2 vols, ed. W.A. Pantin and W.T. Mitchell. Oxford Hist. Soc., NS XIV (1960), XX (1969).

Stephenson, C., *Borough and Town: a Study of Urban Origins in England*. Medieval Academy of America, Cambridge, Mass., 1933.

Tait, J., *The Medieval English Borough: Studies on its Origins and Constitutional History*. Manchester, 1936.

Thornton, G.A., 'A study of the history of Clare, Suffolk: with special reference to its development as a borough', *TRHS*, 4th ser. XI (1928).

Thrupp, S., *The Merchant Class of Medieval London*. Chicago, 1948.

Tierney, B., *Medieval Poor Law: a Sketch of Canonical Theory and its Application in England*. Berkeley, 1959.

Trenholme, N.M., *English Monastic Boroughs*. University of Missouri Studies, II (3), Columbia, 1927.

Unwin, G., *Gilds and Companies of London*. 1908.

Urry, W.J., *Canterbury under the Angevin Kings*. 1966.

Weinbaum, M., *London unter Eduard I und Eduard II*. 2 vols, Stuttgart, 1933.

Weinbaum, M., *The Incorporation of Boroughs*. Manchester, 1937.

Welford, R., *History of Newcastle and Gateshead*. 3 vols, 1884–87.

Willard, J.F., 'Taxation boroughs and parliamentary boroughs, 1294–1336', in J.G. Edwards , V.H. Galbraith and E.F. Jacobs, eds, *Historical Essays in Honour of James Tait*, Manchester, 1933.

Williams, G.A., *Medieval London: from Commune to Capital*. 1963.

(i)   *Money and the money supply*

Bolton, J.L., 'Inflation, economics and politics in thirteenth-century England', *Thirteenth-Century England*, IV (1992).

Challis, C.E., *A New History of the Royal Mint*. Cambridge, 1992.

Craig, J., *The Mint: a History of the London Mint from A.D. 287 to 1948*. Cambridge, 1953.

Harvey, P.D.A., 'The English inflation of 1180–1220', *PP*, no. 61 (1973).

Mate, M.E., 'High prices in early fourteenth-century England: causes and consequences', *EcHR*, 2nd ser. XXVIII (1975).

Mayhew, N.J., 'Numismatic evidence and falling prices in the fourteenth century', *EcHR*, 2nd ser. XXVII (1974).

Mayhew, N.J., ed., *Edwardian Monetary Affairs, 1279–1344*. British Archaeological Reports, 36 (1977).

Mayhew, N.J., 'Money and prices in England from Henry II to Edward III', *AHR*, XXXV (1987).

Metcalf, D.M., 'Continuity and change in English monetary history *c.* 973–1086', *British Numismatic Jnl.*, L–LI(1980–81).

Prestwich, M.C., 'Edward I's monetary policies and their consequences', *EcHR*, 2nd ser. xxii (1969).

(j)   The English economy and society on the eve of the Black Death

Baker, A.R.H., 'Evidence in the *Nonarum Inquisitiones* of contracting arable lands in England during the early fourteenth century', *EcHR*, 2nd ser. xix (1966).

Biddick, K., *The other Economy: Pastoral Husbandry on a Medieval Estate.* Berkeley and Los Angeles, 1989.

Brandon, P.F., 'Cereal yields on the Sussex estates of Battle abbey during the later middle ages', *EcHR*, 2nd ser. xxv (1972).

Campbell, B.M.S., 'Arable productivity in medieval England: some evidence from Norfolk', *Jnl. of Economic History*, xliii (1983).

Campbell, B.M.S., ed., *Before the Black Death: Studies in the 'Crisis' of the Early Fourteenth Century.* Manchester, 1991.

Fox, H.S.A., 'The chronology of enclosure and economic development in medieval Devon', *EcHR*, 2nd ser. xxviii (1975).

Fox, H.S.A., 'The alleged transformation from two-field to three-field systems in medieval England', *EcHR*, 2nd ser. xxxix (1986).

Harriss, G.L., *King, Parliament and Public Finance in Medieval England to 1369.* Oxford, 1975.

Harvey, B.F., 'The population trend in England between 1300 and 1348', *TRHS*, 5th ser. xvi (1966).

Harvey, S.P.J., 'The knight and the knight's fee in England', *PP*, no. 49 (1970).

Hatcher, J., 'A diversified economy: later medieval Cornwall', *EcHR*, 2nd ser. xxii (1969).

Hilton, R.H., 'A crisis of feudalism', in T.H. Aston and C.H.E. Philpin, eds, *The Brenner Debate: Agrarian Class Structure and Economic Development in Pre-Industrial Europe.* Cambridge, 1985.

Kershaw, I., 'The great famine and agrarian crisis in England, 1315–22', *PP*, no. 59 (1973).

Maddicott, J.R., 'The English peasantry and the demands of the crown, 1294–1341', in T.H. Aston, ed., *Landlords, Peasants and Politics in Medieval England.* Cambridge, 1987.

Miller, E., 'War, taxation and the English economy in the late thirteenth and early fourteenth centuries', in J.M. Winter, ed., *War and Economic Development.* Cambridge, 1975.

Plucknett, T.F.T., *The Legislation of Edward I.* Oxford, 1949.

Postan, M.M., 'Investment in medieval agriculture', *Jnl. of Economic History*, xvii (1967).

Postan, M.M. and Hatcher, J., 'Population and class relations in feudal society', *PP*, no. 78 (1978).

Postan, M.M. and Titow, J.Z., 'Heriots and prices on Winchester manors', *EcHR*, 2nd ser. XI(1959).

Powicke, M.R., *Military Obligation in Medieval England: a Study in Liberty and Duty*. Oxford, 1962.

Prestwich, M.C., *War, Politics and Finance under Edward I*. 1972.

Ramsay, J.H., *History of the Revenues of the Kings of England, 1066–1399*. 2 vols, Oxford, 1925.

Saul, N., *Scenes from Provincial Life: Knightly Families in Sussex, 1280–1400*. Oxford, 1986.

Stephenson, M.J., 'Wool yields in the medieval economy', *EcHR*, 2nd ser. XLI (1988).

Titow, J.Z., *Winchester Yields: a Study in Medieval Agricultural Productivity*. Cambridge, 1972.

Index

Aaron of Lincoln, 105, 383, 384, 387
Aaron of York, 383
Abbot's Bromley (Staffs.), 258
Abingdon (Berks.), 118, 237
  abbey, 166
Abington, Little (Cambs.), 78
Acastre, William (York*), 226–7
Acton family (Newcastle), 333, 350
agriculture *see* rural society
Alebrewere, Cristin le (King's Lynn), 379
Alnmouth (Northumb.), 162, 275
Alnwick (Northumb.), 114, 160, 162, 167, 260, 270, 277, 289, 317, 391
Alston (Cumb.), 69, 70
Alsy, John (Leicester), 344
Amyas, William (Nottingham), 244, 245
Andover (Hants.), 118, 140, 229, 232
Appleby (Westmorland), 244
Appleby, Peter (York), 230, 231
apprentices and apprenticeship, 83, 133–4, 331–2, 371–3
Arundel, earl of, 230
Ashbourne (Derbys.), 115–16
Ashburton (Devon), 165
Ashfield Magna (Suffolk), 128
Avening (Gloucs.), 98, 133
Aylsham (Norfolk), 94, 117, 331

Baard, Roger (Newcastle), 347
Baldock (Herts.), 99, 162, 165, 232, 259, 331
Bamburgh (Northumb.), 167, 273, 275, 277
Bampton (Oxon.), 10

Banbury (Oxon.), 270, 275, 317
Barbeflet family (Southampton), 332
Bardi company of Florence, 223, 239, 240
Bardney abbey (Lincs.), 231
Barham (Cambs.), 168
Barnstaple (Devon), 21, 119, 307
Barnwell fair, Cambridge, 162, 166, 168
Barton, Sir William, 230
Barton-on-Humber (Lincs.), 99, 244
Basing, Adam de (London), 228–9
  Thomas de, 229, 230, 232
Basingwerk abbey (Flints.), 145
Basy family (York), 353, 379
Bath (Soms.), 43, 126
Batley (Yorks.), 115
Battle (Sussex), 41, 99, 164, 259, 270
  abbey, 139, 159
Bawsey (Norfolk), 167
Baynard, Ralph, 281
Beaulieu abbey (Hants.), 56, 57, 81, 85, 95, 138
  cloth-making at, 95–8
Beauchamp, Walter de, 184
Beccles (Suffolk), 10, 13, 415
Beckley (Oxon.), 111
Bedford (Beds.), 20, 115, 296, 301, 307, 340
Bedwyn (Wilts.), 18, 99, 103
Bek, Philip (King's Lynn), 337
Bekering, Sir John, 403
Belton, Henry (York), 237, 244, 252, 379
Bentham (Yorks.), 115
Benwell (Northumb.), 64

* The town in brackets denotes place of residence.

Beraud brothers (Cahors), 200
Bere Alston (Devon), 67–8
Berewick, Thomas de (Pocklington), 254
Berkeley (Gloucs.), 275, 307
Berkeley, Thomas and Maurice, 148
Berkhamsted (Herts.), 27, 118, 237, 287
Berwick-upon-Tweed (Northumb.), 148, 164
Betti company of Lucca, 202
Beverley (Yorks.), 12, 57, 117, 237, 244, 293–4, 301, 307
   cloth-making in, 97, 100, 104, 115
Bignor (Sussex), 3
Birdsall (Yorks.), 203
Birland (Devon), 68
Birmingham (Warwicks.), 321
Bitterne (Hants.), 78
Black Death, 429
Bladon (Oxon.), 3
Blake, Roger and John (Bodmin), 72
Blancgernun, Baldwin (Cambridge), 346, 376
Blanket, Thomas (Bristol), 125
Blubberhouses (Yorks.), 69
Bodmin (Cornwall), 72, 165, 349
Bolingbroke, Andrew (York), 379
Bolton (Cumb.), 65, 115n.
Bolton (Lancs.), 258, 262
   fair, 137, 169, 413
Boroughbridge (Yorks.), 287
boroughs
   common seals of, 255, 292, 298, 305–6
   Domesday and origins of, 1, 16–35, 38
   'farm' of revenues from, 281–3, 285–7, 298, 301, 303
   forfeiture of liberties, 318–20
   liberties of, 279–308, 320–2
   parliamentary representation of, 355–6
   royal officials in, 28–30, 31–2, 35–8, 280–1
   taxation of, 280, 285–6, 301
   unification of territories of, 299–300
   see also burgage tenure, burgesses, gilds merchant, municipal government, towns
Boston (Lincs.), 144, 145, 198, 208, 244, 245, 272
   fair, 137, 145, 164, 166, 167, 168, 170–5, 177, 184
   trade of, 60, 71, 108–9, 183, 196, 214
Bothale, Robert de (Nottingham), 244

Box, Martin (London), 231
   William, 229
Brackley (Northants.), 232
Bracknell (Berks.), 245
Bradenham, Lionel de, 141, 142, 148, 403
Bradford on Avon (Wilts.), 411
Bradninch (Devon), 169, 287, 302
Brand, William (Lincoln), 230, 349
Branksea Island (Dorset), 184
Braybrookes of Northamptonshire, 385
Breckland, 401, 412
brewing, 75, 324–30
Bridgham (Norfolk), 79
Bridgnorth (Shrops.), 246
Bridport (Dorset), 84, 147, 336
Brilond, John de (Lübeck), 208
Bristol, 121, 122, 148, 161, 164, 165, 198, 227, 229, 275, 280, 299, 307, 309, 321–2, 331, 333, 342, 349, 350, 364, 368, 371, 382
   cloth-making in, 102–3, 120, 124–5, 126, 408, 415
   map, 266
   trade of, 184, 219, 220
Bromyard (Herefords.), 267
Broomhaugh (Northumb.), 58
Broomley (Northumb.), 58
Brotherlamb, Andrew (Ypres), 198–9
Bruern abbey (Oxon.), 156, 230
Brus, Adam de, 384
Bruton (Soms.), 411
Buckingham (Bucks.), 39, 272
Buckland (Devon), 119
Buckland (Gloucs.), 150
Buckland, Hugh, 281
building
   costs of, 91
   trades, 85–93
   see also earnings and wages
Bukerel, Andrew (London), 185, 284
bullion supply, 191, 193, 213–14, 424–5
   see also money
Bulmer, Sir John, 203
Burcestre, William (Oxford), 350, 354–5, 379
Burford (Oxon.), 232, 275, 287, 289, 291
Burford, John of (London), 177
burgage tenure, 31–2, 301–2
burgesses, 36
   freedom of, 302–3
Burgh, Elizabeth de, 280
   Hubert de, 195
Burnley (Lancs.), 110
Burton, John (Leicester), 344

Burton-on-Trent (Staffs.), 270
Bury St Edmunds (Suffolk), 8, 18, 40, 41, 43, 79, 102, 117, 259, 289, 297–8, 301–2, 317, 322, 337, 338, 362, 363, 412
  abbey, 25, 27, 41
  fair, 118, 150, 161, 167, 170, 172
But, William (Norwich), 243
Byland abbey (Yorks.), 61

Caernarvon castle, 87
Cade, William (St Omer), 192
Calne (Wilts.), 28, 125
Cambois (Northumb.), 131
Cambridge, 18, 20, 21, 23, 25–6, 29, 37, 39, 91, 115, 167, 287–8, 301, 303–4, 307, 313, 316, 328, 337, 344, 351, 359, 364, 382, 387, 388
  cloth-making in, 121
  map, 24
  parishes, 376–8
Cambridge, Reginald of (London), 331–2
Cambridgeshire
  crafsmen in, 131–2
  fairs in, 167–8
Canon family (Corfe), monumental masons, 87
Canterbury (Kent), 8, 12, 18, 19, 23, 32, 36, 37, 43, 225, 227, 266–7, 307, 312, 319, 328, 334, 340, 346, 354, 382
  cloth-making in, 102, 110, 118, 124, 126
Carliol family (Newcastle), 344, 353
  Thomas, 230, 232, 352, 355
Carlisle (Cumb.), 307
Carter, Thomas (Worcester), 250
Castle Bytham (Lincs.), 3
Castle Combe (Wilts.), 125
castles, 39–40
Catsfield (Sussex), 7
Cause, Robert (Lincoln), 105
Cauvel, William (Canterbury), 33, 34, 346
Chagford (Devon), 165
Chaloner, Margery le (Colchester), 56–7
Chaluner, Nicholas (Leicester), 112
Chard (Soms.), 262, 270
Charlbury (Oxon.), 275
Chatton (Northumb.), 162, 167
Chaucer family (London), 332
Chertsey abbey (Surrey), 36
Chester (Cheshire), 12, 14, 18, 23, 32, 165, 184, 219, 266, 290, 295, 307
Chester, earl of, 6, 384

Chesterfield (Derbys.), 71, 337, 338
Chesterton family (Boston), 233
Chichester (Sussex), 40, 287, 291, 337, 338
Chippenham forest (Wilts.), 58
Chilvers Coton (Warwicks.), 84
Chipping Camden (Gloucs.), 169, 177, 275
Chipping Norton (Oxon.), 119, 275
Chipping Sodbury (Gloucs.), 275
Chiriton, Walter (London), 226, 240, 243, 244, 249, 251
Cirencester (Gloucs.), 119, 165, 275, 289–90
Clare (Suffolk), 118, 280, 289, 324, 411
Clarevaus family (York), 353
Clifford (Herefords.), 40
clothing crafts, 81, 326–8
cloth-making, 93–127, 410–11
  locations of the industry, 98–103, 107–11, 114–26, 410–11, 414
  manufacturing costs, 95–7
  manufacturing processes, 94–5
  organization of, 104–7, 111–14, 413–15
  pre-Conquest, 4
  worsteds, 116–17, 122–3, 220–1, 414
  see also craft gilds, exports, fulling mills, prices, trade: internal
Cloune, William (Leicester), 344
cnihtengilds, 31
coal and coal-mining, 58–9, 63–7, 71, 129, 131, 350, 410, 414
Cockermouth (Cumb.), 115, 158, 395
Cokheved, Hugh (Barton-on-Humber), 244, 245, 246, 247
Codicote (Herts.), 77
Coggeshall (Essex), 117
Colchester (Essex), 26, 117, 141, 148, 150, 153, 268, 296, 307, 328, 329, 337, 350, 382, 387
  cloth-making in, 118
  craftsmen and merchants, 53–5, 57, 74, 75, 81
Colchester, Ralph of (Lincoln), 105
Colerne (Wilts.), 119
Colle, Thomas (Shrewsbury), 241, 244, 245, 247, 338
Colne (Lancs.), 62, 110
Combe (Hants.), 140, 156
Combemartin, William (London), 231, 233
Combermere abbey (Cheshire), 145, 174
communications, 11–12, 144–9, 154–5
  see also transport costs

Conduit, Reginald de (London), 238–9, 243, 252, 341
Congleton (Cheshire), 307
Corbridge (Northumb.), 160, 162, 167, 169, 275, 277
    fair, 137, 144, 176, 413
*Corby (Northants.), 3
Cornhill family (London), 345–6, 387
    Stephen, 165
cornmongers, 154, 161
Cossall (Notts.), 67
Costein, Henry (Leicester), 105, 190
Coventry (Warwicks.), 165, 237, 244, 307, 322, 350
    cloth-making in, 100, 116
Cowley (Oxon.), 111
Cowpen (Northumb.), 64, 66, 75
Coxwell (Berks.), 140
craft gilds, 361–75
    and town governments, 361–2, 364–9, 375
    charitable aspects of, 373–4
    of weavers and fullers, 100, 104–9, 112–13, 121, 124–5, 362, 364–7
craftsmen
    rural, 2–4, 128–34
    urban, 8–10, 74–5, 81–5
    see also industries
Cranbrook (Kent), 118
Crane, Nicholas (London), 339
Crassus, Richard (London), 211, 227
Crediton (Devon), 119
Crewkerne (Soms.), 148
Cricklade (Wilts.), 118, 125
Curlevache, Simon (Leicester), 348
Cuxham (Oxon.), 77, 78, 85, 86–7, 122, 140, 142, 277–8

Dalderby, Robert (Lincoln), 245
Danby (Yorks.), 61
Darlington (Durham), 169, 244
Dartford (Kent), 118
Dartmouth (Devon), 122
Dean, Forest of (Gloucs.), 61, 62, 401, 413
Denton, John (Newcastle), 350, 360
Deorman, the moneyer (London), 34
Derby (Derbys.), 8, 20, 26, 71, 102, 165, 301, 337, 338, 349
Derby, Walter (Bristol), 220
Dereham, Elias of, architect, 90n.
Devenish family (Winchester), 353
    John, 351
Devizes (Wilts.), 118
Domesday Inquest and Domesday Book, 1–2, 6–7, 47–8

Domesman, Osbert (Cambridge), 346–7
Doncaster, William (Chester), 231, 349
Dorchester (Dorset), 26, 232
Dorkyng, James (London), 232
Dover (Kent), 38, 40, 149, 164
Downham-in-the-Isle (Cambs.), 80, 423–4
Downton (Wilts.), 78
Draper, Simon (Winchester), 230, 351
Droitwich (Worcs.), 5–6, 12, 76, 148, 177
Duffield Frith (Derbys.), 63
Dukelinton, John (Oxford), 350, 379
Dunfowe, Hugh (Shrewsbury), 338
Dunning family (Cambridge), 344, 346, 351, 354
Dunstable (Beds.), 165, 229, 261, 269, 289
Dunwich (Suffolk), 13, 18, 183, 318
Duraunt, John (Dunstable), 229, 232
Durham, 22, 43, 164, 300, 302
    priory, 64, 137, 145, 156, 165, 166, 246, 411
Durham, William (Darlington), 246, 411
Dursley (Gloucs.), 275

Eadred the weaver (Durham), 4
Earith (Hunts.), 157
Earl Marshal, the, 135, 145, 156
earnings and wages
    in agriculture, 422–3
    of building workers 86, 89–91, 367–8, 370
    of miners, 72–3
Eaton Socon (Beds.), 56
Egremont (Cumb.), 99
Ellel (Lancs.), 115
Elmerugge, Adam de, 230
Elsdon (Northumb.), 62, 167
Ely (Cambs.)
    abbey, 25, 29
    bishopric estates, 135, 150, 404, 423
    cathedral, 60, 64, 85, 87, 89, 90, 91
    fair, 168
Embleton, Richard (Newcastle), 233, 234, 236, 315, 345, 350, 355
Ermine Street, 12
Essex, Wolmar of (London), 229
Eu, Philip de (Oxford), 343
Evesham (Worcs.), 317
Evingham, John (Highworth), 350
Exeter (Devon), 14, 23, 40, 215, 307, 313, 328, 330–1, 338, 351, 382
    cathedral, 87–8, 89, 90, 137, 152
    cloth-making in, 119, 124

exports
  cloth, 15, 104, 108–9, 122–3, 127, 175,
    181, 194, 206, 208–9, 212, 219–21,
  fish, 184–5, 206, 210, 219, 221–2,
    224–5
  grain, 185, 188–9, 192, 206, 210, 219,
    221–2, 224–5
  hides, 185, 203, 219
  salt, 185, 217, 221, 224
  tin and lead, 15, 60, 181, 189, 206,
    208–9, 212, 219, 223
  wool, 15–16, 142–3, 156–7, 164–6,
    174–5, 181–5, 189–93, 197–204,
    209–12, 216–17, 222–4, 229–30
  see also trade: overseas
Eynesbury (Hunts.), 167
Eynsham (Oxon.), 262. 270, 275, 302

Fairfax family (York), 353
Fairford (Gloucs.), 411
fairs, 143, 166–76, 186, 206, 414
  see also markets, trade: internal
Faringdon (Oxon.), 232
Faversham (Kent), 75
Felstead (Essex), 132–3, 150
Fen Ditton (Cambs.), 79, 80
Feteplace, Adam (Oxon.), 164
Fisher, William (Dunstable), 229, 232
fitzAilwin, Henry (London), 284
fitzBerengar, Reiner (London), 346
fitzLefwin, Hugh (York), 347, 354
fitzOsbert, William (London), 284
Fleet (Lincs.), 76
Fleming, Nicholas (York), 354, 355,
    379
Fleming, James le (Southampton), 227,
    331,
  Walter le, 185, 344, 345
Flory, Thomas (London), 172
Flur, Adam (York), 227
Fordwich (Kent), 13, 43
Forz, Isabella de, 141, 172, 202, 395
Fossard, William, 384
Fosse Way, 12, 144
Fountains abbey (Yorks.), 56, 61, 174
Fowey (Cornwall), 196
Framlingham castle (Suffolk), 135
Frescobaldi company of Florence, 201,
    203, 204
Frome (Soms.), 21, 411
fulling mills, 95, 102, 110–11

Galeway, Richard (Newcastle), 244
Galloway family (Newcastle), 350
Gamage, Henry (Oxford), 343
Gegg, Ralph (Scarborough), 236

Geraduci, Hugolino (Lucca), 202
gilds merchant, 105, 112, 226–7, 290–8,
    301, 305–6, 317–18
Glastonbury (Soms.), 3
Glatton (Hunts.), 287
Gloucester, 12–13, 18, 19, 23, 30, 35, 37,
    40, 145, 261, 266, 268, 275, 292, 309,
    319, 350, 359, 382
  cloth-making in, 99, 100, 119–20, 124,
    126
Gloucester, earl of, 173
Godmanchester (Hunts.), 337, 338
Goldbeter, Henry (York), 241, 244, 246,
    247
  John, 244
Golding, Hugh (Ipswich), 117
Gouk, Thomas (Boston), 245
goldsmiths, 82
Gough map, 144
Grandmesnil, Hugh de, 27
Gransden, Little (Cambs.), 80
Grantham (Lincs.), 18, 245
Grantham, John de (London), 243
Graper family (Newcastle), 333, 350
  Peter, 236
Great Bricett (Suffolk), 168
Green's Norton (Northants.), 3
Greystoke, Robert, 230
Grimsby (Lincs.), 183, 196, 307, 359,
    407
Grosseteste, Robert, 138
Guildford (Surrey), 30
Guisborough abbey (Yorks.), 61
Gupil, Henry (Lincoln), 230

Hackforth, William (London), 360–1
Hadleigh (Suffolk), 122
Hadstock (Essex), 162
Halesowen (Worcs.), 128–30, 271, 273,
    289, 333, 334, 350, 420
Halifax (Yorks.), 115
Halstead (Essex), 118
Hamdon Hill (Soms.), 167
Hampton, Bernard de (Southampton),
    229
Haresfield (Gloucs.), 3
Hamwih, 9, 13, 19
  see also Southampton
hanses, 207–8, 224
  see also merchants: German
Harston (Cambs.), 162, 168
Hartlepool (Durham), 307
Hartley (Northumb.), 66
Hastings (Sussex), 12
Haverfordwest (Pembs.), 184
Haverhill (Suffolk), 118, 162

Hawkesbury (Gloucs.), 160–1, 162
Hawkin, Hugh (Newcastle), 414
Hay, Richard de la (Newcastle), 230
Haydon Bridge (Northumb.), 160
Hedon (Yorks.), 262, 302
Helford (Cornwall), 184
Helston-in-Kirrier manor (Cornwall), 287
Helstone-in-Trigg manor (Cornwall), 169
Henley-on-Thames (Oxon.), 140, 150, 165, 277
Henstank (Yorks.), 69
Hereford (Herefords.), 8, 9, 12, 23, 26, 31–2, 35, 164, 382
   St Ethelbert's fair, 149
Herle, William, 314
Heron, William, 273
herrings, 13, 76–7, 148, 150, 269
Hexham (Northumb.), 114, 162, 277
Higham Ferrers (Northants.), 271, 303
Highworth (Wilts.), 329, 350–1
High Wycombe (Bucks.), 118, 121, 267, 271, 295, 296, 328–9, 330
Hinckley (Leics.), 161, 165
Histon (Cambs.), 162
Holm family (Lincoln), 344
Holme, Thomas (Beverley), 237
Honiton (Devon), 119
Hornby (Lancs.), 110
Horsham, Roger (London), 334
Horstead (Norfolk), 133, 150
Houghil, Henry (Leicester), 112, 295
Houghton (Hunts.), 155
Houghton Regis (Beds.), 45
Howard, Sir William, 201
Howden (Yorks.), 168
Hoxne (Suffolk), 168
Hull (Yorks.), 57, 92, 144, 151, 165, 198, 208, 245, 312
   trade of, 60, 77, 183, 211, 214, 217
Hulne priory (Northumb.), 201
Hulton, Richard (Shrewsbury), 338
Huntingdon (Hunts.), 20, 100, 109, 261, 337, 338

Ickleton fair (Cambs.), 162, 168
Icknield Way, 12
Ilchester (Soms.), 10, 287, 304
imports
   cloth, 15, 107–8, 126, 174–5, 181, 186, 193–4, 197–200, 203, 209, 212, 215–16, 222
   dyestuffs, 15, 181, 186, 190, 210, 217–18

fish, 15, 188, 208, 212, 217, 221, 224
furs, 15, 173, 186, 189, 207–8, 224
grain, 224
iron, 62–3, 206, 208–10
pottery, 14, 15
salt, 217, 221
spices, 203, 206, 222
timber, 15, 186, 208, 224
wine, 15, 143, 173–5, 181–2, 185–6, 189, 194–5, 200, 204–6, 211–12, 217–20
see also trade: overseas
industries
   general characteristics of, 52–5
   and regional distribution of wealth, 415–16
   see also apprentices, brewing, building trades, clothing crafts, cloth-making, craftsmen, leather crafts, mills, mining and smelting, pottery manufacture, salt production, servants and journeymen, smiths
Inglesham (Wilts.), 140
Inglewood forest (Cumb.), 56
Inkpenne, Robert (Winchester), 237, 242
   Roger, 351
Ipswich (Suffolk), 13, 14, 26, 27, 102, 163–4, 165, 183, 214, 237, 290–1, 296, 305–6, 311, 314, 315, 316, 319, 337, 338, 360
   cloth-making in, 117
iron and iron-mining, 3, 58, 61–3, 69, 71, 410, 415
Isembard family (Southampton), 344
Islip (Oxon.), 111

Jews, 381–9

Kelsey, Robert (London), 360
Kendal (West.), 115, 145
Kepeharm, John and Lawrence (Oxford), 299
Kidderminster (Worcs.), 119
King's Hall, Cambridge, 146
King's Lynn (Norfolk), 5, 60, 145, 147, 207, 208, 229, 272, 297, 307, 309, 313, 330, 332, 335, 337, 359, 382, 411, 414
   fair, 166, 167, 168
   trade of, 60, 77, 117, 153–4, 165, 183, 196, 214, 224
Kingston, Nicholas (Oxford), 342–3
Kingston on Thames, potteries of, 84
Kirkstall abbey (Yorks.), 156, 202

Knaresborough (Yorks.), 100
  forest of, 61, 62, 415
Knutsford (Cheshire), 258
Kyndecote, John de (Leicester), 232
Kyng, John (Colchester), 357

Lacock (Wilts.), 232
Lagenhoe manor (Essex), 141, 142
Lakenheath (Suffolk), 162
Laleham (Middx.), cloth-making at,
  95–8
Lancaster, earl of, 139
Langton family (York), 349, 353, 379
Launceston (Cornwall), 43, 287
Lavenham (Suffolk), 98, 122, 134, 317,
  411
lawmen, 32–3
lead and lead mining, 3, 15, 58–61, 67–8,
  70–1, 410, 415
leather crafts, 56–7, 74, 81, 83
Lechlade (Gloucs.), 275, 411
Ledbury (Herefords.), 267
Leeds (Yorks.), 113, 115, 270
Leges, Jakemin de (Leicester), 173
Leicester, 20, 26, 27–8, 163, 164, 165,
  166, 288, 289, 291, 292, 293, 294–5,
  300, 312, 313, 322, 328, 330, 331,
  333, 334, 338, 341, 344, 352, 357,
  358, 364–5, 415
  cloth-making in, 100, 106, 111–12,
  116, 121, 126, 174, 407, 415
Leighton Buzzard (Beds.), 134
Leverington, Simon (King's Lynn), 337
Lewes (Sussex), 62, 291
  priory, 201
Limberg, Tidemann (Dortmund), 224
Lincoln, 9, 12, 18, 20, 23, 26, 30, 33, 36,
  38, 40, 163, 196, 244, 245, 266, 286,
  291, 295, 299, 301, 302, 303, 307,
  312, 318, 319, 340, 344, 359, 364,
  374, 382, 383, 388, 407
  bishop of, 161
  cathedral, 87
  cloth-making in, 97, 100, 104, 105,
  111, 113–14, 116, 121, 124, 126,
  415
Lincoln, earl and countess of, 138, 139,
  141, 204, 262
Lincolnshire
  craftsmen in, 133
  markets in, 180
Lindisfarne priory (Northumb.), 64
Lindsey (Lincs.), 151
Linton (Cambs.), 168, 178–9, 328
Littlebourne (Kent), 110
Littleport (Cambs.), 150, 155

London, 12, 13, 15, 16, 17, 19, 20, 21, 30,
  31, 36, 37, 42, 86, 91, 152, 164,
  165–6, 208, 218–19, 258, 262, 263,
  266, 286, 296, 300, 318, 319–20, 330,
  334, 338–9, 340, 342, 345–6, 358,
  362, 378, 382, 390, 391, 392
  Cheapside, 267–8
  cloth-making in, 92, 102, 106, 112–13,
  121, 126, 408, 414
  craftsmen and merchants, 55, 61, 75,
  82, 83, 172, 324–5
  gilds, 362–75
  liberties, development of, 279–84
  market, 63–4, 71–2, 117, 146–7, 148,
  154, 225
  migration to, 331–2
  population of, 264, 274
  ruling circles, 348–9, 360–1
  trade of, 15, 183, 196, 214–15, 219,
  308, 311, 314
  wool merchants, 228–9, 231–2, 242–3
Longbridge Deverill (Wilts.), 58
Long Melford (Suffolk), 134
Long, John le (Bristol), 229
Lopen fair (Soms.), 169
Lostwithiel (Cornwall), 61, 72, 165, 206,
  302, 349
Louth (Lincs.), 407
Louth family (York), 353
Louth Park abbey (Lincs.), 174
Lucca, Luke of, 202
Ludlow (Shrops.), 165, 232, 237, 338
Ludlow, Lawrence of (Shrewsbury), 230,
  235
  Nicholas of, 229–30, 232
Luton (Beds.), 134
Lydford (Devon), 169, 287
Lynleye, John (Shrewsbury), 338
Lyons, Richard (London), 339
Lyons, Nicholas de (Douai), 198

Macclesfield (Cheshire), 307, 318, 322
Madingley, Robert of, 135–6
Magge, Robert (Highworth), 351
Malmesbury (Wilts.), 118
Maldon (Essex), 26–7, 118, 150
Malton (Yorks.), 100
Manchester (Lancs.), 110
Mandeville, Geoffrey de, 37, 258, 281, 283
Market Harborough (Leics.), 244, 245,
  271, 338
markets, 147, 155–66, 178–80
  and urban origins, 177–8
  noticed in Domesday Book, 10
  urban, 163–4, 259–60, 268–9, 277–8,
  280, 324–30

Marlborough (Wilts.), 99, 103, 104, 118
  cloth-making in, 103, 104, 105, 125
Meaux abbey (Yorks.), 156, 172, 174,
  202, 384
Meek, Robert (York), 379
Melbourne castle (Derbys.), 91
Melchebourne brothers (King's Lynn),
  234, 240, 243, 248, 251
Mells (Soms.), 411
Melton Mowbray (Leics.), 10, 244
Mercer, Serlo the (London), 284
merchants, alien, 172–3, 175, 197–210,
  213, 215–25, 379–81
  Brabançon, 108, 184–5, 199–200, 217
  Cahorsin, 184–5, 194–5, 200–1, 204–6,
    380
  Dutch, 183, 217
  Flemish, 15–16, 41–2, 108, 172–3,
    183–6, 190–4, 197–200, 204
  French, 41, 183, 217–18
  Frisian, 13
  Gascon, 184–5, 194–5, 204–7, 218–19
  German, 183–5, 188–9, 204–10, 220–1,
    224–5
  Italian, 172–3, 184, 187, 195, 201–4,
    222–3
  Norman, 16, 184, 190, 217
  Scandinavian, 15, 16, 183–5, 187–8,
    207
  Spanish, 183–5, 223
merchants, English, 13, 16, 156, 185,
  225–54, 344–5, 347–50, 411–16
  as royal financiers, 234–40, 245–51
  assemblies of, 235–49
  'estate' or 'community' of, 226–7, 236,
    240–9
  London, 228–9, 231–2, 242–3
  provincial, 229–32, 242–9
  see also staple
Merlay barony, 178
Merton College, Oxford, 145, 150, 385
Michelmarsh (Hants.), 3
Micklethwaite (Yorks.), 203
Middlewich (Cheshire), 6
mills and milling, 6–7, 77–81, 110–11
  see also fulling mills
Milverton (Soms.), 21
Minchinhampton (Gloucs.), 98, 133,
  165
mining and smelting, 58–74
  organization, 69–74
  output, 59–66
  pre-Conquest, 3
  technology, 66–9
  see also coal, earnings and wages, iron,
    lead, silver, tin

Mitford (Northumb.), 277
money
  mints and moneyers, 17, 33–5, 44–5,
    227, 261, 396
  supply, 44, 396–7, 424–5
  see also bullion supply
Montfort, Simon de, 228
  Eleanor de, 138
Mora, Poncius de (Cahors), 200, 201
Mori company of Florence, 201
Morpeth (Northumb.), 160, 178, 277
Mortain, count of, 5, 43
Mortimer, Edmund and Roger, 230
Moulton (Lincs.), 394
Mowbray, Roger, 347
Moygne, Hugh le (King's Lynn), 337
Much Wenlock (Shrops.), 245
municipal government, 36, 308–16,
  331–2
  aldermen, 282–4, 290, 309–11
  bailiffs, 304–5, 309–11
  borough courts, 37, 282–3, 290–2, 298,
    301, 309–11
  councillors, 309–11
  financial administration, 312–13
  grievances of townsfolk against,
    356–61
  mayorality, 283–4, 299, 306–8
  multiplication of officials, 313–14
  reeves, 29–30, 31–2, 36–8, 285–6, 290,
    298–9, 304–6
  tendency towards oligarchy, 315–16,
    338–9, 356, 359–60
  see also boroughs, craft gilds, gilds mer-
    chant, towns

Nantwich (Cheshire), 6
Needham Market (Suffolk), 334
Nether Wallop (Hants.), 5
Newark (Notts.), 99, 237, 244, 328
  fair, 170
Newbiggin (Northumb.), 275
Newborough (Staffs.), 270–1, 272–3
Newburn (Northumb.), 275
Newbury (Berks.), 102, 164
Newcastle upon Tyne (Northumb.), 64,
  100, 144, 147, 160, 164, 208, 214,
  227, 229, 232, 233, 244, 250, 260,
  264–5, 270, 272, 302, 304, 307, 312,
  314, 315, 332, 333, 347, 349, 350,
  360, 361, 364, 382
  cloth-making in, 113, 114
  trade of, 64, 196
Newminster abbey (Northumb.), 115
Newnham-on-Severn (Gloucs.), 145, 157,
  275

Newport (Essex), 287
Newton, Burghclere (Hants.), 273
Norham (Northumb.), 167, 277, 309
Norman Conquest, economic effects of, 38–43
Northallerton (Yorks.), 115
 fair, 169
Northampton (Northants.), 20, 38, 40, 43, 84, 117, 144, 165, 232, 237, 259, 265, 296, 301, 303, 307, 313, 319, 359, 382, 415
 cloth-making in, 100, 102, 104–5, 108, 110, 116, 121, 126, 408
 fair, 158, 166, 172, 173, 267
Northfleet (Kent), 157
Northleach (Gloucs.), 119, 177, 275
North Shields (Northumb.), 275
Northumberland
 craftsmen in, 131
 fairs in, 167
Northwich (Cheshire), 6
North Walsham (Norfolk), 117, 411
Norwich (Norfolk), 11, 12, 14, 18, 22, 26, 27, 39, 40, 75, 158, 171, 237, 259, 265, 286, 301, 307, 309, 318, 319, 323, 329, 333, 334, 339–40, 357, 361, 365, 373, 374, 382, 387, 388
 cloth-making in, 102, 116–17, 122, 123, 124, 415
 fair, 168
 occupational structure, 325–7
 population of, 274
 priory, 156
Norwich, St William of, 372
Nottingham, 20, 30, 38, 40, 41, 244, 265, 299–300, 319, 334, 382
 cloth-making in, 100, 102, 116, 126

Oakham (Rutland), 168, 287
Orleton, William (Ludlow), 338
Ormskirk (Lancs.), 262
Otterton (Devon), 10
Owen, Henry (Oxford), 343, 344, 351
Oxford, 12, 18, 23, 26, 28, 35, 36, 38, 39, 78, 147, 227, 232, 260, 263, 275, 285, 291–2, 296, 298–9, 304, 306, 307, 309–10, 313, 314, 315, 318, 328, 346, 350, 359, 364, 365, 368, 382, 387, 415
 cloth-making in, 99, 103, 104, 106, 109, 111, 113, 119, 120, 121, 126, 174
 parishes, 376, 379
 ruling circles, 342–4, 349
Oxford, John of (London), 243

Palmer, Thomas (Winchester), 242, 251
parishes and parish churches, 261, 265, 376–9
Passelewe, Edmund, 314
Pavia, fairs of, 14
Penrith (Cumb.), 145
Persun, Henry (Colchester), 337
Peruzzi company of Florence, 223, 239, 240
Pessagno, Antonio (Genoa), 222
Peterborough (Northants.), 111
Pevensey (Sussex), 40
Peverel, William, 41
Pewsey (Wilts.), 411
pewterers, 61
Picard, Henry (London), 243
Pickering (Yorks.), 113, 115
Pilton (Devon), 21
Pipewell abbey (Northants.), 156, 200
Plomer, Ralph le (Oxford), 343
Pole, Richard de la (Hull), 247
 William de la, 145, 151, 238–9, 240, 244, 245, 248, 250, 251–2, 412
Pontefract (Yorks.), 113, 115
poor, *see* towns: poverty in
population, 393–6, 400–2, 419–21, 426–7, 429
 see also towns: populations of
Portsmouth (Hants.), 184
Potterne (Wilts.), 3
Potterton (Yorks.), 3
pottery manufacture, 3–4, 7, 11–13, 84
Prest, Walter (Melton Mowbray), 241, 245, 246, 247, 248
Preston (Lancs.), 307
prices
 cloth, 97–8
 grain, 418, 422–5
 wine, 214, 218
 wool, 198, 214, 239, 422–5
provision trades, 74–5, 327–30, 357–8, 367
Pulteney, John (London), 234, 243, 252, 339, 352
Purbeck (Dorset), 147
Pynson, Robert (Boston), 245

quarries, 3
Queenborough (Kent), 445–6

Ramsey abbey (Hunts.), 25
Ravenser (Yorks.), 208
Reach fair (Cambs.), 150, 167
Reading (Berks.), 118, 289, 294
Reigner, Thomas (Market Harborough), 338

Renger, Richard (London), 284
Retford (Notts.), 245, 258
Rhuddlan (Flints.), 3
Riccardi company of Lucca, 201–2
Riche, Gervase le (Southampton), 193
Richmond (Yorks.), 270
    fair, 170
Rievaulx abbey (Yorks.), 61, 156, 202
Ripon (Yorks.), 100, 145
Rochester (Kent), 168, 285
Rockingham (Northants.), 168
Rodington, Henry (Leicester), 344
Romney (Kent), 184
Rookhope (Durham), 58
Ross (Northumb.), 75
Rossendale (Lancs.), 62
Ross-on-Wye (Herefords.), 267
Rothbury (Northumb.), 277
Rotherham (Yorks.), 411
Rothwell (Yorks.), 165
    park, 62
Roxborough (Scotland), 145
royal households, purchases by, 139, 175,
    185, 216, 230
royal revenues
    of Anglo-Saxon and Norman kings,
    45–9
    levels of medieval taxation, 398–9,
    422–3
Royston (Herts.), 162, 168
rural society
    barriers to agricultural productivity,
    406–7
    famine years in 1315–17, 418–21
    low levels of investment, 404–5
    problems in the early fourteenth
    century, 421–9
    see also craftsmen: rural
Rye (Sussex), 40

Sadlingstones, Hugh (Newcastle), 414
Saffron Walden (Essex), 162
    abbey, 384
St Albans (Herts.), 22, 27, 43, 118, 237
    abbey, 27, 118, 148, 384
St Godric of Finchale, 193
St Ives fair (Hunts.), 104, 118, 119,
    166–7, 168, 170–2, 198
St Neots (Hunts.), 109
    pottery, 3–4, 109
Salford (Lancs.), 258, 262
Salisbury (Wilts.), 118–19, 125, 126, 163,
    232, 237, 260, 262, 288, 289
    cathedral, 89
    Old Sarum, 272
salt production, 5–6, 39, 75–7, 147–8

Saltash (Cornwall), 287
Sampson family (York), 353
    John, 355
Sandwich (Kent), 13, 19, 40, 43, 124,
    184, 198, 203–4, 214, 219, 229
Saxilby (Lincs.), 245
Say, William de, 178
Scarborough (Yorks.), 77, 100, 164, 208,
    337, 338
Scarborough-ware pottery, 84, 410
schools, 260–1
Scott family (Newcastle), 64, 344, 349
Scottow (Norfolk), 117
Seaford (Sussex), 184
Seizevaus, Nicholas (York), 379
Selby family (York), 344, 349, 353, 378
    Hugh, 185, 230–1, 344, 345, 347
    John, 354
self-supply, 135–6, 395, 405–6
Selyman, Robert (Stafford), 338
Seman family (Cambridge), 351
servants and journeymen, 339–42, 370–1,
    375
Servat, William (Cahors and London),
    156, 165, 200, 231, 332, 339, 379
Sevenhampton (Wilts.), 77, 78, 141,
    148
Shaftesbury (Dorset), 30
Sharnford, Robert (Leicester), 173
Sheffield (Yorks.), 289, 411
Shelford, Great and Little (Cambs.), 80,
    140
Shepeye, John de (Coventry), 237, 244
Sherston (Wilts.), 160–1, 162
Shilton, Richard (Leicester), 112
Shoreham (Sussex), 184
Shrewsbury (Shrops.), 23, 31, 35, 38, 40,
    165, 229, 244, 246, 291, 292, 293,
    313, 328, 338
    cloth-making in, 103, 119, 120
Shropshire, craftsmen in, 132
Silchester (Hants.), 232
silver and silver mining, 58, 67–8, 71, 73
Skipton (Yorks.), 63, 113
Sleaford (Lincs.), 177, 270
smiths, 2–4, 87–8, 128–30
Snitterfield (Warwicks.), 177
Southampton (Hants.), 14, 19, 40, 144,
    164, 184, 229, 264, 296, 297, 332,
    338, 339, 344, 349, 356, 358, 360,
    380, 391
    trade of, 147, 196, 214, 219
Southwick, Richard (Southampton), 339
Sowerby (Yorks.), 115
specialization, progress of, 412–16
Spicer, John and Richard (York), 236

Spileman the sword-maker (Winchester), 3

Spini company of Florence, 201

Stafford (Staffs.), 23, 245, 337, 338

Stamford (Lincs.), 8, 18, 20, 26, 32–3, 36, 244, 382, 383, 394
cloth-making in, 100, 108, 111, 116, 126
fair, 119, 166, 172, 173

Stamfordham (Northumb.), 133

Stanham, Stephen de (Lincoln), 171, 236

Stanley (Durham), 65

Stanlow abbey (Cheshire), 174

Stanstead Abbots (Essex), 385

Stanton (Suffolk), 130

staple
Company of the, 246–9, 254
policies, 236–40, 248–9

Steeple Ashton (Wilts.), 411

Stoke, Ralph de (Stamford), 116

Stourbridge fair, Cambridge, 166, 168, 176

Stow (Lincs.), 168

Stowmarket (Suffolk), 341

Stow-on-the-Wold (Gloucs.), 240, 275

Stratford-upon-Avon (Warwicks.), 119, 177, 178, 267, 302, 317, 334

Stratton, Adam of, 77, 141, 169, 385

Studland (Dorset), 5

Sturry (Kent), 110

Stury, Richard de (Shrewsbury), 236

Sudbury (Suffolk), 118, 122

Suffolk, craftsmen in, 130–1

Sutton-under-Brailes (Warwicks.), 156

Swanland, Simon (London), 216

Swanlond, Thomas, 240, 251

Swyncombe fair (Oxon.), 169

Tamworth (Warwicks.), 19, 35

Tarset (Northumb.), 413

Taunton (Soms.), 78, 103, 118, 419

Taverner, John (Bristol), 236

Taverner, Reginald (King's Lynn), 337

Tavistock (Devon), 165, 259–60, 269

taxation *see* revenue: royal

Taynton (Oxon.), 3

technological advances, 7–8, 68–9, 85, 401–2
see also specialization, traditional attitudes and institutions

Terrington (Norfolk), 76

Tetbury (Gloucs.), 275

Tewkesbury (Gloucs.), 10, 40, 232, 275

Thame (Oxon.), 119, 329

Thaxted (Essex), 83–4, 134, 317, 324

Thetford (Norfolk), 8, 9, 11, 12, 18, 23–5, 26, 411

Thirsk (Yorks.), 100

Thornbury (Gloucs.), 275, 350

Thorney abbey (Cambs.), 25

Thornton Parva (Suffolk), 99

Thunderle, Reginald de (London), 156, 231

Tickhill, William (York), 347, 355

tin and tin mining, 15, 58–61, 66, 67–9, 70–3, 410, 414
see also exports: tin

Tintagel (Cornwall), 287

Tintinhull (Soms.), 167

Titchfield (Hants.), 10

Tiverton (Devon), 119

Tortworth (Gloucs.), 177

Totnes (Devon), 31, 39, 43, 119, 297

Toudeby, Gilbert de, 314

Towcester (Northants.), 3

towns
aliens in, 200–2, 208, 332, 379–81
characteristics of, 8–11, 17, 25–7, 255–7, 279–80, 320, 322, 323, 329–30, 333–4, 389–90
distribution of wealth in, 336–42, 353
eleventh-century, 25–38
growth of, 22–5, 30, 263–79, 320
housing in, 29–30, 339, 353–4, 390–2
Jewish communities in, 381–9
lords of towns and townsfolk, 27–30, 41–3, 271–2, 285–90, 297–8, 300–1, 317–18, 320–2
new, 268–74, 320–1
occupational structure of, 258–9, 268–9, 324–30
poverty in, 339–42
quality of life in, 390–2
recruitment of populations of, 330–6
ruling circles in, 342–52
Saxon, 18–25
sokes and enclaves under private lordship in, 28–30, 261–2, 281–2, 286
see also boroughs, burgage tenure, burgesses, craft gilds, craftsmen: urban, gilds merchant, markets, municipal government, parishes

trade, internal, 15, 136–43, 176–80, 228, 234, 253–4, 394–6, 401
charges on, 149
in agricultural produce, 140–2, 144–5, 153–7, 160–1, 169
in cloth, 165, 172
informal transactions in, 155–9
in wool, 164–5, 225–6, 228
see also fairs, markets

trade, overseas, 13–16, 41–2, 181–254, 400–1
  estimates of value of, 195–6, 210–15
  general character of, 186–7, 196–7, 213–15, 408–9, 411
  principal ports for, 196–7, 214–15
  share of English merchants in, 210–25, 233–4
  taxation of, 234–54
  see also exports, imports, merchants
traditional attitudes and institutions, 462–9, 416–17
transport costs, 149–55
  see also communications
Trawden (Lancs.), 66
Trenewith, Michael, 72
Troys, James de (London), 232
Trumpington, Sir Giles of, 351
Truro (Cornwall), 165
Tudeley (Kent), 62
Tunstead (Norfolk), 117
Tutbury castle (Staffs.), 10
Twynham (Gloucs.), 275
Tydeswell, Henry de (Stamford), 245
Tyrewit, Adam (Beverley), 237

Ulseby, Hugh (London), 241, 246, 247–8
Uppingham (Rutland), 245

Valence, Aymer de, 201
Valognes, Roger de, 281
Vaudey abbey (Lincs.), 144, 174
Verdennel, John (York), 349
  Robert, 379
Vere, Aubrey de, 281
Villiers, Gerard de (Lostwithiel), 72

Wainfleet (Lincs.), 147, 225
Wakefield (Yorks), 61, 65, 67, 69, 77, 78, 115, 121, 124, 134, 155
Wallingford (Berks.), 18, 20, 118, 150, 285, 287, 291, 294, 295, 301, 313
Walsoken (Norfolk), 158
Waltham Holy Cross abbey (Essex), 148, 385
Wancy, Roger and Michael de, 385
Warenmouth (Northumb.), 273, 275
Warkworth (Northumb.), 75, 277
Wantage, John of, 156
Warwick (Warwicks.), 12, 43, 237, 317
Watford (Herts.), 232
Watling Street, 12
Weald, the, 62
Wellesthorpe, Roger de (Grantham), 245
Wentlond, John (Huntingdon), 338

Wesenham, John (King's Lynn), 240, 243, 249
Westbury (Wilts.), 3
West Midlands, 176–7, 180
Westminster, 262, 266, 269–70, 335
  abbey of, 139, 156, 281, 404
  fair, 167, 170
Weston, Robert (Shrewsbury), 338
West Whelpington (Northumb.), 84
Whaplode (Lincs.), 394
Whickham and Gateshead coal mines (Durham), 66, 71
Wigmore (Herefords.), 40
Wigston family (Leicester), 333, 334
Wigston Magna (Leics.), 333
Wilton (Wilts.), 26, 94, 118, 125, 287, 291
Wiltshire, craftsmen in, 131
Winchcombe (Gloucs.), 119, 145, 177, 270, 275
  fair, 166, 169
Winchelsea (Sussex), 92, 184, 196, 262, 335
Winchester (Hants.), 8–9, 18, 19, 20, 21, 22–3, 25, 29, 30, 31, 37, 40, 57, 136, 163, 165, 229, 232, 242, 255, 257–8, 259, 261, 263, 264, 267, 268, 280, 286, 288, 300, 307, 309, 310–11, 313, 316, 318–19, 335, 338, 339, 347, 350, 353–4, 365, 376, 382, 387, 389, 390
  cloth-making in, 97, 100, 103, 104, 105, 107, 109–10, 113, 118, 120, 124, 126, 408
  occupational structure, 325–7
  St Giles's fair, 103, 118, 119, 143, 166, 167, 168, 170–2, 174, 175
Winchester bishopric, estates of, 135, 140, 141, 151, 423
Windsor (Berks.), 144
  castle, 87, 90
wine, *see* imports: wine
Winlaton (Durham), 152
Wisbech (Cambs.), 79, 270
Witney (Oxon.), 119, 275
Wodeley, Thomas de (Abingdon), 252–3
women, in crafts, trade and towns, 4, 54–5, 75, 80–1, 102, 129, 132n., 325, 329, 331
Woodkirk (Yorks.), 167
Woodstock (Oxon.), 268–9, 271, 275
wool *see* exports: wool, trade: internal
Wooler (Northumb.), 162, 277
Worcester, 9, 12, 18, 23, 30, 119, 164, 266, 295, 308, 350, 382, 404
  bishop of, 178
Worminghall, Philip (Oxford), 354

Worstead (Norfolk), 117, 134, 411
Wotton-under-Edge (Gloucs.), 275, 307, 411
Wrangle (Lincs.), 76

Yarm (Yorks.), 113, 196, 337, 338
Yarmouth (Norfolk), 117, 121, 122, 138, 148, 411, 414
  trade of, 183, 196, 214, 219, 221
York (Yorks.), 9, 11, 12, 13, 14, 18, 19–20, 23, 26, 33, 36, 39–40, 84, 86, 91, 164, 165, 196, 227, 244, 245, 258, 260–1, 262, 265–6, 280, 286, 295, 296, 300, 302, 307, 312–13, 319, 330, 332, 334, 335, 337, 338, 341, 344, 347, 349, 352–3, 354, 360, 362, 364, 371, 372, 376, 377, 382, 383, 388, 408
  cloth-making in, 100, 106, 107, 108, 110, 115, 124, 126
  craftsmen and merchants, 75, 81, 83
  minster, 87–8, 89–90
  occupational structure of, 325–7
  parishes, 376–9
  ruling circles, 349